Computer-Aided Design: Techniques and Applications

Computer-Aided Design:
Techniques and Applications

Editor: Lamarcus Crowne

New York

Published by NY Research Press
118-35 Queens Blvd., Suite 400,
Forest Hills, NY 11375, USA
www.nyresearchpress.com

Computer-Aided Design: Techniques and Applications
Edited by Lamarcus Crowne

Cataloging-in-Publication Data

Computer-aided design : techniques and applications / edited by Lamarcus Crowne.
   p. cm.
Includes bibliographical references and index.
ISBN 978-1-64725-379-0
1. Computer-aided design. 2. Computer-aided engineering. I. Crowne, Lamarcus.
TA174 .C66 2023
620.004 2--dc23

Contents

Permissions

List of Contributors

Index

Preface

In my initial years as a student, I used to run to the library at every possible instance to grab a book and learn something new. Books were my primary source of knowledge and I would not have come such a long way without all that I learnt from them. Thus, when I was approached to edit this book; I became understandably nostalgic. It was an absolute honor to be considered worthy of guiding the current generation as well as those to come. I put all my knowledge and hard work into making this book most beneficial for its readers.

Coronavirus disease (Covid-19) is a family of viruses, which causes illnesses like Middle East respiratory syndrome (MERS), severe acute respiratory syndrome (SARS) and common cold. Diabetes is a complex chronic disease characterized by dysregulation of blood glucose levels in the body. It is caused by a complete deficiency of insulin or body inability to utilize insulin. There are various factors present in diabetes that are likely to increase the risk and contribute to the development of Covid-19. Some of these factors include a hypercoagulable and proinflammatory state, hyperglycemia, and underlying comorbidities such as chronic kidney disease, hypertension, obesity, and cardiovascular disease. The treatment of a severe Covid-19 infection with steroids can lead to the worsening of hyperglycemia through increased insulin resistance and reduced β-cell secretory function. This book provides significant insights into the associations between Covid-19 and diabetes as well as its possible mechanisms. It consists of researches and studies performed by experts across the globe. The book is appropriate for students seeking detailed information in this area of study as well as for experts.

I wish to thank my publisher for supporting me at every step. I would also like to thank all the authors who have contributed their researches in this book. I hope this book will be a valuable contribution to the progress of the field.

Editor

Reactive Synthesis from Extended Bounded Response LTL Specifications

Alessandro Cimatti [iD], Luca Geatti [iD], Nicola Gigante [iD], Angelo Montanari [iD] and Stefano Tonetta [iD]

Fondazione Bruno Kessler, Trento, Italy,
Email: [cimatti,lgeatti,tonettas]@fbk.eu
University of Udine, Udine, Italy,
Email: [name.surname]@uniud.it

Abstract—**Reactive synthesis is a key technique for the design of correct-by-construction systems and has been thoroughly investigated in the last decades. It consists in the synthesis of a controller that reacts to environment's inputs satisfying a given temporal logic specification. Common approaches are based on the explicit construction of automata and on their determinization, which limit their scalability.**

In this paper, we introduce a new fragment of Linear Temporal Logic, called Extended Bounded Response LTL (LTL_{EBR}), that allows one to combine bounded and universal unbounded temporal operators (thus covering a large set of practical cases), and we show that reactive synthesis from LTL_{EBR} specifications can be reduced to solving a safety game over a deterministic symbolic automaton built directly from the specification. We prove the correctness of the proposed approach and we successfully evaluate it on various benchmarks.

I. Introduction

Since the dawn of computer science, synthesizing correct-by-construction systems starting from a specification is an important and difficult task. A practical algorithm to solve this task would be a big improvement in declarative programming, since it would allow the programmer to write only the specification of the program, freeing her from possible design or implementation errors, that, in many cases, are due to an imperative style of programming. In the context of formal verification and model-based design, the possibility of synthesizing a controller able to comply with the specification for all possible behaviors of the environment would be of great importance as well: all the effort would be directed to improve the quality of the specification for the controller.

Reactive synthesis was first proposed by Church [7] and solved by Büchi and Landweber [5] for S1S specifications with an algorithm of non-elementary complexity. For Linear Temporal Logic (LTL) specifications, the problem has been shown to be 2EXPTIME-complete [21], [22]. In the attempt of making reactive synthesis a practical task, in spite of its very high complexity, research mainly focused on two lines: (i) finding good algorithms for the average case; (ii) restricting the expressiveness of the specification language. Important examples of the first line of research are the contribution by Kupferman and Vardi [15], where the authors devise a procedure to avoid Safra's determinization of Büchi automata (a known bottleneck in all the problems requiring a determinization of a Büchi automaton), and the work by Finkbeiner and

Schewe [11], where the problem is reduced to a sequence of smaller problems on safety automata, obtained by bounding the number of visits to a rejecting state of a co-Büchi automaton. A meaningful example of restrictions to the specification language is the definition of the *Generalized Reactivity(1)* logic [20], whose synthesis problem can be solved in $\mathcal{O}(N^3)$ symbolic steps, where N is the size of the arena. Finally, in [25] Zhu et al. consider reactive synthesis from Safety LTL specifications. Although the complexity remains doubly exponential, the proposed restriction allows one to reason on finite words and thus to exploit efficient tools for finite-state automata, like, for instance, MONA [12].

In this paper, we propose a new fragment of LTL, called *Extended Bounded Response* LTL (LTL_{EBR} for short), which supports *bounded* operators [18], such as $G^{[a,b]}$ and $F^{[a,b]}$, along with universal unbounded temporal operators like G and $\mathcal{R}$. We show that formulas of LTL_{EBR} can be turned into *deterministic symbolic automata* over infinite words, with a translation carried out in a completely symbolic way. Such a result is achieved in two steps: (i) a *pastification* of the subformulas containing only bounded operators by making use of techniques similar to those exploited for MTL [17], [18], and (ii) the construction of *deterministic monitors* for the unbounded temporal operators. These two steps allow the entire procedure to be carried out without ever producing any explicit automaton. Then, we use existing algorithms for safety synthesis to solve the game on the deterministic symbolic automaton. We implemented the proposed solution in a tool, called ebr-ltl-synth, and compared its performance against state-of-the-art synthesizers for full LTL over a set of LTL_{EBR} formulas. The outcomes of the experimental evaluation are encouraging. For lack of space, some of the proofs are reported in [8].

II. Preliminaries

Linear Temporal Logic with Past (LTL+P) is a modal logic interpreted over infinite state sequences. Let Σ be a set of propositions. LTL+P formulas are inductively defined as follows:

$$\phi := p \mid \neg \phi \mid \phi_1 \vee \phi_2 \mid X \phi \mid \phi_1 \mathcal{U} \phi_2 \mid Y \phi \mid \phi_1 \mathcal{S} \phi_2$$

where $p \in \Sigma$. Temporal operators can be subdivided into the *future operators*, next (X) and until ($\mathcal{U}$), and *past operators*, *yesterday* (Y) and *since* ($\mathcal{S}$). We define the following common abbreviations (where $\top$ stands for true): (i) $X^i \phi$ is $X(X^{i-1} \phi)$

if $i > 0$ and X^0 is ; (ii) *release*: $\phi_1 \mathcal{R} \phi_2 \equiv \neg(\neg\phi_1 \mathcal{U} \neg\phi_2)$; (iii) *eventually*: $F\phi_1 \equiv \top\,\mathcal{U}\,\phi_1$; (iv) *globally*: $G\phi_1 \equiv \neg F\neg\phi_1$; (v) *trigger*: $\phi_1 \mathcal{T} \phi_2 \equiv \neg(\neg\phi_1 \mathcal{S} \neg\phi_2)$; (vi) *once*: $O\phi_1 \equiv \top\,\mathcal{S}\,\phi_1$; (vii) *historically*: $H\phi_1 \equiv \neg O\neg\phi_1$.

LTL is obtained from LTL+P by allowing only the *next* and the *until* operators. Conversely, *Full Past* LTL (LTL$_{FP}$) is the fragment of LTL+P that only admits past operators.

LTL can also be enriched with *bounded* temporal operators, such as the *bounded until* ($\phi_1 \mathcal{U}^{[a,b]} \phi_2$) and *bounded eventually* ($F^{[a,b]}\phi_1 \equiv \top\,\mathcal{U}^{[a,b]}\,\phi_1$). *Full Bounded* LTL (LTL$_{FB}$) is the fragment of LTL that includes only the *next*, *bounded until*, and *bounded eventually* operators.

Let us now give the semantics of the above logics. A *state sequence* is an infinite sequence $\sigma = \langle \sigma_0\,\sigma_1\,\dots \rangle \in (2^\Sigma)^\omega$ of sets of propositions $\sigma_i \in 2^\Sigma$, called *states*. Given a sequence σ, a position $i \geq 0$, and a formula ϕ, the satisfaction of ϕ by σ at i, written $\sigma, i \models \phi$, is inductively defined as follows:

$\sigma, i \models p$	iff	$p \in \sigma_i$
$\sigma, i \models \neg\phi$	iff	$\sigma, i \not\models \phi$
$\sigma, i \models \phi_1 \vee \phi_2$	iff	either $\sigma, i \models \phi_1$ or $\sigma, i \models \phi_2$
$\sigma, i \models \phi_1 \wedge \phi_2$	iff	$\sigma, i \models \phi_1$ and $\sigma, i \models \phi_2$
$\sigma, i \models X\phi$	iff	$\sigma, i+1 \models \phi$
$\sigma, i \models Y\phi$	iff	$i > 0$ and $\sigma, i-1 \models \phi$

$$\sigma, i \models \phi_1 \mathcal{U} \phi_2 \quad\text{iff}\quad \text{there exists } j \geq i \text{ such that } \sigma, j \models \phi_2 \text{ and } \sigma, k \models \phi_1 \text{ for all } i \leq k < j$$

$$\sigma, i \models \phi_1 \mathcal{S} \phi_2 \quad\text{iff}\quad \text{there exists } j \leq i \text{ such that } \sigma, j \models \phi_2 \text{ and } \sigma, k \models \phi_1 \text{ for all } j < k \leq i$$

$$\sigma, i \models \phi_1 \mathcal{U}^{[a,b]} \phi_2 \quad\text{iff}\quad \text{there exists } j \in [i+a, i+b] \text{ such that } \sigma, j \models \phi_2 \text{ and } \sigma, k \models \phi_1 \text{ for all } i \leq k < j$$

We say that σ satisfies ϕ, written $\sigma \models \phi$, if and only if $\sigma, 0 \models \phi$. We define the *language* $\mathcal{L}(\phi)$ of a temporal formula ϕ as $\mathcal{L}(\phi) = \{ \sigma \in (2^\Sigma)^\omega \mid \sigma \models \phi \}$.

Symbolic safety automata and safety games

To begin with, we formally define the problems of realizability and reactive synthesis for temporal formulas.

As for realizability, it is convenient to view it as a two-player game between Controller, whose aim is to satisfy the specification, and Environment, who tries to violate it.

Definition 1 (Strategy): Let $\Sigma = \mathcal{C} \cup \mathcal{U}$ be an alphabet partitioned into the set of *controllable* variables $\mathcal{C}$ and the set of *uncontrollable* ones $\mathcal{U}$, such that $\mathcal{C} \cap \mathcal{U} = \varnothing$. A *strategy for Controller* is a function $g : (2^\mathcal{U})^+ \to 2^\mathcal{C}$ that, given the sequence $U = \langle U_0 \dots U_n \rangle$ of choices made by *Environment* so far, determines the current choices $C_n = g(U)$ of *Controller*.

Given a strategy $g : (2^\mathcal{U})^+ \to 2^\mathcal{C}$ and an infinite sequence of uncontrollable choices $U = \langle U_0\,U_1\,\dots \rangle \in (2^\mathcal{U})^\omega$, with some abuse of notation, we denote as $g(U) = \langle U_0 \cup g(\langle U_0 \rangle)\ U_1 \cup g(\langle U_0\,U_1 \rangle)\ \dots \rangle$ the state sequence resulting from reacting to U according to g.

Definition 2 (Realizability and Synthesis): Let ϕ be a temporal formula over the alphabet $\Sigma = \mathcal{C} \cup \mathcal{U}$. We say that ϕ is *realizable* if and only if there exists a strategy $g : (2^\mathcal{U})^+ \to 2^\mathcal{C}$

such that, for any infinite sequence $U = \langle U_0\,U_1\,\dots \rangle \in (2^\mathcal{U})^\omega$, it holds that $g(U) \models \phi$. If ϕ is realizable, the synthesis problem is the problem of computing such a strategy g.

Temporal logic has an intimate relationship with automata on infinite words [24], where different acceptance conditions give rise to different classes of automata. For instance, the acceptance condition of (non-deterministic) Büchi automata allows them to recognize the class of ω-regular languages [4], including all languages definable by LTL+P formulas.

Here, we focus on a restricted type of acceptance condition, called *safety* condition, and we represent automata in a *symbolic* way, as opposed to their common explicit representation.

Definition 3 (Symbolic Safety Automata): A *symbolic safety automaton* (SSA) is a tuple $\mathcal{A} = (V, I, T, S)$, such that (i) $V = X \cup \Sigma$, where X is a set of *state variables* and Σ is a set of *input variables*, and (ii) $I(X)$, $T(X, \Sigma, X')$, and $S(X)$, with $X' = \{x' \mid x \in X\}$, are Boolean formulae which define the set of initial states, the transition relation, and the set of safe states, respectively.

In symbolic automata, states are identified by the values of state variables, and both initial/final states and the transition relation are represented as Boolean formulas. This allows them to be, in many cases, exponentially more succinct than equivalent explicitly represented automata. In particular, the transition relation $T(X, \Sigma, X')$ is built over state variables, input variables, and a *primed* version of state variables that represent the values of state variables at the next state. As an example, if a variable x has to flip at every transition, the transition relation would contain a clause of the form $x \Leftrightarrow \neg x'$.

Definition 4 (Acceptance of SSA): Let $\mathcal{A}$ be an SSA. A *trace* is a sequence $\pi = \langle \pi_0\,\pi_1\,\dots \rangle \in (2^V)^\omega$ of subsets π_i of V that satisfies the transition relation of $\mathcal{A}$, that is, such that for all $i \geq 0$, $T(X, \Sigma, X')$ is satisfied when π_i is used to interpret variables from X and Σ, and π_{i+1} is used to interpret variables from X'. We say that a trace π is *induced* by a word $\sigma = \langle \sigma_0\,\sigma_1\,\dots \rangle \in (2^\Sigma)^\omega$ iff $\sigma_i = \pi_i \cap \Sigma$ for all $i \geq 0$. A trace is *accepting* (or *safe*) iff π_i satisfies $S(X)$ for all $i \geq 0$. The *language* of $\mathcal{A}$, denoted as $\mathcal{L}(\mathcal{A})$, is the set of all $\sigma \in (2^\Sigma)^\omega$ such that there exists an accepting trace induced by σ in $\mathcal{A}$.

For reactive synthesis, a crucial property of an automaton $\mathcal{A}$ is *determinism*, since in order to check if $\sigma \in \mathcal{L}(\mathcal{A})$ it suffices to check if *the* trace induced by σ in $\mathcal{A}$ is accepting.

Definition 5 (Deterministic SSA): An SSA $\mathcal{A} = (V, I, T, S)$ is *deterministic* if:

1) the formula I has exactly one satisfying assignment;
2) the transition relation is of the form:

$$T(X, \Sigma, X') := \bigwedge_{x \in X} (x' \Leftrightarrow \Delta_x(X \cup \Sigma))$$

where each $\Delta_x(X \cup \Sigma)$ is a Boolean formula over X and Σ.

Note that Def. 5 implies that for each $\sigma \in (2^\Sigma)^\omega$, there exists exactly one trace induced by σ for any given deterministic SSA. The realizability and the synthesis problems can be defined over a deterministic automaton as well; this gives rise to a safety game, which is defined as follows.

Definition 6 (Safety Game): Let $\mathcal{A}$ be a deterministic SSA over the alphabet $\Sigma = \mathcal{C} \cup \mathcal{U}$. A safety game is a tuple $G = \langle \mathcal{A}, \mathcal{C}, \mathcal{U} \rangle$, where $\mathcal{C}$ and $\mathcal{U}$ are the sets of controllable and uncontrollable variables, respectively. We say that Controller wins the game if and only if there is a strategy $g : (2^{\mathcal{U}})^+ \to 2^{\mathcal{C}}$ such that for all sequences $U = \langle U_0, U_1, \dots \rangle \in (2^{U})^\omega$, *the* trace induced by $g(U)$ in $\mathcal{A}$ is *accepting*.

III. EXTENDED BOUNDED RESPONSE LTL

In this section, we define *Extended Bounded Response LTL*, abbreviated $\mathsf{LTL}_{\mathsf{EBR}}$. $\mathsf{LTL}_{\mathsf{EBR}}$ extends $\mathsf{LTL}_{\mathsf{FB}}$ (which only features bounded operators) by admitting Boolean combinations of the universal unbounded temporal operators *release* ($\mathcal{R}$) and *globally* (G).

Definition 7 (The logic $\mathsf{LTL}_{\mathsf{EBR}}$): Let $a, b \in \mathbb{N}$. An $\mathsf{LTL}_{\mathsf{EBR}}$ formula α is inductively defined as follows:

$$\psi := p \mid \neg\psi \mid \psi_1 \vee \psi_2 \mid X\psi \mid \psi_1 \mathcal{U}^{[a,b]} \psi_2 \quad \text{Full Bounded Layer}$$
$$\phi := \psi \mid \phi_1 \wedge \phi_2 \mid X\phi \mid G\phi \mid \phi \mathcal{R} \phi \quad \text{Future Layer}$$
$$\alpha := \phi \mid \alpha_1 \vee \alpha_2 \mid \alpha_1 \wedge \alpha_2 \quad \text{Boolean Layer}$$

We refer to Sec. II for the semantics of $\mathsf{LTL}_{\mathsf{EBR}}$ operators. In the next sections, we will show how to build, given an $\mathsf{LTL}_{\mathsf{EBR}}$ formula ϕ, a deterministic symbolic safety automaton $\mathcal{A}(\phi)$ such that $\mathcal{L}(\mathcal{A}(\phi)) = \mathcal{L}(\phi)$.

A. Examples

We now give some simple examples of requirements that can be expressed in the $\mathsf{LTL}_{\mathsf{EBR}}$ logic.

The first one is a typical bounded response requirement: Controller has to answer a grant g at most k time units after the request r of Environment is issued. It can be expressed by the following $\mathsf{LTL}_{\mathsf{EBR}}$ formula:

$$G(r \to F^{[0,k]}g)$$

Another quite common requirement is *mutual exclusion*. As an example, the case of an arbiter that has to grant a resource to at most one client at once can be captured as follows (for each i, g_i means that the resource has been granted to client i):

$$G\left(\bigwedge_{1 \le i < j \le n} \neg(g_i \wedge g_j) \right)$$

When a set of clients with different priorities has to be managed, it is possible to introduce a requirement stating that, whenever two or more clients simultaneously send a request, clients with a higher priority must be granted before those with a lower one ($i < j$ means that the priority of client i is higher than that of client j):

$$\bigwedge_{1 \le i < j \le n} G((r_i \wedge r_j) \to (\neg g_j) \mathcal{U}^{[0,k]} g_i)$$

Finally, in many situations it is important to include requirements about the *configuration* of a system model. Consider the case of a thermostat. One may ask that if the `prog` modality is off, then the controller has to communicate the signal `on` to the boiler for an indefinitely long amount of time, while, in case the `prog` modality is on, it has to do that only for

a specific interval of time, say $[h_1, h_2]$, after which it has to stop the communication with the boiler. This can be expressed in $\mathsf{LTL}_{\mathsf{EBR}}$ by the following formula:

$$(\neg\texttt{prog} \wedge G(\texttt{on})) \vee (\texttt{prog} \wedge G^{[h_1,h_2]}(\texttt{on}) \wedge X^{h_2}G(\texttt{off}))$$

B. Comparison with other temporal logics

Zhu *et al.* [25] studied the synthesis problem for *Safety LTL*, which can be viewed as the *until*-free fragment of LTL in negated normal form (NNF). Every formula ϕ of $\mathsf{LTL}_{\mathsf{EBR}}$ can be turned into a Safety LTL one by (i) transforming ϕ in NNF and (ii) expanding each bounded operator in terms of conjunctions or disjunctions. As an example, the $\mathsf{LTL}_{\mathsf{EBR}}$ formula $\phi := G(p \to F^{[0,5]}q)$ is equivalent to the Safety LTL formula $\phi' := G(p \to \bigvee_{i=0}^{5} X^i q)$. However, since constants in $\mathsf{LTL}_{\mathsf{EBR}}$ are represented by using a logarithmic encoding, $\mathsf{LTL}_{\mathsf{EBR}}$ formulas can be exponentially more succinct than Safety LTL ones. Whether the converse holds as well, *i.e.*, whether any formula of Safety LTL can be translated into an equivalent $\mathsf{LTL}_{\mathsf{EBR}}$ one, is still an open question. As an example, $G(p \vee Gq)$ is a Safety LTL formula but, syntactically, is not an $\mathsf{LTL}_{\mathsf{EBR}}$ one.

Maler *et al.* [18] introduced *Metric Temporal Logic with a Bounded-Horizon* (MTL−B for short) as the metric temporal logic with *only* bounded operators interpreted over dense time. They addressed the problem of reactive synthesis from MTL−B specifications by showing that each MTL−B formula can be transformed into a *deterministic* timed automaton. With respect to this fragment, and ignoring the differences in the underlying temporal structures (in our setting, time is discrete), $\mathsf{LTL}_{\mathsf{EBR}}$ extends MTL−B with Boolean combinations of unbounded universal temporal operators.

IV. FROM $\mathsf{LTL}_{\mathsf{EBR}}$ TO DETERMINISTIC SYMBOLIC SAFETY AUTOMATA

This section focuses on the procedure to turn every $\mathsf{LTL}_{\mathsf{EBR}}$ formula into a deterministic symbolic safety automaton on infinite words (see Def. 5) that recognizes the same language.

In doing that, we apply a few transformation steps on the formula, summarized in Fig. 1, to simplify its syntactic structure and turn it into a form amenable to direct transformation into a deterministic SSA. We define two syntactic restrictions of $\mathsf{LTL}_{\mathsf{EBR}}$ that are the targets of the transformation steps.

Definition 8 (PastLTL$_{\mathsf{EBR}}$): An PastLTL$_{\mathsf{EBR}}$ formula α is inductively defined as follows:

$$\beta := p \mid \neg\beta \mid \beta_1 \vee \beta_2 \mid Y\beta \mid \beta_1 \mathcal{S} \beta_2$$
$$\phi := \beta \mid \phi_1 \wedge \phi_2 \mid X\phi \mid G\phi \mid (X^i\beta)\mathcal{R}\phi$$
$$\alpha := \phi \mid \alpha_1 \vee \alpha_2 \mid \alpha_1 \wedge \alpha_2$$

Definition 9 (Canonical PastLTL$_{\mathsf{EBR}}$): The *canonical form* of PastLTL$_{\mathsf{EBR}}$ formulas is inductively defined as follows:

$$\beta := p \mid \neg\beta \mid \beta_1 \vee \beta_2 \mid Y\beta \mid \beta_1 \mathcal{S} \beta_2$$
$$\phi := \beta \mid G\beta \mid \beta_1 \mathcal{R} \beta_2$$
$$\gamma := \phi \mid X\gamma$$
$$\alpha := \gamma \mid \alpha_1 \vee \alpha_2 \mid \alpha_1 \wedge \alpha_2$$

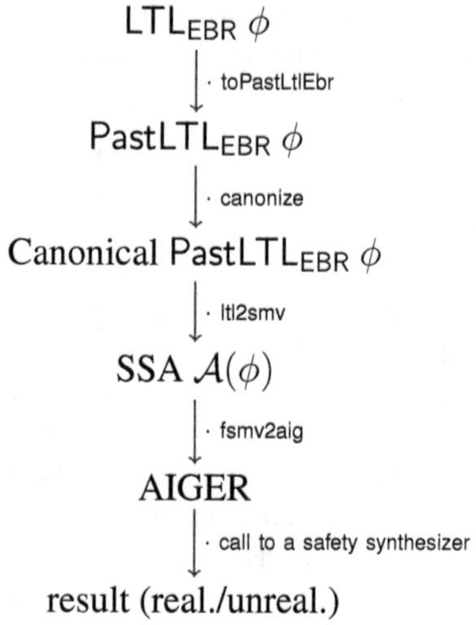

$\mathsf{LTL_{EBR}}\ \phi$

$\downarrow$ · toPastLtlEbr

$\mathsf{PastLTL_{EBR}}\ \phi$

$\downarrow$ · canonize

Canonical $\mathsf{PastLTL_{EBR}}\ \phi$

$\downarrow$ · ltl2smv

SSA $\mathcal{A}(\phi)$

$\downarrow$ · fsmv2aig

AIGER

$\downarrow$ · call to a safety synthesizer

result (real./unreal.)

Figure 1. The overall procedure.

Canonical $\mathsf{PastLTL_{EBR}}$ formulas do not contain nested occurrences of unbounded temporal operators, whose operands can be only full-past formulas, and each of these is prefixed by an arbitrary number of *next* operators.

The transformation of $\mathsf{LTL_{EBR}}$ formulas into deterministic SSAs consists of three steps: (i) a translation from $\mathsf{LTL_{EBR}}$ to $\mathsf{PastLTL_{EBR}}$; (ii) a translation from $\mathsf{PastLTL_{EBR}}$ to its canonical form; (iii) a transformation of canonical $\mathsf{PastLTL_{EBR}}$ formulas into deterministic SSAs. Once a deterministic SSA $\mathcal{A}(\ )$ for the original $\mathsf{LTL_{EBR}}$ formula over $\mathcal{C} \cup \mathcal{U}$ has been obtained, to solve the safety game $\langle \mathcal{A}(\ )\ \mathcal{C}\ \mathcal{U} \rangle$, *i.e.*, to decide the existence of a strategy for Controller in the automaton, we apply an existing safety synthesis algorithm (see Def. 6).

A. From $\mathsf{LTL_{EBR}}$ to $\mathsf{PastLTL_{EBR}}$

Let be an $\mathsf{LTL_{EBR}}$ formula. The first step consists in translating each $\mathsf{LTL_{FB}}$ subformula of into an *equivalent* one, which is of the form X^d, with $\in \mathsf{LTL_{FP}}$ and $d \in \mathbb{N}$. We refer to this process as *pastification* [17], [18]. As we will see, since "the past has already happened", full-past formulas can be represented by deterministic monitors.

In order to pastify each $\mathsf{LTL_{FB}}$ subformula of , we adapt to $\mathsf{LTL_{EBR}}$ a technique developed by Maler *et al.* for MTL$-$B [17], [18]. Intuitively, for each model of a full-bounded formula , there exists a furthermost time point d (the *temporal depth* of) such that the subsequent states cannot be constrained by in any way. The *pastification* of is a formula that uses only past operators and that is equivalent to when interpreted at time point d instead of at the origin.

Definition 10 (Temporal Depth [18]): Let be an $\mathsf{LTL_{FB}}$ formula. The *temporal depth* of , denoted as $D(\ )$, is inductively defined as follows:

- $D(p) = 0$, for all $p \in \Sigma$
- $D(\neg\ _1) = D(\ _1)$
- $D(\ _1 \wedge\ _2) = \max\{D(\ _1)\ D(\ _2)\}$
- $D(X\ _1) = 1 + D(\ _1)$
- $D(\ _1 \mathcal{U}^{[a,b]}\ _2) = b + \max\{D(\ _1)\ D(\ _2)\}$

Let M_ϕ (only M if unambiguous) be the greatest constant in , with $M_\phi = 0$ if has no constants. It can be observed that $D(\ ) \leq M \cdot n$, where $n = |\ |$.

Definition 11 (Pastification [18]): Let be an $\mathsf{LTL_{FB}}$ formula and $d \geq D(\ )$. The pastification of is the formula $\Pi(\ d)$ inductively defined as follows:

- $\Pi(p\ d) = \mathsf{Y}^d p$
- $\Pi(\neg\ d) = \neg \Pi(\ d)$
- $\Pi(\ _1 \wedge\ _2\ d) = \Pi(\ _1\ d) \wedge \Pi(\ _2\ d)$
- $\Pi(X\ d) = \Pi(\ d-1)$
- $\Pi(\ _1 \mathcal{U}^{[a,b]}\ _2\ d) =$
  $\bigvee_{t=0}^{b-a}(\mathsf{Y}^t(\Pi(\ _2\ d-b) \wedge \mathsf{H}^{b-t-1}\mathsf{Y}\Pi(\ _1\ d-b)))$

Note that from Def. 11 we can derive that $\Pi(\mathsf{F}^{[a,b]}\ d) \equiv \Pi(\top\ \mathcal{U}^{[a,b]}\ d) \equiv \bigvee_{t=0}^{b-a} \mathsf{Y}^t\Pi(\ d-b)$, which can be succinctly written using the *once* operator, hence we can define $\Pi(\mathsf{F}^{[a,b]}\ d) = \mathsf{O}^{[0,b-a]}\Pi(\ d-b)$.

Proposition 1 (Soundness of pastification): Let be a $\mathsf{LTL_{FB}}$ formula. For all state sequences $\in (2^\Sigma)^\omega$, all $i \in \mathbb{N}$, and all $d \geq D(\ )$, it holds that:

$$i \models\ \quad \Leftrightarrow \quad\ i \models \mathsf{X}^d\Pi(\ d)$$

From now on, let pastify($\ $) be the formula $X^{D(\phi)}\Pi(\ D(\ ))$. As an example, if $:= \mathsf{F}^{[0,k_1]}(q \wedge \mathsf{F}^{[0,k_2]}p)$, then pastify($\ $) $:= X^{k_1+k_2}\mathsf{O}^{[0,k_1]}(\mathsf{Y}^{k_2}q \wedge \mathsf{O}^{[0,k_2]}p)$. We state the following complexity result about pastification.

Proposition 2: Let be a $\mathsf{LTL_{FB}}$ formula. Then, pastify($\ $) is a formula of size $\mathcal{O}(n^2 \cdot M^{\log_2 n+1})$, where $n = |\ |$ and M is the greatest constant in .

Note that if has no constants, that is, $M = 1$, the size of pastify($\ $) is $\mathcal{O}(n^2)$. Given an $\mathsf{LTL_{EBR}}$ formula , we pastify each of its $\mathsf{LTL_{FB}}$ subformulas with the pastify operator: we call this step toPastLtlEbr. Once it has been completed, the resulting formula belongs to $\mathsf{PastLTL_{EBR}}$.

The toPastLtlEbr algorithm can be improved by observing that there are $\mathsf{LTL_{FB}}$ formulas that already belong to $\mathsf{PastLTL_{EBR}}$. One example is the formula $p \wedge \mathsf{XXX}q$. Obviously, for this kind of formulas there is no need for the algorithm to pastify them. Consider the previous example. Without the proposed trick, the algorithm would have produced the formula $\mathsf{XXX}(\mathsf{YYY}p \wedge q)$, while, by simply noticing that the formula already belongs to $\mathsf{PastLTL_{EBR}}$, it does not need to pastify anything, returning $p \wedge \mathsf{XXX}q$.

Proposition 3: For each $\mathsf{LTL_{EBR}}$ formula , there is an equivalent $\mathsf{PastLTL_{EBR}}$ formula ' of size $\mathcal{O}(n^3 \cdot M^{\log_2 n+1})$, where $n = |\ |$ and M is the greatest constant in .

Proof: Let be an $\mathsf{LTL_{EBR}}$ formula and let ' $:=$ toPastLtlEbr($\ $). By Prop. 1, the toPastLtlEbr algorithm replaces the $\mathsf{LTL_{FB}}$ subformulas of with an equivalent formula, hence $\equiv$ '. Since in there are at most $n = |\ |$ subformulas, then, by Prop. 2, $|$ '$| = n \cdot \mathcal{O}(n^2 \cdot M^{\log_2 n+1})$, that is, $|$ '$| = \mathcal{O}(n^3 \cdot M^{\log_2 n})$. ∎

Note that if there are no constants in , that is, $M = 1$, then, by Prop. 2, $|$toPastLtlEbr($\ $)$| = \mathcal{O}(n^3)$.

B. From PastLTL$_{EBR}$ to Canonical PastLTL$_{EBR}$

The second step is the canonization of the PastLTL$_{EBR}$ formula obtained from the previous step, in order to produce an equivalent formula in canonical form (Def. 9). Canonical PastLTL$_{EBR}$ formulas are Boolean combinations of formulas of the form $X^i \psi_1$, $X^i G \psi_1$, and $X^i(\psi_1 R \psi_2)$, where ψ_1 and ψ_2 are full past formulas. Compared to general PastLTL$_{EBR}$ formulas, those in canonical form do not admit neither nested unbounded operators nor *next* operators in front of the left-hand argument of a *release*. The canonization of a PastLTL$_{EBR}$ formula is obtained by applying a set of rewriting rules.

Definition 12 (Canonization): Given a PastLTL$_{EBR}$ formula ϕ, canonize(ϕ) is the formula obtained by recursively applying the R_1-R_7 rules to the subformulas of ϕ in a bottom-up fashion followed by the application of the R_{flat} rule:

$$R_1 : X(\psi_1 \wedge \psi_2) \rightsquigarrow X\psi_1 \wedge X\psi_2$$

$$R_2 : \psi \, R \, (\psi_1 \wedge \psi_2) \rightsquigarrow \psi \, R \, \psi_1 \wedge \psi \, R \, \psi_2$$

$$R_3 : (X^i \psi_1) \, R \, (X^j \psi_2) \rightsquigarrow$$
$$\begin{cases} X^i(\psi_1 \, R \, (Y^{i-j}\psi_2)) & \text{if } i > j \\ X^j((Y^{j-i}\psi_1) \, R \, \psi_2) & \text{otherwise} \end{cases}$$

$$R_4 : (X^i \psi_1) \, R \, (X^j(\psi_2 \, R \, \psi_3)) \rightsquigarrow$$
$$\begin{cases} X^i(\psi_1 \, R \, ((Y^{i-j}\psi_2) \, R \, (Y^{i-j}\psi_3))) & \text{if } i > j \\ X^j((Y^{j-i}\psi_1) \, R \, (\psi_2 \, R \, \psi_3)) & \text{otherwise} \end{cases}$$

$$R_5 : GX^i G \psi \rightsquigarrow X^i G \psi$$

$$R_6 : GX^i(\psi_1 \, R \, \psi_2) \rightsquigarrow X^i G \psi_2$$

$$R_7 : (X^i \psi_1) \, R \, (X^j G \psi_2) \rightsquigarrow$$
$$\begin{cases} X^i G Y^{i-j}\psi_2 & \text{if } i > j \\ X^j G \psi_2 & \text{otherwise} \end{cases}$$

$$R_{flat} : X^i(\psi_1 \, R \, (\psi_2 \, R \, (\cdots (\psi_{n-1} \, R \, \psi_n) \cdots))) \rightsquigarrow$$
$$X^i((\psi_{n-1} \wedge O(\psi_{n-2} \wedge \cdots O(\psi_1 \wedge Y^i \top) \cdots)) \, R \, \psi_n)$$
for any $n \geq 3$

where ψ, ψ_1, ψ_2, and ψ_3 are full-past formulae.

It is worth noticing that, so far, we do not have rules (preserving equivalence) to deal with the following cases: (i) $(\psi_1 \wedge \psi_2) \, R \, (\cdot)$, (ii) $(G \psi_1) \, R \, (\cdot)$ or (iii) $(\psi_1 \, R \, \psi_2) \, R \, (\cdot)$. This is why, in Def. 7, we restricted the left-hand argument of each *release* operator to be a full-bounded formula.

Lemma 1 (Soundness of canonize($\cdot$)): For any PastLTL$_{EBR}$ formula ϕ, it holds that ϕ and canonize(ϕ) are equivalent and canonize(ϕ) is a Canonical PastLTL$_{EBR}$ formula.

Proposition 4 (Complexity of canonize($\cdot$)): For any PastLTL$_{EBR}$ formula ϕ, canonize(ϕ) can be built in $\mathcal{O}(n)$ time, and the size of canonize(ϕ) is $\mathcal{O}(n)$, where $n = |\phi|$.

C. From Canonical PastLTL$_{EBR}$ to deterministic SSA

The particular shape of canonical PastLTL$_{EBR}$ formulas makes it possible to encode the specification into deterministic SSAs. The key observation is that LTL$_{FP}$ formulas can be encoded into deterministic automata: since these formulas talk exclusively about the past, their truth can be evaluated at any single step depending only on previous steps, without making any guess about the future ("the past already happened"). But LTL$_{FP}$ formulae are not the only ones that can be encoded deterministically. Consider, for instance, the formula $\phi \equiv Xp \vee Xq$. At a first glance, it may seem that ϕ needs a non-deterministic automaton to be encoded, which at the first state makes a choice about whether p or q will hold in the next state. Nevertheless, this formula is equivalent to $X(p \vee q)$ and it corresponds to the *deterministic* automaton that, once arrived in its second state by reading any proposition symbol, proceeds to an accepting state by reading either p or q, or goes to a sink (*error*) state otherwise.

PastLTL$_{EBR}$ in its canonical form combines full past formulas into a broader language that can still be turned into symbolic deterministic automata, extending the above intuition and exploiting the *monitorability* of *universal* temporal operators.

Monitoring is a technique coming from *runtime verification* [16]. Consider the formula $G \phi$. By observing a state sequence, at each step we can decide if a *violation* has occurred; indeed, if ϕ is false at the current step, then the value of $G \phi$ is certainly false for each of the previous steps. More generally, universal temporal formulas, such as $G \phi$ and $\psi_1 \, R \, \psi_2$, are *monitorable*, meaning that a violation of them can be decided on the basis of the observation of a *finite* number of steps. In particular, reporting an error in the next state can be done by considering only the current values. This means that any universal temporal operator can be monitored by adding a Boolean *error variable* with a *deterministic* transition relation.

Therefore, despite not being able to evaluate the truth of a formula such as $G \phi$, as it can be done in the case of past operators, we can nevertheless state in the accepting condition that an error state can never be reached. In this way, if the trace is accepting, that is, an error state can never be reached, then we know that there are no violations, *e.g.*, for $G \phi$, we have forced ϕ to be true in every state. Otherwise, if the trace is not accepting, that is, an error state is reachable, we know that there is a (finite) violation and that the temporal formula was falsified at some step. We therefore introduce an *error bit* for each $X^i \psi_1$, $X^i G \psi_1$, and $X^i(\psi_1 \, R \, \psi_2)$ of a canonical PastLTL$_{EBR}$ formula.

Let ϕ be a canonical PastLTL$_{EBR}$ formula over the alphabet $\Sigma = \mathcal{C} \cup \mathcal{U}$. We define the deterministic SSA $\mathcal{A}(\phi) = (V, I, T, S)$ as follows:

- *Variables.* The set of *state variables* of the automaton is defined as $X = X_P \cup X_F \cup X_C$, where:

$$X_P = \{v_\alpha \mid \alpha \text{ is an LTL}_{FP} \text{ subformula of } \phi\}$$

$$X_F = \left\{ error_\varphi \,\middle|\, \begin{array}{l} \varphi \text{ is subformula of } \phi \text{ of the form} \\ X^i \psi, X^i G \psi, \text{ or } X^i(\psi_1 \, R \, \psi_2) \end{array} \right\}$$

$$X_C = \left\{ counter_i \,\middle|\, \begin{array}{l} i \in \{0 \ldots \log_2 d\} \\ d \text{ max. among all } X^d \text{ in } \phi. \end{array} \right\}$$

Intuitively, variables in X_P track the truth value of all the full-past subformulas, variables in X_F implement the above-described monitoring mechanism, and variables in

X_C are used to encode a binary counter used to monitor nested *tomorrow* operators. In particular, for n nested *tomorrow* operators, a counter with $\log_2(n)$ bits is needed.

- *Initial state.* All the state variables, including the counter bits, are initially false, that is, $I(X) = \bigwedge_{x \in X} \neg x$.
- *Transition relation.* $T(X\ \Sigma\ X')$ is the conjunction of the transition *functions* of the binary counter and the monitors of each subformula of , as will be defined later. Notice that each conjunct is of the form $x' \Leftrightarrow (X \cup \Sigma)$, and thus it is a deterministic transition relation.
- *Safety condition.* $S(X)$ is a Boolean formula obtained from by replacing each formula $\in X_F$ by $\neg error_\varphi$, i.e., $S(X) = [\ \neg error_\varphi]$.

We now define the monitors for the binary counter, used to handle nested *tomorrow* operators, any formula $\in \mathsf{LTL_{FP}}$, and any canonical $\mathsf{PastLTL_{EBR}}$ formula of one of the forms $X^i\ _1$, $X^i G\ _1$, and $X^i(\ _1 \mathcal{R}\ _2)$. We give the definition of the monitors using the SMV language [6], as it provides useful shorthands (like the *switch-case* primitive). Each of the following SMV statement corresponds to the Boolean formula that defines transition functions of our monitors.

The monitor for the counter is defined as follows:

```
next(counter_0) := ¬ counter_0
next(counter_i) := (counter_{i-1} ∨ counter_i) ∧ ¬counter_i
```

If $:= S$ or Y, its monitor is defined as follows:

```
next(v_{Yα}) := v_α ∧ counter > 0
DEFINE
  v_{αSβ} := v_β ∨ (v_α ∧ v_{Y(α)})
```

If is a propositional atom, a negation, or a disjunction of full-past formulas, we define its monitor as follows:

```
DEFINE
  v_p     := p
  v_{¬α}  := ¬v_α
  v_{α∨β} := v_α ∨ v_β
```

For each formula of type X^i, where is a full-past formula, we introduce a new error bit $error_\phi$. Its monitor is defined as follows:

```
next(error_{X^iψ}) := case
  error_{X^iψ}      : TRUE;
  counter = i ∧ ¬v_ψ : TRUE;
  TRUE : FALSE;
esac
```

If $:= X^i G$, where is a full-past formula, we introduce a new error bit $error_\phi$, and we define its monitor as follows:

```
next(error_{X^iGψ}) := case
  counter < i           : FALSE;
  ¬error_{X^iGψ} ∧ v_ψ  : FALSE;
  TRUE : TRUE;
esac
```

The same for $:= X^i(\ _1 \mathcal{R}\ _2)$:

```
next(error_{X^i(ψ_1 R ψ_2)}) := case
  counter < i                              : FALSE;
  ¬error_{X^i(ψ_1 R ψ_2)} ∧ v^i_{ψ_1^P}    : FALSE;
  ¬error_{X^i(ψ_1 R ψ_2)} ∧ v_{ψ_1} ∧ v_{ψ_2} : FALSE;
  ¬error_{X^i(ψ_1 R ψ_2)} ∧ v_{ψ_2}        : FALSE;
  TRUE : TRUE;
esac
```

```
esac
next(v^i_{ψ_1^P}) := case
  counter < i : FALSE;
  v_{ψ_1^P}   : TRUE;
  v^i_{ψ_1^P} : TRUE;
  TRUE  : FALSE;
esac
```

In Fig. 2, we describe the execution of all the steps described so far on a simple formula.

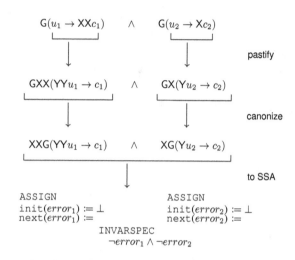

Figure 2. The execution of the sequence of steps: a simple example.

Proposition 5: Let be a canonical $\mathsf{PastLTL_{EBR}}$ formula, with $| | = n$. Then, there exists a deterministic SSA of size $\mathcal{O}(n)$ that accepts the same language.

Theorem 1: Let be an $\mathsf{LTL_{EBR}}$ formula, with $| | = n$, and let M be the greatest constant in . Then, there exists a deterministic SSA of size $\mathcal{O}(n^3 \cdot M^{\log_2 n + 1})$ that accepts the same language.

Corollary 1: Let be an $\mathsf{LTL_{EBR}}$ formula with no constants, with $| | = n$. Then, there exists a deterministic SSA of size $\mathcal{O}(n^3)$ that accepts the same language.

V. SOLVING THE GAME ON THE SYMBOLIC DETERMINISTIC AUTOMATON

Once we have obtained the deterministic SSA $\mathcal{A}(\ )$ for an $\mathsf{LTL_{EBR}}$ formula with the steps described in the previous sections, we can use $\mathcal{A}(\ )$ as the arena of a two-player game between Controller and Environment in order to solve the realizability (and synthesis) problem for .

Let us focus on the *safety game* $G = \langle \mathcal{A}(\ )\ C\ \mathcal{U} \rangle$ (recall Def. 6). Safety games have been extensively studied, as their reachability objective makes the problem simpler than considering -regular objectives, such as, for instance, Büchi and Rabin conditions.

The aim of Controller is to choose an infinite sequence of *controllable* variables in such a way that, no matter what values for the *uncontrollable* variables are chosen by Environment, *the trace induced by the play in* $\mathcal{A}(\ )$ *is safe*, that is, it visits only states s such that $s \models S(X)$ (see Def. 6). Since in our case

$\mathcal{A}(\ )$ recognizes exactly the language of $\ $, the play satisfies $\ $, and thus Controller has a winning strategy for $\ $.

Since the organization of the SYNTCOMP [14], many optimized tools have been proposed in the literature to solve safety games. For this reason, we chose to use a safety synthesizer as a black box. The majority of these tools accept as input a symbolic arena described in terms of and-inverter graphs (or AIGER format [1]), so we provide a simple utility to obtain the AIGER representation of *functional* SMV modules, that is, SMV modules with the transition relation expressed only in terms of ASSIGN statements, such as the ones resulting from our encoding. The AIGER model is then given as input to the chosen safety synthesizer, completing the process outlined in Fig. 1.

The next theorem states the complexity of the procedure.

Theorem 2: The realizability problem for LTL_{EBR} belongs to 2EXPTIME. If no constant is admitted, it belongs to EXPTIME.

Proof: We first show that the proposed algorithm, as described in Fig. 1, belongs to 2EXPTIME for generic LTL_{EBR} formulas. It is easy to see that the time complexity of all the steps matches their space complexity. Therefore, we have an algorithm to turn an LTL_{EBR} formula $\ $ into an equivalent deterministic SSA $\mathcal{A}(\ )$ whose time complexity is $\mathcal{O}(n^3 \cdot M^{\log_2 n+1})$, where $n = |\ |$ and M is the greatest constant in $\ $. Since $\mathcal{A}(\ )$ is symbolically represented, it can be turned into an explicit automaton $\mathcal{A}'(\ )$ of size at most exponential in the size of $\mathcal{A}(\ )$, that is, $|\mathcal{A}'(\ )| \in \mathcal{O}(2^{n^3 \cdot M^{\log_2 n+1}})$. Finally, the time complexity of reachability games is *linear* in the size of the arena [9], and thus the overall time complexity of the realizability problem for LTL_{EBR} is 2EXPTIME. If no constant is admitted, then, by Corollary 1, $|\mathcal{A}'(\ )| \in \mathcal{O}(2^{n^3})$, and the complexity becomes EXPTIME. ∎

Comparison with Safety LTL

It is interesting to brie y compare the proposed procedure for realizability to the one used by the Ssyft tool for Safety LTL specifications [25]. In that tool, the negation of the initial formula is first translated into first-order logic over finite words and then transformed into deterministic automata using the tool MONA [12], which uses the classical subset construction to determinize automata over finite words. Finally, Ssyft uses the classical backward fixpoint iteration to compute the set of winning states over the DFA. It is worth to notice that the way MONA represents automata is *not* fully symbolic: the set of states is explicitly represented, while it uses a BDD for each pair of states in order to represent symbolically the transitions between the two corresponding states. In contrast of subset construction, our solution performs the pastification of full-bounded formulas. Most importantly, our construction of deterministic monitors is carried out in a fully symbolic way.

VI. EXPERIMENTAL EVALUATION

We implemented the proposed procedure (see Fig. 1) in a tool called ebr-ltl-synth.[1] The transformation from LTL_{EBR} to

[1] http://users.dimi.uniud.it/~luca.geatti/tools/ebrltlsynth.html

deterministic SSA together with the translation to AIGER has been implemented inside the nuXmv model checker [6]. As the backend for solving the safety game, we have chosen the SAT-based tool demiurge [2].

We tested our tool on a set of scalable benchmarks divided in four categories (the propositional atoms starting with the letter c are controllable, while those starting with the letter u are uncontrollable):

1) the first category is generated by the realizable formula:

$$G(c_0 \wedge XG(c_1 \wedge \cdots \wedge X^n G(c_n \vee u)\ ))$$

2) the second category is generated by the realizable formula:

$$G((c_0 \vee u_0) \wedge XG((c_1 \vee u_1) \wedge \cdots \wedge X^n G((c_n \vee u_n))\ ))$$

3) the third category is generated by the unrealizable formula:

$$G(c) \wedge \bigvee_{i=1}^{n} G(\bigwedge_{j=0}^{i} u_i)$$

4) the fourth category is generated by the unrealizable formula:

$$c \wedge \bigwedge_{i=1}^{n} X^i(u_i \vee u_{i+1})$$

Each category contains the respective scalable formula for $n \in [1\ 200]$, for a total of 800 benchmarks, half of which is realizable and the other half is unrealizable. We set a timeout of 180 seconds for each benchmark. We compared ebr-ltl-synth with ltlsynt [13], Strix [19] and Ssyft [25]. The first two tools solve the realizability and synthesis problems for full LTL and are based on a translation to parity games. ltlsynt uses SPOT [10] for efficient translation and manipulation of automata. Strix implements several optimizations like specification splitting, that enables to split the initial formula in safety, co-safety, Büchi, and co-Büchi subformulas and speeds up the process of solving of the game. On the contrary, Ssyft solves the realizability problem for specifications written in Safety LTL (see Sec. V for a brief description of the Ssyft tool).

For realizability, we tested all the tools in their sequential configurations. ltlsynt has two sequential configurations, which differ on whether the split of actions into Controller's and Environment's ones is performed before or after the determinization. Strix has two sequential modes as well, depending on the kind of search on the arena (depth-first for the first configuration and with a priority queue for the second). Ssyft and ebr-ltl-synth have only one configuration.

Fig. 3 shows the outcomes of the comparison between ebr-ltl-synth and the best configuration of ltlsynt: it can be clearly seen that, for both realizable and unrealizable formulas, ltlsynt presents an exponential blow-up in the solving time that is avoided by ebr-ltl-synth. Fig. 4 compares ebr-ltl-synth with the best configuration of Strix: while for realizable formulas there is an exponential blow up of Strix avoided by ebr-ltl-synth, it is interesting to note that for the unrealizable benchmarks the difference between the solving time of the two tools is linear, mostly showing a 10x improvement in favor of ebr-ltl-synth.

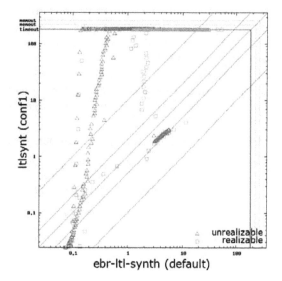

Figure 3. ebr-ltl-synth vs ltlsynt (first conf.) on all scalable benchmarks.

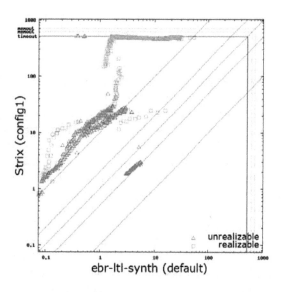

Figure 4. ebr-ltl-synth vs Strix on all scalable benchmarks.

The survival plots for the set of realizable and unrealizable scalable benchmarks are shown in Figs. 5 and 6, respectively.

The outcomes of the comparison between ebr-ltl-synth and Ssyft are shown in Fig. 7. The three lines near the sides of the figure correspond to *timeouts* (the solid black line), *memouts* for unrealizable benchmarks and *memouts* for realizable benchmarks (the dotted lines). It can be noticed that Ssyft reaches a memory out for the vast majority of benchmarks. For instance, on both the realizable categories, Ssyft reaches the first memout with $n = 7$. As for the unrealizable benchmarks, on the third category, Ssyft reaches the first memout with $n = 36$, while for the fourth category with $n = 59$. This is due to MONA, which is not able to build the (explicit) DFA for the

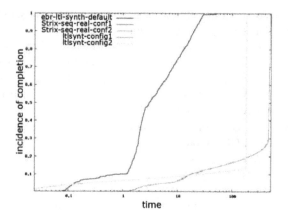

Figure 5. Survival plot for realizable scalable benchmarks.

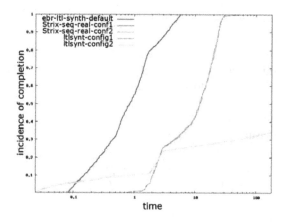

Figure 6. Survival plot for unrealizable scalable benchmarks.

(negation of the) initial specification[2]. This is an important hint about the use of *fully symbolic* techniques for the representation of automata, like the one of ebr-ltl-synth, as in many cases they can avoid an exponential blowup of the automata' state space. The survival plot between ebr-ltl-synth and Ssyft is shown in Fig. 8[3]. The rest of the plots for realizability of scalable benchmarks can be found in [8].

In addition to these scalable formulas, from the benchmarks of SYNTCOMP [14], we filtered the formulas that belong to LTL_{EBR}: this resulted into a set of 29 formulas. The survival plot showing the comparison with ltlsynt and Strix is shown in Fig. 9, while the comparison with Ssyft is shown in Fig. 10. It is interesting to see that, on the SYNTCOMP benchmarks, the results of ebr-ltl-synth and Ssyft are comparable.

As for the synthesis problem, once a specification is found to be realizable, all the tools except for Ssyft produce a strategy as a witness: this strategy is in the form of an and-inverter graph whose input bits are only the starting uncontrollable variables. Often, such a strategy can be minimized by using logic

---

[2]We point out that in some cases, like in the fourth category for $n \geq 60$, MONA's memouts are due to its parser.

[3]The reason why we do not have a single survival plot comparing all the four tools is that Ssyft could not have been compiled for the same platform as the others, due to issues with its source code.

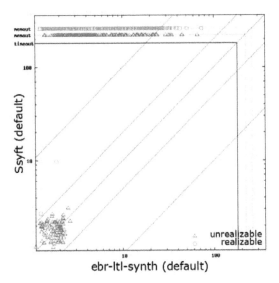

Figure 7. ebr-ltl-synth vs Ssyft on scalable benchmarks.

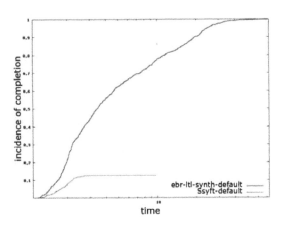

Figure 8. Survival plot for ebr-ltl-synth and Ssyft on scalable benchmarks.

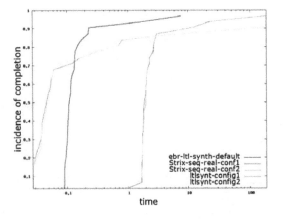

Figure 9. Survival plot for SYNTCOMP benchmarks.

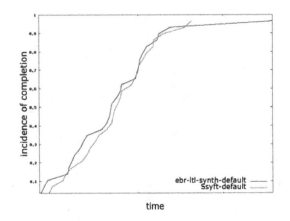

Figure 10. Survival plot for ebr-ltl-synth and Ssyft on SYNTCOMP benchmarks.

synthesis tools (like ABC [3]) as black-box. In the particular case of ebr-ltl-synth, ltlsynt and Strix, they all use a separate logic synthesizer as black box, with different configurations to minimize the strategy. Therefore, we do not compare the size of the resulting strategies, since such a comparison would add nothing about the methods implemented by the tools but would rather compare their backends.

VII. Conclusions

In this paper, we introduce the logic LTL_{EBR}, a fragment of LTL that combines formulas with only bounded operators and a particular combination of universal unbounded temporal operators. We focus on the realizability and reactive synthesis problems for this logic. The main contribution is a *fully symbolic* translation from any LTL_{EBR} formula to a *deterministic* symbolic safety automaton on infinite words. The process applies a pastification step and a set of rules to reach a canonical form for LTL_{EBR} formulas. The realizability is then decided by solving a safety game on the arena represented by the automaton. We first showed that realizability for LTL_{EBR}

belongs to 2EXPTIME, but drops to EXPTIME if no constants are used. Then, we implemented the proposed procedure in a tool, whose experimental evaluation revealed very good performance against tools for realizability and synthesis of full LTL and Safety LTL specifications.

As a future development of this line of work, we believe that the translation from LTL_{EBR} to deterministic SSA may provide many benefits in the context of *symbolic model checking* as well, since the search of the state space could benefit from a deterministic representation of the automaton for the formula [23]. On the automata construction side, an interesting development would be to keep the symbolic bounds during pastification and monitor construction, without, for instance, expanding $X^i\alpha$ into i nested *next* operators. On the expressiveness side, we want to study in which ways *assumptions* can be integrated into LTL_{EBR}. Last but not least, we aim at checking whether the synthesis problem for more expressive logics, like, for instance, LTL, can be reduced to the synthesis problem for LTL_{EBR}, for example checking whether it is possible to use LTL_{EBR} for solving the safety problems originated from *bounded synthesis* techniques.

Acknowledgments: The authors want to thank all the anonymous reviewers of FMCAD 2020 for the insightful comments on a preliminary version of this paper.

REFERENCES

[1] Biere, A., Heljanko, K., Wieringa, S.: Aiger 1.9 and beyond. Available at fmv. jku. at/hwmcc11/beyond1. pdf (2011)

[2] Bloem, R., Könighofer, R., Seidl, M.: Sat-based synthesis methods for safety specs. In: International Conference on Verification, Model Checking, and Abstract Interpretation. pp. 1–20. Springer (2014)

[3] Brayton, R., Mishchenko, A.: ABC: An academic industrial-strength verification tool. In: International Conference on Computer Aided Verification. pp. 24–40. Springer (2010)

[4] Büchi, J.R.: On a decision method in restricted second order arithmetic. In: The collected works of J. Richard Büchi, pp. 425–435. Springer (1990)

[5] Buchi, J.R., Landweber, L.H.: Solving sequential conditions by finite-state strategies. In: The Collected Works of J. Richard Büchi, pp. 525–541. Springer (1990)

[6] Cavada, R., Cimatti, A., Dorigatti, M., Griggio, A., Mariotti, A., Micheli, A., Mover, S., Roveri, M., Tonetta, S.: The nuxmv symbolic model checker. In: International Conference on Computer Aided Verification. pp. 334–342. Springer (2014)

[7] Church, A.: Logic, arithmetic, and automata. In: Proceedings of the international congress of mathematicians. vol. 1962, pp. 23–35 (1962)

[8] Cimatti, A., Geatti, L., Gigante, N., Montanari, A., Tonetta, S.: Reactive synthesis from extended bounded response LTL specifications (2020), https://arxiv.org/abs/2008.05335, Extended Version on *arXiv*

[9] De Alfaro, L., Henzinger, T.A., Kupferman, O.: Concurrent reachability games. Theoretical Computer Science **386**(3), 188–217 (2007)

[10] Duret-Lutz, A., Lewkowicz, A., Fauchille, A., Michaud, T., Renault, E., Xu, L.: Spot 2.0—a framework for LTL and ω-automata manipulation. In: International Symposium on Automated Technology for Verification and Analysis. pp. 122–129. Springer (2016)

[11] Finkbeiner, B., Schewe, S.: Bounded synthesis. International Journal on Software Tools for Technology Transfer **15**(5-6), 519–539 (2013)

[12] Henriksen, J.G., Jensen, J., Jørgensen, M., Klarlund, N., Paige, R., Rauhe, T., Sandholm, A.: Mona: Monadic second-order logic in practice. In: International Workshop on Tools and Algorithms for the Construction and Analysis of Systems. pp. 89–110. Springer (1995)

[13] Jacobs, S., Bloem, R.: The 5th reactive synthesis competition-syntcomp 2018

[14] Jacobs, S., Bloem, R., Brenguier, R., Ehlers, R., Hell, T., Könighofer, R., Pérez, G.A., Raskin, J.F., Ryzhyk, L., Sankur, O., et al.: The first reactive synthesis competition (syntcomp 2014). International journal on software tools for technology transfer **19**(3), 367–390 (2017)

[15] Kupferman, O., Vardi, M.Y.: Safraless decision procedures. In: 46th Annual IEEE Symposium on Foundations of Computer Science (FOCS'05). pp. 531–540. IEEE (2005)

[16] Leucker, M., Schallhart, C.: A brief account of runtime verification. The Journal of Logic and Algebraic Programming **78**(5), 293–303 (2009)

[17] Maler, O., Nickovic, D., Pnueli, A.: Real time temporal logic: Past, present, future. In: International Conference on Formal Modeling and Analysis of Timed Systems. pp. 2–16. Springer (2005)

[18] Maler, O., Nickovic, D., Pnueli, A.: On synthesizing controllers from bounded-response properties. In: International Conference on Computer Aided Verification. pp. 95–107. Springer (2007)

[19] Meyer, P.J., Sickert, S., Luttenberger, M.: Strix: Explicit reactive synthesis strikes back! In: International Conference on Computer Aided Verification. pp. 578–586. Springer (2018)

[20] Piterman, N., Pnueli, A., Sa'ar, Y.: Synthesis of reactive (1) designs. In: International Workshop on Verification, Model Checking, and Abstract Interpretation. pp. 364–380. Springer (2006)

[21] Pnueli, A., Rosner, R.: On the synthesis of an asynchronous reactive module. In: International Colloquium on Automata, Languages, and Programming. pp. 652–671. Springer (1989)

[22] Rosner, R.: Modular synthesis of reactive systems. Ph.D. thesis, PhD thesis, Weizmann Institute of Science (1992)

[23] Sebastiani, R., Tonetta, S.: "More Deterministic" vs. "Smaller" Büchi Automata for Efficient LTL Model Checking. In: Geist, D., Tronci, E. (eds.) CHARME. Lecture Notes in Computer Science, vol. 2860, pp. 126–140. Springer (2003). https://doi.org/10.1007/978-3-540-39724-3_12, https://doi.org/10.1007/978-3-540-39724-3_12

[24] Vardi, M.Y., Wolper, P.: Reasoning about infinite computations. Information and computation **115**(1), 1–37 (1994)

[25] Zhu, S., Tabajara, L.M., Li, J., Pu, G., Vardi, M.Y.: A symbolic approach to safety LTL synthesis. In: Haifa Verification Conference. pp. 147–162. Springer (2017)

2

Automating Compositional Analysis of Authentication Protocols

Zichao Zhang   Arthur Azevedo de Amorim   Limin Jia   Corina S. Pasareanu

Carnegie Mellon University   Carnegie Mellon University   Carnegie Mellon University Carnegie Mellon and NASA Ames

Abstract—**Modern verifiers for cryptographic protocols can analyze sophisticated designs automatically, but require the entire code of the protocol to operate. Compositional techniques, by contrast, allow us to verify each system component separately, against its own guarantees and assumptions about other components and the environment. Compositionality helps protocol design because it explains how the design can evolve and when it can run safely along other protocols and programs. For example, it might say that it is safe to add some functionality to a server without having to patch the client. Unfortunately, while compositional frameworks for protocol verification do exist, they require non-trivial human effort to identify specifications for the components of the system, thus hindering their adoption.**

To address these shortcomings, we investigate techniques for automated, compositional analysis of authentication protocols, using automata-learning techniques to synthesize assumptions for protocol components. We report preliminary results on the Needham-Schroeder-Lowe protocol, where our synthesized assumption was capable of lowering verification time while also allowing us to verify protocol variants compositionally.

I. INTRODUCTION

Cryptographic protocols are notoriously difficult to design, yet their correctness is crucial to ensure the security of software systems. Formal methods are thus valuable, as they can reveal critical bugs before these systems are deployed. Automated tools (ProVerif [1], CryptoVerif [2], Tamarin [3], Maude-NPA [4], etc.) are particularly interesting, as they allow us to focus on modeling the protocol rather than proving its correctness. Although these tools have been applied to ambitious case studies [5], [6], [7], [8], [9], they suffer from one important drawback: they offer little support for compositional reasoning. To verify a property, we must supply the entire protocol model at once, rather than verifying each component of the protocol against self-contained partial specifications. This is unsatisfactory, since a non-compositional analysis works under a *closed-world* assumption that provides few guarantees for when the protocol is itself a component of a larger system—for example, using a private key to sign and encrypt data simultaneously can expose vulnerabilities that are absent if only one of the functionalities is used. Furthermore, decomposition can help speed up verification and guide protocol design when components are modified, or even perhaps *removed*, in case we want to de-bloat an existing protocol without breaking its security.

We envision a future where we can combine the power of compositional reasoning with the convenience of automation. As a first step in this direction, we consider how protocol analysis can benefit from off-the-shelf, automated compositional verification tools. To illustrate, suppose that we have a complex system $M_1 \, M_2$, obtained by composing simpler pieces M_1 and M_2. We would like to show that $M_1 \, M_2$ satisfies a specification P: $M_1 \, M_2 \models P$. Rather than proving P directly, we can resort to the following *assume-guarantee rule*:

$$\frac{Q \, M_1 \, P \qquad true \, M_2 \, Q}{M_1 \, M_2 \models P} \qquad (R1)$$

This rule says that we can prove P by finding an *assumption* Q such that (1) P holds on M_1, assuming that Q holds on the rest of the system; and (2) the component M_2 guarantees that Q holds. Though it can be challenging to craft a suitable Q by hand, prior work [10], [11] shows that it can be inferred with L [12], an automaton learning algorithm, even for systems with multiple components.

We report preliminary results on the analysis of the Needham-Schroeder protocol [13] and its subsequent correction by Lowe [14] (dubbed NS and NSL, for short). We developed models of the protocols for a version of the LTSA model checker [15] extended with automaton learning [10], and used this infrastructure to synthesize assumptions to verify the protocol. Our focus is on *agreement properties*, also known as *correspondence properties* [16], [17], which say that when authentication is complete the participants are indeed talking to whom they think they are talking to.

One obstacle for the formal analysis of security protocols is dealing with rich attacker behavior. A popular threat model is the *symbolic* (or *Dolev-Yao* [18]) paradigm, which says that the attacker has complete control over the network, but is constrained by standard cryptographic assumptions. Thus, the attacker might be able to shuffle, drop or replay messages, but cannot decrypt a message without the corresponding key. To ease the modeling of such threats, we developed *Taglierino*, a domain-specific language for describing protocols and attacker behavior as LTSA automata.

Taglierino requires users to bound the possible attacker behaviors to ensure that its output is finite and it can be analyzed by LTSA. (Any attack can in principle be found with Taglierino if we make this bound large enough.) Though finite, we observed that Dolev-Yao attackers produced in this way require a large number of states (>700k) to cover interesting behaviors. Synthesizing component assumptions directly using such attackers leads to bloated assumptions that are expensive to check and hard to interpret. To facilitate a compositional analysis of NSL, we perform a first decomposition step where we generate assumptions about the behavior of the attacker using *alphabet refinement* [10]. This decomposition shows that we can replace the attacker by a much simpler one (3 rather than 700k states). We use this refined attacker to generate assumptions for the initiator of the protocol. The assumptions are small (10–20 states), so they can be examined by decomposition and used for checking replaced components.

The rest of this paper proceeds as follows. After a quick overview of the NS protocol and how it is modeled in Taglierino (Section II), we present our analysis of the protocol in Section III, explaining how we generated assumptions for the protocol initiator and used them to verify protocol variants and detect bugs. We discuss related work in Section IV and conclude in Section V.

II. AN OVERVIEW OF NS

The Needham-Schroder public key protocol [13] is intended to provide mutual authentication of two agents, Alice (A) and Bob (B). The protocol can be summarized as follows:

$$(1) \quad A \quad S : A \ B$$
$$(2) \quad S \quad A : B \ pk_B \ sk_S$$
$$(3) \quad A \quad B : n_A \ A \ pk_B$$
$$(4) \quad B \quad S : B \ A$$
$$(5) \quad S \quad B : A \ pk_A \ sk_S$$
$$(6^*) \quad B \quad A : n_A \ n_B \ pk_A$$
$$(7) \quad A \quad B : n_B \ pk_B$$

Alice starts by contacting the key server S asking for Bob's public key pk_B. The server returns this information to Alice signed with its own secret key sk_S, to prove that pk_B is authentic. Then, Alice encrypts a fresh cryptographic nonce n_A and sends it to Bob, along her own identity. Bob asks the key server for Alice's public key pk_A, and then sends n_A back to Alice along another fresh nonce n_B, all of this encrypted with Alice's key. Finally, Alice acknowledges the end of the handshake to Bob by sending him n_B back. (The protocol turns out to contain a vulnerability in message (6); we'll come back to this shortly.)

The intended specification for the protocol can be informally stated as follows:

> When Alice receives Message 6, she knows that Bob accepted her connection.
> When Bob receives Message 7, he knows that Alice has tried to contact him.

To formalize this property, we model the behavior of the system as a series of finite automata running in parallel. Each automaton defines a language of traces over the following alphabet:

$send_i(m)$: The agent i has sent the message m over the network.
$recv_i(m)$: The agent i has received the message m from the network.

```
agent "Alice" $ do
  hostX <- receive
  begin "authAB" hostX
  send [alice, hostX]
  sig <- receive
  [pkX, host] <- checkSign spkS sig
  when (host == hostX) $ do
    send $ aenc pkX [na, alice]
    m <- receive
    [nx, ny] <- adec skA m
    if (nx == na) then
        send $ aenc pkX ny
    else fail "nonce_mismatch"
```

Fig. 1: Implementation of Alice in NS.

$begin_i(e \ m)$: The agent i claims that the event e has begun, using the data item m as an identifier.
$end_i(e \ m)$: The agent i claims that the event e has ended, using the data item m as an identifier.

Messages and data items are drawn from a set *Term* that contains an infinite supply of nonces, cryptographic keys, encrypted messages, etc. To keep the models finite, we restrict this set to a finite subset A *Term* of *allowed terms*. Our goal is to prove *agreement* [16], [17]: if an event of the form $end_i(e \ m)$ occurs in an execution trace, then the trace has an earlier occurrence of the event $begin_j(e \ m)$. For instance, Alice might emit $begin_A(auth_{AB} \ B)$ at the beginning of the protocol to signal that she wishes to communicate with Bob, and Bob would emit $end_B(auth_{AB} \ B)$ after receiving $n_B \ pk_B$ to indicate that the connection was successful.

Each protocol participant corresponds to a finite automaton. These automata are specified in Taglierino using a domain-specific language similar to process calculi used in protocol verification [1], [19]. Figure 1 shows the model of Alice in Taglierino. A preamble, not shown in the figure, declares constants such as the nonce na, Alice's identity alice, Alice's private key skA, and Server's public signature key spkS. Alice communicates with the network using send and receive. The first received message (hostX <- receive) means that Alice is willing to run the protocol with any other agent chosen by the network. Upon sending or receiving from the network, Alice can manipulate messages using cryptographic primitives; for example, aenc and adec stand for asymmetric encryption and decryption and checkSign is for checking the signature.

The protocol implementation in Taglierino is compiled down to models for the LTSA model checker [15]. In addition to the honest agents, our compiler generates another automaton that describes how messages are transmitted in the network. This transmission follows the symbolic model of cryptography [18]: an agent i can receive a message m if and only if the predicate $knows(M \ m)$ holds, where M is the set of messages that have been sent to the network up to that point. Intuitively, this amounts to assuming that an attacker can intercept all messages sent in the network and gets to decide what is delivered in the end, potentially tampering with the result. The definition of *knows* is standard; for instance it includes the following clauses

$$\frac{m \in M}{knows(M, m)}$$

$$\frac{knows(M, sk(k)) \qquad knows(M, \{m\}pk(k))}{knows(M, m)},$$

which say that the attacker can always reproduce messages it has previous seen, and also decrypt a message m if it can extract the corresponding decryption key $sk(k)$ from its knowledge. The network automaton does not have *begin* or *end* events in its alphabet, since those are controlled by the honest agents of the system.

III. ANALYZING THE PROTOCOL

When Bob receives $\{n_B\}pk_B$, he thinks that Alice has decided to contact him because there is no other way he could have received this message: the nonce n_B was freshly generated, and only Alice has the power to decrypt the encrypted message $\{n_A, n_B\}pk_B$. Unfortunately, this reasoning is flawed: an attack found by Lowe [14] shows that Alice could have really meant to contact a malicious third party Mallory (M), who uses Alice's messages to trick Bob into believing he is communicating with Alice directly. If Bob implements a banking service, for example, this might allow Mallory to gain access to Alice's account without her permission. The fix found by Lowe is to include Bob's identity in one of the messages:

$$(6) \quad B \to A : \{n_A, n_B, B\}pk_A$$

Lowe's analysis shows that the original sixth message does not have enough information for Alice to know who she is really talking to. This corrected message allows her to stop sending message (7) when she realizes who her contact is.

In this section, we show how we can decompose the resulting NSL protocol in a way that allows us to detect the original flaw and also check the correctness of variants of the protocol, at least in a bounded sense. More precisely, we start by generating an assumption A for Alice in NSL; as a byproduct of this process, we establish the correctness of NSL through the application of (R1). Then, we use A to analyze two variants of the protocol where Alice behaves slightly differently. Since Alice is the only component that changes, we can verify that the variants are correct simply by checking that Alice satisfies the assumption A.

We compare the effort to verify the protocols compositionally and monolithically. Our results (Section III-E) show that compositional verification considerably outperformed monolithic verification when it can reuse the assumption A; if A needs to be regenerated, compositional verification is more

Let M_1 and M_2 be two component in the system and P be the property we want to check. We use αM to denote the alphabet of an component M and Σ_I to denote the interface alphabet, that is, $\Sigma_I = \alpha M_1 \cap \alpha M_2$.

Let σ be an arbitrary trace where σ_n denotes the nth action on trace σ and Σ be a arbitrary set of alphabet, we define

$$find(\Sigma, \sigma) = \begin{cases} \sigma_i, & \text{if } \sigma_i \subseteq \Sigma_I \wedge \sigma_i \not{/} \Sigma \\ \emptyset, & \text{otherwise} \end{cases}$$

where i is the first index scanning from the end of trace σ to the beginning such that the conditions hold.

1) Obtain trace σ from checking $\langle true \rangle M_1 \langle P \rangle$.
2) Initialize $\Sigma = find(\emptyset, \sigma)$.
3) Use the classic learning framework for Σ. If the framework returns true with assumption Q, we report the Q and STOP. When the framework returns false with counterexample trace σ'. This, however, does not necessarily means that $M_1 \parallel M_2$ violates P. Real violations are discovered by the learning framework only if the alphabet is Σ_I and thus we go to the next step.
4) If $find(\Sigma, \sigma')$ returns $\emptyset$, we report false and STOP. If $find(\Sigma, \sigma')$ returns an action a, we update $\Sigma = \Sigma \cup a$ and go to step 3.

Fig. 2: Alphabet refinement process.

Component	#States	#Trans.	Assumption	
			#States	#Trans.
Attacker	775030	4343487	3	178
Alice	14	163	6	69

Fig. 3: Comparison of the original component with its generated assumption, in terms of states and transitions.

expensive. All experiments were performed with a 1.6 GHz Intel Core i5 CPU and 8.0 GB RAM, running 64-bit Ubuntu 18.04 LTS.

A. Generating Assumptions with NSL

Our model of NSL allows all the original messages of the protocol to be exchanged in the network, but includes other terms that enable Lowe's attack in the original NS: $\{n_B\}pk_M$, $\{pk_M, M\}sk_S$, etc. We manually chose these terms by heuristic (i.e.,we took the legitimate messages exchanged by Alice and Bob and scrambled some of the parameters). In total, our model allows 31 messages to be exchanged in the network. When setting up the model, we make sk_M, Mallory's secret key, available to the attacker, while keeping all other private keys secret. We also bounded the attacker to learn at most 4 messages in addition to its initial knowledge.

Attacker	Alice
$send_i(\ n_A\ n_B\ M\ pk_A)$	$send_A(\ n_A\ n_B\ M\ pk_A)$
$send_i(\ n_A\ n_B\ B\ pk_M)$	$send_A(\ n_A\ n_B\ B\ pk_M)$
$send_i(\ n_A\ n_B\ M\ pk_M)$	$send_A(\ n_A\ n_B\ M\ pk_M)$
$send_i(\ n_B\ n_B\ B\ pk_M)$	$send_A(\ n_B\ n_B\ B\ pk_M)$
$send_i(\ n_B\ n_B\ M\ pk_M)$	$send_A(\ n_B\ n_B\ M\ pk_M)$
$send_i(\ n_M\ n_B\ B\ pk_M)$	$send_A(\ n_M\ n_B\ B\ pk_M)$
$send_i(\ n_M\ n_B\ M\ pk_M)$	$send_A(\ n_M\ n_B\ M\ pk_M)$
$send_i(\ n_B\ pk_B)$	$send_A(\ n_B\ pk_B)$
$send_i(\ n_B\ pk_M)$	$send_A(\ n_B\ pk_M)$
$send_i(\ B\ pk_B\ sk_S)$	$send_A(\ B\ pk_B\ sk_S)$
$recv_i(\ n_A\ n_B\ M\ pk_A)$	$recv_A(\ n_A\ n_B\ M\ pk_A)$
$recv_i(\ n_A\ n_B\ B\ pk_M)$	$recv_A(\ n_A\ n_B\ B\ pk_M)$
$recv_i(\ n_A\ n_B\ M\ pk_M)$	$recv_A(\ n_A\ n_B\ M\ pk_M)$
$recv_i(\ n_B\ n_B\ B\ pk_M)$	$recv_A(\ n_B\ n_B\ B\ pk_M)$
$recv_i(\ n_B\ n_B\ M\ pk_M)$	$recv_A(\ n_B\ n_B\ M\ pk_M)$
$recv_i(\ n_M\ n_B\ B\ pk_M)$	$recv_A(\ n_M\ n_B\ B\ pk_M)$
$recv_i(\ n_M\ n_B\ M\ pk_M)$	$recv_A(\ n_M\ n_B\ M\ pk_M)$
$recv_i(\ n_B\ pk_B)$	$recv_A(\ n_B\ pk_B)$
$recv_i(\ n_B\ pk_M)$	$recv_A(\ n_B\ pk_M)$
$recv_i(\ B\ pk_B\ sk_S)$	$recv_A(\ B\ pk_B\ sk_S)$
	$begin_A(auth_{AB}\ B)$
	$begin_A(auth_{AB}\ M)$

Fig. 4: Alphabets of generated assumptions. The identifier i ranges over A and B.

When compiled, our model had a large attacker of more than 700k states. To obtain a more tractable model, we decomposed the system to generate an assumption for the attacker (i.e. letting $M_1 = Alice\ Bob\ Server$ and $M_2 = Attacker$ in rule (R1)). To facilitate learning, we used *alphabet re nement* [10], a technique that generates more compact assumptions by limiting the possible interactions between components. Roughly speaking, alphabet refinement consists in gradually adding actions to the interface of M_1 and M_2 until we successfully generate a sound assumption for the attacker or manage to prove that the property did not hold. (Figure 2 describes this process in more detail.)

After refinement, we further decomposed the system using the assumption on the attacker to generate an assumption for Alice. Figure 3 shows the size of the original components with their generated assumption; Figure 4 shows the alphabets. The fact that we were able to generate an assumption for Alice means that the NSL protocol satisfies agreement. We will now see how this generated assumption facilitates the analysis of protocol variants.

B. Finding Lowe s Flaw in NS

We modified Alice in NSL such that the agent identity in message (6) is not checked. The behavior of the modified protocol is equivalent to the original NS and allows Alice, while

thinking she is contacting Mallory, to accept the message:

$$(6)\ B\quad A:\ n_A\ n_B\ B\ pk_A$$

and continue with:

$$(7)\ A\quad M:\ n_B\ pk_M$$

This behavior enables Lowe's attack on NS, which we rediscovered by checking the modified Alice against the assumption generated in the previous section.

In principle, it is possible this method yields a spurious counterexample. The automaton learning technique generates the weakest assumption for Alice to validate agreement, but the assumption was computed using an *abstraction* that has more behaviors than the original attacker, and thus imposes more restrictions on Alice than would be necessary. To rule out the possibility that our counterexample is spurious, we double-check that it can be produced by this variant of NSL. Even when combined with the time to recheck the counterexample, the time spent to find this bug compositionally was much smaller than the time spent on monolithic bug finding, thus strengthening the case for compositional verification.

C. Serverless NSL

A common simplification of NSL is to assume that Alice knows the keys of the agents she wants to contact from the start. This amounts to removing the communication between Alice and Server (messages (1) and (2)). We were capable of verifying this version of Alice against our previously generated assumption, thus confirming that this serverless variant of NSL is correct.

D. Interpreting the Assumptions

Figure 3 shows that assumption learning with alphabet refinement was capable of significantly abstracting the behavior of the attacker and of Alice, yielding automata that are much smaller in terms of the number of states and the number of transitions. The alphabets of the assumptions (Figure 4) list the actions that must be controlled for the property to hold; removing them from the alphabet has the effect of allowing the attacker to freely perform those actions, regardless of whether a send action was triggered by an honest agent or of whether the attacker had enough knowledge to deliver a message.

The only difference between the alphabet for Alice and for the Attacker is that the Attacker alphabet includes actions for Bob, whereas Alice's includes her *begin* events. Most of the controlled actions are variants of (6) encrypted with pk_M. If the attacker is free to forge such messages indiscriminately, he is capable of learning the nonce n_B even before Bob is contacted by Alice or Mallory. When this is true, the attacker has all the information needed to impersonate Alice and break agreement. (Note that we didn't include n_B in the allowed set of messages, so it is not possible for the attacker to learn this value directly.) Interestingly, the expected message (6)

Protocol	Attack	Compile time(ms)	#States Attacker	Monolithic verification			Compositional verification			
				#States	#Transitions	Time(ms)	#States	#Transitions	Time(ms)	
NSL public key [14]	No	2851	775030	388	2738	8	18	163	1	*
NS public key [13]	Yes [14]	2674	775030	10880	102449	97	19 (3104)	164 (22979)	1 (22)	**
NSL public key (variant)	No	2182	775030	9792	86094	115	13	99	1	

Fig. 5: Experimental results (cf. Section III-E)

in a normal run of the protocol, n_A n_B B pk_A, is not in the alphabet. Intuitively, since the attacker does not control pk_A, the only thing he can do with this message is relaying it to Alice. If Alice meant to talk to Bob anyway, she will eventually trigger *begin* and send her response (7) to Bob, which does not pose any harm for agreement. Otherwise, if she meant to talk to Mallory, receiving this message will trigger a mismatch between Bob's identity and Mallory's; thus, she'll stop running and never send (7) to Bob.

E. Results

Figure 5 summarizes the results of verifying the three variants of NSL above. Each row describes:

whether the variant is vulnerable to an attack;
how long it took to compile the various automata produced by Taglierino;
the number of states in the attacker component;
results for monolithic verification: the number of states and transitions of the compiled automata, as well as the time spent to verify them;
results for compositional verification: the number of states and transitions of the compiled automata used to check that Alice satisfies the generated assumption, as well as the time to perform this check.

Note that the results of compositional verification for the first row (*) are somewhat redundant, since the system is automatically verified as a byproduct of generating the assumptions. We included those numbers for completeness. In each column under the results of compositional verification for the second row (**), the first number refers to the process of generating the counterexample, whereas the second number refers to the process of rechecking it, as explained in Section III-B. In all cases, we observe that compositional verification requires substantially fewer resources than monolithic verification. However, these numbers do not include the time spent to generate Alice's assumption, which amounts to approximately 5 minutes, implying that the benefits of compositional verification mostly apply when we expect to reuse the generated assumptions for several protocol variants.

IV. RELATED WORK

Compositional verification and assume-guarantee reasoning [20], [21], [22], [23], [24] have been studied extensively, as a way to address the state-space explosion problem in model checking [25]. Progress has been made in automating compositional reasoning using learning and abstraction-refinement techniques for iterative building of the necessary assumptions [11], [10], [26]. Other learning-based approaches

for automating assumption generation have been proposed as well, e.g. [27], [28], [29], [30], with many other research works to follow.

All this work was done in the context of applying automated compositional verification to general-purpose software. While there have been many model checkers that target security protocols, for example [31] surveys a number of them and [32], [33] have been applied to Needham-Schroeder protocol, they all verify the entire protocol at once. In fact, there is relatively little research on compositional analysis of security protocols, which pose special challenges due to the complexity introduced by the attacker model. Among the most prominent works in this direction is Protocol Compositional Logic (PCL) [34], a logic and system for proving security properties of network protocols. PCL supports compositional reasoning about complex security protocols and has been applied to a number of industry standards including SSL/TLS, IEEE 802.11 i and Kerberos V5. Despite its success, PCL is limited by the large amount of manual effort that is involved in performing the proofs. Other tools can use the help of humans to guide the proving effort with intermediate lemmas; examples include the Tamarin [3] and the CryptoVerif provers [2]; however, this functionality still requires the entire protocol code. It would be interesting to investigate how to integrate the properties discovered by our framework in such tools. Tamarin is a natural first candidate for experiments in this area, since it works under the symbolic model, just like Taglierion. CryptoVerif, by contrast, is used for proofs in the computational model of cryptography, which would represent a significant departure from our setting.

V. CONCLUSION AND FUTURE WORK

We have carried out a first experiment towards automating the compositional verification of protocols, using the NS and NSL protocols as a case study. Our results show that synthesized assumptions can be used to verify variants of the original protocol and yield faster checks. We see several promising directions for future work. Besides trying out more case studies, we would like to improve the performance of our assumption generation, which right now takes a few minutes to complete ($/$ 5). It would also be interesting to use the generated assumptions to guide the design and simplification of other protocols, or to incorporate those in manual proofs of correctness.

ACKNOWLEDGMENTS

This work was partially funded by ONR award no. N000141812618.

REFERENCES

[1] B. Blanchet, "An efficient cryptographic protocol verifier based on prolog rules," in *Proceedings of the 14th IEEE Workshop on Computer Security Foundations*, ser. CSFW '01, 2001, p. 82.

[2] ——, "A computationally sound mechanized prover for security protocols," in *Proceedings of the 2006 IEEE Symposium on Security and Privacy*, ser. SP '06, 2006, p. 140–154.

[3] B. Schmidt, S. Meier, C. Cremers, and D. Basin, "Automated analysis of Diffie-Hellman protocols and advanced security properties," in *Proceedings of the 2012 IEEE 25th Computer Security Foundations Symposium*, ser. CSF '12, 2012, p. 78–94.

[4] S. Escobar, C. Meadows, and J. Meseguer, "Maude-NPA: Cryptographic protocol analysis modulo equational properties," in *Foundations of Security Analysis and Design V*, 2009, pp. 1–50.

[5] K. Bhargavan, B. Blanchet, and N. Kobeissi, "Verified models and reference implementations for the TLS 1.3 standard candidate," in *2017 IEEE Symposium on Security and Privacy (SP)*, 2017, pp. 483–502.

[6] B. Blanchet, "Symbolic and computational mechanized verification of the ARINC823 avionic protocols," in *2017 IEEE 30th Computer Security Foundations Symposium (CSF)*, 2017, pp. 68–82.

[7] J. Whitefield, L. Chen, R. Sasse, S. Schneider, H. Treharne, and S. Wesemeyer, "A symbolic analysis of ecc-based direct anonymous attestation," in *2019 IEEE European Symposium on Security and Privacy (EuroS&P)*, 2019, pp. 127–141.

[8] D. Basin, J. Dreier, L. Hirschi, S. Radomirovic, R. Sasse, and V. Stettler, "A formal analysis of 5G authentication," in *Proceedings of the 2018 ACM SIGSAC Conference on Computer and Communications Security*, ser. CCS '18, 2018, p. 1383–1396.

[9] N. Kobeissi, K. Bhargavan, and B. Blanchet, "Automated verification for secure messaging protocols and their implementations: A symbolic and computational approach," in *2017 IEEE European Symposium on Security and Privacy (EuroS&P)*, 2017, pp. 435–450.

[10] C. S. Pasareanu, D. Giannakopoulou, M. G. Bobaru, J. M. Cobleigh, and H. Barringer, "Learning to divide and conquer: Applying the L* algorithm to automate assume-guarantee reasoning," *Form. Methods Syst. Des.*, p. 175–205, 2008.

[11] J. M. Cobleigh, D. Giannakopoulou, and C. S. Pasareanu, "Learning assumptions for compositional verification," in *Proceedings of the 9th International Conference on Tools and Algorithms for the Construction and Analysis of Systems*, ser. TACAS'03, 2003, p. 331–346.

[12] D. Angluin, "Learning regular sets from queries and counterexamples," *Inf. Comput.*, p. 87–106, 1987.

[13] R. M. Needham and M. D. Schroeder, "Using encryption for authentication in large networks of computers," *Commun. ACM*, p. 993–999, 1978.

[14] G. Lowe, "Breaking and fixing the Needham-Schroeder public-key protocol using FDR," in *Proceedings of the Second International Workshop on Tools and Algorithms for Construction and Analysis of Systems*, ser. TACAs '96, 1996, p. 147–166.

[15] J. Magee and J. Kramer, *State models and Java programs*, 1999.

[16] T. Y. C. Woo and S. S. Lam, "A semantic model for authentication protocols," in *Proceedings of the 1993 IEEE Symposium on Security and Privacy*, ser. SP '93, 1993, p. 178.

[17] G. Lowe, "A hierarchy of authentication specifications," in *Proceedings of the 10th IEEE Workshop on Computer Security Foundations*, ser. CSFW '97, 1997, p. 31.

[18] D. Dolev and A. Yao, "On the security of public key protocols," *IEEE Trans. Inf. Theor.*, p. 198–208, 2006.

[19] M. Abadi and C. Fournet, "Mobile values, new names, and secure communication," in *Proceedings of the 28th ACM SIGPLAN-SIGACT Symposium on Principles of Programming Languages*, ser. POPL '01, 2001, p. 104–115.

[20] J. Misra and K. M. Chandy, "Proofs of networks of processes," *IEEE Trans. Softw. Eng.*, p. 417–426, 1981.

[21] A. Pnueli, *In Transition from Global to Modular Temporal Reasoning about Programs*, 1989, p. 123–144.

[22] K. L. McMillan, "Verification of an implementation of tomasulo's algorithm by compositional model checking," in *Proceedings of the 10th International Conference on Computer Aided Verication*, ser. CAV '98, 1998, p. 110–121.

[23] ——, "Circular compositional reasoning about liveness," in *Proceedings of the 10th IFIP WG 10.5 Advanced Research Working Conference on Correct Hardware Design and Veri cation Methods*, ser. CHARME '99, 1999, p. 342–345.

[24] K. S. Namjoshi and R. J. Trefler, "On the completeness of compositional reasoning methods," *ACM Trans. Comput. Logic*, 2010.

[25] E. M. Clarke, O. Grumberg, and D. A. Peled, *Model Checking*, 2000.

[26] M. Gheorghiu Bobaru, C. S. Pasareanu, and D. Giannakopoulou, "Automated assume-guarantee reasoning by abstraction refinement," in *Proceedings of the 20th International Conference on Computer Aided Veri cation*, ser. CAV '08, 2008, p. 135–148.

[27] S. Chaki, E. M. Clarke, N. Sinha, and P. Thati, "Automated assume-guarantee reasoning for simulation conformance," in *Computer Aided Veri cation, 17th International Conference, CAV 2005, Edinburgh, Scotland, UK, July 6-10, 2005, Proceedings*, 2005, pp. 534–547.

[28] R. Alur, P. Madhusudan, and W. Nam, "Symbolic compositional verification by learning assumptions," in *Proceedings of the 17th International Conference on Computer Aided Veri cation*, ser. CAV'05, 2005, pp. 548–562.

[29] Y.-F. Chen, E. M. Clarke, A. Farzan, M.-H. Tsai, Y.-K. Tsay, and B.-Y. Wang, "Automated assume-guarantee reasoning through implicit learning," in *Proceedings of the 22nd International Conference on Computer Aided Veri cation*, ser. CAV'10, 2010, p. 511–526.

[30] Y.-F. Chen, A. Farzan, E. M. Clarke, Y.-K. Tsay, and B.-Y. Wang, "Learning minimal separating DFA's for compositional verification," in *Proceedings of the 15th International Conference on Tools and Algorithms for the Construction and Analysis of Systems*, 2009, pp. 31–45.

[31] D. A. Basin, C. Cremers, and C. A. Meadows, "Model checking security protocols," in *Handbook of Model Checking*, 2018, pp. 727–762.

[32] X. Luo, Y. Chen, M. Gu, and L. Wu, "Model checking needham-schroeder security protocol based on temporal logic of knowledge," in *Proceedings of the 2009 International Conference on Networks Security, Wireless Communications and Trusted Computing - Volume 02*, ser. NSWCTC '09, 2009, p. 551–554.

[33] D. Basin, C. Cremers, and M. Horvat, "Actor key compromise: Consequences and countermeasures," in *Proceedings of the 2014 IEEE 27th Computer Security Foundations Symposium*, ser. CSF '14, 2014, p. 244–258.

[34] A. Datta, A. Derek, J. C. Mitchell, and A. Roy, "Protocol composition logic (PCL)," *Electron. Notes Theor. Comput. Sci.*, pp. 311–358, 2007.

3

Automating Modular Verification of Secure Information Flow

Lauren Pick*, Grigory Fedyukovich† (iD), Aarti Gupta*

*Princeton University, Princeton, NJ, USA

†Florida State University, Tallahassee, FL, USA

Abstract—Verifying secure information flow by reducing it to safety verification is a popular approach, based on constructing product programs or self-compositions of given programs. However, most such existing efforts are non-modular, i.e., they do not infer relational specifications for procedures in interprocedural programs. Such relational specifications can help to verify security properties in a modular fashion, e.g., for verifying clients of library APIs. They also provide security contracts at procedure boundaries to aid code understanding and maintenance. There has been recent interest in constructing *modular* product programs, but where users are required to provide procedure summaries and related annotations. In this work, we propose to automatically *infer* relational specifications for procedures in modular product programs. Our approach uses syntax-guided synthesis techniques and grammar templates that target verification of secure information flow properties. This enables automation of modular verification for such properties, thereby reducing the annotation burden. We have implemented our techniques on top of a solver for constrained Horn clauses (CHC). Our evaluation demonstrates that our tool is capable of inferring adequate relational specifications for procedures without requiring annotations. Furthermore, it outperforms an existing state-of-the-art hyperproperty verifier and a modular CHC-based verifier on benchmarks with loops or recursion.

Index Terms—Formal verification, information security, model checking

I. INTRODUCTION

The problem of verifying secure information flow is to check that a program does not leak private inputs to public outputs. To solve this problem, one can verify non-interference [1]: for any two runs of a program with the same public inputs but possibly different private inputs, the public outputs of the program are equal. This property is an instance of a *hyperproperty*, i.e., a relational property involving more than one execution of the same program. In practice, non-interference is often too strong a property to enforce. For example, a password recognizer would have its public output be influenced by whether or not the user-provided private input is the correct password. A common approach is to allow values that need to be leaked to be *declassified* [2].

Barthe *et al.* proposed verifying secure information flow by reducing it to safety verification on a product or self-composed

This material is based upon work supported by the National Science Foundation Graduate Research Fellowship Program under Grant No. DGE-1656466. Any opinions, findings, and conclusions or recommendations expressed in this material are those of the author(s) and do not necessarily reflect the views of the National Science Foundation. This work was supported in part by the National Science Foundation award FMitF 1837030.

program [3]. Despite advancements in automated program verifiers, the ability to perform successful safety verification in practice can depend critically on how the product program is constructed. Construction of product programs has thus been a focus in subsequent efforts [4]–[14]. These efforts encompass various syntactic and semantic transformations, heuristics, and use of reinforcement learning for constructing suitable product programs. Some relational property verifiers avoid explicitly constructing product programs altogether [15]–[19].

A. Motivation

In this paper, we address a related but distinct limitation of existing efforts based on reduction to safety. Most such techniques are non-modular, i.e., they neither leverage nor infer *relational specifications for procedures* in interprocedural programs. In general, modular verification offers significant benefits over non-modular techniques – it is inherently more scalable, can provide procedure interface contracts (not only verification results), and can improve code understanding and maintenance. For example, relational specifications of procedures can provide security contracts for library APIs, such as in the S2N implementation of the TLS protocol [20].

A few existing approaches do leverage relational specifications of procedures, but they either restrict both copies of the program to always follow the same control flow [6] or are not automated [8], [21]. In particular, the work by Eilers *et al.* [21] proposes a *modular product program (MPP)* construction, which is suitable for performing *modular* relational program verification. Intutively, this enables reduction to safety on a per-procedure basis without constructing a monolithic product program. In their implementation, VIPER back-end verifiers checked secure-information-flow properties on benchmarks, but each procedure required user-provided relational invariants and related annotations rather than relying on tools to derive them automatically. Placing this annotation burden on users becomes a barrier to automated verification.

In general, deriving sufficient relational invariants for procedures is a challenging problem, and existing off-the-shelf safety verifiers [22]–[28] may not be able to infer them. As we will show, for verifying secure information flow, such invariants often have a special form that is unlikely to be produced by standard interpolation and existing heuristics in these verifiers. For example, our experimental results (§VII) show that SPACER often fails to infer invariants needed to verify information flow in programs with recursion.

B. Overview of Proposed Approach

In this work, we propose to use Syntax-Guided Synthesis (SyGuS) [29] to automatically infer useful relational specifications about information flow in procedures. The structure in information-flow specifications makes them suitable targets for grammar-based enumerative search and synthesis. We have chosen to work with MPPs because they enable *modular* relational verification *and* they allow leveraging existing techniques for construction of suitable product programs within each procedure. We represent an MPP as a set of constrained Horn clauses (CHCs), and our approach automatically infers relational specifications that are sufficient for verifying the program with respect to given security properties. If there are no given security properties, our approach can still infer relational specifications for procedures that are useful for code understanding or subsequent verification.

Our SyGuS-based approach is based on an enumerative search using grammars extracted from program syntax. Enumerate-and-check approaches have been shown to be effective for synthesis of quantifier-free invariants [27], [30]–[32] and more recently quantified invariants for CHCs handling arrays [33]. We show that such an approach is also effective for information-flow properties.

We propose three templates to generate grammars for invariant synthesis: one that expresses quantifier-free information-flow properties, and two that express quantified properties, which are often difficult to handle by existing automated verifiers. Of the latter two, one infers quantified information-flow properties over *arrays*, and the other infers specifications involving the *context* in which a procedure is called, making this template well-suited for inferring properties where declassification has occurred prior to the procedure being called, since the declassified values will be low-security in the callee.

We have implemented our approach in a tool called FLOWER. An evaluation on available benchmark examples demonstrates that it is effective in inferring useful relational specifications of procedures, without requiring any user-provided annotations. We also compared FLOWER with other state-of-the-art tools: a hyperproperty verifier (DESCARTES [15]) and a modular CHC-based verifier (SPACER [25]). Our experiments demonstrate that our tool generally outperforms them, especially on benchmark examples that contain loops or recursion.

In summary, this paper makes the following contributions:

- We propose a SyGuS-based approach for inference of quantifier-free relational specifications for procedures for verifying secure information flow (§IV, §V).
- We propose grammar templates for inferring such specifications with *quantifiers*, which are challenging for existing verifiers (§VI).
- We have implemented our approach in a prototype tool FLOWER and present an evaluation that shows its effectiveness on several benchmarks[1] (§VII).

---

[1] Our tool and translated benchmarks will be made publicly available.

```
main (int[] a, int n) {        main (b1, b2, a1, a2, n1, n2) {
  a := init(a, 0);               a1, a2 := init(b1, b2, a1,
  outputter(a, 0);                               a2, 0, 0);
  return n;                      assert(outputter(b1, b2, a1,
}                                               a2, 0, 0));
                                 return n1, n2;
                               }

init(a, i) {                   init(b1, b2, a1, a2, i1, i2) {
  if (i ≥ 64) return a;          if (¬(b1 ∧ i1 < 64 ∨
  declassify(a[i] = 0);                 b2 ∧ i2 < 64))
  return init(a, i + 1);           return a1, a2;
}                                l1 := b1 ∧ i1 < 64
                                 l2 := b2 ∧ i2 < 64
                                 assume (l1 ∧ l2 ⇒
                                   (a1[i1] = 0) = (a2[i2] = 0));
                                 return
                                   init(l1, l2, a1,
                                        a2, i1 + 1, i2 + 1);
                               }

outputter(a, i) {              outputter(b1, b2, a1, a2, i1, i2) {
  if (i ≥ 64) return;            if (¬(b1 ∧ i1 < 64 ∨
  if (a[i] = 0) {                      b2 ∧ i2 < 64))
    assert(low(a[i]));             return true;
    print(a[i]);                 l1 := b1 ∧ i1 < 64;
  }                              l2 := b2 ∧ i2 < 64;
  outputter(a, i + 1);           t1 := l1 ∧ a1[i1] = 0;
}                                t2 := l2 ∧ a2[i2] = 0;
                                 print(t1, t2, a1[i1], a2[i2]);
                                 ok := t1 ∧ t2 ⇒ a1[i1] = a2[i2];
                                 ok := ok ∧
                                        outputter(b1, b2, a1, a2,
                                                  i1 + 1, i2 + 1);
                                 return ok;
                               }
```

Fig. 1: Example (**left**: original (P), **right**: modular product program (MP)).

To the best of our knowledge, among methods based on product program construction, our work is the first to *automate modular relational verification* for secure information flow.

II. MOTIVATING EXAMPLE

We demonstrate our approach on an example program P shown in Fig. 1, inspired by a related work [34]. In main, a call to init makes initial assumptions about the array a: for each of the first 64 values in the array, the information about whether or not the value is 0 is declassified recursively. Then, these 64 entries are printed out by the recursive procedure outputter, which contains an assertion that checks that each of the values printed out is public (i.e., low-security) output. Finally, main returns its second argument.

The security primitives used in this example are low, which is a predicate that holds iff its argument is a low-security variable, and declassify, which has the effect of making the value of its argument low-security after the point where declassify is invoked. Without assumptions stating otherwise (i.e., either assume statements that indicate that a value is low-security by using the low primitive or declassify statements), we assume that all inputs are high-security. In the example, after init is called and it declassifies each a[i] = 0 value for i < 64, then the information about whether or not any of the first 64 entries in a is 0 is considered to be public information. The outputter procedure prints out the value of values of a[i] for i < 64 only under the condition that a[i] = 0. This behavior leaks exactly only the declassified information, so the assertion is expected to hold for each call to `outputter`.

The modular product program `MP` for this example is shown in Fig. 1 (right). Note that for *each* variable in `P` (even if irrelevant to verification), `MP` has two copies reflecting the two executions of the program, e.g., `n` is translated to `n1` and `n2`. For each procedure in `P`, two Boolean *activation variables* `b1` and `b2` are added as inputs to the corresponding procedure in `MP`, where they respectively indicate whether the control flow in the corresponding copy of the program has reached the callsite. The idea is that *relational specifications* for procedures hold when both copies of the program have reached the same callsite, i.e., when both activation variables of the callee are true. As a result, all the relational specifications that we infer are implications in which the antecedent contains at least `b1` and `b2` as conjuncts.

The translation to `MP` also shows how the information-flow operation `declassify` is encoded as an assumption, and how the information-flow specification `low(a[i])` is translated into a relational property $t1 \wedge t2 \Rightarrow a1[i1] = a2[i2]$ in `MP`, where `t1` and `t2` were the activation variables under which the specification `low(a[i])` occurred. Finally, note that the assertion in `outputter` has been hoisted to `main` in `MP`, with the return value of `outputter` being *true* if and only if no assertion failed.

We infer quantifier-free information-flow properties[2] for each procedure. For example, we can infer that for `main` of `MP`, the property $b1 \wedge b2 \wedge n1 = n2 \Rightarrow res_1 = res_2$ holds, where res_1 and res_2 represent the return values of `main`. This property says that the output of `main` depends only on its second argument, and it does not rely on any information about whether the second argument or output of `main` is public or private, nor does it express any such information.

We also infer quantified invariants, e.g., $\phi(\texttt{i1})$:

$$\forall j_1, j_2.\, \texttt{i1} \leq j_1 \leq 64 \wedge j_1 = j_2 \Rightarrow (\texttt{a1}[j_1] = 0) = (\texttt{a2}[j_2] = 0)$$

We can then instantiate this property for the call to `init` in `main` to determine that $\phi(0)$ is true when the call to `outputter` is made. However, we cannot yet verify the program because at this point we have not inferred sufficient properties for `outputter`.

Finally, we use the context in which `outputter` is called to influence the guesses that we make for the antecedent in its relational specification. Then we infer the following property for `outputter`, where *res* is the return value of `outputter`: $b1 \wedge b2 \wedge \phi(0) \wedge \texttt{i1} = \texttt{i2} \wedge 0 \leq \texttt{i1} \Rightarrow res$. Note that this property contains quantifiers because $\phi(0)$ does. This property enables us to verify that the assertion for the program holds, leading to a successful conclusion.

III. BACKGROUND AND NOTATION

Here we describe the background on modular product programs and their modeling as CHCs, secure information flow, and relational invariants.

---

[2]We use properties interchangeably with procedure specifications.

```
proc(cond, x) {          proc(b1, b2, cond1, cond2, x1, x2) {
  if (cond)                  t1 = b1 ∧ cond1;  f1 = b1 ∧ ¬ cond1;
    x = x + 1;               t2 = b2 ∧ cond2;  f1 = b2 ∧ ¬ cond2;
  else                       if (t1) x1 = x1 + 1;  if (f1) x1 = 0;
    x = 0;                   if (t2) x2 = x2 + 1;  if (f2) x2 = 0;
  return x;                  return x1, x2;
}                        }
```

Fig. 2: Original (**left**) and modular product (**right**) programs.

A. Modular Product Programs

A k-hyperproperty expresses a property over k runs of the same program. Product programs convert k-hyperproperties into safety properties by creating k renamed versions of all the original variables. In contrast to ordinary product programs, *modular product programs (MPP)* avoid duplicating control structures such as procedure calls by introducing Boolean *activation variables* that indicate whether each program copy has reached a certain execution point [21]. The current activation variable for copy i is *true* if and only if copy i is currently at that location. While the principles of construction of a modular product program are defined in [21], we illustrate it with the following example.

Example 1. Consider the procedure in Fig. 2, for which the activation variables are initially `b1` and `b2`. The activation variables inside the then-branch (resp., else-branch) are `t1` and `t2` (resp., `f1` and `f2`). Each update to variable `x1` (resp., `x2`) is guarded by a condition so that the update is made only when the corresponding current activation variable for the first (resp., second) copy of the program is true. Note that any call to `proc` will also be guarded by a condition that at least one of `b1` or `b2` is *true*. If this doesn't hold, then neither procedure copy has reached the program point at which the procedure is called, so the call should not be made.

For a modular product program with k copies, we define partial functions *idx* and *getIdx* for conveniently handling expressions with renamed copies of variables. For any expression e, $getIdx(e) = i$ iff e represents an expression only over variables from the ith copy; and for any expression e such that $getIdx(e)$ is defined: $getIdx(idx(e, i)) = i$. For example, $idx(\texttt{b1} \wedge \texttt{i1} < 64, 2) = \texttt{b2} \wedge \texttt{i2} < 64$. We also use *idx* to denote the lifting of *idx* to sets of expressions.

B. Secure Information Flow

We use a standard reduction [3] of a (termination-insensitive) secure-information-flow property to a 2-hyperproperty called *non-interference* [1], which ensures that private inputs do not impact public outputs. For a procedure `f`, this is formalized as follows:

$$\forall \bar{li}, \bar{lo}, \bar{hi}, \bar{ho}, \bar{li}', \bar{lo}', \bar{hi}', \bar{ho}'\,.$$

$$\bar{lo}, \bar{ho} = \texttt{f}(\bar{li}, \bar{hi}) \wedge \bar{lo}', \bar{ho}' = \texttt{f}(\bar{li}', \bar{hi}') \wedge \bar{li} = \bar{li}' \Rightarrow \bar{lo} = \bar{lo}'$$

Variables $\bar{li}$ and $\bar{li}'$ represent public inputs to `f` and $\bar{lo}$ and $\bar{lo}'$ represent public outputs. Variables $\bar{hi}$ and $\bar{hi}'$ represent private input variables to `f` and $\bar{ho}$ and $\bar{ho}'$ represent private outputs.

Non-interference states that for any two runs of f, one with inputs $\bar{li}, \bar{hi}$ and one with inputs $\bar{li}', \bar{hi}'$, if their public inputs are equal (i.e., $\bar{li} = \bar{li}'$), then their public outputs should be equal (i.e., $\bar{lo} = \bar{lo}'$) regardless of the private inputs' values.

In a modular product program, relational properties become properties over a single run and take the form of an implication whose antecedent implies the truth of all activation variables, e.g., non-interference takes the following shape:

$$\forall b_1, b_2, \bar{li}, \bar{lo}, \bar{hi}, \bar{ho}, \bar{li}', \bar{lo}', \bar{hi}', \bar{ho}' \ .$$

$$b_1 \land b_2 \land$$

$$\bar{lo}, \bar{ho}, \bar{lo}', \bar{ho}' = f(b_1, b_2, \bar{li}, \bar{li}', \bar{hi}, \bar{hi}') \land \bar{li} = \bar{li}' \Rightarrow \bar{lo} = \bar{lo}'$$

Requiring non-interference can be restrictive since programs may need some amount of leakage to exhibit the desired behavior. *Declassification* can allow secure-information-flow properties to be checked even for programs that leak some information about high-security variables. Declassification is encoded in modular product programs as an assumption that if both programs reach the same `declassify` statement (i.e., if both activation variables are true), then the value being declassified is equal across both copies of the program. Thus `declassify(e)` is encoded as `assume` $b_1 \land b_2 \Rightarrow e_1 = e_2$.

C. Constrained Horn Clauses for Modular Verification

The problem of modular program verification can be expressed as a system of CHCs [35].

Definition 1. A CHC is an implicitly universally-quantified implication, which is of the form $body \Rightarrow head$. Let $\mathcal{R}$ be a set of uninterpreted predicates. The formula $head$ may take either the form $R(\bar{y})$ for $R \in \mathcal{R}$ or else $\bot$. Implications in which $head = \bot$ are called *queries*. The formula $body$ may take the form $\phi(\bar{x})$ or $\phi(\bar{x}) \land R_1(\bar{x}_1) \land \ldots \land R_n(\bar{x}_n)$, where each R_i is an uninterpreted predicate, and $\phi(\bar{x})$ is a fully interpreted formula over $\bar{x}$, which may contain all variables in each $\bar{x}_i$ and (if the head is of the form $R(\bar{y})$) all variables in $\bar{y}$.

A system of CHCs for a particular program can be generated by introducing an uninterpreted predicate per procedure (or a loop head) and encoding the semantics of each procedure (or a loop body) using these predicates. Fig. 3 gives an example encoding of program MP in Fig. 1 (right). Note that *print* is encoded as a nondeterministic procedure with no output.

Definition 2. A *solution* for a system of CHCs is a set of interpretations for predicates in $\mathcal{R}$ that makes all CHC implications valid.

Each interpretation can be viewed as a procedure summary and expresses an invariant for the procedure. In the case of the example program, the following interpretations are sufficient:

$main \qquad \mapsto \lambda \bar{x}.\top \qquad\qquad\qquad print \mapsto \lambda \bar{y}.\top$

$init \qquad\quad \mapsto \lambda b_1, b_2, a_1, a_2, i_1, i_2.\phi(b_1, b_2, a_1, a_2, i_1, i_2)$

$outputter \mapsto \lambda b_1, b_2, a_1, a_2, i_1, i_2, res.\ 0 \le i_1 \Rightarrow res \land$
$\qquad\qquad\qquad i_1 = i_2 \land b_1 \land b_2 \land \phi(b_1, b_2, a_1, a_2, i_1, i_2)$

where $\phi(b_1, b_2, a_1, a_2, i_1, i_2) = \forall j_1, j_2.i_1 \le j_1 < 64 \land i_1 = i_2 \land j_1 = j_2 \Rightarrow (a_1[j_1] = 0) = (a_2[j_2] = 0)$ and $\bar{x}$ and $\bar{y}$ are vectors of variables of lengths 6 and 4, respectively.

Definition 3. For a mapping M of uninterpreted predicates to interpretations, we say that the interpretations of M are *inductive* iff they satisfy all non-query CHCs.

In particular, an M that maps each n-ary predicate R to $\lambda x_1, \ldots, x_n.\top$ is inductive. For a formula F containing uninterpreted predicates, we let $M(F)$ be the result of replacing each predicate with its interpretation in M. For an inductive M, for each predicate R that represents a program procedure r, $M(R)$ is an *overapproximation* of the behavior of procedure r. For a given CHC C in the system of CHCs, where C is of the form $R_1(\bar{x}_1) \land \ldots \land R_n(\bar{x}_n) \land \phi(\bar{x}) \Rightarrow head$, an uninterpreted predicate R_i in its body can be *unfolded* in the CHC by replacing the occurrence of $R_i(\bar{x}_i)$ with $fresh(body_i[\bar{y}_i \mapsto \bar{x}_i], \bar{x}_i, \bar{x})$, where $body_i \Rightarrow R_i(\bar{y}_i)$ is another CHC in the system of CHCs, $body_i[\bar{y}_i \mapsto \bar{x}_i]$ is the simultaneous substitution of variables in $\bar{y}_i$ with variables in $\bar{x}_i$ in $body_i$, and $fresh(e, \bar{x}_i, \bar{x})$ is the result of replacing each variable in e that does not occur in $\bar{x}_i$ with a variable not in $\bar{x}$. We call the result of unfolding a predicate in a CHC C (possibly many times) an *unfolding* of C.

Example 2. An unfolding of *init* in the CHC for *main* in Fig. 3 is as follows: $\neg(b_1 \land k_1 < 64 \lor b_2 \land k_2 < 64) \land i_1 = i_2 = k_1 = k_2 = 0 \land ok \land outputter(b_1, b_2, a_1, a_2, i_1, i_2, ok) \Rightarrow main(b_1, b_2, a_1, a_2, n_1, n_2)$.

For a CHC C of the form $R_1(\bar{x}_1) \land \ldots \land R_n(\bar{x}_n) \land \phi(\bar{x}) \Rightarrow head$, we say that the following formula is the *context* (denoted $ctx(R_i, C)$) for the uninterpreted predicate application $R_i(\bar{x}_i)$:
$$\bigwedge_{\substack{1 \le j \le n \\ j \ne i}} M(R_j)(\bar{x}_j) \land \phi(\bar{x}).$$
We naturally extend the mappings M from uninterpreted predicates to contexts. That is, for the formula above: $M(ctx(R_i, C)) = \bigwedge_{\substack{1 \le j \le n \\ j \ne i}} M(R_j)(\bar{x}_j) \land \phi(\bar{x})$.

IV. SyGuS-based Summary Inference

This section describes our SyGuS-based algorithm for inferring procedure summaries of modular product programs. It takes CHCs as input and maintains a mapping M from uninterpreted predicates in the CHCs to inductive interpretations. The algorithm updates M as it runs and maintains the invariant that M's interpretations are inductive.

Our top-level procedure (Fig. 4) begins with an initial mapping M from each n-ary predicate $R \in \mathcal{R}$ to the coarsest interpretation possible. In pseudocode, we write CHECKGUESSES(G, M, R) to refer to an iterative procedure over all CHCs, where each application $R(\bar{x})$ of symbol R is replaced by formula $\lambda \bar{x}.M(R)(\bar{x}) \land makeGuess(G)(\bar{x})$, where G is a set of guessed interpretations for R based on our grammar templates and $makeGuess(G) = \lambda \bar{x}. \bigwedge \{g(x) \mid g \in G\}$.

The CHCs after the replacement are checked for validity using an SMT solver: if for some CHC C, the corresponding implication does not hold, then the current interpretation for R

$$
\begin{aligned}
&init(b_1, b_2, a_1, a_2, k_1, k_2) \wedge k_1 = 0 \wedge k_2 = 0 \wedge \\
&outputter(b_1, b_2, a_1, a_2, i_1, i_2, ok) \wedge i_1 = 0 \wedge i_2 = 0 \wedge ok && \Rightarrow main(b_1, b_2, a_1, a_2, n_1, n_2) \\
&\neg(b_1 \wedge i_1 < 64 \vee b_2 \wedge i_2 < 64) && \Rightarrow init(b_1, b_2, a_1, a_2, i_1, i_2) \\
&(b_1 \wedge i_1 < 64 \vee b_2 \wedge i_2 < 64) \wedge l_1 = b_1 \wedge i_1 < 64 \wedge l_2 = b_2 \wedge i_2 < 64 \wedge \\
&(l_1 \wedge l_2 \Rightarrow (a_1[i_1] = 0) = (a_2[i_2] = 0)) \wedge init(l_1, l_2, a_1, a_2, i_1 + 1, i_2 + 1) && \Rightarrow init(b_1, b_2, a_1, a_2, i_1, i_2) \\
&\neg(b_1 \wedge i_1 < 64 \vee b_2 \wedge i_2 < 64) && \Rightarrow outputter(b_1, b_2, a_1, a_2, i_1, i_2, \top) \\
&(b_1 \wedge i_1 < 64 \vee b_2 \wedge i_2 < 64) \wedge l_1 = b_1 \wedge i_1 < 64 \wedge l_2 = b_2 \wedge i_2 < 64 \wedge \\
&t_1 = b_1 \wedge a_1[i_1] = 0 \wedge t_2 = b_2 \wedge a_2[i_2] = 0 \wedge print(t_1, t_2, a_1[i_1], a_2[i_2]) \wedge \\
&ok = t_1 \wedge t_2 \Rightarrow a_1[i_1] = a_2[i_2] \wedge outputter(l_1, l_2, a_1, a_2, i_1, i_2, res) && \Rightarrow outputter(b_1, b_2, a_1, a_2, i_1, i_2, ok \wedge res) \\
&\top && \Rightarrow print(l_1, l_2, i_1, i_2) \\
&init(b_1, b_2, a_1, a_2, k_1, k_2) \wedge k_1 = 0 \wedge k_2 = 0 \wedge \\
&outputter(b_1, b_2, a_1, a_2, i_1, i_2, ok) \wedge i_1 = 0 \wedge i_2 = 0 \wedge \neg ok && \Rightarrow \bot
\end{aligned}
$$

Fig. 3: CHC encoding of program M from Fig. 1 (right).

```
1: procedure INFERSUM(CHCs C)
2:     for R ∈ R do M(R) ← λx_1, ..., x_n.⊤
3:     for C ∈ C where C = body ⇒ R(x̄) do
4:         G ← GETQFGUESSES(C) ∪ GETQUANTIFIEDGUESSES(C)
5:         M ← CHECKGUESSES(G, M, R)
6:     while M is not a solution for C do
7:         Q ← GETUNSATISIFIEDQUERY(C)
8:         M ← SOLVE(Q, C, M)
9:     return M
```

Fig. 4: Top-level summary inference procedure.

```
1: procedure SOLVE(Q, C, M)
2:     unfoldings ← ∅
3:     if M(body_Q) is unsatisfiable, then return M
4:     for R in Q's body do
5:         for body ⇒ R(x̄) ∈ C do
6:             G ← GETPDGUESS(Q, body ⇒ R(x̄), M)
7:             M' ← CHECKGUESSES(G, M, R)
8:             if M' ≠ M then return M'
9:             unfoldings ← unfoldings ∪ unfold(R, Q)
10:    for U ∈ unfoldings do
11:        M' ← SOLVE(U, C, M)
12:        if M' ≠ M then return SOLVE(Q, C, M')
```

Fig. 5: Inference procedure for property-directed guesses.

(which must appear in C) is weakened (using, e.g., the HOUDINI algorithm [22]), and the internal loop in CHECKGUESSES is repeated. Note that a new inductive mapping M' is returned as the result of CHECKGUESSES. Note also that M is already inductive whenever CHECKGUESSES is called, so it would be sufficient to weaken $M(R)(\bar{x}) \wedge makeGuess(G)(\bar{x})$ based on G, and CHECKGUESSES would return M in the worst case.

a) General quantifier-free and quantified guesses: For each CHC C, the algorithm generates initial guesses for an uninterpreted predicate in the head of C based on the templates specified later in Sec. V and VI-A.

After M has been updated based on these guesses, M's interpretations will have captured information-flow summaries for each procedure. If M is a solution for the system of CHCs, then these summaries may be sufficient for proving that the assertions of the program hold. Otherwise, the current procedure summaries are not strong enough for proving that

the assertions hold, and the algorithm aims to learn additional property-directed summaries.

b) Property-directed guesses: Additional summaries are generated by our third template, which is described later in Sec. VI-B. Given a query CHC Q that contains an application of some $R \in \mathcal{R}$ to variables $\bar{y}$ in its body, a CHC of the form $body \Rightarrow R(\bar{x})$, and an inductive mapping M, each property-directed guess in $G = \text{GETPDGUESS}(Q, body \Rightarrow R(\bar{x}), M)$ is such that if it is used as an interpretation for R in the query CHC with all the other predicates using their interpretations in M, then the query CHC will be satisfied (i.e., the body of Q will be unsatisfiable).

For such a G, $makeGuess(G)(\bar{y})$ can be viewed as an interpolant separating $body[\bar{x} \mapsto \bar{y}]$ and $M(ctx(R_i, Q))$; to populate G, GETPDGUESS generates guesses that obey the syntactic requirements for such an interpolant and adds them to G only after checking that they maintain the invariant that $makeGuess(G)(\bar{y})$ is an interpolant. The query CHC should be the result of unfolding a currently-unsatisfied query from the original system of CHCs zero or more times. The way in which the algorithm explores unfoldings is shown in Fig. 5. Our algorithm starts with an unsatisfied query Q and tries to infer property-directed summaries for each predicate in Q's body. If no summary can be inferred, it unfolds each predicate in Q and repeats the process on each of these unfoldings, reconsidering Q with each resulting updated interpretation M'.

Let a query U be an unfolding of the query Q. After each update in an interpretation $M'(R)$ of each $R \in \mathcal{R}$ in U, the query Q is reconsidered with M'.

Lemma 1. *If a query U that leads to an interpretation update was obtained by unfolding $R(\bar{y})$ in Q using CHC $body \Rightarrow R(\bar{x})$, then there exists an interpolant I separating $M'(body[\bar{x} \mapsto \bar{y}])$ and $M'(ctx)$.*

Reconsidering Q with the mapping M' allows us to try to guess this interpolant. This finding of interpolants is similar to prior uses of interpolants [36], [37], but in our case, rather than using an interpolating solver, we rely on SyGuS to obtain quantified interpolants that cannot be generated by usual methods used in interpolating solvers.

Example 3. Consider a modification of the system of CHCs for our motivating example in Fig. 3 such that the CHC for $main$ and the query Q are as follows: $outputter(b_1, b_2, a_1, a_2, i_1, i_2, ok) \wedge i_1 = 0 \wedge i_2 = 0 \Rightarrow main(b_1, b_2, a_1, a_2, n_1, n_2, ok)$, $main(b_1, b_2, a_1, a_2, n_1, n_2, ok) \wedge \neg ok \Rightarrow \perp$.

Let U be the unfolding of $main$ in Q, and let M contain the following interpretations: $main \mapsto \lambda \bar{x}.\top$, $outputter \mapsto \lambda \bar{z}.\top$, $print \mapsto \lambda \bar{y}.\top$, $init \mapsto \lambda b_1, b_2, a_1, a_2, i_1, i_2.\phi(b_1, b_2, a_1, a_2, i_1, i_2)$. The result of unfolding of $outputter$ in U allows us to update the summary (using the successfully checked guesses) of $outputter$ to the following:

$$\lambda b_1, b_2, a_1, a_2, i_1, i_2, res.$$
$$b_1 \wedge b_2 \wedge \phi(b_1, b_2, a_1, a_2, i_1, i_2) \wedge i_1 = i_2 \wedge 0 \leq i_1 \Rightarrow res$$

Note that the mapping M' containing this updated interpretation for $outputter$ is such that the following implication holds:

$$M'(outputter(b_1, b_2, a_1, a_2, i_1, i_2, ok) \wedge i_1 = 0 \wedge i_2 = 0) \Rightarrow ok$$

The antecedent of this implication is the interpretation of the body of the CHC for $main$, and the consequent is the negation of $main$'s context in Q. We can thus look for an interpolant that separates the body of $main$ and its context in Q.

Different orders in exploring unfoldings may result in learning different summaries. However, regardless of the order of unfoldings, the summaries discovered constitute a solution for the system of CHCs.

Note that if our templates cannot guess the required invariants, our top-level algorithm may not terminate, either because the second top-level loop may never terminate or because the recursive calls in the algorithm in Fig. 5 may never return. Our algorithm can be terminated early by the user and still return the properties discovered so far, which may be useful for code understanding and can provide hints to the user about manual annotations that may be required. In our experiments (Sect. VII), we did not need any manual annotations in the benchmark examples.

The following theorem implies that if INFERSUM returns a solution for a system of CHCs, the assertions in the original program that are captured by the query CHCs hold.

Theorem 1. INFERSUM *always returns an inductive map* M.

Proof. INFERSUM begins with M being the inductive map that maps each n-ary predicate R to $\lambda x_1, \ldots, x_n.\top$. M can be updated only by assigning it to the result of calls to CHECKGUESS, which always returns an inductive map. It follows that M is inductive when returned by INFERSUM. $\square$

Finally, we note that our proposed SyGuS approach is not inherently limited to verifying secure information flow or to two copies of a program ($k = 2$). It can be adapted to verify k-hyperproperties for $k > 2$ by extending the basic grammar (shown later in Fig. 6) to cover target properties. Furthermore, our ideas on property-directed guesses are not specific to information flow and can apply to other properties.

$$guess ::= \lambda \bar{x}.lhs \Rightarrow rhs$$
$$lhs ::= b_1 \wedge b_2 \mid inEq \wedge lhs \mid inIneq \wedge lhs$$
$$rhs ::= outEq \mid ok \mid declassify$$
$$inEq ::= Eq(inArg) \mid EqArr(inArrArg, ctr)$$
$$outEq ::= Eq(outArg) \mid EqArr(outArrArg, ctr)$$
$$inIneq ::= c < inIntArg \mid c \leq inIntArg \mid c > inIntArg \mid c \geq inIntArg$$

Fig. 6: Grammar for generating quantifier-free guesses for information flow.

V. GRAMMAR TEMPLATES WITHOUT QUANTIFIERS

Fig. 6 lists the grammar used in the INFERSUM algorithm (Fig. 4) to generate quantifier-free guesses that represent information-flow properties. Each guess has the form of an implication and corresponds to a relational property because the activation variables b1 and b2 always occur positively in the antecedent. The antecedent (lhs) allows additional conjuncts expressing equalities ($inEq$) and inequalities ($inIneq$) over input arguments of procedures ($inArg$), including arrays ($inArrArg$) indexed by expressions (ctr). The consequent (rhs) allows conjuncts expressing equalities ($outEq$) over output arguments of procedures ($outArg$, $outArrArg$), the results of assertions (ok), or declassify expressions ($declassify$). In the equalities, the expression $Eq(e)$ represents the equality $e = idx(e, 2)$, and $EqArr(e, i)$ represents the equality $e[i] = idx(e[i], 2)$. The inequalities allow comparison of input integer arguments ($inIntArgs$) against constants (c).

The terminals in our grammar are populated from a combination of variable types and a syntactic analysis of the CHC encoding of the body of the target procedure. The candidate variables include input/output parameters of procedure and outputs that store the result of assertions. We extract various expressions, e.g., representing indices in array accesses, or consequents in declassify assertions. The complete set of terminals is listed in Appendix A. Other than activation variables and the results of assertions, all terminals e in our grammar are such that $getIdx(e) = 1$ to reduce redundancy among guesses due to symmetry resulting from indices, e.g., in equality expressions.

VI. GRAMMAR TEMPLATES WITH QUANTIFIERS

In this section, we present two templates for generating guesses with quantifiers – one for arrays and the other for property-directed invariants.

A. Quantified Templates for Arrays

We generate guesses for quantified invariants for a given procedure by adapting a technique from prior work [33] to target *relational* properties. We consider here the task of generating a quantified invariant for a CHC $body(\bar{x}) \Rightarrow R(\bar{x})$. We construct guess for a quantified invariant from four parts:

- a set of quantified variables $qVars$ not in $\bar{x}$,
- a *range* formula over the variables in $inIntArgs \cup qVars$,
- a set of *equalities* over variables in $qVars \cup inIntArgs \cup idx(inIntArgs, 2)$,

- a *cell property* formula over the variables in $\bar{x} \cup qVars$. All these components except *equalities* come directly from prior work [33], which combined them to form a candidate invariant: $\forall qVars.range \Rightarrow cell\ property$. We take a similar approach but use *equalities* to guess invariants over both program copies. We also use activation variables in the antecedent of the implication so that the candidate invariant only applies when both program copies are aligned. Here we only generate *range* formulas over variables for the first program copy and use the equalities to ensure that the corresponding variables in the second copy are equal to those in the first.

Quantified variables and range variables are determined similarly to previous work [33]. For each variable i in $inIntArgs \cap ctrs$ used to access an array index, two fresh quantified variables $q1$ and $q2$ are added to $qVars$, where $idx(q1, 2) = q2$. We let $quant(i) = q1$. For each such variable, we also generate a range formula that is an inductive invariant for R of the form:

$$range ::= i \le q1 < boundGt \mid boundLt < q1 \le i$$

Here, $boundGt$ is the set of expressions e over variables $\bar{x}$ for which $i < e$ or $e > i$ occurs as a subexpression of *body*, the body of a procedure. Similarly, $boundLt$ is the set of expressions e over variables $\bar{x}$ for which $e < i$ or $i > e$ occurs as a subexpression of *body*. Let the set *ranges* denote the set of such *range* expressions that are inductive for R (which we first check for each such candidate).

For each variable i in $inIntArgs \cap ctrs$, we generate the equality $quant(i) = idx(quant(i), 2)$ and the equality $i = idx(i, 2)$ and add them to the set *equalities*.

Finally, to generate cell properties, we consider the subset of expressions generated by the grammar in Fig. 6 that contain accesses to array cells (also known as *select*-terms and denoted $[\cdot]$) with indices Idx such that for each $i \in Idx$, *ranges* contains an expression containing $idx(i, 1)$. We take each such expression e and substitute each occurrence of any variable $i \in inIntArg \cap ctr$ with $quant(i)$ and then add the resulting expression to the set *cellProps*.

For each $cellProp \in cellProps$, we generate the following candidate invariant:

$$\lambda\bar{x}.\forall qVars. \bigwedge ranges \wedge \bigwedge equalities \wedge b_1 \wedge b_2 \Rightarrow cellProp$$

B. Property-Directed Templates

The final template allows us to generate property-directed guesses for a particular procedure r given a mapping M to inductive interpretations. This template consists of two parts: a *context guess* and a *quantifier-free guess*. As mentioned previously, we aim to find interpolants using SyGuS rather than an interpolating solver. The context guess is used to incorporate relevant properties from the context into the guess, and the quantifier-free guess is used to strengthen it.

We first describe how to generate the context guess given a CHC C that is an unfolding of a *query* Q, a predicate application $R(\bar{y})$ for procedure r that occurs in the body of the unfolding, and a CHC $body \Rightarrow R(\bar{x})$. Let ctx be the context for $R(\bar{y})$ in the unfolding of Q.

```
1: procedure FILTER(Ands, R(ȳ), C, M)
2:     M' ← M[R ↦ λȳ. ⋀ Ands]
3:     for body ⇒ R(x̄) ∈ C do
4:         for application R(x̄') in body, context ctx do
5:             query ← M'(R)(x̄) ∧ M'(ctx) ∧ ¬M'(R)(x̄')
6:             if query satisfiable then
7:                 m ← GETMODEL(query)
8:                 FC ← FALSECONJS(m, M'(R)(x̄'), Ands)
9:                 return FILTER(Ands \ FC, R, C, M)
10:    return Ands
```

Fig. 7: Procedure to find largest useful element in $\mathcal{P}(Ands)$.

Let $Ands$ be the set of conjuncts in $M(ctx)$. Each element of the powerset $\mathcal{P}(Ands)$ can become a context guess. We are interested only in elements p in $\mathcal{P}(Ands)$ that represent properties that, while initially not guaranteed to be true whenever r is called, are guaranteed to hold for any subsequent recursive calls to r provided that they held at the initial invocation of r. We discover the largest set $conseqAnds \subseteq \mathcal{P}(Ands)$ that represents such properties through a procedure based on the Houdini algorithm [22] (as shown in the algorithm in Fig. 7).

The procedure in Fig. 7 examines each CHC in $\mathcal{C}$ with an application of R to variables $\bar{x}$ in its head. The mapping M' maps R to the interpretation $\lambda\bar{y}. \bigwedge Ands$ but is otherwise the same as the current mapping M. For each such CHC, it checks if $M(R)$ is inductive (line 5) and uses a model (called a counterexample-to-induction) to weaken $Ands$. We can now use $\mathcal{P}(conseqAnds)$ as the set of context guesses.

We generate quantifier-free guesses $QFGuesses$ for $body \Rightarrow R(\bar{x})$ as shown in Sec. V, except now the set c of integer constants also includes all integer constants in ctx.

The algorithm in Fig. 8 describes how the context and quantifier-free guesses are combined to make a guess for R with context ctx and the current set of interpretations M. For each $\lambda\bar{x}.lhs \Rightarrow rhs \in QFGuess$ and $p \in \mathcal{P}(conseqAnds)$, we consider the mapping $M' = M[R \mapsto \lambda\bar{x}.M(R)(\bar{x}) \wedge rhs]$, which is the same as the mapping M except the interpretation for R is updated to $\lambda\bar{x}.M(R)(\bar{x}) \wedge rhs$. If $M'(ctx)$ is unsatisfiable and $lhs \wedge p$ is satisfiable (line 5), we generate the following guess: $\lambda\bar{x}.lhs \wedge p \Rightarrow rhs$. We only consider guesses such that $M'(ctx)$ is unsatisfiable because these guesses are such that if they are treated as an interpretation for R in $\mathcal{C}$, they make $M'(\mathcal{C})$ satisfiable. This requirement ensures that the guesses considered help make progress toward proving the assertion in the original program corresponding to query Q. The checks on line 5 guarantee that each element added to $Guesses$, when applied to $\bar{y}$, is an interpolant separating $body[\bar{x} \mapsto \bar{y}]$ and $M'(ctx)$. If all guesses in $Guesses$ are interpolants separating these formulas, then it follows that $makeGuess(Guesses)(\bar{y})$ is also such an interpolant. Note that these guesses may contain quantifiers if the interpretations in M contain quantifiers.

VII. IMPLEMENTATION AND EVALUATION

We have implemented our technique in a prototype tool called FLOWER, developed on top of the CHC solver FREQ-

```
1: procedure COMBINEGUESS(QFGuess, conseqAnds, M, R, ctx)
2:     for λx̄.lhs ⇒ rhs ∈ QFGuess do
3:         for p ∈ P(conseqAnds) do
4:             M' ← M[R ↦ λx̄.M(R)(x̄) ∧ rhs]
5:             if M'(ctx) unsat, lhs ∧ p sat then
6:                 Guesses ← Guesses ∪ {λx̄.lhs ∧ p ⇒ rhs}
```

Fig. 8: Inference procedure for property-directed guesses.

HORN [27], [38]. We evaluated it on a suite of benchmarks[3] from the literature and real-world examples.

In our implementation, all candidate guesses allowed by our grammars are enumerated and checked, i.e., there is no further heuristic selection (currently) in our tool. Although this can be problematic if there are too many guesses, we did not encounter this issue in practice. For property-directed guesses, the unfoldings are explored in a breadth-first like manner.

a) Benchmarks: Of our 29 benchmarks, 15 are based on a subset[4] of the evaluation set for MPPs [4], [6], [19], [21], [34], [39]–[42]. While small in size, with the original programs ranging from 24-70 lines of VIPER [43] code, these programs include non-trivial features such as arrays and declassification that are challenging for automated verifiers. We added two benchmarks based on code from Amazon Web Service's S2N [20], about 160 lines of SMT-LIB2 code that involve reading/writing from buffers. We also translated six benchmarks based on BLAZER's "Literature" and "STAC" benchmarks [19], which ranged from 41-208 lines of Java.

The VIPER benchmarks contained many manual annotations of information-flow specifications for both procedures and loops. We treated the specification for the apparent top-level procedure as an assertion, and eliminated the remaining annotations. Loops were encoded as recursion, as is typical in CHC encodings. Memory locations and memory-related annotations in the benchmarks were not encoded in CHCs; structures were either flattened or encoded as arrays.

The BLAZER benchmarks considered were written in Java and originally checked for timing side channels. This can be reduced to checking for noninterference with appropriate instrumentation [44]. We manually instrumented and encoded these benchmarks into CHCs.

b) Evaluation: We also compared our tool against a state-of-the-art relational verifier DESCARTES [15] and a modular CHC-based verifier SPACER[5] [25]. For DESCARTES, we translated CHC benchmarks to intraprocedural Java programs.

Results from experiments on our suite of 29 benchmarks with a timeout of 10 minutes are shown in Table I. BLAZER benchmarks are prefixed with "B" and S2N benchmarks are prefixed with "s2n." A timeout is indicated with **TO** and an unknown result with **U**. N/A indicates that DESCARTES was unable to handle the benchmark because of the presence of arrays or declassification. Benchmarks were run on a MacBook Pro, with a 2.7GHz Intel Core i5 processor and 8GB RAM.

---

[3] Available at https://github.com/lmpick/flower-benchmarks

[4] We left out termination-related properties; automation would require synthesis of ranking functions, which we do not currently support.

[5] SPACER outperformed all tools in CHC-Comp'19 in all LIA categories [45].

TABLE I: Results for 29 benchmarks. Times shown in seconds.

Example	Recursive	Flower Time	Spacer Time	Descartes Time
Banerjee		8.00	0.04	N/A
B GPT14	✓	73.91	**TO**	**U**
B K96	✓	12.60	**TO**	**U**
B Login	✓	18.20	**TO**	N/A
B ModPow1	✓	60.86	**TO**	**U**
B ModPow2	✓	104.59	**TO**	**U**
B PWCheck	✓	18.04	**TO**	N/A
Costanzo (2)	✓	3.94	0.65	N/A
Costanzo (4)	✓	3.85	7.10	N/A
Costanzo (8)	✓	3.85	62.50	N/A
Costanzo (16)	✓	4.08	**TO**	N/A
Costanzo (32)	✓	3.88	**TO**	N/A
Costanzo (64)	✓	3.93	**TO**	N/A
Costanzo (unbounded)	✓	8.17	**TO**	N/A
Darvas		2.04	0.03	N/A
Declassification	✓	4.91	0.03	N/A
Joana Fig. 1 top left		0.96	0.03	N/A
Joana Fig. 2 bottom left		0.90	0.02	0.06
Joana Fig. 2 top		0.58	0.02	0.08
Joana Fig. 13 left		0.25	0.03	0.07
Kusters		8.07	0.03	0.09
Main Example	✓	135.90	**U**	N/A
Main Example (det.)	✓	13.98	**TO**	N/A
s2n Ex. 1	✓	352.70	0.06	N/A
s2n Ex. 2	✓	30.95	**TO**	N/A
Smith	✓	23.26	**TO**	N/A
Terauchi Fig. 1		0.40	0.03	0.08
Terauchi Fig. 2		0.84	0.03	N/A
Terauchi Fig. 3	✓	3.55	**TO**	**U**

Our tool FLOWER is able to solve all 29 benchmarks, including all 15 benchmarks originally used to assess the usefulness of MPPs. Note that our tool successfully solved all these examples *without the annotations required by* VIPER [43]. This demonstrates the effectiveness of our approach in reducing the annotation burden for verifying secure information flow.

SPACER is able to solve 14 of the 29 benchmarks, timing out for 14, and reporting **U** for one. DESCARTES cannot handle the majority of the benchmarks; of the 10 benchmarks it can take as input, DESCARTES solves 5. Out of the 20 examples with recursion (marked in Column 2), SPACER can only solve 5, whereas our tool can handle all 20. SPACER finds invariants via interpolation, which is unlikely to directly capture relational properties, so it is unable to find suitable invariants for these recursive procedures. For recursion-free examples, relational invariants are less crucial; invariants capturing precise behaviors are easier to find and are often sufficient for verification.

DESCARTES is similarly unable to find appropriate invariants. For each of the 5 recursive benchmarks that it can take as input, it is unable to find the required loop invariant to verify the program. Although DESCARTES also uses a template-based approach for generating candidate invariants, the templates are insufficient for these benchmarks.

To evaluate scalability, we considered versions of the Costanzo benchmark with different array bounds (shown in parentheses in Table I). Fig. 9 shows the performance comparison against SPACER as the array bound increases. SPACER's behavior indicates its inability to find relational properties; it

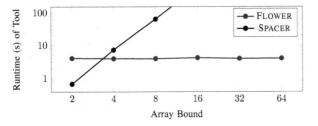

Fig. 9: Timing results for Costanzo benchmark with different array bounds.

learns properties for each array index individually, rendering it unable to solve the Costanzo benchmark within 10 minutes after the array bound reaches 16 (note that the original Costanzo benchmark has bound 64). Although it was run in a mode that allows it to learn quantified properties, SPACER is unable to find the desired relational property. In contrast, our approach solves all the bounded Costanzo benchmarks in about the same time because the quantified guesses are the same except for the constant bound. Our approach is also able to solve the Costanzo benchmark in which the array is *unbounded*, which SPACER is unable to do.

VIII. RELATED WORK

There are many related efforts in relational program verification, information-flow checkers, and syntax-guided synthesis.

a) Relational Program Verification: While this work focuses on modular product programs [21], many other approaches also reduce relational program verification to safety verification [3]–[9], including those that employ a reduction to systems of CHCs [10], [46]. *However, most do not perform modular reasoning over procedures but inline them, and do not generate relational specifications for procedures.* One modular approach restricts both copies of the program to always follow the same control flow [6]. Another uses *mutual* summaries but does not provide an automatic procedure for inferring summaries as we do [8].

Other relational verifiers avoid explicitly constructing a product program. Some use program logics to work with Hoare triples [15]–[17], construct product programs implicitly [18], use decomposition instead of composition [19], or employ reinforcement learning [12]. These approaches also do not modularly reason about nor infer relational specifications for procedures, though they may modularly handle loops [15].

b) Information-Flow Checkers: Most automatic hyperproperty verifiers can handle information-flow properties by constructing product programs either implicitly [15], [18], or by lazily performing self-composition [13], [14] or synchronization [10], [46]. However, most of these techniques do not perform modular reasoning over the product programs or results of self-composition. One synchronization approach uses property-directed reachability and use modular reasoning for inference of relational procedure summaries [25], [46], [47], but our experiments show that the property-directed reachability tool SPACER upon which this tool was built often fails to infer the needed invariants in programs with recursion.

Other efforts focus on verifying *resource* leakage, such as the presence of timing side channels [11], [19], [44]. With appropriate instrumentation for resource leakage [11], [44], checking for timing leakage can be reduced to hyperproperty verification. As seen in our evaluation, our tool can be used to check the absence of timing side channels after appropriate resource usage instrumentation.

Approaches based on types and abstract interpretation can modularly infer information-flow properties of procedures. There are many type-inference-based approaches for checking secure information flow [48]–[51]. Such approaches employ a security type system such that terms only type check if they do not have any illegal information flows (e.g., from low-security to high-security variables). There are also approaches based on dynamic taint analysis [52]–[57], which involves instrumenting code with taint variables and code to track taint. However, type-inference-based and taint analysis approaches suffer from imprecision (e.g., due to path-insensitivity or an inability to infer invariants over arrays) that may lead to failure in type inference even for leakage-free programs. In contrast, our approach is path-sensitive and requires only the annotations that specify the property to be verified. One abstract-interpretation-based approach can infer possible information-flow dependencies, indicating which variables' values may depend on others' [58]. This approach, like ours, does not require annotations indicating which inputs and outputs are public or private. However, unlike our approach, it does not handle programs with procedures, arrays, or declassification.

c) Syntax-Guided Synthesis: Our approach is also related to a wide range of guess-and-check SyGuS techniques [27], [29]–[33], [38]. Especially relevant are enumerate-and-check approaches to solve CHCs [27], [33], [38]. Our template for guessing quantified invariants for arrays adapts a previous technique [33] to the setting of reasoning about secure information flow. As far as we know, such techniques have not been applied to inferring or verifying information-flow properties. The structure of information-flow properties makes them ideal targets for grammar-based enumerative search and synthesis.

IX. CONCLUSIONS

We have introduced a SyGuS-based technique for automatic inference of modular relational specifications that are useful for verifying secure information flow in interprocedural programs. Our technique relies on three grammar templates to infer procedure summaries in modular product programs, where these procedure summaries are of a particular form. The first template guesses quantifier-free summaries for information flow, the second guesses quantified summaries for expressing properties over arrays, and the third template guesses summaries that depend on the calling context of a procedure. An implementation of our techniques on top of a CHC solver and an experimental evaluation on benchmarks demonstrates that our approach finds useful procedure summaries to verify secure information flow, thereby reducing the annotation burden in prior work. Our tool outperforms a state-of-the-art hyperproperty verifier and a modular CHC-based verifier on several benchmark examples.

REFERENCES

[1] J. A. Goguen and J. Meseguer, "Security policies and security models," in *1982 IEEE Symposium on Security and Privacy*, 1982, pp. 11–20.

[2] A. Sabelfeld and D. Sands, "Dimensions and principles of declassification," in *CSFW*. IEEE Computer Society, 2005, pp. 255–269.

[3] G. Barthe, P. R. D'Argenio, and T. Rezk, "Secure information flow by self-composition," in *CSFW*. IEEE Computer Society, 2004, pp. 100–114.

[4] T. Terauchi and A. Aiken, "Secure information flow as a safety problem," in *SAS*, ser. Lecture Notes in Computer Science, vol. 3672. Springer, 2005, pp. 352–367.

[5] G. Barthe, J. M. Crespo, and C. Kunz, "Product programs and relational program logics," *J. Log. Algebraic Methods Program.*, vol. 85, no. 5, pp. 847–859, 2016.

[6] ——, "Relational verification using product programs," in *FM*, ser. Lecture Notes in Computer Science, vol. 6664. Springer, 2011, pp. 200–214.

[7] ——, "Beyond 2-safety: Asymmetric product programs for relational program verification," in *LFCS*, ser. Lecture Notes in Computer Science, vol. 7734. Springer, 2013, pp. 29–43.

[8] C. Hawblitzel, M. Kawaguchi, S. K. Lahiri, and H. Rebêlo, "Towards Modularly Comparing Programs Using Automated Theorem Provers," in *CADE*, ser. LNCS, vol. 7898. Springer, 2013, pp. 282–299.

[9] M. R. Clarkson and F. B. Schneider, "Hyperproperties," *Journal of Computer Security*, vol. 18, no. 6, pp. 1157–1210, 2010.

[10] E. De Angelis, F. Fioravanti, A. Pettorossi, and M. Proietti, "Relational verification through horn clause transformation," in *SAS*, ser. Lecture Notes in Computer Science, vol. 9837. Springer, 2016, pp. 147–169.

[11] J. Chen, Y. Feng, and I. Dillig, "Precise detection of side-channel vulnerabilities using quantitative cartesian hoare logic," in *ACM Conference on Computer and Communications Security*. ACM, 2017, pp. 875–890.

[12] J. Chen, J. Wei, Y. Feng, O. Bastani, and I. Dillig, "Relational verification using reinforcement learning," *Proc. ACM Program. Lang.*, vol. 3, no. OOPSLA, pp. 141:1–141:30, 2019.

[13] W. Yang, Y. Vizel, P. Subramanyan, A. Gupta, and S. Malik, "Lazy self-composition for security verification," in *CAV (2)*, ser. Lecture Notes in Computer Science, vol. 10982. Springer, 2018, pp. 136–156.

[14] R. Shemer, A. Gurfinkel, S. Shoham, and Y. Vizel, "Property directed self composition," in *CAV (1)*, ser. Lecture Notes in Computer Science, vol. 11561. Springer, 2019, pp. 161–179.

[15] M. Sousa and I. Dillig, "Cartesian hoare logic for verifying k-safety properties," in *PLDI*. ACM, 2016, pp. 57–69.

[16] G. Barthe, B. Köpf, F. Olmedo, and S. Z. Béguelin, "Probabilistic relational reasoning for differential privacy," in *POPL*. ACM, 2012, pp. 97–110.

[17] N. Benton, "Simple relational correctness proofs for static analyses and program transformations," in *POPL*. ACM, 2004, pp. 14–25.

[18] A. Farzan and A. Vandikas, "Automated hypersafety verification," in *CAV (1)*, ser. Lecture Notes in Computer Science, vol. 11561. Springer, 2019, pp. 200–218.

[19] T. Antonopoulos, P. Gazzillo, M. Hicks, E. Koskinen, T. Terauchi, and S. Wei, "Decomposition instead of self-composition for proving the absence of timing channels," in *PLDI*. ACM, 2017, pp. 362–375.

[20] Amazon Web Services, "https://github.com/awslabs/s2n," 2019.

[21] M. Eilers, P. Müller, and S. Hitz, "Modular product programs," in *ESOP*, ser. Lecture Notes in Computer Science, vol. 10801. Springer, 2018, pp. 502–529.

[22] C. Flanagan, R. Joshi, and K. R. M. Leino, "Annotation inference for modular checkers," *Inf. Process. Lett.*, vol. 77, no. 2-4, pp. 97–108, 2001.

[23] A. Albarghouthi, A. Gurfinkel, and M. Chechik, "From under-approximations to over-approximations and back," in *TACAS*, ser. LNCS, vol. 7214. Springer, 2012, pp. 157–172.

[24] P. Rümmer, H. Hojjat, and V. Kuncak, "Disjunctive interpolants for Horn-Clause verification," in *CAV*, ser. LNCS, vol. 8044. Springer, 2013, pp. 347–363.

[25] A. Komuravelli, A. Gurfinkel, and S. Chaki, "Smt-based model checking for recursive programs," *Formal Methods in System Design*, vol. 48, no. 3, pp. 175–205, 2016.

[26] O. Padon, K. L. McMillan, A. Panda, M. Sagiv, and S. Shoham, "Ivy: safety verification by interactive generalization," in *PLDI*. ACM, 2016, pp. 614–630.

[27] G. Fedyukovich, S. J. Kaufman, and R. Bodík, "Sampling invariants from frequency distributions," in *FMCAD*. IEEE, 2017, pp. 100–107.

[28] H. Zhu, S. Magill, and S. Jagannathan, "A data-driven CHC solver," in *PLDI*. ACM, 2018, pp. 707–721.

[29] R. Alur, R. Bodík, G. Juniwal, M. M. K. Martin, M. Raghothaman, S. A. Seshia, R. Singh, A. Solar-Lezama, E. Torlak, and A. Udupa, "Syntax-guided synthesis," in *FMCAD*. IEEE, 2013, pp. 1–8.

[30] S. Padhi, R. Sharma, and T. D. Millstein, "Data-driven precondition inference with learned features," in *PLDI*. ACM, 2016, pp. 42–56.

[31] R. Alur, A. Radhakrishna, and A. Udupa, "Scaling Enumerative Program Synthesis via Divide and Conquer," in *TACAS, Part I*, ser. LNCS, vol. 10205, 2017, pp. 319–336.

[32] A. Reynolds, H. Barbosa, A. Nötzli, C. W. Barrett, and C. Tinelli, "cvc4sy: Smart and Fast Term Enumeration for Syntax-Guided Synthesis," in *CAV, Part II*, ser. LNCS, vol. 11562. Springer, 2019, pp. 74–83.

[33] G. Fedyukovich, S. Prabhu, K. Madhukar, and A. Gupta, "Quantified invariants via syntax-guided synthesis," in *CAV (1)*, ser. Lecture Notes in Computer Science, vol. 11561. Springer, 2019, pp. 259–277.

[34] D. Costanzo and Z. Shao, "A separation logic for enforcing declarative information flow control policies," in *POST*, ser. Lecture Notes in Computer Science, vol. 8414. Springer, 2014, pp. 179–198.

[35] S. Grebenshchikov, N. P. Lopes, C. Popeea, and A. Rybalchenko, "Synthesizing software verifiers from proof rules," in *PLDI*. ACM, 2012, pp. 405–416.

[36] K. L. McMillan, "Lazy abstraction with interpolants," in *CAV*, ser. Lecture Notes in Computer Science, vol. 4144. Springer, 2006, pp. 123–136.

[37] ——, "Lazy annotation revisited," in *CAV*, ser. Lecture Notes in Computer Science, vol. 8559. Springer, 2014, pp. 243–259.

[38] G. Fedyukovich, S. Prabhu, K. Madhukar, and A. Gupta, "Solving Constrained Horn Clauses Using Syntax and Data," in *FMCAD*. ACM, 2018, pp. 170–178.

[39] A. Banerjee and D. A. Naumann, "Secure information flow and pointer confinement in a java-like language," in *CSFW*. IEEE Computer Society, 2002, p. 253.

[40] Á. Darvas, R. Hähnle, and D. Sands, "A theorem proving approach to analysis of secure information flow," in *SPC*, ser. Lecture Notes in Computer Science, vol. 3450. Springer, 2005, pp. 193–209.

[41] D. Giffhorn and G. Snelting, "A new algorithm for low-deterministic security," *Int. J. Inf. Sec.*, vol. 14, no. 3, pp. 263–287, 2015.

[42] G. Smith, "Principles of secure information flow analysis," in *Malware Detection*, ser. Advances in Information Security. Springer, 2007, vol. 27, pp. 291–307.

[43] P. Müller, M. Schwerhoff, and A. J. Summers, "Viper: A verification infrastructure for permission-based reasoning," in *VMCAI*, ser. Lecture Notes in Computer Science, vol. 9583. Springer, 2016, pp. 41–62.

[44] K. Athanasiou, B. Cook, M. Emmi, C. MacCárthaigh, D. Schwartz-Narbonne, and S. Tasiran, "Sidetrail: Verifying time-balancing of cryptosystems," in *VSTTE*, ser. Lecture Notes in Computer Science, vol. 11294. Springer, 2018, pp. 215–228.

[45] CHC-Comp, "https://chc-comp.github.io," 2019.

[46] D. Mordvinov and G. Fedyukovich, "Property directed inference of relational invariants," in *FMCAD*. IEEE, 2019, pp. 152–160.

[47] K. Hoder and N. Bjørner, "Generalized property directed reachability," in *SAT*, ser. Lecture Notes in Computer Science, vol. 7317. Springer, 2012, pp. 157–171.

[48] D. E. Denning and P. J. Denning, "Certification of programs for secure information flow," *Commun. ACM*, vol. 20, no. 7, pp. 504–513, 1977.

[49] D. M. Volpano, C. E. Irvine, and G. Smith, "A sound type system for secure flow analysis," *Journal of Computer Security*, vol. 4, no. 2/3, pp. 167–188, 1996.

[50] A. C. Myers, "Jflow: Practical mostly-static information flow control," in *POPL*. ACM, 1999, pp. 228–241.

[51] M. Patrignani, P. Agten, R. Strackx, B. Jacobs, D. Clarke, and F. Piessens, "Secure compilation to protected module architectures," *ACM Trans. Program. Lang. Syst.*, vol. 37, no. 2, pp. 6:1–6:50, 2015.

[52] G. Sarwar, O. Mehani, R. Boreli, and M. A. Kâafar, "On the effectiveness of dynamic taint analysis for protecting against private information leaks on android-based devices," in *SECRYPT*. SciTePress, 2013, pp. 461–468.

[53] M. Costa, J. Crowcroft, M. Castro, A. I. T. Rowstron, L. Zhou, L. Zhang, and P. Barham, "Vigilante: end-to-end containment of internet worms," in *SOSP*. ACM, 2005, pp. 133–147.

[54] J. R. Crandall and F. T. Chong, "Minos: Control data attack prevention orthogonal to memory model," in *MICRO*. IEEE Computer Society, 2004, pp. 221–232.

[55] M. G. Kang, S. McCamant, P. Poosankam, and D. Song, "DTA++: dynamic taint analysis with targeted control-flow propagation," in *NDSS*. The Internet Society, 2011.

[56] E. J. Schwartz, T. Avgerinos, and D. Brumley, "All you ever wanted to know about dynamic taint analysis and forward symbolic execution (but might have been afraid to ask)," in *IEEE Symposium on Security and Privacy*. IEEE Computer Society, 2010, pp. 317–331.

[57] D. X. Song, D. Brumley, H. Yin, J. Caballero, I. Jager, M. G. Kang, Z. Liang, J. Newsome, P. Poosankam, and P. Saxena, "Bitblaze: A new approach to computer security via binary analysis," in *ICISS*, ser. Lecture Notes in Computer Science, vol. 5352. Springer, 2008, pp. 1–25.

[58] M. Zanioli and A. Cortesi, "Information leakage analysis by abstract interpretation," in *SOFSEM*, ser. Lecture Notes in Computer Science, vol. 6543. Springer, 2011, pp. 545–557.

APPENDIX

A. *Terminals in SyGuS Grammar for Secure Information Flow*

The terminals in our grammar to generate quantifier-free guesses (Fig. 6) are populated by a combination of tagging types of variables and a syntactic analysis of the CHC encoding of the body of the target procedure under consideration.

a) Tagging the types: For a CHC with head $R(\bar{x})$ that encode a modular product procedure r, each $x \in \bar{x}$ is tagged as follows:

- `in`: if x corresponds to a non-activation input argument x in r with $getIdx(x) = 1$;
- `out`: if x corresponds to an output *ret* in r with $getIdx(ret) = 1$;
- `arr`: if x is an array;
- `int`: if x is an integer;
- `ok`: if x is an output value storing the result of assertions.

The following metavariables specify what the terminals based on tags range over:

- *inArg*: the set *inArgs* of variables tagged `in`;
- *inArrArg*: the set *inArrArgs* of variables tagged both `in` and `arr`;
- *outArg*: the set of variables *outArgs* tagged `out`;
- *outArrArg*: the set of variables *outArrArgs* of variables tagged both `out` and `arr`;
- *inIntArg*: the set of variables *inIntArg* tagged `in` and `int`;
- *ok*: the set of variables tagged `ok`.

The activation variables in $\bar{x}$ are denoted b_1 and b_2.

b) Syntactic Analysis: The terminal *ctr* is based on a syntactic analysis of the body of the CHC. It ranges over a set *ctrs* comprising the following:

- all expressions e with $getIdx(e) = 1$ that occur in the procedure body within subexpressions of the form $a[e]$ for some a;
- terminals that c ranges over, consisting of all integer constants that occur as the right- or left-hand side of equalities or inequalities in the body of the procedure;
- terminals that *declassify* ranges over, which consists of the consequents $e_1 = e_2$ of any implications of the form $b_1 \wedge b_2 \Rightarrow e_1 = e_2$, where b_1 and b_2 are Boolean variables, $getIdx(e_1) = 1$, and $getIdx(e_2) = 2$.

4

Using Model Checking Tools to Triage the Severity of Security Bugs in the Xen Hypervisor

Byron Cook*†, Björn Döbel*, Daniel Kroening*‡ (iD), Norbert Manthey*,
Martin Pohlack*, Elizabeth Polgreen§‖ (iD), Michael Tautschnig*¶ (iD), Pawel Wieczorkiewicz*

*Amazon Web Services   †University College London   ‡University of Oxford
§UC Berkeley   ¶Queen Mary University of London
‖University of Edinburgh

Abstract—In practice, few security bugs found in source code are urgent, but quickly identifying which ones are is hard. We describe the application of bounded model checking to triaging reported issues quickly at the cloud service provider Amazon Web Services (AWS). We focus on the job of reactive security experts who need to determine the severity of bugs found in the Xen hypervisor. We show that, using our publicly available extensions to the model checker CBMC, a security expert can obtain traces to construct security tests and estimate the severity of the reported finding within 15 minutes. We believe that the changes made to the model checker, as well as the methodology for using tools in this scenario, will generalise to other organisations and environments.

I. INTRODUCTION

Some bugs have serious security implications. For well-engineered systems most bugs do not. The reason is that these systems are built with *defense in depth* [1], meaning that the average bug found usually just temporarily reduces the depth of the defense provided until the bug is fixed, but does not present an immediate security concern that nullifies assumed defenses.

At Amazon Web Services (AWS), a key challenge we face is quickly categorising each bug report, which requires answering the question whether the bug is reachable through all security layers. Determining vulnerability severity is performed under intense time-pressure, as Amazon s first priority is the continuous security of its customers. The key to success in these situations is access to quick and accurate answers to questions about state-space reachability. Our case study focuses on determining the severity of bugs in Xen [2], an open-source hypervisor used throughout the industry. AWS uses a customised Xen version on some of its Elastic Compute Cloud (EC2) servers. While this case study focuses on Xen, we believe the results generalise to other large-scale systems: based on our experience with Xen and other systems, after an initial effort to ensure successful builds of the code base, the system-specific effort to apply the approach reported on in this case study is low.

For each security finding, the Xen Project publishes a *Xen Security Advisory* (XSA) [3]. A typical XSA comes with a description of the problem and a source-code patch to mitigate the issue. Before full publication, the XSA is shared with the members of Xen s pre-disclosure list, as is common in responsible disclosure processes. At AWS, members of 24/7 security operations triage potential security bugs as they are discovered or reported. They may find themselves in the following quandary: should they wake the engineering team from their beds to investigate? Or do the existing layers of defense mitigate against the consequences of the bug? Often the same code is used in multiple products, where the defenses will differ from service to service.

In order to assess the severity of a given XSA, the security expert will manually determine whether the vulnerability is reachable in the AWS-customised version of Xen. Engineers construct *security tests* to reproduce the vulnerability, thereby answering the reachability question. This reachability question fundamentally is a global question about the interaction amongst details across the entire EC2 system. It includes complex custom hardware, software, protocols, and networks that implement the layers of security defense, as well as enabling high compute utilization and scalability needed for one of the world s largest cloud providers.

In this case study we describe our use of bounded model checking to help our security experts make faster and more accurate assessments of severity. The complexity of the overall environment is well beyond the capacity of today s formal methods tools. We automate the part of the process that was previously most time-consuming for security experts using an extended version of CBMC [4]. For a given XSA, we use the source-code patch provided with the XSA to write an assertion, which we insert into the patched source-code area. Reachability and violation of this assertion indicates a possible exploitation of the vulnerability. We analyse the Xen source code in the context of a potential security bug and generate traces that are helpful for test construction.

These tests will be executed in the overall EC2 environment, and help the security experts among us understand which defenses remain intact, or else help find a complete proof-of-concept test, which will be used to confirm any mitigation. In our experience, we can perform work in minutes that would previously have taken weeks or months. Because weeks is unacceptably long, before the use of our methodology, additional developers were enlisted as needed in order to reach a more timely analysis conclusion. Now, we are able to more rapidly make high-confidence calls using the high-fidelity answers produced by our methodology. The result is that the rare critical security bugs get fixed even faster than before, with fewer human resources.

Related work: We integrate our extensions into CBMC [5], [6], a bit-precise bounded model checking tool for C programs. Model checking is frequently applied to security problems: Gallagher et al. [7] use security patches to generate verification assertions, and use CBMC and Frama-C to verify these. UQBTng [8] automatically finds integer over ows in Win32 binaries using CBMC. Vasudevan et al. [9] use CBMC in the verification of a small hypervisor framework. Automated verification techniques have been applied to the address translation subsystem [10] of the Xen hypervisor, using a parametric verification technique to reduce the model size. A small custom hypervisor is analysed by Alkassar [11] and [12]. Dahlin et al. [13] develop a simple but fully verified hypervisor. None of these approaches scales to the size of Xen (cf. Section III).

Frama-C has been applied to verify a subset of the Xen hypervisor code [14], using modelling of assembly code, harness functions and manually picking hypercalls. The considered properties are shallower than required for analysing security issues. In contrast, we aim to automatically select hypercalls, and focus on the interaction between the guest and the hypervisor. KLEE [15] cannot be applied, as Xen does not compile to LLVM [16]. This rules out tools built on top of KLEE, such as the automatic exploit generation tool of [17], and also the concolic execution approach that Chen et al. presented for Linux kernel modules [18].

II. CBMC AND BOUNDED MODEL CHECKING

CBMC [6] is a bounded model checker [19] which can check for the violations of assertions in C programs, or prove absence of violations given a specific bound. The default behaviour of CBMC is that it unwinds any loops or recursion in the program to a given unwinding limit but unrolls the rest of the program fully. CBMC performs a bit-precise translation of the source program into a Boolean formula, which is then passed to a SAT solver. If the formula is satisfiable, then a counterexample trace that leads to a violated assertion exists, and CBMC translates the model returned from the SAT solver back into assignments to program state variables for each state in this trace.

CBMC s code base also provides for a number of text-book data- ow analyses. These include precise slicers as discussed in Section III-B. In Section IV we explain as to why we had to add approximate slicing to complement the precise ones.

III. THE XEN HYPERVISOR

In cloud computing, one physical *host machine* is partitioned into several parts, called *virtual machines*. Virtual machines behave like complete computers with their own operating system, and each virtual machine serves a single *guest* (serving as a host in nested virtualisation [20]). The software that provides this illusion is called a hypervisor [21], [22]. Xen [2] is a bare-metal hypervisor, as it runs directly on the hardware of the host and manages all the host s resources. A similar hypervisor is KVM [23], for which this work would apply as well.

1) Virtual machines: Every guest virtual machine in Xen has its own guest kernel and operating system. A system call from a program of a guest, e.g., a request for access to I/O devices, reaches the guest kernel. In most configurations of Xen, the guest kernel does not have direct control of the physical machine. Hence, the guest kernel issues a *hypercall* or accesses a predefined memory range to request the service from the hypervisor. Xen is event-driven: after booting and once a guest runs, Xen waits for guest code to execute and takes actions on hypercalls, or host interrupts. The hypervisor handles hardware exceptions and interrupts, which may be raised by the CPU when guests issue privileged instructions.

2) Memory: Xen uses *virtual memory* for isolation and to give guests the impression they are working with contiguous sections of memory, when the physical memory could be spread across different locations. Virtual memory is split into fixed-length contiguous blocks called *pages* and each *virtual address*, describing a location in a page, is mapped to a physical address in a *page frame*. This mapping is stored in a *page table*. There are several ways Xen can virtualise memory; most commonly Xen uses hardware support in the form of nested paging and extended page tables.

A. Example Vulnerability and Security Test

In the presence of an adversarial guest, security issues can result in information leaks, guest denial of service (DoS), privilege escalation to or DoS of the host machine. We discuss XSA 227 [24] as an example of a potential vulnerability.

1) Security vulnerablity XSA 227: A guest can share memory with, e.g., other guests, or devices. When setting up a new shared memory area, the guest passes the memory location to be shared to the hypervisor, by giving the *guest-physical address* of an entry in one of its page tables. To share the page, the hypervisor modifies this page table entry. Before the modification, Xen checks several properties. XSA 227 reported that Xen did not check whether the entry address starts at the beginning of a page table entry, i.e., whether the address is *aligned*. Since Xen writes exactly one page table entry, the hypervisor can write beyond an unaligned page table entry, allowing the guest to partially overwrite the next page table entry. Writing to the page table in this unprotected way is sufficient to allow a guest to grant itself additional permissions and gain full system access.

2) Security test for XSA 227: To establish the severity of an XSA for AWS, an engineer develops tests to trigger the vulnerability in the EC2 environment. For XSA 227, the test performs a hypercall from a guest that shares memory at a non-aligned address. If the hypercall returns with success, the vulnerability is reachable. Else, if the hypercall returns an error code—and if no other mistakes have been made when invoking the hypercall—the vulnerability is unreachable.

3) Equivalent reachability problem: For XSA 227, part of the XSA patch provided is the following macro that checks whether the page-table entry of a page is aligned:

```
#define IS_ALIGNED(val, align) \
  (((val) & ((align) - 1)) == 0)
```

We use this macro to add an assertion that, if violated, indicates the vulnerability is exploitable. For XSA 227, we insert the following `assert` statement over local variables `pte_addr` and `nl1e` into the source-code area patched in the XSA:

```
assert(IS_ALIGNED(pte_addr, sizeof(nl1e)));
```

We can thus use software model checking to verify whether the above assertion can be violated, starting from the hypercall entry point. Such a counterexample can be used to construct the above mentioned test.

B. Challenges in Applying Automated Program Analyses

Existing program analysis techniques, however, cannot be applied out-of-the-box to the Xen code base: (1) Xen uses C code with systems extensions and assembly code throughout the codebase, for example interfacing with hardware. In Xen 4.8, there remain more than 700 lines of assembly in the code base. To the best of our knowledge, there is no symbolic verification tool that can handle this combination of C and assembly code on such a large code base. (2) Modelling behaviour of an adversarial guest precisely would require modelling the exact start state of the machine, which is determined in boot code, the exact interaction history with other guests, and maintaining a full model of the memory layout and system registers. We cannot do this, due to both the proliferation of low-level assembly code in the boot code and the scalability demands of a full memory model. (3) Xen is configurable, due to its requirement to have full control of a machine regardless of architecture. Thus, Xen contains code that emulates CPU instructions for multiple different architecture avours. During boot time, the architecture avour is determined and function pointers are set to point to the correct implementations. (4) The size of the code base exceeds the scalability limits of existing software model checkers: Xen 4.8 is comprised of $\sim$300,000 lines of code. Benchmarks in the TACAS Competition on Software Verification [25] are smaller. The largest tasks feature $\sim$100,000 lines of code. However, in 2019, large solved benchmarks in this competition typically had either short counterexample traces or simple proofs of safety. For Xen, we expect long counterexample traces of instructions to refute safety, due to the steps involved in the interaction with hypervisors. For all XSAs we have investigated, unpatched CBMC failed to complete analysis within an 8 hour time window, even after using all available program slicers. Program slicing [26] uses dependence analysis to remove instructions that cannot affect a property of interest. CBMC includes a reachability slicer, which removes instructions that cannot affect any assertion, and a slicer to remove code that initialises unused global variables. These slicers are fast but do not remove enough code for the analysis of Xen to become feasible. CBMC also contains a full-program slicer, which computes the cone-of-in uence [27]. Full slicing is precise but, owing to the cost of points-to analyses, not scalable and does not complete on the Xen codebase within 8 hours.

```c
void do_hypercall()
{
  int nondet;
  switch(nondet)
  {
  case 1:
    XEN_GUEST_HANDLE (const_trap_info_t) traps1;
    do_set_trap_table(traps1);
    break;
  case 2:
    XEN_GUEST_HANDLE (mmu_update_t) ureqs2;
    unsigned int count2;
    XEN_GUEST_HANDLE (uint) pdone2;
    unsigned int foreigndom2;
    do_mmu_update(ureqs2, count2, pdone2, foreigndom2);
    break;
  case 3:
    XEN_GUEST_HANDLE (ulong) frame_list3;
    unsigned int entries3;
    do_set_gdt(frame_list3, entries3);
  ...
```

Figure 1. Model of the hypercall table. This is modelled as a non-deterministic switch over all possible hypercalls, called with non-deterministic arguments.

IV. EXTENDING CBMC TO HANDLE XEN

We address these four challenges using automated approximations with hooks for expert-provided refinement, implemented in an extended version of CBMC [4].

A. Assembly Code

When the lack of interpretation of assembly code adversely affects precision, we model it in C, most importantly the hypercall table of Xen, which contains the hypercalls a guest may use. We model this as a non-deterministic choice over hypercalls, entered with non-deterministic arguments, to allow all possible guest behaviour. Figure 1 shows a snippet from this model. While this model is currently constructed manually, it is reused across XSAs. Future work on CBMC includes adding native support for assembly code, which will avoid the need for expert-provided input for this stage.

B. Environment Modelling

We start our analysis either at a start point known to be relevant to the XSA or at the hypercall entry-point. To over-approximate the state of the machine at the point the guest makes a hypercall, we automatically generate an environment that assumes non-deterministic values for all input parameters to the start function, and constrains all pointers to refer to valid areas of memory. To enforce the latter, we add harness functions into the code at analysis time, as shown in Figure 3. These functions initialise the pointers to point to valid but non-deterministic objects. By starting from this set of states, we over-approximate the potential behaviour of the adversary between boot and the first hypercall we model.

C. Function Pointer Removal

By default, CBMC expands function pointers to a case statement over a set of functions determined using an over-approximating signature-based analysis. For the configurable

```
#define ARGS(x, n)                        \
    [__HYPERVISOR_ ## x ]={n, n}
#define COMP(x, n, c)                     \
    [__HYPERVISOR_ ## x ]={n, c}

const hypercall_args_t
  hypercall_args_table[NR_hypercalls] =
{
    ARGS(set_trap_table, 1),
    ARGS(mmu_update, 4),
    ARGS(set_gdt, 2),
    ...

#define HYPERCALL(x)                      \
    [ __HYPERVISOR_ ## x ] =              \
      { (hypercall_fn_t *) do_ ## x,  \
        (hypercall_fn_t *) do_ ## x }
#define COMPAT_CALL(x)                    \
    [ __HYPERVISOR_ ## x ] =              \
        {(hypercall_fn_t *) do_ ## x, \
         (hypercall_fn_t *) compat_ ## x }
    ...

static const hypercall_table_t
    pv_hypercall_table[] = {
    COMPAT_CALL(set_trap_table),
    HYPERCALL(mmu_update),
    COMPAT_CALL(set_gdt),
    ...
```

Figure 2. Fragments of the original code that builds the hypercall table

```
int main()
{
    struct x86_emulate_ctxt harness_ctxt;
    struct x86_emulate_ops harness_ops;
    int nondet;
    // instantiate read function pointer
    switch(nondet)
    {
    case 1:
        harness_ops.read = EXAMPLE;
        break;
    case 2:
        harness_ops.read = EXAMPLE2;
        break;
    }
    // expert restricts possible vendor values
    __CPROVER_assume(harness_ctxt.vendor < 3);

    x86_emulate(&harness_ctxt, &harness_ops);
}
```

Figure 3. Harness for x86_emulate. An expert can provide restrictions over the input space, such as the restriction on the values of vendor variable shown in the assumption here. Uninitialised variables such as nondet are considered free variables to be assigned any non-deterministic value by the underlying SAT solver.

code base of Xen, the signature-based analysis yields up to 300 functions for a single function pointer. CBMC determines the precise set of function calls, i.e., the subset of feasible cases, during symbolic execution. As our analysis running on Xen uses non-deterministic initial states, symbolic execution would typically deem *all* cases feasible, even though most of them are spurious. To reduce the candidate set per pointer, we now use CBMC s existing ow-insensitive points-to analysis [28] in place of the signature-based analysis. This ow-insensitive analysis is field-sensitive, therefore the analysis distinguishes the fields of every object, while merging the values of them for different program locations. If the ow-insensitive points-to analysis yields an empty set as, e.g., caused by pointers depending on boot code, we fall back to the original behaviour. With this change, we introduce 20k fewer function calls, about 114k instead of 134k, and hence reduce the likelihood of spurious counterexamples.

Con gurable harnesses: Xen code supports several architectures. For our analysis we pick a single set of architectures, i.e., Intel 64bit CPUs. This allows us to restrict the set of functions considered for handling architecture specifics, while still using a non-deterministic machine state. We thus support adding expert-provided code into the harnesses described in Section IV-B to restrict the candidates of these function pointers to a specific function or a non-deterministic choice over a constrained set of functions, e.g., excluding all AMD-specific functions.

The example given in Figure 3, x86_emulate contains several function pointers and an expert engineer specifies two possible function pointers for the read function.

D. Approximating Program Slicer

In order to focus analysis on the relevant part of the hypervisor, we introduce a more aggressive slicing approach following the algorithm of Figure 4: we first compute an approximation of the call graph using the function-pointer removal as described above. Using this call graph, the slicer computes the set of paths from the entry point to the target property. From this set, we select *direct paths*, which we define as the paths without cycles on the call graph. We then take these direct paths and remove all function calls that return back to the calling function and replace these function calls with an approximation of their behaviour by *havocking* the function body, as explained in Section IV-D1. This produces an approximation of the cone of in uence, which may be sufficiently small to analyse with CBMC.

If the resulting program slice is still too large to analyse, the approximating slicer can be configured to keep only functions on the shortest direct path. To increase precision, we can preserve all functions within a given distance of function calls from the direct paths, illustrated in Figure 5. To obtain scalability and precision, we run multiple analyses with varying degrees of precision in parallel to find the configuration that completes within the timeout with maximum precision.

1) Approximating behaviour of missing code: If a function is removed, we must approximate the behaviour of that function in order to avoid missing counterexamples. A coarse approximation is to *havoc* the function, i.e., assume the function may return a non-deterministic value and may assign a non-deterministic value to any arguments passed by pointer. This approximation is not strictly an over-approximation, because it may under-approximate behaviour as described below. We chose this simplification, because computing and refining a sound over-approximation is computationally intensive, and missing some

---

Approximating_Slice (CFG g, node entry, node target, bool direct, int distance)

S1 FP := remove_function_pointers(g)

S2 CG := compute_call_graph(FP)

S3 DP := get_direct_paths(CG, entry, target)

S4 DP := shortest_path(DP) **if** $\neg$ direct **else** DP

S5   mark_for_havoc = $\emptyset$

S6   **for** node n **in** FP:

S7   **if** distance(FP, DP, n) > distance:

S8   mark_for_havoc := mark_for_havoc $\cup \{n\}$

S9   **for** node n **in** mark_for_havoc:

S10   havoc_object(n)

Figure 4. Approximating slicing is applied to input program represented by its control- ow graph g, and configurable in the entry- and target nodes, whether or not to consider all direct paths, and the maximum distance.

counterexamples due to under-approximation is acceptable for our use case as we strive to support the security expert in constructing tests.

2) Potential under-approximation: The first source of under-approximation are global variables written to by a function that we removed. We partly mitigate the absence of modelling this behaviour by starting our analysis in a non-deterministic initial state, including non-deterministic global variables. It is, however, possible that a trace requires a global variable to take different values during the trace; such counterexamples would thus be missed.

The second source of under-approximation is not havocking pointers to pointers. When a function receives a pointer A as argument that points to pointer B, we do not havoc pointer B. When a function receives a pointer A that points to a **struct** B that contains a pointer C, we do not havoc pointer C. We choose not to havoc these pointers, as this can change any memory to any value, and introduces spurious counterexamples. There are 84 functions in Xen that accept pointers to pointers, and experts

did not find any to be relevant to the XSAs we analysed.

V. DETERMINING SEVERITY OF VULNERABILITIES

Our aim is to assist experts in determining the severity of a security vulnerability, within a specific version of Xen. To illustrate this use case, we selected a few XSAs with different properties: 200, 212, 213, 227, and 238 [3]. We build our modifications on top of CBMC version 5.10, which uses Mini-Sat 2.2.1 [29]. We disable MiniSAT s pre-processor, as it usually consumes more run time than the actual verification task for the given problems. We pick Xen release 4.8 [30], as none of the selected XSAs have been mitigated in this version, and fixed handling comments in assembly to allow us to compile the code with CBMC. Next, we added the assertions and harness functions for each XSA. This is a required setup step the complexity of which varies between adding a single assertion, and adding a full harness for the hypercall table (about 300 instructions), depending on the XSA. When starting from our provided package, these harnesses are already present, and hence, future harnesses require less effort. To speed-up overall time, and precision, we run multiple configurations of the slicer and analysis options in parallel via AWS Batch [31], to obtain first results quickly. Our Xen and CBMC packages including all scripting are available for download[1] and the aggressive slicer is available in the main CBMC branch[2].

The counterexample trace contains all function entries and exits, arguments and relevant variable assignments. We add an option to CBMC to print the trace in HTML with options to expand function calls.

A. Results

The experiments were run on AWS Batch using the EC2 r5 instance family, with a memory limit of 110 GiB and an overall timeout of 8 hours per job. The original Xen binary contains 103,662 effective program locations, i.e., code statements that affect the state of the program. We ran CBMC out-the-box on each of the XSAs with all combinations of the CBMC program slicers, with a loop unwinding limit of 0, i.e., executing the

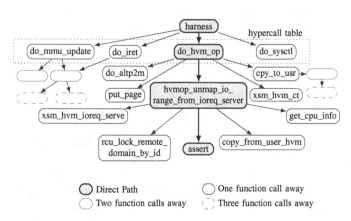

Figure 5. Xen s call graph from the harness function to an assertion representing XSA 238. The thick framed nodes show the *direct path*; these functions are always preserved by the approximating slicer. The thin, solid framed nodes show functions which will be approximated, as described in Section IV-D1, by default. If we preserve functions up to one function call away from the direct paths, the light grey nodes will be preserved, and the unlabelled nodes represent functions which will be approximated.

---

[1]https://github.com/nmanthey/xen/tree/FMCAD2020
[2]https://github.com/diffblue/cbmc

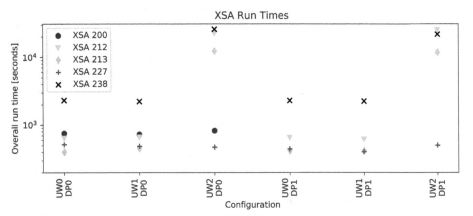

Figure 6. Run time of the overall approach for selected configurations that finish within 8 hours. We fixed the parameters to distance=2, and advanced function pointer removal as well as run full slicing after approximating slicing. Keeping all direct paths (DP1), as well as unwinding loops (UW) during search are altered.

loop body just once. The reachability slicer and global slicer reduce the instruction count by up to 20 %. CBMC cannot produce a results for any of the combinations, and the full slicer does not finish within the 8 h timeout.

We vary the input parameters to approximating slicing (cf. Figure 4) to preserve all direct paths, or shortest paths only, or preserve functions with a distance of up to 2 calls. We limit loop unwinding to 0, 1 or 2 iterations, and use both function pointer removal approaches. These limits were chosen since they were large enough to produce precise enough results to create tests from the traces. It is possible to increase these limits and still obtain traces, but substantially large values may result in a binary too large to analyse in reasonable time (for instance, increasing the depth to 10 or greater).

Slicing is crucial, as it reduces the size of the input program to less than 5 % of its original size in under 10 minutes. Overall run times of the more precise configurations (distance=2) are presented in Figure 6. For smaller distances, the run times are typically smaller. The figure shows that run times depend on the XSA, as well as on the unwinding parameter – for more unwinding the run time for XSAs 213, 212 and 238 increases. For XSA 200, no direct-path based traces can be produced within 8 hours in case all direct paths are kept, because XSA 200 is located in instruction emulation code, which introduces many direct paths.

For all five selected XSAs, an initial result for at least one configuration is returned within 10 minutes. This time allows engineers to refine the harness to improve the result for test generation quickly. Within the first hour, more than 30 configurations produce traces.

B. Turning a Trace To a Test

To make the results of this work consumable for future XSAs, we also discuss how to turn a counterexample trace from CBMC into a security test that could be executed inside the guest. The required information is

1) the configuration of Xen
2) the type of the guest that can hit the security issue

3) the interaction the guest has to perform to trigger the security issue

A typical XSA description provides data for item 1 and 2, because it scopes the security issue. In case CBMC produces a valid trace for an assertion, this trace provides information about item 3, namely the relevant data that comes from the guest. This data is forwarded to Xen via a few interfaces:

1) hypercalls, namely the call to perform, as well as the arguments for the hypercall
2) copy_from_guest, a function which copies data from the guest into the hypervisor
3) hardware interaction, e.g., content of packages that are generated by interaction with the (emulated) hardware

In the XSAs we analysed, we only see interaction via hypercalls and the function copy_from_guest. No devices are involved in these XSAs.

Finally, to turn the relevant parts of the trace into an actual security test, we need the basic building blocks to interact with the hypervisor, for example being able to compile a kernel module or the required C header files to use the definitions of structures that are passed as arguments to the hypercall. We use the Xen Testing Framework [32], which provides these building blocks, supports many hypercalls and allows the user to create a security test easily. XTF also already has tests for past XSAs. For the XSAs we use, actual tests can be found via the following URL: https:/xenbits.xen.org/gitweb/ ?p=xtf.git;a=blob_plain;f=tests/xsa-200/main.c.[3]

1) Extract Guest Interaction From Traces: To extract the guest interaction, we have to follow the variables that are used as parameters for hypercalls and the copy_from_guest function.[4] Given our abstraction, CBMC is allowed to choose arbitrary values for the parameters and returns from copy_from_guest, which matches that adversarial model: an adversarial guest can write arbitrary data to those.

We now use an example trace that has been generated for XSA 227, with the relevant parts shown in Figure 7, to turn it into

---

[3]Replace the 200 with the any of the XSA numbers 200, 212, 213 or 227.
[4]In Xen 4.8, copy_from_guest is a macro, which is expanded to copy_from_user_hvm.

the basic building blocks for a security test. Note, CBMC traces first list the function call, and then show how the parameters are evaluated.[5]

We implemented a harness that calls the hypercall do_grant_table_op (line 4), and which allows CBMC to choose arguments for this hypercall. CBMC picks cmd=0 (step 3), which is equivalent of the operation GNTTABOP_map_grant_ref.

CBMC also generates a pointer value for the variable uop (step 3), which is likely to be wrong. A wrong value is chosen, because the trace starts in the middle of a running Xen, and the initialization of the data structures for the guest in the hypervisor has not been done yet. To make the security test complete, a grant table map would have to be created first, and then the correct value would have been known. This work does not take the preparation of the environment into account yet, as that step requires further expert knowledge. In the same spurious way, the value for variable count is set to 258, but the trace actually consumes only a single element. Therefore, this value should be set to 1 in the actual code.

Next, in step 6 we call the function gnttab_map_grant_ref, following the value of the parameter cmd. This function then issues the call to copy_from_guest (step 7), and looks for data of the type "struct gnttab_map_grant_ref". The result of this operation should contain the value 4089, or 0xFF9, for the member host_addr. The rest of the trace then shows how this value is used and propagated forward until the assertion is violated in step 13. The assertion basically checks whether the lower bits of the address are set to 0, which fails, because the least significant bit is set in the representation of 0xFF9.

Now that the relevant information is extracted from the trace, the corresponding block in a security test for the fix of XSA 238 should contain the following lines:

```
struct gnttab_map_grant_ref map = {
    .host_addr = 0xFF9,
    .flags = 21,
    .ref = 0,
    .dom = 0,
};
hypercall_grant_table_op(
        GNTTABOP_map_grant_ref, &map, 1);
```

Again, due to the abstraction, there are values from the trace that might be invalid, because the aggressive slicing drops calls to functions that might have checked these properties. Furthermore, values to be used might depend on the system setup, so that the values CBMC reports might only be used as a guideline. Still, the trace highlights that it is possible to trigger the security issue from the guest, and furthermore provides candidate data that can be used to generate a security test for the issue.

C. Practical Relevance

EC2 launched in 2006. The Xen project reported its first XSA in March 2011, and has since announced more than 300

XSAs—about three per month. AWS Xen security team has provided feedback to the Xen security team on several occasions and reported four follow-up XSAs. Using this experience, we analyzed the five XSAs above as examples. The generated traces for four out of those proved to be good enough as building blocks for tests: the relevant hypercall, as well as relevant input values for the hypercall are present in the trace. When there are multiple traces, we use the trace with most precision, i.e. highest unwinding, distance, and direct paths included. Ultimately this runnable test is used to avoid future security regressions. Only the trace for XSA 213 requires further work, as CBMC only reports the second half of the trace, and skips setting the hypervisor into a specific mode first, because we start the analysis from a non-deterministic machine state.

Compared to the manual assessments that we performed, the automated approach is often faster. If we take setting up Xen for the analysis into account, i.e. adapting available harnesses and packaging for AWS Batch, we are usually in the same ball-park. While AWS security experts can often quickly assess reachability of a location in the code base, for a specific configuration and version of the hypervisor, finding input values to bypass checks and doing this analysis for all different production configurations is more challenging. For these cases, the presented approach is a win, as the amount of engineering time spent can be reduced from engineering days to hours.

We note that failing to find a trace is not sufficient to allow the security team to ignore an issue, and the security team makes risk-based assessments based on their experience and judgment. In some cases in this scenario it is necessary to fall back to the traditional techniques to establish high confidence that a potential issue does not require a fix. In these scenarios, our tool can, nevertheless, still be a useful datapoint that, combined with other information, can give the security team confidence that additional investigation is not urgent.

The recent XSA 296 reported the vulnerability for PV and HVM guests. After about a day of manual work, AWS experts could rule out HVM guests. The new approach would have been helpful, as all reported traces would have relied on PV guest features, helping to rule out HVM faster.

For similarly complex software projects, the presented technique will provide valuable insight into reachability and produce sample input values to trigger a software bug. Less experienced teams might benefit from the automated approach to speed up response time for security incidents.

1) Limitations and open challenges: Our approach has a number of limitations which reduce the precision of our results. We may miss traces for several reasons: CBMC has an incomplete understanding of assembly code; we do not consider whether functions we remove modify globals; we unwind loops to a finite bound; and CBMC does not maintain a full model of memory. We may produce spurious traces because we start from a mid-point in the code using a non-deterministic start state. Addressing these limitations and running bit-precise analysis on large code bases remains an open challenge. We feel that the natural next step towards this would be refinement of our

```
-----------------------------------------------------------------
Function call: my_granttable_init (depth 1)
-----------------------------------------------------------------
Function call: textbf{do_grant_table_op} (depth 2)
-----------------------------------------------------------------
State 943: textbf{cmd=0u} (0x0)
State 944: uop={ .p=INVALID-65535 } ({ 0xFFFF8200 80000002 })
State 945: count=258u (0x102)
-----------------------------------------------------------------
Function call: gnttab_map_grant_ref (depth 3)
-----------------------------------------------------------------
State 999: copy_from_user_hvm(_d, (_s + i),
(sizeof(textbf{struct gnttab_map_grant_ref}) * 1));
 op={ textbf{.host_addr=4089ul}, .flags=21u, .ref=0u, .dom=0,
                .status=0, .handle=0u, .dev_bus_addr=0ul }
            ({ 0xFF9, 0x15, 0x0, 0x0, 0x0, 0x0, 0x0 })
-----------------------------------------------------------------
Function call: __gnttab_map_grant_ref (depth 4)
Function call: create_grant_host_mapping (depth 5)
-----------------------------------------------------------------
State 1144: {addr=4089ul} (0xFF9)
-----------------------------------------------------------------
Function call: create_grant_pte_mapping (depth 6)
-----------------------------------------------------------------
State 1194: {pte_addr=4089ul} (0xFF9)
-----------------------------------------------------------------
Violated property: assert((pte_addr & sizeof(l1_pgentry_t)-1)==0)
-----------------------------------------------------------------
```

Figure 7. The relevant parts of the CBMC trace for XSA 227 that guides test generation.

approximations.

There are cases where security issues can only be triggered if there are two guest CPUs available. Analysis would have to scale for parallel interaction, including parallel hypercalls, and modification of guest data.

Finally, automation would benefit from an incremental approach of the technique. The investigating engineer might receive the initial results, and then modify the harness to restrict the search space. Today, the complete process has to be triggered again, and the whole search has to be repeated. We expect starting analysis from a state similar to a given trace to significantly reduce the run time of subsequent iterations, similarly to incremental SAT solving [33].

VI. CONCLUSION

We have described the application of bounded model checking and slicing to the Xen hypervisor used in triaging reported security concerns. By introducing improved handling of function pointers and approximating program slicing in combination with havocking functions we are able to use bounded model checking to construct counterexample traces that reproduce security issues and ultimately, determine their severity. Despite the open challenges listed in the previous section, we have shown that we can use automation to help generate security tests from patches today, which supports more rapid security analysis and also leads to a more secure cloud environment for customers. This tooling assists experts in determining the severity of security vulnerabilities, constructing security tests for these scenarios, and helping on-call security experts quickly decide whether they should wake up developers or allow them to enjoy their well-deserved sleep.

Acknowledgments: E. Polgreen is supported by NSF grants 739816 and 183713.

REFERENCES

[1] A. Follner, A. Bartel, H. Peng, Y. Chang, K. K. Ispoglou, M. Payer, and E. Bodden, "PSHAPE: automatically combining gadgets for arbitrary method execution," in *Security and Trust Management - 12th International Workshop, STM 2016, Heraklion, Crete, Greece, September 26-27, 2016, Proceedings*, ser. Lecture Notes in Computer Science, vol. 9871. Springer, 2016, pp. 212–228. [Online]. Available: https://doi.org/10.1007/978-3-319-46598-2_15

[2] P. Barham, B. Dragovic, K. Fraser, S. Hand, T. L. Harris, A. Ho, R. Neugebauer, I. Pratt, and A. Warfield, "Xen and the art of virtualization," in *SOSP*. ACM, 2003, pp. 164–177.

[3] Xenproject.org Security Team, "Xen security advisories," 2019, accessed: 2019-12-17. [Online]. Available: https://xenbits.xenproject.org/xsa/

[4] E. Polgreen, "CBMC extensions," 2018, accessed: 2019-12-19. [Online]. Available: https://github.com/polgreen/cbmc/tree/xen_extended_cbmc

[5] E. M. Clarke, D. Kroening, and F. Lerda, "A tool for checking ANSI-C programs," in *TACAS*, ser. Lecture Notes in Computer Science, vol. 2988. Springer, 2004, pp. 168–176.

[6] D. Kroening and M. Tautschnig, "CBMC – C bounded model checker (competition contribution)," in *TACAS*, ser. Lecture Notes in Computer Science, vol. 8413. Springer, 2014, pp. 389–391.

[7] J. Gallagher, R. Gonzalez, and M. E. Locasto, "Verifying security patches," in *Workshop on Privacy & Security in Programming*. ACM, 2014, pp. 11–18.

[8] R. Wojtczuk, "UQBTng: A tool capable of automatically finding integer overflows in Win32 binaries," in *CCC*. Chaos Communication Congress, 2005.

[9] A. Vasudevan, S. Chaki, L. Jia, J. M. McCune, J. Newsome, and A. Datta, "Design, implementation and verification of an extensible and modular hypervisor framework," in *IEEE Symposium on Security and Privacy*. IEEE Computer Society, 2013, pp. 430–444.

[10] J. Franklin, S. Chaki, A. Datta, J. M. McCune, and A. Vasudevan, "Parametric verification of address space separation," in *POST*, ser. Lecture Notes in Computer Science, vol. 7215. Springer, 2012, pp. 51–68.

[11] E. Alkassar, M. A. Hillebrand, W. J. Paul, and E. Petrova, "Automated verification of a small hypervisor," in *VSTTE*, ser. Lecture Notes in Computer Science, vol. 6217. Springer, 2010, pp. 40–54.

[12] W. J. Paul, S. Schmaltz, and A. Shadrin, "Completing the automated verification of a small hypervisor – assembler code verification," in *SEFM*, ser. Lecture Notes in Computer Science, vol. 7504. Springer, 2012, pp. 188–202.

[13] M. Dahlin, R. Johnson, R. B. Krug, M. McCoyd, and W. D. Young, "Toward the verification of a simple hypervisor," in *ACL2*, ser. EPTCS, vol. 70, 2011, pp. 28–45.

[14] A. Puccetti, "Static analysis of the XEN kernel using Frama-C," *J. UCS*, vol. 16, no. 4, pp. 543–553, 2010.

[15] C. Cadar, D. Dunbar, and D. R. Engler, "KLEE: unassisted and automatic generation of high-coverage tests for complex systems programs," in *OSDI*. USENIX Association, 2008, pp. 209–224.

[16] C. Lattner and V. Adve, "LLVM: A compilation framework for lifelong program analysis & transformation," in *Proceedings of the International Symposium on Code Generation and Optimization: Feedback-Directed and Runtime Optimization*, ser. CGO 04. USA: IEEE Computer Society, 2004, p. 75.

[17] T. Avgerinos, S. K. Cha, A. Rebert, E. J. Schwartz, M. Woo, and D. Brumley, "Automatic exploit generation," *Commun. ACM*, vol. 57, no. 2, pp. 74–84, 2014. [Online]. Available: https://doi.org/10.1145/2560217.2560219

[18] B. Chen, Z. Yang, L. Lei, K. Cong, and F. Xie, "Automated bug detection and replay for COTS linux kernel modules with concolic execution," in *27th IEEE International Conference on Software Analysis, Evolution and Reengineering, SANER 2020, London, ON, Canada, February 18-21, 2020*, K. Kontogiannis, F. Khomh, A. Chatzigeorgiou, M. Fokaefs, and M. Zhou, Eds. IEEE, 2020, pp. 172–183. [Online]. Available: https://doi.org/10.1109/SANER48275.2020.9054797

[19] A. Biere, A. Cimatti, E. M. Clarke, and Y. Zhu, "Symbolic model checking without BDDs," in *TACAS*, ser. Lecture Notes in Computer Science, vol. 1579. Springer, 1999, pp. 193–207.

[20] M. Ben-Yehuda, M. D. Day, Z. Dubitzky, M. Factor, N. Har El, A. Gordon, A. Liguori, O. Wasserman, and B. Yassour, "The turtles project: Design and implementation of nested virtualization," in *9th USENIX Symposium on Operating Systems Design and Implementation, OSDI 2010, October 4-6, 2010, Vancouver, BC, Canada, Proceedings*. USENIX Association, 2010, pp. 423–436. [Online]. Available: http://www.usenix.org/events/osdi10/tech/full_papers/Ben-Yehuda.pdf

[21] H. Katzan Jr., "Operating systems architecture," in *AFIPS*, ser. AFIPS Conference Proceedings, vol. 36. AFIPS Press, 1970, pp. 109–118.

[22] G. J. Popek and R. P. Goldberg, "Formal requirements for virtualizable third generation architectures," *Commun. ACM*, vol. 17, no. 7, pp. 412–421, 1974.

[23] A. Kivity, "KVM: Kernel-based virtual machine," 2006, accessed: 2019-12-19. [Online]. Available: http://lkml.iu.edu/hypermail/linux/kernel/0610.2/1369.html

[24] Xenproject.org Security Team, "Advisory XSA-227," 2018, accessed: 2019-12-19. [Online]. Available: https://xenbits.xenproject.org/xsa/advisory-227.html

[25] D. Beyer, "Software verification with validation of results - (report on SV-COMP 2017)," in *TACAS*, ser. Lecture Notes in Computer Science, vol. 10206, 2017, pp. 331–349.

[26] M. Weiser, "Program slicing," in *ICSE*. IEEE Computer Society, 1981, pp. 439–449.

[27] A. Biere, E. M. Clarke, R. Raimi, and Y. Zhu, "Verifiying safety properties of a power PC microprocessor using symbolic model checking without bdds," in *CAV*, ser. Lecture Notes in Computer Science, vol. 1633. Springer, 1999, pp. 60–71.

[28] M. Shapiro and S. Horwitz, "Fast and accurate ow-insensitive points-to analysis," in *Conference Record of POPL 97: The 24th ACM SIGPLAN-SIGACT Symposium on Principles of Programming Languages, Papers Presented at the Symposium, Paris, France, 15-17 January 1997*. ACM Press, 1997, pp. 1–14. [Online]. Available: https://doi.org/10.1145/263699.263703

[29] N. Eén and N. Sörensson, "An extensible SAT-solver," in *SAT*, ser. Lecture Notes in Computer Science, vol. 2919. Springer, 2003, pp. 502–518.

[30] Xen Project, "Xen project 4.8.0," 2018, accessed: 2019-12-19. [Online]. Available: https://xenproject.org/downloads/xen-project-archives/xen-project-4-8-series/xen-project-4-8-0/

[31] "AWS Batch," 2016, accessed: 2019-12-19. [Online]. Available: https://aws.amazon.com/batch

[32] "Xen test framework," http://xenbits.xen.org/docs/xtf/, accessed: 2018-09-10.

[33] N. Eén and N. Sörensson, "Temporal induction by incremental SAT solving," *Electr. Notes Theor. Comput. Sci.*, vol. 89, no. 4, pp. 543–560, 2003.

5

Ternary Propagation-Based Local Search for more Bit-Precise Reasoning

Aina Niemetz ⓘD
Stanford University

Mathias Preiner ⓘD
Stanford University

Abstract—**Current state of the art for reasoning about quantifier-free bit-vector constraints in Satisfiability Modulo Theories (SMT) is a technique called bit-blasting, an eager translation into propositional logic (SAT). While efficient in practice, it may not scale for large bit-widths when the input size cannot be sufficiently reduced with preprocessing techniques. A recent propagation-based local search procedure was shown to be effective on hard satisfiable instances, in particular in combination with bit-blasting in a sequential portfolio setting. However, a major weakness of this approach is its obliviousness to bits that can be simplified to constant values. In this paper, we generalize propagation-based local search with respect to such constant bits to ternary values. We further extend the procedure to handle more bit-vector operators, and introduce heuristics for more precise inverse value computation via bound tightening for inequality constraints. We provide an extensive experimental evaluation and show that the presented techniques yield a considerable improvement in performance.**

I. INTRODUCTION

Satisfiability Modulo Theories (SMT) solvers for the theory of fixed-width bit-vectors provide bit-precise reasoning for many applications in hardware and software verification. In particular the quantifier-free fragment of this theory has received a lot of interest in recent years, as witnessed by the high and increasing number of participants in the corresponding divisions of the annual SMT competition [35]. Current state of the art for solving quantifier-free bit-vector formulas in SMT is a technique called bit-blasting, where the input formula is first simplified and then eagerly translated into propositional logic (SAT). While efficient in practice, it does not necessarily scale for large bit-widths, in particular if the size of the input cannot be sufficiently reduced during preprocessing.

In [24], we attacked the problem from a different angle and proposed a complete propagation-based local search procedure for quantifier-free bit-vector formulas. It is based on propagating target values from the outputs to the inputs, does not require bit-blasting, brute-force randomization or restarts, and lifts the concept of *backtracing* of Automatic Test Pattern Generation (ATPG) [19] to the word-level. Even though it only allows to determine satisfiability (as expected for local search), it is particularly effective in a sequential portfolio [36] combination with bit-blasting. One of its main weaknesses, however, is its obliviousness to bits that can be simplified to constant values [22]. For example, consider

a formula $(1110 \mathbin{\&} x) \not\approx 0000$, where the left operand of the *bitwise and* ($\&$) operation forces its least significant bit (LSB) to constant 0. The procedure in [24] is oblivious to this information and may select invalid target values for $(1110 \mathbin{\&} x)$ where the LSB is set to 1. Propagating such values that are invalid due to constant bits and can therefore never be assumed may introduce significant overhead.

In this paper, we generalize the propagation-based local search approach presented in [24] with respect to constant bits to ternary values. We extract constant bit information from the bit-level circuit representation of the input formula, use ternary bit-vectors to represent this information and propagate target values with respect to these constant bits. This allows us to propagate more precise target values since we can guarantee that we only propagate target values that can actually be assumed. We show in our experiments that this considerably reduces redundant work and improves performance.

Down-propagating values as in [24] utilizes inverse value (and its less restrictive variant, consistent value) computation. Computing inverse values is, however, not always possible. For example, finding an inverse value for x in multiplication $x \cdot s$ such that it produces value t given value s, i.e., $x \cdot s \approx t$, is only possible if the value of t has at least as many rightmost zeroes in its binary representation as the value of s, i.e., if the *invertibility condition* $(s \mid -s) \mathbin{\&} t \approx t$ is true. A consistent value for x, on the other hand, is any value that produces t disregarding value s, i.e., there exists a value v such that $x \cdot v \approx t$. Finding consistent values for x is in general always possible. When considering constant bits in x, however, inverse and consistent value computation is further restricted, and the latter becomes conditional. In [24] we defined invertibility conditions without considering constant bits in x in pseudocode, which we then formalized and verified in [26]. In this paper, we provide and verify invertibility conditions and *consistency conditions* with respect to constant bits in the operand to solve for. We further extend the set of natively supported bit-vector operators, and introduce heuristics for more precise inverse value computation via bound tightening for inequality constraints. To summarize, this paper makes the following *contributions*.

- We introduce the notion of *consistency condition*. We further derive and present invertibility conditions and consistency conditions *with respect to constant bits* for a representative set of bit-vector operators that allows us to model all bit-vector operators defined in SMT-LIB [4].

This work was supported in part by DARPA (award no. FA8650-18-2-7861) and ONR (award no. N68335-17-C-0558).

- We verify the correctness of all presented conditions up to a certain bit-width.
- We present a (probabilistically approximately) complete [17] generalization of the propagation-based local search procedure in [24] with respect to constant bits.
- We extend the set of bit-vector operators from [24] with bit-wise xor, signed less than, sign extension and arithmetic right shift, and provide invertibility and consistency conditions modulo constant bits for all of them.
- We introduce two heuristics for inequality predicates that allow us to infer more precise inverse values based on tightening bounds with respect to its operands and satisfied top-level inequalities.

Related Work. In previous years, a new generation of SAT solvers implementing Stochastic Local Search (SLS) achieved remarkable results in SAT competitions [2, 3, 6]. Hybrid combinations of SLS and CDCL [30] SAT procedures aim to get more than the best out of both worlds by tightly integrating SLS strategies into the CDCL approach, with promising results in last year's SAT race [8, 31, 33]. Attempts to utilize SLS techniques in SMT by integrating an SLS SAT solver into the DPLL(T)-framework of the SMT solver MathSAT [12], on the other hand, were not able to compete with bit-blasting [16]. In [15], Fröhlich et al. lifted stochastic local search (SLS) from the bit-level to the word-level without bit-blasting, with promising results. Their approach, however, does not fully exploit the word-level structure but rather simulates bit-level local search by focusing on single bit flips. In [25], we proposed a propagation-based extension of [15], which introduced an additional strategy to propagate assignments from the outputs to the inputs. Our propagation-based local search approach in [24] expands on this idea and does not employ any SLS strategies. Invertibility conditions have been formalized, verified and utilized for quantified bit-vector formulas to generate symbolic instantiations in [26]. Recently, in [10] the concept of invertibility conditions has been lifted to the theory of floating-points by means of Syntax-Guided Synthesis (SyGuS) [1].

II. Preliminaries

We assume the usual notions and terminology of many-sorted first-order logic with equality (denoted by $\approx$) (see, e.g., [14, 20]). We will focus on the quantifier-free fragment of the theory of fixed-size bit-vectors $T_{BV} = (\Sigma_{BV}, I_{BV})$ as defined by the SMT-LIB 2 standard [4]. The signature Σ_{BV} includes a unique sort $\sigma_{[w]}$ for each bit-width w, function symbols overloaded for every $\sigma_{[w]}$, all *bit-vector constants* of sort $\sigma_{[w]}$ for each w, and a sort Bool and the Boolean constants $\top$ (true) and $\bot$ (false). We further assume that Σ_{BV} includes the Boolean operators $\neg$ (not) and $\wedge$ (and). Without loss of generality, we will interpret Boolean expressions as bit-vector expressions of size one. The non-empty class of Σ_{BV}-interpretations I_{BV} (the *models* of T_{BV}) interpret sort and functions symbols as specified in SMT-LIB 2.

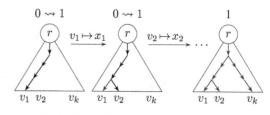

Fig. 1: Basic idea of propagation-based local search.

We denote a Σ_{BV}-term (or *bit-vector term*) a of width w as $a_{[w]}$ when we want to specify its bit-width explicitly. The width of a bit-vector sort or term is given by the function κ, e.g., $\kappa(\sigma_{[w]}) = w$ and $\kappa(t_{[w]}) = w$. We will omit the bit-width from the notation when it is clear from the context.

We represent a bit-vector constant $c_{[w]}$ as a bit-string of 0s and 1s, with the most significant bit (MSB) as the left-most bit $c[msb]$ at index $msb = w - 1$, and the least significant bit (LSB) as the right-most bit $c[lsb]$ at index $lsb = 0$. We use $\text{smax}_{[w]}$ or $\text{smin}_{[w]}$ for the *maximum or minimum signed value* of width w, e.g., $\text{smax}_{[4]} = 0111$ and $\text{smin}_{[4]} = 1000$, and $\text{ones}_{[w]}$ for the maximum unsigned value, e.g., $\text{ones}_{[4]} = 1111$. We refer to the bit at index i of a bit-vector t as $t[i]$ and use $ctz(t)$ to denote the *count of trailing zeros* of a bit-vector t. Similarly, $clz(t)$ and $clo(t)$ denote the count of *leading zeros* and *leading ones* in t. When interpreting t as signed value, we use $cnt(t)$ to denote $clo(t)$ when $t[msb] \approx 1$, and $clz(t)$ when $t[msb] \approx 0$. We further use function min to determine the unsigned minimum value of two bit-vectors, and functions $addo$ and $mulo$, which return true if the addition and multiplication of two bit-vectors overflows, respectively.

Without loss of generality, for a given input formula we consider a restricted set of bit-vector function symbols (or *bit-vector operators*) as listed in Table I. The selection in this set is arbitrary but complete in the sense that it suffices to express all bit-vector operators defined in SMT-LIB 2. This means that our approach is not restricted to this particular set of operators and can be lifted to any other set of bit-vector operators.

Note that we extend the set of operators considered in [24] with $<_s$, $\oplus$, $\gg_a$ and sign extension. Further, we sometimes use the logical connectives $\vee$ (or), $\Rightarrow$ (implication) and $\Leftrightarrow$ (if and only if), and the bit-vector operators $\not\approx$ (disequality), $|$ (bit-wise or) and (un)signed inequalities $\leq_u$, $\geq_u$, $\leq_s$ and $\geq_s$ as shorthand when convenient.

III. Propagation-Based Local Search

The basic idea of the propagation-based local search procedure for quantifier-free bit-vector constraints as presented in [24] is illustrated in Figure 1 and lifts the concept of backtracing from ATPG [19] from the bit-level to the word-level. The procedure iteratively moves from a non-satisfying to a satisfying assignment by propagating target values from the outputs towards the inputs as follows.

Given a quantifier-free bit-vector formula as a directed acyclic graph (DAG) with a single root node r. We start from a random initial assignment to the inputs that does not satisfy r, i.e., root r evaluates to 0, and assume that its target value is 1 (this desired transition from actual to target value is indicated in Figure 1 by $0 \rightsquigarrow 1$). Starting from the root, this target value is then propagated along a single path towards an input, and this process is repeated until the root is satisfied, i.e., a solution is found. Down-propagation of target values is performed as a down-traversal where each traversal step represents a *propagation step*. In each propagation step, we first select the *propagation path*, i.e., the operand of the current node (representing a bit-vector operation) for which we want to compute the next target value. After selecting the propagation path, we then select the *propagation value* (the new target value) for the selected operand.

Propagation path and value selection are the two main sources of *non-determinism* of this procedure. Paths are non-deterministically selected with a preference to *essential inputs*. The concept of essential inputs was introduced in [24] to lift the notion of *controlling* inputs from the bit-level to the word-level, e.g., for $00 \cdot 01 \approx t$ with target value $t = 10$, the left operand of the multiplication is essential since t can not be assumed without changing its value. Target values are determined via *inverse* and (its less strict variant) *consistent value computation*, and non-deterministically chosen if multiple possible values exist. An *inverse value* for an operand x allows to immediately produce a given target value assuming that the current value of the other operand (if any) does not change, e.g., for $x \cdot 10 \approx t$ with target value $t = 10$, both 01 and 11 are inverse values for x. A *consistent value* for x, on the other hand, allows to produce a given target value after changing the value of the other operand (if necessary), e.g., for $x \cdot 00 \approx t$ with target value $t = 10$, any value greater than zero is a consistent value for x. Notice that for every bit-vector literal $x \diamond s \approx t$ (with $\diamond$ a bit-vector operator as listed in Table I), any inverse value is also a consistent value for x.

When down-propagating values, inverse value computation can only be applied if such an inverse value exists. Computing a consistent value, on the other hand, is always possible (if constant bits are not considered, as in [24]). Inverse value computation is usually preferred over consistent value computation if possible. If no inverse value exists, the procedure falls back to consistent value computation. However, even if an inverse value exists, it is necessary to non-deterministically select between inverse and consistent value computation in order to guarantee completeness, as shown in [24].

Propagation-based local search as in [24] is not able to determine unsatisfiability, as expected for local search. However, when determining satisfiability it is probabilistically approximately complete (PAC) [17], i.e., it is guaranteed to (eventually) find a solution if there exists one.

IV. PROPAGATING CONSTANT BITS

In this section, we generalize the propagation-based local search procedure as presented in [24] with respect to constant bits to ternary values. Figure 2 describes the generalized algorithm in pseudocode, with all parts of the original algorithm (as given in [24]) that are affected by the generalization indicated

Symbol	SMT-LIB Syntax	Sort
$\approx, <_u, <_s$	=, bvult, bvslt	$\sigma_{[w]} \times \sigma_{[w]} \to$ Bool
$\sim$	bvnot	$\sigma_{[w]} \to \sigma_{[w]}$
$\&, \oplus$	bvand, bvxor	$\sigma_{[w]} \times \sigma_{[w]} \to \sigma_{[w]}$
$\ll, \gg, \gg_a$	bvshl, bvlshr, bvashr	$\sigma_{[w]} \times \sigma_{[w]} \to \sigma_{[w]}$
$+, \cdot$	bvadd, bvmul	$\sigma_{[w]} \times \sigma_{[w]} \to \sigma_{[w]}$
mod, $\div$	bvurem, bvudiv	$\sigma_{[w]} \times \sigma_{[w]} \to \sigma_{[w]}$
$\circ$	concat	$\sigma_{[w]} \times \sigma_{[m]} \to \sigma_{[w+m]}$
$\langle m \rangle$	sign_extend	$\sigma_{[w]} \to \sigma_{[m+w]}$
$[u:l]$	extract ($l \le u < w$)	$\sigma_{[w]} \to \sigma_{[u-l+1]}$

TABLE I: Set of considered bit-vector operators.

```
function sat(r, 𝒜_t, 𝒜_b):
1    while 𝒜_b(r) ≉ 1:
2        n = r, t = 1
3        while ¬isLeaf(n):
4            n_x = select(n, t, 𝒜_b)
5            if ¬isConsistent(n, n_x, t, 𝒜_t):
6                break   // conflict
7                v = value(n, n_x, t, 𝒜_t, 𝒜_b)
8            t = v, n = n_x
9            if ¬const(n):
10               𝒜_b = 𝒜_b{n ↦ t}
11   return true
```

Fig. 2: The propagation-based local search algorithm generalized with respect to constant bits to ternary values. Parts affected and lifted are indicated in blue.

in blue (with boxed line numbers). In the following, we first introduce notation, and then describe how to lift all relevant parts of the procedure to ternary values.

Without loss of generality and as in [24], we assume that a quantifier-free bit-vector formula ϕ is represented as a single-rooted DAG with root r of bit-width one. Its set of nodes $\mathcal{N}$ includes r and is partitioned into a set of *bit-vector operations* and a set of *leaf* nodes, the latter consisting of bit-vector constants and bit-vector variables (the *primary inputs*).

In the following, given a bit-vector literal $\diamond x \approx t$ or $x \diamond s \approx t$ (with $\diamond$ a bit-vector operator as listed in Table I), we will use t for the target value of the bit-vector operation, x to identify the operand we compute a value for, and s for the value of the other operand (if any).

We define a *binary bit-vector* as introduced above, and a *ternary bit-vector* x as a vector of three-valued bits where each bit can assume the values true (1), false (0) and undetermined (•). We either use a string representation or a range-based representation for x, where the latter is a pair of binary bit-vectors $\langle x^{lo}, x^{hi} \rangle$ that determine the lower and upper bound of x, respectively. If $x[i] = •$, then $x^{lo}[i] = 0$ and $x^{hi}[i] = 1$, and $x[i]$ otherwise. For example, a ternary bit-vector of size 4 with a true MSB and all other bits undetermined is represented as 1••• when represented as a string, and as the pair of two binary bit-vectors $\langle 1000, 1111 \rangle$ when represented as a bit-vector range. In the following, we only consider *valid* range representations for ternary bit-vectors, i.e., pairs $\langle x^{lo}, x^{hi} \rangle$ for which the validity check ($\sim x^{lo} \mid x^{hi} \approx$ ones) from [21] evaluates to true. For example, a range $\langle 1100, 1000 \rangle$ is invalid since $x^{lo}[2] >_u x^{hi}[2]$, and thus $\sim 1100 \mid 1000 \approx 1011 \not\approx 1111$. We use function $valid(x^{lo}, x^{hi})$ to check if x is valid.

In the following, we will use x for ternary bit-vectors, and s, t and v for binary bit-vectors. Further, to simplify notation, we will frequently use bit-vector literal patterns $\diamond x \approx t$ and $x \diamond s \approx t$ ($s \diamond x \approx t$) for unary and binary literals, where we mix ternary and binary bit-vectors. We use x in these patterns as a placeholder, which represents constant bits in the operand we want to compute a binary bit-vector value for. Further, we sometimes give definitions only for one binary case (e.g., $x \diamond s \approx t$) when the other case is treated symmetrically.

We define assignment $\mathcal{A}_b : \mathcal{N} \mapsto \{0, 1\}^+$ of formula ϕ as a complete function that maps nodes $n \in \mathcal{N}$ to binary bit-vector values. We use $\mathcal{A}_b\{n \mapsto t\}$ to update node n to map to the new binary bit-vector value t, and assume that such an update propagates with respect to the semantics of the operators listed in Table I, e.g., $\mathcal{A}_b(n_x + n_s) = \mathcal{A}_b(n_x) + \mathcal{A}_b(n_s)$ for $n_x, n_s \in \mathcal{N}$. We further define assignment $\mathcal{A}_t : \mathcal{N} \mapsto \{0, 1, \bullet\}^+$ as a complete function that represents constant bits and maps nodes $n \in \mathcal{N}$ to ternary bit-vectors. Assignment $\mathcal{A}_t$ is precomputed as described in Section IV-B.

Definition 1 (Matching Constant Bits). *Given a ternary bit-vector x represented as a pair of binary bit-vectors $\langle x^{lo}, x^{hi} \rangle$. A binary bit-vector v matches the constant bits in x if and only if $(x^{hi}\ \&\ v \approx v) \wedge (x^{lo} \mid v \approx v)$.*

We use function mcb to check for matching constant bits, i.e., $mcb(x, v)$ (alternatively, $mcb(x^{lo}, x^{hi}, v)$) is true if v matches the constant bits in x.

Given a bit-vector operation $\diamond n_x$ or $n_x \diamond n_s$ ($n_s \diamond n_x$) with operand $n_s \in \mathcal{N}$, operand $n_x \in \mathcal{N}$ the operand to solve for, and $\diamond$ an operator as defined in Table I. As a first step, we lift the notion of random, inverse and consistent values from [24] to consider constant bits in n_x as follows.

Definition 2 (Random Value). *A binary bit-vector v is a random value for a ternary bit-vector $x = \mathcal{A}_t(n_x)$ if $\kappa(v) \approx \kappa(x) \wedge mcb(x, v)$.*

Definition 3 (Consistent Value). *Given a bit-vector literal $\diamond x \approx t$ or $x \diamond s \approx t$, with $x = \mathcal{A}_t(n_x)$ a ternary bit-vector representing constant bits in n_x, and $s = \mathcal{A}_b(n_s)$ and t binary bit-vectors. Given a target value t, a random value v is a consistent value for x if (there exists a binary bit-vector value s' such that) $\diamond v \approx t$ or $v \diamond s' \approx t$ evaluates to $\top$.*

Definition 4 (Inverse Value). *Given a bit-vector literal and x, s and t as above. Given a target value t (and a value s), a consistent value v is called an inverse value for x if $\diamond v \approx t$ or $v \diamond s \approx t$ evaluates to $\top$.*

As an example, consider a ternary bit-vector $x_{[2]} = 1\bullet$ with $x^{lo} = 10$ and $x^{hi} = 11$. For $x \cdot 11 \approx 01$, $v = 11$ is an inverse value for x. For $x \cdot 00 \approx 01$, there exists no inverse value, but $v = 11$ is a consistent value for x since $11 \cdot s' \approx 01$ with

$s' = 11$. A random value for x that is neither an inverse value nor a consistent value for both examples is $v = 10$.

Given a binary bit-vector operation $n = n_x \diamond n_s$ with $n \in \mathcal{N}$ and $\diamond$ an operator as defined in Table I. We lift the notion of essential input of n from [24] to consider constant bits in its operands $n_x, n_s \in \mathcal{N}$ as follows.

Definition 5 (Essential Input). *Let n_x be an operand of a node $n \in \mathcal{N}$ with $n = n_x \diamond n_s$ and $\mathcal{A}_b(n) = \mathcal{A}_b(n_x) \diamond \mathcal{A}_b(n_s)$. Further, let t be the target value of n. We say that n_x is an essential input with respect to t if there exists no value v for n_s with respect to constant bits in n_s such that $\mathcal{A}_b(n_x) \diamond v \approx t$.*

For example, consider inequality $n_x <_u n_s$ with target value $t = 1$, $\mathcal{A}_b(n_x) = 1011$, $\mathcal{A}_b(n_s) = 1000$ and $\mathcal{A}_t(n_s) = 100\bullet$. When only considering the current assignment of n_x and n_s in $\mathcal{A}_b$, neither of the operands is essential—operand n_x would be if $\mathcal{A}_b(n_x) = \text{ones}_{[4]}$, and n_s if $\mathcal{A}_b(n_s) = 0_{[4]}$. However, considering constant bits in n_s, operand n_x is essential since n_s can not assume a value greater than $\mathcal{A}_b(n_x)$. More generally, for any $n_x <_u n_s$ with $\mathcal{A}_t(n_x) = \langle x^{lo}, x^{hi} \rangle$ and $\mathcal{A}_t(n_s) = \langle s^{lo}, s^{hi} \rangle$, n_x is essential if $\mathcal{A}_b(n_x) \approx \text{ones} \vee \mathcal{A}_b(n_x) \geq_u s^{hi}$, and n_s is essential if $\mathcal{A}_b(n_s) \approx 0 \vee x^{lo} \geq_u \mathcal{A}_b(n_s)$.

As an interesting general observation, an operand n_x is essential if there exists no inverse value for the other operand n_s given $\mathcal{A}_b(n_x)$, $\mathcal{A}_t(n_s)$ and target value t. Operands to unary bit-vector operations are always essential.

Algorithm Overview. Function sat in Figure 2 determines the satisfiability of a given input formula, and takes as input root r, an initial assignment $\mathcal{A}_b$, and a precomputed fixed assignment $\mathcal{A}_t$. Assignment $\mathcal{A}_b$ is updated in each iteration of the outer loop (lines 1–8), whereas $\mathcal{A}_t$ is determined before function sat is called. Each iteration of the outer loop represents a move, i.e., the down propagation of target value $t = 1$ for root r along a single path until a primary input is reached, which then triggers an update of assignment $\mathcal{A}_b$ (lines 9–10) where input n is mapped to the new value t. Each iteration of the inner loop (lines 3–8) represents a single down propagation (a propagation step), which mainly consists of two phases: path selection (line 4) and value selection (line 7).

Path Selection. In each propagation step, on line 4, we first select the next leg of the propagation path as follows. For a bit-vector operation n, function $select$ first determines which of its operands are essential with respect to target value t and constant bits in the other operand (if any). If all or none of the operands are essential, we non-deterministically select one of them. Else, the essential operand is selected.

To determine if an operand n_x is essential, we check if it is possible to find an inverse value for the other operand n_s given t, $\mathcal{A}_b(n_x)$ and $\mathcal{A}_t(n_s)$, i.e., we check if the corresponding invertibility condition when solved for n_s is false. For example, for $n_x + n_s$ with $t = 11$, $\mathcal{A}_b(n_x) = 10$ and $\mathcal{A}_t(n_s) = \bullet 0$, n_x is essential since $mcb(\bullet 0, 11 - 10)$ is false.

Value Selection. After selecting the path, we then propagate t as target value for n to its selected operand n_x by computing an inverse or consistent value for n_x. An inverse value, however, does not always exist, even when constant bits in the selected operand are not considered. And while it is always possible to find a consistent value when constant bits are not considered, this is not the case when they are. We therefore generalize the notion of *invertibility conditions* [24, 26] and introduce the new notion of *consistency conditions* to determine if there exists a value for n_x with respect to $\mathcal{A}_t(n_x)$ such that target value t can be assumed. These conditions are utilized when selecting the propagation value as follows.

In each propagation step in Figure 2, before selecting a value with respect to constant bits for operand n_x (line 7), function *isConsistent* tests the corresponding *consistency condition* for bit-vector operation n and its operand n_x with respect to target value t and $x = \mathcal{A}_t(n_x)$ (line 5). If this determines that no consistent value exists, the current target value for n can never be assumed (notice that every inverse value is also consistent) and we stop the current down propagation by breaking out of the inner loop to restart from the root (line 6). Note that this is in contrast to the original procedure, where it was *always* possible to find a consistent value for n_x.

If the consistency condition is true, in function *value* on line 5, we select a consistent value if no inverse value exists, i.e., if the *invertibility condition* for n with respect to n_x, t, $s = \mathcal{A}_b(n_s)$ (if any other operand n_s) and $x = \mathcal{A}_t(n_x)$ is false. Else, we non-deterministically choose between inverse and consistent values (with a preference for inverse values). As shown in [24], the latter non-deterministic choice between inverse and consistent values (as opposed to always choosing inverse values if possible) is necessary for the sake of completeness. Note that if multiple possible inverse or consistent values exist, we non-deterministically select one of them.

Invertibility Conditions. Given target value t for bit-vector operation n and the current assignment $s = \mathcal{A}_b(n_s)$ of its operand other than n_x (if any), computing an *inverse* value is in general *not* always possible, even when not considering constant bits in n_x. As in [26], we refer to the exact condition under which an inverse value can be computed for x given s and t as *invertibility condition* (IC), e.g., for bit-vector literal $x \diamond s \approx t$ we have that $\forall s, t. (IC(s, t) \Leftrightarrow \exists y. (y \diamond s \approx t))$. We lift this to consider constant bits in n_x by interpreting x as a ternary bit-vector $x = \mathcal{A}_t(n_x)$, and yield generalized invertibility conditions for all operators in Table I as given in Tables II–III. Thus, for literal $x \diamond s \approx t$ we now have that

$$\forall x, s, t. (IC(x, s, t) \Leftrightarrow \exists y. (y \diamond s \approx t \wedge mcb(x, y))). \quad (1)$$

The unary case is defined analogously. Note that invertibility conditions without considering constant bits in n_x were first given in pseudocode in [24], and formalized and verified for up to 65 bits in [26]. In Tables II and III, we indicate the part of an invertibility condition that is the condition without considering constant bits in n_x in blue. For cases that do not include such a condition, this condition is $\top$. For example, for $x \cdot s \approx t$, the blue part of the invertibility condition ensures that $ctz(s) \leq_u ctz(t)$, and the remainder determines if possible solutions match constant bits in x.

Consistency Conditions. Computing a *consistent* value when *not* considering constant bits is *always* possible, and thus in the procedure in [24], it was never possible to encounter a case where no inverse *and* no consistent value exists. In contrast, when considering constant bits in n_x, it is *not always* possible to determine a consistent value for n_x, e.g., for $\bullet 0 \cdot s \approx 01$ there is no value that x can assume such that t can be produced for some s. We therefore introduce the new notion of *consistency condition* when considering constant bits in n_x as follows.

Definition 6. *(Consistency Condition) Given a bit-vector literal $\diamond x \approx t$ or $x \diamond s \approx t$, we refer to the exact condition under which a consistent value can be computed for x given t as* consistency condition *(CC)*.

For unary operations, any invertibility condition is also a consistency condition. For $x \diamond s \approx t$, we have that

$$\forall x, t. (CC(x, t) \Leftrightarrow \exists y, s. (y \diamond s \approx t \wedge mcb(x, y))) \quad (2)$$

and the other binary case is defined analogously. The consistency conditions with respect to constant bits in x for bit-vector operators in Table I are given in Tables IV and V.

Synthesizing Conditions. Previous work utilized SyGuS techniques to synthesize invertibility conditions for bit-vector [26] and floating-point [10] literals. For this work, we adopted the SyGuS approach from [26] to find invertibility and consistency conditions with respect to constant bits. We encoded Equations 1 and 2 as SyGuS problems to synthesize functions IC and CC and defined a general grammar that includes all bit-vector operators from Table I (excl. concatenation and sign extension), common logical connectives and the additional operators mcb, clz, ctz, and clo. For the invertibility condition problems, we further added the corresponding condition that must hold without considering constant bits (indicated in blue in Tables II–III) as pre-condition. In total, we generated 30 (15 invertibility, 15 consistency) SyGuS problems and used the SyGuS solver in CVC4 [29] with a time limit of 7200 seconds and 8GB memory limit. Overall, CVC4 was able to synthesize 10 conditions (3 invertibility and 7 consistency conditions). Unfortunately, all three invertibility conditions were trivial and we were not successful in synthesizing any complex invertibility conditions. Of the seven consistency conditions, on the other hand, three were significantly simpler than the manually crafted ones (marked with ★ in Table V).

Completeness (PAC). As in [24], the two main sources of non-determinism of our procedure are path and value selection when down-propagating target values. However, we now aim to only propagate target values that can actually be assumed, i.e., $mcb(\mathcal{A}_t(n_x), \mathcal{A}_b(n_x)) = \top$. Path selection still implements the same strategy as in [24], i.e., essential inputs are selected over non-essential inputs. The notion of essential input has been lifted to constant bits, however, this only excludes values that can never be assumed. Generalizing value selection to ternary values, as intended, significantly changes the behavior of the algorithm compared to [24]. Since we compute consistent and inverse values with respect to

$(x \approx s) \approx t$	$(t \Rightarrow mcb(x,s)) \wedge (\sim t \Rightarrow (x^{hi} \not\approx x^{lo} \vee x^{hi} \not\approx s))$
$(x <_u s) \approx t$	$(t \Rightarrow s \not\approx 0 \wedge x^{lo} <_u s) \wedge (\sim t \Rightarrow (s \geq_u x) \approx t)$
$(s <_u x) \approx t$	$(t \Rightarrow s \not\approx ones \wedge x^{hi} >_u s) \wedge (\sim t \Rightarrow x^{lo} \leq_u s)$
$(x <_s s) \approx t$	$(t \Rightarrow (s \not\approx smin \wedge ((x[msb] \approx 0 \wedge x^{lo} <_s s) \vee (x[msb] \in \{1,\bullet\} \wedge (smin \mid x^{lo}) <_s s)))) \wedge (\sim t \Rightarrow (((x[msb] \approx 1 \wedge x^{hi} \geq_s s) \vee (x[msb] \in \{0,\bullet\} \wedge (smax \,\&\, x^{hi}) \geq_s s))))$
$(s <_s x) \approx t$	$(t \Rightarrow (s \not\approx smax \wedge ((x[msb] \approx 1 \wedge s <_s x^{hi}) \vee (x[msb] \in \{0,\bullet\} \wedge s <_s (smax \,\&\, x^{hi}))))) \wedge (\sim t \Rightarrow (((x[msb] \approx 0 \wedge s \geq_s x^{lo}) \vee (x[msb] \in \{1,\bullet\} \wedge s \geq_s (smin \mid x^{lo})))))$

TABLE II: Invertibility conditions for bit-vector predicates modulo constant bits in x.

constant bits and break on conflict when no consistent value exists, it is guaranteed that every target value that is propagated down all the way to the primary inputs can be assumed with respect to constant bits in the inputs. As a consequence, we only exclude target values that can never be part of a satisfying assignment of the input formula. Our procedure is thus still probabilistically approximately complete (PAC), following the same line of argument as in [24].

A. Verifying Invertibility and Consistency Conditions

The invertibility and consistency conditions in Tables II–V are utilized in our procedure to determine whether a given target value can be down-propagated. Incorrect conditions will not result in unsoundness of the procedure, but may affect completeness (PAC). To verify the correctness of these conditions we check for each literal and bit-width up to 65 if the negation of the corresponding quantified formula as defined above is unsatisfiable. For unary literals, consistency conditions are also invertibility conditions and we only have to check the unsatisfiability of

$$\exists x^{lo}, x^{hi}, t.\, valid(x^{lo}, x^{hi}) \wedge \neg(IC(x,t) \Leftrightarrow \exists y.\, (\diamond y \approx t \wedge mcb(x^{lo}, x^{hi}, y))).$$

Note that we do not test the conditions for extracts since they can essentially be reduced to the checks for equality, which makes tests for all combinations of upper and lower indices redundant. Further, in order to keep the number of queries manageable, we only check for signed extensions of up to 4 bits. For binary literals, we check each of the formulas

$$\exists x^{lo}, x^{hi}, s, t.\, valid(x^{lo}, x^{hi}) \wedge \neg(IC(x,s,t) \Leftrightarrow \exists y.\, (y \diamond s \approx t \wedge mcb(x^{lo}, x^{hi}, y)))$$

$$\exists x^{lo}, x^{hi}, t.\, valid(x^{lo}, x^{hi}) \wedge \neg(CC(x,t) \Leftrightarrow \exists y, s.\, (y \diamond s \approx t \wedge mcb(x^{lo}, x^{hi}, y)))$$

The other binary case is defined analogously. Note that for the sake of simplicity, we only use operands of the same bit-width (from 1 to 65) for concatenation. Concatenation can again be seen as a special case of equality, i.e., $x \circ s \approx t$ can be interpreted as $x \circ s \approx t_x \circ t_s$, and the check can be reduced to checking the condition $IC((x \approx t_x) \approx 1) \wedge s \approx t_s$. Hence,

$x + s \approx t$	$mcb(x, t-s)$
$x \cdot s \approx t$	$(-s \mid s) \,\&\, t \approx t \wedge (s \approx 0 \vee ((odd(s) \Rightarrow mcb(x, t \cdot s^{-1})) \wedge (\neg odd(s) \Rightarrow mcb(x \ll c, y \ll c))))$ with $c = ctz(s)$ and $y = (t \gg c) \cdot (s \gg c)^{-1}$
$x \bmod s \approx t$	$\sim(-s) \geq_u t \wedge ((s \approx 0 \vee t \approx ones) \Rightarrow mcb(x,t)) \wedge ((s \not\approx 0 \wedge t \not\approx ones) \Rightarrow \exists y.\, (mcb(x, s \cdot y + t) \wedge \neg mulo(s,y) \wedge \neg addo(s \cdot y, t)))$
$s \bmod x \approx t$	$(t+t-s) \,\&\, s \geq_u t \wedge (s \approx t \Rightarrow (x^{lo} \approx 0 \vee x^{hi} >_u t)) \wedge (s \not\approx t \Rightarrow \exists y.\, (mcb(x,y) \wedge y >_u t \wedge (s-t) \bmod y \approx 0))$
$x \div s \approx t$	$(s \cdot t) \div s \approx t \wedge (t \approx 0 \Rightarrow x^{lo} <_u s) \wedge ((t \not\approx 0 \wedge s \not\approx 0) \Rightarrow \exists y.\, (mcb(x,y) \wedge (\neg c \Rightarrow y <_u s \cdot t + 1) \wedge (c \Rightarrow y \leq_u ones)))$ with $c = mulo(s, t+1) \vee addo(t,1)$
$s \div x \approx t$	$s \div (s \div t) \approx t \wedge (t \not\approx ones \Rightarrow x^{hi} >_u 0) \wedge ((s \not\approx 0 \vee t \not\approx 0) \Rightarrow (s \div x^{hi} \leq_u t \wedge \exists y.\, (mcb(x,y) \wedge (t \approx ones \Rightarrow y \geq_u 0 \wedge y \leq_u s \div t) \wedge (t \not\approx ones \Rightarrow y >_u t + 1 \wedge y \leq_u s \div t))))$
$x \,\&\, s \approx t$	$t \,\&\, s \approx t \wedge ((s \,\&\, x^{hi}) \,\&\, c) \approx (t \,\&\, c)$ with $c = \sim(x^{lo} \oplus x^{hi})$
$x \oplus s \approx t$	$mcb(x, s \oplus t)$
$x \ll s \approx t$	$(t \gg s) \ll s \approx t \wedge mcb(x \ll s, t)$
$s \ll x \approx t$	$ctz(s) \leq_u ctz(t) \wedge (t \not\approx 0 \Rightarrow s \ll c \approx t) \wedge (t \approx 0 \Rightarrow (x^{hi} \geq_u c \vee s \approx 0)) \wedge (t \not\approx 0 \Rightarrow mcb(x,c))$ with $c = ctz(t) - ctz(s)$
$x \gg s \approx t$	$(t \ll s) \gg s \approx t \wedge mcb(x \gg s, t)$
$s \gg x \approx t$	$clz(s) \leq_u clz(t) \wedge (t \not\approx 0 \Rightarrow s \gg c \approx t) \wedge (t \approx 0 \Rightarrow (x^{hi} \geq_u c \vee s \approx 0)) \wedge (t \not\approx 0 \Rightarrow mcb(x,c))$ with $c = clz(t) - clz(s)$
$x \gg_a s \approx t$	$(s <_u \kappa(s) \Rightarrow ((t \ll s) \gg_a s \approx t)) \wedge (s \geq_u \kappa(s) \Rightarrow (t \approx ones \vee t \approx 0)) \wedge mcb(x \gg_a s, t)$
$s \gg_a x \approx t$	$s[msb] \approx 0 \Rightarrow IC(s \gg x = t) \wedge s[msb] \approx 1 \Rightarrow IC(\sim s \gg x = \sim t)$
$x \circ s \approx t$	$s \approx t^s \wedge mcb(x, t^x)$ with $t^x = t[msb : \kappa(s)]$ and $t^s = t[\kappa(s) - 1 : lsb]$
$s \circ x \approx t$	$s \approx t^s \wedge mcb(x, t^x)$ with $t^s = t[msb : \kappa(s)]$ and $t^x = t[\kappa(s) - 1 : lsb]$
$x\langle n \rangle \approx t$	$(t^n \approx 0 \vee t^n \approx ones) \wedge mcb(x, t^x)$ with $t^n = t[msb : \kappa(x) - 1]$ and $t^x = t[\kappa(x) - 1 : lsb]$
$x[u : l] \approx t$	$mcb(x[u : l], t)$

TABLE III: Invertibility conditions for non-predicate bit-vector operators modulo constant bits in x.

$(x \approx s) \approx t$	$\top$
$(x <_u s) \approx t$	$\sim t \vee x^{lo} \not\approx ones$
$(s <_u x) \approx t$	$\sim t \vee x^{hi} \not\approx 0$
$(x <_s s) \approx t$	$\sim t \vee (x^{lo} \approx x^{hi} \Rightarrow x^{lo} \not\approx smax)$
$(s <_s x) \approx t$	$\sim t \vee (x^{lo} \approx x^{hi} \Rightarrow x^{lo} \not\approx smin)$

TABLE IV: Consistency conditions for bit-vector predicates modulo constant bits in x.

$x + s \approx t$	$\top$
$x \cdot s \approx t$	$(t \not\approx 0 \Rightarrow x^{hi} \not\approx 0) \wedge (odd(t) \Rightarrow x^{hi}[lsb] \not\approx 0) \wedge$ $(\neg odd(t) \Rightarrow \exists y. (mcb(x,y) \wedge ctz(t) \geq_u ctz(y)))$
$x \bmod s \approx t$	$(t \approx \text{ones} \Rightarrow mcb(x, \text{ones})) \wedge$ $(t \not\approx \text{ones} \Rightarrow (t >_u (\text{ones} - t) \Rightarrow mcb(x,t)) \wedge$ $(t \leq_u (\text{ones} - t) \Rightarrow (mcb(x,t) \vee$ $\exists y. (mcb(x,y) \wedge y >_u 2 \cdot t))))$
★ $s \bmod x \approx t$	$(x^{lo} \gg (t \div x^{hi})) \approx x^{lo}$
$x \div s \approx t$	$(t \not\approx \text{ones} \Rightarrow x^{hi} \geq_u t) \wedge (t \approx 0 \Rightarrow x^{lo} \not\approx \text{ones}) \wedge$ $((t \not\approx 0 \wedge t \not\approx \text{ones} \wedge t \not\approx 1 \wedge \neg mcb(x,t)) \Rightarrow$ $(\neg mulo(2,t) \wedge \exists y, o. (mcb(x, y \cdot t + o) \wedge y \geq_u 1 \wedge$ $o \leq_u c \wedge \neg mulo(y,t) \wedge \neg addo(y \cdot t, o))))$ with $c = min(y - 1, x^{hi} - y \cdot t)$
$s \div x \approx t$	$(t \approx \text{ones} \Rightarrow (mcb(x, 0) \vee mcb(x, 1))) \wedge$ $(t \not\approx \text{ones} \Rightarrow (\neg mulo(x^{lo}, t) \wedge$ $\exists y. (y >_u 0 \wedge mcb(x,y) \wedge \neg mulo(y,t))))$
$x \mathbin{\&} s \approx t$	$t \mathbin{\&} x^{hi} \approx t$
$x \oplus s \approx t$	$\top$
$x \ll s \approx t$	$\exists y. (y \leq_u ctz(t) \wedge mcb(x \ll y, t))$
★ $s \ll x \approx t$	$((\text{ones} \ll x^{lo}) \mathbin{\&} t) \approx t$
$x \gg s \approx t$	$\exists y. (y \leq_u clz(t) \wedge mcb(x \gg y, t))$
★ $s \gg x \approx t$	$((\text{ones} \gg x^{lo}) \mathbin{\&} t) \approx t$
$x \gg_a s \approx t$	$(t \approx 0 \vee t \approx \text{ones}) \Rightarrow$ $\exists y. (y[msb] \approx t[msb] \wedge mcb(x,y)) \wedge$ $(t \not\approx 0 \wedge t \not\approx \text{ones}) \Rightarrow$ $(\exists y. (c \Rightarrow y \leq_u clo(t) \wedge \sim c \Rightarrow y \leq_u clz(t) \wedge$ $mcb(x \gg_a y, t)))$ with $c = (t \ll y)[msb] \approx 1$
$s \gg_a x \approx t$	$t \approx 0 \vee t \approx \text{ones} \vee \exists y. (c \Rightarrow y <_u clo(t) \wedge$ $\sim c \Rightarrow y <_u clz(t)) \wedge mcb(x,y))$ with $c = t[msb] \approx 1$
$x \circ s \approx t$	$mcb(x, t[msb : \kappa(s)])$
$s \circ x \approx t$	$mcb(x, t[msb - \kappa(s) : lsb])$
$x\langle n \rangle \approx t$	$IC(x\langle n \rangle = t)$
$x[u : l] \approx t$	$IC(x[u : l] = t)$

TABLE V: Consistency conditions for non-predicate bit-vector operators modulo constant bits in x. Conditions marked with ★ are conditions synthesized with SyGuS.

it is not necessary to check the condition for concatenation for all possible combinations of bit-widths of the operands.

We split the conditions for the predicates by the value of t and generated in total 3575 quantified bit-vector verification problems for 55 conditions (30 invertibility and 25 consistency conditions). To verify these problems, we used our SMT solver Bitwuzla [23] and the solvers CVC4 [5] and Z3 [13]. Note that we had to exclude Q3B [18] due to disagreements with all three other solvers on 2/3 of the commonly solved instances. We used a time limit of 3600 seconds and a memory limit of 8GB and ran this verification task on a cluster with Intel Xeon CPU E5-2620 CPUs with 2.1GHz and 128GB memory.

We consider a condition to be verified for a certain bit-width, if all solvers that don't run into the time limit agree on its status, and the status is unsat. Overall we were able to verify 2867 out of 3575 instances (80.2%). For operators $\{\approx, <_u, \&, \oplus, \ll, \gg, \gg_a, +, \circ, \langle\rangle, [:]\}$ we were able to verify *all invertibility conditions*, and for operators $\{\approx, <_u, \&, +, \cdot, \circ\}$

we were able to verify *all consistency conditions* for all bit-widths up to 65. For $x <_s s$, no solver was able to verify the invertibility condition for bit-width 36, and for $x \oplus s$ no solver was able to verify the consistency condition for bit-widths 32, 49, 52 and 58. The remaining conditions were verified at least for bit-widths up to (and including) 7.

Verifying the correctness of the presented invertibility and consistency conditions up to some bit-width establishes a certain level of trust but does not prove that they are correct for all possible bit-widths. Proving the correctness for all bit-widths is more involved since it requires bit-width independent proofs [27] and is left to future work.

B. Computing Assignment $\mathcal{A}_t$

Assignment $\mathcal{A}_t : \mathcal{N} \mapsto \{0, 1, \bullet\}^+$ maps each node $n \in \mathcal{N}$ to a ternary bit-vector, which represents constant bits in n. We determine these constant bits upfront by utilizing the And-Inverter Graph (AIG) circuit representation of the input formula. Rewriting on the AIG layer during the translation [11] allows to simplify gates to constants, which are then mapped back to the word-level and represented as the constant bits of the corresponding ternary bit-vectors in $\mathcal{A}_t$.

Bit-blasting the input formula to AIGs introduces additional overhead, both in terms of time and memory, in particular for large bit-widths. In [21], the authors proposed word-level propagators based on ternary bit-vectors for a limited set of bit-vector operators, which was later extended in [34]. These propagators might allow to determine constant bits without the additional overhead of bit-blasting to AIGs. We leave utilizing these propagators to compute $\mathcal{A}_t$ to future work.

V. EXTENSIONS

Tables III and V include invertibility conditions and consistency conditions for the bit-vector operators $\oplus, \gg_a, <_s$ and sign extension, which are not considered in [24]. Instead, they are rewritten in terms of a smaller set of base operators. For example, signed bit-vector operators are encoded by means of unsigned operations only, and bit-wise operations are mostly expressed in terms of $\&$ and $\sim$. As a consequence, the overall size of the formula (in terms of number of nodes) increases. This can have a negative impact on our local search procedure, since the number of paths that need to be considered when propagating target values potentially increases. Further, eliminating bit-vector operators can introduce multiple occurrences of their operands, which can make it harder to find a value that is part of a satisfying assignment. For example, the bit-vector exclusive or operation $t_1 = x \oplus s$ can be represented as $t_2 = ((x \mid s) \mathbin{\&} \sim(x \mathbin{\&} s))$. Selecting an inverse value for x in t_1 only requires one propagation step, whereas for x in t_2 we have to find a value that is also consistent with $x \mid s$ and $\sim(x \mathbin{\&} s)$, which may take multiple propagation steps.

We extended the set of operators in [24] to natively support bit-vector operators $\oplus, \gg_a, <_s$, and sign extension since they are widely used in SMT-LIB benchmarks. Other operators such as signed division and remainder operators do not occur as frequently and we leave the native support for these operators to future work.

A. Tightening Bounds for Inequalities

Given a bit-vector inequality literal $x \diamond s \approx t$ $(s \diamond x \approx t)$ with $\diamond \in \{<_u, <_s\}$, an inverse value for x is a random value within a certain range. The lower (upper) bound is determined by s, whereas the other bound is at least the (un)signed minimum (at most the (un)signed maximum) value, depending on constant bits in x. For example, for $x <_u s$ with target value $t = 1$, the range of possible inverse values v for x is $x^{lo} \leq_u v <_u s$. When such a range is large and only few values within this range are part of a satisfying assignment, randomly picking the right value can have a very low probability. For example, for $x_0 <_u s$ with target value $t = 1$ and $x_0 = x_1\langle w \rangle$, we first compute an inverse value v_0 for x_0 within range $x^{lo} \leq_u v_0 <_u s$, and then propagate v_0 to $x_1\langle w \rangle$. The sign extension of x_1 requires that the $w + 1$ left-most bits of v_0 are either $0_{[w+1]}$ or ones$_{[w+1]}$, i.e., the value of bit $v_0[\kappa(x_1) - 1]$ determines the w left-most bits. However, this information is not known when computing an inverse value for x_0 since we do not consider its kind. As a consequence, we may select inverse values where the $w+1$ left-most bits are neither ones$_{[w+1]}$ or $0_{[w+1]}$, which will immediately produce a conflict in the next propagation step.

In the following, we discuss heuristics that address this weakness and further tighten the bounds based on the currently satisfied top-level inequality constraints.

Inequalities with Sign Extension. Consider an unsigned inequality over sign extension $x\langle w \rangle <_u s$ with target value $t = 1$. We can define the following two ranges when computing an inverse value v for $x\langle w \rangle$.

$$\text{ones}_{[w+1]} \circ 0_{[\kappa(x)-1]} \leq_u v <_u s \tag{3}$$

$$0 \leq_u v <_u min(s, 0_{[w]} \circ \text{smin}_{[\kappa(x)]}) \tag{4}$$

Each of these ranges can only be considered if it is valid, i.e., if the lower bound is strictly less than the upper bound. Further, range (3) is only applicable if $x[msb] \in \{1, \bullet\}$, and range (4) if $x[msb] \in \{0, \bullet\}$. Picking an inverse value v with $mcb(x, v)$ from any of these two ranges guarantees that the $w + 1$ left-most bits are either $0_{[w+1]}$ or ones$_{[w+1]}$. Similar ranges can be derived for $t = 0$ and $<_s$.

Satisfied Inequality Constraints. An additional, more general way to tighten the bounds of inverse value computation for an inequality literal with operand n_x is to determine these bounds with respect to other inequality constraints on n_x that are currently satisfied in $\mathcal{A}_b$. We consider all satisfied inequalities on n_x that are conjuncts reachable from the root. If this results in an invalid range, i.e., if the lower bound is greater than the upper bound, we fall back to computing a consistent value without this bound tightening strategy.

We only consider this heuristic for inverse values and not for consistent values in order to maintain completeness. For example, consider formula $n_x <_u 100 \wedge n_a <_u n_x$ with $\mathcal{A}_b(n_x) = 110$ and $\mathcal{A}_b(n_a) = 101$. Assignment $\mathcal{A}_b$ satisfies

inequality $n_a <_u n_x$, but falsifies $n_x <_u 100$. We select node $n_x <_u 100$, assume $x <_u 100 \approx 1$ with $x = \mathcal{A}_t(n_x)$, and determine 100 as upper and $\mathcal{A}_b(n_x)$ as lower bound of the inverse value for x. Since this range is invalid, we fall back to computing a consistent value. If we compute a consistent value with the bound tightening strategy above, we would ignore the upper bound and use $\mathcal{A}_b(n_x)$ as lower bound. However, this would result in getting stuck in computing consistent values greater than $\mathcal{A}_b(n_x)$, which will never satisfy $n_x <_u 100$ and would therefore be incomplete.

Note that in our implementation, we currently only consider inequality constraints that have the same signedness as the inequality we currently compute an inverse for. Further, this heuristic can be generalized to apply to inverse value computation in general (not only for inequality literals), which requires to incorporate ranges into all inverse value computations. We leave these extensions to future work.

VI. Evaluation

We implemented our techniques in our SMT solver Bitwuzla [23], which is the successor of our SMT solver Boolector [28]. It supports the theories of arrays, bit-vectors, floating-points and uninterpreted functions and their combinations. We first evaluate our generalized procedure and the proposed extensions in comparison to the base procedure presented in [24]. We then show the performance of a sequential portfolio combination of our procedure with state-of-the-art bit-blasting as implemented in Bitwuzla. We performed all experiments on a cluster with Intel Xeon CPU E5-2620 CPUs with 2.1GHz and 128GB memory. We use an 8GB memory limit for each solver/benchmark pair and count memory out as time out. We consider the following configurations:

1) **base** The propagation-based local search procedure presented in [24], which serves as a baseline for our propagation-based local search configurations.
2) **prop-c** Our ternary propagation-based local search procedure (Section IV).
3) **prop-c+** Configuration **prop-c** with additional propagators for $\oplus$, $\gg_a$, and sign extension enabled.
4) **prop-cb+** Configuration **prop-c+** with all bound tightening heuristics from Section V and $<_s$ propagator enabled.
5) **bb** The bit-blasting engine of Bitwuzla with CaDiCaL [8] version 1.2.1, CryptoMiniSat [32] version 5.7.0, Kissat [9] version sc2020 (winner of SAT competition 2020), and Lingeling [7] version bcj as SAT back ends.
6) **bb-prop-cb+** Sequential portfolio of **bb** and **prop-cb+**, where **prop-cb+** is run prior to invoking **bb** with a limit of 10k propagation steps and 2M steps for updating $\mathcal{A}_b$.

We evaluated configurations **base**, **prop-c**, **prop-c+**, and **prop-cb+** on all 14,382 QF_BV benchmarks from SMT-LIB with status "sat". We ran each configuration with 20 different seeds for the random number generator and a time limit of 60 seconds. Figure 3 shows the number of solved instances of **base**, **prop-c**, **prop-c+**, and **prop-cb+** over all 20 runs with different seeds as box-and-whiskers plots. The box of a plot shows the interquartile range (IQR), and the

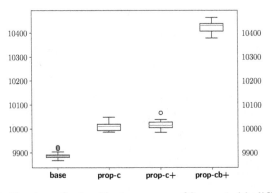

Fig. 3: Number of solved instances over 20 runs (with different seeds) of configurations **base**, **prop-c**, **prop-c+**, and **prop-cb+**.

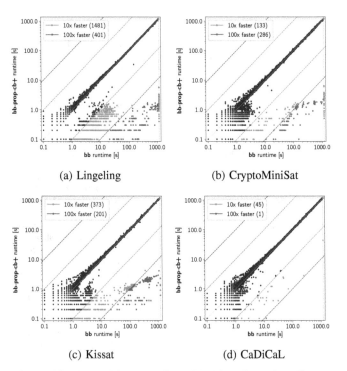

(a) Lingeling   (b) CryptoMiniSat

(c) Kissat   (d) CaDiCaL

Fig. 4: **bb** versus **bb-prop-cb+** with Lingeling (4a), Crypto-MiniSat (4b), Kissat (4c), and CaDiCaL (4d) with a time limit of 1200 seconds.

orange line indicates the median value over all runs of a configuration. The ends of the whiskers indicate minimum and maximum values excluding outliers, which are shown as circles. IQR measures the distance between the lower and upper quartile. Additionally, we also determine the median absolute deviation (MAD), which is a measure for how much one run deviates from the median. Configuration **prop-c** (IQR: 26.5, MAD: 13.4) clearly outperforms **base** (IQR: 10.3, MAD: 9.0) with +120 (median) solved instances. Enabling additional propagators for $\oplus$, $\gg_a$, and sign extension in **prop-c+** (IQR: 23.0, MAD: 14.5) increases the number of solved instances by +3 (median) in comparison to **prop-c**. Enabling the bound tightening heuristics achieves the best results, with over 400 additional solved instances (median) compared to **prop-c+** (IQR: 31.3, MAD: 18.9).

Value computation in **prop-c** is expected to propagate more precise values than **base**, i.e., we expect the number of moves required to solve a problem to decrease. In an additional experiment, we compare the runs of **base** and **prop-c** that are closest to their median on commonly solved instances. As expected, configuration **prop-c** requires 70% less moves, 63% less propagations and 44% less updates of $\mathcal{A}_b$ than **base** while being 9% faster in terms of solving time.

By enabling the additional operators $\oplus$, $\gg_a$, and sign extension (as discussed in Section V), we observed that the median of configuration **prop-c+** increased by 3 solved instances. Further, enabling $<_s$ for configuration **prop-c+** resulted in a considerable loss of 262 median solved instances. This is due to the *uclid* benchmark family, which contains many signed inequalities that effectively define (small) ranges over positive/unsigned values only. For these instances, rewriting $<_s$ in terms of $<_u$ thus significantly reduces the number of possible values for its operands[1]. However, natively handling $<_s$ in combination with our bound tightening heuristics in configuration **prop-cb+** solves all 262 *uclid* benchmarks. Generally, natively handling different sets of operators yields (sometimes significantly) different results. Identifying a minimal set that

allows for best performance may simplify the implementation and is an interesting direction for future work.

Figure 4 shows the performance of the sequential portfolio combination **bb-prop-cb+** in comparison to configuration **bb** with a time limit of 1200 seconds on *all* QF_BV benchmarks (41,713 total). We compare **bb-prop-cb+** against bit-blasting with CaDiCaL, CryptoMiniSat, Kissat, and Lingeling as SAT back ends. Our sequential portfolio combination clearly compensates weaknesses of CryptoMiniSat, Kissat, and Lingeling on satisfiable instances. The bit-blasting engine with CaDiCaL as a back end significantly improves over the other configurations, but **bb-prop-cb+** still improves over the configuration with CaDiCaL in terms of runtime. Overall, the overhead introduced on unsatisfiable instances is negligible.

All experimental data is available at https://bitwuzla.github.io/papers/fmcad2020.

VII. CONCLUSION

We have presented a generalization of propagation-based local search for quantifier-free bit-vector formulas with respect to constant bits to ternary values. We have derived and verified invertibility and consistency conditions modulo constant bits for a majority of the bit-vector operators defined in SMT-LIB 2. We have shown that our approach yields more precise value propagation and considerably improves the performance.

Our sequential portfolio utilizes propagation-based local search and improves over pure bit-blasting. When falling back to the bit-blasting engine, however, it does not share any information, which is an interesting direction for future work.

---

[1]Bitwuzla rewrites $a <_s b$ to $(a[msb] > b[msb]) \vee (a[msb] \approx b[msb] \wedge a[msb-1:0] <_u b[msb-1:0])$.

REFERENCES

[1] R. Alur, R. Bodík, G. Juniwal, M. M. K. Martin, M. Raghothaman, S. A. Seshia, R. Singh, A. Solar-Lezama, E. Torlak, and A. Udupa. Syntax-guided synthesis. In *Formal Methods in Computer-Aided Design, FMCAD 2013, Portland, OR, USA, October 20-23, 2013*, pages 1–8. IEEE, 2013.

[2] A. Balint, A. Belov, M. J. H. Heule, and M. Järvisalo, editors. *SAT Competition 2013*, volume B-2013-1 of *Department of Computer Science Series of Publications B*. University of Helsinki, 2013.

[3] A. Balint, A. Belov, M. Järvisalo, and C. Sinz. Overview and analysis of the SAT challenge 2012 solver competition. *Artificial Intelligence*, 223:120–155, 2015.

[4] C. Barrett, A. Stump, and C. Tinelli. The SMT-LIB Standard: Version 2.0. In A. Gupta and D. Kroening, editors, *Proceedings of the 8th International Workshop on Satisfiability Modulo Theories (Edinburgh, UK)*, 2010.

[5] C. W. Barrett, C. L. Conway, M. Deters, L. Hadarean, D. Jovanovic, T. King, A. Reynolds, and C. Tinelli. CVC4. In G. Gopalakrishnan and S. Qadeer, editors, *Computer Aided Verification - 23rd International Conference, CAV 2011, Snowbird, UT, USA, July 14-20, 2011. Proceedings*, volume 6806 of *Lecture Notes in Computer Science*, pages 171–177. Springer, 2011.

[6] A. Belov, M. J. H. Heule, and M. Järvisalo, editors. *SAT Competition 2014*, volume B-2014-2 of *Department of Computer Science Series of Publications B*. University of Helsinki, 2014.

[7] A. Biere. CaDiCaL, Lingeling, Plingeling, Treengeling and YalSAT Entering the SAT Competition 2018. In M. Heule, M. Järvisalo, and M. Suda, editors, *Proc. of SAT Competition 2018 – Solver and Benchmark Descriptions*, volume B-2018-1 of *Department of Computer Science Series of Publications B*, pages 13–14. University of Helsinki, 2018.

[8] A. Biere. CaDiCaL at the SAT Race 2019. In M. Heule, M. Järvisalo, and M. Suda, editors, *Proc. of SAT Race 2019 – Solver and Benchmark Descriptions*, volume B-2019-1 of *Department of Computer Science Series of Publications B*, pages 8–9. University of Helsinki, 2019.

[9] A. Biere, K. Fazekas, M. Fleury, and M. Heisinger. CaDiCaL, Kissat, Paracooba, Plingeling and Treengeling entering the SAT Competition 2020. In *Proc. of SAT Competition 2020 – Solver and Benchmark Descriptions*, page 49, 2020. To appear.

[10] M. Brain, A. Niemetz, M. Preiner, A. Reynolds, C. W. Barrett, and C. Tinelli. Invertibility conditions for floating-point formulas. In I. Dillig and S. Tasiran, editors, *Computer Aided Verification - 31st International Conference, CAV 2019, New York City, NY, USA, July 15-18, 2019, Proceedings, Part II*, volume 11562 of *Lecture Notes in Computer Science*, pages 116–136. Springer, 2019.

[11] R. Brummayer and A. Biere. Local Two-Level And-Inverter Graph Minimization without Blowup. In *2nd Doctoral Workshop on Mathematical and Engineering Methods in Computer Science (MEMICS'06), Mikulov, Czechia, October 2006, Proceedings*, 2006.

[12] A. Cimatti, A. Griggio, B. J. Schaafsma, and R. Sebastiani. The mathsat5 SMT solver. In N. Piterman and S. A. Smolka, editors, *Tools and Algorithms for the Construction and Analysis of Systems - 19th International Conference, TACAS 2013, Held as Part of the European Joint Conferences on Theory and Practice of Software, ETAPS 2013, Rome, Italy, March 16-24, 2013. Proceedings*, volume 7795 of *Lecture Notes in Computer Science*, pages 93–107. Springer, 2013.

[13] L. M. de Moura and N. Bjørner. Z3: an efficient SMT solver. In C. R. Ramakrishnan and J. Rehof, editors, *Tools and Algorithms for the Construction and Analysis of Systems, 14th International Conference, TACAS 2008, Held as Part of the Joint European Conferences on Theory and Practice of Software, ETAPS 2008, Budapest, Hungary, March 29-April 6, 2008. Proceedings*, volume 4963 of *Lecture Notes in Computer Science*, pages 337–340. Springer, 2008.

[14] H. B. Enderton. *A Mathematical Introduction to Logic*. Academic Press, 2nd edition, 2001.

[15] A. Fröhlich, A. Biere, C. M. Wintersteiger, and Y. Hamadi. Stochastic local search for satisfiability modulo theories. In B. Bonet and S. Koenig, editors, *Proceedings of the Twenty-Ninth AAAI Conference on Artificial Intelligence, January 25-30, 2015, Austin, Texas, USA.*, pages 1136–1143. AAAI Press, 2015.

[16] A. Griggio, Q. Phan, R. Sebastiani, and S. Tomasi. Stochastic local search for SMT: combining theory solvers with walksat. In C. Tinelli and V. Sofronie-Stokkermans, editors, *Frontiers of Combining Systems,*

8th International Symposium, FroCoS 2011, Saarbrücken, Germany, October 5-7, 2011. Proceedings, volume 6989 of *Lecture Notes in Computer Science*, pages 163–178. Springer, 2011.

[17] H. H. Hoos. On the run-time behaviour of stochastic local search algorithms for SAT. In *AAAI/IAAI*, pages 661–666. AAAI Press / The MIT Press, 1999.

[18] M. Jonás and J. Strejcek. Q3B: an efficient bdd-based SMT solver for quantified bit-vectors. In I. Dillig and S. Tasiran, editors, *Computer Aided Verification - 31st International Conference, CAV 2019, New York City, NY, USA, July 15-18, 2019, Proceedings, Part II*, volume 11562 of *Lecture Notes in Computer Science*, pages 64–73. Springer, 2019.

[19] W. Kunz and D. Stoffel. *Reasoning in Boolean Networks: Logic Synthesis and Verification Using Testing Techniques*. Kluwer Academic Publishers, Norwell, MA, USA, 1997.

[20] M. Manzano. Introduction to many-sorted logic. In *Many-sorted logic and its applications*, pages 3–86. John Wiley & Sons, Inc., New York, NY, USA, 1993.

[21] L. D. Michel and P. V. Hentenryck. Constraint satisfaction over bit-vectors. In M. Milano, editor, *Principles and Practice of Constraint Programming - 18th International Conference, CP 2012, Québec City, QC, Canada, October 8-12, 2012. Proceedings*, volume 7514 of *Lecture Notes in Computer Science*, pages 527–543. Springer, 2012.

[22] A. Niemetz. *Bit-Precise Reasoning Beyond Bit-Blasting*. PhD thesis, Johannes Kepler University Linz, 2017.

[23] A. Niemetz and M. Preiner. Bitwuzla at the SMT-COMP 2020. *CoRR*, abs/2006.01621, 2020.

[24] A. Niemetz, M. Preiner, and A. Biere. Propagation based local search for bit-precise reasoning. *Formal Methods in System Design*, 51(3):608–636, 2017.

[25] A. Niemetz, M. Preiner, A. Biere, and A. Fröhlich. Improving local search for bit-vector logics in SMT with path propagation. In *Proceedings of the Fourth International Workshop on Design and Implementation of Formal Tools and Systems, Austin, TX, USA, September 26-27, 2015.*, pages 1–10, 2015.

[26] A. Niemetz, M. Preiner, A. Reynolds, C. Barrett, and C. Tinelli. Solving quantified bit-vectors using invertibility conditions. In H. Chockler and G. Weissenbacher, editors, *Computer Aided Verification - 30th International Conference, CAV 2018, Held as Part of the Federated Logic Conference, FloC 2018, Oxford, UK, July 14-17, 2018, Proceedings, Part II*, volume 10982 of *Lecture Notes in Computer Science*, pages 236–255. Springer, 2018.

[27] A. Niemetz, M. Preiner, A. Reynolds, Y. Zohar, C. W. Barrett, and C. Tinelli. Towards bit-width-independent proofs in SMT solvers. In P. Fontaine, editor, *Automated Deduction - CADE 27 - 27th International Conference on Automated Deduction, Natal, Brazil, August 27-30, 2019, Proceedings*, volume 11716 of *Lecture Notes in Computer Science*, pages 366–384. Springer, 2019.

[28] A. Niemetz, M. Preiner, C. Wolf, and A. Biere. Btor2 , btormc and boolector 3.0. In H. Chockler and G. Weissenbacher, editors, *Computer Aided Verification - 30th International Conference, CAV 2018, Held as Part of the Federated Logic Conference, FloC 2018, Oxford, UK, July 14-17, 2018, Proceedings, Part I*, volume 10981 of *Lecture Notes in Computer Science*, pages 587–595. Springer, 2018.

[29] A. Reynolds, H. Barbosa, A. Nötzli, C. W. Barrett, and C. Tinelli. cvc4sy: Smart and fast term enumeration for syntax-guided synthesis. In I. Dillig and S. Tasiran, editors, *Computer Aided Verification - 31st International Conference, CAV 2019, New York City, NY, USA, July 15-18, 2019, Proceedings, Part II*, volume 11562 of *Lecture Notes in Computer Science*, pages 74–83. Springer, 2019.

[30] J. P. M. Silva, I. Lynce, and S. Malik. Conflict-driven clause learning SAT solvers. In A. Biere, M. Heule, H. van Maaren, and T. Walsh, editors, *Handbook of Satisfiability*, volume 185 of *Frontiers in Artificial Intelligence and Applications*, pages 131–153. IOS Press, 2009.

[31] M. Soos and A. Biere. CryptoMiniSat 5.6 with YalSAT at the SAT Race 2019. In M. Heule, M. Järvisalo, and M. Suda, editors, *Proc. of SAT Race 2019 – Solver and Benchmark Descriptions*, volume B-2019-1 of *Department of Computer Science Series of Publications B*, pages 14–15. University of Helsinki, 2019.

[32] M. Soos, K. Nohl, and C. Castelluccia. Extending SAT solvers to cryptographic problems. In O. Kullmann, editor, *Theory and Applications of Satisfiability Testing - SAT 2009, 12th International Conference, SAT 2009, Swansea, UK, June 30 - July 3, 2009. Proceedings*, volume 5584 of *Lecture Notes in Computer Science*, pages 244–257. Springer, 2009.

[33] M. Soos, B. Selman, and H. Kautz. CryptoMiniSat 5.6 with WalkSAT at the SAT Race 2019. In M. Heule, M. Järvisalo, and M. Suda, editors, *Proc. of SAT Race 2019 – Solver and Benchmark Descriptions*, volume B-2019-1 of *Department of Computer Science Series of Publications B*, pages 12–13. University of Helsinki, 2019.

[34] W. Wang, H. Søndergaard, and P. J. Stuckey. Wombit: A portfolio bit-vector solver using word-level propagation. *J. Autom. Reasoning*, 63(3):723–762, 2019.

[35] T. Weber, S. Conchon, D. Déharbe, M. Heizmann, A. Niemetz, and G. Reger. The SMT competition 2015-2018. *J. Satisf. Boolean Model. Comput.*, 11(1):221–259, 2019.

[36] L. Xu, F. Hutter, H. H. Hoos, and K. Leyton-Brown. Satzilla: Portfolio-based algorithm selection for SAT. *Journal of Artificial Intelligence Research (JAIR)*, 32:565–606, 2008.

6

Trace Logic for Inductive Loop Reasoning

Pamina Georgiou[ID], Bernhard Gleiss[ID], Laura Kovács[ID]
TU Wien, Austria

Abstract—We propose trace logic, an instance of many-sorted first-order logic, to automate the partial correctness verification of programs containing loops. Trace logic generalizes semantics of program locations and captures loop semantics by encoding properties at arbitrary timepoints and loop iterations. We guide and automate inductive loop reasoning in trace logic by using generic trace lemmas capturing inductive loop invariants. Our work is implemented in the RAPID framework, by extending and integrating superposition-based first-order reasoning within RAPID. We successfully used RAPID to prove correctness of many programs whose functional behavior are best summarized in the first-order theories of linear integer arithmetic, arrays and inductive data types.

I. INTRODUCTION

One of the main challenges in automating software verification comes with handling inductive reasoning over programs containing loops. Until recently, automated reasoning in formal verification was the primary domain of satisfiability modulo theory (SMT) solvers [1], [2], yielding powerful advancements for inferring and proving loop properties with linear arithmetic and limited use of quantifiers, see e.g. [3], [4], [5]. Formal verification however also requires reasoning about unbounded data types, such as arrays, and inductively defined data types. Specifying, for example as shown in Figure 1, that every element in the array b is initialized by a non-negative array element of a requires reasoning with quantifiers and can be best expressed in many-sorted extensions of first-order logic. Yet, the recent progress in automation for quantified reasoning in first-order theorem proving has not yet been fully integrated in formal verification. In this paper we address such a use of first-order reasoning and propose trace logic $\mathcal{L}$, an instance of many-sorted first-order logic, to automate the partial correctness verification of program loops, by expressing program semantics in $\mathcal{L}$, and use $\mathcal{L}$ in combination with superposition-based first-order theorem proving.

Contributions: In our previous work [6], an initial version of trace logic $\mathcal{L}$ was introduced to formalize and prove relational properties. In this paper, we go beyond [6] and turn trace logic $\mathcal{L}$ into an efficient approach to loop (safety) verification. We propose trace logic $\mathcal{L}$ as a unifying framework to reason about both relational and safety properties expressed in full first-order logic with theories. We bring the following contributions.

(i) We generalize the semantics of program locations by treating them as functions of execution timepoints. In essence, unlike other works [7], [8], [9], [10], we formalize program properties at arbitrary timepoints of locations.

(ii) Thanks to this generalization, we provide a non-recursive axiomatization of program semantics in trace logic $\mathcal{L}$ and prove completeness of our axiomatization with respect to

```
1   func main() {
2     const Int[] a;
3
4     Int[] b;
5     Int i = 0;
6     Int j = 0;
7     while (i < a.length) {
8       if (a[i] ≥ 0) {
9         b[j] = a[i];
10        j = j + 1:
11      }
12      i = i + 1;
13    }
14  }
15  assert (∀k_I.∃l_I.((0 ≤ k <j ∧ a.length ≥ 0)
                → b(k) = a(l)))
16
```

Fig. 1. Program copying positive elements from array a to b.

Hoare logic. Our semantics in trace logic $\mathcal{L}$ supports arbitrary quantification over loop iterations (Section V).

(iii) We guide and automate inductive loop reasoning in trace logic $\mathcal{L}$, by using generic trace lemmas capturing inductive loop invariants (Section VI). We prove soundness of each trace lemma we introduce.

(iv) We bring first-order theorem proving into the landscape of formal verification, by extending recent results in superposition-based reasoning [11], [12], [13] with support for trace logic properties, complementing SMT-based verification methods in the area (Section VI). As logical consequences of our trace lemmas are also loop invariants, superposition-based reasoning in trace logic $\mathcal{L}$ enables to automatically find loop invariants that are needed for proving safety assertions of program loops.

(v) We implemented our approach in the RAPID framework and combined RAPID with new extensions of the first-order theorem prover VAMPIRE. We successfully evaluated our work on more than 100 benchmarks taken from the SV-Comp repository [14], mainly consisting of safety verification challenges over programs containing arrays of arbitrary length and integers (Section VII). Our experiments show that RAPID automatically proves safety of many examples that, to the best of our knowledge, cannot be handled by other methods.

II. RUNNING EXAMPLE

We illustrate and motivate our work with Figure 1. This program iterates over a constant integer array a of arbitrary length and copies positive values into a new array b. We are interested in proving the safety assertion given at line 15: given that the length `a.length` of a is not negative, every element in b is an element from a. Expressing such a property requires alternations of quantifiers in the first-order theories of linear integer arithmetic and arrays, as formalized in line 15. We write $k_{\mathbb{I}}$ and $l_{\mathbb{I}}$ to specify that k, l are of sort integer $\mathbb{I}$. While the safety assertion of line 15 holds, proving correctness of Figure 1 is challenging for most state-of-the-art approaches, such as e.g. [15], [3], [4], [5]. The reason is that proving safety of Figure 1 needs inductive invariants with existential/alternating quantification and involves inductive reasoning over arbitrarily bounded loop iterations/timepoints. In this paper we address these challenges as follows.

(i) We extend the semantics of program locations to describe locations parameterized by timepoints, allowing us to express values of program variables at arbitrary program locations within arbitrary loop iterations. We write for example $i(l_{12}(it))$ to denote the value of program variable i at location l_{12} in a loop iteration it, where the location l_{12} corresponds to the program line 12. We reserve the constant end for specifying the last program location l_{15}, that is line 15, corresponding to a terminating program execution of Figure 1. We then write $b(end, k)$ to capture the value of array b at timepoint end and position k. For simplicity, as a is a constant array, we simply write $a(k)$ instead of $a(end, k)$.

(ii) Exploiting the semantics of program locations, we formalize the safety assertion of line 15 in trace logic $\mathcal{L}$ as follows:

$$\forall k_{\mathbb{I}}.\exists l_{\mathbb{I}}.\big((0 \leq k < j(end) \wedge a.length \geq 0) \to b(end, k) \simeq a(l)\big) \tag{1}$$

(iii) We express the semantics of Figure 1 as a set $\mathcal{S}$ of first-order formulas in trace logic $\mathcal{L}$, encoding values and dependencies among program variables at arbitrary loop iterations. To this end, we extend $\mathcal{S}$ with so-called trace lemmas, to automate inductive reasoning in trace logic $\mathcal{L}$. One such trace lemma exploits the semantics of updates to j, allowing us to infer that *every* value of j between 0 to $j(end)$, and thus each position at which the array b has been updated, is given by *some* loop iteration. Moreover, updates to j happen at different loop iterations and thus a position j at which b is updated is visited uniquely throughout Figure 1.

(iv) We finally establish validity of (1), by deriving (1) to be a logical consequence of $\mathcal{S}$.

III. PRELIMINARIES

We assume familiarity with standard first-order logic with equality and sorts. We write $\simeq$ for equality and x_S to denote that a logical variable x has sort S. We denote by $\mathbb{I}$ the set of integer numbers and by $\mathbb{B}$ the boolean sort. The term algebra of natural numbers is denoted by $\mathbb{N}$, with constructors 0 and successor suc. We also consider the symbols pred and $\leq$ as part of the signature of $\mathbb{N}$, interpreted respectively as the predecessor function and less-than-equal relation. Let P be a first-order formula with one free variable x of sort $\mathbb{N}$. We recall the standard (step-wise) induction schema for natural numbers as being

$$\Big(P(0) \wedge \forall x'_{\mathbb{N}}.\big(P(x') \to P(\mathrm{suc}(x'))\big)\Big) \to \forall x_{\mathbb{N}}.P(x) \tag{2}$$

```
    program := function
    function := func main(){ context }
 subprogram := statement | context
  statement := atomicStatement
             | if( condition ){ context } else { context }
             | while( condition ){ context }
    context := statement; ... ; statement
```

Fig. 2. Grammar of $\mathcal{W}$.

In our work, we use a variation of the induction schema (2) to reason about intervals of loop iterations. Namely, we use the following schema of *bounded induction*

$$\left(P(bl) \wedge \right. \quad \text{(base case)}$$
$$\left. \forall x'_{\mathbb{N}}.\Big(\big(bl \leq x' < br \wedge P(x')\big) \to P(\mathrm{suc}(x'))\Big)\right) \quad \text{(inductive case)}$$
$$\to \forall x_{\mathbb{N}}.\Big(bl \leq x \leq br \to P(x)\Big),$$

where $bl, br \in \mathbb{N}$ are term algebra expressions of $\mathbb{N}$, called respectively as left and right bounds of bounded induction.

IV. PROGRAMMING MODEL $\mathcal{W}$

We consider programs written in an imperative while-like programming language $\mathcal{W}$. This section recalls terminology from [6], however adapted to our setting of safety verification. Unlike [6], we do not consider multiple program traces in $\mathcal{W}$. In Section V, we then introduce a generalized program semantics in trace logic $\mathcal{L}$, extended with reachability predicates. Figure 2 shows the (partial) grammar of our programming model $\mathcal{W}$, emphasizing the use of contexts to capture lists of statements. An input program in $\mathcal{W}$ has a single main-function, with arbitrary nestings of if-then-else conditionals and while-statements. We consider *mutable and constant variables*, where variables are either integer-valued numeric variables or arrays of such numeric variables. We include standard *side-effect free expressions over booleans and integers*.

A. Locations and Timepoints

A program in $\mathcal{W}$ is considered as sets of locations, with each location corresponding to positions/lines of program statements in the program. Given a program statement s, we denote by l_s its (program) location. We reserve the location l_{end} to denote the end of a program. For programs with loops, some program locations might be revisited multiple times. We therefore model locations l_s corresponding to a statement s as functions of *iterations* when the respective location is visited. For simplicity, we write l_s also for the functional representation of the location l_s of s. We thus consider locations as timepoints of a program and treat them l_s as being functions l_s over iterations. The target sort of locations l_s is $\mathbb{L}$. For each enclosing loop of a statement s, the function symbol l_s takes arguments of sort $\mathbb{N}$, corresponding to loop iterations. Further, when s is a loop itself, we also introduce a function symbol n_s with argument and target sort $\mathbb{N}$; intuitively, n_s corresponds to the last loop iteration of s. We denote the set of all function symbols l_s as S_{Tp}, whereas the set of all function symbols n_s is written as S_n.

Example 1: We refer to program statements s by their (first) line number in Figure 1. Thus, l_5 encodes the timepoint corresponding to the first assignment of i in the program (line 5). We write $l_7(0)$ and $l_7(n_7)$ to denote the timepoints of the first and last loop iteration, respectively. The timepoints $l_8(\text{suc}(0))$ and $l_8(it)$ correspond to the beginning of the loop body in the second and the it-th loop iterations, respectively. $\square$

B. Expressions over Timepoints

We next introduce commonly used expressions over timepoints. For each while-statement w of $\mathcal{W}$, we introduce a function it^w that returns a unique variable of sort $\mathbb{N}$ for w, denoting loop iterations of w. Let $w_1, \ldots, w_k$ be the enclosing loops for statement s and consider an arbitrary term it of sort $\mathbb{N}$. We define tp_s to be the expressions denoting the timepoints of statements s as

$$tp_s := l_s(it^{w_1}, \ldots, it^{w_k}) \qquad \text{if s is non-while statement}$$
$$tp_s(it) := l_s(it^{w_1}, \ldots, it^{w_k}, it) \qquad \text{if s is while-statement}$$
$$lastIt_s := n_s(it^{w_1}, \ldots, it^{w_k}) \qquad \text{if s is while-statement}$$

If s is a while-statement, we also introduce $lastIt_s$ to denote the last iteration of s. Further, consider an arbitrary subprogram p, that is, p is either a statement or a context. The timepoint $start_p$ (parameterized by an iteration of each enclosing loop) denotes the timepoint when the execution of p has started and is defined as

$$start_p := \begin{cases} tp_p(0) & \text{if p is while-statement} \\ tp_p & \text{if p is non-while statement} \\ start_{s_1} & \text{if p is context } s_1;\ldots;s_k \end{cases}$$

We also introduce the timepoint end_p to denote the timepoint upon which a subprogram p has been completely evaluated and define it as

$$end_p := \begin{cases} start_s & \text{if s occurs after p in a context} \\ end_c & \text{if p is last statement in context c} \\ end_s & \text{if p is context of if-branch or} \\ & \text{else-branch of s} \\ tp_s(\text{suc}(it^s)) & \text{if p is context of body of s} \\ l_{end} & \text{if p is top-level context} \end{cases}$$

Finally, if s is the topmost statement of the top-level context in main(), we define

$$start := start_s.$$

C. Program Variables

We express values of program variables v at various timepoints of the program execution. To this end, we model (numeric) variables v as functions $v : \mathbb{L} \mapsto \mathbb{I}$, where $v(tp)$ gives the value of v at timepoint tp. For array variables v, we add an

additional argument of sort $\mathbb{I}$, corresponding to the position where the array is accessed; that is, $v : \mathbb{L} \times \mathbb{I} \mapsto \mathbb{I}$. The set of such function symbols corresponding to program variables is denoted by S_V.

Our framework for constant, non-mutable variables can be simplified by omitting the timepoint argument in the functional representation of such program variables, as illustrated below.

Example 2: For Figure 1, we denote by $i(l_5)$ the value of program variable i before being assigned in line 5. As the array variable a is non-mutable (specified by const in the program), we write $a(i(l_8(it)))$ for the value of array a at the position corresponding to the current value of i at timepoint $l_8(it)$. For the mutable array b, we consider timepoints where b has been updated and write $b(l_9(it), j(l_9(it)))$ for the array b at position j at the timepoint $l_9(it)$ during the loop. $\square$

We emphasize that we consider (numeric) program variables v to be of sort $\mathbb{I}$, whereas loop iterations it are of sort $\mathbb{N}$.

D. Program Expressions

Arithmetic constants and program expressions are modeled using integer functions and predicates. Let e be an arbitrary program expression and write $[\![e]\!](tp)$ to denote the value of the evaluation of e at timepoint tp. Let $v \in S_V$, that is a function v denoting a program variable v. Consider e, e_1, e_2 to be program expressions and let tp_1, tp_2 denote two timepoints. We define

$$Eq(v, tp_1, tp_2) :=$$
$$\begin{cases} \forall pos_{\mathbb{I}}. \ v(tp_1, pos) \simeq v(tp_2, pos), & \text{if v is an array} \\ v(tp_1) \simeq v(tp_2), & \text{otherwise} \end{cases}$$

to denote that the program variable v has the same values at tp_1 and tp_2. We further introduce

$$EqAll(tp_1, tp_2) := \bigwedge_{v \in S_V} Eq(v, tp_1, tp_2)$$

to define that all program variables have the same values at timepoints tp_1 and tp_2. We also define

$$Update(v, e, tp_1, tp_2) :=$$
$$v(tp_2) \simeq [\![e]\!](tp_1) \wedge \bigwedge_{v' \in S_V \setminus \{v\}} Eq(v', tp_1, tp_2),$$

asserting that the numeric program variable v has been updated while all other program variables v' remain unchanged. This definition is further extended to array updates as

$$UpdateArr(v, e_1, e_2, tp_1, tp_2) :=$$
$$\forall pos_{\mathbb{I}}. \ (pos \not\simeq [\![e_1]\!](tp_1) \rightarrow v(tp_2, pos) \simeq v(tp_1, pos))$$
$$\wedge \ v(tp_2, [\![e_1]\!](tp_1)) \simeq [\![e_2]\!](tp_1)$$
$$\bigwedge_{v' \in S_V \setminus \{v\}} Eq(v', tp_1, tp_2).$$

Example 3: In Figure 1, we refer to the value of i+1 at timepoint $l_{12}(it)$ as $i(l_{12}(it))+1$. Let S_V^l be the set of function symbols representing the program variables of Figure 1. For an update of j in line 10 at some iteration it, we derive

$$Update(j, j+1, l_9(it), l_{10}(it)) := j(l_{10}(it)) \simeq (j(l_9(it)) + 1)$$
$$\wedge \bigwedge_{v' \in S_V^l \setminus \{j\}} Eq(v', l_9(it), l_{10}(it)).$$

V. Axiomatic Semantics in Trace Logic $\mathcal{L}$

Trace logic $\mathcal{L}$ has been introduced in [6], yet for the setting of relational verification. In this paper we generalize the formalization of [6] in three ways. First, (i) we define program semantics in a non-recursive manner using the *Reach* predicate to characterize the set of reachable locations within a given program context (Section V-B). Second, and most importantly, (ii) we prove completeness of trace logic $\mathcal{L}$ with respect to Hoare Logic (Theorem 2), which could have not been achieved in the setting of [6]. Finally, (iii) we introduce the use of logic $\mathcal{L}$ for safety verification (Section VI).

A. Trace Logic $\mathcal{L}$

Trace logic $\mathcal{L}$ is an instance of many-sorted first-order logic with equality. We define the signature $\Sigma(\mathcal{L})$ of trace logic as

$$\Sigma(\mathcal{L}) := S_{\mathbb{N}} \cup S_{\mathbb{I}} \cup S_{Tp} \cup S_V \cup S_n,$$

containing the signatures of the theory of natural numbers (term algebra) $\mathbb{N}$ and integers $\mathbb{I}$, as well the respective sets of timepoints, program variables and last iteration symbols as defined in section IV.
We next define the semantics of $\mathcal{W}$ in trace logic $\mathcal{L}$.

B. Reachability and its Axiomatization

We introduce a predicate $Reach : \mathbb{L} \mapsto \mathbb{B}$ to capture the set of timepoints reachable in an execution and use *Reach* to define the axiomatic semantics of $\mathcal{W}$ in trace logic $\mathcal{L}$. We define reachability *Reach* as a predicate over timepoints, in contrast to defining reachability as a predicate over program configurations such as in [16], [7], [5], [10].
We axiomatize *Reach* using trace logic formulas as follows.
Definition 1 (Reach-predicate): For any context c, any statement s, let $Cond_s$ be the expression denoting a potential branching condition in s. We define

$$Reach(start_c) := \begin{cases} true, \\ \quad \text{if } c \text{ is top-level context} \\ Reach(start_s) \wedge Cond_s(start_s), \\ \quad \text{if } c \text{ is context of if-branch of } s \\ Reach(start_s) \wedge \neg Cond_s(start_s), \\ \quad \text{if } c \text{ is context of else-branch of } s \\ Reach(start_s) \wedge it^s < lastIt_s, \\ \quad \text{if } c \text{ is context of body of } s. \end{cases}$$

For any non-while statement s' occurring in context c, let

$$Reach(start_{s'}) := Reach(start_c),$$

and for any while-statement s' occurring in context c, let

$$Reach(tp_{s'}(it^{s'})) := Reach(start_c) \wedge it^{s'} \leq lastIt_{s'}.$$

Finally let $Reach(end) := true$. □
Note that our reachability predicate *Reach* allows specifying properties about intermediate timepoints (since those properties can only hold if the referred timepoints are reached) and supports reasoning about which locations are reached.

C. Axiomatic Semantics of $\mathcal{W}$

We axiomatize the semantics of each program statement in $\mathcal{W}$, and define the semantics of a program in $\mathcal{W}$ as the conjunction of all these axioms.

a) Main-function: Let p_0 be an arbitrary, but fixed program in $\mathcal{W}$; we give our definitions relative to p_0. The semantics of p_0, denoted by $[\![p_0]\!]$, consists of a conjunction of one implication per statement, where each implication has the reachability of the start-timepoint of the statement as premise and the semantics of the statement as conclusion:

$$[\![p_0]\!] := \bigwedge_{s \text{ statement of } p_0} \forall enclIts. \big(Reach(start_s) \rightarrow [\![s]\!] \big)$$

where $enclIts$ is the set of iterations $\{it^{w_1}, \ldots, it^{w_n}\}$ of all enclosing loops $w_1, \ldots, w_n$ of some statement s in p_0, and the semantics $[\![s]\!]$ of program statements s is defined as follows.

b) Skip: Let s be a statement **skip**. Then

$$[\![s]\!] := EqAll(end_s, start_s) \tag{3}$$

c) Integer assignments: Let s be an assignment $v = e$, where v is an integer-valued program variable and e is an expression. The evaluation of s is performed in one step such that, after the evaluation, the variable v has the same value as e before the evaluation. All other variables remain unchanged and thus

$$[\![s]\!] := Update(v, e, end_s, start_s) \tag{4}$$

d) Array assignments: Consider s of the form $a[e_1] = e_2$, with a being an array variable and e_1, e_2 being expressions. The assignment is evaluated in one step. After the evaluation of s, the array a contains the value of e_2 before the evaluation at position pos corresponding to the value of e_1 before the evaluation. The values at all other positions of a and all other program variables remain unchanged and hence

$$[\![s]\!] := UpdateArr(v, e_1, e_2, end_s, start_s) \tag{5}$$

e) Conditional if-then-else Statements: Let s be **if**(Cond){ c_1} **else** {c_2}. The semantics of s states that entering the if-branch and/or entering the else-branch does not change the values of the variables and we have

$$[\![s]\!] := \quad [\![Cond]\!](start_s) \rightarrow EqAll(start_{c_1}, start_s) \tag{6a}$$
$$\wedge \quad \neg[\![Cond]\!](start_s) \rightarrow EqAll(start_{c_2}, start_s) \tag{6b}$$

where the semantics $[\![Cond]\!]$ of the expression Cond is according to Section IV-D.

f) While-Statements: Let s be the while-statement **while**(Cond){c}. We refer to Cond as the *loop condition*. The semantics of s is captured by conjunction of the following three properties: (7a) the iteration $lastIt_s$ is the first iteration where Cond does not hold, (7b) entering the loop body does not change the values of the variables, (7c) the values of the variables at the end of evaluating s are the same as the variable values at the loop condition location in iteration $lastIt_s$. As such, we have

$$\llbracket s \rrbracket := \quad \forall it^s_{\mathbb{N}}. \, (it^s < lastIt_s \rightarrow \llbracket \mathrm{Cond} \rrbracket(tp_s(it^s)))$$

$$\wedge \quad \neg \llbracket \mathrm{Cond} \rrbracket(tp(lastIt_s)) \tag{7a}$$

$$\wedge \quad \forall it^s_{\mathbb{N}}. \, (it^s < lastIt_s \rightarrow EqAll(start_c, tp_s(it^s))) \tag{7b}$$

$$\wedge \quad EqAll(end_s, tp_s(lastIt_s)) \tag{7c}$$

D. Soundness and Completeness.

The axiomatic semantics of $\mathcal{W}$ in trace logic is sound. That is, given a program p in $\mathcal{W}$ and a trace logic property $F \in \mathcal{L}$, we have that any interpretation in $\mathcal{L}$ is a model of F according to the small-step operational semantics of $\mathcal{W}$. We conclude the next theorem - and refer to [17] for details.

Theorem 1 ($\mathcal{W}$-Soundness): Let p be a program. Then the axiomatic semantics $\llbracket p \rrbracket$ is sound with respect to standard small-step operational semantics.   □

Next, we show that the axiomatic semantics of $\mathcal{W}$ in trace logic $\mathcal{L}$ is complete with respect to Hoare logic [18], as follows. Intuitively, a Hoare Triple $\{F_1\}p\{F_2\}$ corresponds to the trace logic formula

$$\forall enclIts. \big(Reach(start_p) \rightarrow ([F_1](start_p) \rightarrow [F_2](end_p))\big) \tag{8}$$

where the expressions $[F_1](start_p)$ and $[F_2](end_p)$ denote the result of adding to each program variable in F_1 and F_2 the timepoints $start_p$ respectively end_p as first arguments. We therefore define that the axiomatic semantics of $\mathcal{W}$ is *complete with respect to Hoare logic*, if for any Hoare triple $\{F_1\}p\{F_2\}$ valid relative to the background theory $\mathcal{T}$, the corresponding trace logic formula (8) is derivable from the axiomatic semantics of $\mathcal{W}$ in the background theory $\mathcal{T}$. With this definition at hand, we get the following result, proved formally in [17].

Theorem 2 ($\mathcal{W}$-Completeness with respect to Hoare logic): The axiomatic semantics of $\mathcal{W}$ in trace logic is complete with respect to Hoare logic.   □

VI. TRACE LOGIC FOR SAFETY VERIFICATION

We now introduce the use of trace logic $\mathcal{L}$ for verifying safety properties of $\mathcal{W}$ programs. We consider safety properties F expressed in first-order logic with theories, as illustrated in line 15 of Figure 1. Thanks to soundness and completeness of the axiomatic semantics of $\mathcal{W}$, a partially correct program p with regard to F can be proved to be correct using the axiomatic semantics of $\mathcal{W}$ in trace logic $\mathcal{L}$. That is, we assume termination and establish partial program correctness. Assuming the existence of an iteration violating the loop condition can be help backward reasoning and, in particular, automatic splitting of loop iteration intervals.

However, proving correctness of a program p annotated with a safety property F faces the reasoning challenges of the underlying logic, in our case of trace logic. Due to the presence of loops in $\mathcal{W}$, a challenging aspect in using trace logic for safety verification is to handle inductive reasoning as induction cannot be generally expressed in first-order logic. To circumvent the challenge of inductive reasoning and automate

verification using trace logic, we introduce a set of first-order lemmas, called *trace lemmas*, and extend the semantics of $\mathcal{W}$ programs in trace logic with these trace lemmas. Trace lemmas describe generic inductive properties over arbitrary loop iterations and any logical consequence of trace lemmas yields a valid program loop property as well. We next summarize our approach to program verification using trace logic and then address the challenge of inductive reasoning in trace logic $\mathcal{L}$.

A. Safety Verification in Trace Logic

Given a program p in $\mathcal{W}$ and a safety property F,

(i) we express program semantics $\llbracket p \rrbracket$ in trace logic $\mathcal{L}$, as given in Section V;

(ii) we formalize the safety property in trace logic $\mathcal{L}$, that is we express F by using program variables as functions of locations and timepoints (similarly as in (1)). For simplicity, let us denote the trace logic formalization of F also by F;

(iii) we introduce instances $\mathcal{T}^p_{\mathcal{L}}$ of a set $\mathcal{T}_{\mathcal{L}}$ of trace lemmas, by instantiating trace lemmas with program variables, locations and timepoints of p;

(iv) to verify F, we then show that F is a logical consequence of $\llbracket p \rrbracket \wedge \mathcal{T}^p_{\mathcal{L}}$;

(v) however to conclude that p is partially correct with regard to F, two more challenges need to be addressed. First, in addition to Theorem 1, soundness of our trace lemmas $\mathcal{T}_{\mathcal{L}}$ needs to be established, implying that our trace lemma instances $\mathcal{T}^p_{\mathcal{L}}$ are also sound. Soundness of $\mathcal{T}^p_{\mathcal{L}}$ implies then validity of F, whenever F is proven to be a logical consequence of sound formulas $\llbracket p \rrbracket \wedge \mathcal{T}^p_{\mathcal{L}}$. However, to ensure that F is provable in trace logic, as a second challenge we need to ensure that our trace lemmas $\mathcal{T}_{\mathcal{L}}$, and thus their instances $\mathcal{T}^p_{\mathcal{L}}$, are strong enough to prove $\llbracket p \rrbracket \wedge \mathcal{T}^p_{\mathcal{L}} \implies F$. That is, proving that F is a safety assertion of p in our setting requires finding a suitable set $\mathcal{T}_{\mathcal{L}}$ of trace lemmas.

In the remaining of this section, we address (v) and show that our trace lemmas $\mathcal{T}_{\mathcal{L}}$ are sound consequences of bounded induction (Section VI-B). Practical evidence for using our trace lemmas are further given in Section VII-B.

B. Trace Lemmas $\mathcal{T}_{\mathcal{L}}$ for Verification

Trace logic properties support arbitrary quantification over timepoints and describe values of program variables at arbitrary loop iterations and timepoints. We therefore can relate timepoints with values of program variables in trace logic $\mathcal{L}$, allowing us to describe the value distributions of program variables as functions of timepoints throughout program executions. As such, trace logic $\mathcal{L}$ supports

(1) reasoning about the *existence* of a specific loop iteration, allowing us to split the range of loop iterations at a particular timepoint, based on the safety property we want to prove. For example, we can express and derive loop iterations corresponding to timepoints where one program variable takes a specific value for *the first time during loop execution*;

(2) universal quantification over the array content and range of loop iterations bounded by two arbitrary left and right bounds, allowing us to apply instances of the induction scheme (3) within a range of loop iterations bounded, for example, by it and $lastIt_s$ for some while-statement s.

Addressing these benefits of trace logic, we express generic patterns of inductive program properties as *trace lemmas*. Identifying a suitable set $\mathcal{T_L}$ of trace lemmas to automate inductive reasoning in trace logic $\mathcal{L}$ is however challenging and domain-specific. We propose three trace lemmas for inductive reasoning over arrays and integers, by considering

(A1) one trace lemma describing how values of program variables change during an interval of loop iterations;

(B1-B2) two trace lemmas to describe the behavior of loop counters.

We prove soundness of our trace lemmas - below we include only one proof and refer to [17] for further details.

(A1) Value Evolution Trace Lemma: Let w be a while-statement, let v be a mutable program variable and let ∘ be a reflexive and transitive relation - that is $\simeq$ or $\leq$ in the setting of trace logic. The *value evolution trace lemma of w, v, and* ∘ is defined as

$$\forall bl_{\mathbb{N}}, br_{\mathbb{N}}.$$
$$\left(\forall it_{\mathbb{N}}.\left((bl \leq it < br \wedge v(tp_w(bl)) \circ v(tp_w(it))) \right.\right.$$
$$\left. \rightarrow v(tp_w(bl)) \circ v(tp_w(\text{suc}(it))) \right) \qquad \text{(A1)}$$
$$\left. \rightarrow \left(bl \leq br \rightarrow v(tp_w(br)) \circ v(tp_w(br)) \right) \right)$$

In our work, the value evolution trace lemma is mainly instantiated with the equality predicate $\simeq$ to conclude that the value of a variable does not change during a range of loop iterations, provided that the variable value does not change at any of the considered loop iterations.

Example 4: For Figure 1, the value evaluation trace lemma (A1) yields the property

$$\forall j_{\mathbb{I}}. \; \forall bl_{\mathbb{N}}. \; \forall br_{\mathbb{N}}.$$
$$\left(\forall it_{\mathbb{N}}.\left((bl \leq it < br \; \wedge \; b(l_8(bl), j) = b(l_8(it), j)) \right.\right.$$
$$\left. \rightarrow b(l_8(bl), j) = b(l_8(s(it)), j) \right)$$
$$\left. \rightarrow \left(bl \leq br \rightarrow b(l_8(bl), j) = b(l_8(br), j) \right) \right),$$

which allows to prove that the value of b at some position j remains the same from the timepoint it the value was first set until the end of program execution. That is, we derive $b(l_9(end), j(l_9(it))) = a(i(l_8(it)))$. □

We next prove soundness of our trace lemma (A1).

Proof *(Soundness Proof of Value Evolution Trace Lemma (A1))* Let bl and br be arbitrary but fixed and assume that the premise of the outermost implication of (A1) holds. That is,

$$\forall it_{\mathbb{N}}.((bl \leq it < br \wedge v(tp_w(bl)) \circ v(tp_w(it)))$$
$$\rightarrow v(tp_w(bl)) \circ v(tp_w(\text{suc}(it)))) \qquad \text{(9)}$$

We use the induction axiom scheme (3) and consider its

instance with $P(it) := v(tp_w(bl)) \circ v(tp_w(it))$, yielding the following instance of (3):

$$\left(v(tp_w(bl)) \circ v(tp_w(it)) \quad \wedge \right. \qquad \text{(10a)}$$
$$\forall it_{\mathbb{N}}.\left((bl \leq it < br \wedge v(tp_w(bl)) \circ v(tp_w(it))) \right. \qquad \text{(10b)}$$
$$\left. \rightarrow v(tp_w(bl)) \circ v(tp_w(\text{suc}(it))) \right) \Big)$$
$$\rightarrow \forall it_{\mathbb{N}}.\Big(bl \leq it \leq br \rightarrow v(tp_w(bl)) \circ v(tp_w(it)) \Big) \qquad \text{(10c)}$$

Note that the base case property (10a) holds since ∘ is reflexive. Further, the inductive case (10b) holds also since it is implied by (9). We thus derive property (10c), and in particular $bl \leq br \leq br \rightarrow v(tp_w(bl)) \circ v(tp_w(br))$. Since $\leq$ is reflexive, we conclude $bl \leq br \rightarrow v(tp_w(bl)) \circ v(tp_w(br))$, proving thus our trace lemma (A1). □

(B1) Intermediate Value Trace Lemma: Let w be a while-statement and let v be a mutable program variable. We call v to be *dense* if the following holds:

$$Dense_{w,v} := \forall it_{\mathbb{N}}.\Big(it < lastIt_w \rightarrow$$
$$\big(v(tp_w(\text{suc}(it))) = v(tp_w(it)) \vee$$
$$v(tp_w(\text{suc}(it))) = v(tp_w(it)) + 1 \big) \Big)$$

The *intermediate value trace lemma of w and v* is defined as

$$\forall x_{\mathbb{I}}.\Big(\big(Dense_{w,v} \wedge v(tp_w(0)) \leq x < v(tp_w(lastIt_w)) \big) \rightarrow$$
$$\exists it_{\mathbb{N}}.\big(it < lastIt_w \wedge v(tp_w(it)) \simeq x \wedge \qquad \text{(B1)}$$
$$v(tp_w(\text{suc}(it))) \simeq v(tp_w(it)) + 1 \big) \Big)$$

The intermediate value trace lemma (B1) allows us conclude that if the variable v is dense, and if the value x is between the value of v at the beginning of the loop and the value of v at the end of the loop, then there is an iteration in the loop, where v has exactly the value x and is incremented. This trace lemma is mostly used to find specific iterations corresponding to positions x in an array.

Example 5: In Figure 1, using trace lemma (B1) we synthesize the iteration it such that $b(l_9(it), j(l_9(it))) = a(i(l_8(it)))$. □

(B2) Iteration Injectivity Trace Lemma: Let w be a while-statement and let v be a mutable program variable. The *iteration injectivity trace lemma of w and v* is

$$\forall it_{\mathbb{N}}^1, it_{\mathbb{N}}^2.\Big(\big(Dense_{w,v} \wedge v(tp_w(\text{suc}(it^1))) = v(tp_w(it^1)) + 1$$
$$\wedge \; it^1 < it^2 \leq lastIt_w \big) \qquad \text{(B2)}$$
$$\rightarrow v(tp_w(it^1)) \not\simeq v(tp_w(it^2)) \Big)$$

The trace lemma (B2) states that a strongly-dense variable visits each array-position at most once. As a consequence, if each array position is visited only once in a loop, we know that its value has not changed after the first visit, and in particular the value at the end of the loop is the value after the first visit.

Example 6: Trace lemma (B2) is necessary in Figure 1 to apply the value evolution trace lemma (A1) for b, as we need to make sure we will never reach the same position of j twice. □

Based on the soundness of our trace lemmas, we conclude the next result.

Theorem 3 (*Trace Lemmas and Induction*): Let p be a program. Let L be a trace lemma for some while-statement w of p and some variable v of p. Then L is a consequence of the bounded induction scheme (3) and of the axiomatic semantics of $[\![p]\!]$ in trace logic $\mathcal{L}$.   □

VII. Implementation and Experiments

A. Implementation

We implemented our approach in the RAPID tool, written in C++ and available at https://github.com/gleiss/rapid. RAPID takes as input a program in the while-language $\mathcal{W}$ together with a property expressed in trace logic $\mathcal{L}$ using the SMT-LIB syntax [19]. RAPID outputs (i) the program semantics as in Section V, (ii) instantiations of trace lemmas for each mutable variable and for each loop of the program, as discussed in Section VI-B, and (iii) the safety property, expressed in trace logic $\mathcal{L}$ and encoded in the SMT-LIB syntax.

For establishing safety, we pass the generated reasoning task to the first-order theorem prover VAMPIRE [20] to prove the safety property from the program semantics and the instantiated trace lemmas[1], as discussed in Section VI-A. VAMPIRE searches for a proof by refuting the negation of the property based on saturation of a set of clauses with respect to a set of inference rules such as resolution and superposition.

In our experiments, we use a custom version[2] of VAMPIRE with a timeout of 60 seconds, in two different configurations. On the one hand, we use a configuration RAPID⁻, where we tune VAMPIRE to the trace logic domain using (i) existing options and (ii) domain-specific implementation to guide the high-level proof search. On the other hand, we use a configuration RAPID*, which extends RAPID⁻ with recent techniques from [11], [12] improving theory reasoning in equational theories. As such, RAPID* represents the result of a fundamental effort to improve VAMPIRE's reasoning for software verification. In particular, theory split queues [12] present a partial solution to the prevalent challenge of combining quantification and *light-weight* theory reasoning, drastically improving first-order reasoning in applications of software verification, as shown next.

B. Experimental Results

We considered challenging Java- and C-like verification benchmarks from the SV-Comp repository [14], containing the combination of loops and arrays. We omitted those examples for which the task is to find bugs in form of counterexample traces, as well as those examples that cannot be expressed in our programming model $\mathcal{W}$, such as examples with explicit memory management. In order to improve the set of benchmarks, we also included additional challenging programs and functional properties. As a result, we obtained benchmarks ranging over

45 unique programs with a total of 103 tested properties. Our benchmarks are available in the RAPID repository[3].

We manually transformed those benchmarks into our input format. SV-Comp benchmarks encode properties featuring universal quantification by extending the corresponding program with an additional loop containing a standard C-like assertion. For instance, the property

$$\forall i_\mathbb{I}.\ 0 \le i < a.length \to P(a(i, end))$$

would be encoded by extending the program with a loop

```
for(int i = 0; i < a.length; i++)
assert(P(a[i]))
```

While this encoding loses explicit structure and results in a harder reasoning task, it is necessary as other tools do not support explicit universal quantification in their input language. In contrast, our approach can handle arbitrarily quantified properties over unbounded data structures. We, thus, directly formulate universally quantified properties, without using any program transformations.

The results of our experiments are presented in Table 1. We divided the results in four segments in the following order: the first eleven problems are quantifier-free, the largest part of 62 problems are universally quantified, seven problems are existentially quantified, while the last 23 problems contain quantifier alternations. First, we are interested in the overall number of problems we are able to prove correct. In the configuration RAPID*, which represents our main configuration, VAMPIRE is able to prove 78 out of 103 encodings. In particular, we verify Figure 1, corresponding to benchmark `copy_positive_1`, as well as other challenging properties that involve quantifier alternations, such as `partition_5`.

Second, we are interested in comparing the results for configurations RAPID⁻ and RAPID*, in order to understand the importance of recently developed techniques from [11] and [12] for reasoning in the trace logic domain. While RAPID⁻ is only able to prove 15 out of 103 properties, RAPID* is able to prove 78 properties, that is, RAPID* improves over RAPID⁻ by 63 examples. Moreover, only RAPID* is able to prove advanced properties involving quantifier alternations. We therefore see that RAPID* drastically outperforms RAPID⁻, suggesting that the recently developed techniques are essential for efficient reasoning in trace logic.

Third, we are interested in what kinds of properties RAPID can prove. It comes with no surprise that all quantifier-free instances could be proved. Out of 62 universally quantified properties, RAPID could establish correctness of 53 such properties. More interestingly, RAPID proves 14 out of 30 benchmarks containing either existentially quantified properties or such with quantifier alternations. The benchmarks that could not be solved by RAPID are primarily universally and alternatingly quantified properties that need additional trace lemmas relating values of multiple program variables.

---

[1] We also established the soundness of each trace lemma instance separately by running additional validity queries with VAMPIRE.

[2] https://github.com/vprover/vampire/tree/gleiss-rapid

[3] https://github.com/gleiss/rapid/tree/master/examples/arrays

TABLE I
EXPERIMENTAL RESULTS

Benchmark	RAPID⁻	RAPID*	Benchmark	RAPID⁻	RAPID*	Benchmark	RAPID⁻	RAPID*
atleast_one_iteration_0	✓	✓	in_place_max	-	✓	swap_1	-	✓
atleast_one_iteration_1	✓	✓	inc_by_one_0	-	✓	vector_addition	-	✓
find_sentinel	✓	✓	inc_by_one_1	-	✓	vector_subtraction	-	✓
find1_0	-	✓	inc_by_one_harder_0	-	✓	check_equal_set_flag_0	✓	✓
find1_1	-	✓	inc_by_one_harder_1	-	✓	find_max_1	-	-
find2_0	-	✓	init	-	✓	find_max_from_second_1	-	-
find2_1	✓	✓	init_conditionally_0	-	✓	find1_2	✓	✓
indexn_is_arraylength_0	✓	✓	init_conditionally_1	-	✓	find1_3	✓	✓
indexn_is_arraylength_1	-	✓	init_non_constant_0	-	✓	find2_2	✓	✓
set_to_one	✓	✓	init_non_constant_1	-	✓	find2_3	✓	✓
str_cpy_3	✓	✓	init_non_constant_2	-	✓	collect_indices_eq_val_2	-	✓
both_or_none	-	✓	init_non_constant_3	-	✓	collect_indices_eq_val_3	-	-
check_equal_set_flag_1	-	✓	init_non_constant_easy_0	-	✓	copy_nonzero_1	-	✓
collect_indices_eq_val_0	-	✓	init_non_constant_easy_1	-	✓	copy_positive_1	-	✓
collect_indices_eq_val_1	-	✓	init_non_constant_easy_2	-	✓	find_max_local_0	-	-
copy	-	✓	init_non_constant_easy_3	-	✓	find_max_local_1	-	-
copy_absolute_0	-	✓	init_partial	-	✓	find_max_up_to_1	-	-
copy_absolute_1	-	✓	init_prev_plus_one_0	-	✓	find_min_1	-	-
copy_nonzero_0	-	✓	init_prev_plus_one_1	-	✓	find_min_local_0	-	-
copy_partial	-	✓	init_prev_plus_one_alt_0	-	✓	find_min_local_1	-	-
copy_positive_0	-	✓	init_prev_plus_one_alt_1	-	✓	find_min_up_to_1	-	-
copy_two_indices	-	✓	max_prop_0	-	✓	merge_interleave_2	-	-
find_max_0	-	✓	max_prop_1	-	✓	partition_2	-	✓
find_max_2	-	✓	merge_interleave_0	-	-	partition_3	-	✓
find_max_from_second_0	-	-	merge_interleave_1	-	-	partition_4	-	-
find_max_local_2	-	-	min_prop_0	-	✓	partition_5	-	✓
find_max_up_to_0	-	-	min_prop_1	-	✓	partition_6	-	-
find_max_up_to_2	-	-	partition_0	-	✓	partition-harder_0	-	✓
find_min_0	-	✓	partition_1	-	✓	partition-harder_1	-	✓
find_min_2	-	✓	push_back	-	✓	partition-harder_2	-	-
find_min_local_2	-	-	reverse	-	✓	partition-harder_3	-	-
find_min_up_to_0	-	-	str_cpy_0	-	✓	partition-harder_4	-	-
find_min_up_to_2	-	-	str_cpy_1	-	✓	str_len	✓	✓
find1_4	-	✓	str_cpy_2	✓	✓			
find2_4	✓	✓	swap_0	-	✓	**Total solved**	**15**	**78**

Comparing with other tools. We compare our work against other approaches in VIII. Here, we omit a direct comparison of RAPID with other tools for the following reasons:

(1) Our benchmark suite includes 62 universally quantified and 11 non-quantified properties that could technically be supported by state-of-the-art tools such as SPACER/SEAHORN and FREQHORN. Our benchmarks, however, also include 30 benchmarks with existential (7 examples) and alternating quantification (23 examples) that these tools cannot handle. As these examples depend on invariants that are alternatingly or at least existentially quantified, we believe these other tools cannot solve these benchmarks, while RAPID* could solve 14 examples in this domain.

(2) In our preliminary work [6], we already compared our reasoning within RAPID against Z3 and CVC4. These experiments showed that due to the fundamental difference in handling variables as functions over timepoints in our semantics, RAPID outperformed SMT-based reasoning approaches.

(3) Our program semantics is different than the one used in Horn clause verification techniques.

Concerning previous approaches with first-order reasoners, the benchmarks of [21] represent a subset of 55 examples from our current benchmark suite: only 21 examples from our benchmark suite could be proved by [21]. For instance, our example in Figure 1 could not be proven in [21]. We believe that our work can be combined with approaches from [22], [21] to non-trivial invariants and loop bounds from saturation-based proof search. Our work can, thus, complement existing tools in proving complex quantified properties.

VIII. RELATED WORK

Our work is closely related to recent efforts in using first-order theorem provers for proving software properties [22], [21]. While [21] captures programs semantics in the first-order language of extended expressions over loop iterations, in our work we further generalize the semantics of program locations and consider program expressions over loop iterations and arbitrary timepoints. Further, we introduce and prove trace lemmas to automate inductive reasoning based on bounded induction over loop iterations. Our generalizations in trace logic proved to be necessary to automate the verification of properties with arbitrary quantification, which could not be effectively achieved in [21]. Our work is not restricted to reasoning about single loops as in [21].

Compared to [6], we provide a non-recursive generalization of the axiomatic semantics of programs in trace logic, prove completeness of our axiomatization in trace logic, ensure soundness of our trace lemmas and use trace logic for safety verification.

In comparison to verification approaches based on program transformations [8], [9], [23], we do not require user-provided functions to transform program states to smaller-sized states [10], nor are we restricted to universal properties generated by symbolic executions [9]. Rather, we use only three trace lemmas that we prove sound and automate the verification of first-order properties, possibly with alternations of quantifiers.

The works [24], [25] consider expressive abstract domains and limit the generation of universal invariants to these domains, while supporting potentially more generic program grammars than our $\mathcal{W}$ language. Our work however can verify universal and/or existential first-order properties with theories, which is not the case in [8], [9], [24], [25]. Verifying universal loop properties with arrays by implicitly finding invariants is addressed in [4], [5], [26], [27], [28], [29], and by using constraint horn clause reasoning within property-driven reachability analysis in [16], [30].

Another line of research proposes abstraction and lazy interpolation [31], [32], as well as recurrence solving with SMT-based reasoning [33]. Synthesis-based approaches, such as [5], are shown to be successful when it comes to inferring universally quantified invariants and proving program correctness from these invariants. Synthesis-based term enumeration is used also in [23] in combination with user-provided invariant templates. Compared to these works, we do not consider programs only as a sequence of states, but model program values as functions of loop iterations and timepoints. We synthesize bounds on loop iterations and infer first-order loop invariants as logical consequences of our trace lemmas and program semantics in trace logic.

IX. Conclusion

We introduced trace logic to reason about safety loop properties over arrays. Trace logic supports explicit timepoint reasoning to allow arbitrary quantification over loop iterations. We use trace lemmas as consequences of bounded induction to automated inductive loop reasoning in trace logic. We formalize the axiomatic semantics of programs in trace logic and prove it to be both sound and complete. We report on our implementation in the RAPID framework, allowing us to use superposition-based reasoning in trace logic for verifying challenging verification examples. Generalizing our work to termination analysis and extending our programming language, and its semantics in trace logic, with more complex constructs are interesting tasks for future work.

Acknowledgements. This work was funded by the ERC Starting Grant 2014 SYMCAR 639270, the ERC Proof of Concept Grant 2018 SYMELS 842066, the Wallenberg Academy Fellowship 2014 TheProSE, and the Austrian FWF research project W1255-N23.

References

[1] L. De Moura and N. Bjørner, "Z3: An Efficient SMT Solver," in *TACAS*, 2008, pp. 337–340.

[2] C. Barrett, C. L. Conway, M. Deters, L. Hadarean, D. Jovanović, T. King, A. Reynolds, and C. Tinelli, "CVC4," in *CAV*, 2011, pp. 171–177.

[3] A. Karbyshev, N. Bjørner, S. Itzhaky, N. Rinetzky, and S. Shoham, "Property-directed inference of universal invariants or proving their absence," pp. 583–602, 2015.

[4] A. Gurfinkel, S. Shoham, and Y. Vizel, "Quantifiers on demand," in *ATVA*, 2018, pp. 248–266.

[5] G. Fedyukovich, S. Prabhu, K. Madhukar, and A. Gupta, "Quantified invariants via syntax-guided synthesis," in *CAV*, 2019, pp. 259–277.

[6] G. Barthe, R. Eilers, P. Georgiou, B. Gleiss, L. Kovács, and M. Maffei, "Verifying relational properties using trace logic," in *FMCAD*, 2019, pp. 170–178.

[7] N. Bjørner, A. Gurfinkel, K. McMillan, and A. Rybalchenko, "Horn Clause Solvers for Program Verification," in *Fields of Logic and Computation II*, 2015, pp. 24–51.

[8] N. Kobayashi, G. Fedyukovich, and A. Gupta, "Fold/unfold transformations for fixpoint logic," in *TACAS*, 2020, pp. 195–214.

[9] S. Chakraborty, A. Gupta, and D. Unadkat, "Verifying array manipulating programs with full-program induction," in *TACAS*, 2020, pp. 22–39.

[10] O. Ish-Shalom, S. Itzhaky, N. Rinetzky, and S. Shoham, "Putting the squeeze on array programs: Loop verification via inductive rank reduction," in *VMAI*, 2020, pp. 112–135.

[11] B. Gleiss, L. Kovács, and J. Rath, "Subsumption demodulation in first-order theorem proving," in *IJCAR*, 2020.

[12] B. Gleiss and M. Suda, "Layered clause selection for theory reasoning," in *IJCAR*, 2020.

[13] L. Kovács, S. Robillard, and A. Voronkov, "Coming to Terms with Quantified Reasoning," in *POPL*, 2017, pp. 260–270.

[14] D. Beyer, "Automatic verification of c and java programs: Sv-comp 2019," in *TACAS*, 2019, pp. 133–155.

[15] A. Gurfinkel, T. Kahsai, A. Komuravelli, and J. A. Navas, "The seahorn verification framework," in *CAV*, 2015, pp. 343–361.

[16] K. Hoder and N. Bjørner, "Generalized property directed reachability," in *SAT*, 2012, pp. 157–171.

[17] P. Georgiou, B. Gleiss, and L. Kovács, "Trace Logic for Inductive Loop Reasoning," 2020, arXiv:2008.01387.

[18] C. A. R. Hoare, "An axiomatic basis for computer programming," *Communications of the ACM*, vol. 12, no. 10, pp. 576–580, 1969.

[19] C. Barrett, P. Fontaine, and C. Tinelli, "The SMT-LIB Standard: Version 2.6," Department of Computer Science, The University of Iowa, Tech. Rep., 2017, available at www.SMT-LIB.org.

[20] L. Kovács and A. Voronkov, "First-Order Theorem Proving and Vampire," in *CAV*, 2013, pp. 1–35.

[21] B. Gleiss, L. Kovács, and S. Robillard, "Loop Analysis by Quantification over Iterations," in *LPAR*, 2018, pp. 381–399.

[22] L. Kovács and A. Voronkov, "Finding loop invariants for programs over arrays using a theorem prover," in *FASE*, 2009, pp. 470–485.

[23] W. Yang, G. Fedyukovich, and A. Gupta, "Lemma synthesis for automating induction over algebraic data types," in *CP*, 2019, pp. 600–617.

[24] I. Dillig, T. Dillig, and A. Aiken, "Fluid Updates: Beyond Strong vs. Weak Updates," in *ESOP*, 2010, pp. 246–266.

[25] P. Cousot, R. Cousot, and F. Logozzo, "A Parametric Segmentation Functor for Fully Automatic and Scalable Array Content Analysis," in *POPL*, 2011, pp. 105–118.

[26] A. Komuravelli, N. Bjorner, A. Gurfinkel, and K. L. McMillan, "Compositional verification of procedural programs using horn clauses over integers and arrays," in *FMCAD*, 2015, pp. 89–96.

[27] G. Fedyukovich, S. J. Kaufman, and R. Bodík, "Sampling invariants from frequency distributions," in *FMCAD*, 2017, pp. 100–107.

[28] G. Fedyukovich and R. Bodík, "Accelerating syntax-guided invariant synthesis," in *TACAS*, 2018, pp. 251–269.

[29] Y. Matsushita, T. Tsukada, and N. Kobayashi, "Rusthorn: Chc-based verification for rust programs," in *ESOP*, 2020, pp. 484–514.

[30] A. Cimatti and A. Griggio, "Software model checking via ic3," in *CAV*, 2012, pp. 277–293.

[31] F. Alberti, R. Bruttomesso, S. Ghilardi, S. Ranise, and N. Sharygina, "Lazy abstraction with interpolants for arrays," in *LPAR*, 2012, pp. 46–61.

[32] M. Afzal, S. Chakraborty, A. Chauhan, B. Chimdyalwar, P. Darke, A. Gupta, S. Kumar, C. Babu, D. Unadkat, and R. Venkatesh, "Veriabs: Verification by abstraction and test generation (competition contribution)," in *TACAS*, 2020, pp. 383–387.

[33] P. Rajkhowa and F. Lin, "Extending viap to handle array programs," in *VSTTE*, 2018, pp. 38–49.

7

Thread-modular Counter Abstraction for Parameterized Program Safety

Thomas Pani (iD)
TU Wien, Vienna, Austria
pani@forsyte.at

Georg Weissenbacher (iD)
TU Wien, Vienna, Austria
weissenb@forsyte.at

Florian Zuleger (iD)
TU Wien, Vienna, Austria
zuleger@forsyte.at

Abstract—Automated safety proofs of parameterized software are hard: State-of-the-art methods rely on intricate abstractions and complicated proof techniques that often impede automation. We replace this heavy machinery with a clean abstraction framework built from a novel combination of *counter abstraction*, *thread-modular reasoning*, and *predicate abstraction*. Our fully automated method proves parameterized safety for a wide range of classically challenging examples in a straight-forward manner.

Index Terms—parameterized program, parameterized safety, counter abstraction, thread-modular reasoning, predicate abstraction

I. Introduction

In this paper, we present a novel method for automatically proving safety of programs that are executed by an unbounded number of concurrent threads.

Running example. Consider the program template $T[N]$ over global variables s and t and parameter N shown in Fig. 1a[1]. Assume that T is executed by an arbitrary number of n threads, where each thread runs the program $P = T[N/n]$ obtained by replacing N by n in T (Fig. 1b). We write $P(n) = P_1 \parallel \cdots \parallel P_n$ for this *parameterized program*. In this paper, we show how to automatically prove that the error location ℓ_{err} is unreachable from an initial state of $s = t = 0$ for all $n > 0$.

Despite the seemingly simple structure of the program, automatically constructing such a safety proof is hard: Note that the value of global variable t equals the number of threads at either control location ℓ_1, ℓ_2, or ℓ_{err}. Similarly, the value of s equals the number of threads at control location ℓ_2. In addition, the assertion not only refers to variables, but also to the parameter n. Thus, a safety proof for this program needs to relate the unboundedly many local states of all threads, the arbitrary number of threads n, and the global variables s and t in a meaningful way.

A. Tackling dimensions of infinity

A parameterized program – like the one above – induces an infinite family of concurrent programs, one for each instantiation of the parameter n. Together, this family of concurrent programs exhibits the following *dimensions of infinity* that any automated procedure has to deal with:

(I) **Unbounded replication of local state.** The program template's control structure and local variables are replicated for each of the unboundedly many threads.

(II) **Infinite data domain.** As for sequential software, the program variables range over an infinite data domain.

State-of-the-art methods rely on heavy proof machinery to tackle these dimensions (cf. Section III). In contrast, our method is a novel combination of well-known techniques. Significantly improving the start of the art, we build a powerful and cleanly structured two-step abstraction framework. Our method is fully automated and treats the infinity dimensions in dedicated abstraction layers:

The first step of our method, *thread-modular counter abstraction* (TMCA), deals with dimension (I) and is inspired by the well-known techniques counter abstraction [2] and thread-modular reasoning [3], [4]. TMCA uses symmetry reduction to track the number of threads in a specific local state, encodes this information in the (already infinite) data domain, and abstracts the unbounded local state into a stateless thread-modular summary. TMCA models are sequential programs that can be checked using off-the-shelf software verifiers. However, our experiments show that state-of-the-art techniques diverge on them. We thus tackle infinity dimension (II) by presenting a *novel predicate refinement heuristic* for predicate abstraction [5], [6].

II. Motivating Example

Fig. 2 gives an overview of our approach. We briefly discuss its structure and demonstrate it on our introductory example.

A. Counter instrumentation

Our method keeps one thread concrete and computes an abstraction of the $n - 1$ other threads. We call these $n - 1$ threads *the environment*. Our method starts by instrumenting the program $P = T[N/n]$ from Fig. 1b to track the local state of the $n - 1$ environment threads in additional global counter variables. This introduction of auxiliary state serves to retain some information about the local state of all threads in the subsequent abstraction step.

Running example. In our motivating example (Fig. 1b), each thread's local state is given entirely by the valuation of its program counter, which ranges over the finite domain of program locations $\{\ell_0, \ell_1, \ell_2\}$. Our method introduces fresh global variables $\{c_0, c_1, c_2\}$ and instruments the program such

---

[1]This slightly abstracted version of a ticket lock is adapted from the introductory example in [1]. We extend their version with an upper bounds check $s - t \leq N$. This allows us to bound $s - t$ by the number of threads n.

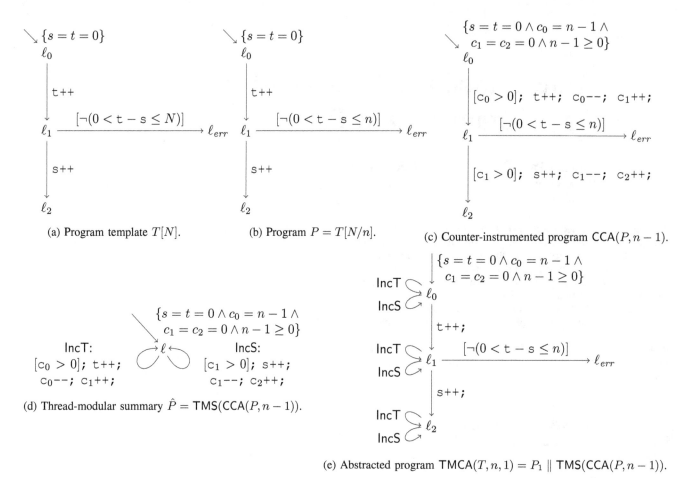

(a) Program template $T[N]$.   (b) Program $P = T[N/n]$.   (c) Counter-instrumented program $\mathsf{CCA}(P, n-1)$.

(d) Thread-modular summary $\hat{P} = \mathsf{TMS}(\mathsf{CCA}(P, n-1))$.

(e) Abstracted program $\mathsf{TMCA}(T, n, 1) = P_1 \parallel \mathsf{TMS}(\mathsf{CCA}(P, n-1))$.

Fig. 1: Running example illustrating the thread-modular abstraction TMCA. Adapted from the introductory example in [1] by extending the assertion with an upper bounds check $s - t \leq N$ on the parameter.

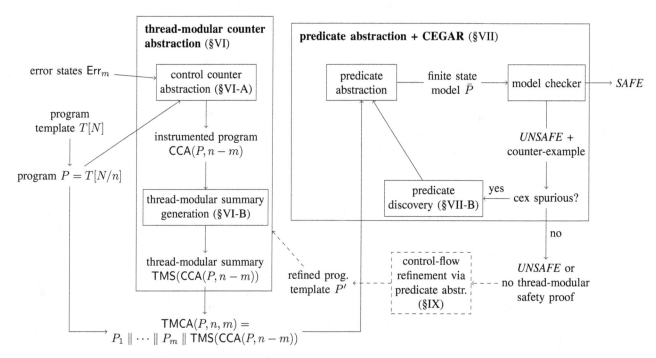

Fig. 2: Overall structure of our method. Dashed parts are beyond the scope of this work and sketched in Section IX.

that variable c_i tracks the number of threads at location ℓ_i. The resulting instrumented program $\mathsf{CCA}(P, n-1)$ is shown in Fig. 1c.

B. Thread-modular summary generation

In this step, our method uses thread-modular reasoning to project away the unboundedly many local variables of the $n-1$ environment threads. Our method generates a thread-modular summary $\hat{P}$ of the instrumented program $\mathsf{CCA}(P, n-1)$, such that $\hat{P}$ over-approximates the reachable global state space of the environment threads for all $n > 0$.

Running example. In our example, the only local variable of $\mathsf{CCA}(P, n-1)$ (Fig. 1c) is the program counter. By projecting it away, we obtain $\hat{P} = \mathsf{TMS}(\mathsf{CCA}(P, n-1))$ as the thread-modular summary in Fig. 1d: Abstract transition IncT corresponds to transition $\ell_0 \to \ell_1$, while IncS corresponds to transition $\ell_1 \to \ell_2$. It is easy to see that from its initial state

$$\{s = t = 0 \wedge c_0 = n-1 \wedge c_1 = c_2 = 0 \wedge n-1 \geq 0\},$$

$\hat{P}$ over-approximates the globally visible behavior of $n-1$ environment threads for all $n > 0$. Thus, instead of analyzing the parameterized program $P(n)$, we instead consider its over-approximation $\mathsf{TMCA}(T, n, 1) = P_1 \parallel \hat{P}$ (shown in Fig. 1e), where $\hat{P}$ over-approximates the behavior of $P_2 \parallel \cdots \parallel P_n$.

C. Invariant generation (predicate abstraction + CEGAR)

The abstracted program $\mathsf{TMCA}(T, n, 1)$ from above is just a sequential program that could be checked by off-the-shelf software verifiers, e.g., based on predicate abstraction. Our experiments (Section VIII) show that our abstraction already allows state-of-the-art methods to prove safety for *some* examples. However, due to the uncommon structure of our abstract models, standard predicate discovery heuristics often diverge. Again improving the state of the art, we thus introduce a novel predicate selection heuristic in Section VII.

Running example. For our abstracted example $\mathsf{TMCA}(T, n, 1)$ in Fig. 1e, this predicate selection procedure finds the following invariant at control location ℓ_1:

$$c_1 < t - s \wedge t - s \leq n - c_0 \wedge$$
$$c_0 \geq 0 \wedge c_1 \geq 0 \wedge c_2 \geq 0 \wedge n > 0 \wedge s \geq 0 \wedge t > 0$$

Obviously, this implies that $0 < t - s \leq n$ and thus proves the error location ℓ_{err} unreachable.

III. RELATED WORK

There exists extensive research on the automated verification of *parameterized systems*, i.e., the unbounded replication of *finite-state* components. The survey in [7] gives an overview. In contrast, we are interested in the safety verification of *parameterized programs*, where already the individual components are *infinite-state*. Several works discuss their verification, among them approaches orthogonal to ours such as *cutoff detection* [8], [9], semi-automatic *deductive techniques* [10], or those based on *small model properties* [11], [12]. In the following, we discuss the works most closely related to ours.

Ganjei et al. [13], [14] prove parameterized program safety by combining two nested CEGAR loops: Their method applies *symmetric predicate abstraction* [15], a specialization of predicate abstraction for symmetric concurrent programs, to obtain a program template's finite-state abstraction as a boolean program. The method then uses counter abstraction to encode the parallel composition of n copies of the boolean program into a monotonic counter machine (essentially a vector addition system, i.e., more threads lead to more behavior). Since some wide-spread synchronization constructs have *non-monotonic* behavior, these tests are lost in the monotonic abstraction[2]. The authors strengthen their abstraction using a thread-modular analysis and check the resulting, now non-monotonic counter machine with the inner CEGAR loop running *constrained monotonic abstraction* [16], again abstracting the non-monotonic system into a monotonic one for which state reachability is decidable.

Kaiser et al. [17] present another combination of monotonic abstraction nested inside a specialized predicate abstraction. They introduce a symbolic representation for tracking inter-thread predicates, extending those of [15]. The resulting system is again non-monotonic and the authors force monotonicity as above. It is however unclear how to construct these inter-thread predicates or how to refine the monotonic abstraction.

Following a different approach, Farzan et al. [1] introduce *control flow nets*, a hybrid of Petri nets and control flow graphs, as their program model. The proof procedure alternates between synthesizing a candidate *counting automaton* (a kind of restricted counter machine) and checking language inclusion with the underlying control flow net. While the method is explained in theory, no implementation is given. In addition, the Petri net program model has several shortcomings. First, it is unclear how to encode a given parameterized program: even the authors present a program where "it does not seem possible to encode the verification problem for mutual exclusion by a control flow net" [1]. Second, it is unclear how to express the additional upper-bounds check on N added to our running example (Fig. 1b) given that the parameter is not symbolically represented in the control flow net.

In summary, state-of-the-art methods rely on tightly coupled, specialized abstractions and heavy, non-standard proof machinery. Many times, implementation questions are unclear and the possibility of automation is questionable. However, our experiments show that many practical examples can be proven in a more straight-forward way: We replace the heavy machinery of previous work with a *clean, two-step abstraction framework built from a novel combination of well-known techniques*, thus significantly improving the state of the art.

In particular, we start from a *standard program model* by encoding our program templates as transition systems. To these, our method first applies a novel thread-modular counter abstraction adapted to infinite-state systems that tracks and

---

[2]Synchronization mechanisms such as the *dynamic barriers* considered by Ganjei et al. [13], [14] test the number of threads in a specific state. In essence, their counter abstraction would then have to encode a counter machine with zero tests, making state reachability checking undecidable.

projects away the unboundedly replicated local state. In the subsequent step, we apply *standard predicate abstraction* to deal with the infinite data domain. The discovery of counting arguments is left entirely to the predicate refinement phase. We show in Section VIII that this straight-forward method is powerful enough for many examples from the literature. In addition, our two-step abstraction follows a clean design by applying the *separation of concerns* design principle: each dimension of infinity is dealt with in a dedicated component. While our upfront thread-modular abstraction may be too coarse in some cases, it could be strengthened by an outer refinement loop, again running *predicate abstraction*. This additional refinement step is beyond the scope of this work; we sketch it in Section IX and leave its detailed investigation for future work.

IV. CONTRIBUTIONS

We introduce a novel framework for parameterized software verification. Its advantages over state-of-the-art methods lie in its clean design and simplicity, while being powerful enough to tackle a superset of benchmarks compared to previous work. In particular, we make the following contributions:

1) Our framework is presented as a novel layered proof system of well-understood and pluggable components. The power of our method stems from adapting, combining, and extending established methods without introducing complicated new proof machinery or non-standard concepts (Sections VI and VII). To our knowledge, we are the first to suggest this combination of techniques for safety proofs of parameterized programs. In particular, we contribute the following technical advancements:

   a) We adapt counter abstraction to infinite-state systems by introducing auxiliary state to track the number of threads in a specific local state (Section VI). To our knowledge we are the first to propose such a counter abstraction and to apply it to parameterized programs.

   b) Predicate abstraction with standard predicate selection heuristics diverges on our abstract models (Section VIII). We present novel predicate selection heuristics to guide a CEGAR loop in the presence of these counter-abstracted summaries (Section VII).

2) We implement our method based on constrained Horn clauses (CHCs) and demonstrate its efficacy on a combined benchmark set from various sources (Section VIII).

3) The individual components of our framework lend themselves to tweaking and adaptation, both on the theoretical side (e.g., by providing new heuristics or refinement methods) and on the practical side (e.g., through new and improved backend solvers) (Section IX).

V. PROGRAM MODEL AND PROBLEM STATEMENT

In this section, we start to formally develop the technique illustrated above by formalizing our program model and problem statement.

Definition 1 (Program model). Let $\mathbf{g} = (g_1, \ldots, g_k)$ and $\mathbf{l} = (l_1, \ldots, l_j)$ be disjoint tuples of *global* and *local program variables*. Let N be a *symbolic parameter*. A *guarded command* $gc \in \mathsf{GC}$ over $\mathbf{l}, \mathbf{g}, N$ has the form

$$gc : [cond] \mid v := e \mid gc_1; \ gc_2$$

where $[cond]$ is an assume statement over $\mathbf{l}, \mathbf{g}, N$, and $v := e$ is an assignment of expression e over $\mathbf{l}, \mathbf{g}, N$ to a local or global variable v. We write $\nu(\mathbf{g}, \mathbf{l})$ for the valuation of global and local variables and omit its arguments wherever clear from the context. We denote by $[\![gc]\!](\nu) = \nu'$ the *effect* of a guarded command gc and write $\varphi(\mathbf{g}, \mathbf{g}', \mathbf{l}, \mathbf{l}')$ for its standard encoding as a formula over primed and unprimed variables.

A *program template* $T[N]$ over global and local variables $\mathbf{g}$ and $\mathbf{l}$ and a parameter N is a directed labeled graph $T[N] = (Loc, \delta, \ell_0, Init)$ where Loc is a finite set of *control locations*, $\ell_0 \in Loc$ is the *initial location*, $\delta \subseteq Loc \times \mathsf{GC} \times Loc$ is a finite set of *transitions*, and $Init$ is a predicate over $\mathbf{g}, \mathbf{l}, N$ describing the initial valuations of variables. From template $T[N]$, we obtain *program* $P = T[N/n] = (Loc, \delta', \ell_0, Init')$ by replacing each occurrence of N in T (i.e., in δ and $Init$) with the expression n. We call a pair (ℓ, ν) of a control location $\ell \in Loc$ and a valuation $\nu(\mathbf{g}, \mathbf{l})$ a *program state*. We represent *runs* of P as interleaved sequences of states and transitions and write $(\ell_0, \nu_0) \xrightarrow{gc_0} (\ell_1, \nu_1) \xrightarrow{gc_1} \ldots$ such that ν_0 satisfies $Init'$, and for all $i \geq 0$ we have that $(\ell_i, gc_i, \ell_{i+1}) \in \delta'$ and $\nu_{i+1} = [\![gc_i]\!](\nu_i)$.

We define the *interleaving* of two programs $P_1 = (Loc_1, \delta_1, \ell_{1,0}, Init_1)$ and $P_2 = (Loc_2, \delta_2, \ell_{2,0}, Init_2)$ over joint global variables $\mathbf{g}$ and disjoint local variables $\mathbf{l}_1$ and $\mathbf{l}_2$ as the program $P_1 \parallel P_2 = (Loc_1 \times Loc_2, \rho, (\ell_{1,0}, \ell_{2,0}), Init_1 \wedge Init_2)$ over global and local variables $\mathbf{g}$ and $\mathbf{l}_1 \cup \mathbf{l}_2$ where $((\ell_1, \ell_2), gc, (\ell'_1, \ell'_2)) \in \rho$ iff either $(\ell_1, gc, \ell'_1) \in \delta_1$ and $\ell'_2 = \ell_2$, or $(\ell_2, gc, \ell'_2) \in \delta_2$ and $\ell'_1 = \ell_1$. Let $P = (Loc, \delta, \ell_0, Init)$ be a program. For *thread identifiers* $i = 1, \ldots, k$ we obtain the *instantiation* P_i of P by replacing each local variable l_j with its i-th copy $l_{j,i}$. We define the k-*times interleaving* of P as $P^k = P_1 \parallel \cdots \parallel P_k$. Finally, a program template $T[N]$ induces a *parameterized program* $P(n) = (T[N/n])^n$.

Following [18], [19], we define *safety* of a parameterized program in the style of coverability:

Definition 2 (Safety). Let $T[N]$ be program template, and let $P(n)$ be its induced parameterized program over vectors of global and local variables $(\mathbf{g}, \mathbf{l}_1, \ldots, \mathbf{l}_n)$. Recall that a state of $P(n)$ has the form $((\ell_1, \ldots, \ell_n), \nu)$. We define *safety* relative to a generator set of error states Err_m of $(T[N/n])^m$ for a fixed $m > 0$. $P(n)$ is *safe* iff for all $n > 0$, no run of $P(n)$ reaches an error state from the system error states Err, where

$$\mathsf{Err} \stackrel{\text{def}}{=} \{((\ell_1, \ldots, \ell_n), \nu) \mid ((\ell_{i_1}, \ldots, \ell_{i_m}), \nu') \in \mathsf{Err}_m \text{ s.t.}$$
$$\nu'(\mathbf{g}) = \nu(\mathbf{g}), \nu'(\mathbf{l}_j) = \nu(\mathbf{l}_{i_j}) \text{ for } 1 \leq j \leq m$$
$$\text{and some } i_1, \ldots, i_m \text{ s.t. } 1 \leq i_1 < \cdots < i_m \leq n\}. \quad (1)$$

Intuitively, $P(n)$ is unsafe if it contains m pairwise distinct threads that reach an error state from Err_m while the remaining

$n - m$ symmetric threads may take arbitrary control locations and local states. Note that for a concrete parameterized verification problem, m is a scalar value but n is universally quantified: Given a program template $T[N]$ and a generator set Err_m, our goal is to prove safety of the induced parameterized program $P(n)$, i.e., to show that reaching an error state from Err is infeasible for all parameter instantiations $n > 0$. Our method follows a two-step process that we explain in the next two sections.

VI. TACKLING INFINITY DIMENSION I: THREAD-MODULAR COUNTER ABSTRACTION (TMCA)

As outlined in Section I, there are two main challenges in proving safety of a parameterized program $P(n)$: its *unboundedly replicated local state*, and the *infinite data domain*. The first step of our method, *thread-modular counter abstraction* (TMCA), tackles the first aspect. We deal with the second dimension, infinite data, in Section VII.

TMCA is inspired both by the work on *counter abstraction* [2] and *thread-modular reasoning* [3], [4]. Starting from a program template $T[N]$, its induced parameterized program $P(n) = T[N/n]_1 \parallel \cdots \parallel T[N/n]_n$, and a generator set of error states Err_m, our goal is to construct an abstraction $\hat{P}$ such that $\text{TMCA}(T, n, m) = T[N/n]_1 \parallel \cdots \parallel T[N/n]_m \parallel \hat{P}$ over-approximates the reachable state space of $P(n)$, but has only finitely many control locations and variables. In the following, we explain both aspects of TMCA in further detail.

A. Control counter abstraction (CCA)

Counter abstraction [2] was introduced to abstract the parallel execution of an unbounded number of *finite-state* processes: For each state, a counter is introduced to track how many processes reside in their respective copy of the state. Counter values are then projected onto a finite domain to obtain a finite-state system that is model-checked. This idea has been adapted to parameterized software [13], [17] by first predicate-abstracting the program template into a boolean program, and then counting the number of threads residing in one of the finitely many abstract states.

In contrast, our method instruments counters as *auxiliary variables* [20], [21] into an *infinite-state* system: It is well-known that thread-modular reasoning is incomplete [22], but can be made more expressive by adding auxiliary state [10], [20]. Thus, in contrast to earlier work on counter abstraction, our goal is not to finitize the entire parameterized system, but to express the unboundedly replicated local state of a parameterized program $P(n)$ in the already infinite data domain. To this end, we first instrument the corresponding program P with fresh *counter variables*, one for each program location, that count the number of threads in (their copy of) the respective control state. We formalize this idea:

Definition 3 (Auxiliary variable instrumentation). Let $P = (Loc, \delta, \ell_0, Init)$ be a program over global and local variables $\mathbf{g}$ and $\mathbf{l}$. We extend the set of global variables with a set of fresh auxiliary variables, one for each program location: for global variables $\mathbf{g} = (g_1, \ldots, g_i)$ and control locations

$Loc = \{\ell_0, \ell_1, \ldots, \ell_j\}$, let $\mathbf{g}' = (g_1, \ldots, g_i, c_0, c_1, \ldots, c_j)$. The *instrumented program* $\text{CCA}(P, k) = (Loc, \delta', \ell_0, Init')$ is defined over the extended global variables $\mathbf{g}'$ and local variables $\mathbf{l}$ where the instrumented transition relation δ' is

$$\ell_{src} \xrightarrow{gc'} \ell_{tgt} \in \delta' \quad \text{iff} \quad \ell_{src} \xrightarrow{gc} \ell_{tgt} \in \delta \quad \text{where}$$

$$gc' \stackrel{\text{def}}{=} [c_{src} > 0]; \, gc; \, c_{src} := c_{src} - 1; \, c_{tgt} := c_{tgt} + 1;$$

and $Init' \stackrel{\text{def}}{=} Init \wedge c_0 = k \wedge c_1 = \cdots = c_j = 0 \wedge k \geq 0.$

Proposition 1. *Let P be a program and let P^k be its k-times interleaving. Up to the instrumented counter variables, $\text{CCA}(P, k)^k$ has the same reachable states as P^k for all $k > 0$.*

Note that CCA's second argument k can be symbolic. We use this below to obtain a summary for an arbitrary number of threads.

B. Thread-modular summary generation (TMS)

The parameterized program instrumented as outlined above still contains unboundedly many local variables. To tackle this second aspect of unboundedly replicated local state, our method computes a *thread-modular summary*. Originally conceived as an extension of Hoare logic to concurrency, *thread-modular reasoning* [3], [4] picks one *reference thread* and models the interleaved steps of all other threads (the *environment*) in an *environment assumption*. This environment assumption is a binary relation over global program states and over-approximates the environment's transition relation.

We compute thread-modular summaries by projecting away all local state (i.e., the control locations and valuations of local variables) from the program's transition relation[3]:

Definition 4 (Thread-modular summary). Let $P = (Loc, \delta, \ell_0, Init)$ be a program over global and local variables $\mathbf{g}$ and $\mathbf{l}$. We define the *thread-modular summary* $\text{TMS}(P) = (\{\ell\}, \delta', \ell, Init')$ for a fresh program location $\ell \notin Loc$ where $Init' \stackrel{\text{def}}{=} \exists \mathbf{l}. Init$ and δ' is defined as

$$\ell \xrightarrow{\exists \mathbf{l}, \mathbf{l}'. \varphi(\mathbf{g}, \mathbf{g}', \mathbf{l}, \mathbf{l}')} \ell \in \delta' \quad \text{iff} \quad \ell_{src} \xrightarrow{\varphi(\mathbf{g}, \mathbf{g}', \mathbf{l}, \mathbf{l}')} \ell_{tgt} \in \delta.$$

Proposition 2. *Let P be a program. $\text{TMS}(P)$ over-approximates the reachable global states of P's k-times interleaving P^k for all $k > 0$.*

C. Putting it together: Thread-modular counter abstr. (TMCA)

The combination of control counter abstraction (Section VI-A) and thread-modular reasoning (Section VI-B) yields a control- and local-stateless thread-modular summary that over-approximates the reachable states of the original program. In addition, it retains the number of threads in a specific control location in the instrumented counter variables.

---

[3]We choose this definition because it is sufficiently fine-grained for our benchmarks. In general, stronger notions of a thread-modular summary (e.g., restricting the transition relation to reachable states) can be adopted [23].

As we motivated in Section I, this is essential for constructing counting proofs. Observe the following property of the combination of CCA and TMS:

Proposition 3. *Let P be a program. Up to instrumentation variables,* $\mathsf{TMS}(\mathsf{CCA}(P, k))$ *over-approximates the reachable global states of P^k for all $k > 0$.*

Recall from Definition 2 that safety of a parameterized program $P(n)$ is defined with respect to a generator set of error states Err_m. For deciding if a program state belongs to Err_m, the control locations and valuations of local variables of the $n - m$ other symmetric threads are irrelevant. We thus use the following generalization of thread-modular reasoning: We pick a finite set of m reference threads (recall that the parallel composition of finitely many threads is again a sequential program) and apply a combination of control counter abstraction and thread-modular summary generation to abstract all $n - m$ other threads.

Definition 5 (Thread-modular counter abstraction). *Let $T[N]$ be a program template and let $P(n)$ be the induced parameterized program. Let Err_m be a generator set of error states. We define the thread-modular control abstraction $\mathsf{TMCA}(T, n, m)$ as the program*

$$\mathsf{TMCA}(T[N], n, m) \stackrel{\text{def}}{=} \text{let } P = T[N/n] \text{ in}$$
$$P_1 \parallel \cdots \parallel P_m \parallel \mathsf{TMS}(\mathsf{CCA}(P, n - m)). \quad (2)$$

Proposition 4. *Let $T[N]$ be a program template, let $P(n)$ be its induced parameterized program, and let Err_m be a generator set of error states. We define R to be the set of reachable states of $P(n)$ projected to its first m components, i.e., let*

$$R = \{((\ell_1, \ldots, \ell_m), \nu(\mathbf{g}, \mathbf{l}_1, \ldots, \mathbf{l}_m)) \mid s.t.$$
$$((\ell_1, \ldots, \ell_n), \nu(\mathbf{g}, \mathbf{l}_1, \ldots, \mathbf{l}_n)) \text{ is reachable in } P(n)\}. \quad (3)$$

Then, the states reachable by $\mathsf{TMCA}(T, n, m)$ are a superset of R.

Note that by symmetry of Err, R contains an error state if and only if an error state is reachable by $P(n)$.

Theorem 1. *Let $T[N]$ be a program template, let $P(n)$ be its induced parameterized program, and let Err_m be a generator set of error states. If $\mathsf{TMCA}(T, n, m)$ is safe with respect to Err_m, then so is $P(n)$ for all $n > 0$.*

VII. TACKLING INFINITY DIMENSION II: PREDICATE ABSTRACTION (PA)

The parameterized program $P(n)$ induced by a program template $T[N]$ refers to an *infinite family of programs*. In contrast, consider its *thread-modular counter abstraction* $\mathsf{TMCA}(T, n, m)$: if its parameter n remains symbolic, we obtain an abstraction of the parameterized program in the form of a sequential program with finitely many control locations and local variables, while over-approximating the infinite family of programs induced by $P(n)$. Standard software verification

methods could be applied to prove safety, thus tackling infinity dimension (II) from Section I: the *infinite data domain*.

However, our experiments show that standard methods often fail on our models: We encode the TMCA abstraction of our benchmarks as a set of constrained Horn clauses (CHCs) [24]. Both state-of-the-art solvers ELDARICA [25] and Z3 [26] diverge on many of our examples (Table I, columns 1c and 1d; cf. Section VIII for details). We speculate that this is due to the uncommon structure of our TMCA models. In this section, we discuss how to guide a predicate abstraction-based solver to converge on TMCA models.

A. Predicate selection for TMCA models

A standard method for building predicate abstractions is to iteratively use an interpolating theorem prover to find new predicates that rule out spurious counter-examples [27]: We encode the error path in a logical formula in the usual way and split it into partitions $A \wedge B$. If the formula is unsatisfiable, the solver returns an *interpolant* I over the common symbols of A and B such that $A \rightarrow I$ and $I \rightarrow \neg B$. Intuitively, the interpolant I gives a reason why the path $A \wedge B$ is infeasible, and can thus be used as a predicate to refine the abstraction.

The key to converging predicate abstraction CEGAR loops is to chose the "right" interpolants. Conventional wisdom holds that referring to *loop counters*, which frequently appear on infeasible error paths, is best avoided in abstract models: tracking their values leads to loop unrolling and divergence of the CEGAR loop [28], [29]. This poses a challenge for thread-modular summaries:

Running example. Recall the TMCA abstraction of our example in Fig. 1e: Due to product construction with the thread-modular summary $\mathsf{TMS}(\mathsf{CCA}(P, n - 1))$, *all* variables are loop counters: the self-loops IncS and IncT at each program location increment or decrement c_0, c_1, c_2, s, and t. Tracking the value of either one leads to useless loop unrollings.

Even more elaborate predicates, e.g., tracking the difference expression in the assertion do not lead to convergence: Assume that we already applied predicate abstraction and the model checker returned the following spurious counter-example[4] (starting in an initial state where $s = t = 0$):

$$\texttt{t++; IncT; IncS; [0 >= t-s];}$$

The formula representing this error path is shown in Fig. 3a. If we partition the formula between IncT and IncS, an interpolating theorem prover is likely to find the new predicate $2 \leq t - s$. This rules out the spurious counter-example above, but leads to another, longer one:

$$\texttt{t++; IncT; IncT; IncS; IncS; [0 >= t-s];}$$

This again can be ruled out by the additional predicate $3 \leq t - s$ but only leads to further unrollings of IncS and IncT and to further invariants of this shape; the CEGAR loop diverges.

---

[4]One can reproduce the behavior of this running example in the model checker ELDARICA (v2.0.2) [25] and the interpolating theorem prover PRINCESS (v2020-03-12) [30].

$$s = 0 \wedge t = 0 \wedge c_0 = n - 1 \wedge c_1 = 0 \wedge c_2 = 0 \wedge n > 0 \wedge \qquad \text{(initial state)}$$
$$s' = s \wedge t' = t + 1 \wedge c_0' = c_0 \wedge c_1' = c_1 \wedge c_2' = c_2 \wedge \qquad (\ell_0 \to \ell_1\text{: t++})$$
$$c_0' > 0 \wedge s'' = s' \wedge t'' = t' + 1 \wedge c_0'' = c_0' - 1 \wedge c_1'' = c_1' + 1 \wedge c_2'' = c_2' \wedge \qquad (\ell_1 \to \ell_1\text{: IncT})$$
$$c_1'' > 0 \wedge s''' = s'' + 1 \wedge t''' = t'' \wedge c_0''' = c_0'' \wedge c_1''' = c_1'' - 1 \wedge c_2''' = c_2'' + 1 \wedge \qquad (\ell_1 \to \ell_1\text{: IncS})$$
$$0 < t''' - s''' \qquad \text{(assertion)}$$

(a) Concrete interpolation query.

$$s = 0 \wedge t = 0 \wedge c_0 = n - 1 \wedge c_1 = 0 \wedge c_2 = 0 \wedge n > 0 \qquad \text{(initial state)}$$
$$s' = s \wedge t' = t + 1 \wedge c_0' = c_0 \wedge c_1' = c_1 \wedge c_2' = c_2 \wedge \qquad (\ell_0 \to \ell_1\text{: t++})$$
$$c_0' > 0 \wedge s^A = s' \wedge t^A = t' + 1 \wedge c_0^A = c_0' - 1 \wedge c_1^A = c_1' + 1 \wedge c_2^A = c_2' \wedge \;(s^A = \dot{s} \wedge t^A - c_1^A = \dot{t} - \dot{c}_1)\; \wedge \qquad (\ell_1 \to \ell_1\text{: IncT})$$
$$c_1^B > 0 \wedge s''' = s^B + 1 \wedge t''' = t^B \wedge c_0''' = c_0^B \wedge c_1''' = c_1^B - 1 \wedge c_2''' = c_2^B + 1 \wedge \;(s^B = \dot{s} \wedge t^B - c_1^B = \dot{t} - \dot{c}_1)\; \wedge \qquad (\ell_1 \to \ell_1\text{: IncS})$$
$$0 < t''' - s''' \qquad \text{(assertion)}$$

(b) Abstract interpolation query.

Fig. 3: Interpolation queries for our running example.

Instead, we want to find an invariant that relates the location counters c_0, c_1, c_2 to the values of the global variables s and t. The next section explains how to achieve this.

B. An interpolation abstraction heuristic for TMCA models

As we argued above, interpolating predicate abstraction is always driven by heuristics to prevent divergence. We now present a heuristic that we find useful for the considered problem domain and later show that it outperforms several existing ones. *Interpolation abstraction* [31] is a state-of-the-art method to implement predicate selection. Indeed, EL-DARICA with its default interpolation abstraction heuristic (Table I, column 1b) fares better than without (column 1c) but still diverges on some benchmarks. We introduce a dedicated heuristic for TMCA models to remedy this shortcoming.

Interpolation abstraction uses a set of *template terms* to abstract the interpolation query and thus guide the theorem prover in its search for an interpolant. We briefly introduce the method on our running example and refer the interested reader to the canonical description [31] for further reading.

Running example. As explained in Section I, the valuations of s and t correspond to the number of threads in specific control locations, and thus to sums over the instrumented location counters. In particular, at ℓ_1 we have that

$$t = c_1 + c_2 + 1 \quad \text{and} \quad s = c_2 \quad \text{and thus} \qquad (6)$$
$$t - s = (c_1 + c_2 + 1) - (c_2) = c_1 + 1 \qquad (7)$$

Assume that we choose template terms $\{t - c_1, s\}$. The abstracted query is shown in Fig. 3b: Common symbols have been renamed and limited knowledge about them is reintroduced via equalities over the template terms in the shaded subformulae: in particular, the concrete values of t'' and c_1'' are lost, and only relational knowledge about their difference is reintroduced. Thus, $2 \leq \dot{t} - \dot{s}$ is no longer an interpolant. Instead, our interpolation procedure finds the new predicate $c_1 < t - s$, which is inductive at ℓ_1 and rules out further unrollings of the thread-modular summary. Note that this predicate $c_1 < t - s$ is implied by the invariant in

Equation (7) and, together with $0 \leq c_1$, implies the assertion $0 < t - s$.

It remains to define how our method computes the set of template terms for interpolation abstraction.

Definition 6 (Interpolation abstraction template terms). Let $T[N]$ be a program template over global and local variables **g** and **l**, let $P = T[N/n]$ be the program obtained by replacing N with n in T, and let $P(n)$ be the induced parameterized program. We start by computing a set of template terms for the thread-modular abstraction $\mathsf{TMS}(\mathsf{CCA}(P, n - m))$. For each variable x, we compute a stride set

$$S(x) = \{\alpha \mid x \text{ is incremented by } \alpha \text{ on some transition}$$
$$\text{of } \mathsf{TMS}(\mathsf{CCA}(P, n - m))\}.$$

We then define difference terms

$$T_{\mathsf{TMS}} = \{\alpha x - \beta c \mid x \text{ is a global program variable},$$
$$c \text{ is a location counter introduced by CCA},$$
$$\alpha \in S(c) \text{ and } \beta \in S(x)\}$$

We define the set of interpolation abstraction template terms *Templ* as the union of the following:
1) all global variables **g**,
2) the parameter n,
3) the set of difference terms T_{TMS}.

We replace the template term heuristics of [31] with our set *Templ* but still use their search algorithm: It explores the powerset lattice $\langle \mathcal{P}(Templ), \subseteq \rangle$ to find the largest subsets of *Templ* for which the abstracted interpolation query is still unsat. Of these, it picks the smallest ones and computes interpolants to refine the predicate abstraction.

Intuitively, this search behavior explores relational abstractions, such as $t - c_1$, early while still allowing us to track the value of global variables and to introduce the parameter n if necessary. In cases where there is no relationship between the global variables and location counters as captured by T_{TMS}, our templates may still be useful by ruling out interpolants that track concrete variable values and would lead to loop unwinding. Finally, it is worth pointing out that even though our template terms are linear relations, interpolation abstraction is semantic in nature and does not restrict the prover to only find such interpolants [31].

VIII. EXPERIMENTS

We implement our TMCA abstraction and predicate discovery engine [32] inside the ELDARICA Horn solver [25], [31]. It takes as input a program template $T[N]$ and the error states Err_m in a C-like language and outputs the abstracted program $TMCA(T, n, m)$ as a set of constrained Horn clauses (CHCs) [24] in the standard SMT-LIB format.

Our benchmarks and results are shown in Table I. The first group of benchmarks consists of program templates that sequentially increment and decrement a global variable. At each program location we assert the tightest possible lower and upper bounds; given that the number of increments and decrements depends on the number of concurrent threads n, these assertions are parameterized by the number of concurrent threads. The second group of benchmarks is a set of programs using unbounded thread creation taken from the software verification competition SV-COMP [33]. In its latest three editions (2018–2020), no sound verification tool proved these benchmarks safe. In addition, fkp2014 and the bluetooth driver qw2004 are the introductory and running example of [1]. The third group of benchmarks from [14] includes non-monotonic synchronization barriers (cf. Section III).

The columns of Table I compare the two main contributions of this work:

1) TMCA (Section VI), compared in sub-columns (1a)–(1d) to other approaches in columns (2) and (3), and
2) our predicate selection heuristic (Section VII) applied to TMCA models, compared in sub-column (1a) to other predicate selection heuristics in sub-columns (1b)–(1d).

In particular, we first compare TMCA abstraction with different backend solvers (column 1) to PACMAN [14] (col. 2) and ELDARICA's unbounded thread encoding[5] [18] (col. 3). The last two benchmarks, parent-child and as-many, use dynamic thread creation which is currently not supported by ELDARICA. ELDARICA times out on the remaining ones. Unfortunately, we were unable to compile PACMAN (even with the authors' help), due to outdated and commercial software dependencies. We are thus limited to citing previous results from [14] (recall from Section III that our main objective is to replace their dedicated abstraction techniques with a cleaner framework of well-established ones).

Second, we compare different backend solvers on our TMCA-abstracted models in column (1): our predicate selection heuristic from Section VII (1a), ELDARICA's default heuristic [31] (1b), ELDARICA without interpolation abstraction (1c) and the CHC solver in Z3 [26] (1d). Of the

benchmarks, only maximum does not have a thread-modular proof and thus cannot be proved safe by our method. On the remaining benchmarks, our predicate selection heuristic is the only one to solve all tasks and does so well below the timeout limit of 15 minutes. Meanwhile, ELDARICA with default heuristics encounters 5 timeouts, ELDARICA without interpolation abstraction 10, and Z3 even 11. This shows how important an appropriate predicate discovery algorithm is for our thread-modular abstractions.

In summary, a combination of both contributions (TMCA abstraction and our predicate selection heuristic) is necessary to tackle all benchmarks.

IX. FUTURE WORK

Our framework for parameterized program safety is designed to be modular and pluggable. As such, there are many directions for future work. We discuss several promising ones in this section and invite further ideas and suggestions from the community.

a) Thread-modular reasoning: [19] investigates *k-thread modular* proofs, a method orthogonal to auxiliary state introduction, to make thread-modular proofs more expressive. Another new approach to thread-modular verification is presented in [34], where a reflective abstraction is computed iteratively in a fixed point process. Integrating these approaches with our method makes an interesting area for future work.

In addition, we sketch how to further refine our thread-modular abstraction by closing the outer CEGAR loop. This corresponds to the dashed parts of Fig. 2. If the model checker reports a genuine counter-example, this may mean that the parameterized program is in fact unsafe, or that our upfront thread-modular abstraction was too coarse. If simulation on the original program finds the counter-example to be spurious, one can use predicate abstraction to refine the program's original control structure. This results in additional counters in our thread-modular abstraction. These counters are then not only capable of tracking control state, but also arbitrary predicates.

b) Predicate selection: The interpolation abstraction approach to predicate selection is highly semantic, in that the interpolant search is left to the underlying theorem prover. While this provides a lot of freedom, it would be interesting to see how a more syntactic approach – e.g., based on syntax-guided synthesis [35] – performs.

c) Solving: While currently limited to CHC solvers, we plan to evaluate our abstraction with further sound software verification tools as backend solvers.

X. CONCLUSION

In this work, we present a method for proving parameterized safety of infinite-state programs. Our method cleanly separates different abstraction concerns and, in contrast to related work, is built from well-established methods. Finally, we demonstrated its efficacy on a number of benchmarks from the literature.

---

[5]This encoding is usually unaware of the parameter n. We therefore slightly modify our benchmarks such that the encoding's implicitly introduced local thread id variable is bounded by n.

TABLE I: Benchmark results: Time to solve the respective encoding. ⊙ indicates a timeout after 15 minutes, the fastest tool for our TMCA encoding is highlighted in bold.

	(1) TMCA abstraction (Section VI)				(2) PACMAN	(3) ELDARICA
Benchmark	(a) our heuristic (Section VII)	(b) ELDARICA -abstract:relIneqs	(c) ELDARICA -abstract:off	(d) Z3 [26]	[14]	[18]
pp	1.5s	1.5s	1.4s	**0.1s**		⊙
mm	1.5s	1.7s	1.4s	**0.1s**		⊙
ppmm	2.5s	**2.3s**	⊙	⊙		⊙
mmpp	2.6s	**2.3s**	⊙	⊙		⊙
ppmmpp	**95.5s**	179.1s	⊙	⊙		⊙
fkp2014 [1]	**2.0s**	⊙	⊙	⊙		⊙
fkp2014 extd. (Fig. 1b)	**2.0s**	⊙	⊙	⊙		⊙
qw2004 [1]	**2.7s**	5.5s	⊙	⊙		⊙
locals [14]	**124.6s**	⊙	⊙	⊙	16s	⊙
shareds [14]	23.8s	**10.9s**	⊙	⊙	160s	⊙
readflag [14]	**25.5s**	⊙	⊙	⊙	34s	⊙
semaphore [14]	**36.4s**	⊙	⊙	⊙	68s	⊙
cyclic [14]	7.3s	**4.5s**	4.9s	⊙	30s	⊙
maximum [14]	——————— no thread-modular proof ———————				489s	⊙
parent-child [14]	——————— dynamic thread creation ———————				76s	dyn.thr.c.
as-many [14]	——————— dynamic thread creation ———————				68s	dyn.thr.c.

REFERENCES

[1] A. Farzan, Z. Kincaid, and A. Podelski, "Proofs that count," in *POPL*. ACM, 2014, pp. 151–164.

[2] A. Pnueli, J. Xu, and L. D. Zuck, "Liveness with (0, 1, infty)-counter abstraction," in *CAV*, ser. Lecture Notes in Computer Science, vol. 2404. Springer, 2002, pp. 107–122.

[3] C. B. Jones, "Specification and design of (parallel) programs," in *IFIP Congress*. North-Holland/IFIP, 1983, pp. 321–332.

[4] C. Flanagan and S. Qadeer, "Thread-modular model checking," in *SPIN*, ser. Lecture Notes in Computer Science, vol. 2648. Springer, 2003, pp. 213–224.

[5] S. Graf and H. Saïdi, "Construction of abstract state graphs with PVS," in *CAV*, ser. Lecture Notes in Computer Science, vol. 1254. Springer, 1997, pp. 72–83.

[6] T. Ball, A. Podelski, and S. K. Rajamani, "Boolean and cartesian abstraction for model checking C programs," in *TACAS*, ser. Lecture Notes in Computer Science, vol. 2031. Springer, 2001, pp. 268–283.

[7] L. D. Zuck and A. Pnueli, "Model checking and abstraction to the aid of parameterized systems (a survey)," *Comput. Lang. Syst. Struct.*, vol. 30, no. 3-4, pp. 139–169, 2004.

[8] A. Kaiser, D. Kroening, and T. Wahl, "Dynamic cutoff detection in parameterized concurrent programs," in *CAV*, ser. Lecture Notes in Computer Science, vol. 6174. Springer, 2010, pp. 645–659.

[9] S. La Torre, P. Madhusudan, and G. Parlato, "Model-checking parameterized concurrent programs using linear interfaces," in *CAV*, ser. Lecture Notes in Computer Science, vol. 6174. Springer, 2010, pp. 629–644.

[10] L. P. Nieto, "Completeness of the owicki-gries system for parameterized parallel programs," in *IPDPS*. IEEE Computer Society, 2001, p. 150.

[11] A. Pnueli, S. Ruah, and L. D. Zuck, "Automatic deductive verification with invisible invariants," in *TACAS*, ser. Lecture Notes in Computer Science, vol. 2031. Springer, 2001, pp. 82–97.

[12] T. Arons, A. Pnueli, S. Ruah, J. Xu, and L. D. Zuck, "Parameterized verification with automatically computed inductive assertions," in *CAV*, ser. Lecture Notes in Computer Science, vol. 2102. Springer, 2001, pp. 221–234.

[13] Z. Ganjei, A. Rezine, P. Eles, and Z. Peng, "Abstracting and counting synchronizing processes," in *VMCAI*, ser. Lecture Notes in Computer Science, vol. 8931. Springer, 2015, pp. 227–244.

[14] ——, "Counting dynamically synchronizing processes," *STTT*, vol. 18, no. 5, pp. 517–534, 2016.

[15] A. F. Donaldson, A. Kaiser, D. Kroening, and T. Wahl, "Symmetry-aware predicate abstraction for shared-variable concurrent programs," in *CAV*, ser. Lecture Notes in Computer Science, vol. 6806. Springer, 2011, pp. 356–371.

[16] P. A. Abdulla, Y. Chen, G. Delzanno, F. Haziza, C. Hong, and A. Rezine, "Constrained monotonic abstraction: A CEGAR for parameterized verification," in *CONCUR*, ser. Lecture Notes in Computer Science, vol. 6269. Springer, 2010, pp. 86–101.

[17] A. Kaiser, D. Kroening, and T. Wahl, "Lost in abstraction: Monotonicity in multi-threaded programs," in *CONCUR*, ser. Lecture Notes in Computer Science, vol. 8704. Springer, 2014, pp. 141–155.

[18] H. Hojjat, P. Rümmer, P. Subotic, and W. Yi, "Horn clauses for communicating timed systems," in *HCVS*, ser. EPTCS, vol. 169, 2014, pp. 39–52.

[19] J. Hoenicke, R. Majumdar, and A. Podelski, "Thread modularity at many levels: a pearl in compositional verification," in *POPL*. ACM, 2017, pp. 473–485.

[20] S. S. Owicki, "Axiomatic proof techniques for parallel programs," Ph.D. dissertation, Cornell University, 1975.

[21] S. S. Owicki and D. Gries, "An axiomatic proof technique for parallel programs I," *Acta Inf.*, vol. 6, pp. 319–340, 1976.

[22] K. R. Apt, F. S. de Boer, and E. Olderog, *Verification of Sequential and Concurrent Programs*, ser. Texts in Computer Science. Springer, 2009.

[23] T. A. Henzinger, R. Jhala, R. Majumdar, and S. Qadeer, "Thread-modular abstraction refinement," in *CAV*, ser. Lecture Notes in Computer Science, vol. 2725. Springer, 2003, pp. 262–274.

[24] S. Grebenshchikov, N. P. Lopes, C. Popeea, and A. Rybalchenko, "Synthesizing software verifiers from proof rules," in *PLDI*. ACM, 2012, pp. 405–416.

[25] H. Hojjat and P. Rümmer, "The ELDARICA horn solver," in *FMCAD*. IEEE, 2018, pp. 1–7.

[26] L. M. de Moura and N. Bjørner, "Z3: an efficient SMT solver," in *TACAS*, ser. Lecture Notes in Computer Science, vol. 4963. Springer, 2008, pp. 337–340.

[27] K. L. McMillan, "Lazy abstraction with interpolants," in *CAV*, ser. Lecture Notes in Computer Science, vol. 4144. Springer, 2006, pp. 123–136.

[28] P. Rümmer and P. Subotic, "Exploring interpolants," in *FMCAD*. IEEE, 2013, pp. 69–76.

[29] D. Beyer, S. Löwe, and P. Wendler, "Refinement selection," in *SPIN*, ser. Lecture Notes in Computer Science, vol. 9232. Springer, 2015, pp. 20–38.

[30] P. Rümmer, "A constraint sequent calculus for first-order logic with linear integer arithmetic," in *LPAR*, ser. Lecture Notes in Computer Science, vol. 5330. Springer, 2008, pp. 274–289.

[31] J. Leroux, P. Rümmer, and P. Subotic, "Guiding craig interpolation with domain-specific abstractions," *Acta Inf.*, vol. 53, no. 4, pp. 387–424, 2016.

[32] "ELDARICA with TMCA," https://github.com/thpani/eldarica/tree/tmca, 2020.

[33] D. Beyer, "Advances in automatic software verification: SV-COMP 2020," in *TACAS (2)*, ser. Lecture Notes in Computer Science, vol. 12079. Springer, 2020, pp. 347–367.

[34] A. Sánchez, S. Sankaranarayanan, C. Sánchez, and B. E. Chang, "Invariant generation for parametrized systems using self-reflection - (extended version)," in *SAS*, ser. Lecture Notes in Computer Science, vol. 7460. Springer, 2012, pp. 146–163.

[35] R. Alur, R. Bodík, G. Juniwal, M. M. K. Martin, M. Raghothaman, S. A. Seshia, R. Singh, A. Solar-Lezama, E. Torlak, and A. Udupa, "Syntax-guided synthesis," in *FMCAD*. IEEE, 2013, pp. 1–8.

8

A Theoretical Framework for Symbolic Quick Error Detection

Florian Lonsing ⓘ, Subhasish Mitra, and Clark Barrett ⓘ
Computer Science Department, Stanford University, Stanford, CA 94305, USA
E-mail: {lonsing, subh, barrett}@stanford.edu

Abstract—Symbolic quick error detection (SQED) is a formal pre-silicon verification technique targeted at processor designs. It leverages bounded model checking (BMC) to check a design for counterexamples to a self-consistency property: given the instruction set architecture (ISA) of the design, executing an instruction sequence twice on the same inputs must always produce the same outputs. Self-consistency is a universal, implementation-independent property. Consequently, in contrast to traditional verification approaches that use implementation-specific assertions (often generated manually), SQED does not require a full formal design specification or manually-written properties. Case studies have shown that SQED is effective for commercial designs and that SQED substantially improves design productivity. However, until now there has been no formal characterization of its bug-finding capabilities. We aim to close this gap by laying a formal foundation for SQED. We use a transition-system processor model and define the notion of a bug using an abstract specification relation. We prove the soundness of SQED, i.e., that any bug reported by SQED is in fact a real bug in the processor. Importantly, this result holds regardless of what the actual specification relation is. We next describe conditions under which SQED is complete, that is, what kinds of bugs it is guaranteed to find. We show that for a large class of bugs, SQED can always find a trace exhibiting the bug. Ultimately, we prove full completeness of a variant of SQED that uses specialized state reset instructions. Our results enable a rigorous understanding of SQED and its bug-finding capabilities and give insights on how to optimize implementations of SQED in practice.

I. Introduction

Pre-silicon verification of HW designs given as models in a HW description language (e.g., Verilog) is a critical step in HW design. Due to the steadily increasing complexity of designs, it is crucial to detect logic design bugs before fabrication to avoid more difficult and costly debugging in post-silicon validation.

Formal techniques such as bounded model checking (BMC) [1] have an advantage over traditional pre-silicon verification techniques such as simulation in that they are exhaustive up to the BMC bound. Hence, formal techniques provide valuable guarantees about the correctness of a design under verification (DUV) with respect to the checked properties. However, in traditional assertion-based formal verification techniques, these properties are implementation-specific and must be written manually based on expert knowledge about the DUV. Moreover, it is a well-known, long-standing challenge that sets of manually-written, implementation-specific properties might be insufficient to detect all bugs present in a DUV [2]–[6].

This work was supported by the Defense Advanced Research Projects Agency, grant FA8650-18-2-7854.

Symbolic quick error detection (SQED) [7]–[10] is a formal pre-silicon verification technique targeted at processor designs. In sharp contrast to traditional formal approaches, SQED does not require manually-written properties or a formal specification of the DUV. Instead, it checks whether a self-consistency [11] property holds in the DUV. The self-consistency property employed by SQED is universal and implementation-independent. Each instruction in the instruction set architecture (ISA) of the DUV is interpreted as a function in a mathematical sense. The self-consistency check then amounts to checking whether the outputs produced by executing a particular instruction sequence match if the sequence is executed twice, assuming the inputs to the two sequences also match.

SQED leverages BMC to exhaustively explore all possible instruction sequences up to a certain length starting from a set of initial states. Several case studies have demonstrated that SQED is highly effective at producing short bug traces by finding counterexamples to self-consistency in a variety of processor designs, including industrial designs [9]. Moreover, SQED substantially increases verification productivity.

However, until now there has been no rigorous theoretical understanding of (A) whether counterexamples to self-consistency found by SQED always correspond to actual bugs in the DUV—the *soundness* of SQED—and (B) whether for each bug in the DUV there exists a counterexample to self-consistency that SQED can find—the *completeness* of SQED. This paper makes significant progress towards closing this gap.

We model a processor as a transition system. This model abstracts away implementation-level details, yet is sufficiently precise to formalize the workings of SQED. To prove soundness and (conditional) completeness of SQED, we need to establish a correspondence between counterexamples to self-consistency and bugs in a DUV. In our formal model we achieve this correspondence by first defining the correctness of instruction executions by means of a general, abstract specification. A bug is then a violation of this specification. The abstract specification expresses the following general and natural property we expect to hold for actual DUVs: an instruction writes a correct output value into a destination location and does not modify any other locations.

As **our main results**, we prove soundness and conditional completeness of SQED. For soundness, we prove that if SQED reports a counterexample to the universal self-consistency property, then the processor has a bug. This result shows that SQED does not produce spurious counterexamples. Importantly, this result holds regardless of the actual specification, confirming that SQED does not depend on such implementation-specific details. For completeness, we prove that if the processor has a bug then, under modest assumptions, there exists a counterexample to self-consistency that can be found by SQED. We also show that SQED can be made fully (unconditionally) complete with additional HW support in the form of specialized state reset instructions. Our results enable a rigorous understanding of SQED and its bug-finding capabilities in actual DUVs and provide insight on how to optimize implementations of SQED.

In the following, we first present an overview of SQED from a theoretical perspective (Section II). Then we define our transition system model of processors (Section III) and formalize the correctness of instruction executions in terms of an abstract specification relation (Section IV). After establishing a correspondence between the abstract specification and the self-consistency property employed by SQED (Section V), we prove soundness and (conditional) completeness of SQED (Section VI). We conclude with a discussion of related work and future research directions (Sections VII and VIII).

II. OVERVIEW OF SQED

We first informally introduce the basic concepts and terminology related to SQED. Fig. 1a shows an overview of the high-level workflow. Given a processor design $\mathcal{P}$, i.e., the DUV, SQED is based on symbolic execution of instruction sequences using BMC. We assume that an *instruction* $i = (op, l, (l, l))$ consists of an opcode op, an output location l, and a pair (l, l) of input locations.[1] *Locations* are an abstraction used to represent registers and memory locations.

The self-consistency check is based on executing two instructions that should always produce the same result. The two instructions are called an *original* and a *duplicate instruction*, respectively. The duplicate instruction has the *same opcode* as the original one, i.e., it implements the same functionality, but it operates on different input and output locations. The locations on which the duplicate instruction operates are determined by an *arbitrary but fixed bijective function* $L_D : \mathcal{L}_O \quad \mathcal{L}_D$ between two subsets $\mathcal{L}_O$, the *original locations*, and $\mathcal{L}_D$, the *duplicate locations*, that form a partition of the set $\mathcal{L}$ of all locations in $\mathcal{P}$. An original instruction can only use locations in $\mathcal{L}_O$. An *instruction duplication function* Dup then maps any original instruction i_O to its duplicate i_D by copying the opcode and then applying L_D to its locations.

Example 1. *Let* $\mathcal{L} = 0, \ldots, 31$ *be the identifiers of 32 registers of a processor* $\mathcal{P}$, *and consider the partition* $\mathcal{L}_O = 0, 1, \ldots, 15$ *and* $\mathcal{L}_D = 16, 17, \ldots, 31$. *Let* $i_O = (ADD, l_{12}, (l_4, l_8))$ *be an original register-type ADD instruction operating on registers* $4, 8,$ *and* 12. *Using* $L_D(k) = k + 16$, *we obtain* $Dup(i_O) = i_D = (ADD, l_{28}, (l_{20}, l_{24}))$.

Consider a different partition $\mathcal{L}_O = 0, 2, 4, \ldots, 30$ *and* $\mathcal{L}_D = 1, 3, 5, \ldots, 31$ *and function* $L_D(k) = k + 1$. *For this function,* $Dup(i_O) = (ADD, l_{13}, (l_5, l_9))$.

Self-consistency checking is implemented using *QED tests*. A QED test is an instruction sequence $i = i_O :: i_D$ consisting of a sequence i_O of n original instructions followed by a corresponding sequence $i_D = Dup(i_O)$ of n duplicate instructions (where operator "::" denotes concatenation). A QED test i is symbolically executed from a *QED-consistent state*, that is, a state where the value stored in each original location l is the same as the value stored in its corresponding duplicate location $\mathcal{L}_D(l)$. The resulting final state after executing i should then also be QED-consistent. Fig. 1a illustrates the workflow. A QED test i *succeeds* if the final state that results from executing i is QED-consistent; otherwise it *fails*. Starting the execution in a QED-consistent state guarantees that original and duplicate instructions receive the same input values. Thus, if the final state is not QED-consistent, then this indicates that some pair of original and duplicate instructions behaved differently.

Example 2. *Consider Fig. 1b and the QED test* $i = i_O :: i_D$ *consisting of one original instruction* i_O *and its duplicate* $Dup(i_O) = i_D$ *for some function* L_D. *Suppose that* i *is executed in a QED-consistent state* s_0 *(denoted by* $QEDcons(s_0)$ *and* $s_0(\mathcal{L}_O) = s_0(\mathcal{L}_D))$ *and both* i_O *and* i_D *execute correctly. Instruction* i_O *produces state* s_1, *where the values at duplicate locations remain unchanged, i.e.,* $s_0(\mathcal{L}_D) = s_1(\mathcal{L}_D)$, *because* i_O *operates on original locations only. When instruction* i_D *is executed in state* s_1, *it modifies only duplicate locations. The final state* s_2 *is QED-consistent (denoted by* $QEDcons(s_2)$ *and* $s_2(\mathcal{L}_O) = s_2(\mathcal{L}_D))$, *and thus QED test* i *succeeds.*

Example 3 (Bug Detection). *Consider processor* $\mathcal{P}$ *and* $\mathcal{L}_O$ *and* $\mathcal{L}_D$ *from Example 1. Let* $i_{O,1} = (ADD, l_{12}, (l_4, l_{15}))$ *and* $i_{O,2} = (MUL, l_{15}, (l_{12}, l_{12}))$ *be original register-type addition and multiplication instructions. Using* $L_D(k) = k+16$, *we obtain* $Dup(i_{O,1}) = i_{D,1} = (ADD, l_{28}, (l_{20}, l_{31}))$ *and* $Dup(i_{O,2}) = i_{D,2} = (MUL, l_{31}, (l_{28}, l_{28}))$. *Assume that* $\mathcal{P}$ *has a bug that is triggered when two MUL instructions are executed in subsequent clock cycles, resulting in the corruption of the output location of the second MUL instruction.[2] Note that executing the QED test* $i = i_{O,1}, i_{O,2} :: i_{D,1}, i_{D,2}$ *in a QED-consistent initial state produces a QED-consistent final state: the bug is not triggered by* i *because* $i_{D,1}$ *is executed between* $i_{O,2}$ *and* $i_{D,2}$. *A slightly longer test* $i = i_{O,2}, i_{O,1}, i_{O,2} :: i_{D,2}, i_{D,1}, i_{D,2}$ *does trigger the bug, however, because the subsequence* $i_{O,2}, i_{D,2}$ *of two back-to-back MULs causes the first duplicate instruction* $i_{D,2}$ *in* i *to produce an incorrect result at* l_{31}. *This incorrect result then propagates through the next two instructions, resulting in a QED-inconsistent final state since the values at* l_{15} *and* l_{31}, *i.e., the output locations of* $i_{O,2}$ *and* $i_{D,2}$, *differ.*

QED-consistency is the universal, implementation-independent property that is checked in SQED. In practice, the property must refer to some basic information about the design such as, e.g., symbolic register names, but this can be generated automatically from a high-level ISA description [10]. BMC

---

[1]This model is used for simplicity, but it could easily be extended to allow instructions with additional inputs or outputs.

[2]This scenario corresponds to a real bug in an out-of-order RISC-V design detected by SQED: https://github.com/ridecore/ridecore/issues/4.

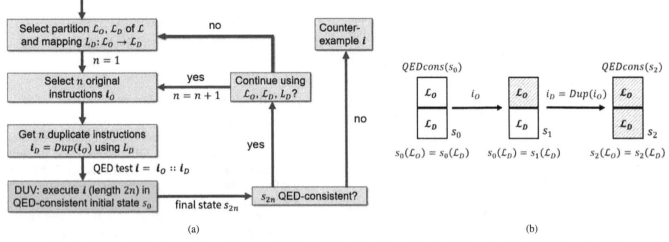

Fig. 1. SQED workflow from a theoretical perspective (a) and illustration of executing the QED test $i = i_O :: i_D$ in Example 2 (b).

is used to symbolically and exhaustively generate all possible QED tests up to a certain length $2n$ (the BMC bound). BMC ensures that SQED will find the shortest possible failing QED test first. The high-level workflow shown in Fig. 1a allows for flexibility in choosing the partition and mapping between original and duplicate locations. We rely on this flexibility for the results in this paper (Theorems 1 and 2). Current SQED implementations use a predefined partition and mapping, based on which BMC enumerates all possible QED tests. Extending implementations to have the BMC tool also choose a partition and mapping could be explored in future work.

We refer to related work [7], [9], [12] for case studies that demonstrate the effectiveness of BMC-based SQED on a variety of processor designs. The scalability of SQED in practice is determined by the scalability of the BMC tool being used. Thus, approaches for improving scalability of BMC can also be applied to SQED, e.g. abstraction, decomposition, and partial instantiation techniques [7].

III. INSTRUCTION AND PROCESSOR MODEL

We model a processor as a transition system containing an abstract set of locations. The set of locations includes registers and memory locations. A state of a processor consists of an *architectural* and a *non-architectural* part. In a state transition that results from executing an instruction, the architectural part of a state is modified explicitly by updating the value at the output location of the executed instruction. The architectural part of a state is also called the *software-visible* state of the processor. It comprises those parts of the state that can be updated by executing instructions of the user-level ISA of the processor, such as memory locations and general-purpose registers. The non-architectural part of a state comprises the remaining parts that are updated only implicitly by executing an instruction, such as pipeline or status registers.

Instructions are functions that take inputs from locations and write an output to a location. We assume that every instruction produces its result in one transition. In our model, we abstract away implementation details of complex processor designs

(e.g., pipelined, out-of-order, multi-processor systems). This is for ease of presentation and reasoning. However, many of these complexities can be viewed as refinements of our abstraction, meaning that our formal results still hold on complex models (i.e., our results can be lowered to more detailed models such as those described in [7], [8]). Working out the details of such refinements is one important avenue for future work.

Definition 1 (Transition System). *A processor is a* transition system *[13], [14]* $\mathcal{P} = (\mathcal{V} \ \mathcal{L} \ S_{\overline{a}} \ s_{\overline{a} \ I} \ Op \ I \ T)$, *where*

- $\mathcal{V}$ *is a set of* abstract data values,
- $\mathcal{L}$ *is a set of* memory locations *(from which we define the set S_a of architectural states as the set of total functions from locations to values, i.e. $S_a = \{s_a \mid s_a : \mathcal{L} \to \mathcal{V}\}$),*
- $S_{\overline{a}}$ *is a set of* non-architectural states *(from which we further define the set of all states as $S = S_a \times S_{\overline{a}}$),*
- $s_{\overline{a} \ I} \in S_{\overline{a}}$ *is a* unique *initial non-architectural state (from which we define the set of initial states as $S_I = S_a \times \{s_{\overline{a} \ I}\}$,*
- Op *is a set of* operation codes (opcodes),
- $I = Op \times \mathcal{L} \times \mathcal{L}^2$ *is the set of* instructions, *and*
- $T : S \times I \to S$ *is the* transition function, *which is total.*

A state $s \in S$ with $s = (s_a \ s_{\overline{a}})$ consists of an architectural part $s_a \in S_a$ and a non-architectural part $s_{\overline{a}} \in S_{\overline{a}}$. In the architectural part $s_a : \mathcal{L} \to \mathcal{V}$, $\mathcal{L}$ represents all possible registers and memory locations, i.e., in practical terms, $\mathcal{L}$ is the address space of $\mathcal{P}$. An initial state $s_I \in S_I$ with $s_I = (s_a \ s_{\overline{a} \ I})$ is defined by a unique non-architectural part $s_{\overline{a} \ I} \in S_{\overline{a}}$ and an arbitrary architectural part $s_a \in S_a$. We assume that $s_{\overline{a} \ I} \in S_{\overline{a}}$ is unique to make the exposition simpler. Our model could easily be extended to a set of initial non-architectural states. The number $|\mathcal{L}|$ of memory locations is arbitrary but fixed. We write $v = s(l)$ to denote the value $v = s_a(l)$ at location $l \in \mathcal{L}$ in state $s = (s_a \ s_{\overline{a}})$. We also write $(v \ v') = s(l \ l')$ as shorthand for $v = s(l)$ and $v' = s(l')$.

To formally define instruction duplication, we need to reason about *original* and *duplicate* memory locations. To this end, we partition the set $\mathcal{L}$ of memory locations into two sets of equal size, the *original* and *duplicate locations* $\mathcal{L}_O$ and $\mathcal{L}_D$, respectively, i.e., $\mathcal{L}_O \cap \mathcal{L}_D = \emptyset$, $\mathcal{L}_O \cup \mathcal{L}_D = \mathcal{L}$, and $|\mathcal{L}_O| = |\mathcal{L}_D|$. Given $\mathcal{L}_O$ and $\mathcal{L}_D$, we define an **arbitrary but fixed** *bijective function* $L_D : \mathcal{L}_O \to \mathcal{L}_D$ that maps an original location $l_O \in \mathcal{L}_O$ to its corresponding duplicate location $l_D = L_D(l_O)$. The inverse of L_D is denoted by L_D^{-1} and is uniquely defined. We write $(l_D, l_D') = L_D(l_O, l_O')$ as shorthand for $l_D = L_D(l_O)$ and $l_D' = L_D(l_O')$. Function L_D implements a correspondence between original and duplicate locations, which we need to define QED-consistency (Definition 11 below).

An instruction $i \in I$ with $i = (op, l, (l', l''))$ is defined by an opcode $op \in Op$, an output location $l \in \mathcal{L}$, and a pair of input locations $(l', l'') \in \mathcal{L}^2$. Function $op : I \to Op$ maps an instruction to its opcode $op(i)$. Functions $L_{out} : I \to \mathcal{L}$ and $L_{in} : I \to \mathcal{L}^2$ map an instruction i to its output and input locations $L_{out}(i) = l$ and $L_{in}(i) = (l', l'')$, respectively. Given a state $s = (s_a, s_{\overline{a}})$, instruction i reads values in s from its input locations $L_{in}(i)$ and writes a value to its output location $L_{out}(i)$, resulting in a transition to a new state $s' = (s'_a, s'_{\overline{a}})$, written as $s' = T(s, i)$. The transition function T is total, i.e., for every instruction i and state s, there exists a successor state $s' = T(s, i)$. As mentioned above, we have kept the model simple in order to make the presentation more accessible, but our results can be lifted to many extensions, including, e.g., more complicated kinds of instructions or instructions with enabledness conditions cf. [15].

We write $\boldsymbol{i} \in I^n$ and $\boldsymbol{s} \in S^n$ to denote sequences $\boldsymbol{i} = i_1, \ldots, i_n$ and $\boldsymbol{s} = s_1, \ldots, s_n$ of n instructions and n states, respectively. We will use :: for sequence concatenation and extend the transition function T to sequences as follows.

Definition 2 (Path). *Given sequences $\boldsymbol{i} = i_1, \ldots, i_n$ and $\boldsymbol{s} = s_1, \ldots, s_n$ of n instructions and states, $\boldsymbol{s}$ is a path from state $s_0 \in S$ to s_n via $\boldsymbol{i}$, written $\boldsymbol{s} = T(s_0, \boldsymbol{i})$, iff $\bigwedge_{k=0}^{n-1} s_{k+1} = T(s_k, i_{k+1})$.*

If $\boldsymbol{s} = T(s_0, \boldsymbol{i})$, then for convenience we also write $s_n = T(s_0, \boldsymbol{i})$ to denote the final state s_n.

Definition 3 (Reachable State). *A state s is reachable, written $reach(s)$, iff $s = T(s_0, \boldsymbol{i})$ for some $s_0 \in S_I$ and instruction sequence $\boldsymbol{i}$.*

The set I of instructions contains as proper subsets the sets of *original* and *duplicate* instructions, I_O and I_D, respectively. Original (duplicate) instructions operate only on original (duplicate) locations, i.e., $i_O \in I_O . L_{in}(i_O) \in \mathcal{L}_O^2 \wedge L_{out}(i_O) \in \mathcal{L}_O$ and $i_D \in I_D . L_{in}(i_D) \in \mathcal{L}_D^2 \wedge L_{out}(i_D) \in \mathcal{L}_D$. Given these definitions, we formalize instruction duplication as follows.

Definition 4 (Instruction Duplication). *Let $Dup : I_O \to I_D$ be an instruction duplication function that maps an original instruction $i_O = (op, l_O, (l_O, l_O'))$ to a duplicate instruction $i_D = Dup(i_O) = (op, L_D(l_O), L_D(l_O, l_O'))$ with respect to the bijective function L_D.*

An original instruction and its duplicate have the same opcode. We write $\boldsymbol{i_O} \in I_O^n$ and $\boldsymbol{i_D} \in I_D^n$ to denote sequences $\boldsymbol{i_O} = i_{O,1}, \ldots, i_{O,n}$ and $\boldsymbol{i_D} = i_{D,1}, \ldots, i_{D,n}$ of n original and duplicate instructions, respectively. We lift Dup in the natural way also to sequences of instructions as follows.

Definition 5 (Instruction Sequence Duplication). *Let $\boldsymbol{i_O} = i_{O,1}, \ldots, i_{O,n}$ be a sequence of original instructions. Then $Dup(\boldsymbol{i_O}) = Dup(i_{O,1}), \ldots, Dup(i_{O,n})$.*

IV. Formalizing Correctness

We formalize the correctness of instruction executions in a processor $\mathcal{P}$ using an abstract specification relation. We then link this abstract specification to QED-consistency, the self-consistency property employed by SQED (Section V below).

For our formalization, we assume that every opcode $op \in Op$ has a *specification function* $Spec_{op} : \mathcal{V}^2 \to \mathcal{V}$ that specifies how the opcode computes an output value from input values. Using this family of functions, we define an overall *abstract specification relation* $Spec \subseteq S \times I \times S$, which expresses when an instruction $i \in I$ can transition to a state $s' \in S$ from a state $s \in S$ while respecting the opcode specification.

Definition 6 (Abstract Specification). $\forall s, s' \in S, i \in I.$

$$
\begin{aligned}
Spec(s, i, s') &\Leftrightarrow \forall l \in \mathcal{L}. \\
&(l \neq L_{out}(i) \Rightarrow s(l) = s'(l)) \quad (1) \\
&\wedge (l = L_{out}(i) \Rightarrow s'(l) = Spec_{op(i)}(s(L_{in}(i))))
\end{aligned}
$$

Equation (1) states general and natural properties that we expect to hold for a processor $\mathcal{P}$. If an instruction i executes according to its specification, then the values at locations that are not output locations of i are unchanged. Additionally, the value produced at the output location of the instruction must agree with the value specified by function $Spec_{op(i)}$. Note that the specification relation $Spec$ specifies only how the architectural part of a state is updated by a transition (not the non-architectural part). Consequently, there might exist multiple states whose non-architectural parts satisfy the right-hand side of (1). This is why $Spec$ is a relation rather than a function. As special cases of (1), original and duplicate instructions have the following properties:

$$
\begin{aligned}
\forall s, s' \in S, i_O \in I_O, &l_O \in \mathcal{L}_O, i_D \in I_D, l_D \in \mathcal{L}_D. \\
(Spec(s, i_O, s') &\Rightarrow s(l_D) = s'(l_D)) \quad (2) \\
\wedge (Spec(s, i_D, s') &\Rightarrow s(l_O) = s'(l_O)) \quad (3)
\end{aligned}
$$

Equations (2) and (3) express that the execution of an original (duplicate) instruction does not change the values at duplicate (original) locations if the instruction executes according to its specification. The following *functional congruence* property of instructions also follows from (1):

$$
\begin{aligned}
\forall s_0, s_1, s', s'' &\in S, i, i' \in I. \\
[op(i) = op(i') &\wedge Spec(s_0, i, s') \wedge Spec(s_1, i', s'') \quad (4) \\
\wedge s_0(L_{in}(i)) = s_1(L_{in}(i'))] &\Rightarrow s'(L_{out}(i)) = s''(L_{out}(i'))
\end{aligned}
$$

By functional congruence, if two instructions with the same opcode are executed on inputs with the same values, then the output values are the same. We next define the correctness of a processor $\mathcal{P}$ based on the abstract specification $Spec$.

Definition 7 (Correctness). *A processor $\mathcal{P}$ is* correct *with respect to specification Spec iff $\forall i \in I, s \in S.\ reach(s) \Rightarrow Spec(s, i, T(s, i))$.*

Correctness requires every instruction to execute according to the abstract specification *Spec* in every reachable state of $\mathcal{P}$.

A *bug* in $\mathcal{P}$ is a counterexample to correctness, i.e., an instruction that fails in at least one (not necessarily initial) reachable state and may or may not fail in other states.

Definition 8 (Bug). *A bug with respect to specification Spec in a processor $\mathcal{P}$ is defined by a pair $\mathcal{B} = \langle i_b, S_b \rangle$ consisting of an instruction $i_b \in I$ and a non-empty set $S_b \subseteq S$ of states such that $S_b = \{s \in S \mid reach(s) \wedge \neg Spec(s, i_b, T(s, i_b))\}$.*

The above definitions rely on the notion of an abstract specification relation. Having *some* abstract specification is a *theoretical* construct that is necessary to formally characterize instruction failure and establish formal proofs about SQED. However, it is important to note that to apply SQED in *practice*, we do not need to know what the abstract specification relation is.

A bug $\langle i_b, S_b \rangle$ is precisely characterized by the set S_b of all reachable states in which i_b fails. The following proposition follows from Definitions 7 and 8.

Proposition 1. *A processor $\mathcal{P}$ has a bug with respect to specification Spec iff it is not correct with respect to Spec.*

As special cases of processor correctness and bugs, respectively, we define correctness and bugs with respect to instructions that are executed in an initial state only.

Definition 9 (Single-Instruction Correctness). *Processor $\mathcal{P}$ is* single-instruction correct *iff:*
$$\forall i \in I, s_0 \in S_I.\ Spec(s_0, i, T(s_0, i)).$$

Single-instruction correctness implies that all instructions, i.e., all opcodes and all combinations of input and output locations, execute correctly in all initial states. A *single-instruction bug* is a counterexample to single-instruction correctness.

Definition 10 (Single-Instruction Bug). *Processor $\mathcal{P}$ has a* single-instruction bug *with respect to specification Spec iff $\exists i \in I, s_0 \in S_I.\ \neg Spec(s_0, i, T(s_0, i)).$*

Several approaches exist for single-instruction checking of a processor, which is complementary to SQED (cf. Section VII).

V. Self-Consistency as QED-Consistency

We now define QED-consistency (cf. Section II) as a property of states of a processor $\mathcal{P}$ based on function L_D. Then we formally define the notion of QED test and show that for correct processors, QED tests preserve QED-consistency. This result is key to the proof of the soundness in Section VI below.

Definition 11 (QED-Consistency). *A state s is* QED-consistent, *written $QEDcons(s)$, iff $\forall l_O \in \mathcal{L}_O.\ s(l_O) = s(L_D(l_O))$.*

QED-consistency is based on checking the architectural part of a state. An equivalent condition can be formulated in terms of duplicate locations: $\forall l_D \in \mathcal{L}_D.\ s(l_D) = s(L_D^{-1}(l_D))$.

Definition 12 (QED test). *An instruction sequence i is a QED test if $i = i_O :: Dup(i_O)$ for some sequence i_O of original instructions.*

We link the abstract specification *Spec* to the semantics of original and duplicate instructions. This way, we obtain a notion of functional congruence that readily follows as a special case from (4).

Corollary 1 (Functional Congruence: Duplicate Instructions). *Given $i_O \in I_O$ and $i_D \in I_D$ with $i_D = Dup(i_O)$, the following holds for all states s_0, s_1, s, and s':*
$$\big[Spec(s_0, i_O, s) \wedge Spec(s_1, i_D, s') \wedge$$
$$s_0(L_{in}(i_O)) = s_1(L_D(L_{in}(i_O)))\big] \Rightarrow$$
$$s(L_{out}(i_O)) = s'(L_D(L_{out}(i_O)))$$

Corollary 1 states that an original instruction i_O produces the same value at its output location as its duplicate instruction $i_D = Dup(i_O)$, provided that these instructions execute in states where the values at the respective input locations match.

We generalize Corollary 1 to show that after executing a pair of original and duplicate instructions, the values at *all* original locations match the values at the corresponding duplicate locations, assuming those values also matched before executing the instructions.

Lemma 1 (cf. Corollary 1). *Given $i_O \in I_O$ and $i_D \in I_D$ with $i_D = Dup(i_O)$, the following holds for all states s_0, s_1, s, and s':*
$$\big[Spec(s_0, i_O, s) \wedge Spec(s_1, i_D, s') \wedge$$
$$\forall l_O \in \mathcal{L}_O.\ s_0(l_O) = s_1(L_D(l_O))\big] \Rightarrow$$
$$\forall l_O \in \mathcal{L}_O.\ s(l_O) = s'(L_D(l_O))$$

Proof. See online appendix [16]. □

Lemma 1 leads to an important result that we need to prove soundness of SQED (Lemma 3 below): executing a QED test i starting in a QED-consistent state results in a QED-consistent final state if all instructions in i execute according to the abstract specification *Spec* (cf. Fig. 1b).

Lemma 2 (QED-Consistency and QED tests). *Let $i = i_1, \ldots, i_{2n}$ be a QED test, let $s_0, \ldots, s_{2n}$ be a sequence of $2n + 1$ states, and let Spec be some abstract specification relation. Then,*
$$QEDcons(s_0) \wedge \left(\bigwedge_{j:=0}^{2n-1} Spec(s_j, i_{j+1}, s_{j+1}) \right)$$
$$\Rightarrow QEDcons(s_{2n})$$

Proof. Assuming the antecedent, let $l_O \in \mathcal{L}_O$ be arbitrary but fixed with $l_D = L_D(l_O)$. By repeated application of (2), we derive $s_0(l_D) = s_1(l_D) = \ldots = s_n(l_D)$, and hence:
$$s_0(l_D) = s_n(l_D) \qquad (5)$$

by transitivity. By repeated application of (3), we derive:
$$s_n(l_O) = s_{2n}(l_O) \qquad (6)$$

Now, $QEDcons(s_0)$ implies $s_0(l_O) = s_0(L_D(l_O))$, from which it follows by (5) that $s_0(l_O) = s_n(L_D(l_O))$. By repeated application of Lemma 1, we can next derive $s_j(l_O) = s_{n+j}(L_D(l_O))$ for $1 \le j \le n$, and in particular, $s_n(l_O) = s_{2n}(L_D(l_O))$. Finally, by applying (6), we get $s_{2n}(l_O) = s_{2n}(L_D(l_O))$. Since l_O was chosen arbitrarily, $QEDcons(s_{2n})$ holds. $\qquad\square$

VI. SOUNDNESS AND CONDITIONAL COMPLETENESS

SQED checks a processor $\mathcal{P}$ for self-consistency by executing QED tests and checking QED-consistency (cf. Fig 1a). We now define the correctness of $\mathcal{P}$ in terms of QED tests that, when executed, always result in QED-consistent states. This way, we establish a correspondence between counterexamples to QED-consistency and bugs in $\mathcal{P}$. We then prove our main results (Theorem 1) related to the bug-finding capabilities of SQED, i.e., soundness and conditional completeness.

Definition 13 (Failing and Succeeding QED Tests). *Let i be a QED test, $s_0 \in S_I$ an initial state such that $QEDcons(s_0)$ holds, and let $s = T(s_0, i)$. We say that:*

> *QED test i fails if $\neg QEDcons(s)$.*
> *QED test i succeeds if $QEDcons(s)$.*

Definition 14 (Processor QED-Consistency). *A processor $\mathcal{P}$ is QED-consistent if all possible QED tests succeed.*

Definition 15 (Processor QED-Inconsistency). *A processor $\mathcal{P}$ is QED-inconsistent if some QED test fails.*

Lemma 3. *Let $\mathcal{P}$ be a processor. If $\mathcal{P}$ is QED-inconsistent, then $\mathcal{P}$ is not correct with respect to any abstract specification relation.*

Proof. Let i be a failing QED test for $\mathcal{P}$ and assume that processor $\mathcal{P}$ is correct with respect to some abstract specification relation $Spec$. By Lemma 2, we conclude $QEDcons(s_{2n})$, which contradicts the assumption that i is a failing QED test. $\quad\square$

Importantly, Lemma 3 holds regardless of what the actual specification relation $Spec$ is, i.e., it is independent of $Spec$ and the opcode specification function $Spec_{op}$ (Definition 6).

Lemma 3 shows that SQED is a *sound* technique: any error reported by a failing QED test is in fact a real bug in the system. It is more challenging to determine the degree to which SQED is *complete*, that is, for which bugs do there exist failing QED tests? We address this question next.

Suppose that $\mathcal{B} = \langle i_b, S_b \rangle$ is a bug with respect to a specification $Spec$ in a processor $\mathcal{P}$, where $i_b = (op_b, l_{out}^b, (l_{in1}^b, l_{in2}^b))$. A *bug-specific QED test* for $\mathcal{B}$ is a QED test that sets up the conditions for and includes the activation of the bug. By Definition 8, if i_b is executed in $\mathcal{P}$ starting from any state in S_b, the specification is violated. That is, for each $s_b \in S_b$, $\neg Spec(s_b, i_b, T(s_b, i_b))$. Let $s = T(s_b, i_b)$. According to (1), there are two ways the specification can be violated. Either: (A) the value in the output location of i_b is different from that required by $Spec$, i.e.: $s(l_{out}^b) \ne Spec_{op_b}(s_b(l_{in1}^b), s_b(l_{in2}^b))$, which we call a *type-A bug*; or (B) the value in some other, non-output location l_{bad} is not preserved, i.e.: $s(l_{bad}) \ne s_b(l_{bad})$

for some $l_{bad} \ne l_{out}^b$, which we call a *type-B bug*. We now define a bug-specific QED test formally.

Definition 16 (Bug-Specific QED Test). *Let $\mathcal{B} = \langle i_b, S_b \rangle$ be a bug in $\mathcal{P}$ with respect to Spec, where $i_b = (op_b, l_{out}^b, (l_{in1}^b, l_{in2}^b))$. The instruction sequence $i = i_1, \ldots, i_n, i_{n+1}, \ldots, i_{2n}$ is a bug-specific QED test for $\mathcal{B}$ if the following conditions hold:*

1) $i_{n+1} = i_b$.
2) *i is a QED test for some L_D, i.e. for $1 \le k \le n$, $i_{n+k} = Dup(i_k)$. In particular, $i_1 = (op_b, l_{out}, (l_{in1}, l_{in2}))$, with $(l_{in1}, l_{in2}, l_{out}) = L_D^{-1}((l_{in1}^b, l_{in2}^b, l_{out}^b))$.*
3) *There exists a path $s \in S^{2n}$ from $s_0 \in S_I$ with $QEDcons(s_0)$, such that $s = T(s_0, i) = s_1, \ldots, s_n, s_{n+1}, \ldots, s_{2n}$, where $s_n \in S_b$.*
4) $Spec(s_0, i_1, s_1)$.
5) *Additionally, we need three more conditions that depend on the bug types:*

Case A: *If i_b is a type-A bug with respect to s_n, i.e. $s_{n+1}(l_{out}^b) \ne Spec_{op_b}(s_n(l_{in1}^b), s_n(l_{in2}^b))$, then let $l_{orig} = l_{out}$ and $l_{dup} = l_{out}^b$. We then require:*

- $s_{n+1}(l_{dup}) = s_{2n}(l_{dup})$,
- $s_1(l_{orig}) = s_{2n}(l_{orig})$,
- $s_0(L_{in}(i_b)) = s_n(L_{in}(i_b))$.

Case B: *If i_b is a type-B bug with respect to s_n, i.e. $s_n(l_{bad}) \ne s_{n+1}(l_{bad})$ for some $l_{bad} \ne l_{out}^b$, then let $l_{orig} = L_D^{-1}(l_{bad})$ with $l_{orig} \ne l_{out}$ and $l_{dup} = l_{bad}$. We then require:*

- $s_{n+1}(l_{dup}) = s_{2n}(l_{dup})$,
- $s_1(l_{orig}) = s_{2n}(l_{orig})$.
- $s_1(l_{dup}) = s_n(l_{dup})$,

Clearly, it is always possible to satisfy the first two conditions by declaring the buggy instruction i_b to be the duplicate of i_1 with respect to some function L_D. Moreover, if we restrict our attention to single-instruction correct processors, then the fourth condition always holds as well. This fits in well with the stated intended role of SQED which is to find sequence-dependent bugs, rather than single-instruction bugs.

Understanding when the remaining conditions 3 and 5 hold is more complicated. We must find some instruction sequence $i' = i_2 \ldots i_n$ that can transition $\mathcal{P}$ from the state s_1 following the execution of i_1 to one of the bug-triggering states in S_b, i.e., s_n. Often it is reasonable to assume that $\mathcal{P}$ is *strongly connected*, i.e., that there always exists an instruction sequence that can transition from one reachable state to another. This is almost enough to ensure the existence of i'. However, there are a few other restrictions on i' to satisfy Definition 16.

First, i' must consist of only original instructions to satisfy the definition of a QED test. We are free to choose L_D to be anything that works, so the main restriction is that i' cannot use any instructions referencing locations that are used by i_b, i.e., l_{in1}^b, l_{in2}^b, or l_{out}^b. Note that we defined $i_{n+1} = i_b$ to be the first duplicate instruction. This ends up being the most severe restriction on i' because it means that instructions in i'

cannot write to the locations used as inputs by i_b. We discuss some mitigations to this restriction in Section VI-A.

Somewhat surprisingly, the three requirements in condition 5 are not very severe, as we now explain. For both type-A and type-B bugs, locations l_{orig} and l_{dup} are an original location and its duplicate, respectively, that will hold inconsistent values when the QED test i fails. For type-A bugs, l_{orig} holds the correct output value of i_1 and l_{dup} holds the incorrect output value of i_b. For type-B bugs, l_{dup} holds the value of location l_{bad} that is incorrectly modified when i_b is executed in state s_n, and l_{orig} is the original location that corresponds to $l_{dup} = l_{bad}$.

The first requirement $s_{n+1}(l_{dup}) = s_{2n}(l_{dup})$ means that the duplicate sequence $Dup(i)$ of i in the QED test has to preserve the value of l_{dup} in s_{n+1} also in the final state s_{2n}. Further, since $l_{orig} = L_D^{-1}(l_{dup})$, this also imposes restrictions on the modifications that i can make to l_{orig}. However, as this is just one original location, it is unlikely that every possible i would need to modify it to get to some bug-triggering state s_n.

The second requirement is $s_1(l_{orig}) = s_{2n}(l_{orig})$. For similar reasons, it is unlikely that i would need to modify l_{orig}, and the duplicate sequence $Dup(i)$ of i should not modify it either, since it is an original location and original locations should be left alone by duplicate instructions. Although the buggy instruction i_b might modify l_{orig} if it has more than one bug effect, we may be able to choose the locations of i_1 and L_D differently to avoid this.

Finally, the last requirement of condition 5 depends on the two cases A and B. In both cases, we require that i does not modify certain duplicate locations: the input locations $L_{in}(i_b)$ of i_b (A) and location l_{dup} that is incorrectly modified by i_b (B). Sequence i should not modify any duplicate locations as it is composed of original instructions. Note that we do not have to make the strong assumption that i executes according to its specification, only that it avoids corrupting a few key locations. Given that we have a lot of freedom in choosing L_D and hence the locations of i_1, these requirements are likely to be satisfiable if there are some degrees of freedom in choosing a path to one of the bug-triggering states.

We now prove our conditional completeness property, namely that if a bug-specific QED test i exists, then i fails.

Lemma 4. *Let $\mathcal{P}$ be a processor with a bug $\mathcal{B} = i_b, S_b$ with respect to specification Spec, for which there exists a bug-specific QED test i. Then i fails.*

Proof. Let $\mathcal{B} = i_b, S_b$ be a bug and i be a bug-specific QED test for $\mathcal{B}$. By Definition 16 we have $i = i_1, \ldots, i_n, i_{n+1}, \ldots, i_{2n}$ and $s = T(s_0, i) = s_0, s_1, \ldots, s_n, s_{n+1}, \ldots, s_{2n}$, where $s_n \in S_b$ and $i_b = i_{n+1}$, and $QEDcons(s_0)$ holds. We show that $QEDcons(s_{2n})$ holds by showing that $s_{2n}(l_{orig}) = s_{2n}(l_{dup})$. We distinguish the two cases A and B in Definition 16.

Case A. Since $QEDcons(s_0)$ and $Dup(i_1) = i_b$, we have

$$s_0(L_{in}(i_1)) = s_0(L_{in}(i_b)) \tag{7}$$

From the third requirement of Case A in Definition 16, we have $s_0(L_{in}(i_b)) = s_n(L_{in}(i_b))$, so it follows that,

$$s_0(L_{in}(i_1)) = s_n(L_{in}(i_b)) \tag{8}$$

By (8) and since $op(i_1) = op(i_b)$, also

$$Spec_{op(i_1)}(s_0(L_{in}(i_1))) = Spec_{op(i_b)}(s_n(L_{in}(i_b))) \tag{9}$$

Since $Spec(s_0, i_1, s_1)$ by Definition 16, we have

$$s_1(L_{out}(i_1)) = Spec_{op(i_1)}(s_0(L_{in}(i_1))) \tag{10}$$

Since we are in Case A, we have from Definition 16 that $l_{orig} = L_{out}(i_1)$, and from the second requirement of Case A, we have $s_1(l_{orig}) = s_{2n}(l_{orig})$, so it follows that,

$$s_{2n}(l_{orig}) = Spec_{op(i_1)}(s_0(L_{in}(i_1))) \tag{11}$$

Since i_b fails in state s_n, we have that,

$$s_{n+1}(L_{out}(i_b)) = Spec_{op(i_b)}(s_n(L_{in}(i_b))) \tag{12}$$

Again, from Case A in Definition 16, we have $l_{dup} = L_{out}(i_b)$, and from the first requirement of Case A, we have $s_{n+1}(l_{dup}) = s_{2n}(l_{dup})$, so it follows that,

$$s_{2n}(l_{dup}) = Spec_{op(i_b)}(s_n(L_{in}(i_b))) \tag{13}$$

Finally, (9) and (11) give us,

$$s_{2n}(l_{orig}) = Spec_{op(i_b)}(s_n(L_{in}(i_b))) \tag{14}$$

But then (13) and (14) imply $s_{2n}(l_{orig}) = s_{2n}(l_{dup})$, and hence $QEDcons(s_{2n})$.
Case B. See online appendix [16]. $\qquad\square$

Theorem 1.

> *SQED is sound (Lemma 3).*
> *SQED is complete for bugs for which a bug-specific QED test exists (Lemma 4).*

Theorem 1 is relevant for practical applications of SQED. Referring to the high-level workflow shown in Fig. 1a, BMC symbolically explores all possible QED tests up to bound n for a particular fixed mapping L_D. If a failing QED test i is found, then by the soundness of SQED, i corresponds to a bug in the processor. By completeness, if there exists a bug for which a bug-specific QED test i exists, then with a sufficiently large bound n, BMC will find a sequence i that will fail.

A. Extensions

We now consider variants of QED tests that cover a larger class of bugs (i.e. bugs that cannot be detected by a bug-specific QED test). Ultimately, with hardware support we obtain a family of QED tests which, together with single-instruction correctness, results in a complete variant of SQED (Theorem 2).

The main limitation of bug-specific QED tests arises from the fact that QED tests consist of a sequence of original instructions followed by duplicate ones. This makes it impossible to set up a bug-specific QED test for an important class of forwarding-logic bugs (a simple refinement of our model can be used for the important case of pipelined systems). To see why, consider that a bug-triggering state $s_n \in S_b$ must be reached by executing a sequence of original instructions. The buggy instruction, which is a *duplicate*, is executed in state s_n and would have to read a value from some *original* location written previously.

To resolve this limitation, first note that there is another way that SQED can find bugs, namely by finding QED tests for which the bug occurs during the original sequence, but not during the duplicate one. This kind of QED test is much more effective with a simple extension to allow no-operation instructions (a trick also employed in [11]). To formalize this, we first define a set $\mathcal{N}$ of no-operation instructions (NOPs).

Definition 17. *Let $\mathcal{N}$ be the set of instructions such that, for every state $(s_a, s_{\overline{a}})$, if $i_{nop} \in \mathcal{N}$, then $T((s_a, s_{\overline{a}}), i_{nop}) = (s_a, s_{\overline{a}}')$ for some $s_{\overline{a}}' \in S_{\overline{a}}$.*

An instruction in $\mathcal{N}$ may change the non-architectural part of a state, but not the architectural part.

Definition 18. *An* extended QED test *is any sequence of instructions obtained from a standard QED test by inserting zero or more instructions from $\mathcal{N}$ anywhere in the sequence.*

Extended QED tests enjoy the same properties as standard QED tests. In particular, an appropriately lifted version of Lemma 2 holds and the notions of failing and succeeding QED tests can be lifted to extended QED tests in the obvious way.

Definition 19 (Bug-Hunting Extended QED Test). *Let $\mathcal{P}$ be a single-instruction correct processor with at least one bug. The instruction sequence $\boldsymbol{i}$ is a bug-hunting extended QED test with a bug-prefix of size k and initial state s_0 for $\mathcal{P}$ if the following conditions hold:*

1) *There is some bug $\mathcal{B} = \langle i_b, S_b \rangle$ in $\mathcal{P}$ such that $T(s_0, i_1, \ldots, i_{k-1}) \in S_b$ and $i_k = i_b$*
2) *$\boldsymbol{i}$ is an extended QED test*
3) *i_k is an original instruction, and $i_{k+1} = Dup(i_1)$*

Unlike a bug-specific QED test, a bug-hunting extended QED test is not guaranteed to fail. It starts with a bug-triggering sequence of length k, and then finishes with a modified duplicate sequence which may add (or subtract) NOPs from $\mathcal{N}$. The NOPs can be used to change the timing between any interdependent instructions, making it more likely that the duplicate sequence will produce a correct result, especially if the bug depends on forwarding-logic. One can show (omitted for lack of space) that for a general class of forwarding-logic bugs, there does always exist an extended QED test that fails.

Another QED test extension is to allow original and duplicate instructions to be *interleaved* [10], rather than requiring that all original instructions precede all duplicate instructions [8].[3] Again, it is straightforward to show that this extension preserves Lemma 2. Clearly, the set of bugs that can be found by adding

interleaving are a strict superset of those that can be found without. In practice, implementations of SQED search for all possible extended QED tests with interleaving. Empirically, case studies have not turned up any (non-single-instruction) bugs that cannot be found with this combination. However, one can construct pathological systems with bugs that cannot be found by such QED tests. We address these cases next.

B. Hardware Extensions

With hardware support, stronger guarantees can be achieved that lead to our final completeness result (Theorem 2). We first introduce a *soft-reset* instruction, which transitions the non-architectural part of a state to the initial non-architectural state $s_{\overline{a},I}$ without changing the architectural part. Then we define a variant of bug-hunting extended QED tests where we insert soft-reset instructions in the sequence of duplicate instructions. This way, all duplicate instructions execute in an initial state and hence execute according to the specification for single-instruction correct processors. The resulting QED test always fails, in contrast to a bug-hunting extended QED test.

Definition 20. *i_r is a soft-reset instruction for $\mathcal{P}$ if for every state $(s_a, s_{\overline{a}})$, $T((s_a, s_{\overline{a}}), i_r) = (s_a, s_{\overline{a},I})$.*

It is easy to see that $i_r \notin \mathcal{N}$.

Definition 21 (Bug-Specific Soft-Reset QED Test). *Let $\mathcal{P}$ be single-instruction correct with at least one bug $\mathcal{B} = \langle i_b, S_b \rangle$. The instruction sequence $\boldsymbol{i} = i_1, \ldots i_n$ is a bug-specific soft-reset QED test for $\mathcal{P}$ if the following conditions hold:*

1) *$\boldsymbol{i}$ is a bug-hunting extended QED test for $\mathcal{P}$ with a minimal bug-prefix of size $k \geq 2$ and initial state s_0*
2) *Let $\boldsymbol{s} = T(s_0, \boldsymbol{i})$. Then, $\forall l \in \mathcal{L}_D. s_{k-1}(l) = s_k(l)$, i.e., $i_b = i_k$ does not corrupt any duplicate location*
3) *$n = 3k$*
4) *For each $1 \le j \le k$, $i_{k+2j-1} = i_r$*

Lemma 5. *If $\mathcal{P}$ is single-instruction correct and has a bug-specific soft-reset QED test $\boldsymbol{i}$, then $\boldsymbol{i}$ fails.*

Proof. See online appendix [16]. $\square$

There are still a few (pathological) ways in which a bug may be missed by searching for all possible soft-reset QED tests. First, there may be no triggering sequence starting from any QED-consistent state. Second, it could be that the triggering sequence for a bug requires using more than half of all the locations, making it impossible to divide the locations among original and duplicate instructions. Finally, it could be that the bug always corrupts duplicate locations for every possible candidate sequence. These can all be remedied by adding *hard reset* instructions, which reset $\mathcal{P}$ to a specific initial state.

Definition 22. *The set $\{ i_{R, s_I} \mid s_I \in S_I \}$ is a family of hard reset instructions for $\mathcal{P}$ if for every state s, $T(s, i_{R, s_I}) = s_I$.*

Definition 23. *Let $\mathcal{P}$ be a processor. Then $\boldsymbol{i} = i_1 \ldots i_{2k+2}$ is a bug-specific hard-reset QED test with bug-prefix size k and initial state s_I for $\mathcal{P}$ if the following conditions hold:*

1) *$k \geq 2$*

---

[3] The bug in Example 3 can be detected by executing the QED test $\boldsymbol{i} = i_{O,1}, i_{D,1} :: i_{O,2}, i_{D,2}$, which interleaves original and duplicate instructions. The subsequence $i_{O,2}, i_{D,2}$ of two back-to-back MULs causes $i_{D,2}$ to produce an incorrect result at its output location l_{31}. The final state is QED-inconsistent since the output location l_{15} of $i_{O,2}$ holds the correct value, while l_{31} holds an incorrect one.

2) $i_1 \ldots i_k$ *reach and trigger a bug* $\mathcal{B} = \langle i_b, S_b \rangle$ *in* $\mathcal{P}$ *starting from* s_I, *where* $i_k = i_b$

3) $i_{k+1} = i_{R,s_I}$

4) $i_{k+2} \ldots i_{2k} = i_1 \ldots i_{k-1}$

5) $i_{2k+1} = i_r$

6) $i_{2k+2} = i_k$

Notice that there is no notion of duplication for a hard-reset QED test. Instead, the exact same sequence is executed twice except that there is a hard reset in between and a soft reset right before the last instruction. Hard-reset QED tests also use a slightly different notion of success and failure.

Definition 24. *Let i be a bug-specific hard-reset QED test with bug-prefix size k and initial state s_I, and let $s = T(s_I, i)$.*

i succeeds if $s_k(l) = s_{2k+2}(l)$ for every location $l \in \mathcal{L}$.
i fails if $s_k(l) \neq s_{2k+2}(l)$ for some location $l \in \mathcal{L}$.

The combination of single-instruction correctness checking and exhaustive search for hard-reset QED tests is complete.

Theorem 2. *If $\mathcal{P}$ is single-instruction correct and has no failing bug-specific hard-reset QED tests, then it is correct.*

Proof. See online appendix [16]. □

VII. RELATED WORK

Assertion-based formal verification techniques using theorem proving or (bounded) model checking, e.g., [1], [17]–[19], require implementation-specific, manually-written properties. In contrast to that, *symbolic quick error detection (SQED)* [7]–[10] is based on a universal self-consistency property.

In an early application of self-consistency checking for processor verification without a specification [11], given instruction sequences are transformed by, e.g., inserting NOPs. The original and the modified instruction sequence are expected to produce the same result. As a formal foundation, this approach relies on formulating and explicitly computing an equivalence relation over states, which is not needed with SQED.

SQED originates from *quick error detection (QED)*, a post-silicon validation technique [20]–[22]. QED is highly effective in reducing the length of existing bug traces (i.e., instruction sequences) in post-silicon debugging of processor cores. To this end, existing bug traces are systematically transformed into *QED tests* by techniques that (among others) include instruction duplication [23]. SQED exhaustively searches for minimal-length QED tests using BMC for pre-silicon verification. It is also applicable to post-silicon validation. SQED was extended to operate with symbolic initial states [12], [24] to overcome the potential limitations of BMC when unrolling the transition relation of a design starting in a concrete initial state.

SQED employs the principle of self-consistency based on a mathematical interpretation of instructions as functions. That principle is also applied by *accelerator quick error detection (A-QED)* [25], a formal pre-silicon verification technique for HW accelerator designs. A-QED checks the functions implemented by an accelerator for functional consistency and, like SQED, does not require a formal specification.

Unique program execution checking [26] relies on a particular variant of self-consistency to check security vulnerabilities of processor designs for covert channel attacks. In the context of security, self-consistency is also applied to verify secure information flow by self-composition of programs [27]–[30].

Several approaches, including both formal and simulation-based approaches, exist for checking *single-instruction (SI) correctness* cf. [9], [24], [31]. Checking SI correctness is complementary to checking self-consistency using SQED and is also much more tractable. In a formal approach, a property corresponding to $Spec_{op}$ (based on the ISA) is written for each opcode $op \in Op$, and the model checker is used to ensure that the property holds when starting from any initial state. Because the approach is restricted to initial states and only a single instruction execution, it is much simpler to specify and check than would be a property specifying the full correctness of $\mathcal{P}$. Efficient specialized approaches exist for checking multiplier units [32]–[35], which is computationally hard.

VIII. CONCLUSION AND FUTURE WORK

We laid a formal foundation for symbolic quick error detection (SQED) and presented a theoretical framework to reason about its bug-finding capabilities. In our framework, we proved soundness as well as (conditional) completeness, thereby closing a gap in the theoretical understanding of SQED. Soundness implies that SQED does not produce spurious counterexamples, i.e., any counterexample to QED-consistency reported by SQED corresponds to an actual bug in the design. For completeness, we characterized a large class of bugs that can be detected by failing QED tests under modest assumptions about these bugs. We also identified several QED test extensions based on executing no-operation and reset instructions. For these extensions, we proved even stronger completeness guarantees, ultimately leading to a variant of SQED that, together with single-instruction correctness, is complete.

As future work, it would be valuable to extend our framework to consider variants of SQED that operate with more fully symbolic initial states [12], [24]. The challenge will be to identify how this can be done while guaranteeing no spurious counterexamples. For practical applications, our theoretical results provide valuable insights. For example, in present implementations of SQED [9], [10], the flexibility to partition register/memory locations into sets of original and duplicate locations and to select the bijective mapping between these two sets has not yet been explored. Similarly, it is promising to combine standard QED tests and the specialized extensions we presented in a uniform practical tool framework. Features like soft/hard reset instructions could either be implemented in HW in a design-for-verification approach or in software inside a model checker. In another research direction, we plan to extend our framework to model the detection of deadlocks using SQED, cf. [7], and prove related theoretical guarantees.

Acknowledgments. We thank Karthik Ganesan and John Tigar Humphries for helpful initial discussions and the anonymous reviewers for their feedback.

REFERENCES

[1] A. Biere, A. Cimatti, E. M. Clarke, and Y. Zhu, "Symbolic Model Checking without BDDs," in *Proc. TACAS*, ser. LNCS, vol. 1579. Springer, 1999, pp. 193–207.

[2] S. Katz, O. Grumberg, and D. Geist, ""Have I written enough Properties?" - A Method of Comparison between Specification and Implementation," in *Proc. CHARME*, ser. LNCS, vol. 1703. Springer, 1999, pp. 280–297.

[3] H. Chockler, O. Kupferman, and M. Y. Vardi, "Coverage Metrics for Temporal Logic Model Checking," in *Proc. TACAS*, ser. LNCS, vol. 2031. Springer, 2001, pp. 528–542.

[4] K. Claessen, "A Coverage Analysis for Safety Property Lists," in *Proc. FMCAD*. IEEE, 2007, pp. 139–145.

[5] D. Große, U. Kühne, and R. Drechsler, "Estimating functional coverage in bounded model checking," in *Proc. DATE*. EDA Consortium, San Jose, CA, USA, 2007, pp. 1176–1181.

[6] H. Chockler, D. Kroening, and M. Purandare, "Coverage in interpolation-based model checking," in *Proc. DAC*. ACM, 2010, pp. 182–187.

[7] D. Lin, E. Singh, C. Barrett, and S. Mitra, "A structured approach to post-silicon validation and debug using symbolic quick error detection," in *Proc. ITC*. IEEE, 2015, pp. 1–10.

[8] E. Singh, D. Lin, C. Barrett, and S. Mitra, "Logic bug detection and localization using symbolic quick error detection," *IEEE Transactions on Computer-Aided Design of Integrated Circuits and Systems*, pp. 1–1, 2018.

[9] E. Singh, K. Devarajegowda, S. Simon, R. Schnieder, K. Ganesan, M. R. Fadiheh, D. Stoffel, W. Kunz, C. W. Barrett, W. Ecker, and S. Mitra, "Symbolic QED Pre-Silicon Verification for Automotive Microcontroller Cores: Industrial Case Study," in *Proc. DATE*. IEEE, 2019, pp. 1000–1005.

[10] F. Lonsing, K. Ganesan, M. Mann, S. S. Nuthakki, E. Singh, M. Srouji, Y. Yang, S. Mitra, and C. W. Barrett, "Unlocking the Power of Formal Hardware Verification with CoSA and Symbolic QED: Invited Paper," in *Proc ICCAD*. ACM, 2019, pp. 1–8.

[11] R. B. Jones, C. H. Seger, and D. L. Dill, "Self-Consistency Checking," in *Proc. FMCAD*, ser. LNCS, vol. 1166. Springer, 1996, pp. 159–171.

[12] M. R. Fadiheh, J. Urdahl, S. S. Nuthakki, S. Mitra, C. Barrett, D. Stoffel, and W. Kunz, "Symbolic quick error detection using symbolic initial state for pre-silicon verification," in *Proc. DATE*. IEEE, 2018, pp. 55–60.

[13] R. M. Keller, "A Fundamental Theorem of Asynchronous Parallel Computation," in *Parallel Processing, Proc. Sagamore Computer Conference*, ser. LNCS, vol. 24. Springer, 1974, pp. 102–112.

[14] R. M. Keller, "Formal Verification of Parallel Programs," *Commun. ACM*, vol. 19, no. 7, pp. 371–384, 1976.

[15] B. Huang, H. Zhang, P. Subramanyan, Y. Vizel, A. Gupta, and S. Malik, "Instruction-Level Abstraction (ILA): A Uniform Specification for System-on-Chip (SoC) Verification," *ACM Trans. Design Autom. Electr. Syst.*, vol. 24, no. 1, pp. 10:1–10:24, 2019.

[16] F. Lonsing, S. Mitra, and C. W. Barrett, "A Theoretical Framework for Symbolic Quick Error Detection," *CoRR*, vol. abs/2006.05449, 2020, FMCAD 2020 proceedings version with appendix. [Online]. Available: https://arxiv.org/abs/2006.05449

[17] W. A. Hunt Jr., "Microprocessor design verification," *J. Autom. Reasoning*, vol. 5, no. 4, pp. 429–460, 1989.

[18] J. R. Burch and D. L. Dill, "Automatic Verification of Pipelined Microprocessor Control," in *Proc. CAV*, ser. LNCS, vol. 818. Springer, 1994, pp. 68–80.

[19] A. Biere, E. M. Clarke, R. Raimi, and Y. Zhu, "Verifiying Safety Properties of a Power PC Microprocessor Using Symbolic Model Checking without BDDs," in *Proc. CAV*, ser. LNCS, vol. 1633. Springer, 1999, pp. 60–71.

[20] T. Hong, Y. Li, S. Park, D. Mui, D. Lin, Z. A. Kaleq, N. Hakim, H. Naeimi, D. S. Gardner, and S. Mitra, "QED: Quick Error Detection tests for effective post-silicon validation," in *Proc. ITC*. IEEE, 2010, pp. 154–163.

[21] D. Lin, T. Hong, Y. Li, F. Fallah, D. S. Gardner, N. Hakim, and S. Mitra, "Overcoming post-silicon validation challenges through quick error detection (QED)," in *Proc. DATE*. EDA Consortium San Jose, CA, USA / ACM DL, 2013, pp. 320–325.

[22] D. Lin, T. Hong, Y. Li, E. S, S. Kumar, F. Fallah, N. Hakim, D. S. Gardner, and S. Mitra, "Effective Post-Silicon Validation of System-on-Chips Using Quick Error Detection," *IEEE Trans. on CAD of Integrated Circuits and Systems*, vol. 33, no. 10, pp. 1573–1590, 2014.

[23] N. Oh, P. P. Shirvani, and E. J. McCluskey, "Error detection by duplicated instructions in super-scalar processors," *IEEE Trans. Reliability*, vol. 51, no. 1, pp. 63–75, 2002.

[24] K. Devarajegowda, M. R. Fadiheh, E. Singh, C. Barrett, S. Mitra, W. Ecker, D. Stoffel, and W. Kunz, "Gap-free Processor Verification by S^{2}QED and Property Generation," in *Proc. DATE*. IEEE, 2020.

[25] E. Singh, F. Lonsing, S. Chattopadhyay, M. Strange, P. Wei, X. Zhang, Y. Zhou, D. Chen, J. Cong, P. Raina, Z. Zhang, C. Barrett, and S. Mitra, "A-QED Verification of Hardware Accelerators," in *Proc. DAC, to appear*. ACM, 2020.

[26] M. R. Fadiheh, D. Stoffel, C. W. Barrett, S. Mitra, and W. Kunz, "Processor Hardware Security Vulnerabilities and their Detection by Unique Program Execution Checking," in *Proc. DATE*. IEEE, 2019, pp. 994–999.

[27] G. Barthe, P. R. D Argenio, and T. Rezk, "Secure Information Flow by Self-Composition," in *Proc. CSFW-17*. IEEE, 2004, pp. 100–114.

[28] G. Barthe, J. M. Crespo, and C. Kunz, "Relational Verification Using Product Programs," in *Proc. FM*, ser. LNCS, vol. 6664. Springer, 2011, pp. 200–214.

[29] J. B. Almeida, M. Barbosa, G. Barthe, F. Dupressoir, and M. Emmi, "Verifying Constant-Time Implementations," in *Proc. USENIX*. USENIX Association, 2016, pp. 53–70.

[30] W. Yang, Y. Vizel, P. Subramanyan, A. Gupta, and S. Malik, "Lazy Self-composition for Security Verification," in *Proc. CAV*, ser. LNCS, vol. 10982. Springer, 2018, pp. 136–156.

[31] A. Reid, R. Chen, A. Deligiannis, D. Gilday, D. Hoyes, W. Keen, A. Pathirane, O. Shepherd, P. Vrabel, and A. Zaidi, "End-to-End Verification of Processors with ISA-Formal," in *Proc. CAV*, ser. LNCS, vol. 9780. Springer, 2016, pp. 42–58.

[32] U. Krautz, M. Wedler, W. Kunz, K. Weber, C. Jacobi, and M. Pflanz, "Verifying full-custom multipliers by Boolean equivalence checking and an arithmetic bit level proof," in *ASP-DAC*. IEEE, 2008, pp. 398–403.

[33] A. A. R. Sayed-Ahmed, D. Große, U. Kühne, M. Soeken, and R. Drechsler, "Formal verification of integer multipliers by combining Gröbner basis with logic reduction," in *Proc. DATE*, 2016, pp. 1048–1053.

[34] D. Ritirc, A. Biere, and M. Kauers, "Column-wise verification of multipliers using computer algebra," in *Proc. FMCAD*, 2017, pp. 23–30.

[35] D. Kaufmann, A. Biere, and M. Kauers, "Verifying Large Multipliers by Combining SAT and Computer Algebra," in *Proc. FMCAD*. IEEE, 2019, pp. 28–36.

9

Reductions for Strings and Regular Expressions Revisited

Andrew Reynolds* , Andres Nötzli† , Clark Barrett† , and Cesare Tinelli*

*The University of Iowa, †Stanford University

Abstract—The theory of strings supported by solvers in formal methods contains a large number of operators. Instead of implementing a semi-decision procedure that reasons about all the operators directly, string solvers often reduce operators to a core fragment and implement a semi-decision procedure over that fragment. These reductions considerably increase the number of constraints and thus have to be done carefully to achieve good performance. We propose novel reductions from regular expressions to string constraints and a framework for minimizing the introduction of new variables in current reductions of string constraints. The reductions of regular expression constraints enable string solvers to handle a significant fragment of such constraints without using dedicated reasoning over regular expressions. Minimizing the number of variables in the reduced constraints makes those constraints significantly cheaper to solve by the core solver. An experimental evaluation of our implementation of both techniques in CVC4, a state-of-the-art SMT solver with extensive support for the theory of strings, shows that they significantly improve the solver's performance.

I. INTRODUCTION

Most software processes strings in some fashion, and as a result, modern programming languages include functionality to manipulate strings in various ways. The semantics of these string manipulations are often complex, which makes automated reasoning about programs that use them challenging. In recent years, researchers have proposed various approaches to tackle this challenge with dedicated solvers for string constraints [18], [20], [5], [11], [4], [3]. Dedicated solvers have been successfully used in a wide range of applications such as finding or proving the absence of SQL injections and XSS vulnerabilities in web applications [25], [23], [30], reasoning about access policies in cloud infrastructure [7], [6], and generating database tables from SQL queries for unit testing [28].

Modern string solvers natively support an extensive set of high-level string operations commonly found in programming languages, such as regular language membership, string replacement, and computing the index of one string in another. Reasoning about string constraints can be roughly divided into three areas: (i) reasoning about basic word equations with length constraints, (ii) reasoning about extended string constraints, and (iii) reasoning about regular membership constraints. One common approach to handling extended string constraints is to reduce the high-level operators to a set of basic operators and implement a semi-decision procedure for the latter. In such a design, the overall performance of a string solver depends on the efficiency of those reductions.

In particular, these reductions tend to introduce fresh string variables, which affect the difficulty of the problem for the solver for basic constraints.

The expressive power of the signature for string constraints often enables the user to write the same constraints in multiple equivalent ways. As a simple example, consider the following three formulas, each stating in effect that string y is the result of removing the first character from another string x:

$$\exists z.\, x \approx z \cdot y \wedge |z| \approx 1 \tag{1}$$
$$\mathsf{substr}(x, 1, |x| - 1) \approx y \tag{2}$$
$$x \in \mathsf{rcon}(\Sigma, \mathsf{to\_re}(y)) \tag{3}$$

Equation (1) states that there exists some string z of length one such that x is the result of concatenating that string and y. Equation (2) uses the extended string function substr to state that y is the substring of x starting at position one and having length $|x| - 1$. Equation (3) states that x is in the regular language consisting of the set of strings obtained by concatenating (rcon) the regular language of single character strings (Σ) with the (singleton) regular language containing just y. In this work, we observe that many string constraints like those above share common properties and can be handled based on reductions that lead to a more effective collaboration between the various subsolvers in current string solvers.

The contributions of this paper are as follows:

- We introduce *witness sharing*, a novel technique that can significantly reduce the number of variables introduced by string solvers that reason about combinations of word equations, extended string constraints, and regular expressions.
- We verify the correctness of our technique by generating verification conditions that encode some of its soundness properties and solve them using multiple string solvers.
- We describe new techniques for encoding regular expressions using extended functions whose reductions take advantage of witness sharing.
- We implement these techniques in the state-of-the-art string subsolver of the SMT solver CVC4 [9], showing that they lead to significant performance improvements.

In the remainder of this section, we discuss related work. We discuss preliminaries in Section II, introduce the concept of witness sharing in Section III, and discuss the reduction of regular expression constraints to extended string functions in Section IV. Finally, we evaluate our approach in Section V.

$n :$ Int for all $n \in \mathbb{N}$

$+ :$ Int $\times$ Int $\to$ Int $\quad - :$ Int $\to$ Int

$\_ \cdot \ldots \cdot \_ :$ Str $\times \cdots \times$ Str $\to$ Str

$l :$ Str for all $l \in \mathcal{A}^*$

$\geqslant :$ Int $\times$ Int $\to$ Bool

$|\_| :$ Str $\to$ Int

substr : Str $\times$ Int $\times$ Int $\to$ Str $\quad$ ctn : Str $\times$ Str $\to$ Bool

indexof : Str $\times$ Str $\times$ Int $\to$ Int $\quad$ replace : Str $\times$ Str $\times$ Str $\to$ Str

$\_ \in \_ :$ Str $\times$ Lan $\to$ Bool $\quad \Sigma :$ Lan

rcon : Lan $\times \cdots \times$ Lan $\to$ Lan $\quad$ to_re : Str $\to$ Lan

inter : Lan $\times \cdots \times$ Lan $\to$ Lan $\quad$ star : Lan $\to$ Lan

union : Lan $\times \cdots \times$ Lan $\to$ Lan $\quad$ range$_{c_1, c_2} :$ Lan

Fig. 1. Functions in the signature of the theory of strings T_S.

Related Work String solvers typically reduce the input constraints to a basic representation. Common basic representations include finite automata [24], [16], [17], [27], [14]; a variation of word equations and length constraints [22], [12], [31], [25]; bit-vectors [18]; and arrays [19]. The reductions to word equations and length constraints are similar to those studied in this work, and our techniques would apply there in a similar manner.

To the best of our knowledge, improving the efficiency of reductions themselves was not a major factor in previous work, although there is work on avoiding unnecessary reductions. Reynolds et al. [21] propose the use of aggressive rewriting to eliminate or simplify extended string constraints before performing reductions. In earlier work, Reynolds et al. [22] describe an approach to perform reductions lazily after simplifying extended functions based on other constraints in the current solving context. The general approach proposed here tackles the cost of reductions from a different angle and can be combined with these approaches.

Backes et al. [7] reduce a fragment of regular expression constraints to extended string constraints. In contrast to our approach, their technique is not integrated within a solver and is restricted to a smaller fragment.

II. PRELIMINARIES

We work in the context of many-sorted first-order logic with equality and assume the reader is familiar with the notions signature, term, literal, (quantified) formula, and free variable. We consider many-sorted signatures Σ that contain an (infix) logical symbol $\approx$ for equality—which has type $\sigma \times \sigma$ for all sorts σ in Σ and is always interpreted as the identity relation. A *theory* is a pair $T = (\Sigma, \mathbf{I})$, where Σ is a signature and $\mathbf{I}$ is a class of Σ-interpretations, the *models* of T. A Σ-formula φ is *satisfiable* (resp., *unsatisfiable*) *in* T if it is satisfied by some (resp., no) interpretation in $\mathbf{I}$. We write $\models_T \varphi$ to denote that the Σ-formula φ is T-*valid*, i.e., is satisfied in every model of T. By convention and unless otherwise stated, we use letters x, y, z to denote variables and s, t to denote terms.

We consider an (extended) theory T_S of strings whose signature Σ_S is given in Figure 1. We fix a totally ordered finite alphabet $\mathcal{A}$ of characters. The signature includes the sorts Str, Lan, and Int denoting $\mathcal{A}^*$, regular languages over $\mathcal{A}$, and integers, respectively. The *core* signature is given on the first three lines in the figure. It includes the usual symbols

of linear integer arithmetic, interpreted as expected. We will write $t_1 \bowtie t_2$, with $\bowtie \in \{>, <, \leqslant\}$, as syntactic sugar for the equivalent inequality between t_1 and t_2 expressed using only $\geqslant$. The core string symbols are given on the first and third line. They consist of a constant symbol, or *string constant*, for each word of $\mathcal{A}^*$ (including ϵ for the empty word), interpreted as that word; a variadic function symbol $\_ \cdot \ldots \cdot \_ :$ Str$\times \ldots \times$ Str $\to$ Str, interpreted as word concatenation; and a function symbol $|\_| :$ Str $\to$ Int, interpreted as the word length function.

The four function symbols in the next two lines of Figure 1 encode operations on strings that often occur in applications. We refer to these function symbols as *extended functions*. Informally, their semantics are as follows. A *position* in a string x is a non-negative integer smaller than the length of x that identifies a character in x—with 0 identifying the first character, 1 the second, and so on. For all x, y, z, n, m, the term substr(x, n, m) is interpreted as the maximal substring of x starting at position n with length at most m, or the empty string if n is an invalid position or m is negative; the predicate ctn(x, y) is interpreted as true if and only if x contains y, i.e., if y is a substring of x (every string contains the empty string); indexof(x, y, n) is interpreted as the position of the first occurrence of y in x starting at position n, or -1 if y is empty, n is an invalid position, or if no such occurrence exists; replace(x, y, z) is interpreted as the result of replacing the first occurrence in x of y by z, or just x if x does not contain y. We write substr(x, n) as a shorthand for substr$(x, n, |x| - n)$.

The signature includes an infix binary predicate symbol $\_ \in \_ :$ Str $\times$ Lan $\to$ Bool, which denotes word membership in the given regular language. The remaining symbols are used to construct regular expressions. In particular, Σ denotes (the language of) all strings of length one; to_re(s) denotes the singleton language containing just the word denoted by s; rcon$(R_1, \ldots, R_n)$ denotes all strings that are a concatenation of the strings in the languages denoted by $R_1, \ldots, R_n$; the Kleene star operator star(R) denotes all strings that are obtained as the concatenation of zero or more repetitions of the strings denoted by R; inter$(R_1, \ldots, R_n)$ and union$(R_1, \ldots, R_n)$ denote respectively the intersection and the union of the languages denoted by their arguments; Finally, we include the class of indexed regular expression symbols of the form range$_{c_1, c_2}$ where c_1 and c_2 are strings of length one. We call this a *regular expression range*, which is interpreted as the language containing all strings of length one that are between c_1 and c_2 (inclusive) in the ordering associated with $\mathcal{A}$. We refer to atomic or negated atomic formulas over the signature above as *string constraints*.

III. WITNESS SHARING FOR STRING SOLVING

In this section, we introduce a technique we call *witness sharing*, which can be used to improve the performance of string solvers that reason in logics that combine: (i) word equations with length constraints; (ii) extended string constraints (with operators like ctn, replace, and so on); and (iii) regular membership constraints. The goal of this technique is to reduce the number of variables introduced internally by SMT solvers when solving various kinds of string constraints. Our key observation is that these variables have common properties, and consequently they can often be shared across multiple inferences, according to a policy that preserves the soundness of the solver. Before describing the technique, it is helpful to review how $CDCL(T)$-based string solvers operate.

CDCL(T) A CDCL(T)-based solver [10] with support for string constraints works via a cooperation between a propositional SAT solver and a *theory solver*. A theory solver checks the satisfiability of constraints in a background theory T such as arithmetic or strings (the theory solver may consist of multiple cooperating solvers when T is a combination of theories). For a given input formula F, the SAT solver is responsible for determining whether F is propositionally unsatisfiable, that is, unsatisfiable when treating its atomic subformulas as propositional variables. In that case, F is also T-unsatisfiable. Otherwise, the SAT solver generates a propositionally satisfying assignment for the atoms of F in the form of a set of theory literals M. The theory solver then tries to determine if M is consistent with the theory T. If so, F is T-satisfiable; otherwise, the theory solver adds a new (T-valid) formula φ to F, and the above loop repeats.

The formula φ, usually called a *theory lemma*, may correspond to a *conflict clause*, that is, a clause of the form $\ell_1 \vee \ldots \vee \ell_n$, where each literal ℓ_i is forced to be false by M. The addition of a conflict clause causes the SAT solver to choose a new satisfying assignment. Note that not all theory lemmas are conflict clauses. Some are simply T-valid formulas added to F to help the SAT solver refocus its search to assignments that satisfy those lemmas too. The theory solvers for strings we describe next produce this sort of lemmas.

Theory Solvers for String Constraints In this section, we focus on the behavior of the theory solver for strings in a CDCL(T) loop. Such solvers are often designed with sub-solvers that handle word equations, extended string constraints, and regular expressions over the signature for T_S provided in Figure 1, or some variant of it. Their design and implementation have been thoroughly described in previous work [20], [5], [26]. For the purposes of this paper, it suffices to view a theory solver for strings as a method that takes as input a set M_S of string constraints, which we also refer to as the *context*, and either (a) returns (a set of) theory lemmas φ to be added to the set of constraints F maintained by the SAT solver, or (b) returns sat, indicating that M_S is T_S-satisfiable.

We can view a string solver abstractly as a set S of *inference schemas*. An inference schema is a mapping from T_S-literals ℓ (called its *premise*) to a list of the form $(C_1 \Rightarrow \varphi_1), \ldots, (C_n \Rightarrow \varphi_n)$ where $C_1, \ldots, C_n$ and $\varphi_1, \ldots, \varphi_n$ are formulas. We assume without loss of generality that all models of T_S satisfy exactly one of $C_1, \ldots, C_n$. Intuitively, an inference schema specifies that a list of conclusions $\varphi_1, \ldots, \varphi_n$ are implied by literal ℓ under the conditions $C_1, \ldots, C_n$ respectively. An abstract procedure for a theory solver for strings can be summarized by the following definition.

Definition 1 (Theory Solver for Strings). *A theory solver*

for T_S based on an inference schema set S takes as input a set of T_S-literals M_S and adds formulas to an initially empty set F as follows. For each inference schema of the form $\ell \mapsto (C_1 \Rightarrow \varphi_1, \ldots, C_n \Rightarrow \varphi_n)$ and literal $\ell\sigma \in M_S$, where σ is a substitution mapping the variables of ℓ to ground terms:

1) *if $M_S \models C_i\sigma$ for some i, then add $((\ell \wedge C_i) \Rightarrow \varphi_i)\sigma$ to F unless this lemma is already in F;*
2) *otherwise, add $(C_1 \vee \ldots \vee C_n)\sigma$ to F.*

If no formulas were added to F, return sat.

In other words, for each inference schema for which there exists a ground T_S-literal $\ell\sigma$ contained in (or, more generally, entailed by) the current context M_S that matches the premise ℓ, if any condition C_i is implied by the current assertions, we add a theory lemma stating that the conclusion φ_i must hold when the premise and its condition hold (under substitution σ). The theory lemma is added to the set of formulas F known by the SAT solver if it does not already occur in F. If none of the conditions $C_1, \ldots, C_n$ are implied, the solver adds the *splitting lemma* $(C_1 \vee \ldots \vee C_n)\sigma$, which will force the SAT solver to pick a condition to satisfy, which in turn will force the theory solver to derive one of the conclusions $\varphi_1\sigma, \ldots, \varphi_n\sigma$. A theory solver for strings is *refutation-sound* if it adds only T_S-valid formulas to F. It is *model-sound* if it returns sat only when M_S is T_S-satisfiable. We do not provide the details on the strategies used by a theory solver for strings in this paper and instead refer the reader to previous work [20], [5], [26].

It is important to note that, in contrast to traditional theory solvers, many state-of-the-art theory solvers for strings generate lemmas that do not necessarily correspond to conflict clauses. In fact, the generated lemmas may contain new literals or even literals with new (string) variables. A common example is the lemma for handling equality between two string concatenations.

Example 1. *Consider the T_S-literal ℓ of the form $x \cdot x' \approx y \cdot y'$, where x, y, x', y' are variables. A possible inference schema maps ℓ to:*

$$((|x| \approx |y| \Rightarrow x \approx y), (|x| > |y| \Rightarrow \exists k_1.\, x \approx y \cdot k_1),$$
$$(|x| < |y| \Rightarrow \exists k_2.\, x \cdot k_2 \approx y))$$

When $x \cdot x' \approx y \cdot y'$ holds, if x and y have the same length then they must be equal. If x is longer than y then y is a prefix of x, a fact expressed by the formula $\exists k_1.\, x \approx y \cdot k_1$, stating that x is the concatenation of y with some other string k_1. The case for when y is longer than x is analogous.

Notice that conclusions in the inference schema described above contain existentially quantified variables. In practice, existential quantifiers are eliminated eagerly by *Skolemization*, i.e., by instantiating them by fresh variables before the theory lemma is added to the set F. Thus, in the above example, a theory solver for strings may return $(x \cdot x' \approx y \cdot y' \wedge |x| > |y|) \Rightarrow x \approx y \cdot v_1$ where v_1 is a fresh variable. Later in this section, we argue that variables introduced in lemmas such as this one can be shared amongst multiple theory lemmas based on a careful analysis of the inference schemas.

	Premise	Conclusion	Condition	Witness Terms
(V-Split)	$x \cdot x' \approx y \cdot y'$	$x \approx y \wedge x' \approx y'$	$\lvert x \rvert \approx \lvert y \rvert$	
		$\exists k_1. x \approx y \cdot k_1 \wedge k_1 \cdot x' \approx y'$	$\lvert x \rvert > \lvert y \rvert$	$k_1 \mapsto \mathsf{suf}(x, \lvert y \rvert)$
		$\exists k_2. y \approx x \cdot k_2 \wedge x' \approx k_2 \cdot y'$	$\lvert x \rvert < \lvert y \rvert$	$k_2 \mapsto \mathsf{suf}(y, \lvert x \rvert)$
(C-Split)	$x \cdot x' \approx c \cdot y'$	$x \approx c \wedge x' \approx y'$	$\lvert x \rvert \approx 1$	
		$\exists k_1. x \approx c \cdot k_1 \wedge k_1 \cdot x' \approx y'$	$\lvert x \rvert > 1$	$k_1 \mapsto \mathsf{suf}(x, 1)$
		$x' \approx c \cdot y'$	$\lvert x \rvert \approx 0$	
(Deq-V-Split)	$x \cdot x' \not\approx y \cdot y'$	$x \not\approx y \vee x' \not\approx y'$	$\lvert x \rvert \approx \lvert y \rvert$	
		$\exists k_1 k_2. x \approx k_1 \cdot k_2 \wedge \lvert k_1 \rvert \approx \lvert y \rvert$	$\lvert x \rvert > \lvert y \rvert$	$k_1 \mapsto \mathsf{pre}(x, \lvert y \rvert)$ $k_2 \mapsto \mathsf{suf}(x, \lvert y \rvert)$
		$\exists k_3 k_4. y \approx k_3 \cdot k_4 \wedge \lvert k_3 \rvert \approx \lvert x \rvert$	$\lvert x \rvert < \lvert y \rvert$	$k_3 \mapsto \mathsf{pre}(y, \lvert x \rvert)$ $k_4 \mapsto \mathsf{suf}(y, \lvert x \rvert)$
(Deq-C-Split)	$x \cdot x' \not\approx c \cdot y'$	$x \not\approx c \vee x' \not\approx y'$	$\lvert x \rvert \approx 1$	
		$\exists k_1 k_2. x \approx k_1 \cdot k_2 \wedge \lvert k_1 \rvert \approx 1$	$\lvert x \rvert > 1$	$k_1 \mapsto \mathsf{pre}(x, 1)$
		$x' \not\approx c \cdot y'$	$\lvert x \rvert \approx 0$	$k_2 \mapsto \mathsf{suf}(x, 1)$

Fig. 2.   Inference schemas that introduce existential variables in string solvers for word equations.

Inference Schemas for String Solvers To give further context for how theory solvers for strings operate, we describe a representative list of inference schemas that introduce new variables in theory lemmas in a typical state-of-the-art string solver. Figures 2 to 4 list commonly applied inferences in the core equation solver (Figure 2), the solver for extended string functions (Figure 3), and the solver for regular expression memberships (Figure 4). In these figures, the first column gives the premise of the inference, and the second column gives (possibly multiple) conclusions that can be derived from that premise, given the conditions in the third column. We will address the fourth column in later parts of this section.

In Figure 2, the first inference schema V-Split is used when we have inferred an equality between two string terms of the form $x \cdot x'$ and $y \cdot y'$. Given this constraint, the string solver may be also able to infer whether x is equal to y, y is a prefix of x or vice versa, as discussed in Example 1. Based on these three cases, a (set of) equalities can be inferred possibly involving a new existentially quantified variable k_1 or k_2. The inference schema C-Split is similar to V-Split and handles the case where one side of an equality begins with a character constant c. There are two analogous schemas for string disequalities. The schema Deq-V-Split handles disequalities where both sides of the disequality begin with a variable (x and y). As in the equality case, the conditions split on the subcases where the length of x is equal, greater, or less than that of y. If they have equal length, the disequality is satisfied if and only if x and y differ or their remainders differ. If x is longer than y, then x can be decomposed into two parts k_1 and k_2 where k_1 has the same length as y. The case when y is longer than x is analogous. Schema Deq-C-Split is similar and handles the case where one side of the disequality begins with a constant. These four schemas do case-splitting based on the *first* argument of concatenation terms; although not shown here, four analogous inference schemas are used for splitting based on the *last*

argument of concatenation terms. In practice, when splitting a string in the schemas for disequalities, there is no need to include the literal ℓ in the lemma since it is valid without ℓ.

The inference schemas in Figure 3 cover the support for reducing the extended string functions ctn, substr, replace, and indexof respectively. To simplify the exposition, we assume with no loss of generality that for every extended string term t in the input set M_S of constraints, M_S contains an equality of the form $t \approx x$ for some variable x, which we call the *purification variable* for term t. The schema R-Ctn states that if x contains y then it must be equal to the concatenation term $k_1 \cdot y \cdot k_2$ for some (possibly empty) k_1 and k_2. The schema R-Substr relates the purification variable y for a substring term $\mathsf{substr}(x, n, m)$ with its arguments. Namely, the first conclusion holds when n is a valid position and m is positive, as expressed by its condition. It states that x must be of the form $k_1 \cdot y \cdot k_2$, where k_1 must have length n (to ensure y is a substring of x starting at position n). The remainder of the conclusion ensures that the length of y matches the semantics of substr. The length of the remainder string k_2 must equal either the length of the remaining portion of x after position $n + m$, or 0 (in the case that $n + m \geqslant \lvert x \rvert$). Moreover, unless y equals the empty string, it must have length at most m.[1] The schema R-Replace applies to premise $\mathsf{replace}(x, y, z) \approx w$ and introduces a conclusion with existential variables when x contains a non-empty string y. In that case, the first occurrence of y in x is immediately preceded by some prefix k_1 of x. This is expressed by the constraint $x \approx k_1 \cdot y \cdot k_2 \wedge \neg\mathsf{ctn}(k_1 \cdot \mathsf{pre}(y, \lvert y \rvert - 1), y)$, where $\mathsf{pre}(y, \lvert y \rvert - 1)$ is shorthand for $\mathsf{substr}(y, 0, \lvert y \rvert - 1)$, which denotes the result of removing the last character from y. If y is empty, the result of replace is to prepend z to x. If x does not contain y at all, the result of replace is the original string x. The schema R-Indexof introduces one conclusion with

---

[1] Note that the form of the conclusion here is slightly different from that found in analagous rules provided in previous work [22].

	Premise	Conclusion	Condition	Witness Terms
(R-Ctn)	$\mathsf{ctn}(x,y)$	$\exists k_1 k_2.\, x \approx k_1 \cdot y \cdot k_2$	$\top$	$k_1 \mapsto \mathsf{pre}_C(x,y)$ $k_2 \mapsto \mathsf{suf}_C(x,y)$
(R-Substr)	$\mathsf{substr}(x,n,m) \approx y$	$\begin{cases} \exists k_1 k_2.\, x \approx k_1 \cdot y \cdot k_2 \wedge \lvert k_1 \rvert \approx n \wedge \lvert y \rvert \leqslant m \\ \quad \wedge\, (\lvert k_2 \rvert \approx \lvert x \rvert - (n+m) \vee \lvert k_2 \rvert \approx 0) \\ y \approx \epsilon \end{cases}$	$\begin{array}{l} 0 \leqslant n < \lvert x \rvert \\ \wedge\, m > 0 \\ \text{otherwise} \end{array}$	$k_1 \mapsto \mathsf{pre}(x,n)$ $k_2 \mapsto \mathsf{suf}(x,n+m)$
(R-Replace)	$\mathsf{replace}(x,y,z) \approx w$	$\begin{cases} \exists k_1 k_2.\, w \approx k_1 \cdot z \cdot k_2 \wedge x \approx k_1 \cdot y \cdot k_2 \wedge \\ \quad \neg\mathsf{ctn}(k_1 \cdot \mathsf{pre}(y, \lvert y \rvert - 1), y) \\ w \approx z \cdot x \\ w \approx x \end{cases}$	$\begin{array}{l} \mathsf{ctn}(x,y) \wedge \\ y \not\approx \epsilon \\ y \approx \epsilon \\ \neg\mathsf{ctn}(x,y) \end{array}$	$k_1 \mapsto \mathsf{pre}_C(x,y)$ $k_2 \mapsto \mathsf{suf}_C(x,y)$
(R-Indexof)	$\mathsf{indexof}(x,y,n) \approx m$	$\begin{cases} \exists k_1 k_2.\, \neg\mathsf{ctn}(k_1 \cdot \mathsf{pre}(y, \lvert y \rvert - 1), y) \\ \quad \wedge\, m \approx n + \lvert k_1 \rvert \wedge \mathsf{suf}(x,n) \approx k_1 \cdot y \cdot k_2 \\ m \approx n \\ m \approx -1 \end{cases}$	$\begin{array}{l} 0 \leqslant n \leqslant \lvert x \rvert \wedge y \not\approx \epsilon \\ \quad \wedge\, \mathsf{ctn}(\mathsf{suf}(x,n),y) \\ 0 \leqslant n \leqslant \lvert x \rvert \wedge y \approx \epsilon \\ \text{otherwise} \end{array}$	$k_1 \mapsto$ $\mathsf{pre}_C(\mathsf{suf}(x,n),y)$ $k_2 \mapsto$ $\mathsf{suf}_C(\mathsf{suf}(x,n),y)$

Fig. 3. Inference schemas that introduce existential extended functions.

existential variables for premise $\mathsf{indexof}(x,y,n) \approx m$ when n is a valid position in x and the substring of x after position n (written $\mathsf{suf}(x,n)$) contains a non-empty string y. In this case, the variable k_1 is introduced as the prefix of $\mathsf{suf}(x,n)$ before the first occurrence of y in $\mathsf{suf}(x,n)$. If y is empty and n is a valid position in x, the result is n. If n is an invalid position, the result is -1.

The inference schemas in Figure 4 introduce existential variables when reasoning about regular expressions. U-RCon is applied to reduce (positively asserted) membership constraints in a language expressed as the concatenation of two regular expressions R_1 and R_2. In this case, x must consist of two strings k_1 and k_2 that occur in R_1 and R_2, respectively. Finally, the rule for Kleene star U-RStar is similar to the rule U-RCon: if x occurs in R or is empty, then $x \in R^*$ holds trivially (so the conclusion is just $\top$). Otherwise x must be decomposable into three pieces k_1, k_2 and k_3, where k_1 and k_3 occur in R, and k_2 occurs in R^*.

Example 2. *Using double quotes to denote string constants, let M_S be $\{x \approx \text{``}a\text{''} \cdot y, x \in \mathsf{rcon}(\Sigma, R), y \notin R, \lvert x \rvert > 1\}$. We may apply U-RCon to literal $x \in \mathsf{rcon}(\Sigma, R)$, which matches the premise of that schema, to obtain its conclusion:*

$$\exists k_1 k_2.\, (x \approx k_1 \cdot k_2 \wedge k_1 \in \Sigma \wedge k_2 \in R) \tag{4}$$

Similarly we may C-Split[2] for literal $x \approx \text{``}a\text{''} \cdot y$ to obtain:

$$\exists k_3.\, x \approx \text{``}a\text{''} \cdot k_3 \wedge k_3 \approx y \tag{5}$$

After passing theory lemmas with these conclusions to the SAT solver, where existential variables k_1, k_2, k_3 are Skolemized respectively with fresh variables v_1, v_2, v_3, the string solver will be invoked again with a context extended with the set $\{x \approx v_1 \cdot v_2, v_1 \in \Sigma, v_2 \in R, x \approx \text{``}a\text{''} \cdot v_3, v_3 \approx y\}$.

[2] We assume matching is modulo empty strings in concatenation terms, so that string t matches $x \cdot x'$ under the substitution $\{x \mapsto t, x' \mapsto \epsilon\}$.

In the above example, observe that both v_2 and v_3 represent the result of removing the first character from x. Thus, it is sound to use the same Skolem variable to witness both k_2 and k_3. This can easily be inferred based on a policy that we describe in the following, which will make it easier for the string solver to conclude that sets of assertions like the one above are unsatisfiable.

A. Witness Sharing by Smart Quantifier Elimination

In total, there are 22 places where the string solver in CVC4 introduces existentially quantified variables in its inference schemas (9 for word equations, 8 for extended string functions, 5 for regular expressions). A naive approach for Skolemizing those variables would replace each of them by a fresh Skolem variable for each derived conclusion. However, in the following, we argue that the witnesses for existential quantified formulas in these rules can be *shared* across multiple formulas. A majority of the 22 kinds of variables fall into one of four categories: (i) the prefix of a string s up to some fixed position n; (ii) the suffix of a string s after some fixed position n; (iii) the prefix of a string s up to the position of a substring t; and (iv) the suffix of a string s after the position of a substring t.

One way to view it is that the quantified formulas introduced by the various inference schemas admit quantifier elimination in the extended string signature. For example, in the second conclusion of schema V-Split, the formula

$$\exists k_1.\, x \approx y \cdot k_1 \wedge k_1 \cdot x' \approx y'$$

is equivalent to

$$x \approx y \cdot \mathsf{substr}(x, \lvert y \rvert) \wedge \mathsf{substr}(x, \lvert y \rvert) \cdot x' \approx y'\,,$$

when the premise and corresponding condition for that schema hold. In principle, we could eliminate those quantifiers instead of Skolemizing them. This would not be efficient, however, because of the cost of processing terms with extended functions such as $\mathsf{substr}(x, \lvert y \rvert)$. Instead, we observe that each existential variable in a inference schema conclusion has a *witness term*,

	Premise	Conclusion	Condition	Witness Terms
(U-RCon)	$x \in \mathrm{rcon}(R_1, R_2)$	$\exists k_1 k_2.\, x \approx k_1 \cdot k_2 \wedge k_1 \in R_1 \wedge k_2 \in R_2$ $\top$		$k_1 \mapsto \mathrm{pre}(x, \|R_1\|)$ $k_2 \mapsto \mathrm{suf}(x, \|R_1\|)$
(U-RStar)	$x \in R^*$	$\begin{cases} \exists k_1 k_2 k_3.\, x \approx k_1 \cdot k_2 \cdot k_3 \\ \quad \wedge\, k_1 \in R \wedge k_2 \in R^* \wedge k_3 \in R \\ \top \end{cases}$	$x \not\approx \epsilon \wedge x \notin R$ otherwise	$k_1 \mapsto \mathrm{pre}(x, \|R\|)$ $k_2 \mapsto \mathrm{substr}(x, \|R\|, |x| - 2 * \|R\|)$ $k_3 \mapsto \mathrm{suf}(x, |x| - \|R\|)$

Fig. 4.   Inference schemas that introduce existential variables in string solvers for regular expressions.

i.e., can be equivalently replaced by a term over the extended string signature, as is the case for k_1 above.

Based on this observation, instead of eliminating existential variables by instantiating them with their witness term t, we instantiate them with a *witness variable*, a Skolem variable that is associated with t. We do that by constructing and maintaining a mapping from witness terms to Skolem variables with the goal of mapping pairs of witness terms to the *same* Skolem variable whenever we recognize (inexpensively, as described in Section III-B) that the two witness terms are equivalent. This way, we can *recycle* Skolem variables introduced earlier, and keep their number low, without loss of generality.

Witness Terms   For variables that represent the prefix (resp., suffix) of string x before (resp., after) a given position n, the corresponding witness term can be expressed using the substring operator, namely with terms of the form $\mathrm{substr}(s, 0, n)$ and $\mathrm{substr}(s, n)$. For convenience, we write $\mathrm{pre}(s, n)$ and $\mathrm{suf}(s, n)$ as shorthand for these terms. Furthermore, we write $\mathrm{pre}_C(s, t)$ to abbreviate $\mathrm{pre}(s, \mathrm{indexof}(s, t, 0))$ which denotes the term equivalent to the prefix of s before the first occurrence of t in s when one exists. We additionally write $\mathrm{suf}_C(s, t)$ to denote the suffix of s after the first occurrence of t in s if one exists, which abbreviates $\mathrm{suf}(s, |\mathrm{pre}_C(s, t)| + |t|)$.

The last column in Figures 2 to 4 lists the witness terms for each inference schema. The justifications for most witness terms are straightforward. R-Ctn, R-Replace, and R-Indexof use pre_C and suf_C because they involve reasoning about the occurrence of one string in another. Witness terms for the regular expression schema U-RCon can be constructed for regular expressions R for which there exists a term of integer type, which we denote by $\|R\|$ here, such that all strings that belong to R have length $\|R\|$. For example, $\|\mathrm{to\_re}(x)\| = |x|$. We call $\|R\|$ the *regular expression length* of R. We use a simple (incomplete) recursive method, summarized in Figure 5, to infer $\|R\|$ for a regular expression R when possible. For U-RCon, which applies to the premise $x \in \mathrm{rcon}(R_1, R_2)$, multiple choices for witness terms may exist. If a regular expression length can be computed for R_1, then we know that k_1 and k_2 can be given witness terms $\mathrm{pre}(x, \|R_1\|)$ and $\mathrm{suf}(x, \|R_1\|)$ respectively. Although not shown in the figure, witness terms $\mathrm{pre}(x, |x| - \|R_2\|)$ and $\mathrm{suf}(x, |x| - \|R_2\|)$ can be given when $\|R_2\|$ can be inferred. For U-RStar, we assume witness terms are used only when $\|R\|$ can be inferred. For this rule, k_1 is the prefix of x whose length is $\|R\|$, k_3 is the suffix of x whose length is $\|R\|$, and k_2 is remaining string after removing these

$$
\begin{aligned}
\|\Sigma\| &= 1 \\
\|\mathrm{range}(c_1, c_2)\| &= 1 \\
\|\mathrm{to\_re}(s)\| &= |s| \\
\|\mathrm{union}(R_1, \cdots, R_k)\| &= u, \text{if } \forall i.\, \|R_i\| = u \\
\|\mathrm{inter}(R_1, \cdots, R_k)\| &= u, \text{if } \exists i.\, \|R_i\| = u \\
\|\mathrm{rcon}(R_1, \cdots, R_k)\| &= \|R_1\| + \cdots + \|R_k\|
\end{aligned}
$$

Fig. 5.   Definition of $\|R\|$ for cases in which a regular expression R only accepts strings of a fixed length.

two substrings.

Example 3. *We revisit the inference schemas applied for Example 2. In that example, we applied U-RCon to $x \in \mathrm{rcon}(\Sigma, R)$ to obtain the conclusion given by (4) over existentially quantified variables k_1 and k_2. According to Figure 4, since $\|\Sigma\| = 1$, the witness terms for k_1 and k_2 are $\mathrm{pre}(x, 1)$ and $\mathrm{suf}(x, 1)$ respectively. Similarly, we applied C-Split to the equality $x \approx \text{"}a\text{"} \cdot y$ to obtain the conclusion given by (5) over the existentially quantified variable k_3. According to Figure 2, the witness term for k_3 is $\mathrm{suf}(x, 1)$. Since k_2 and k_3 have the same witness term, they can be witnessed by the same variable $v_{\mathrm{suf}(x,1)}$. Using this (shared) variable results in a context where the string solver is given as input the set of assertions $\{v_{\mathrm{suf}(x,1)} \in R, v_{\mathrm{suf}(x,1)} \approx y, y \notin R\}$, which can be easily shown to be unsatisfiable: the first two constraints imply that $y \in R$ which contradicts the third constraint.*

In the above example, the string solver was able to derive a contradiction in the state resulting from the application of two inference schemas. This was made possible by witnessing existential variables for two inference schemas with the same variable $v_{\mathrm{suf}(x,1)}$. A solver without witness sharing requires further case splitting before finding a similar contradiction. In practice, the use of witness sharing to minimize the number of witness variables leads to significant performance improvements, as we show in Section V.

B. Implementation Details

We list some of the important optimizations and implementation details for witness sharing in the following.

Witness Sharing based on Term Rewriting   Two existential variables can be witnessed by the same variable when their witness terms s and t are equivalent. String solvers implement aggressive rewriting techniques on string terms (see, e.g., [21]), which we can leverage to perform fast but incomplete checks of the validity of the constraint $s \approx t$. We write $s\!\downarrow$ to denote the *rewritten form* of term s, which in practice is computed by a component of the SMT solver we call the *rewriter*. A rewriter is designed to be sound, that is, $s{\downarrow} = t{\downarrow}$ implies $s \approx t$. It is, however, typically incomplete for performance reasons, which means that two equivalent terms may have different rewritten forms. We apply the rewriter to witness terms before mapping them to witness variables to obtain improved sharing of witness variables.

Relaxing the Witness for the First Occurrence It is important to note that the witness variable v_t corresponding to witness term m is not necessarily constrained to be equal to t in the solver, which allows models where they indeed differ. This is not a problem because the value of a witness variable in any model is guaranteed to be a witness for the corresponding existentially quantified variable. We can use this fact to avoid introducing additional constraints on witness variables. Recall that term $\mathsf{pre}_C(x, y)$ is the prefix of x before the *first* occurrence of y in x if there is one. Constraints for witness variables are derived from the conclusions of rules. Indeed, R-Replace from Figure 3 introduces the constraint $\neg\mathsf{ctn}(v_{\mathsf{pre}_C(x,y)} \cdot \mathsf{substr}(y, 0, |y| - 1), y)$ to insist that $v_{\mathsf{pre}_C(x,y)}$ be the prefix of x before the first occurrence. It is, however, not necessary to add the same constraint in the conclusion of R-Ctn. Instead, it is sufficient to insist that $v_{\mathsf{pre}_C(x,y)}$ be the prefix of x before *any* such occurrence. Applying the latter schema in isolation may permit models where $v_{\mathsf{pre}_C(x,y)}$ corresponds to a prefix of x prior to an occurrence of y in x other than the first one. Nevertheless, the inference schema R-Ctn may use $\mathsf{pre}_C(x, y)$ as a witness term because $v_{\mathsf{pre}_C(x,y)}$ can be assumed (when necessary, and without loss of generality) to be the prefix before the first occurrence. Avoiding additional constraints is important in practice because negative containment constraints like the one above are notoriously expensive to reason about. This can be seen as constraining the witness variables lazily.

Equivalence of Witness Variables and Substring Terms If we have a constraint of the form $y \approx t$ in the context where y is a variable and t is a witness term t, we can use y as the witness variable for t instead of introducing a fresh variable v_t. This insight is particularly useful for applications of substring. Recall that we assume that we purify extended string terms, so applications of substring only appear in assertions of the form $\mathsf{substr}(x, n, m) \approx y$ where y is the purification variable. As a result, we can use y as the witness variable if we have a witness term of the form $\mathsf{substr}(x, n, m)$. This means that witness variables are entailed to be equal to existing substring terms that occur in M_S whenever applicable.

Propagation Based on Adjacent Literals While not shown in Figure 2, a solver for word equations can be optimized by inferring when a string must contain a constant prefix. This can be inferred for equalities where one side has the form $x \cdot l_1 \cdot x'$, and the other side begins with a constant that cannot overlap with l_1. We demonstrate this in the following example.

Example 4. *Let ℓ be the literal $x \cdot \text{``b''} \cdot x' \approx \text{``aaaa''} \cdot y'$. Since x is followed by "b" on the left-hand side of ℓ, it must be the case that x begins with "aaaa" or otherwise "b" would*

overlap with "aaaa" and the two strings would be disequal. Thus, the conclusion $\exists k_1. x \approx \text{``aaaa''} \cdot k_1$ is implied by ℓ.

CVC4 implements an inference schema where $\exists k_1. x \approx l_1 \cdot k_1$ is derived as a conclusion from the premise $x \cdot l_2 \cdot x' \approx l_1 \cdot l_3 \cdot y'$ under the condition that no non-empty prefix of l_2 is a suffix of l_1, nor is l_2 contained in l_1. While the justification of this conclusion is complex, witness sharing can be applied in a straightforward way. Namely, k_1 in the above conclusion can be mapped to the witness term $\mathsf{suf}(x, |l_1|)$ and shared with variables from other inference schemas as explained earlier.

C. Checking Soundness for Witness Terms

As we have seen, witness sharing derives (implicit) equivalences between witnesses for existential variables. It is critical that the implementation of witness sharing preserve the soundness of the solver. To verify that this is indeed the case, we have constructed a set of 8 benchmarks expressing the correctness of inference schemas that leverage witness sharing. In particular, for each inference schema from Figures 2 and 3 with premise ℓ and conclusion $\exists k_1, \ldots, k_n. \varphi$ under condition C_i, we have generated a formula that expresses the entailment:

$$\ell \wedge C_i \models_{T_\mathsf{S}} \varphi\{k_1 \mapsto t_1, \ldots, k_n \mapsto t_n\},$$

where $t_1, \ldots, t_n$ are the witness terms for $k_1, \ldots, k_n$. If this entailment does not hold, then there is a case where adding the conclusion with the witness terms to a set of assertions makes them unsatisfiable despite the original set of assertions being satisfiable, that is, the schema makes the solver refutation-unsound. On the other hand, if this entailment holds, then the soundness of the inference schema (using witness sharing) is confirmed. To see why this is the case, notice the entailment check with witness terms is strictly stronger than the same check with witness variables. This is because every model for the variant with witness terms $\varphi\{k_1 \mapsto t_1, \ldots, k_n \mapsto t_n\}$ can be extended to a model for the variant with witness variables $\varphi\{k_1 \mapsto v_{t_1} \ldots, k_n \mapsto v_{t_n}\}$ by interpreting witness variables $v_{t_1}, \ldots, v_{t_n}$ the same way as the corresponding witness terms. This is always possible because the variables themselves are unconstrained. In other words, $\varphi\{k_1 \mapsto t_1, \ldots, k_n \mapsto t_n\}$ entails $\varphi\{k_1 \mapsto v_{t_1}, \ldots, k_n \mapsto v_{t_n}\}$.

We generated one benchmark for each of the inference schemas in Figures 2 and 3. We generated only one benchmark for schemas that have multiple (symmetric) conclusions. We did not consider the verification of the regular expression rules, since neither of the solvers we used for the analysis, CVC4 and Z3 [15], currently support reasoning over regular expression variables. Overall, CVC4 (with witness sharing disabled) and Z3 are capable of showing that the entailment expressed by each of the 8 benchmarks holds, thus corroborating the correctness of our approach.

IV. REGULAR EXPRESSION ELIMINATION

In this section, we discuss an alternate approach to solving regular membership constraints by reducing them to extended string operators. The key insight is that instead of using the

$$x \in \mathsf{rcon}(R_1, R_2) \rightarrow \mathsf{pre}(x, \|R_1\|) \in R_1 \, \wedge$$
$$\mathsf{suf}(x, \|R_1\|) \in R_2$$

$$x \in \mathsf{rcon}(R_1, R_2) \rightarrow \mathsf{pre}(x, |x| - \|R_2\|) \in R_1 \, \wedge$$
$$\mathsf{suf}(x, |x| - \|R_2\|) \in R_2$$

$$x \in \mathsf{rcon}(\Sigma^*, \mathsf{to\_re}(y), \Sigma^*, R) \rightarrow \mathsf{indexof}(x, y, 0) \not\approx -1 \, \wedge$$
$$\mathsf{suf}_C(x, y) \in \mathsf{rcon}(\Sigma^*, R)$$

$$x \in \mathsf{rcon}(R_1, \mathsf{to\_re}(y), R_2) \rightarrow$$
$$\exists i. \ 0 \leqslant i < |x| - |y| \, \wedge$$
$$\mathsf{pre}(x, i) \in R_1 \wedge$$
$$\mathsf{substr}(x, i, |y|) \approx y \, \wedge \, \mathsf{suf}(x, i + |y|) \in R_2$$

$$x \in R^* \rightarrow \forall k. \ 0 \leqslant k < \mathsf{div}(|x|, \|R\|) \implies$$
$$\mathsf{substr}(x, k * \|R\|, \|R\|) \in R$$

Fig. 6. Rules for regular expression elimination

inference schemas from the previous section to generate theory lemmas while solving, we can specialize them and apply them eagerly to eliminate certain types of regular membership constraints. The advantage of this eager elimination is that we do not need to rely on cooperation between the regular membership subsolver and the other subsolvers. The techniques from the previous section can then be applied more readily. The following example demonstrates this point.

Example 5. *Consider the constraint:*

$$x \in \mathsf{rcon}(\Sigma, \Sigma^*, \mathsf{to\_re}(\text{``}abc\text{''}), \Sigma^*)$$

If we applied the rule U-RCon, we would introduce variables that are matched by the Σ^* components. If we look at this constraint through the lens of extended string operators, it is straightforward to show that it is equivalent to $\mathsf{ctn}(\mathsf{substr}(x, 1), \text{``}abc\text{''})$. Our techniques for regular expression elimination may eagerly replace the membership constraint above with this extended string constraint, which can be subsequently processed while leveraging our strategy for witness terms described in the previous section.

To start, all membership constraints with a regular expression whose top symbol is not concatenation or Kleene star can be eliminated eagerly by rewriting. For example, $x \in \mathsf{inter}(\Sigma, \mathsf{union}(R, \mathsf{to\_re}(\text{``}abc\text{''})))$ is equivalent to $|x| \approx 1 \wedge (x \in R \vee x \approx \text{``}abc\text{''})$. We have extended CVC4 with a set of rules for reducing the other kinds of regular expression memberships (for rcon and Kleene star) to constraints involving extended functions. The most prominent of these rules are given in Figure 6. We give these rules in a form $x \in R \rightarrow \varphi$ where φ is a constraint involving extended string constraints that is equivalent to $x \in R$ and does not contain the top symbol of R.

The first two rules can be applied to constraints of the form $x \in \mathsf{rcon}(R_1, R_2)$ when all strings belonging to R_1 or R_2 are of a fixed length. These rules parallel the use of witness terms for U-RCon when $\|R_1\|$ or $\|R_2\|$ is defined. The next rule applies to the case where the regular expression requires a string y followed by arbitrary characters in some prefix of x. Its conclusion assumes the suffix x after the *first* occurrence of y in x occurs in R. This is with no loss of generality since the regular expression allows us to match an arbitrary number

of characters after the position y occurs in x. The final rule for rcon is applicable to a larger set of regular expressions, where it cannot be assumed that the occurrence of $\mathsf{to\_re}(y)$ matches the position where it occurs in x. It says that if the membership constraint requires some string y to appear in x, we can split x in three parts: the prefix before the match on y (which occurs at some position i between 0 and $|x| - |y|$), the match itself, and the suffix after the match. In practice, the rules for regular expression concatenation are ordered with decreasing order of precedence: to reduce a constraint, we apply the first rule among those listed that matches a given membership constraint. For $x \in R^*$, if $\|R\|$ is defined, we can turn such constraints into a (bounded) quantifier that ensures that each substring of x at positions that are multiples of $\|R\|$ and have length $\|R\|$ are in R.

We observe in our evaluation in Section V that regular expression elimination leads to further performance improvements when combined with witness sharing. We attribute this to the fact that replacing regular expression membership constraints with extended string constraints may lead to a reduction in the number of unique constraints that must be processed by the SMT solver for inputs that combine regular expressions and extended functions. In other words, eliminating regular expressions may in some cases enable the solver to detect conflicts at the propositional level or by using high-level theory reasoning even before shared witness variables are introduced, in particular for input constraints that combine regular expression memberships and extended string functions.

V. EVALUATION

In this section, we evaluate the impact of witness sharing and regular expression elimination. To this end, we have implemented our approach in CVC4, a state-of-the-art SMT solver with extensive support for the theory of strings.

We evaluate our implementation on three benchmark sets: PYEX, a benchmark set originating from the symbolic execution of Python code [22]; FSTRINT, a benchmark set [1] originating from the concolic execution of Python code with Py-Conbyte [29]; and TRANSF, which consists of industrial benchmarks that were transformed using StringFuzz [13]. From TRANSF, we omit 438 benchmarks that use regular expression ranges with non-constant bounds and benchmarks that define functions over regular expression arguments. Both of those features are not supported by CVC4.

We compare four configurations of CVC4: **cvc4+wr** uses both regular expression elimination and witness sharing; **cvc4+r** uses just regular expression elimination; **cvc4+w** uses witness sharing only; and **cvc4** does not use the new techniques. As a point of reference, we compare our approach against Z3 4.8.8, another state-of-the-art string solver. We omit a comparison with Z3STR3 4.8.8 and Z3-TRAU 1.1 [2] (the new version of TRAU) because our experiments have shown that these versions

Set		cvc4+wr	cvc4+r	cvc4+w	cvc4	z3	R%
	sat	**21256**	20117	21254	20116	20214	
PYEX	unsat	**3866**	3847	**3866**	3847	3691	10%
	×	299	1457	301	1458	1516	
	sat	4403	4410	4404	**4412**	4323	
FSTRINT	unsat	**17095**	17085	**17095**	17089	16834	8%
	×	75	78	74	72	416	
	sat	3690	3688	3670	3663	**3771**	
TRANSF	unsat	**4796**	4780	4769	4771	4780	7%
	×	259	277	306	311	194	
	sat	**29349**	28215	29328	28191	28308	
Total	unsat	**25757**	25712	25730	25707	25305	
	×	633	1812	681	1841	2126	

TABLE I

NUMBER OF SOLVED PROBLEMS PER BENCHMARK SET. BEST RESULTS ARE IN BOLD. ALL BENCHMARKS RAN WITH A TIMEOUT OF 300 SECONDS.

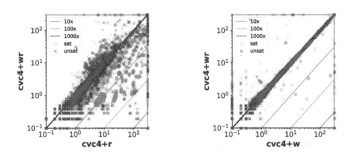

Fig. 7. Scatter plots of runtimes showing the impact of disabling witness sharing and regular expression elimination. All benchmarks ran with a timeout of 300 seconds.

are unsound.[3]

We ran our experiments on a cluster with Intel Xeon CPU E5-2620 v4 CPUs running Ubuntu 16.04 and allocated a physical CPU core, 8 GB of RAM, and 300 seconds for each job.

Table I summarizes our results. It lists the number of satisfiable and unsatisfiable answers as well as timeouts (×) for each configuration and benchmark set. For solved problems, we report the cumulative decrease in fresh variables introduced in the column "R%." To measure this, we instrument the code of **cvc4+wr** to record how many fresh variables were created by the inference schemas discussed in Section III using witness sharing, and compare it to the number of variables that would have been created with witness sharing disabled. Note that this measurement does not take into account compounding effects: Generating fewer variables at an earlier stage may prevent the introduction of fresh variables later in the solving process. Figure 7 shows the impact of disabling witness sharing and regular expression elimination by providing scatter plots that compare the performance of **cvc4+wr** with **cvc4+r** and **cvc4+w**. It differentiates between satisfiable and unsatisfiable instances. Overall, **cvc4** performs better than z3 and the other configurations only improve on that, which shows that our

[3]Overall, CVC4 and z3STR3 disagreed on 440 FSTRINT and 22 TRANSF benchmarks whereas CVC4 and z3-TRAU disagreed on 416 TRANSF benchmarks. Out of those cases, z3STR3 accepted all 325 models produced by CVC4 and rejected all 137 of its own models while z3-TRAU accepted all 343 models produced by CVC4 and rejected all 73 of its own models.

approach has the potential of improving a solver that is already competitive with the state-of-the-art.

Witness sharing has a major impact on performance, especially for satisfiable instances as the scatter plot in Figure 7 visualizes. Without witness sharing, **cvc4+r** solves significantly fewer satisfiable problems from PYEX and increases the number of timeouts by over four times. The impact is less pronounced on the other benchmark sets, although it makes a noticeable impact on unsatisfiable benchmarks from the TRANSF set. As expected, the performance impact depends on the structure of the problem. The benchmarks in TRANSF primarily consist of regular expression membership constraints, so there are fewer opportunities for witness sharing. On the FSTRINT benchmarks, **cvc4+wr** does not improve performance over **cvc4+r** despite eliminating a similar amount of variables. Nevertheless, witness sharing cumulatively over these three sets decreases the number of timeouts of CVC4 from 1812 to 633. We believe this indicates the importance of the use of witness sharing for advancing the state of the art in current string solvers.

Although less impactful, comparing **cvc4+wr** and **cvc4+w** indicates that our techniques for regular expression elimination lead to gains in both the overall number of satisfiable and unsatisfiable benchmarks. Regular expression elimination has no impact on the PYEX benchmarks because they lack regular expression membership constraints. Regular expression elimination has the biggest positive impact on the TRANSF benchmarks, where it decreases the number of unsolved instances from 306 to 259. Notice those benchmarks are generated with a fuzzing tool. Thus, they include regular expressions such as $rcon([to\_re("Q")]^*, to\_re("q"))^*$ that are less amendable to regular expression elimination than real-world benchmarks. Overall, we believe these results demonstrate the value of exploring alternate encodings of regular expressions in combination with extended string function constraints.

VI. CONCLUSION

We have presented an approach for $CDCL(T)$ theory solvers for strings that leverages the observation that many variables introduced by these solvers can be shared. Our implementation in the SMT solver CVC4 of witness sharing for these variables, as well as related techniques for recasting regular expressions as extended string constraints, leads to significant performance gains with respect to the state of the art, both in terms of number of benchmarks solved and run times.

As ongoing work, we are further investigating optimizations to the reductions used in this paper. We believe that the principle of witness sharing can be applied even more aggressively to infer when (pairs of) *input* variables are constrained to be equivalent to witness terms and hence can be equated as a preprocessing step. More generally, it can be used as a way of optimizing other $CDCL(T)$ theory solvers that introduce fresh variables within theory lemmas they generate. For example, some procedures for reasoning about finite sets [8] use fresh variables to witness when two sets are disequal. We conjecture that witness sharing can be applied fruitfully there as well.

REFERENCES

[1] str_int_benchmarks. https://github.com/plfm-iis/str_int_benchmarks, 2019.

[2] Z3-TRAU. https://github.com/guluchen/z3/tree/new_trau, 2019.

[3] P. A. Abdulla, M. F. Atig, Y. Chen, B. P. Diep, J. Dolby, P. Janku, H. Lin, L. Holík, and W. Wu. Efficient handling of string-number conversion. In A. F. Donaldson and E. Torlak, editors, *Proceedings of the 41st ACM SIGPLAN International Conference on Programming Language Design and Implementation, PLDI 2020, London, UK, June 15-20, 2020*, pages 943–957. ACM, 2020.

[4] P. A. Abdulla, M. F. Atig, Y. Chen, B. P. Diep, L. Holík, A. Rezine, and P. Rümmer. Flatten and conquer: a framework for efficient analysis of string constraints. In A. Cohen and M. T. Vechev, editors, *Proceedings of the 38th ACM SIGPLAN Conference on Programming Language Design and Implementation, PLDI 2017, Barcelona, Spain, June 18-23, 2017*, pages 602–617. ACM, 2017.

[5] P. A. Abdulla, M. F. Atig, Y. Chen, L. Holík, A. Rezine, P. Rümmer, and J. Stenman. String constraints for verification. In *Computer Aided Verification - 26th International Conference, CAV 2014, Held as Part of the Vienna Summer of Logic, VSL 2014, Vienna, Austria, July 18-22, 2014. Proceedings*, pages 150–166, 2014.

[6] J. Backes, U. Berrueco, T. Bray, D. Brim, B. Cook, A. Gacek, R. Jhala, K. S. Luckow, S. McLaughlin, M. Menon, D. Peebles, U. Pugalia, N. Rungta, C. Schlesinger, A. Schodde, A. Tanuku, C. Varming, and D. Viswanathan. Stratified abstraction of access control policies. In S. K. Lahiri and C. Wang, editors, *Computer Aided Verification - 32nd International Conference, CAV 2020, Los Angeles, CA, USA, July 21-24, 2020, Proceedings, Part I*, volume 12224 of *Lecture Notes in Computer Science*, pages 165–176. Springer, 2020.

[7] J. Backes, P. Bolignano, B. Cook, C. Dodge, A. Gacek, K. S. Luckow, N. Rungta, O. Tkachuk, and C. Varming. Semantic-based automated reasoning for AWS access policies using SMT. In N. Bjørner and A. Gurfinkel, editors, *2018 Formal Methods in Computer Aided Design, FMCAD 2018, Austin, TX, USA, October 30 - November 2, 2018*, pages 1–9. IEEE, 2018.

[8] K. Bansal, A. Reynolds, C. W. Barrett, and C. Tinelli. A new decision procedure for finite sets and cardinality constraints in SMT. In *Proceedings of IJCAR'16*, volume 9706 of *LNCS*, pages 82–98. Springer, 2016.

[9] C. Barrett, C. L. Conway, M. Deters, L. Hadarean, D. Jovanovic, T. King, A. Reynolds, and C. Tinelli. CVC4. In G. Gopalakrishnan and S. Qadeer, editors, *Computer Aided Verification - 23rd International Conference, CAV 2011, Snowbird, UT, USA, July 14-20, 2011. Proceedings*, volume 6806 of *Lecture Notes in Computer Science*, pages 171–177. Springer, 2011.

[10] C. Barrett and C. Tinelli. Satisfiability modulo theories. In E. Clarke, T. Henzinger, H. Veith, and R. Bloem, editors, *Handbook of Model Checking*. Springer, 2018.

[11] M. Berzish, V. Ganesh, and Y. Zheng. Z3str3: A string solver with theory-aware heuristics. In D. Stewart and G. Weissenbacher, editors, *2017 Formal Methods in Computer Aided Design, FMCAD 2017, Vienna, Austria, October 2-6, 2017*, pages 55–59. IEEE, 2017.

[12] N. Bjørner, N. Tillmann, and A. Voronkov. Path feasibility analysis for string-manipulating programs. In S. Kowalewski and A. Philippou, editors, *Tools and Algorithms for the Construction and Analysis of Systems, 15th International Conference, TACAS 2009, Held as Part of the Joint European Conferences on Theory and Practice of Software, ETAPS 2009, York, UK, March 22-29, 2009. Proceedings*, volume 5505 of *Lecture Notes in Computer Science*, pages 307–321. Springer, 2009.

[13] D. Blotsky, F. Mora, M. Berzish, Y. Zheng, I. Kabir, and V. Ganesh. Stringfuzz: A fuzzer for string solvers. In H. Chockler and G. Weissenbacher, editors, *Computer Aided Verification - 30th International Conference, CAV 2018, Held as Part of the Federated Logic Conference, FloC 2018, Oxford, UK, July 14-17, 2018, Proceedings, Part II*, volume 10982 of *Lecture Notes in Computer Science*, pages 45–51. Springer, 2018.

[14] T. Chen, M. Hague, A. W. Lin, P. Rümmer, and Z. Wu. Decision procedures for path feasibility of string-manipulating programs with complex operations. *PACMPL*, 3(POPL):49:1–49:30, 2019.

[15] L. M. de Moura and N. Bjørner. Z3: an efficient SMT solver. In C. R. Ramakrishnan and J. Rehof, editors, *Tools and Algorithms for the Construction and Analysis of Systems, 14th International Conference, TACAS 2008, Held as Part of the Joint European Conferences on Theory and Practice of Software, ETAPS 2008, Budapest, Hungary, March 29-April 6, 2008. Proceedings*, volume 4963 of *Lecture Notes in Computer Science*, pages 337–340. Springer, 2008.

[16] X. Fu and C. Li. A string constraint solver for detecting web application vulnerability. In *Proceedings of the 22nd International Conference on Software Engineering and Knowledge Engineering*, SEKE'2010. Knowledge Systems Institute Graduate School, 2010.

[17] P. Hooimeijer and M. Veanes. An evaluation of automata algorithms for string analysis. In *Proceedings of the 12th international conference on Verification, model checking, and abstract interpretation*, pages 248–262. Springer-Verlag, 2011.

[18] A. Kiezun, V. Ganesh, S. Artzi, P. J. Guo, P. Hooimeijer, and M. D. Ernst. HAMPI: A solver for word equations over strings, regular expressions, and context-free grammars. *ACM Trans. Softw. Eng. Methodol.*, 21(4):25:1–25:28, 2012.

[19] G. Li and I. Ghosh. Pass: string solving with parameterized array and interval automaton. In *Haifa Verification Conference*, pages 15–31. Springer, 2013.

[20] T. Liang, A. Reynolds, C. Tinelli, C. Barrett, and M. Deters. A DPLL(T) theory solver for a theory of strings and regular expressions. In *Computer Aided Verification - 26th International Conference, CAV 2014, Held as Part of the Vienna Summer of Logic, VSL 2014, Vienna, Austria, July 18-22, 2014. Proceedings*, pages 646–662, 2014.

[21] A. Reynolds, A. Nötzli, C. W. Barrett, and C. Tinelli. High-level abstractions for simplifying extended string constraints in SMT. In I. Dillig and S. Tasiran, editors, *Computer Aided Verification - 31st International Conference, CAV 2019, New York City, NY, USA, July 15-18, 2019, Proceedings, Part II*, volume 11562 of *Lecture Notes in Computer Science*, pages 23–42. Springer, 2019.

[22] A. Reynolds, M. Woo, C. W. Barrett, D. Brumley, T. Liang, and C. Tinelli. Scaling up DPLL(T) string solvers using context-dependent simplification. In R. Majumdar and V. Kuncak, editors, *Computer Aided Verification - 29th International Conference, CAV 2017, Heidelberg, Germany, July 24-28, 2017, Proceedings, Part II*, volume 10427 of *Lecture Notes in Computer Science*, pages 453–474. Springer, 2017.

[23] P. Saxena, D. Akhawe, S. Hanna, F. Mao, S. McCamant, and D. Song. A symbolic execution framework for javascript. In *31st IEEE Symposium on Security and Privacy, S&P 2010, 16-19 May 2010, Berleley/Oakland, California, USA*, pages 513–528. IEEE Computer Society, 2010.

[24] D. Shannon, S. Hajra, A. Lee, D. Zhan, and S. Khurshid. Abstracting symbolic execution with string analysis. In *Testing: Academic and Industrial Conference Practice and Research Techniques-MUTATION (TAICPART-MUTATION 2007)*, pages 13–22. IEEE, 2007.

[25] M. Trinh, D. Chu, and J. Jaffar. S3: A symbolic string solver for vulnerability detection in web applications. In G. Ahn, M. Yung, and N. Li, editors, *Proceedings of the 2014 ACM SIGSAC Conference on Computer and Communications Security, Scottsdale, AZ, USA, November 3-7, 2014*, pages 1232–1243. ACM, 2014.

[26] M. Trinh, D. Chu, and J. Jaffar. Progressive reasoning over recursively-defined strings. In *Computer Aided Verification - 28th International Conference, CAV 2016, Toronto, ON, Canada, July 17-23, 2016, Proceedings, Part I*, pages 218–240, 2016.

[27] M. Veanes, N. Bjørner, and L. De Moura. Symbolic automata constraint solving. In *Proceedings of the 17th International Conference on Logic for Programming, Artificial Intelligence, and Reasoning*, LPAR'10, pages 640–654. Springer-Verlag, 2010.

[28] M. Veanes, N. Tillmann, and J. de Halleux. Qex: Symbolic SQL query explorer. In E. M. Clarke and A. Voronkov, editors, *Logic for Programming, Artificial Intelligence, and Reasoning - 16th International Conference, LPAR-16, Dakar, Senegal, April 25-May 1, 2010, Revised Selected Papers*, volume 6355 of *Lecture Notes in Computer Science*, pages 425–446. Springer, 2010.

[29] Wei-Cheng Wu. Py-Conbyte. https://github.com/spencerwuwu/py-conbyte, 2019.

[30] F. Yu, M. Alkhalaf, and T. Bultan. Stranger: An automata-based string analysis tool for PHP. In *Tools and Algorithms for the Construction and Analysis of Systems, 16th International Conference, TACAS 2010, Held as Part of the Joint European Conferences on Theory and Practice of Software, ETAPS 2010, Paphos, Cyprus, March 20-28, 2010. Proceedings*, pages 154–157, 2010.

[31] Y. Zheng, X. Zhang, and V. Ganesh. Z3-str: a z3-based string solver for web application analysis. In B. Meyer, L. Baresi, and M. Mezini, editors, *Joint Meeting of the European Software Engineering Conference and the ACM SIGSOFT Symposium on the Foundations of Software Engineering, ESEC/FSE'13, Saint Petersburg, Russian Federation, August 18-26, 2013*, pages 114–124. ACM, 2013.

10

Verifying Properties of Bit-Vector Multiplication using Cutting Planes Reasoning

Vincent Liew[1], Paul Beame[2], Jo Devriendt[3], Jan Elffers[4] and Jakob Nordström[5]

[1,2]Allen School of Computer Science & Engineering
University of Washington
Seattle, WA, USA
[1]vliew@cs.washington.edu, [2]beame@cs.washington.edu
[3,4]Department of Computer Science
Lund University & University of Copenhagen
Lund, Sweden and Copenhagen, Denmark
[3]jo.devriendt@cs.lth.se, [4]jan.elffers@cs.lth.se
[5]Department of Computer Science
University of Copenhagen & Lund University
Copenhagen, Denmark and Lund, Sweden
jn@di.ku.dk

Abstract—Systems mixing Boolean logic and arithmetic have been a long-standing challenge for verification tools such as SAT-based bit-vector solvers. Though SAT solvers can be highly efficient for Boolean reasoning, they scale poorly once multiplication is involved. Algebraic methods using Gröbner basis reduction have recently been used to efficiently verify multiplier circuits in isolation, but generally do not perform well on problems involving bit-level reasoning.

We propose that pseudo-Boolean solvers equipped with cutting planes reasoning have the potential to combine the complementary strengths of the existing SAT and algebraic approaches while avoiding their weaknesses.

Theoretically, we show that there are optimal-length cutting planes proofs for a large class of bit-level properties of some well known multiplier circuits. This scaling is significantly better than the smallest proofs known for SAT and, in some instances, for algebraic methods. We also show that cutting planes reasoning can extract bit-level consequences of word-level equations in exponentially fewer steps than methods based on Gröbner bases.

Experimentally, we demonstrate that pseudo-Boolean solvers can verify the word-level equivalence of adder-based multiplier architectures, as well as commutativity of bit-vector multiplication, in times comparable to the best algebraic methods. We then go further than previous approaches and also verify these properties at the bit-level. Finally, we find examples of simple nonlinear bit-vector inequalities that are intractable for current bit-vector and SAT solvers but easy for pseudo-Boolean solvers.

Index Terms—Multiplier circuits, bit-vector arithmetic, verification, pseudo-Boolean solving, cutting planes, SAT solving, Gröbner bases

I. INTRODUCTION

While there has been great progress in verification tools since the 1980s, current methods still cannot efficiently deal with problems that combine multiplication and Boolean operations. These problems are encapsulated in the theory of *bit-vector arithmetic*, which supports both common bit-level operations like shifting and word-level arithmetic operations like addition and multiplication of bit-vectors. Thus, bit-vector formulas can express the behavior of a program or arithmetic circuit in a natural, yet bit-precise, manner.

Though deciding bit-vector formulas is NEXPTIME-complete in general [31], current bit-vector solvers are fairly efficient on many problems arising in practice ([12], [18], [22], [27], [38], [41], [47]). However, for instances that involve multiplication these solvers must often rely on the *bit-blasting* approach [32], which determines the satisfiability of a bit-vector formula by converting it into an equisatisfiable CNF formula to be fed into a conflict-driven clause learning (CDCL) SAT solver ([4], [39], [42]).

While CDCL SAT solvers effectively handle bit-level operations, they tend to perform poorly when multiplication is involved, with running times scaling exponentially in the bit-width on such problems ([8], [14], [30]). CDCL solvers are based on *resolution* ([11], [46]), in the sense that a *resolution proof* can be extracted from the execution trace for an unsatisfiable formula [5]. Thus, weaknesses of this proof system impose hard limits on solver performance. Resolution is very poor at tasks like counting [24] and mod-2 reasoning [52], and though degree-2 multiplier identities were recently shown to have polynomial-size proofs [7], these proofs are quite large. To unlock the ability to solve even more complicated formulas that mix bit-level reasoning with multiplication, we need to fundamentally improve the back-end reasoning.

Two natural approaches for strengthening resolution-based reasoning are embodied by the proof systems *polynomial calculus* [16], which reasons with polynomials instead of clauses, and *cutting planes* [17], which operates on 0-1 linear inequalities. Both of these proof systems can efficiently simulate resolution, and can be exponentially stronger.

Computer algebra has recently emerged as a powerful tool for verifying isolated gate-level multiplier circuits ([10], [15], [36], [37], [44], [45], [50], [51], [54]). A major advantage of

Gröbner basis methods, which perform algebraic reasoning that is captured by the polynomial calculus proof system, is that they operate with polynomials instead of disjunctive clauses. This makes it possible to encode the *correctness* of a multiplier with input bit-vectors $\mathbf{x}, \mathbf{y}$ and output bit-vector $(\mathbf{xy})$ through the word-level *specification equation*:

$$\left(\sum_{i=0}^{n-1} 2^i x_i \right) \left(\sum_{i=0}^{n-1} 2^i y_i \right) - \left(\sum_{i=0}^{2n-1} 2^i (xy)_i \right) = 0.$$

Unfortunately, for the non-algebraic parts of circuits, Gröbner basis methods are typically orders of magnitude slower than SAT solvers and scale poorly on general reasoning. We provide an explanation for this by showing, drawing on [25], that Gröbner basis methods require an exponential number of steps to derive bit-level consequences of word-level properties. Hence, these methods are unlikely to supplant the role of SAT solvers for bit-vector arithmetic.

We propose instead that *conflict-driven pseudo-Boolean solvers* [13] that take advantage of the *cutting planes* method for 0-1 linear inequalities [17] have the potential to achieve the "best of both worlds", combining the strengths of Gröbner basis methods for polynomials with the efficiency of CDCL SAT solvers for Boolean reasoning. Cutting planes reasoning can easily express word-level properties and does not suffer the same obstacles as polynomial calculus, since only a linear number of steps are needed to derive *all* of the individual bit-equalities from a word-level equality.

An essential aspect of this approach in improving on SAT-based methods is that one can express the correctness of 1-bit adders, basic building blocks of arithmetic circuits, directly via pairs of inequalities, instead of using sets of clauses, and one can similarly directly express word-level properties of circuit outputs. Together, these yield a higher-level fully precise form of "bit-blasting".

The main theoretical contribution of this paper is the construction of optimal, $O(n^2)$-length cutting planes proofs for a large class of n-bit ring identities, including commutativity and distributivity. We emphasize that these identities can be proven not only at the word level, but also for individual bits.

While $O(n^2)$-length polynomial calculus proofs are known for some of these properties at the word level [29], this algebraic method cannot efficiently extract the bit-equalities. As a consequence, for example, the best known polynomial calculus proof for the bit-level property "the middle bit of xy equals the middle bit of yx" is still the $O(n^5 \log n)$-length resolution proof given by [7], which is much larger than our $O(n^2)$-length cutting planes proof.

These ring identities appeared previously as testbed instances representing the gap between word-level and bit-level methods of reasoning. For example, it was observed in 2016 that proving the commutativity of a multiplier circuit is already intractable for SAT solving at 16 bits [9]. While bit-vector solvers try to overcome this shortcoming of SAT by implementing word-level preprocessing and inprocessing, the verification of larger systems containing multiplication and bit-logic (that appear for instance, in cryptography) remains a

key weakness. The ability to verify these ring identities at the bit level, rather than through preprocessing, is a good test for the potential of any method for verifying these more complex systems.

Experimentally, we are able to use pseudo-Boolean solvers to verify the word-level equivalence of several different multiplier circuits of up to 256 bits in similar times to those of the best algebraic methods. We find that these solvers can be particularly efficient at extracting all of the bit-level equalities from a word-level equality, which neither CDCL solvers nor Gröbner basis reduction can do efficiently.

We also show that pseudo-Boolean solvers can be used to efficiently verify a number of bit-vector inequalities combining multiplication with bit-wise operations. In contrast, these inequalities are much harder or intractable for the top bit-vector solvers Boolector ([12], [43]), Z3 [18], Yices2 [19] and CVC4 [2]. Our examples demonstrate some of the potential of pseudo-Boolean solvers for reasoning with nonlinear, bit-precise systems that are out of reach of current methods. These bit-vector inequalities are inspired by the combinations of arithmetic and bit-wise operations that naturally arise in embedded systems or high-performance computation, where "bit hacks" can be used to implement methods such as absolute value or "reverse the bits in a byte" (see [1] and [26]) and more complicated mixtures of arithmetic and bit-wise operations are used in cryptographic and hashing computations.

II. NOTATION AND PRELIMINARIES

We write the i-th entry of a bit-vector $\mathbf{x}$ as a Boolean variable x_i. We typically refer to circuits by the output bit-vectors that they produce — for example we use $\mathbf{C}$ to refer to both a circuit and its output bit-vector, depending on the context. Often we write this output bit-vector in terms of the inputs, so that a multiplier circuit denoted by $\mathbf{xy}$ is understood to take input bit-vectors $\mathbf{x}, \mathbf{y}$ and output a bit-vector labeled $\mathbf{xy}$. We label the internal variables of a circuit $\mathbf{C}$ using the superscript C, for example: $t_{i,j}^C$.

Definition Given a set of polynomials Φ over a set of variables $\{x_1, x_2, \ldots, x_n\}$ and a field K, a *polynomial calculus refutation* of Φ is a sequence of polynomials ending with the polynomial 1 such that each line is either in Φ or is derived from the previous lines using the inference rules of linear combination and multiplication by a monomial m:

$$\frac{p \qquad q}{\alpha p + \beta q} \, (\alpha, \beta \in K), \qquad \frac{p}{m \cdot p} \, .$$

The polynomials $x^2 - x$ are also included as axioms for each variable x so that it only takes Boolean values. The polynomial p is interpreted to mean the equation $p = 0$.

Definition Given a set of 0-1 linear inequalities Φ over a set of variables $\{x_1, x_2, \ldots, x_n\}$, a *cutting planes* refutation of Φ is a sequence of 0-1 linear inequalities ending with the inequality $0 \geq 1$ such that each line is either in Φ or is derived from the previous lines using the inference rules of positive linear combination

$$\frac{\sum_i a_i x_i \geq b \qquad \sum_i a_i' x_i \geq b'}{\sum_i (\alpha a_i + \beta b_i) x_i \geq \alpha b + \beta b'}$$

where $\alpha, \beta \geq 0$, and the *division rule*

$$\frac{\sum_i (c \cdot a_i) x_i \geq b}{\sum_i a_i x_i \geq \lceil \frac{b}{c} \rceil} .$$

The *literal axioms* $-x \geq -1$ and $x \geq 0$ are also included for each variable x. Throughout this paper we will use "=" as shorthand for the two equivalent "$\leq, \geq$" inequalities.

A. A polynomial calculus lower bound for bit-extraction

The bit-extraction lower bound discussed in the introduction follows directly from the following polynomial calculus lower bound for *subset-sum equations* due to Impagliazzo, Pudlak and Sgall.

Theorem II.1 ([25]). *Let $c_1, \ldots, c_n$ be nonzero real numbers such that no subset sums to the real number m. Then the equation $m - \sum_{i=1}^{n} c_i x_i = 0$ has no polynomial calculus refutation of degree $\lceil n/2 \rceil$ in the field of real numbers.*

Theorem II.2 ([25]). *Suppose that Φ is a set of polynomials of degree at most $\sqrt{n}$, where n is the number of variables appearing in Φ. Let d denote the minimum refutation degree of Φ, and M denote the minimum number of monomials in a refutation of Φ, and assume that $M \geq 3$. Then $M \geq \exp\left((d-1)^2/4n\right)$.*

We combine Theorems II.1 and II.2 to demonstrate the weakness of polynomial calculus in extracting bit-level properties from word-level ones.

Corollary II.3. *For a fixed integer k, any polynomial calculus refutation of the system of two polynomials:*

$$f := \sum_{i=0}^{n-1} 2^i (s_i - s_i')$$

$$g := s_k - s_k' - 1$$

contains at least $e^{n/4-1} \approx 2^{0.36n}$ monomials.

Proof. Define the polynomial $f' := \sum_{i \neq k} 2^i (s_i - s_i') + 2^k$. Observe that Theorem II.1 gives us a degree lower bound of $n - 1$ on refutations of the polynomial $\{f'\}$. Theorem II.2 translates this into a monomial size lower bound of $e^{n/4-1}$. The reduction below lifts this lower bound on $\{f'\}$ to the polynomials $\{f, g\}$.

We show that a length l polynomial calculus refutation of the polynomials $\{f, g\}$ may be converted into a length l refutation of the polynomial $\{f'\}$ without increasing the number of monomials in each line as follows: First notice that the polynomials f, f' are equivalent modulo the polynomial $g = s_k - s_k' - 1$. Given a PC refutation of $\{f, g\}$, we reduce each line by g (which effectively sets $s_k = 1$ and $s_k' = 0$), only reducing the number of monomials, to produce a refutation of $\{f'\}$. $\square$

As a consequence of this corollary, polynomial calculus cannot derive $s_k = s_k'$ from the first equation using fewer than $e^{n/4-1}$ monomials. In comparison, cutting planes has small derivations that produce all of the bit-equalities.

Proposition II.4. *There is an $O(n)$-length cutting planes derivation of all n bit-equalities $s_i = s_i'$ from the equation $\sum_{i=0}^{n-1} 2^i s_i - \sum_{i=0}^{n-1} 2^i s_i' = 0$.*

Proof. We extract the individual bit-equalities in the low-to-high sequence $s_0 = s_0', s_1 = s_1', \ldots s_{n-1} = s_{n-1}'$. Recall that in cutting planes, the equation $\sum_{i=0}^{n-1} 2^i s_i - \sum_{i=0}^{n-1} 2^i s_i' = 0$ is represented by two inequalities. Take the inequality $\sum_{i=0}^{n-1} 2^i s_i - \sum_{i=0}^{n-1} 2^i s_i' \geq 0$, and use the literal axioms on s_0, s_0' to get $\sum_{i=1}^{n-1} 2^i s_i - \sum_{i=1}^{n-1} 2^i s_i' \geq -1$. Divide this by 2 to get $\sum_{i=1}^{n-1} 2^{i-1} s_i - \sum_{i=1}^{n-1} 2^{i-1} s_i' \geq 0$. Finally, use linear combination to multiply this by 2 and add it to the equation $\sum_{i=0}^{n-1} 2^i s_i' - \sum_{i=0}^{n-1} 2^i s_i \geq 0$ to obtain the result $s_i' - s_i \geq 0$. A symmetric derivation gives $s_i - s_i' \geq 0$. $\square$

B. Adder and multiplier circuit constructions

Definition A *ring identity* $L = R$ denotes a pair of ring expressions L, R that can be transformed into each other using commutativity, distributivity and associativity.

To prove that a given ring identity $L = R$ holds for some choice of circuit implementations for $+$ and $\times$, we use these implementations to build a circuit $\mathbf{L}$ representing the expression L and another circuit $\mathbf{R}$ for the expression R. The goal of our cutting planes proofs is to show that the resulting output bit-vectors $\mathbf{L}, \mathbf{R}$ are equal bit-by-bit, i.e., that $L_i = R_i$ holds for every i.

Circuits for addition and multiplication

The circuits that we will consider are built using *adders* that output, in binary, the sum of three input bits. A (1-bit) adder is encoded as follows:

Definition For an adder A with inputs a_0, a_1, a_2, the outputs c, d are determined by the equation $a_0 + a_1 + a_2 - 2c - d = 0$. We call c the *carry-bit* and d the *sum-bit*.

In our circuits, each variable belongs to a column, i. The variables in column i have a *weight* of 2^i. Each adder is also assigned to a column. An adder A belonging to the i-th column takes three input bits from column i and outputs a *sum-bit* into column i and a *carry-bit* into column $i+1$. The equation associated with A ensures that the weight of its outputs is equal to the weight of its inputs.

a) Ripple-Carry Adder: Figure 1 shows the design of a ripple-carry adder $\mathbf{x} + \mathbf{y}$, which takes in two bitvectors $\mathbf{x}, \mathbf{y}$ and outputs their sum in binary.

b) Multiplier circuits: Figure 2 shows the design of an array multiplier and our labeling of the internal circuit variables. The first phase of an array multiplier is a common part of many multiplier designs: the circuit computes a *tableau* of partial products $t_{i,j} = x_i \wedge y_j$ for each pair of input bits x_i and y_j. In the second phase, n ripple-carry adders are arranged

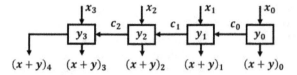

Fig. 1. A 4-bit ripple-carry adder adding $\mathbf{x}, \mathbf{y}$. Each box represents a full adder with incoming arrows and the labels in the boxes representing inputs and outgoing arrows representing outputs.

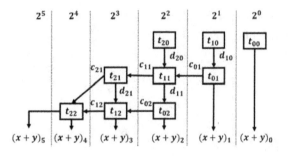

Fig. 2. 3-bit array multiplier.

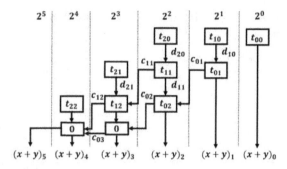

Fig. 3. 3-bit diagonal multiplier.

in a grid-like fashion in order to sum the n rows of the tableau. A closely related variant of the array multiplier is the diagonal multiplier, shown in Figure 3, which routes its carry bits to the next row instead of the same row.

Wallace-tree multipliers sum the tableau by arranging a network of adders in a tree-like structure. This log-depth structure reduces the number of rows in the tableau to 2, then uses an adder circuit to compute the final sum. In hardware implementations, this final stage adder is typically a *carry-lookahead adder*, so that the full multiplier has logarithmic depth. However, carry-lookahead adders use non full-adder components, which will lie outside the scope of this paper. The Wallace-tree multipliers in this paper will use ripple-carry adders for this final stage, so that the multiplier contains only full adder components.

III. ARRAY MULTIPLIER COMMUTATIVITY IN $O(n^2)$ STEPS

In this section, we give $O(n^2)$-length derivations for the word-level equivalence of the output bit-vectors $\mathbf{xy}$ and $\mathbf{yx}$ for both polynomial calculus and cutting planes. For polynomial calculus, this proof was, in essence, previously written down in [44].

Swapping the order of inputs $\mathbf{x}, \mathbf{y}$ to a multiplier has the effect of reversing the order of tableau values in each column. In particular we have the equalities $t_{i,j}^{xy} = t_{j,i}^{yx}$ between tableau variables. The next lemma shows that from these bit-level equalities we can derive the word-level equality of the output bit-vectors $\mathbf{xy}$ and $\mathbf{yx}$ using only $O(n^2)$ linear combination steps. As both polynomial calculus and cutting planes can carry out such steps (recall that cutting planes represents "=" using two inequalities), they can both perform this proof.

Lemma III.1. *Suppose that we have two n-bit array multipliers $\mathbf{xy}$ and $\mathbf{yx}$ implementing the two sides of the commutativity relation $xy = yx$. Further, suppose that we are given the*

n^2 *equalities between the tableau variables $t_{i,j}^{xy} = t_{j,i}^{yx}$. Then there is a derivation in degree 1 and length $3n^2 + 1$ of the equation $\sum_{i=0}^{n-1} 2^i(xy)_i - \sum_{i=0}^{n-1} 2^i(yx)_i = 0$ that only uses linear combinations.*

Proof. We first derive two "conservation of weight" equations for the circuits $\mathbf{xy}$ and $\mathbf{yx}$ that state that the total weight of a multiplier's output bits is the same as the total weight of its tableau bits. We obtain these by adding up the adder constraints, weighting them so that the internal circuit variables cancel. For an adder in column i corresponding to a constraint $a_0 + a_1 + a_2 - 2c - d = 0$, this weighting simply scales the constraint up by a factor of 2^i. Once all the n^2 adder equations for an array multiplier $\mathbf{xy}$ have been summed together, we will arrive at an equation stating that the weight of tableau variables $t_{i,j}^{xy}$ is the same as the weight of the output variables $\mathbf{xy}$. After repeating the same steps for the multiplier $\mathbf{yx}$, we arrive at the two equations

$$\left(\sum_{i,j=0}^{n-1} 2^{i+j} t_{i,j}^{xy} \right) - \left(\sum_{i=0}^{2n-1} 2^i(xy)_i \right) = 0$$

$$\left(\sum_{i,j=0}^{n-1} 2^{i+j} t_{j,i}^{yx} \right) - \left(\sum_{i=0}^{2n-1} 2^i(yx)_i \right) = 0$$

having used $2n^2$ linear combination steps. We then use a total of n^2 further derivation steps to replace $t_{j,i}^{yx}$ by $t_{i,j}^{xy}$ for each pair $i, j \in [0, n-1]$ in the latter equation. Finally, we subtract the two equations to finish the derivation. $\square$

Theorem III.2. *There is a polynomial calculus derivation in length $4n^2 + 1$, and also a cutting planes derivation in length $14n^2 + 2$, of the equation $\sum_{j=0}^{n-1} 2^i(xy)_i - \sum_{j=0}^{n-1} 2^i(yx)_i = 0$ from the array multiplier circuits $\mathbf{xy}$ and $\mathbf{yx}$.*

Proof. Given the previous lemma, to complete our derivation we need to obtain the tableau equalities $t_{i,j}^{xy} = t_{j,i}^{yx}$. In polynomial calculus, we get each equality with one subtraction step with the equations $t_{i,j}^{xy} = x_i y_j$ and $t_{j,i}^{yx} = y_j x_i$. So deriving these equalities takes an additional n^2 polynomial calculus steps.

In cutting planes, it takes 3 linear inequalities (clauses) to represent a constraint $t_{i,j}^{xy} = x_i y_j$. From these, we can derive that $t_{i,j}^{xy} = t_{j,i}^{yx}$ in eight steps. Hence, deriving the tableau equalities takes $8n^2$ cutting planes steps. Afterwards, it takes two cutting planes steps to carry out each of the $3n^2 + 1$ linear combination steps of Lemma III.1. $\qquad\square$

In cutting planes we can use proposition II.4 to prove bit-level equality from the equation $\sum_{i=0}^{n-1} 2^i(xy)_i - \sum_{i=0}^{n-1} 2^i(yx)_i = 0$, which gives the following corollary.

Corollary III.3. *There is a length-$O(n^2)$ cutting planes derivation yielding all of the $2n$ equalities $(xy)_i = (yx)_i$ from the array multiplier circuits* **xy** *and* **yx**.

For other ring identities such as distributivity, we no longer have straightforward equalities between the tableau variables on either side of the identity. For distributivity, the natural generalization of these tableau variable equalities contains nonlinear terms. Before we give our cutting planes proofs, we introduce the (k, d)-cutting planes proof system in the next section as a convenient way to work with nonlinear terms within cutting planes.

IV. (k, d)-Cutting Planes Proofs

Our cutting planes multiplier proofs will be written in a more convenient format that allows for a limited number of nonlinear terms in each inequality. Although cutting planes proofs only allow the use of linear inequalities, we will also be able to efficiently represent a large class of *nonlinear* Boolean inequalities using sets of linear inequalities.

Definition We say that a polynomial inequality ϕ on the Boolean variables X is (k, d)-*nonlinear* if is written in the form

$$\ell(X) + \sum_{i=1}^{k} \ell_i m_i \geq b$$

where $\ell(X)$ is an integer linear form (i.e., $\ell(X) = \sum_i c_i x_i$), each $\ell \in \{\ell_1, \dots, \ell_k\}$ is a non-negative integer linear form (i.e., $\ell = \sum_i c_i x_i$ and each $c_i \geq 0$), each m_i is a degree at most $d - 1$ monomial with coefficient $+1$ or -1, containing only variables disjoint from ℓ_i, and lastly, b is an integer.

We emphasize that this proof system distinguishes between inequalities ϕ and ϕ' that are semantically equivalent, but are syntactically different due to different factorizations. For example, the inequality $(x_1 + x_2)y_1 \geq b$ is *not* considered to be the same as the inequality $x_1 y_1 + x_2 y_1 \geq b$. The first inequality is $(1, 2)$-nonlinear while the second is $(2, 2)$-nonlinear. In simulating (k, d)-nonlinear inequalities by ordinary linear ones, these two inequalities will be represented by two different (though semantically equivalent) sets of linear inequalities.

Definition Let $\mathcal{CP}^{+(k,d)}$ denote the (k, d)-*cutting planes* proof system. Each line is a (k, d)-nonlinear inequality on a set of Boolean variables $\{x_i\}$. Its rules are as follows. The *literal axioms* are the same as in $\mathcal{CP}$: for each variable x_i we have $x_i \geq 0$ and $-x_i \geq -1$. The division rule and linear combination rule from $\mathcal{CP}$ generalize as one would expect. Writing $\ell(X) = \sum_i (c \cdot a_i) x_i$:

$$\frac{\sum_i (c \cdot a_i) x_i + \sum_i (c \cdot \ell_i) m_i \geq b}{\sum_i a_i x_i + \sum_i \ell_i m_i \geq \lceil \frac{b}{c} \rceil}$$

And for any $\alpha, \beta \in \mathbb{N}$, as long as the result is (k, d)-nonlinear:

$$\frac{\sum_i \ell_i m_i + \ell(X) \geq b, \quad \sum_j \ell'_j m'_j + \ell'(X) \geq b'}{\sum_i \alpha \ell_i m_i + \alpha \ell(X) + \sum_j \beta \ell'_j m'_j + \beta \ell'(X) \geq \alpha b + \beta b'}$$

The *factoring rule* is that if the (k, d)-nonlinear inequality ϕ contains two terms $\ell m, \ell' m$ with the same monomial m, then we can factor these into term $(\ell + \ell')m$. Syntactically:

$$\frac{\ell(X) + \sum_i \ell_i m_i + \ell m + \ell' m \geq b}{\ell(X) + \sum_i \ell_i m_i + (\ell + \ell')m \geq b}.$$

The *distributing rule* is the reverse of the factoring rule, except we can only distribute "one at a time". For example, rewriting $(10y_1 + 8y_2)x_1 x_2 x_3 \rightarrow 10y_1 x_1 x_2 x_3 + 8y_2 x_1 x_2 x_3$ would require 8 applications of the distributing rule below. For a non-negative linear form $\ell = \sum_i c_i x_i$, where each $c_i \geq 0$, define $\max(\ell) = \sum_i c_i$. Because of a technical detail related to the simulation size, we require that the two inequalities $\max(\ell) \geq \ell \geq 0$ have been derived from the literal axioms before making this inference:

$$\frac{\ell(X) + \sum_i \ell_i m_i + (\ell + y_r)m_p \geq b \qquad \max(\ell) \geq \ell \geq 0}{\ell(X) + \sum_i \ell_i m_i + \ell m_p + y_r m_p \geq b}.$$

The *multiplication rule* permits the multiplication of an inequality ϕ by a variable z, provided that the resulting inequality ϕz is (k, d)-nonlinear. Decomposing $\ell(X) = \ell(X)^+ - \ell(X)^-$ into a sum of positive terms $\ell(X)^+$ and negative terms $\ell(X)^-$:

$$\frac{\ell(X)^+ - \ell(X)^- + \sum_i \ell_i m_i \geq b}{\ell(X)^+ z - \ell(X)^- z + \sum_i \ell_i m_i z - bz \geq 0}.$$

Theorem IV.1. *Fix a pair of positive integers $k \geq 1$ and $d \geq 2$. The cutting planes proof system $\mathcal{CP}$ p-simulates the $\mathcal{CP}^{+(k,d)}$ proof system. In particular, a $\mathcal{CP}^{+(k,d)}$ proof of s lines can be simulated by a cutting planes proof of at most $(k + 4)d^k s$ lines.*

The idea of the proof of Theorem IV.1 is to find a tight set of at most d linear upper bounds for each degree d nonlinear term. To simulate an inequality with k nonlinear terms of degree at most d, we use the set of at most d^k linear inequalities obtained by plugging in every combination of upper bounds for each nonlinear term. The full details of this simulation can be found in [34].

V. Optimal Cutting Planes Multiplier Proofs

In the previous proof of commutativity, we were able to give cutting planes proofs without including nonlinear terms. However, when giving proofs for distributivity and other larger identities, nonlinear terms are difficult to avoid. This is where the (k, d)-cutting planes format is convenient for expressing $O(n^2)$ length cutting planes proofs of distributivity. We generalize these proofs for distributivity to obtain $O(n^2)$ length proofs for a large class of degree two ring identities.

In the first half of these proofs, we sum up the adder-constraints in each ripple-carry adder circuit $\mathbf{x} + \mathbf{y}$ to derive the "conservation of weight" equation $\sum_i 2^i (x_i + y_i) = \sum_i 2^i (x + y)_i$, and also in each multiplication circuit $\mathbf{xy}$ to derive the "conservation of weight" equation $\sum_{i,j} 2^{i+j} t_{i,j}^{xy} = \sum_i 2^i (xy)_i$.

This section focuses on the second half of the proof, where the goal is to show that both sides hold equal weight in their multiplier tableau variables. The idea is to derive an equation $\rho(i, j)$ relating the (i, j)-th tableau entry of each multiplier. Fixing j and summing these equations along i gives an equation $\rho(j)$ relating the j-th rows of each multiplier. Finally, adding together the equations $\rho(j)$ yields the desired equation for the full multiplier tableaus.

A. Distributivity

Theorem V.1. *There is a length $O(n^2)$ $\mathcal{CP}$ proof that the circuits $(\mathbf{x} + \mathbf{y})\mathbf{z}$ and $\mathbf{xz} + \mathbf{yz}$ for length n bit-vectors $\mathbf{x}, \mathbf{y}, \mathbf{z}$ have equal outputs.*

Proof. We will give a length $O(n^2)$ proof in $\mathcal{CP}^{+(5,2)}$. By Theorem IV.1, this implies that there is an equivalent cutting planes proof that is only a constant factor larger. We begin with the following lemma, which gives a small derivation that the weight of the j-th row of the multiplier $(\mathbf{x} + \mathbf{y})\mathbf{z}$ is the same as the combined weight of the j-th rows of multipliers $\mathbf{xz}$ and $\mathbf{yz}$.

Lemma V.2. *For each $j \in [0, n-1]$ there is a length $O(n)$ derivation in $\mathcal{CP}^{+(5,2)}$ of the equality $\rho(j)$, defined as: $\sum_{i=0}^{n} 2^{i+j} \cdot t_{i,j}^{(x+y)z} = \sum_{i=0}^{n-1} 2^{i+j} \cdot (t_{i,j}^{xz} + t_{i,j}^{yz})$. from the circuits $(\mathbf{x} + \mathbf{y})\mathbf{z}$ and $\mathbf{xz} + \mathbf{yz}$.*

Proof. Fix $j \in [0, n-1]$. We give a constant length derivation for each cell-wise constraint $\rho(i, j)$, defined for $i \in [1, n-1]$ as

$$t_{i,j}^{(x+y)z} = t_{i,j}^{xz} + t_{i,j}^{yz} + c_{i-1}^{x+y} z_j - 2 c_i^{x+y} z_j$$

and defined for $i = 0$ and $i = n$ the same way, absent the non-existing variables c_{-1}^{x+y}, c_n^{x+y}, $t_{n,j}^{xz}$ and $t_{n,j}^{yz}$. Adding up the constraints $\rho(i, j)$ will yield $\rho(j)$.

Start with the equation $x_i + y_i + c_{i-1}^{x+y} - 2 c_i^{x+y} - (x + y)_i = 0$, given by the i-th adder in the ripple-carry adder $(\mathbf{x} + \mathbf{y})$. Multiplying this equation by z_j, we obtain the $(5, 2)$-nonlinear equation $x_i z_j + y_i z_j + c_{i-1}^{x+y} z_j - 2 c_i^{x+y} z_j - (x + y)_i z_j = 0$. Substituting in the tableau variables $t_{i,j}^{(x+y)z}, t_{i,j}^{xz}, t_{i,j}^{yz}$ gives us $\rho(i, j)$.

To derive $\rho(j)$ we add together the constraints $\rho(i, j)$ so that the carry terms telescope: We start with $\rho(n, j)$. Use linear combination to derive the equation $2\rho(n, j) + \rho(n - 1, j)$:

$$2 t_{n,j}^{(x+y)z} + t_{n-1,j}^{(x+y)z} = t_{n-1,j}^{xz} + t_{n-1,j}^{yz} + c_{n-1}^{x+y} z_j.$$

Repeating this step for $\rho(n-2, j), \ldots, \rho(0, j)$ gives $\rho(j)$. $\square$

The rest of the proof combines equations $\rho(j)$ given by Lemma V.2 with the conservation of weight equations. We first observe that combining the conservation of weight equations gives us, in a constant number of steps, the two equations

$$\sum_{i=0}^{2n} 2^i \cdot (xz + yz)_i = \sum_{j=0}^{n-1} \sum_{i=0}^{n-1} 2^{i+j} \cdot (t_{i,j}^{xz} + t_{i,j}^{yz}) \quad (1)$$

$$\sum_{i=0}^{2n} 2^i \cdot ((x + y)z)_i = \sum_{j=0}^{n-1} \sum_{i=0}^{n} 2^{i+j} \cdot t_{i,j}^{(x+y)z}. \quad (2)$$

Sum all of the equalities $\rho(j)$ to derive the equation ρ, stating that both sides have equal weight in their tableau variables: $\sum_{i,j} 2^{i+j} \cdot (t_{i,j}^{xz} + t_{i,j}^{yz}) = \sum_{i,j} 2^{i+j} \cdot t_{i,j}^{(x+y)z}$. Combine this with equations 1 and 2 to obtain the final result: $\sum_i 2^i \cdot (xz + yz)_i = \sum_i 2^i \cdot ((x + y)z)_i$. $\square$

Notice that we only used the structure of the multipliers $(\mathbf{x} + \mathbf{y})\mathbf{z}$, $\mathbf{xz}$ and $\mathbf{yz}$ to derive the conservation of weight equations relating the sum of tableau variables to the output of the multiplier. The above proof is thereby compatible with any integer multiplier for which we can efficiently derive these conservation of weight equations. For example, we obtain $O(n^2)$ length proofs for Wallace tree multipliers using a final stage ripple-carry adder. In comparison, the best prior proof known for, say, checking that the middle pair of bits of an array multiplier and a Wallace tree multiplier are equal, was the quasi-polynomial size $n^{O(\log n)}$ resolution proof given in [6].

Reversing the order of multiplier inputs only has the effect of permuting the order of tableau variables, so the above proof also immediately generalizes to identities like $z(x + y) = zx + xz$ that mix distributivity and commutativity.

B. 2-Colorable identities

In this section we state some theorems that we can obtain by generalizing the ideas behind the proofs for the identity $(x + y)z = xz + yz$ to provide $O(n^2)$ length cutting planes proofs for larger instances of distributivity. The proofs of these theorems may be found in [34].

Theorem V.3. *Let $\mathbf{x_1}, \mathbf{x_2}, \ldots, \mathbf{x_s}$ and $\mathbf{y_1}, \mathbf{y_2}, \ldots, \mathbf{y_{s'}}$ be length n bit-vectors. Define the circuit $\mathbf{L}$ as $(\mathbf{x_1} + \mathbf{x_2} + \ldots + \mathbf{x_s})(\mathbf{y_1} + \mathbf{y_2} + \ldots + \mathbf{y_{s'}})$. Also define the circuit $\mathbf{R}$ as $\left(\sum_{\alpha,\beta} \mathbf{x_\alpha y_\beta}\right)$, representing the fully expanded version of $\mathbf{L}$. There is a length $O(n^2)$ cutting planes proof that circuits L and R have equal outputs.*

Theorem V.3 gives us $O(n^2)$ cutting planes proofs for fixed ring identities that can be written as sum of independent bit-vector distributing or factoring steps. However, there exist identities such as $x(y + z) + wz = xy + (x + w)z$ which cannot be decomposed into a sum of independent distributing and factoring components. Nevertheless, we can still give an $O(n^2)$ length proof of this identity. We define the notion of a *2-colorable* degree two identity to identify the general class of ring identities for which our technique can derive $O(n^2)$ length proofs.

Definition Let $L = R$ be a degree two ring identity. A *2-coloring* for $L = R$ is an assignment of either the color red or blue to each bit-vector, with multiplicity (so a bit-vector may appear twice with different colors), such that: (1) each bit-vector in a sub-expression $(\mathbf{x_1} + \mathbf{x_2} + \ldots + \mathbf{x_r})$ has the same color as the bit-vector representing the sub-expression, (2) two sub-expressions that are multiplied together have opposite colors, and (3) the colored version of $L = R$, where a blue input bit-vector colored blue $\mathbf{x_i}$ is distinguished from its red counterpart $\mathbf{x_i}$, is still a valid ring identity.

For example, $(\mathbf{x} + \mathbf{y})\mathbf{z} = \mathbf{xz} + \mathbf{zy}$ has the 2-coloring $(\mathbf{x} + \mathbf{y})\mathbf{z} = \mathbf{xz} + \mathbf{zy}$. The more general form of distributivity in Theorem V.3 clearly always has an 2-coloring. Lastly, the identity $\mathbf{x}(\mathbf{y} + \mathbf{z}) + \mathbf{wz} = \mathbf{xy} + \mathbf{z}(\mathbf{x} + \mathbf{w})$ has the 2-coloring $\mathbf{x}(\mathbf{y} + \mathbf{z}) + \mathbf{wz} = \mathbf{xy} + \mathbf{z}(\mathbf{x} + \mathbf{w})$. An example of an identity without a 2-coloring is $\mathbf{x}(\mathbf{y} + \mathbf{z}) + \mathbf{w}(\mathbf{x} + \mathbf{y}) = \mathbf{y}(\mathbf{x} + \mathbf{w}) + \mathbf{x}(\mathbf{z} + \mathbf{w})$.

Theorem V.4. *Let $L = R$ be a 2-colorable degree two ring identity on length n bit-vectors $\mathbf{x_1}, \ldots, \mathbf{x_s}$. There is a length $O(n^2)$ cutting planes proof that the circuits $\mathbf{L}$ and $\mathbf{R}$ have equivalent outputs.*

VI. Experiments

The goal of our experiments was to evaluate the potential of using cutting planes solvers to reason with mixtures of multiplication and bit-level logic. Such problems are a key weakness of using a SAT-based approach to "bit-blasting". We found several types of problems where pseudo-Boolean solvers performed well out-of-the-box. These include checking the word-level equivalence, commutativity, or correctness of different multipliers, extracting bit-equalities from word-level equalities, and verifying nonlinear bit-vector inequalities.

In our experiments, we used an Intel Core i7-6700K CPU at 4.00GHz with a memory limit of 8GB. The wall-clock time limit was set to 1200 seconds. We list experiment times in seconds (wall-clock time) and write TO if the time limit of 1200 seconds was exceeded. Our benchmarks are available at [35].

We used two pseudo-Boolean solvers, each equipped with a different form of cutting planes reasoning. The first, Sat4j-CP [33], employs *saturation* in its conflict analysis. The second solver, RoundingSat [21], [48], instead uses division; we used the new multi-precision version of the solver for which we could also log and separately verify the derivations it used.

Our experiments focused on integer multipliers with n-bit inputs and $2n$ bits of output. We report results on three different circuits to represent multiplication: array, diagonal, and Wallace-tree multipliers with final stage ripple-carry adder. As noted in the introduction, we directly represent the adder constraints as two inequalities instead of as a set of clauses and define a "spec-equation multiplier" without a circuit by simply using the specification equation

$$\sum_{i,j=0}^{n-1} 2^{i+j} t_{i,j}^{xy} - \sum_{i=0}^{2n-1} 2^i (xy)_i = 0$$

TABLE I
Time to prove equivalences between multipliers using Sat4j and RoundingSat. We give the time to prove equivalence the word-level, the time to extract the individual bits of the word-level equivalence, and the sum of these gives the total time to prove bit-level equivalence. We compare performance to the algebraic approach of [28]

Instance	n	Sat4j-CP Word-level	RoundingSat Extract	Bit-level
array $x \cdot y = y \cdot x$	32	6	1	7
	64	8	6	14
	128	25	41	66
	256	171	158	329
diagonal $x \cdot y = y \cdot x$	32	7	1	8
	64	7	6	13
	128	25	41	66
	256	172	158	330
array spec-eqn	32	6	1	7
	64	18	6	24
	128	135	41	176
	256	TO	N/A	TO
diagonal spec-eqn	32	4	1	5
	64	18	6	24
	128	129	41	170
	256	TO	N/A	TO
diagonal $\equiv$ array	32	2	1	3
	64	5	6	11
	128	16	41	57
	256	102	158	260
Instance	n	Gröbner [28] Word-level	Extract	Bit-level
gate-array $x \cdot y = y \cdot x$	32	1	N/A	N/A
	64	3	N/A	N/A
	128	27	N/A	N/A
	256	273	N/A	N/A
gate-array spec-eqn	32	1	N/A	N/A
	64	2	N/A	N/A
	128	14	N/A	N/A
	256	136	N/A	N/A

Pseudo-Boolean benchmarks with array, diagonal, or spec-eqn used our generator. Gate-level array multipliers were generated by Boolector [43].

TABLE II
Time to prove equivalences with Wallace tree multipliers using Sat4j and RoundingSat.

Instance	n	Sat4j-CP Word-level	RoundingSat Extract	Bit-level
Wallace $x \cdot y = y \cdot x$	16	1	1	2
	32	5	1	6
	48	TO	N/A	TO
	64	TO	N/A	TO
Wallace $\geq$ spec-eqn	16	1	N/A	N/A
	32	5	N/A	N/A
	48	65	N/A	N/A
	64	360	N/A	N/A
array $\equiv$ Wallace	16	1	1	2
	32	2	1	3
	48	45	3	48
	64	41	6	47

along with the partial product constraints $t_{i,j}^{xy} = x_i y_j$. In these two ways, the pseudo-Boolean format allows us to "bit-blast" multiplication, along with other word-level functions, to a higher-level description than CNF while maintaining full bit-precision.

Our first set of experiments, presented in Table I, uses

the pseudo-Boolean solvers Sat4j-CP and RoundingSat to verify the word-level and bit-level equivalence of different multiplier circuits. More precisely, we use Sat4j-CP to prove an equation of the form $\sum_i 2^i(s_i - s_i') = 0$ stating that the total weight of the outputs $\mathbf{s}, \mathbf{s}'$ is the same for the two multipliers. Then we have RoundingSat deduce, from this equation, each equality $s_i = s_i'$ individually in order to prove equivalence at the bit-level. Performance on bit-extraction scaled particularly well with the right choice of pseudo-Boolean solver, as shown in Table III, which also includes a comparison with the theoretical lower bound we showed for algebraic methods. Using these two steps, we can efficiently check the commutativity of array, diagonal, and Wallace-tree multipliers, as well as several equivalences between array, diagonal, and spec-equation multipliers. We can also check some of these properties of Wallace-tree multipliers for up to 32 or 64 bits.

An important step for showing word-level equivalence was to do some basic pre-processing to find equivalent partial products ($t_{i,j}^{xy}$ variables). Adding these equivalences was key to obtaining efficient solve times in Sat4j-CP. In contrast, we found that adding these equivalences did not help SAT-based solvers. We note that most bit-vector solvers, and many SAT solvers, already perform similar pre-processing to find equivalent variables; current pseudo-Boolean solvers based on cutting planes do not yet have such pre-processing.

To provide some context for these results, we compared the performance of our pseudo-Boolean approach to the algebraic approach of [28], which is currently the fastest method for verifying these properties. We replicated their verification of the commutativity and correctness of a simple gate-level array multiplier "btor", generated by Boolector, by using their tool, AMulet, in our environment to obtain the solve times at the bottom of Table I. We note that AMulet, is also capable of similarly fast solve times for more complicated gate-level multipliers such as Booth-encoded Wallace-tree multipliers. We direct interested readers to [28] for further experiments using the algebraic approach to verify commutativity, correctness, and equivalence of these other gate-level multiplier architectures.

Current pseudo-Boolean solvers have limited reasoning capabilities for these lower level multipliers. In particular, these solvers degenerate to SAT-based reasoning when given a CNF input. Our focus is not so much on verifying a large spectrum of multiplier circuits as on bit-vector solving, where we are free to choose the most efficient way to represent bit-vector multiplication.

We see that for simple array and diagonal multipliers, our approach (on adder-level multipliers) achieves comparable times to the algebraic approach (on gate-level multipliers) for proving commutativity and word-level equivalence. Furthermore, we are able to efficiently extract each of the individual bit-level equalities that a word-level equality implies.

For Wallace-tree multipliers with a final stage ripple-carry adder (wt-rca), we could check its equivalence with an array for 64 bits within 1 minute. We could also check commutativ-

TABLE III

Time in seconds to prove the equality $s_0 = s_0'$ from the equation $\sum_{i=0}^{n-1} 2^i(s_i - s_i') = 0$ for the cutting planes solvers RoundingSat (RS) and Sat4j-CP, compared to the SAT-based solvers Sat4j-Res and NaPS [49]. We also compare with the polynomial calculus lower bound given by Corollary II.3.

n	RS	Sat4j-CP	Sat4j-Res	NaPS	#monomials
12	.001	7	.4	.1	7
16	.001	TO	3	2	20
20	.001		81	39	54
24	.001		TO	208	148
28	.002			Error	403
32	.002				1096
64	.009				3×10^6
128	.04				2×10^{13}
256	.2				2×10^{27}
512	.4				1×10^{55}

ity for 32 bits in 5 seconds. However, we hit time-out on larger instances of 48 or 64 bits. We were also unable to completely verify the equivalence of a wt-rca and spec equation multiplier for 32-bit instances, though we could show that the the output of the wt-rca is at least as large as the output of the spec equation in 5 seconds. We see that Sat4j-CP has a harder time with these more complicated multiplier architectures.

Our other experiments, presented in Table IV, use the solver RoundingSat to verify some nonlinear bit-vector inequalities involving untruncated multiplication and the operations "|" for bit-wise OR, "&" for bit-wise AND. We use these bit-wise operations to apply the *bit masks* "$| k$" and "$\& k$", where k is set to the constant alternating bit-string $(10)^{(n/2)}$. (This value was an arbitrary choice that contains a mix of 1s and 0s; we observed similar performance across all solvers with other values of k.) The inequalities listed follow from thinking of "|" and "&" as, respectively, computing the bit-wise maximum and minimum of their inputs.

We compare RoundingSat's performance on these inequalities against the bit-vector solvers Boolector, Yices2, Z3 and CVC4. Our inputs to these bit-vector solvers used the word-level format SMT-LIB2 [3] to allow for full use of word-level reasoning and other non-SAT capabilities. We found that these bit-vector solvers (with the exception of Boolector) generally exceeded the time limit at 20 bits. On the other hand, when we "bit-blasted" multiplication using the spec-equation, RoundingSat outperformed all of the bit-vector solvers, with the exception of last inequality $(x \mid k)(y+1) \geq ky + x$, where Boolector won out by a few bits.

VII. CONCLUSIONS & DIRECTIONS

In this paper, we have described a new approach to deciding nonlinear bit-vector formulas: include 1-bit adders among the set of essential building blocks along with the usual Boolean operations and express properties using pseudo-Boolean formulas rather than CNF formulas during "bit-blasting". We have shown, both experimentally and in principle, how pseudo-Boolean solvers based on cutting planes reasoning, when given these new bit-blasted formulas, can achieve levels of performance comparable to, or better than, the best alterna-

TABLE IV
Time to prove bit-vector inequalities containing both multiplication and bit-level operations. We compare RoundingSat (RS), Boolector 3.2.0 (Btor), Z3 4.8.7, Yices 2.6.2 and CVC4.

Inequality	n	RS	Btor	Z3	Yices2	CVC4
$(x \mid k)z \geq kz$	16	17	14	21	31	44
	20	11	136	TO	TO	TO
	24	16	TO			
	28	501				
	32	TO				
$kz \geq (x\&k)z$	16	.06	10	15	172	31
	20	.5	117	1154	TO	TO
	24	.7	TO	TO		
	28	.6				
	32	.6				
$(x \mid k)z \geq (x\&k)z$	16	.2	14	22	31	44
	20	7	TO	TO	TO	TO
	24	2				
	28	629				
	32	TO				
$(x \mid z)(z \mid k) \geq kx$	16	.008	19	43	114	50
	20	.05	351	TO	TO	TO
	24	.1	TO			
	28	.2				
	32	.2				
$kx \geq (x\&z)(z\&k)$	16	.04	10	32	100	48
	20	.07	243	TO	TO	TO
	24	.1	TO			
	28	23				
	32	7				
$(x \mid k)(y+1)$ $\geq ky + x$	16	.4	25	29	38	118
	20	TO	342	TO	TO	TO
	24		TO			

Bit-vector k is the value $(10)^{(n/2)}$. & is bit-wise AND, $\mid$ is bit-wise OR.

tive methods on a number of natural multiplier verification examples.

In particular, we have given $O(n^2)$-length cutting planes proofs for a broad class of properties of multipliers, matching the optimal efficiency of the best Gröbner basis algorithms for these properties at the word level, while also being able to extract bit-level properties. Importantly, Gröbner basis algorithms are not known to be able to extract such bit-level properties efficiently: We have shown that such methods require exponential time to extract bit-level consequences from word-level properties.

An interesting open question is whether polynomial size cutting planes proofs can be found for degree three identities such as associativity. Although word-level associativity has an $O(n^2)$ length proof in polynomial calculus, this cannot be used to show the individual bit-level equalities.

We also have shown experimentally that for several of these properties on inputs of up to 256 bits — namely, commutativity, correctness, and equivalence — pseudo-Boolean solvers can achieve performance comparable to that of the best algebraic solvers at the word-level, and, in contrast to algebraic methods, also solve these problems at the bit-level.

Finally, we have experimentally verified a number of crafted bit-vector inequalities, each involving a mixture of multiplication and bit-wise operations and have shown that our pseudo-Boolean approach can achieve much better verification performance than several of the best current bit-vector solvers.

The idea of using pseudo-Boolean solving for verifying nonlinear bit-vector formulas appears not to have been explored previously. One possible explanation for this is that when pseudo-Boolean solvers are run purely on CNF inputs, their reasoning collapses to that of CDCL SAT solvers, only much less efficient ones because of the more involved data structures and algorithms required in the pseudo-Boolean case. Our use of 1-bit adders as fundamental structures is critical to achieving the performance that we obtain.

Conflict-driven pseudo-Boolean solvers are still at a relatively early stage of development, especially compared to the 25+ years of concerted effort directed at optimizing Gröbner basis algorithms and CDCL solvers. In particular, there is quite some variation in the different forms of conflict analysis methods used, and some of these methods have been shown to be quite weak. In fact, many solvers, such as NaPS [49] and Open-WBO [40], do not use any cutting planes reasoning and instead reduce the problem to SAT. Other shortcomings in the cutting planes reasoning used in current solvers are discussed in ([20], [23], [53]). In our experiments, different conflict analysis methods worked best on different problems. For example, we found that the saturation-based solver Sat4j-CP worked much better than RoundingSat for checking word-level equalities. On the other hand, the division-based solver RoundingSat significantly outperformed Sat4j-CP when tasked with extracting bit-equalities, and also for checking bit-vector inequalities. This is in contrast with CDCL solvers where the best ideas for conflict analysis have largely converged on a single method that is used by all of the currently best solvers.

We view this work as providing a "call to arms" for pseudo-Boolean solver development, focusing especially on features that will be useful in verification of these kinds of bit-vector problems. In particular, though our experiments validate the pseudo-Boolean approach in principle, none of the solvers we used allowed us to verify the properties for which we provided more complex cutting planes proofs in Section V. Thus, there is substantial scope for developing new methods and heuristics for pseudo-Boolean solving that can carry out much more of this cutting planes reasoning in practice.

ACKNOWLEDGMENTS

Paul Beame and Vincent Liew's research was supported in part by NSF-SHF grant CCF-1714593. Jo Devriendt, Jan Elffers, and Jakob Nordström were funded by the Swedish Research Council (VR) grant 2016-00782, and Jakob Nordström was also supported by the Independent Research Fund Denmark (DFF) grant 9040-00389B. Some development work on RoundingSat was done using computational resources provided by the Swedish National Infrastructure for Computing (SNIC) at the High Performance Computing Center North (HPC2N) at Umeå University.

References

[1] S. Anderson, "Bit twiddling hacks," https://graphics.stanford.edu/~seander/bithacks.html, accessed: 2020-05-15.

[2] C. Barrett, C. L. Conway, M. Deters, L. Hadarean, D. Jovanovi'c, T. King, A. Reynolds, and C. Tinelli, "CVC4," in *Proceedings of the 23rd International Conference on Computer Aided Verification (CAV '11)*, ser. Lecture Notes in Computer Science, G. Gopalakrishnan and S. Qadeer, Eds., vol. 6806. Springer, Jul. 2011, pp. 171–177, snowbird, Utah. [Online]. Available: http://www.cs.stanford.edu/~barrett/pubs/BCD+11.pdf

[3] C. Barrett, P. Fontaine, and C. Tinelli, "The SMT-LIB standard: Version 2.5," Department of Computer Science, The University of Iowa, Tech. Rep., 2015.

[4] R. J. Bayardo Jr. and R. Schrag, "Using CSP look-back techniques to solve real-world SAT instances," in *Proceedings of the 14th National Conference on Artificial Intelligence (AAAI '97)*, Jul. 1997, pp. 203–208.

[5] P. Beame, H. A. Kautz, and A. Sabharwal, "Towards understanding and harnessing the potential of clause learning," *J. Artif. Intell. Res. (JAIR)*, vol. 22, pp. 319–351, 2004.

[6] P. Beame and V. Liew, "Towards verifying nonlinear integer arithmetic," in *Computer Aided Verification*, R. Majumdar and V. Kunčak, Eds. Cham: Springer International Publishing, 2017, pp. 238–258.

[7] ——, "Toward verifying nonlinear integer arithmetic," *J. ACM*, vol. 66, no. 3, pp. 22:1–30, June 2019. [Online]. Available: https://doi.org/10.1145/3319396

[8] A. Biere, "Collection of Combinational Arithmetic Miters Submitted to the SAT Competition 2016," in *Proc. of SAT Competition 2016 – Solver and Benchmark Descriptions*, ser. Department of Computer Science Series of Publications B, T. Balyo, M. Heule, and M. Järvisalo, Eds., vol. B-2016-1. University of Helsinki, 2016, pp. 65–66.

[9] ——, "Weaknesses of CDCL solvers," in *Fields Institute Workshop on Theoretical Foundations of SAT Solving*, August 2016, http://www.fields.utoronto.ca/talks/weaknesses-cdcl-solvers.

[10] A. Biere, M. Kauers, and D. Ritirc, "Challenges in verifying arithmetic circuits using computer algebra," in *19th International Symposium on Symbolic and Numeric Algorithms for Scientific Computing (SYNASC '17)*, 2017.

[11] A. Blake, "Canonical expressions in Boolean algebra," Ph.D. dissertation, University of Chicago, 1937.

[12] R. Brummayer and A. Biere, "Boolector: An efficient SMT solver for bit-vectors and arrays," in *Proceedings of the 15th International Conference on Tools and Algorithms for the Construction and Analysis of Systems: Held As Part of the Joint European Conferences on Theory and Practice of Software, ETAPS 2009*, ser. TACAS '09. Berlin, Heidelberg: Springer-Verlag, 2009, pp. 174–177. [Online]. Available: http://dx.doi.org/10.1007/978-3-642-00768-2-16

[13] D. Chai and A. Kuehlmann, "A fast pseudo-Boolean constraint solver," *IEEE Transactions on Computer-Aided Design of Integrated Circuits and Systems*, vol. 24, no. 3, pp. 305–317, March 2005.

[14] S. Chakraborty, A. Gupta, and R. Jain, "Matching multiplications in bit-vector formulas," in *Verification, Model Checking, and Abstract Interpretation*, A. Bouajjani and D. Monniaux, Eds. Cham: Springer International Publishing, 2017, pp. 131–150.

[15] M. Ciesielski, T. Su, A. Yasin, and C. Yu, "Understanding algebraic rewriting for arithmetic circuit verification: a bit-flow model," *IEEE Transactions on Computer-Aided Design of Integrated Circuits and Systems*, pp. 1–1, 2019.

[16] M. Clegg, J. Edmonds, and R. Impagliazzo, "Using the Groebner basis algorithm to find proofs of unsatisfiability," in *Proceedings of the Twenty-eighth Annual ACM Symposium on Theory of Computing*, ser. STOC '96. New York, NY, USA: ACM, 1996, pp. 174–183. [Online]. Available: http://doi.acm.org/10.1145/237814.237860

[17] W. Cook, C. Coullard, and G. Turán, "On the complexity of cutting-plane proofs," *Discrete Applied Mathematics*, vol. 18, no. 1, pp. 25 – 38, 1987. [Online]. Available: http://www.sciencedirect.com/science/article/pii/0166218X87900394

[18] L. de Moura and N. Bjørner, "Z3: An efficient SMT solver," in *Tools and Algorithms for the Construction and Analysis of Systems*, C. R. Ramakrishnan and J. Rehof, Eds. Berlin, Heidelberg: Springer Berlin Heidelberg, 2008, pp. 337–340.

[19] B. Dutertre, "Yices 2.2," in *Computer-Aided Verification (CAV' 14)*, ser. Lecture Notes in Computer Science, A. Biere and R. Bloem, Eds., vol. 8559. Springer, July 2014, pp. 737–744.

[20] J. Elffers, J. Giráldez-Cru, J. Nordström, and M. Vinyals, "Using combinatorial benchmarks to probe the reasoning power of pseudo-Boolean solvers," in *Theory and Applications of Satisfiability Testing – SAT 2018*, O. Beyersdorff and C. M. Wintersteiger, Eds. Cham: Springer International Publishing, 2018, pp. 75–93.

[21] J. Elffers and J. Nordström, "Divide and conquer: Towards faster pseudo-Boolean solving," in *Proceedings of the Twenty-Seventh International Joint Conference on Artificial Intelligence, IJCAI-18*. International Joint Conferences on Artificial Intelligence Organization, 7 2018, pp. 1291–1299. [Online]. Available: https://doi.org/10.24963/ijcai.2018/180

[22] A. Franzén, A. Cimatti, A. Nadel, R. Sebastiani, and J. Shalev, "Applying SMT in symbolic execution of microcode," in *Proceedings of the 2010 Conference on Formal Methods in Computer-Aided Design*, ser. FMCAD '10. Austin, TX: FMCAD Inc, 2010, pp. 121–128. [Online]. Available: http://dl.acm.org.offcampus.lib.washington.edu/citation.cfm?id=1998496.1998520

[23] S. Gocht, J. Nordström, and A. Yehudayoff, "On division versus saturation in pseudo-Boolean solving," in *Proceedings of the Twenty-Eighth International Joint Conference on Artificial Intelligence, IJCAI-19*. International Joint Conferences on Artificial Intelligence Organization, 7 2019, pp. 1711–1718. [Online]. Available: https://doi.org/10.24963/ijcai.2019/237

[24] A. Haken, "The intractability of resolution," *Theoretical Computer Science*, vol. 39, pp. 297 – 308, 1985, third Conference on Foundations of Software Technology and Theoretical Computer Science. [Online]. Available: http://www.sciencedirect.com/science/article/pii/0304397585901446

[25] R. Impagliazzo, P. Pudlák, and J. Sgall, "Lower bounds for the polynomial calculus and the Gröbner basis algorithm," *Computational Complexity*, vol. 8, no. 2, pp. 127–144, 1999.

[26] H. S. W. Jr., *Hacker's Delight, Second Edition*. Pearson Education, 2013. [Online]. Available: http://www.hackersdelight.org/

[27] M. Katelman and J. Meseguer, "vlogsl: A strategy language for simulation-based verification of hardware," in *Hardware and Software: Verification and Testing*, S. Barner, I. Harris, D. Kroening, and O. Raz, Eds. Berlin, Heidelberg: Springer Berlin Heidelberg, 2011, pp. 129–145.

[28] D. Kaufmann, "Formal verification of multiplier circuits using computer algebra," Ph.D. dissertation, Johannes Kepler University Linz, 2020.

[29] D. Kaufmann, A. Biere, and M. Kauers, "SAT, computer algebra, multipliers," in *Vampire 2018 and Vampire 2019. The 5th and 6th Vampire Workshops*, ser. EPiC Series in Computing, L. Kovács and A. Voronkov, Eds., vol. 71. EasyChair, 2020, pp. 1–18.

[30] D. Kaufmann, M. Kauers, A. Biere, and D. Cok, "Arithmetic verification problems submitted to the SAT Race 2019," in *Proc. of SAT Race 2019 – Solver and Benchmark Descriptions*, ser. Department of Computer Science Series of Publications B, M. Heule, M. Järvisalo, and M. Suda, Eds., vol. B-2019-1. University of Helsinki, 2019, p. 49.

[31] G. Kovásznai, A. Fröhlich, and A. Biere, "Complexity of fixed-size bit-vector logics," *Theory of Computing Systems*, vol. 59, no. 2, pp. 323–376, Aug 2016. [Online]. Available: https://doi.org/10.1007/s00224-015-9653-1

[32] D. Kroening and O. Strichman, *Decision Procedures: An Algorithmic Point of View*. Springer, 2008.

[33] D. Le Berre and A. Parrain, "The Sat4j library, release 2.2," *JSAT*, vol. 7, pp. 59–6, 01 2010.

[34] V. Liew, "A path paved by proof complexity towards verifying nonlinear integer arithmetic," Ph.D. dissertation, University of Washington, 2020.

[35] ——, "Ring Benchmarks," Aug. 2020. [Online]. Available: https://doi.org/10.5281/zenodo.3987457

[36] A. Mahzoon, D. Große, and R. Drechsler, "Polycleaner: Clean your polynomials before backward rewriting to verify million-gate multipliers," in *2018 IEEE/ACM International Conference on Computer-Aided Design (ICCAD)*, Nov 2018, pp. 1–8.

[37] ——, "Revsca: Using reverse engineering to bring light into backward rewriting for big and dirty multipliers," in *2019 56th ACM/IEEE Design Automation Conference (DAC)*, June 2019, pp. 1–6.

[38] F. Marić and P. Janičić, "Urbiva: Uniform reduction to bit-vector arithmetic," in *Automated Reasoning*, J. Giesl and R. Hähnle, Eds. Berlin, Heidelberg: Springer Berlin Heidelberg, 2010, pp. 346–352.

[39] J. P. Marques-Silva and K. A. Sakallah, "GRASP: A search algorithm for propositional satisfiability," *IEEE Transactions on Computers*, vol. 48, no. 5, pp. 506–521, May 1999, preliminary version in *ICCAD '96*.

[40] R. Martins, V. Manquinho, and I. Lynce, "Open-WBO: A modular MaxSAT solver,," in *Theory and Applications of Satisfiability Testing – SAT 2014*, C. Sinz and U. Egly, Eds. Cham: Springer International Publishing, 2014, pp. 438–445.

[41] R. Michel, A. Hubaux, V. Ganesh, and P. Heymans, "An SMT-based approach to automated configuration," in *SMT 2012. 10th International Workshop on Satisfiability Modulo Theories*, ser. EPiC Series in Computing, P. Fontaine and A. Goel, Eds., vol. 20. EasyChair, 2013, pp. 109–119. [Online]. Available: https://easychair.org/publications/paper/bKGs

[42] M. W. Moskewicz, C. F. Madigan, Y. Zhao, L. Zhang, and S. Malik, "Chaff: Engineering an efficient SAT solver," in *Proceedings of the 38th Design Automation Conference (DAC '01)*, Jun. 2001, pp. 530–535.

[43] A. Niemetz, M. Preiner, and A. Biere, "Boolector 2.0 system description," *Journal on Satisfiability, Boolean Modeling and Computation*, vol. 9, pp. 53–58, 2014 (published 2015).

[44] D. Ritirc, A. Biere, and M. Kauers, "Column-wise verification of multipliers using computer algebra," in *Formal Methods in Computer-Aided Design, FMCAD 2017, Vienna, Austria, October 02-06, 2017.*, D. Stewart and G. Weissenbacher, Eds. IEEE, 2017, pp. 23–30.

[45] ——, "Improving and extending the algebraic approach for verifying gate-level multiplies," in *Design, Automation and Test in Europe (DATE'18)*, 2018.

[46] J. A. Robinson, "A machine-oriented logic based on the resolution principle," *Journal of the ACM*, vol. 12, no. 1, pp. 23–41, Jan. 1965.

[47] A. Romano and D. Engler, "Expression reduction from programs in a symbolic binary executor," in *Model Checking Software*, E. Bartocci and C. R. Ramakrishnan, Eds. Berlin, Heidelberg: Springer Berlin Heidelberg, 2013, pp. 301–319.

[48] "RoundingSat," https://gitlab.com/miao_research/roundingsat.

[49] M. Sakai and H. Nabeshima, "Construction of an ROBDD for a PB-constraint in band form and related techniques for PB-solvers," *IEICE Transactions on Information and Systems*, vol. E98.D, no. 6, pp. 1121–1127, 2015.

[50] A. A. R. Sayed-Ahmed, D. Große, U. Kühne, M. Soeken, and R. Drechsler, "Formal verification of integer multipliers by combining Gröbner basis with logic reduction," in *2016 Design, Automation & Test in Europe Conference & Exhibition, DATE 2016*, Dresden, Germany, March 2016, pp. 1048–1053. [Online]. Available: http://ieeexplore.ieee.org/xpl/freeabs_all.jsp?arnumber=7459464

[51] M. Temel, A. Slobodová, and W. A. Hunt, "Automated and scalable verification of integer multipliers," in *Computer Aided Verification - 32nd International Conference, CAV 2020, Los Angeles, CA, USA, July 21-24, 2020, Proceedings, Part I*, ser. Lecture Notes in Computer Science, vol. 12224. Springer, 2020, pp. 485–507. [Online]. Available: https://doi.org/10.1007/978-3-030-53288-8_23

[52] A. Urquhart, "Hard examples for resolution," *J. ACM*, vol. 34, no. 1, p. 209–219, Jan. 1987. [Online]. Available: https://doi.org/10.1145/7531.8928

[53] M. Vinyals, J. Elffers, J. Giráldez-Cru, S. Gocht, and J. Nordström, "In between resolution and cutting planes: A study of proof systems for pseudo-Boolean SAT solving," in *Theory and Applications of Satisfiability Testing – SAT 2018*, O. Beyersdorff and C. M. Wintersteiger, Eds. Cham: Springer International Publishing, 2018, pp. 292–310.

[54] C. Yu, M. Ciesielski, and A. Mishchenko, "Fast algebraic rewriting based on and-inverter graphs," *IEEE Transactions on Computer-Aided Design of Integrated Circuits and Systems*, vol. 37, no. 9, pp. 1907–1911, Sep. 2018.

11

ART: Abstraction Refinement-Guided Training for Provably Correct Neural Networks

Xuankang Lin*, He Zhu†, Roopsha Samanta* and Suresh Jagannathan*

*Purdue University, West Lafayette, IN 47907

†Rutgers University, Piscataway, NJ 08854

Abstract—**Artificial Neural Networks (ANNs) have demonstrated remarkable utility in various challenging machine learning applications. While formally verified properties of their behaviors are highly desired, they have proven notoriously difficult to derive and enforce. Existing approaches typically formulate this problem as a *post facto* analysis process. In this paper, we present a novel learning framework that ensures such formal guarantees are *enforced by construction*. Our technique enables training provably correct networks with respect to a broad class of safety properties, a capability that goes well-beyond existing approaches, *without* compromising much accuracy. Our key insight is that we can integrate an optimization-based abstraction refinement loop into the learning process and operate over dynamically constructed partitions of the input space that considers accuracy and safety objectives synergistically. The refinement procedure iteratively splits the input space from which training data is drawn, guided by the efficacy with which such partitions enable safety verification. We have implemented our approach in a tool (ART) and applied it to enforce general safety properties on unmanned aviator collision avoidance system ACAS Xu dataset and the Collision Detection dataset. Importantly, we empirically demonstrate that realizing safety does not come at the price of much accuracy. Our methodology demonstrates that an abstraction refinement methodology provides a meaningful pathway for building both accurate and correct machine learning networks.**

I. INTRODUCTION

Artificial neural networks (ANNs) have emerged in recent years as the primary computational structure for implementing many challenging machine learning applications. Their success has been due in large measure to their sophisticated architecture, typically comprised of multiple layers of connected neurons (or *activation functions*), in which each neuron represents a possibly non-linear function over the inputs generated in a previous layer. In a supervised setting, the goal of learning is to identify the proper coefficients (i.e., *weights*) of these functions that minimize differences between the outputs generated by the network and ground truth, established via training samples. The ability of ANNs to identify fine-grained distinctions among their inputs through the execution of this process makes them particularly useful in a variety of diverse domains such as classification, image recognition, natural language translation, or autonomous driving.

However, the most *accurate* ANNs may still be *incorrect*. Consider, for instance, the ACAS Xu (Airborne Collision Avoidance System) application that targets avoidance of midair collisions between commercial aircraft [1], whose system is controlled by a series of ANNs to produce horizontal

maneuver advisories. One example *safety property* states that if a potential intruder is far away and is significantly slower than one's own vehicle, then regardless of the intruder's and subject's direction, the ANN controller should output a Clear-of-Con ict advisory (as it is unlikely that the intruder can collide with the subject). Unfortunately, even a sophisticated ANN handler used in the ACAS Xu system, although well-trained, has been shown to violate this property [2]. Thus, ensuring the reliability of ANNs, especially those adopted in safety-critical applications, is increasingly viewed as a necessity.

The programming languages and formal methods community has responded to this familiar, albeit challenging, problem with increasingly sophisticated and scalable *veri cation* approaches [2]–[5] — given a trained ANN and a property, these approaches either certify that the ANN satisfies the property or identify a potential violation of the property. Unfortunately, when verification fails, these approaches provide no insight on how to effectively leverage verification counterexamples to *repair* complex, uninterpretable networks and ensure safety. Further, many verification approaches focus on a popular, but ultimately, narrow class of properties — *local robustness* — expressed over *some, but not all* of a network's input space.

In this paper, we address the limitations of existing verification approaches by proposing a novel *training* approach for *generation of ANNs that are correct-by-construction with respect to a broad class of correctness properties expressed over the network s inputs*. Our training approach integrates correctness properties into the training objective through a *correctness loss function* that quantifies the violation of the correctness properties. Further, to enable certification of correctness of a possibly infinite set of network behaviors, our training approach employs abstract interpretation methods [4], [6] to generate sound abstractions of both the *input space* and the *network itself*. Finally, to ensure the trained network is both correct *and* accurate with respect to training data, our approach iteratively refines the precision of the input abstraction, guided by the value of the correctness loss function. Our approach is sound — if the correctness loss reduces to 0, the generated ANN is guaranteed to satisfy the associated correctness properties.

The work ow of this overall approach — Abstraction Refinement-guided Training (ART) — is shown in Fig. 1. ART takes as input a correctness property (in out) that prescribes desired network output behavior using logic constraints

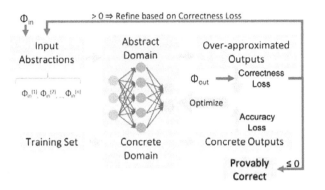

Fig. 1: The ART framework.

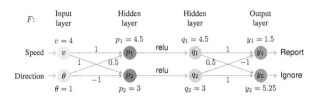

Fig. 2: A monitoring system using 2-layer ReLU network.

Φ_{out} when the inputs to the network are within a domain described by Φ_{in}. ART is parameterized by an abstract domain $\mathcal{D}$ that yields an abstraction over inputs in Φ_{in}. Additionally, ART takes a set of labeled training data. The correctness loss function quantifies the *distance* of the abstract network output from the correctness constraint Φ_{out}. In each training iteration, ART both updates the network weights and refines the input abstraction. The network weights are updated using classical gradient descent optimization to mitigate the correctness loss (upper loop of Fig. 1) and the standard accuracy loss (lower loop of Fig. 1). The abstraction refinement utilizes information provided by the correctness loss to improve the precision of the abstract network output (the top arrow of Fig. 1). As we show in Section V, the key novelty of our approach - exploiting the synergy between refinement and approximation - (a) often leads to, at worst, *mild* impact on accuracy compared to a safe oracle baseline; and (b) provides significantly higher assurance on network correctness than existing verification or training [7] methods which do not exploit abstraction refinement.

This paper makes the following contributions. (1) We present an abstract interpretation-guided training strategy for building correct-by-construction neural networks, defined with respect to a rich class of safety properties, including functional correctness properties that relate input and output structure. (2) We define an input space abstraction refinement loop that reduces training on input data to training on input space partitions, where the precision of the abstraction is, in turn, guided by a notion of correctness loss as determined by the correctness property. (3) We formalize soundness claims that capture correctness guarantees provided by our methodology; these results characterize the ability of our approach to ensure correctness with respect to domain-specific correctness properties. (4) We have implemented our ideas in a tool (ART) and applied it to challenging benchmarks including the ACAS Xu collision avoidance dataset [1], [2] and the Collision Detection dataset [8]. We provide a detailed evaluation study quantifying the effectiveness of our approach and assess its utility to ensure correctness guarantees without compromising accuracy. We additionally provide a comparison of our approach with *post facto* counterexample-guided verification strategies to demonstrate the benefits of ART's methodology compared to

such techniques.

The remainder of the paper is organized as follows. In the next section, we provide a detailed motivating example that illustrates our approach. Section III provides background and Section IV formalizes our approach. Details about ART's implementation and evaluation are provided in Section V. Related work and conclusions are presented in Section VI and VII, resp.

II. ILLUSTRATIVE EXAMPLE

We illustrate and motivate the key components of our approach by starting with a realistic, albeit simple, end-to-end example. We consider the construction of a learning-enabled system for autonomous driving. The learning objective is to identify potentially dangerous objects within a prescribed range of the vehicle's current position.

Problem Setup. For the purpose of this example, we simplify our scenario by assuming that we track only a single object and that the information given by the vehicle's radar is a feature vector of size two, containing (a) the object's normalized relative speed $v \in [-5, 5]$ where the positive values mean that the objects are getting closer; and (b) the object's relative angular position $\theta \in [-\pi, \pi]$ in a polar coordinate system with our vehicle located in the center. Either action **Report** or action **Ignore** is advised by the system for this object given the information.

Consider an implementation of an ANN for this problem that uses a 2-layer ReLU neural network F with initialized weights as depicted in Fig. 2. The network takes an input vector $x = (v, \theta)$ and outputs a prediction score vector $y = (y_1, y_2)$ for actions **Report** and **Ignore**, respectively. The action with higher prediction score is picked by the advisory system. For simplicity, both layers in F are linear layers with 2 neurons and without bias terms. An element-wise ReLU activation function $relu(x) = \max(x, 0)$ is applied after the first layer.

Correctness Property. To serve as a useful advisory system, we can ascribe some correctness properties that we would like the network to always satisfy. While our approach generalizes to an arbitrary number of the correctness properties that one may wish to enforce, we focus on one such correctness property Φ in this example: *Objects in front of the vehicle that are stationary or moving closer should not be ignored.* The meaning of "*stationary or moving closer*" and "*in front of*" can be interpreted in terms of predicates Φ_{in} and Φ_{out} over feature vector components such as $v \geq 0$ and $\theta \leq [0.5\ 2.5]^1$, respectively. Using such representations and recalling that $v \in [-5\ 5]$, $\phi = (\phi_{in}, \phi_{out})$ can be precisely formulated as:

$$\phi: \underbrace{v \geq -v \wedge \theta \geq [0.5] \wedge \theta \leq [0.5\ 2.5]}_{\Phi_{in}} \implies y = F(v, \theta) \implies \underbrace{y_1 > y_2}_{\Phi_{out}}$$

Observe that this property is violated with the network and the example input shown in Fig. 2.

Concrete Correctness Loss Function. To quantify how *correct* F is on inputs satisfying predicate ϕ_{in}, we define a *correctness loss function*, denoted $dist_g$, over the output y of the neural network and the output predicate ϕ_{out}:

$$dist_g(y, \phi_{out}) = \min_{q \models \Phi_{out}} g(y, q)$$

parameterized on a distance function g over the input space such as the Manhattan distance (L_1-norm), Euclidean distance ($Euclid$-norm), etc. The correctness distance function is intentionally defined to be semantically meaningful—when $dist_g(y, \phi_{out}) = 0$, it follows that y satisfies the output predicate ϕ_{out}. This function can then be used as a loss function, among other training objectives to train the neural network towards satisfying (ϕ_{in}, ϕ_{out}). For this example, we can compute the correctness distance of the network output $y = (y_1, y_2)$ from $\phi_{out} = y_1 > y_2$ to be $dist_{Euclid}(y, \phi_{out}) = \max\left((y_2 - y_1), \frac{1}{\sqrt{2}}, 0\right)$ which is calculated based on the Euclidean distance between point (y_1, y_2) and line $y_2 - y_1 = 0$.

Abstract Domain. A general correctness property like ϕ is often defined over an infinite set of data points; however, since training necessarily is performed using only a finite set of samples, we cannot generalize observations made on just these samples to assert the validity of ϕ on the trained network. Our approach, therefore, leverages abstract interpretation techniques to generate sound abstractions of both the network input space and the network itself. By training on these abstractions, our method obtains a finite approximation of the infinite set of possible network behaviors, enabling correct-by-construction training.

We parameterize our approach on any abstract domain that serves as a sound over-approximation of a neural network's behavior, i.e., abstractions in which an abstract output is guaranteed to subsume all possible outputs for the set of abstract inputs. In the example, we consider the *interval* abstract domain $\mathcal{I}$ that is simple enough to motivate the core ideas of our approach. We note that ART is not bound to specific abstract domains, the interval domain is used only for illustrative purposes here, our experiments in Section V are conducted using more precise abstractions.

An interval abstraction of our 2-layer ReLU network, denoted $F_{\mathcal{I}}$, is shown in Fig. 3. The concrete neural network

---

^{1}We pick $[0.5, 2.5]$ because it is slightly wider than the front view angle of $[\frac{\pi}{4}, \frac{3\pi}{4}]$.

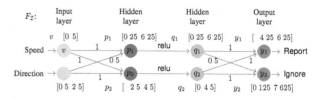

Fig. 3: The 2-layer ReLU network over interval domain.

computation F is abstracted by maintaining the lower and upper bounds $[\underline{u}, \overline{u}]$ of each neuron u. For neuron p_2 in this example, following interval arithmetic [9], the lower bound of neuron is computed by $\underline{p_2} = 1 \cdot \underline{v} + (-1) \cdot \overline{\theta} = -2.5$ and the upper bound $\overline{p_2} = 1 \cdot \overline{v} + (-1) \cdot \underline{\theta} = 4.5$. For ReLU activation function, $F_{\mathcal{I}}$ resets negative lower bounds to 0 and preserves everything else. Consider neurons p_2, q_2, lower bound $\underline{q_2}$ is reset to 0 while its upper bound $\overline{q_2}$ remains unchanged. In this way, $F_{\mathcal{I}}$ soundly over-approximates all possible outputs generated by the network given any inputs satisfying ϕ_{in}. Applying $F_{\mathcal{I}}$, the neural network's *abstract output* is $y_1 \in [-4.25\ 6.25]$ and $y_2 \in [0.125\ 7.625]$, which fails to show that $y_1 > y_2$ always holds. As a counterexample depicted in Fig. 2, the input $v = 4, \theta = 1$ leads to violation.

Abstract Correctness Loss Function. Given ϕ_{in}, to quantify how correct F is based on the abstract output $y^{\#}$, we can also define an abstract correctness loss function, denoted L_g, over $y^{\#}$ and the output predicate ϕ_{out}:

$$L_g(y^{\#}, \phi_{out}) = \max_{y \in \gamma(y^{\#})} dist_g(y, \phi_{out})$$

where $\gamma(y^{\#})$ maps $y^{\#}$ to the set of values it represents in the concrete domain and g is a distance function over the input space as before. In our example, $L_{Euclid}(y^{\#}, \phi_{out}) = \max\left((\overline{y_2} - \underline{y_1}), \frac{1}{\sqrt{2}}, 0\right) = 11.875\sqrt{2}$.

Measuring the worst-case distance of possible outputs to ϕ_{out}, L_g is also semantically meaningful — when $L_g(y^{\#}, \phi_{out}) = 0$, it follows that all possible values represented by $y^{\#}$ satisfy the output predicate ϕ_{out}. In other words, the trained neural network F is certified safe w.r.t. the correctness property ϕ.

L_g can be leveraged as the objective function during optimization. The min and max units in L_g can be implemented using MaxPooling and MinPooling units, and hence is differentiable. Then we can use off-the-shelf automatic differentiation libraries [10] in the usual fashion to derive and backpropagate the gradients and readjust F's weights towards minimizing L_g.

Input Space Abstraction Refinement. The abstract correctness loss function L_g provides a direction for neural network weight optimization. However, L_g could be overly imprecise since the amount of spurious cases introduced by the neural network abstraction is correlated with the size of the abstract input *region*. This kind of imprecision leads to sub-optimal optimization, ultimately hurting the feasibility of correct-by-construction as well as the model accuracy.

Such imprecision arises easily when using less precise abstract domains like the interval domain. For our running example, by bisecting the input space along each dimension, the resulting abstract correctness loss values of each region range from $3\,125\sqrt{2}$ to $9\,125\sqrt{2}$. If the original abstract correctness loss $11\,875\sqrt{2}$ pertains to a real input, it should be reflected in some sub-region as well. Now that $9\,125\sqrt{2} < 11\,875\sqrt{2}$, the original abstract correctness loss must be spurious and thus suboptimal for optimization.

To use more accurate gradients for network weight optimization, our approach leverages the above observation to also iteratively partition the input region Φ_{in} during training. In other words, we seek for an input space abstraction refinement mechanism that reduces imprecise abstract correctness loss introduced by abstract interpretation. Notably, incorporating input space abstraction refinement with the gradient descent optimizer does not compromise the soundness of our approach. As long as all sub-regions of Φ_{in} are provably correct, the network's correctness with respect to Φ_{in} trivially holds.

Iterative Training. Our training algorithm interweaves input space abstraction refinement and gradient descent training on a network abstraction in each training iteration by leveraging the correctness loss function produced by the network abstract interpreter (as depicted in Fig. 1), until a provably correct ANN is trained. The refined input abstractions computed in an iteration are used for training over the abstract domain in the next iteration.

For our illustrative example, we set the learning rate of the optimizer to be $0\,01$. In our experiment, the maximum correctness loss among all refined input space abstractions drops to 0 after 11 iterations. Convergence was achieved by heuristically partitioning the input space Φ_{in} into 76 regions. The trained ANN is guaranteed to satisfy the correctness property $(\Phi_{in} \Rightarrow \Phi_{out})$.

III. BACKGROUND

Definition III.1 (Neural network). Neural networks are functions $F : \mathbb{R}^d \to \mathbb{R}^e$ composed of Q layers and $Q-1$ activation functions. Each layer is a function $f_k(\cdot) : \mathbb{R}^{m_{k-1}} \to \mathbb{R}^{m_k}$ for $k = 1 \dots Q$ where $m_0 = d$ and $m_Q = e$. Each activation function is of the form $\sigma_k(\cdot) : \mathbb{R}^{m_k} \to \mathbb{R}^{m_k}$ for $k = 1 \dots Q-1$. Then, $F = f_Q \circ \sigma_{Q-1} \circ f_{Q-1} \circ \dots \circ \sigma_1 \circ f_1$.

Definition III.2 (Abstraction). An abstraction $\mathcal{D}$ is defined as a tuple: $\langle \mathcal{D}_c, \mathcal{D}_a, \alpha, \gamma, T \rangle$ where

- $\mathcal{D}_c : \{x \mid x \in \mathbb{R}^d\}$ and where $d \in \mathbb{Z}^+$ is the concrete domain;
- $\mathcal{D}_a$ is the abstract domain of interest;
- $\alpha(\cdot)$ is an *abstraction* function that maps a set of concrete elements to an abstract element;
- $\gamma(\cdot)$ is a *concretization* function that maps an abstract element to a set of concrete elements;

- $T = \{(T_c, T_a) \mid T_c(\cdot) : \mathcal{D}_c \to \mathcal{D}_c, T_a(\cdot) : \mathcal{D}_a \to \mathcal{D}_a\}$ is a set of transformer pairs over $\mathcal{D}_c$ and $\mathcal{D}_a$.

An abstraction is sound if for all $S \subseteq \mathcal{D}_c$, $S \subseteq \gamma(\alpha(S))$ holds and given $(T_c, T_a) \in T$,

$$\forall c \in \mathcal{D}_c, a \in \mathcal{D}_a, c \in \gamma(a) \implies T_c(c) \in \gamma(T_a(a))$$

Definition III.3 ($\mathcal{D}$-compatible). Given a sound abstraction $\mathcal{D} = \langle \mathcal{D}_c, \mathcal{D}_a, \alpha, \gamma, T \rangle$, a neural network F is $\mathcal{D}$-compatible iff for every layer or activation function $\phi(\cdot)$ in F, there exists an abstract transformer T_a such that $(\phi(\cdot), T_a) \in T$, and T_a is differentiable at least almost everywhere.

For a $\mathcal{D}$-compatible neural network F, we denote by $F_{\mathcal{D}} : \mathcal{D}_a \to \mathcal{D}_a$ the over-approximation of F where every layer $f_k(\cdot)$ and activation function $\sigma_k(\cdot)$ in F are replaced in $F_{\mathcal{D}}$ by their corresponding abstract transformers in $\mathcal{D}$.

Although our approach is parametric over abstract domains, we do require every abstract transformer T_a associated with these domains to be differentiable, so as to enable training using the worst cases over-approximated over $\mathcal{D}$ via gradient-descent style optimization algorithms.

To reason about a neural network over an abstraction $\mathcal{D}$, we need to first characterize what it means for an ANN to operate over $\mathcal{D}$.

Definition III.4 (Evaluation over Abstract Domain). Given a $\mathcal{D}$-compatible neural network F, the evaluation of F over $\mathcal{D}$ and a range of inputs $X \in \mathcal{D}_a$ is $F_{\mathcal{D}}(X)$ where $F_{\mathcal{D}}(X)$ over-approximates all possible outputs in the concrete domain corresponding to any input covered by X.

Theorem III.1 (Over-approximation Soundness). *For sound abstraction $\mathcal{D}$, given a $\mathcal{D}$-compatible neural network F, a range of inputs $X \in \mathcal{D}_a$,*

$$\forall x, x \in \gamma(X) \implies F(x) \in \gamma(F_{\mathcal{D}}(X))$$

Proofs of all theorems are provided in the supplemental material [11].

IV. CORRECT-BY-CONSTRUCTION TRAINING

Our approach aims to train an ANN F with respect to a *correctness property* Φ, which is formally defined in Section IV-A. The abstraction of F w.r.t. Φ based on abstract domain $\mathcal{D}$ essentially can be seen as a function parameterized over the weights of F, which can nonetheless be trained to fit Φ using standard optimization algorithms. Section IV-B formally defines the abstract *correctness loss* function $L_{\mathcal{D}}$ to guide the optimization of F's weights over $\mathcal{D}$. Such an abstraction inevitably introduces spurious data samples into training due to over-approximation. Section IV-C introduces the idea of *input space abstraction and refinement* as a mechanism that can reduce such spuriousness during optimization over $\mathcal{D}$. The detailed pseudocode of ART algorithm, including the refinement procedure, is presented in Section IV-D.

A. Correctness Property

The correctness properties we consider are expressed as logical propositions over the network's inputs and outputs. We assume that an ANN correctness property expresses constraints on the outputs, given assumptions on the inputs.

Definition IV.1 (Correctness Property). Given a neural network $F : \mathbb{R}^d \to \mathbb{R}^e$, a correctness property $\varphi = (\varphi_{in}, \varphi_{out})$ is a tuple in which φ_{in} defines a bounded input domain over $\mathbb{R}^d$ in the form of an interval $[\underline{x}, \overline{x}]$ where $\underline{x}, \overline{x} \in \mathbb{R}^d$, are lower, upper bounds, resp., on the network input; and φ_{out} is a quantifier-free Boolean combination of linear inequalities over the network output vector $y \in \mathbb{R}^e$:

$$\varphi_{out} ::= P \mid \neg P \mid P \wedge P \mid P \vee P ;$$

$$P ::= A\, y \leq b \text{ where } A \in \mathbb{R}^e, b \in \mathbb{R};$$

An input vector $x \in \mathbb{R}^d$ is said to satisfy $\varphi_{in} = [\underline{x}, \overline{x}]$, denoted $x \models \varphi_{in}$, iff $\underline{x} \leq x \leq \overline{x}$. An output vector $y \in \mathbb{R}^e$ satisfies φ_{out}, denoted $y \models \varphi_{out}$, iff $\varphi_{out}(y)$ is true. A neural network $F : \mathbb{R}^d \to \mathbb{R}^e$ satisfies φ, denoted $F \models \varphi$, iff $\forall x . x \models \varphi_{in} \Rightarrow F(x) \models \varphi_{out}$.

Definition IV.2 (Concrete Correctness Loss Function). For an atomic output predicate P, the concrete correctness loss function, $dist_g(y, P)$, quantifies the *distance* from an output vector $y \in \mathbb{R}^e$ to P:

$$dist_g(y, P) = \min_{q \models P} g(y, q)$$

where $g : \mathbb{R}^d \times \mathbb{R}^d \to \mathbb{Z}^{\geq 0}$ is a differentiable distance function over the inputs. Similarly, $dist_g(y, \varphi_{out})$, the "*distance*" from an output vector $y \in \mathbb{R}^e$ to general output predicate φ_{out}, can be computed efficiently by induction as long as $g(\cdot)$ can be computed efficiently:

- $dist_g(y, P)$ and $dist_g(y, \neg P)$ can be computed using basic arithmetic;
- $dist_g(y, P_1 \wedge P_2) = \max(dist_g(y, P_1), dist_g(y, P_2))$;
- $dist_g(y, P_1 \vee P_2) = \min(dist_g(y, P_1), dist_g(y, P_2))$.

Note that $dist_g(y, \varphi_{out})$ may not represent the minimum distance for arbitrary φ_{out}, but it is efficient to compute while still retaining the following soundness theorem.

Theorem IV.1 (Zero Concrete Correctness Loss Soundness). *Given output predicate φ_{out} over $\mathbb{R}^e$ and output vector $y \in \mathbb{R}^e$,*

$$dist_g(y, \varphi_{out}) = 0 \iff y \models \varphi_{out}$$

B. Over-approximation

To reason about correctness properties defined over an infinite set of data points, our approach generates sound abstractions of both the network input space and the network itself, obtaining a finite approximation of the infinite set of possible network behaviors. We start by quantifying the abstract correctness loss of over-approximated outputs.

Definition IV.3 (Abstract Correctness Loss Function). Given a sound abstraction $\mathcal{D} = \langle \mathcal{D}_c, \mathcal{D}_a, T \rangle$, a $\mathcal{D}$-compatible neural network F, and a correctness property $\varphi = (\varphi_{in}, \varphi_{out})$, the abstract correctness loss function is defined as:

$$L_{\mathcal{D},g}(F, \varphi) = \max_{p \in \gamma(Y_\mathcal{D})} dist_g(p, \varphi_{out})$$

$$\text{where } Y_\mathcal{D} = F_\mathcal{D}(\alpha(\varphi_{in}))$$

Here $g : \mathbb{R}^d \times \mathbb{R}^d \to \mathbb{Z}^{\geq 0}$ is a differentiable distance function over concrete inputs as before.

The abstract correctness loss function measures the worst-case distance to φ_{out} of any neural network outputs subsumed by the abstract network output. It is designed to extend the notion of concrete correctness loss to the abstract domain with a similar soundness guarantee, as formulated in the following theorem.

Theorem IV.2 (Zero Abstract Correctness Loss Soundness). *Given a sound abstraction $\mathcal{D}$, a $\mathcal{D}$-compatible neural network F, and a correctness property φ,*

$$L_{\mathcal{D},g}(F, \varphi) = 0 \iff F \models \varphi$$

In what follows, we fix the distance function g over concrete inputs and denote the abstract correctness loss function simply as $L_\mathcal{D}$.

C. Abstraction Refinement

Recall that in Section II we illustrated how imprecision in the correctness loss for a coarse abstraction can be mitigated using an input space abstraction refinement mechanism. Our notion of refinement is formally defined below.

Definition IV.4 (Input Space Abstraction). An input space abstraction S refines a correctness property $\varphi = (\varphi_{in}, \varphi_{out})$ into a set of correctness properties $S = \left\{ (\varphi_{in}^i, \varphi_{out}) \right\}$ such that $\varphi_{in} = \bigcup_i \varphi_{in}^i$. Given a neural network F and an input space abstraction S, $F \models S \iff \bigwedge_{\Phi \in S} F \models \varphi$.

Definition IV.5 (Input Space Abstraction Refinement). A well-founded abstraction refinement $\hookrightarrow$ is a binary relation over a set of input abstractions $\mathcal{S} = S_1 \times S_2$ such that:

- (reflexivity): $\forall S_i \in \mathcal{S}, S_i \hookrightarrow S_i$;
- (refinement): $\forall S_i \hookrightarrow S \in \mathcal{S}$ and correctness property $(\varphi_{in}, \varphi_{out})$,

$$\left(\varphi_{in} = \bigcup_{(\Phi_{in}^j, \_) \in S_i} \varphi_{in}^j \right) \wedge \left(\bigwedge_{(\_, \Phi_{out}^j) \in S_i} \varphi_{out}^j \Rightarrow \varphi_{out} \right)$$
$$\Rightarrow S_i \models (\varphi_{in}, \varphi_{out}) ;$$

- (transitivity): $\forall S_1 \hookrightarrow S_2 \hookrightarrow S_3 \in \mathcal{S}, S_1 \hookrightarrow S_2 \wedge S_2 \hookrightarrow S_3 \Rightarrow S_1 \hookrightarrow S_3$;
- (composition): $\forall S_1, S_2, S_3, S_4 \in \mathcal{S}, S_1 \hookrightarrow S_3 \wedge S_2 \hookrightarrow S_4 \Rightarrow S_1 \cup S_2 \hookrightarrow S_3 \cup S_4$.

The *reflexivity*, *transitivity*, and *compositional* requirements for a well-founded refinement are natural. The *refinement* rule states that an input space abstraction S refines some correctness property $(\varphi_{in}, \varphi_{out})$ if the union of all input domains in S is equivalent to φ_{in} and all output predicates in

S are logically equivalent to Ψ_{out}. This rule enables Ψ_{in} to be safely decomposed into a set of sub-domains. As a result, the problem of enforcing coarse-grained correctness properties on neural networks can be converted into one that enforces multiple fine-grained properties, an easier problem to tackle because much of the imprecision introduced by the coarse-grained abstraction can now be eliminated.

Theorem IV.3 (Sufficient Condition via Refinement).

$$F \vDash S_1 \wedge S_2 \wedge S_1 \wedge S_2 \wedge F \models S_1 \Longrightarrow F \models S_2$$

To do this, we naturally extend the notion of abstract correctness loss over one property to an input space abstraction.

Definition IV.6 (Abstract Correctness Loss Function for Input Space Abstraction). Given a sound abstraction $\mathcal{D}$, $\mathcal{D}$-compatible neural network F, and input space abstraction S, the *abstract correctness loss* of F with respect to S is denoted by[2]

$$L_{\mathcal{D}}(F \vDash S) = \sum_{\Phi \in S} L_{\mathcal{D}}(F \vDash \Phi)$$

Theorem IV.4 (Zero Abstract Correctness Loss for Input Space Abstraction). *Given a sound abstraction $\mathcal{D}$, a $\mathcal{D}$-compatible neural network F, and an input space abstraction S,*

$$L_{\mathcal{D}}(F \vDash S) = 0 \Longrightarrow F \models S$$

D. The ART Algorithm

The goal of our ANN training algorithm, given in Fig. 4, is to optimize the network to have $L_{\mathcal{D}}(F \vDash S)$ reduce to 0, thereby ensuring a correct-by-construction network. The algorithm takes as input both an initial input space abstraction S and a set of labeled training data $\{(x_{\text{train}}, y_{\text{label}})\}$ in order to achieve correctness while maintaining high accuracy on the trained model. The abstract correctness loss, denoted $\ell_{\mathcal{D}}$, is computed at Line 4 according to Def. IV.3 and checked correctness by comparing against 0. If $\ell_{\mathcal{D}} = 0$, as long as the accuracy loss, denoted $\ell_{\mathcal{A}}$, is also satisfactory, ART returns a correct and accurate network following Thm. IV.4.

The joint loss of $\ell_{\mathcal{D}}$ and $\ell_{\mathcal{A}}$ is used to guide the optimization of neural network parameters using standard gradient-descent algorithms. The requirement of abstract transformers being differentiable at least almost anywhere in Def. III.3 enables computation of gradients $\ell_{\mathcal{D}}$ using off-the-shelf automatic differentiation libraries [10].

Starting from Line 10, abstractions in S that have the largest $\ell_{\mathcal{D}}$ values represent the potentially most imprecise cases and thus are chosen for refinement. During refinement, ART first picks a dimension to refine using heuristic scores similar to [3]. The heuristic coarsely approximates the cumulative gradient over one dimension, with a larger score suggesting greater potential of decreasing correctness loss. The input abstraction is then bisected along the picked dimension as refinement.

---

[2]We can refine the definition to have positive weighted importance of each correctness property in S; ascribing different weights to different correctness properties does not affect soundness.

Fig. 4: ART correct-by-construction training algorithm.

Require: Abstract domain $\mathcal{D}$, $\mathcal{D}$-compatible neural network F, input space abstraction S, learning rate $\eta \in \mathbb{R}^+$, training data set $(x_{\text{train}}, y_{\text{label}})$, accuracy loss function $L_{\mathcal{A}}$, accuracy loss bound $\epsilon_{\mathcal{A}} \in \mathbb{R}^+$, hyper-parameter k.

Ensure: Return the optimized F whose correctness properties are enforced and accuracy loss bounded by $\epsilon_{\mathcal{A}}$.

```
1:  procedure ART
2:      W ← all weights in F to optimize
3:      while true do
4:          ℓ_D, ℓ_A ← L_D(F ⊨ S), L_A(F(x_train, y_label))
5:          if ℓ_D = 0 ∧ ℓ_A ≤ ε_A then
6:              return F
7:          end if
                                                        ▷ optimization
8:          F ← ∂(ℓ_D + ℓ_A)/∂W̃
9:          W ← W ∘ F
                                                        ▷ refinement
10:         T ← Subset of S with k largest ℓ_D values
11:         S' ← S \ T
12:         for all (Ψ_in^i, Ψ_out^i) ∈ T do
13:             for all Ψ_in^j ∈ REFINE(Ψ_in^i, ℓ_D) do
14:                 S' ← S' ∪ (Ψ_in^j, Ψ_out^i)
15:             end for
16:         end for
17:         S ← S'
18:     end while
19: end procedure

20: procedure REFINE(Ψ_in, ℓ_D)
21:     for all dimension i of Ψ_in do
22:         score_i = ∂ℓ_D/∂{Ψ_in}_i · Ψ_in^i
23:     end for
24:     dim ← arg max score_i          ▷ pick dimension
25:     Ψ_in^1, Ψ_in^2 ← Ψ_in bisected along dimension dim
26:     return { Ψ_in^1, Ψ_in^2 }
27: end procedure
```

Corollary 1 (ART Soundness). *Given a sound abstraction $\mathcal{D}$, a $\mathcal{D}$-compatible neural network F, and an initial input space abstraction S of correctness properties, if the ART algorithm in Fig. 4 generates a neural network F', $L_{\mathcal{D}}(F' \vDash S) = 0$ and $F' \models S$.*

V. Evaluation

We have performed an evaluation of our approach to validate the feasibility of building neural networks that are correct-by-construction over a range of correctness properties.[3] All experiments reported in this section were performed on a Ubuntu 16.04 system with 3.2GHz CPU and NVidia GTX 1080 Ti GPU with 11GB memory. All experiments uses the

---

[3]The code is available at https://github.com/XuankangLin/ART.

DeepPoly abstract domain [12] implemented on Python 3.7 and PyTorch 1.4 [10].

A. ACAS Xu Dataset

Our first evaluation study centers around the network architecture and correctness properties described in the Airborne Collision Avoidance System for Unmanned Aircraft (ACAS Xu) dataset [1], [2]. A family of 45 neural networks are used in the avoidance system; each of these networks consists of 6 hidden layers with 50 neurons in each hidden layer. ReLU activation functions are applied to all hidden layer neurons. All 45 networks take a feature vector of size 5 as input that encodes various aspects of an airborne environment. The outputs of the networks are prediction scores over 5 advisory actions to select the advisory action.

In the evaluation, we reason about sophisticated correctness conditions of the ACAS Xu system in terms of its aggregated ability to preserve up to 10 correctness properties [2] among all 45 networks. Each network is supposed to satisfy some subset of these 10 properties. All correctness properties can be formulated in terms of input (ϕ_{in}) and output (ϕ_{out}) predicates as in Section IV-A.

Setup. Among the 45 provided networks, 36 are reported with safety property violations and 9 are reported safe [2]. We evaluate ART on those 36 unsafe networks to demonstrate the effectiveness of generating correct-by-construction networks. The test sets from unsafe networks may contain unsafe points and are thus unauthentic, so we apply ART on those 9 already safe networks to demonstrate the accuracy overhead when enforcing the safety properties. Unfortunately, the training and test sets to build these ACAS Xu networks are not publicly available online. In spite of that, the ACAS Xu dataset provides the state space of input states that is used for training and over which the correctness properties are defined. We, therefore, uniformly sample a total of 10k training set and 5k test set data points from the state space. The labels are collected by evaluating each of the provided 45 networks on these sampled inputs, with those ACAS Xu networks serving as oracles. Each network is then trained by ART using its safety specification and the prepared training set, starting with the provided weights when available or otherwise randomly initialized weights. We record whether the trained network is correct-by-construction, as well as their accuracy evaluated on the prepared test set and the overall training time.

Applying ART. During each training epoch (i.e., each iteration of the outermost while loop in Fig. 4), our implementation refines up to $k = 200$ abstractions at a time that expose the largest correctness losses. Larger k leads to finer-grained abstractions but incurs more training cost. The Adam optimizer [13] is used in both training tasks and runs up to 100 epochs with learning rate 0.001 and a learning rate decay policy if the loss has been stable for some time. Cross entropy loss is used as the loss function for accuracy. For all experiments with refinement enabled, refinement operations are applied to

TABLE I: Applying ART to ACAS Xu Dataset.

	Refinement	Safe%	Min Accu.	Mean Accu.	Max Accu.
36 unsafe nets	Yes	**100%**	90.38%	96.10%	98.70%
	No	94.44%	87.88%	94.45%	98.22%
9 safe nets	Yes	**100%**	93.82%	96.25%	99.92%
	No	88.89%	86.32%	94.29%	99.92%

Fig. 5: Correctness rate and accuracy change of *post facto* training using sampled points or counterexamples. Results are normalized based on the baseline networks.

derive up to 5k refined input space abstractions before weight update starts. The detailed results are shown in Table I.

To demonstrate the importance of abstraction refinement mechanism, we also compare between the results with and without refinement (as done in existing work [6]). For completeness, we record the correct-by-construction enforced rate (**Safe%**) and the evaluated accuracy statistics for both tasks among multiple runs. Observe that ART successfully generates correct-by-construction networks for all scenarios with only minimal loss in accuracy. On the other hand, if refinement is disabled, it fails to generate correct-by-construction networks for all cases, and displays lower accuracy than the refinement-enabled instantiations. The average training time for each network is 69.39s if with refinement and 57.85s if without.

Comparison with post facto *training loop.* We also consider a comparison of our abstraction refinement-guided training for correct-by-construction networks against a *post facto* training loop that feed concrete correctness related data points to training loops. Such concrete points may be sampled from the provided specification or the collected counterexamples from an external solver. We show the results on 8 representative networks comparing to the same baseline in Figure 5. These 8 networks belong to a representative set of networks that cover all 10 provided safety properties.

For the experiment using sampled data points, 5k points sampled from correctness properties are used during training. For the experiment using counterexamples, all counterexamples from correctness queries to external verifier **ReluVal** [3] are collected and used during training. In both experiments, the points from original training set are used for jointly training to preserve accuracy and the correctness distance functions following that in Section IV-B are used as loss functions.

TABLE II: Applying ART to Collision Detection Dataset.

	Refinement	Enforced	Accuracy	Time
Original [8]	N/A	328/500	99.87%	N/A
ART	Yes	481/500	96.83%	583s
	No	420/500	86.3%	419s

We concluded the experiments using counterexamples after 20 epochs since no improvement was seen after this point. Both experiments fail to enforce correctness properties in most cases and they may impose great impact to model accuracy compared to the baseline network. We believe this result demonstrates the difficulty of applying a counterexample-guided training loop strategy for generating safe networks compared an abstraction-guided methodology.

B. Collision Detection Dataset

Our second evaluation task focuses on the Collision Detection Dataset [8] where a neural network controller is used to predict whether two vehicles running curve paths at different speeds would collide. The network takes as input a feature vector of size 6, containing the information of distances, speeds, and directions of the two vehicle. The network output prediction score are used to classify the scenario as a colliding or non-colliding case.

A total of 500 correctness properties are proposed in the Collision Detection dataset that identify the safety margins around particular data points. The network presented in the dataset respects 328 such properties. In our evaluation, we use a 3-layer fully-connected neural network controller with 50, 128, 50 neurons in different hidden layers. Using the same training configurations as in Section V-A and evaluating on the same training and test sets provided in the dataset, the results are shown in Table II. After 100 epochs, ART converged to a local minimum and managed to certify 481 out of all 500 safety properties. Although it did not achieve zero correctness loss, ART can produce a solution that satisfies significantly more correctness properties than the oracle neural network, at the cost of only a small accuracy drop.

VI. RELATED WORK

Neural Network Verication. Inspired by the success of applying program analysis to large software code bases, abstract interpretation-based techniques have been adapted to reason about ANNs by developing efficient abstract transformers that relax nonlinearity of activation functions into linear inequality constraints [4], [6]–[8], [12], [14], [15]. Similar approaches [16]–[19] encode nonlinearity via linear outer bounds of activation functions and may delegate the verification problem to SMT solvers [2], [20] or Mixed Integer Programming solvers [21]–[23]. Most of those verifiers focus on robustness properties only and do not support verifiable training of network-wide correctness properties. For example, [12] encodes concrete ANN operations into ELINA [24], a numeric abstract transformer, and therefore disables opportunities for training or optimization thereafter.

Correctness properties may also be retrofitted onto a trained neural network for safety concerns [25]–[28]. These approaches usually synthesize a reactive system that monitors the potentially controller network and corrects any potentially unsafe actions. Comparing to correct-by-construction methods, runtime overheads are inevitable for such *post facto* shielding techniques.

Correctness Properties in Neural Networks. There have been a large number of recent efforts that have explored verifying the *robustness* of networks against adversarial attacks [29]–[31]. Recent work has shown how symbolic reasoning approaches [3], [4] can be used to help validate network robustness; other efforts combine optimization techniques with symbolic reasoning to guide symbolic analysis [5]. Our approach looks at the problem of verification and certification from the perspective of general safety specifications that are typically richer than notions of robustness governing these other techniques and provide the correct-by-construction guarantee upon training termination. Encoding logical constraints other than robustness properties into loss functions has been explored in [32]–[35]. However, they operate only on concrete sample instances and do not provide any correct-by-construction guarantees.

Training over Abstract Domains. The closest approach to our setting is the work in [6], [36]. They introduced geometric abstractions that bound activations as they propagate through the network via abstract interpretation. Importantly, since these convex abstractions are differentiable, neural networks can optimize towards much tighter bounds to improve the verified accuracy. A simple bounding technique based on interval bound propagation was also exploited in [7] (similar to the interval domain from [6]) to train verifiably robust neural networks that even beat the state-of-the-art networks in image classification tasks, demonstrating that a correct-by-construction approach can indeed save the need of more expensive verification procedures in challenging domains. They did not, however, consider verification in the context of global safety properties as discussed here, in which the over-approximation error becomes non-negligible; nor did they formulate their approach to be parametric in the specific form of the abstractions chosen. Similar ideas have been exploited in provable defenses works [36]–[39], however, they apply best-effort adversarial defenses only and provide no guarantee upon training termination.

VII. CONCLUSIONS

This paper presents a correct-by-construction toolchain that can train neural networks with provable guarantees. The key idea is to optimize a neural network over the abstraction of both the input space and the network itself using abstraction refinement mechanisms. Experimental results show that our technique realizes trustworthy neural network systems for a variety of properties and benchmarks with only mild impact on model accuracy.

ACKNOWLEDGMENT

This work was supported by C-BRIC, one of six centers in JUMP, a Semiconductor Research Corporation (SRC) program sponsored by DARPA; NSF under award CCF-1846327; and NSF under Grant No. CCF-SHF 2007799.

REFERENCES

[1] K. D. Julian, J. Lopez, J. S. Brush, M. P. Owen, and M. J. Kochenderfer, "Policy compression for aircraft collision avoidance systems," in *2016 IEEE/AIAA 35th Digital Avionics Systems Conference (DASC)*, Sep. 2016, pp. 1–10.

[2] G. Katz, C. W. Barrett, D. L. Dill, K. Julian, and M. J. Kochenderfer, "Reluplex: An efficient SMT solver for verifying deep neural networks," in *Computer Aided Veri cation - 29th International Conference, CAV 2017, Heidelberg, Germany, July 24-28, 2017, Proceedings, Part I*, 2017, pp. 97–117. [Online]. Available: https://doi.org/10.1007/978-3-319-63387-9_5

[3] S. Wang, K. Pei, J. Whitehouse, J. Yang, and S. Jana, "Formal security analysis of neural networks using symbolic intervals," in *27th USENIX Security Symposium, USENIX Security 2018, Baltimore, MD, USA, August 15-17, 2018.*, 2018, pp. 1599–1614. [Online]. Available: https://www.usenix.org/conference/usenixsecurity18/presentation/wang-shiqi

[4] T. Gehr, M. Mirman, D. Drachsler-Cohen, P. Tsankov, S. Chaudhuri, and M. T. Vechev, "AI2: safety and robustness certification of neural networks with abstract interpretation," in *2018 IEEE Symposium on Security and Privacy, SP 2018, Proceedings, 21-23 May 2018, San Francisco, California, USA*, 2018, pp. 3–18. [Online]. Available: https://doi.org/10.1109/SP.2018.00058

[5] G. Anderson, S. Pailoor, I. Dillig, and S. Chaudhuri, "Optimization and abstraction: a synergistic approach for analyzing neural network robustness," in *Proceedings of the 40th ACM SIGPLAN Conference on Programming Language Design and Implementation, PLDI 2019, Phoenix, AZ, USA, June 22-26, 2019.*, 2019, pp. 731–744. [Online]. Available: https://doi.org/10.1145/3314221.3314614

[6] M. Mirman, T. Gehr, and M. T. Vechev, "Differentiable abstract interpretation for provably robust neural networks," in *Proceedings of the 35th International Conference on Machine Learning, ICML 2018, Stockholmsmässan, Stockholm, Sweden, July 10-15, 2018*, 2018, pp. 3575–3583. [Online]. Available: http://proceedings.mlr.press/v80/mirman18b.html

[7] S. Gowal, K. D. Dvijotham, R. Stanforth, R. Bunel, C. Qin, J. Uesato, R. Arandjelovic, T. Mann, and P. Kohli, "Scalable verified training for provably robust image classification," in *The IEEE International Conference on Computer Vision (ICCV)*, October 2019.

[8] R. Ehlers, "Formal verification of piece-wise linear feed-forward neural networks," in *Automated Technology for Veri cation and Analysis - 15th International Symposium, ATVA 2017, Pune, India, October 3-6, 2017, Proceedings*, 2017, pp. 269–286. [Online]. Available: https://doi.org/10.1007/978-3-319-68167-2_19

[9] R. E. Moore, R. B. Kearfott, and M. J. Cloud, *Introduction to Interval Analysis*. SIAM, 2009. [Online]. Available: https://doi.org/10.1137/1.9780898717716

[10] A. Paszke, S. Gross, F. Massa, A. Lerer, J. Bradbury, G. Chanan, T. Killeen, Z. Lin, N. Gimelshein, L. Antiga, A. Desmaison, A. Köpf, E. Yang, Z. DeVito, M. Raison, A. Tejani, S. Chilamkurthy, B. Steiner, L. Fang, J. Bai, and S. Chintala, "Pytorch: An imperative style, high-performance deep learning library," in *Advances in Neural Information Processing Systems 32: Annual Conference on Neural Information Processing Systems 2019, NeurIPS 2019, 8-14 December 2019, Vancouver, BC, Canada*, 2019, pp. 8024–8035. [Online]. Available: http://papers.nips.cc/paper/9015-pytorch-an-imperative-style-high-performance-deep-learning-library

[11] X. Lin, H. Zhu, R. Samanta, and S. Jagannathan, "ART: abstraction refinement-guided training for provably correct neural networks," *CoRR*, vol. abs/1907.10662, 2019. [Online]. Available: http://arxiv.org/abs/1907.10662

[12] G. Singh, T. Gehr, M. Püschel, and M. T. Vechev, "An Abstract Domain for Certifying Neural Networks," *PACMPL*, vol. 3, no. POPL, pp. 41:1–41:30, 2019. [Online]. Available: https://dl.acm.org/citation.cfm?id=3290354

[13] D. P. Kingma and J. Ba, "Adam: A method for stochastic optimization," in *3rd International Conference on Learning Representations, ICLR 2015, San Diego, CA, USA, May 7-9, 2015, Conference Track Proceedings*, 2015. [Online]. Available: http://arxiv.org/abs/1412.6980

[14] G. Singh, T. Gehr, M. Mirman, M. Püschel, and M. T. Vechev, "Fast and effective robustness certification," in *Advances in Neural Information Processing Systems 31: Annual Conference on Neural Information Processing Systems 2018, NeurIPS 2018, 3-8 December 2018, Montréal, Canada.*, 2018, pp. 10 825–10 836. [Online]. Available: http://papers.nips.cc/paper/8278-fast-and-effective-robustness-certification

[15] G. Singh, T. Gehr, M. Puschel, and M. Vechev, "Robustness certification with refinement," in *International Conference on Learning Representations*, 2019. [Online]. Available: https://openreview.net/forum?id=HJgeEh09KQ

[16] H. Zhang, T. Weng, P. Chen, C. Hsieh, and L. Daniel, "Efficient neural network robustness certification with general activation functions," in *Advances in Neural Information Processing Systems 31: Annual Conference on Neural Information Processing Systems 2018, NeurIPS 2018, 3-8 December 2018, Montréal, Canada.*, 2018, pp. 4944–4953. [Online]. Available: http://papers.nips.cc/paper/7742-efficient-neural-network-robustness-certification-with-general-activation-functions

[17] T. Weng, H. Zhang, H. Chen, Z. Song, C. Hsieh, L. Daniel, D. S. Boning, and I. S. Dhillon, "Towards fast computation of certified robustness for relu networks," in *Proceedings of the 35th International Conference on Machine Learning, ICML 2018, Stockholmsmässan, Stockholm, Sweden, July 10-15, 2018*, 2018, pp. 5273–5282. [Online]. Available: http://proceedings.mlr.press/v80/weng18a.html

[18] S. Wang, Y. Chen, A. Abdou, and S. Jana, "Mixtrain: Scalable training of formally robust neural networks," *CoRR*, vol. abs/1811.02625, 2018. [Online]. Available: http://arxiv.org/abs/1811.02625

[19] S. Wang, K. Pei, J. Whitehouse, J. Yang, and S. Jana, "Efficient formal safety analysis of neural networks," in *Advances in Neural Information Processing Systems 31: Annual Conference on Neural Information Processing Systems 2018, NeurIPS 2018, 3-8 December 2018, Montréal, Canada.*, 2018, pp. 6369–6379. [Online]. Available: http://papers.nips.cc/paper/7873-efficient-formal-safety-analysis-of-neural-networks

[20] G. Katz, D. A. Huang, D. Ibeling, K. Julian, C. Lazarus, R. Lim, P. Shah, S. Thakoor, H. Wu, A. Zeljic, D. L. Dill, M. J. Kochenderfer, and C. W. Barrett, "The marabou framework for verification and analysis of deep neural networks," in *Computer Aided Veri cation - 31st International Conference, CAV 2019, New York City, NY, USA, July 15-18, 2019, Proceedings, Part I*, 2019, pp. 443–452. [Online]. Available: https://doi.org/10.1007/978-3-030-25540-4_26

[21] C. Cheng, G. Nührenberg, and H. Ruess, "Maximum resilience of artificial neural networks," in *Automated Technology for Veri cation and Analysis - 15th International Symposium, ATVA 2017, Pune, India, October 3-6, 2017, Proceedings*, 2017, pp. 251–268. [Online]. Available: https://doi.org/10.1007/978-3-319-68167-2_18

[22] S. Dutta, S. Jha, S. Sankaranarayanan, and A. Tiwari, "Output range analysis for deep feedforward neural networks," in *NASA Formal Methods - 10th International Symposium, NFM 2018, Newport News, VA, USA, April 17-19, 2018, Proceedings*, 2018, pp. 121–138. [Online]. Available: https://doi.org/10.1007/978-3-319-77935-5_9

[23] V. Tjeng, K. Y. Xiao, and R. Tedrake, "Evaluating robustness of neural networks with mixed integer programming," in *International Conference on Learning Representations*, 2019. [Online]. Available: https://openreview.net/forum?id=HyGIdiRqtm

[24] G. Singh, M. Püschel, and M. T. Vechev, "Fast polyhedra abstract domain," in *Proceedings of the 44th ACM SIGPLAN Symposium on Principles of Programming Languages, POPL 2017, Paris, France, January 18-20, 2017*, 2017, pp. 46–59. [Online]. Available: http://dl.acm.org/citation.cfm?id=3009885

[25] H. Zhu, Z. Xiong, S. Magill, and S. Jagannathan, "An Inductive Synthesis Framework for Verifiable Reinforcement Learning," in *Proceedings of the 40th ACM SIGPLAN Conference on Programming Language Design and Implementation, PLDI 2019, Phoenix, AZ, USA, June 22-26, 2019*, 2019, pp. 686–701. [Online]. Available: https://doi.org/10.1145/3314221.3314638

[26] M. Alshiekh, R. Bloem, R. Ehlers, B. Könighofer, S. Niekum, and U. Topcu, "Safe Reinforcement Learning via Shielding," *AAAI*, 2018.

[27] R. Bloem, B. Könighofer, R. Könighofer, and C. Wang, "Shield synthesis: - runtime enforcement for reactive systems," in *Tools and Algorithms*

for the Construction and Analysis of Systems - 21st International Conference, TACAS 2015, 2015, pp. 533–548.

[28] C. Fan, U. Mathur, S. Mitra, and M. Viswanathan, "Controller synthesis made real: Reach-avoid specifications and linear dynamics," pp. 347–366, 2018.

[29] A. Madry, A. Makelov, L. Schmidt, D. Tsipras, and A. Vladu, "Towards Deep Learning Models Resistant to Adversarial Attacks," in *6th International Conference on Learning Representations, ICLR 2018, Vancouver, BC, Canada, April 30 - May 3, 2018, Conference Track Proceedings*, 2018. [Online]. Available: https://openreview.net/forum?id=rJzIBfZAb

[30] K. Pei, Y. Cao, J. Yang, and S. Jana, "Deepxplore: Automated whitebox testing of deep learning systems," in *Proceedings of the 26th Symposium on Operating Systems Principles, Shanghai, China, October 28-31, 2017*, 2017, pp. 1–18. [Online]. Available: https://doi.org/10.1145/3132747.3132785

[31] I. J. Goodfellow, J. Shlens, and C. Szegedy, "Explaining and harnessing adversarial examples," in *3rd International Conference on Learning Representations, ICLR 2015, San Diego, CA, USA, May 7-9, 2015, Conference Track Proceedings*, 2015. [Online]. Available: http://arxiv.org/abs/1412.6572

[32] M. Fischer, M. Balunovic, D. Drachsler-Cohen, T. Gehr, C. Zhang, and M. Vechev, "DL2: Training and querying neural networks with logic," in *Proceedings of the 36th International Conference on Machine Learning*, ser. Proceedings of Machine Learning Research, K. Chaudhuri and R. Salakhutdinov, Eds., vol. 97, Long Beach, California, USA, 09–15 Jun 2019, pp. 1931–1941. [Online]. Available: http://proceedings.mlr.press/v97/fischer19a.html

[33] J. Xu, Z. Zhang, T. Friedman, Y. Liang, and G. V. den Broeck, "A semantic loss function for deep learning with symbolic knowledge," in *Proceedings of the 35th International Conference on Machine Learning, ICML 2018, Stockholmsmässan, Stockholm, Sweden, July 10-15, 2018*, 2018, pp. 5498–5507. [Online]. Available: http://proceedings.mlr.press/v80/xu18h.html

[34] P. Minervini and S. Riedel, "Adversarially regularising neural NLI models to integrate logical background knowledge," in *Proceedings of the 22nd Conference on Computational Natural Language Learning, CoNLL 2018, Brussels, Belgium, October 31 - November 1, 2018*, 2018, pp. 65–74. [Online]. Available: https://aclanthology.info/papers/K18-1007/k18-1007

[35] Z. Hu, X. Ma, Z. Liu, E. H. Hovy, and E. P. Xing, "Harnessing deep neural networks with logic rules," in *Proceedings of the 54th Annual Meeting of the Association for Computational Linguistics, ACL 2016, August 7-12, 2016, Berlin, Germany, Volume 1: Long Papers*, 2016. [Online]. Available: http://aclweb.org/anthology/P/P16/P16-1228.pdf

[36] M. Balunovic and M. Vechev, "Adversarial training and provable defenses: Bridging the gap," in *International Conference on Learning Representations*, 2020. [Online]. Available: https://openreview.net/forum?id=SJxSDxrKDr

[37] E. Wong and J. Z. Kolter, "Provable defenses against adversarial examples via the convex outer adversarial polytope," in *Proceedings of the 35th International Conference on Machine Learning, ICML 2018, Stockholmsmässan, Stockholm, Sweden, July 10-15, 2018*, 2018, pp. 5283–5292. [Online]. Available: http://proceedings.mlr.press/v80/wong18a.html

[38] E. Wong, F. R. Schmidt, J. H. Metzen, and J. Z. Kolter, "Scaling provable adversarial defenses," in *Advances in Neural Information Processing Systems 31: Annual Conference on Neural Information Processing Systems 2018, NeurIPS 2018, 3-8 December 2018, Montréal, Canada.*, 2018, pp. 8410–8419. [Online]. Available: http://papers.nips.cc/paper/8060-scaling-provable-adversarial-defenses

[39] A. Raghunathan, J. Steinhardt, and P. Liang, "Certified defenses against adversarial examples," in *6th International Conference on Learning Representations, ICLR 2018, Vancouver, BC, Canada, April 30 - May 3, 2018, Conference Track Proceedings*, 2018. [Online]. Available: https://openreview.net/forum?id=Bys4ob-Rb

12

SYSLITE: Syntax-Guided Synthesis of PLTL Formulas from Finite Traces

M. Fareed Arif, Daniel Larraz (ID), Mitziu Echeverria, Andrew Reynolds (ID), Omar Chowdhury (ID), Cesare Tinelli (ID)
Department of Computer Science, The University of Iowa

Abstract—We present an ef cient approach to learn past-time linear temporal logic formulas (PLTL) from a set of propositional variables and a sample of nite traces over those variables. The ef ciency of our approach can be attributed to a careful encoding of the PLTL formula learning problem as a bit-vector function synthesis problem, and the use of an enhanced Syntax-Guided Synthesis (SyGuS) engine to solve the latter. We implemented our approach in a tool called SYSLITE and empirically evaluated its ef cacy with two case studies. In these case studies, we observe that SYSLITE on average enjoys a speedup of 44x over current learning approaches for temporal formulas while learning the expected formulas in the vast majority of cases.

I. INTRODUCTION

We are interested in the problem of synthesizing past-time, propositional linear temporal logic (PLTL) formulas when given an alphabet (*i.e.,*, a set of propositional variables) and a sample of finite traces as inputs. The input sample consists of a set of *positive traces* and a disjoint set of *negative traces*. The synthesized PLTL formulas — containing the usual logical connectives, past-time temporal operators, and propositional variables from the input alphabet — are required to be satisfied by each of the positive traces and falsified by each of the negative traces. In machine learning terms, our goal is to learn classifiers for the input traces. However, in contrast to statistical learning approaches, our setting requires an *exact classi er* for the sample traces, that is, one that rejects no positive traces and accepts no negative ones [1], [2].

The synthesis of PLTL formulas from finite samples has a variety of applications, including security policy mining from logs [3], [4], debugging or understanding the behavior of a system [5], and identifying the root cause of a protocol's misbehavior [6], [7]. The PLTL fragment we consider represents safety properties amenable to efficient runtime verification [8]–[12]. This fragment or its variants have been used to represent security, privacy, and safety properties of systems which can be efficiently enforced through runtime monitoring [11]–[15].

We use PLTL formula synthesis to learn attack signatures for cellular networks such as 3G, 4G LTE, and 5G from a set of *benign* (*i.e.,* positive) and attack (*i.e.,* negative) traces. The cellular network attacks we consider are possible due to the protocol state machine's inability to handle particular out-of-order packets injected over-the-air by an adversary [6], [16]–[20]. Such attack signatures can be characterized by PLTL formulas when considering the relative ordering of packets and their payloads received/sent by the cellular device. One can envision a protocol monitor installed on a mobile device that captures messages from the cellular modem with the goal of detecting particular attack signatures, and notifies the user when such attacks are detected. To our knowledge, there exist no attack notification mechanisms of this kind currently. Efficiently solving the PLTL formula synthesis problem is the first technical step towards building such mechanisms.

Prior work. The prior work most relevant to ours is the one by Neider and Gavran [5]. They present two methods for synthesizing propositional, future-only linear temporal logic (LTL) formulas given an alphabet and a sample of (finitely representable) infinite traces. The first method formulates the LTL formula synthesis problem as a Boolean satisfiability problem and then uses an off-the-shelf SAT solver to solve that problem. Because such SAT-based approach does not scale well, the authors then develop a second method based on decision tree learning where the SAT-based method is used as an oracle to generate predicates for the decision tree. More recently, Riener [21] improves on Neider and Gavran's SAT-based method by precomputing models for shape constraints required by the original method. The approaches followed in these works are not directly applicable to attack signature generation due to one or more of the following reasons: (1) they consider samples with infinite traces only; (2) they synthesize LTL formulas containing only future temporal operators, which are not necessarily monitorable at runtime; (3) they impose certain shape restrictions on the synthesized formula which lead to lengthy formulas.

Exploring possible approaches. Since the prior methods above [5], [21] are not directly applicable to our problem domain, we started by first adapting them to the synthesis of *PLTL* formulas from nite traces. In our evaluation, we observed that they either do not scale or do not yield succinct formulas. We then tried to reduce the synthesis problem to a Satisfiability Modulo Theory (SMT) problem where the PLTL syntax is encoded as an algebraic data-type (ADT) and the formula to synthesize is represented by a free variable f with that type. We encoded the requirements of acceptance of the positive traces and rejection of the negative traces as constraints on f and used an SMT solver with finite model finding capabilities [22], [23] to obtain models of the ADT problem. Such models assign to f a datatype value representing a candidate solution to the synthesis problem. Unfortunately, this SMT-based approach is not scalable either, which prompted us to consider an encoding of our synthesis problem as a Syntax-Guided Synthesis (SyGuS) problem [24] over ADTs. Similarly to previous approach, however, the

SyGuS approach proved to be not scalable. The main reason in both cases seems to be that ADTs are user-defined and hence do not benefit from the sort of specialized optimizations that SMT solvers employ for other builtin theories.

Our approach. This brings us to our final approach in which we encode the problem as a SyGuS problem with fixed-size bit-vectors and use a specific SyGuS engine [25] to solve it. In our encoding, we view the projection of a trace of length n over a propositional variable as a bit-vector of size n and then lift the semantics of logical and past temporal connectives to operate over bit-vectors. Such an encoding has the following advantages: (1) since fixed-size bit-vectors are natively supported by the SyGuS solver, we benefit from the solver's various optimization techniques (e.g., rewrite rules) for them; (2) restrictions on the shape of the formula to be learned can be readily added as syntactic constraints on the SyGuS problem; (3) semantics constraints capturing the formula's consistency with sample traces can be efficiently evaluated through direct bit-vector operations on whole traces, unlike prior approaches which operate on each individual state in a trace; (4) with an appropriate term enumeration strategy within the SyGuS solver, it is possible to obtain candidate formulas of minimal size together with other candidates; (5) thanks to the SyGuS solver's symmetry breaking criteria (*i.e.*, agreement over the sample traces), our approach can enumerate different shapes of formulas while maintaining scalability.

Implementation and evaluation. We have implemented our approach in a novel tool called SYSLITE[1] which uses the CVC4SY SyGuS engine [25]. We also adapted to our setting and implemented the prior methods [5], [21] mentioned earlier and considered them as baselines in our experiments. We evaluated the various approaches based on their scalability and ability to synthesize succinct PLTL formulas.

To verify the generality of our SyGuS approach, in a first case study, we collected a number of PLTL formulas from the literature and considered the behavior they represent as our learning target. For each target formula, we generated random traces and classified them as positive or negative based on whether they satisfied or falsified the formula. We then fed a subset of these classified random traces to both SYSLITE and our implementation of the baseline approaches, and compared the synthesized formulas with the corresponding target formulas. We observed that SYSLITE exhibits an average 60x speedup over the baseline while synthesizing a formula logically equivalent to the target formula in most cases.

In a second case study, we used real-world cellular network traces for 11 known attacks [6], [16]–[20]. We observed that SYSLITE can learn the attack signatures 28x times faster on average than the baseline while still being able to generate succinct attack signatures.

Contributions. To summarize, this paper makes the following technical contributions:

1) We explored a number of possible approaches for PLTL formula learning from samples, including extensions of

---

prior SAT-based approaches originally applied to learning LTL formulas with future operators only. Our empirical evaluation show that none of these approaches scale to realistic trace lengths and numbers of input traces.

2) We propose a new, more scalable learning approach which formulates the learning problem as a SyGuS problem and relies on a high-performance SyGuS engine to generate candidate solutions. Our encoding uses the theory of fixed-size bit-vectors which is natively supported by the underlying SyGuS solver, enabling us to benefit from several specific optimizations.

3) Our PLTL formula learning approach is implemented in a new tool, SYSLITE, which uses the CVC4SY SyGuS engine as a backend. We have empirically evaluated its efficacy on two case studies while considering previous state-of-the-art methods as baselines. The case studies show that SYSLITE on-average enjoys a 44x speed-up over the baselines while, at the same time, being able to learn the expected behavior in almost all cases.

II. TECHNICAL PRELIMINARIES

Many-Sorted First-Order Logic. We rely on the usual notions and terminology of many-sorted first-order logic with equality ($\simeq$). We assume the usual definitions of signature, well-sorted terms, literals, and formulas [26]. A *theory* is a pair $T = (\Sigma, I)$ where Σ is a signature and I is a non-empty class of Σ-interpretations, the *models of T*, that is closed under variable reassignment and isomorphism. A Σ-formula φ is T-*satis able* (respectively, T-*unsatis able*) if it is satisfied by some (resp., no) interpretation in I. A satisfying interpretation for φ, *models* φ. A formula φ is *valid in* T (or, T-*valid*), written $\models_T \varphi$, if every model of T is a model of φ.

Theory of Fixed-size bit-vectors. The theory $T_{\mathrm{BV}} = (\Sigma_{\mathrm{BV}}, I_{\mathrm{BV}})$ of fixed-size bit-vectors as defined in the SMT-LIB 2 standard [27] consists of the class of interpretations I_{BV} and signature Σ_{BV}, which includes a unique sort for each positive integer n, representing the bit-vector width. We assume that Σ_{BV} includes all *bit-vector constants* for each n, represented here as bit-strings or, to simplify the notation, by the corresponding natural number in $\{0, \ldots, 2^{n-1}\}$. We write a Σ_{BV}-term (or, *bit-vector term*) t of width n as $t_{[n]}$ when we want to specify its bit-width explicitly. We refer to the i-th bit of $t_{[n]}$ as $t[i]$ with $0 \leq i < n$. We consider $t[0]$ as the least significant bit, and $t[n-1]$ as the most significant bit of t, and denote the subvector of t from index j down to i as $t[j : i]$. We will use the following arithmetic bit-vector operators: addition ($+$), arithmetic negation ($-$), and unsigned shift to the left ($\ll$), as well as the following bitwise operators: logical negation ($\sim$), conjunction ($\&$), and disjunction ($|$).

SyGuS Problem. A SyGuS problem for a function f in a theory T consists of (1) *semantic restrictions*, or a specification, given by a (second-order) T-formula of the form $\exists f. \varphi$, and (2) *syntactic restrictions* on the definitions for f, given by a context-free grammar R. A *solution for* f is a lambda term $\lambda x. e$ of the same type as f, such that (i) the formula

---

[1]SYSLITE is available at https://github.com/CLC-UIowa/SySLite.

$\varphi\{f \mapsto \lambda \boldsymbol{x}. e\}$ is T-valid (modulo beta-reductions) and (ii) the term e is in the language generated by R.

Past-Time Propositional Linear Temporal Logic (PLTL).
The formulas we learn are of the form $\square_f \Phi$ where Φ is a PLTL formula and $\square_f$ is a future temporal operator over finite traces (discussed below).

Definition 1 (Syntax). *The set of well-formed PLTL formulas, denoted as Φ and Ψ, is generated by the following grammar:*

$$\Phi, \Psi \quad ::= \quad \top \mid \bot \mid p \mid \circ^1 \Phi \mid \Phi \circ^2 \Psi$$

where p belongs to a non-empty set, or alphabet, $\mathcal{A}$ of propositional variables, $\circ^1 \in \{\neg, \ominus, \diamondsuit, \square\}$, and $\circ^2 \in \{\wedge, \vee, \mathcal{S}\}$. A core formula is a formula that does not contain the operators $\vee, \diamondsuit,$ and $\square$. The size of a formula Φ, denoted with $|\Phi|$, is the number of its proper subformulas.

Informally, $\top$ and $\bot$ are the universally true and the universally false formulas, respectively, and $\wedge, \vee$, and $\neg$ are the usual Booleans operators. On the other hand, $\ominus, \diamondsuit, \square,$ and $\mathcal{S}$ are past temporal operators, respectively read as "yesterday", "once", "historically", and "since. Unary operators have a higher precedence than binary operators, and temporal operators have a higher precedence than logical operators.

We fix an alphabet $\mathcal{A}$ for the PLTL formulas in the rest of the paper. The standard PLTL semantics is defined over infinite traces in a Kripke structure [28]. For our purposes, however, it is more useful to define a semantics of PLTL over finite traces. A finite trace σ (of length $n \in \mathbb{N}$ over $\mathcal{A}$) is a sequence $(\sigma_0, \ldots, \sigma_{n-1})$ of states where a state is a total mapping from $\mathcal{A}$ to the set $\{\mathbf{t}, \mathbf{f}\}$ of Boolean values. Let $\sigma = (\sigma_0, \ldots, \sigma_{n-1})$ be a trace of length n. For a propositional variable $p \in \mathcal{A}$ and we denote by $\sigma(p)$ the *projection* of σ over p, that is, the sequence of Boolean values $(\sigma_0(p), \ldots, \sigma_{n-1}(p))$.

Definition 2 (Semantics). *The semantics of PLTL is provided by a ternary satisfiability relation $\models$ defined inductively over core PLTL formulas as follows for all finite traces $\sigma = (\sigma_0, \ldots, \sigma_{n-1})$ and positions $i \in [0, n-1]$.*

- $\sigma, i \models \top$
- $\sigma, i \models p \ \ if \ \sigma_i(p) = \mathbf{t}$
- $\sigma, i \models \neg\Phi \ \ if \ (\sigma, i) \not\models \Phi$
- $\sigma, i \models \Phi \wedge \Psi \ \ if \ (\sigma, i) \models \Phi \ and \ (\sigma, i) \models \Psi$
- $\sigma, i \models \ominus\Phi \ \ if \ i > 0 \ and \ (\sigma, i-1) \models \Phi$
- $\sigma, i \models \Phi \mathcal{S} \Psi \ \ if \ there \ is \ an \ j \in [0, i] \ such \ that \ (\sigma, j) \models \Psi \ and \ (\sigma, k) \models \Phi \ for \ all \ k \in [j+1, i].$

This semantics is extended to the full language of PLTL by treating the additional operators as syntactic sugar according to the following equivalences: $\bot \equiv \neg\top$; $\Phi \vee \Psi \equiv \neg(\neg\Phi \wedge \neg\Psi)$; $\diamondsuit\Phi \equiv \top \mathcal{S} \Phi$; $\square\Phi \equiv \neg \diamondsuit \neg\Phi$. We write $\sigma \models \Phi$ as a shorthand for $\sigma, 0 \models \Phi$. Finally, we write $\sigma \models \square_f \Phi$ to indicate that $\sigma, i \models \Phi$ for all $i \in [0, n-1]$ where n is the length of σ.

III. Problem Definition and Possible Approaches

In this section, we formalize the problem of PLTL formula synthesis from finite samples and discuss potential but inef-

ficient approaches for solving it. We start by introducing the auxiliary notion of *consistency* used in our problem definition.

Definition 3 (Consistency). *A PLTL formula Φ is consistent with a finite sample $\mathcal{D} = (\mathcal{P}, \mathcal{N})$ of positive finite traces $\mathcal{P}$ and negative finite traces $\mathcal{N}$ with $\mathcal{P} \cap \mathcal{N} = \emptyset$ if and only if the following two conditions hold.*

1) $\sigma^+ \models \square_f\Phi$ *for all traces $\sigma^+ \in \mathcal{P}$.*
2) $\sigma^- \not\models \square_f\Phi$ *for all traces $\sigma^- \in \mathcal{N}$.*

A formula Φ consistent with $\mathcal{D}$ is *minimal* if no PLTL formula Ψ with $|\Psi| < |\Phi|$ is consistent with $\mathcal{D}$.

Problem Definition 1 (PLTL Formula Synthesis from Finite Samples). *The PLTL formula synthesis problem for a given sample $\mathcal{D} = (\mathcal{P}, \mathcal{N})$ is the problem of finding one or more PLTL formulas Φ that are consistent with $\mathcal{D}$.*

A. Possible Approaches

We considered several natural approaches to the PLTL synthesis problem. Unfortunately, our experimental evaluation revealed that they do not scale well. It is, however, valuable to discuss them here because their weaknesses point to potential performance bottlenecks which any synthesis algorithm must overcome to be effective in practice. We describe a better approach in Section IV.

SAT-based Approaches. We adapted to our context prior SAT-based approaches for learning LTL formulas from samples containing only infinite traces [5], [21]. These approaches look for formulas of increasing size, measured as the *depth* of the formula's abstract syntax tree (AST) which, in essence, guarantees the identification of minimal formulas consistent with a given sample $\mathcal{D}$. As in the approach by Neider and Gavran [5], for a given depth d, the PLTL formula synthesis problem can be posed as the problem of checking the satisfiability of a formula γ^d of propositional logic. The reduction is meant to be such that, γ^d is satisfiable exactly when the original synthesis problem is solvable. Moreover, it is possible to construct a PLTL solution to the synthesis problem from any propositional model of γ^d. The formula γ^d has the form $\gamma^d_{\text{syn}} \wedge \gamma^d_{\text{sem}}$ where γ^d_{syn} tries to captures syntactic restrictions on the expected solution (a well-formed PLTL formula with depth d) whereas γ^d_{sem} captures the semantic restriction that the extracted solution is consistent with the sample.[2] In turn, γ^d_{syn} has the form $\gamma^d_{\text{shape}} \wedge \gamma^d_{\text{label}}$ where models of γ^d_{shape} determine possible AST shapes of depth d (including some infeasible ones) and models of γ^d_{label} assign labels (*i.e.,*, propositions, logical or temporal operators) to the AST nodes. To identify different feasible formulas, this SAT-based approach can be executed in *enumerative* mode by blocking a returned model of γ^d and reissuing a call to the SAT solver with γ^d as well as the blocking formula. Similarly to the original work, this approach does not scale to realistically sized traces or large numbers of them, as we discuss in our evaluation section.

---

[2]In practice, models of γ^d_{syn} can lead to an overabundance of PLTL solutions since the syntactic restrictions are not strong enough to rule out certain redundancies. Thus, some *a posteriori* filtering is required.

Riener [21] improved on Neider and Gavran's work by precomputing the models of the formula γ_{shape}^d for a given depth d and supplying them with the rest of the formulas in γ^d, in effect trading off input size for execution time. The improved method essentially breaks a number of symmetries, greatly reducing the number of solutions that differ in an insignificant way from each other. It can generate stronger syntactic restrictions by relying on an underlying representation based on chains instead of directed acyclic graphs as in Neider and Gavran. We adapted the method to our context but observed that scalability issues persist, especially, when the alphabet size is larger than 3.

Finally, we also considered a second approach by Neider and Gavran [5] which combines a classical decision tree learning algorithm with their SAT-based approach. In a first phase, the SAT-based algorithm is executed over k positive and k negative traces to obtain a candidate formula. The approach keeps choosing randomly from $2k$ traces until all the example traces can be separated or a timeout is reached. At that point, it invokes the decision tree learning algorithm which essentially uses the candidate formulas generated in the first phase as possible predicates for the decision tree. Because the decision tree learning algorithm combines these predicates into if-then-else clauses, it only applies to logical languages that are closed under negation. Unfortunately, the presence of the outermost $_f$ operator in our PLTL fragment of interest, makes this fragment not closed under negation and hence this second approach is not applicable to our case.

SMT-based Approach. One of the scalability challenges of SAT-based algorithms can be attributed to the inefficient enumeration of the well-formed PLTL formulas. This is particularly apparent in the approach of Riener [21] who attempts to address this challenge through precomputation. A natural potential solution is to move to an SMT-based approach where the formula to be synthesized is a value of an algebraic data type (ADT) Δ that captures the abstract syntax of well-formed PLTL formulas directly. Each PLTL propositional constant and (logical and temporal) operator is modeled by a corresponding constructor of Δ with the same arity. Traces can be encoded as (partially defined) Boolean maps from propositional constants and trace positions. The PLTL semantics is captured by an *evaluation function*, a recursively defined total function that takes a trace t and a data type d as input and returns true if and only if t satisfies the formula represented by d. The synthesis problem is then encoded by a set of constraints on a fresh constant φ of type Δ, standing for the formula to be synthesized, stating that the evaluation of φ is true for all the positive traces and false for all the negative ones. Synthesizing the PLTL formula thus reduces to asking the SMT solver to find a model of the ADT problem. If it succeeds, the ADT value assigned to φ describes a possible solution. In our evaluation, we observed that such an approach is unfortunately also not scalable, possibly due to the inherent complexity of solving SMT problems over ADTs.

SyGuS-based Approach. We explored next a SyGuS-based

approach where the PLTL syntax is encoded as a context-free grammar whereas the consistency with the sample set is given as the specification. Although more scalable than the SMT-based one, this approach is still not sufficiently scalable for our case studies. An analysis of our SyGuS encoding revealed the following two weaknesses whose mitigation led us to our final approach, discussed in the next section. First, since algebraic data types are user-defined, reasoning about them does not benefit from the specialized optimizations (*e.g.,*, rewrite rules, symmetry breaking) available to SMT solvers for other builtin theories such as bit-vectors or linear integer arithmetic. Second, both this and the SMT-based approach require evaluating a candidate solution at each position of each trace in order to guarantee consistency with the sample. Expressing such a constraint requires the use of quantified formulas (with quantification over traces and positions) and recursive function definitions (for the evaluation function) both of which are expensive to reason about.

B. Lessons learned

After analyzing the different approaches above to the PLTL synthesis problem, we identified the following performance bottlenecks, which we tried to address in our final approach. First, the SAT-based approaches produce constraints with a lot of symmetries and hence many redundant solutions, a substantial bottleneck. Except for the SyGus-based approach, none of these approches apply symmetry breaking optimizations to rule out or reduce the generation of formulas similar to previously generated ones, substantially hampering the generation of truly diverse PLTL formulas consistent with the input sample. Finally, all the approaches attempt to achieve sample-consistency through (quantified or explicit) constraints on *individual* trace positions, thus missing out on full-trace-level optimizations, which are crucial to scalability.

Examples of our SMT-based and SyGuS-based encodings can be found in the longer version of this paper [29].

IV. PLTL SYNTHESIS WITH SYGUS

In this section, we present an efficient approach for synthesizing a PLTL formula consistent with a finite sample $\mathcal{D}$ using a SyGuS solver over the theory of fixed-sized bit-vectors. It relies on the observation that a PLTL formula over finite traces of length at most n can be encoded as a function over bit-vectors of size n. Thus, the problem of synthesizing a PLTL formula is reduced to the synthesis of a bit-vector function.

Similarly to a bit-vector encoding presented by Baresi et al. [30], we use bit-vectors of size $n > 0$ to represent the truth values of PLTL formulae at positions $[0, n-1]$ of a given trace of length n. More precisely, for each atomic proposition $p \in \mathcal{A}$, we use a bit-vector variable $\overleftarrow{p}_{[n]}$ such that $\overleftarrow{p}_{[n]}[i]$ captures the value of proposition p at all instants i from 0 to $n-1$. The bit-vector representation of $\perp$ for length n, denoted with $\overleftarrow{\perp}_{[n]}$, is the bit-vector constant 0 of size n, while the bit-vector representation of $\top$, denoted with $\overleftarrow{\top}_{[n]}$, is the value of $\sim\overleftarrow{\perp}_{[n]}$. For any other PLTL formula Φ, we describe the value of Φ at positions 0 through $n-1$ in a trace by the bit-vector obtained by recursively performing operations on the bit-vectors corresponding to the sub-formulas of Φ. The operations performed depend on the structure of Φ and follow the transformations shown in Table I.

TABLE I.   Translation of a PLTL formulas to bit-vector terms.

Φ	Φ	unfolded bit-vector encoding
Ψ	Ψ	Ψ
$\Psi_1 \;\; \Psi_2$	$\Psi_1 \,\&\, \Psi_2$	$\Psi_1 \,\&\, \Psi_2$
$\Psi_1 \;\; \Psi_2$	$\Psi_1 \mid \Psi_2$	$\Psi_1 \mid \Psi_2$
Ψ	Ψ	$\ll \Psi$
Ψ	Ψ	$\Psi \;\; \Psi$
Ψ	Ψ	$(1 + \Psi) \,\&\, \Psi$
$\Psi_1 \, \mathcal{S} \, \Psi_2$	$\Psi_1 \, \mathcal{S} \, \Psi_2$	$\Psi_2 \;\; (\;\; ((\Psi_1 \;\; \Psi_2) + \Psi_2) \,\&\, \Psi_1)$

Table I also introduces new bit-vector operators, , , , and $\overleftarrow{\mathcal{S}}$ denoting, respectively, the bit-vector encodings for the temporal operators , , , and $\mathcal{S}$. To establish the correctness of the connection between the bit-vector encoding and the semantics of PLTL (see Theorem 1) and to explain the example we use the following notation: for a propositional variable $p \in \mathcal{A}$ and a trace σ of length n, $\overleftarrow{\sigma(p)}$ denotes the bit-vector representation of $\sigma(p)$, that is, for all $i \in [0, n-1]$, $\overleftarrow{\sigma(p)}[i] = 1$ if $\sigma_i(p) = \mathbf{t}$, and $\overleftarrow{\sigma(p)}[i] = 0$ if $\sigma_i(p) = \mathbf{f}$.

To see more concretely how the translation works we explain, for instance, the correspondence between the unary PLTL operator (read: true at least once in the present or past) and its bit-vector counterpart with an example.

Example 1. Let σ be a trace of length 6 where propositional variable p is true only at positions 3 and 4. The projection $\sigma(p)$ is represented by the bit vector 011000 with the most significant (i.e., leftmost) bit corresponding to $\sigma_5(p)$, the next most significant bit corresponding to $\sigma_4(p)$, and so on. So $\overleftarrow{\sigma(p)} = 011000$. Intuitively, the valuation of p over σ should then be represented by the bit-vector 111000. To verify that let $\overleftarrow{p}_{[6]}$ be the bit-vector variable corresponding to p. According to our translation, $\overleftarrow{p} = (\overleftarrow{p}) = -\overleftarrow{p} \mid \overleftarrow{p} = -\overleftarrow{p}_{[6]} \mid \overleftarrow{p}_{[6]}$ where $\mid$ is bitwise disjunction and $-$ is arithmetic negation (two's complement). If we evaluate the resulting bit-vector term with the valuation $\alpha = \{\overleftarrow{p}_{[6]} \mapsto 011000\}$ we get

$$\begin{aligned} \alpha(-\overleftarrow{p}_{[6]} \mid \overleftarrow{p}_{[6]}) &= -011000 \mid 011000 \\ &= 101000 \mid 011000 = 111000 \end{aligned}$$

as expected. $\square$

Theorem 1. *Let Φ be a PLTL formula over the alphabet $\mathcal{A} = \{p_1, \ldots, p_m\}$ and let σ be a trace of length n over $\mathcal{A}$. Then,*

$$\sigma \models_f \Phi \quad \text{iff} \quad \models_{T_{\mathrm{BV}}} \overleftarrow{\Phi} \{\bar{p} \mapsto \bar{\sigma}\} \simeq \overleftarrow{\top}_{[n]}$$

where $\bar{p} = (\overleftarrow{p_1}_{[n]}, \ldots, \overleftarrow{p_m}_{[n]})$ and $\bar{\sigma} = (\overleftarrow{\sigma(p_1)}, \ldots, \overleftarrow{\sigma(p_m)})$.

Proof. By induction on the structure of Φ. See Arif et al. [29] for a full proof. $\square$

We now describe how we use the bit-vector encoding above to reduce the problem of synthesizing a PLTL formula consistent with a sample into a SyGuS problem over bit-vectors. More precisely, given propositional variables $p_i \in \mathcal{A}$, with $1 \le i \le m$, and a sample $\mathcal{D} = (\mathcal{P}, \mathcal{N})$ whose longest trace has length n, we seek to synthesize a bit-vector function $f(\overleftarrow{p_1}_{[n]}, \ldots, \overleftarrow{p_m}_{[n]})$ such that if $\lambda \overleftarrow{p_1}_{[n]}, \ldots, \lambda \overleftarrow{p_m}_{[n]}. \, e$ is a solution for the SyGuS problem, then there exists a PLTL formula Φ consistent with $\mathcal{D}$ whose bit-vector encoding is e (that is, $\overleftarrow{\Phi} = e$).

To meet the requirements on f, we start by imposing the syntactic restrictions expressed by this context-free grammar:

$$\Psi \;\; ::= \;\; \overleftarrow{\top}_{[n]} \;\mid\; \overleftarrow{\bot}_{[n]} \;\mid\; \overleftarrow{p}_{[n]} \;\mid\; \circ^1 \Psi \;\mid\; \Psi \circ^2 \Psi$$

where $\overleftarrow{p}$ is $\overleftarrow{p_j}_{[n]}$ for some $j \in [0, m]$, $\circ^1 \in \{\sim, \; , \; , \; \}$ are the unary operators, and $\circ^2 \in \{\&, \mid, \overleftarrow{\mathcal{S}}\}$ are the binary operators. Notice that, although , , , and $\overleftarrow{\mathcal{S}}$ do not belong to the theory of bit-vectors, they can be defined using a bit-vector function in the SyGuS problem (see Table I).

In addition, the function f is subject to the following semantic restrictions where $|\sigma|$ denotes the length of trace σ:

$$1) \quad \bigwedge_{\sigma \in \mathcal{P}} f(\overleftarrow{\sigma(p_1)}, \ldots, \overleftarrow{\sigma(p_m)})[|\sigma| - 1 : 0] \simeq \overleftarrow{\top}_{[n]}[|\sigma| - 1 : 0]$$

$$2) \quad \bigwedge_{\sigma \in \mathcal{N}} f(\overleftarrow{\sigma(p_1)}, \ldots, \overleftarrow{\sigma(p_m)})[|\sigma| - 1 : 0] \not\simeq \overleftarrow{\top}_{[n]}[|\sigma| - 1 : 0]$$

The two constraints enforce the consistency of the solution respectively with the positive traces and the negative traces. Notice that, since an input may include traces of different length, we compare only the relevant positions for each trace.

V. IMPLEMENTATION AND EVALUATION OF SYSLITE

In this section, we discuss the implementation of SYSLITE and our empirical evaluation of it based on two case studies.

A. SYSLITE *Implementation*

SYSLITE is a wrapper around the syntax-guided synthesis solver CVC4SY which is part of the SMT solver CVC4 [31] and now incorporates additional optimizations for PLTL synthesis. CVC4SY supports various theories, including that of fixed-size bit-vectors, used in our encoding, and implements several specialized synthesis algorithms for various types of synthesis conjectures [32]. We rely on its support for enumerative counterexample-guided inductive synthesis (CEGIS) which was recently improved with several novel strategies [33].

In enumerative CEGIS [34], candidate solutions are generated based on some ordering, typically on term size. In our setting, a candidate solution is a function whose definition involves the bit-vector symbols from Section IV. CVC4SY uses advanced techniques to aggressively reduce the number of candidate solutions it generates. In particular, it uses fast incomplete techniques based on term rewriting to avoid generating candidate solutions s' that are logically equivalent to some previous candidate s. This form of *symmetry breaking*, is critical for the scalability of enumerative approaches [32]. Our encoding of PLTL formulas as bit-vector constraints was motivated by the intention to capitalize on CVC4SY's infrastructure for establishing the equivalence of bit-vector terms developed to accelerate SyGuS enumeration [35].

For synthesis conjectures (*i.e.,*, semantic restrictions) $\exists f. \varphi$ where all applications of f in φ have concrete values as arguments, CVC4SY can apply a stronger version of symmetry breaking that considers *equivalence under examples*. Suppose the concrete inputs for f in φ are $c_1, \ldots, c_n$. Using this technique, while constructing a new candidate solution for f, the solver disregards any term t' that over the inputs $c_1, \ldots, c_n$ evaluates exactly as some previously disregarded term t. For example, the terms $x \,\&\, y$ and x take the same value over the inputs $(0001, 0001), (0000, 0001), (1010, 1110)$ for (x, y). Hence, one of them ($x \,\&\, y$, due to its larger size) will be excluded from consideration in candidate solutions since it is equivalent to x for all relevant inputs as specified in the conjecture. In practice, this heuristic is traditionally applied when the synthesis conjecture specifies a set of input/output pairs for the function f to synthesize (with constraints of the form $f(c_i) = o_i$). We have generalized symmetry breaking in CVC4SY to apply the heuristics to any conjecture $\exists f. \varphi$ where f is applied to concrete inputs, even when φ is not just a conjunction of input/output constraints. In our specific context, this enables symmetry breaking constraints for the negative traces, and also allows us to have traces of different length in the same problem.

Since the evaluation of terms on concrete examples is a major bottleneck in syntax-guided synthesis solvers, we have additionally implemented in CVC4SY several low-level optimizations for quickly computing the result of PLTL terms on concrete inputs. Thanks to our encoding of PLTL formulas as bit-vector constraints, we can capitalize on the data structures in the core of CVC4 for representing and efficiently evaluating bit-vectors terms. Our experiments confirm that this is critical to achieving scalability for the synthesis tasks in question.

The enumeration strategy itself (by formula size) remains a major bottleneck in our approach when behavior consistent with the training set cannot be captured by a small formula. In contrast, capturing behavior that spans distant states on a trace is not, per se, problematic because evaluation times for a given candidate solution grow linearly with trace length.

B. Empirical Analysis Criteria and Con guration

Research questions. In our evaluation of SYSLITE, we aimed to answer two research questions. Compared to a baseline:

RQ_1. How effective is SYSLITE in synthesizing succinct, diverse, and accurate PLTL formulas?

RQ_2. How scalable is SYSLITE?

Case studies. We address the above questions in the context of the two case studies presented in Sections V-C and V-D, respectively. The first focuses on RQ_1 whereas the second focuses on RQ_2 based on SYSLITE's ability to synthesize attack signatures from real cellular network traces.

Baseline. We compare SYSLITE against a baseline represented by our own implementation of the (first) SAT-based method by Neider and Gavran [5]. We use our own implementation and not theirs because the latter applies to traditional LTL, as opposed to PLTL. We do not discuss here the other approaches we tried, that is, Reiner's SAT-based approach [21], our encodings to algebraic data types, as well as DFA learning approaches, specifically, RPNI [36], since they proved either not scalable or ineffective. We point out that, in the second case study (V-D), the passive DFA learning approach does scale significantly better than SYSLITE with trace length and number of traces. However, the produced signatures are of significantly worse quality in all considered benchmarks (e.g., have F1 score as low as 0.35 for RLF report attack). Moreover, the quality of the DFA signatures does not necessarily improve with a larger set of traces or longer traces over the signatures produced by SYSLITE. In other words, SYSLITE can learn better quality signatures with fewer and shorter traces. Furthermore, recall that in this case study the objective is to generate attack monitors that execute on a mobile phone. A PLTL formula of size n can be monitored with just $2n$ *bits* of memory [8]. In contrast, the learned DFA equivalent to a PLTL formula can have $O(2^n)$ states [37]–[39]. The memory footprint of such a high number of states per signature makes DFA-based monitors infeasible in practice, especially, when many attacks are being monitored at the same time.

Sample sizes. For both of our case studies, we considered sample sizes 50, 100, 250, 500, and 1250. For Case Study I, traces were generated randomly and have length 10 whereas for Case Study II the traces were collected from a cellular network and have length 100. We chose on purpose data sets with an equal number of positive and negative traces. An imbalanced dataset, due for example to an uneven distribution of positive and negative traces for the target behavior (which we did observe in some of the benchmarks), can negatively impact the quality of the synthesized formula by not restricting the search space enough to learn the desired behavior early in the search. Oversampling, on the other hand, does not impact the quality of the synthesized formula, although it can obviously impact training time.

Training and testing con guration. We used the standard Pareto-principle of classifier evaluation which suggests an (80%, 20%) partition of the provided sample set into training and testing datasets, respectively. By considering a synthesized PLTL formula Φ as a classifier for the traces in the testing set, its quality can be measured in terms of *precision* (the percentage of correctly classified traces among all traces classified as positive by Φ), *recall* (the ratio of correctly classified positive traces over the total number of positive traces) and their harmonic mean (F1 score). Moreover, the evaluation method also performs cross-validation. It considers the first five solutions generated by SYSLITE and by the baseline, selecting the formula (or formulas, in case of ties) with the highest F1 score.

In Case Study I, one could imagine directly comparing the *closeness* of a synthesized formula to the target formula, for instance by considering the Jaccard distance of the sets of satisfying traces, up to some fixed length n, for each formula. We did not do it since it is prohibitively expensive for requiring the enumeration of all such traces. A better approach might be to estimate closeness by adapting model counting techniques to this setting, something we leave to future work.

Evaluation infrastructure. We performed all our evaluations on a 3.40GHz Intel(R) Xeon(R) E3-1240 CPU running CentOS (Linux Kernel 3.10.0-1062.9.1) on 16GB RAM. We set a 3600 second timeout for each learning task.

C. Case Study I: PLTL Formulae from Literature

The purpose of this case study was to measure SYSLITE's effectiveness in synthesizing succinct and accurate formulas from a sample set of traces. For this, we first collected a few representative PLTL formulas from the literature (see Table II). For each of them, we collected a sample consisting of randomly generated traces and then checked if SYSLITE and the baseline were able to learn the original formula or a logically equivalent one. We had both synthesis approaches generate up to 5 candidate formulas before a given timeout.

TABLE II. target formulas from the literature.

Literature Formula	PLTL Formula
Chinese Wall Policy [11]	$f((\text{access\_org1\_records} \quad (\text{access\_org2\_records})) \quad (\text{access\_org2\_records} \quad (\text{access\_org1\_records})))$
Bank Transaction Policy [11]	$f(\text{Transaction\_over\_threshold\_performed} \quad (\text{Transaction\_over\_threshold\_approved}))$
Secure File [11]	$f((\text{secure\_le\_open} \quad (\quad (\text{secure\_le\_open})) \quad (\text{secure\_le\_open} \, S \, \text{secure\_le\_closed})))$
Financial Institute Policy [11]	$f(\text{grant} \quad (\text{grant} \, S \, \text{request}))$
GLBA-6802 [12], [15]	$f(\text{institution\_discloses\_to\_a} \quad \text{liate\_customers\_npi} \quad (\text{customer\_opt\_out} \, S \, \text{notice\_of\_disclosure}))$
HIPPA-164508A2 [12], [15]	$f(\text{covered\_entity\_discloses\_patient\_psych\_notes} \quad (\text{authorization\_psych\_notes\_revoked}) \, S \, \text{receive\_patient\_authorization\_psych\_notes})$
HIPPA-164508A3 [12], [15]	$f(\text{covered\_entity\_discloses\_patient\_info\_for\_marketing} \quad (\text{receive\_patient\_authorization\_marketing}))$
Dynamic Separ. of Duty [11]	$f(\text{member\_activates\_role1} \quad (\quad (\quad \text{member\_activates\_role2})) \quad (\text{member\_activates\_role2} \, S \, \text{member\_deactivates\_role2})))$

Trace generation: Given a target formula φ from Table II, a desired trace length ℓ, and a desired sample size $2n$, our trace generation process uses a cryptographically-secure pseudorandom number generator to produce a sample set $\mathcal{P}$ of n positive traces and a sample set $\mathcal{N}$ of n negative traces, all of length ℓ. It generates a trace σ of length ℓ by randomly assigning truth values to φ's propositional variables for each of the ℓ states of σ. The trace goes in the set $\mathcal{P}$ or $\mathcal{N}$ depending on whether it satisfies φ or not, as long as the set in question contains less than n traces; otherwise, it is discarded. Note that, depending on the target formula φ, we may have to oversample for positive or negative traces.

Measuring quality of synthesized formulas. To evaluate the quality of the synthesized formulas, in addition to relying on the usual statistical measures (i.e., precision, recall, and F1 score) on the test dataset, we considered logical equivalence with the target formula (i.e., being satisfied by exactly the same set of possible traces) as another metric of effectiveness. We used the GOAL tool [40] to check for equivalence in PLTL.

Quality of synthesized formulas. Our results on the synthesized formulas' quality (i.e., equivalence to target formula) and count are summarized in Table III. For each run of SYSLITE

TABLE III. Case Study I: Quality of Synthesis Methods.

target Formula	SYSLITE		SAT	
	Count	Quality	Count	Quality
Chinese Wall Policy [11]	5/5	1/5	4/5	0/5
Bank Transaction Policy [11]	5/5	5/5	4/5	4/5
Secure File [11]	5/5	5/5	0/5	0/5
Financial Institute [11]	5/5	5/5	2/5	1/5
GLBA-6802 [12], [15]	5/5	5/5	1/5	2/5
HIPPA-164508A2 [12], [15]	5/5	5/5	1/5	0/5
HIPPA-164508A3 [12], [15]	5/5	5/5	4/5	4/5
Dynamic Separation of Duty [11]	2/5	0/5	2/5	0/5
Total:	37/40 (92%)	31/40 (76%)	18/40 (45%)	11/40 (27%)

and the baseline for a particular dataset and a target formula, we select the highest-ranked formula after cross validation[3] among those synthesized in the allotted time, if any. For each original (target) formula, column **Count** reports the total of number selected formulas across the 5 training sets of different size. For instance, a value of $2/5$ indicates that the algorithm was able to synthesize formulas for 2 of the 5 training sets. Column **Quality** reports how many of the selected formulas are logically equivalent to the target formula.

Our evaluation confirms that SYSLITE can learn the target formula or an equivalent one for each of the five random sample sets in almost all cases. The only exceptions are the Dynamic Separation of Duty formula, for which SYSLITE generates two formulas neither of which is equivalent to the target formula, and the Chinese Wall Policy formula, for which it generates one formula and only for the sample set of size 1250. To put things in perspective, however, note that since the Chinese Wall Policy formula has two variables and traces have length 10, a set of 1250 traces covers just 0.1% of the set of all possible 4^{10} traces. Remarkably, SYSLITE is able to learn the right formula with much smaller sample sets in all the other cases, with perfect precision, recall, and F1 scores.

Looking at the baseline approach, it performs gracefully with a few simple target formulas such as Bank Transaction Policy and HIPAA-164508A3. However, it cannot synthesize any candidates for the Secure File target formula. Moreover, its synthesized formulas for HIPPA-164508A2, Dynamic Separation of Duty, and Chinese Wall Policy are not equivalent to the target. See Arif et al. [29] for detailed results.

Scalability. The training results for case study I are shown in Figure 1. The X-axis of the graph represents the different training set sizes: 80% of 50, 100, 250, 500, and 1250, while the Y-axis (in log-scale) represents the training time in seconds. Cross validation times are not shown because they are uniform and negligible. The horizontal red line on the top of the graph represents the timeout (3600 seconds). In the graph, we only show results for the 3 target formulas for which the SAT-method performs best. See [29] for complete results.

In our evaluation, SYSLITE was able to generate results for almost all combinations of target formula and training set size while exhibiting an average 60x speedup over the baseline. The exception, already mentioned, is the Dynamic Separation of Duty formula where it timed-out on the training sets with more than 100 traces. This is likely due to the large size of the formulas to be synthesized which requires

---

[3]In this case study, we did not observe any ties after cross-validation.

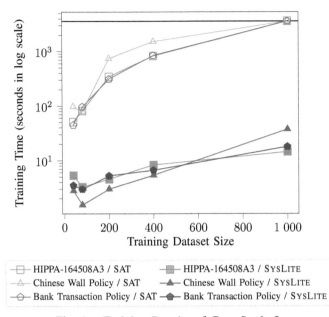

Fig. 1. Training Results of Case Study I.

TABLE IV. Table summarizing the attacks used for evaluation of 4G LTE Attack Signature Generation. (● = NAS Protocol Layer, ○ = RRC Protocol Layer)

Name of Attack	SYSLITE-synthesized Attack Signature	PL
Numb Attack [6]	$\Box_f$(authentication_reject ⇒ ⊖(authentication_response))	●
Authentication Failure [6]	$\Box_f$(¬(authentication_failure))	●
IMSI Cracking Attack Against 4G [16]	$\Box_f$(¬(paging_IMSI_and_TMSI))	●
IMSI Catching [16]	$\Box_f$(¬(identity_request_IMSI))	●
Measurement Report [17]	$\Box_f$(measurementReport ⇒ (¬(rrcConnectionSetup) S securityModeComplete))	○
RLF Report [17]	$\Box_f$(ueInformationResponse ⇒ (¬(rrcConnectionRequest) S securityModeCommand))	○
AKA Bypass Attack [18]	$\Box_f$(rrcConnectionReconfiguration ⇒ (¬(rrcConnectionSetupComplete) S securityModeCommand))	○
Malformed Identity Request [19]	$\Box_f$(¬(identity_request_malformed))	●
Null Encryption Chosen by MME	$\Box_f$(¬(MME_null_encryption_chosen))	●
EMM Information Spoofing [20]	$\Box_f$(¬(emm_information_insecure))	○
Paging with IMSI [16]	$\Box_f$(¬(paging_IMSI ∨ paging_IMSI_and_TMSI))	●

SYSLITE to enumerate internally a very large number of terms. The baseline method was unable to generate any formula and timed-out, even for the smallest sample (of 50 traces) for the Secure File formula. For a few of the other target formulas, it failed to synthesize a candidate even for the small sample sets (of size 50 and 100). For example, in HIPPA-164508A2 policy it failed to synthesize any formula for sample size larger than 50 traces; for the Dynamic Separation of Duty and Financial Institute it was unable to deal with sample sets with more than 100 traces. These scalability problems are the main cause of its low formula-quality scores (shown in Table III) and low statistical measures scores (not shown).

D. Case Study II: 4G LTE Attack Signature Generation

Our second case study focused on synthesizing *attack signatures*, represented as PLTL formulas, for cellular networks from a set of *benign* (i.e., positive) and *attack* (i.e., negative) traces. Once again, we considered the scalability and effectiveness of SYSLITE versus the SAT-based baseline. The choice of this application domain was motivated by the vital role cellular networks play in a modern nation's infrastructure, which makes them a frequent target for malicious attacks [6], [16]–[18], [41], [42].

As with any protocol, the cellular network protocol allows only specific orderings of messages (packets) sent or received by a cellular device, and predicates over their payload (e.g., the sequence number is in a range). For a given type of attack, the synthesized attack signature is expected to be satisfied, ideally, by *all and only* the benign protocol executions, those not containing an attack. This way, one can deploy a runtime monitor [43] for each attack type that checks whether the current execution violates (i.e., falsifies) the attack signature and issues an alert as soon as it detects a violation. Currently, there are no mechanisms that can achieve this goal

efficiently. Being able to automatically synthesize effective attack signatures is the natural first step towards that. In light of this, our case study focused on 11 known, representative attacks that are detectable from the vantage point of a cellular device (see Table IV). These attacks target weaknesses of the cellular network protocol in the Non-Access Stratum (NAS) layer, responsible for communication between a cellular device and the core network, and the Radio Resource Control (RRC) layer, responsible for the communication between a device and the base station [6], [16]–[20]. While other attacks exist [7], [16]–[18], [44]–[51], they are not detectable from a device's point of view and thus are not relevant to our case study.

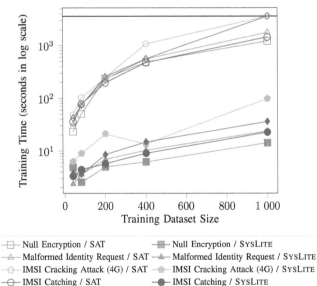

Fig. 2. Training Results of Case Study II.

Trace gathering. We now discuss how we gathered benign

traces and generated attack traces through testbed experiments.

Benign Traces: We collected benign traces by random sampling traces from a crowd-sourced platform to which users world-wide submit their cellular network traces through an Android app called MobileInsight [52]. Our collected traces include 1892 NAS layer traces containing about 52K messages and 2045 RRC layer traces containing about 1.5M messages. We cleaned up the traces so that each contained 100 states as this is sufficient for the attacks we considered.

Malicious Traces: To collect malicious traces, we first implemented each attack and its variants using srsLTE [53] and software-defined radios in a testbed. srsLTE is an open-source cellular network stack which permits the modification of different components of the network. We then extracted the attack traces with SCAT [54], a desktop application capable of extracting 4G LTE modem traffic exposed by certain devices through a USB interface. Finally, we inserted one or more copies of the attack traces at arbitrary positions of some arbitrarily chosen benign traces to obtain our set of malicious traces. The latter is meant to mimic real-world scenarios in which attacks span a few sessions of the protocol.

Quality of the synthesized attack signatures. In this case study, our quality criteria were signature succinctness and correctness in capturing the attack. We consider an attack signature to be succinct if it can concisely capture the attack's root cause without including super uous events (e.g., messages received/sent) or conditions (e.g., predicates over message payload). Visual inspection of the signatures returned by SYSLITE and the baseline shows that those generated by SYSLITE, shown in Table IV, are more succinct.

Looking at correctness, all the attack signatures synthesized by either the SAT-based baseline or SYSLITE for the NAS layer have a perfect (100%) precision, recall and F1 on the testing set. However, the baseline is able to synthesize signature only with samples of small size. For all the RRC layer attacks, SYSLITE is able to score perfectly on the test dataset based on the statistical measures. The baseline, however, does not achieve a 100% precision, recall, and F1 score as it cannot synthesize any signature for the Measurement Report attack. We have manually vetted the synthesized attack signatures by both SYSLITE and the baseline based on our expertise in cellular security and observed that the generated signatures correctly identified (i.e., rejected) traces containing attacks.

Scalability. The scalability results for Case Study II are shown in Figure 2. The graph's X-axis shows the sizes of the different training sets we used whereas the Y-axis (in log-scale) reports the corresponding training time in seconds. The timeout value is shown as a red horizontal line. For ease of exposition, we show only the training results for 3 NAS and 2 RRC layers attacks. For the rest of attacks, the results follow a similar trend. See Arif et al. [29] for complete results.

We conjecture that the performance of the baseline is comparable with that of SYSLITE when learning attack signatures on the NAS protocol layer because it induces attacks spanning only a single protocol session. Thus, the patterns are relatively easier to learn. On the other hand, for the RRC layer attacks, the sequences of attack steps can be complex and spread over multiple sessions, thus making it challenging to learn (see [29]). Indeed, the baseline timed out more frequently while synthesizing multi-session attacks from RRC traffic. In case of the Measurement Report attack, the baseline timed out for all sample sizes and did not yield any signature. In contrast, and as illustrated in Figure 2, we observed that the SYSLITE is scalable and efficient in synthesizing multi-session attacks signatures, exhibiting on average a 28x speedup over the baseline. We stress that scalability is essential in this context to promptly generate attack signatures for newly discovered attacks before attackers can cause substantial damage.

VI. RELATED WORK

The problem of Learning LTL formulas consistent with a given set of traces is an instance of the so called language learning from the informant problem [1], [5], [21]. Unlike prior approaches for Signal Temporal Logic (STL) formula learning [55]–[58] and LTL specification mining [59], [60], these exact learning methods do not require any user-provided templates. Alternatively, for attack monitor synthesis, one can envision using active/passive learning to learn a regular language representation (e.g., DFA [61]–[64], NFA [65], alternating automaton [66]) of attack signatures. Monitoring such regular language representations with language recognizers (e.g., DFA) may require exponentially more states than PLTL.

Also, these regular language learning methods are not scalable as an automaton requires an explicit state representation of the behavior to-be-learned. LTL formulas, in contrast, are an efficient alternative for capturing behavior as it offers a more succinct and interpretable representation. Efforts on synthesis of reactive synthesis design [67] and counterexample-guided inductive synthesis [68] are complementary to the approaches we discuss here.

VII. CONCLUSION

We have presented an efficient approach for synthesizing PLTL formulas from a set of finite traces. The approach reduces the problem to a bit-vector function synthesis problem and then uses an enhanced version of the CVC4SY SyGuS solver to solve the latter. The reduction to bit-vector function synthesis proves critical for performance not only because CVC4SY implements specific optimization for bit-vectors but also because it allows us to efficiently express the requirements capturing the consistency of the solution with the samples. The conventional wisdom that SyGuS solvers are more efficient for problems over natively supported theories compared to reductions to other SMT theories (such as algebraic datatypes) or to SAT is corroborated by our experimental evaluation.

Possible directions for future work include understanding the impact of grammar representation (i.e., which temporal operators to be included in the syntactic specification of the SyGuS problem) in the efficiency of PLTL formula synthesis as well as extending the current approach to synthesizing past, propositional metric temporal logic.

ACKNOWLEDGMENTS

This work was partially funded by DARPA YFA contract
no. D19AP00039 and by NSF grant no. 1656926. The authors
are grateful to Daniel Nader, Ivan Gravan, Rajarshi Roy, and
the anonymous reviewers for their helpful feedback.

REFERENCES

[1] Colin De la Higuera. *Grammatical inference: learning automata and grammars.* Cambridge University Press, 2010.

[2] Nader H Bshouty. Exact learning via the monotone theory. In *Proceedings of 1993 IEEE 34th Annual Foundations of Computer Science,* pages 302–311. IEEE, 1993.

[3] Scott D. Stoller and Thang Bui. Mining hierarchical temporal roles with multiple metrics. *Journal of Computer Security,* 26(1):121–142, 2018.

[4] Zhongyuan Xu and Scott D. Stoller. Mining attribute-based access control policies from logs. In Vijay Atluri and Guenther Pernul, editors, *Proceedings of the 28th Annual IFIP WG 11.3 Working Conference on Data and Applications Security and Privacy (DBSec 2014),* volume 8566 of *Lecture Notes in Computer Science,* pages 276–291. Springer-Verlag, 2014.

[5] Daniel Neider and Ivan Gavran. Learning linear temporal properties. In *2018 Formal Methods in Computer Aided Design (FMCAD),* pages 1–10. IEEE, 2018.

[6] Syed Rafiul Hussain, Omar Chowdhury, Shagufta Mehnaz, and Elisa Bertino. LTEInspector: A Systematic Approach for Adversarial Testing of 4G LTE. In *25th Annual Network and Distributed System Security Symposium, NDSS, San Diego, CA, USA, February 18-21,* 2018.

[7] Syed Rafiul Hussain, Mitziu Echeverria, Imtiaz Karim, Omar Chowdhury, and Elisa Bertino. 5greasoner: A property-directed security and privacy analysis framework for 5g cellular network protocol. In *Proceedings of the 2019 ACM SIGSAC Conference on Computer and Communications Security,* pages 669–684, 2019.

[8] Klaus Havelund and Grigore Roşu. Synthesizing monitors for safety properties. In *International Conference on Tools and Algorithms for the Construction and Analysis of Systems,* pages 342–356. Springer, 2002.

[9] Andreas Bauer, Martin Leucker, and Christian Schallhart. Comparing ltl semantics for runtime verification. *Journal of Logic and Computation,* 20(3):651–674, 2010.

[10] Shaohui Wang, Anaheed Ayoub, Oleg Sokolsky, and Insup Lee. Runtime verification of traces under recording uncertainty. In *International Conference on Runtime Veri cation,* pages 442–456. Springer, 2011.

[11] David Basin, Felix Klaedtke, and Samuel Müller. Monitoring security policies with metric first-order temporal logic. In *Proceedings of the 15th ACM Symposium on Access Control Models and Technologies,* SACMAT '10, page 23–34, New York, NY, USA, 2010. Association for Computing Machinery.

[12] Omar Chowdhury, Limin Jia, Deepak Garg, and Anupam Datta. Temporal mode-checking for runtime monitoring of privacy policies. In Armin Biere and Roderick Bloem, editors, *Computer Aided Veri cation,* pages 131–149, Cham, 2014. Springer International Publishing.

[13] Deepak Garg, Limin Jia, and Anupam Datta. Policy auditing over incomplete logs: Theory, implementation and applications. In *Proceedings of the 18th ACM Conference on Computer and Communications Security,* CCS '11, page 151–162, New York, NY, USA, 2011. Association for Computing Machinery.

[14] Omar Chowdhury, Andreas Gampe, Jianwei Niu, Jeffery von Ronne, Jared Bennatt, Anupam Datta, Limin Jia, and William H. Winsborough. Privacy promises that can be kept: A policy analysis method with application to the hipaa privacy rule. In *Proceedings of the 18th ACM Symposium on Access Control Models and Technologies,* SACMAT '13, page 3–14, New York, NY, USA, 2013. Association for Computing Machinery.

[15] Henry DeYoung, Deepak Garg, Limin Jia, Dilsun Kaynar, and Anupam Datta. Experiences in the logical specification of the hipaa and glba privacy laws. In *Proceedings of the 9th Annual ACM Workshop on Privacy in the Electronic Society,* WPES '10, page 73–82, New York, NY, USA, 2010. Association for Computing Machinery.

[16] Syed Rafiul Hussain, Mitziu Echeverria, Omar Chowdhury, Ninghui Li, and Elisa Bertino. Privacy Attacks to the 4G and 5G Cellular Paging Protocols Using Side Channel Information. In *26th Annual Network and Distributed System Security Symposium, NDSS, San Diego, CA, USA, February 24-27, 2019,* 2019.

[17] Altaf Shaik, Jean-Pierre Seifert, Ravishankar Borgaonkar, N. Asokan, and Valtteri Niemi. Practical Attacks Against Privacy and Availability in 4G/LTE Mobile Communication Systems. In *23nd Annual Network and Distributed System Security Symposium, NDSS, San Diego, CA, USA, February 21-24,* 2016.

[18] Hongil Kim, Jiho Lee, Lee Eunkyu, and Yongdae Kim. Touching the Untouchables: Dynamic Security Analysis of the LTE Control Plane. In *Proceedings of the IEEE Symposium on Security & Privacy (SP).* IEEE, 2019.

[19] Benoit Michau and Christophe Devine. How to Not Break LTE Crypto. In *ANSSI Symposium sur la sécurité des technologies de l information et des communications (SSTIC),* 2016.

[20] Shinjo Park, Altaf Shaik, Ravishankar Borgaonkar, and Jean-Pierre Seifert. White Rabbit in Mobile: Effect of Unsecured Clock Source in Smartphones. In *Proceedings of the 6th Workshop on Security and Privacy in Smartphones and Mobile Devices,* pages 13–21. ACM, 2016.

[21] Heinz Riener. Exact synthesis of LTL properties from traces. In *2019 Forum for Speci cation and Design Languages (FDL),* pages 1–6. IEEE, 2019.

[22] Andrew Reynolds, Cesare Tinelli, Amit Goel, and Sava Krstić. Finite model finding in smt. In *International Conference on Computer Aided Veri cation,* pages 640–655. Springer, 2013.

[23] Andrew Reynolds, Jasmin Christian Blanchette, Simon Cruanes, and Cesare Tinelli. Model finding for recursive functions in smt. In *International Joint Conference on Automated Reasoning,* pages 133–151. Springer, 2016.

[24] Rajeev Alur, Rastislav Bodik, Garvit Juniwal, Milo MK Martin, Mukund Raghothaman, Sanjit A Seshia, Rishabh Singh, Armando Solar-Lezama, Emina Torlak, and Abhishek Udupa. *Syntax-guided synthesis.* IEEE, 2013.

[25] Andrew Reynolds, Haniel Barbosa, Andres Nötzli, Clark Barrett, and Cesare Tinelli. cvc 4 sy: smart and fast term enumeration for syntax-guided synthesis. In *International Conference on Computer Aided Veri cation,* pages 74–83. Springer, 2019.

[26] Herbert B. Enderton. *A mathematical introduction to logic.* Academic Press, 2 edition, 2001.

[27] Clark Barrett, Aaron Stump, and Cesare Tinelli. The SMT-LIB Standard: Version 2.0. In A. Gupta and D. Kroening, editors, *Proceedings of the 8th International Workshop on Satis ability Modulo Theories (Edinburgh, UK),* 2010.

[28] S. Kripke. Semantical Considerations on Modal Logic. *Acta Phil. Fennica,* 16:83–94, 1963.

[29] M. Fareed Arif, Daniel Larraz, Mitziu Echeverria, Andrew Reynolds, Omar Chowdhury, and Cesare Tinelli. SYSLITE: syntax-guided synthesis of PLTL formulas from finite traces. Technical report, Department of Computer Science, The University of Iowa, August 2020. Available at https://github.com/CLC-UIowa/SySLite.

[30] Luciano Baresi, Mohammad Mehdi Pourhashem Kallehbasti, and Matteo Rossi. Efficient scalable verification of LTL specifications. In *2015 IEEE/ACM 37th IEEE International Conference on Software Engineering,* volume 1, pages 711–721. IEEE, 2015.

[31] Clark Barrett, Christopher L. Conway, Morgan Deters, Liana Hadarean, Dejan Jovanovic, Tim King, Andrew Reynolds, and Cesare Tinelli. CVC4. In *Computer Aided Veri cation - 23rd International Conference, CAV 2011, Snowbird, UT, USA, July 14-20, 2011. Proceedings,* pages 171–177, 2011.

[32] Andrew Reynolds, Morgan Deters, Viktor Kuncak, Cesare Tinelli, and Clark W. Barrett. Counterexample-guided quantifier instantiation for synthesis in SMT. In *Computer Aided Veri cation - 27th International Conference, CAV 2015, San Francisco, CA, USA, July 18-24, 2015, Proceedings, Part II,* pages 198–216, 2015.

[33] Andrew Reynolds, Haniel Barbosa, Andres Nötzli, Clark W. Barrett, and Cesare Tinelli. cvc4sy: Smart and fast term enumeration for syntax-guided synthesis. In *Computer Aided Veri cation - 31st International Conference, CAV 2019, New York City, NY, USA, July 15-18, 2019, Proceedings, Part II,* pages 74–83, 2019.

[34] Armando Solar-Lezama, Liviu Tancau, Rastislav Bodik, Sanjit Seshia, and Vijay Saraswat. Combinatorial sketching for finite programs. *SIGPLAN Not.,* 41(11):404–415, October 2006.

[35] Andres Nötzli, Andrew Reynolds, Haniel Barbosa, Aina Niemetz, Mathias Preiner, Clark W. Barrett, and Cesare Tinelli. Syntax-guided rewrite rule enumeration for SMT solvers. In *Theory and Applications of Satis ability Testing - SAT 2019 - 22nd International Conference, SAT*

2019, Lisbon, Portugal, July 9-12, 2019, Proceedings, pages 279–297, 2019.

[36] José Oncina and Pedro Garcia. Inferring regular languages in polynomial updated time. In *Pattern recognition and image analysis: selected papers from the IVth Spanish Symposium*, pages 49–61. World Scientific, 1992.

[37] Shufang Zhu, Geguang Pu, and Moshe Y. Vardi. First-order vs. second-order encodings for ltlf-to-automata translation, 2019.

[38] Ashok K. Chandra, Dexter C. Kozen, and Larry J. Stockmeyer. Alternation. *J. ACM*, 28(1):114–133, January 1981.

[39] Giuseppe De Giacomo and Moshe Y. Vardi. Linear temporal logic and linear dynamic logic on finite traces. In *Proceedings of the Twenty-Third International Joint Conference on Artificial Intelligence*, IJCAI '13, page 854–860. AAAI Press, 2013.

[40] Yih-Kuen Tsay, Yu-Fang Chen, Ming-Hsien Tsai, Kang-Nien Wu, and Wen-Chin Chan. Goal: A graphical tool for manipulating büchi automata and temporal formulae. In *International Conference on Tools and Algorithms for the Construction and Analysis of Systems*, pages 466–471. Springer, 2007.

[41] Adrian Dabrowski, Nicola Pianta, Thomas Klepp, Martin Mulazzani, and Edgar Weippl. Imsi-catch me if you can: Imsi-catcher-catchers. In *Proceedings of the 30th annual computer security applications Conference*, pages 246–255, 2014.

[42] Syed Rafiul Hussain, Mitziu Echeverria, Ankush Singla, Omar Chowdhury, and Elisa Bertino. Insecure connection bootstrapping in cellular networks: the root of all evil. In *Proceedings of the 12th Conference on Security and Privacy in Wireless and Mobile Networks*, pages 1–11, 2019.

[43] Viktor Schuppan and Armin Biere. Shortest counterexamples for symbolic model checking of ltl with past. In *International Conference on Tools and Algorithms for the Construction and Analysis of Systems*, pages 493–509. Springer, 2005.

[44] Iosif Androulidakis. Intercepting mobile phone calls and short messages using a gsm tester. In *International Conference on Computer Networks*, pages 281–288. Springer, 2011.

[45] Myrto Arapinis, Loretta Mancini, Eike Ritter, Mark Ryan, Nico Golde, Kevin Redon, and Ravishankar Borgaonkar. New privacy issues in mobile telephony: fix and verification. In *Proceedings of the 2012 ACM conference on Computer and communications security*, pages 205–216, 2012.

[46] Byeongdo Hong, Sangwook Bae, and Yongdae Kim. Guti reallocation demystified: Cellular location tracking with changing temporary identifier. In *NDSS*, 2018.

[47] Katharina Kohls, David Rupprecht, Thorsten Holz, and Christina Pöpper. Lost traffic encryption: fingerprinting lte/4g traffic on layer two. In *Proceedings of the 12th Conference on Security and Privacy in Wireless and Mobile Networks*, pages 249–260, 2019.

[48] Denis Foo Kune, John Koelndorfer, Nicholas Hopper, and Yongdae Kim. Location leaks on the gsm air interface. *ISOC NDSS (Feb 2012)*, 2012.

[49] Ulrike Meyer and Susanne Wetzel. A man-in-the-middle attack on umts. In *Proceedings of the 3rd ACM workshop on Wireless security*, pages 90–97, 2004.

[50] David Rupprecht, Katharina Kohls, Thorsten Holz, and Christina Pöpper. Breaking lte on layer two. In *2019 IEEE Symposium on Security and Privacy (SP)*, pages 1121–1136. IEEE, 2019.

[51] David Rupprecht, Katharina Kohls, Thorsten Holz, and Christina Pöpper. Imp4gt: Impersonation attacks in 4g networks. In *ISOC Network and Distributed System Security Symposium (NDSS)*. ISOC, February 2020.

[52] Yuanjie Li, Chunyi Peng, Zengwen Yuan, Jiayao Li, Haotian Deng, and Tao Wang. Mobileinsight: Extracting and analyzing cellular network information on smartphones. In *Proceedings of the 22nd Annual International Conference on Mobile Computing and Networking*, MobiCom '16, pages 202–215, New York, NY, USA, 2016. ACM.

[53] Ismael Gomez-Miguelez, Andres Garcia-Saavedra, Paul D Sutton, Pablo Serrano, Cristina Cano, and Doug J Leith. srsLTE: An Open-source Platform for LTE Evolution and Experimentation. In *Proceedings of the Tenth ACM International Workshop on Wireless Network Testbeds, Experimental Evaluation, and Characterization*, pages 25–32, 2016.

[54] Byeongdo Hong, Shinjo Park, Hongil Kim, Dongkwan Kim, Hyunwook Hong, Hyunwoo Choi, Jean-Pierre Seifert, Sung-Ju Lee, and Yongdae Kim. Peeking over the cellular walled gardens-a method for closed network diagnosis. *IEEE Transactions on Mobile Computing*, 17(10):2366–2380, 2018.

[55] Eugene Asarin, Alexandre Donzé, Oded Maler, and Dejan Nickovic. Parametric identification of temporal properties. In *International Conference on Runtime Verification*, pages 147–160. Springer, 2011.

[56] Zhaodan Kong, Austin Jones, and Calin Belta. Temporal logics for learning and detection of anomalous behavior. *IEEE Transactions on Automatic Control*, 62(3):1210–1222, 2016.

[57] Prashant Vaidyanathan, Rachael Ivison, Giuseppe Bombara, Nicholas A DeLateur, Ron Weiss, Douglas Densmore, and Calin Belta. Grid-based temporal logic inference. In *2017 IEEE 56th Annual Conference on Decision and Control (CDC)*, pages 5354–5359. IEEE, 2017.

[58] Ezio Bartocci, Luca Bortolussi, and Guido Sanguinetti. Learning temporal logical properties discriminating ecg models of cardiac arrhytmias. *arXiv preprint arXiv:1312.7523*, 2013.

[59] Wenchao Li, Lili Dworkin, and Sanjit A Seshia. Mining assumptions for synthesis. In *Ninth ACM/IEEE International Conference on Formal Methods and Models for Codesign (MEMPCODE2011)*, pages 43–50. IEEE, 2011.

[60] Caroline Lemieux, Dennis Park, and Ivan Beschastnikh. General ltl specification mining (t). In *2015 30th IEEE/ACM International Conference on Automated Software Engineering (ASE)*, pages 81–92. IEEE, 2015.

[61] Dana Angluin. Learning regular sets from queries and counterexamples. *Information and computation*, 75(2):87–106, 1987.

[62] Georgios Giantamidis, Stavros Tripakis, and Stylianos Basagiannis. Learning moore machines from input–output traces. *International Journal on Software Tools for Technology Transfer*, pages 1–29, 2019.

[63] Marijn J. H. Heule and Sicco Verwer. Exact dfa identification using sat solvers. In *Proceedings of the 10th International Colloquium Conference on Grammatical Inference: Theoretical Results and Applications*, page 66–79, Berlin, Heidelberg, 2010. Springer-Verlag.

[64] Daniel Neider and Nils Jansen. Regular model checking using solver technologies and automata learning. In *NASA Formal Methods Symposium*, pages 16–31. Springer, 2013.

[65] Benedikt Bollig, Peter Habermehl, Carsten Kern, and Martin Leucker. Angluin-style learning of nfa. In *Twenty-First International Joint Conference on Artificial Intelligence*, 2009.

[66] Dana Angluin, Sarah Eisenstat, and Dana Fisman. Learning regular languages via alternating automata. In *Twenty-Fourth International Joint Conference on Artificial Intelligence*, 2015.

[67] Nir Piterman, Amir Pnueli, and Yaniv Sa'ar. Synthesis of reactive (1) designs. In *International Workshop on Verification, Model Checking, and Abstract Interpretation*, pages 364–380. Springer, 2006.

[68] Rajeev Alur, Rishabh Singh, Dana Fisman, and Armando Solar-Lezama. Search-based program synthesis. *Communications of the ACM*, 61(12):84–93, 2018.

13

Selecting Stable Safe Configurations for Systems Modelled by Neural Networks with ReLU Activation

Franz Brauße
Department of Computer Science
University of Manchester, UK
franz.brausse@manchester.ac.uk

Zurab Khasidashvili
Product Enablement Solutions Group
Intel Israel Development Center
zurab.khasidashvili@intel.com

Konstantin Korovin
Department of Computer Science
University of Manchester, UK
konstantin.korovin@manchester.ac.uk

Abstract—**Combining machine learning with constraint solving and formal methods is an interesting new direction in research with a wide range of safety critical applications. Our focus in this work is on analyzing Neural Networks with Rectified Linear Activation Function (`NN-ReLU`). The existing, very recent research works in this direction describe multiple approaches to satisfiability checking for constraints on `NN-ReLU` output. Here we extend this line of work in two orthogonal directions: We propose an algorithm for finding configurations of `NN-ReLU` that are (1) safe and (2) stable. We assume that the inputs of the `NN-ReLU` are divided into existentially and universally quantified variables, where the former represent the parameters for configuring the `NN-ReLU` and the latter represent (possibly constrained) free inputs. We are looking for (1) values of the configuration parameters for which the `NN-ReLU` output satisfies a given constraint for any legal values of the input variables (the safety requirement); and (2) such that the entire family of configurations with configuration variable values close to a safe configuration is also safe (the stability requirement). To our knowledge this is the first work that proposes SMT-based algorithms for searching safe and stable configuration parameters for systems modelled using neural networks. We experimentally evaluate our algorithm on `NN-ReLUs` trained on a set of real-life datasets originating from an industrial CAD application at Intel.**

I. INTRODUCTION

Neural Networks (NN) are widely used in modeling real life systems and processes, including safety critical ones. Formal analysis of NN models is therefore becoming increasingly important for exploration, validation and optimisation of complex systems, and for a much wider range of applications. Multiple recent research works have partly addressed this emerging need: they propose satisfiability checking algorithms for the constraints defined by an `NN-ReLU` and by inequality constraints on its inputs and outputs by encoding this problem into Satisfiability Modulo Theories (SMT) [3] or Mixed-Integer Linear Programming (MILP) [28], [4], [16], [6], [9], [17]. In this work, by a constraint we will mean a Boolean combination of inequality constraints on the inputs of a `NN-ReLU` or its outputs. Given an `NN-ReLU` and constraints on inputs most of these algorithms can verify whether output constraints are satisfied and provide a tight over-approximation (guarantee) on the outputs' range if required; the former capability is called

robustness to adversarial examples in [4] for classification models, and the latter is called *range estimation* in [9] for regression models; and both are studied for extensions of `NN-ReLU` called *Piecewise Linear* NN [25] in [6] and [9], respectively.

In this paper we are looking into a related but quite different problem. In many applications we have analog systems which do not have explicit representations and are modelled using NNs based on some experimental test data. An important part of such systems are parameters that are usually configured manually to obtain a desired system behaviour. In this paper we propose several algorithms for finding safe, stable and close to optimal parameters for such systems. An atomic building block in our algorithm is the capability of an SMT solver to check that the output satisfies safety constraints for inputs restricted by input constraints. The problem of finding parameter configurations is more general than the safety problem and requires solving problems with quantifier alternations which are notoriously difficult for SMT solvers.

In a nutshell, we assume that the inputs of an `NN-ReLU` are divided into two groups: the *configuration parameters* that are used to configure the system, and the regular inputs to the system for interacting with the environment. Values of the configuration parameters should be fixed before the system starts operating to perform the task it is designed and configured for, in a safe and close to optimal fashion. A *configuration* is then an assignment of values to the configuration parameters. We assume that the `NN-ReLU` output o is a numeric variable that ranges between 0 and 1, and we are looking for assignments to the configuration parameters such that for all legal values of inputs the output satisfies one or more range constraints like $o \geq 0.9$. Such an assignment is then a *safe* assignment and so is the corresponding configuration. In addition, assuming that, say, the high values of the `NN-ReLU` output are considered as a better performance, then *optimisation* in the context of this work would mean finding safe configuration of the `NN-ReLU` for a constraint $o \geq th$ with a threshold value $th > 0.9$, e.g., constraint $o \geq 0.95$. Since we do not aim to always find a maximal possible threshold for which a safe configuration exists, "close to optimal" is used in this work informally.

To avoid any confusion, we remark straightaway that by configuring a NN-ReLU we do not mean configuring the NN-ReLU training parameters themselves to aid a faster convergence of the training or to improve the modeling accuracy. Configuring parameters that control the training procedure of NNs is an important problem that in principle can be approached heuristically with the procedure proposed in this work to search for close to optimal configurations but this application is outside of the scope of this paper. In this paper we consider configuration parameters which are a part of the analog system which is modelled by a NN-ReLU.

We propose to formalise the problem of configuration selection for NN-ReLU modelled in first-order logic or quantified SMT, where the configuration parameters correspond to the existentially quantified variables and the inputs correspond to universally quantified variables. The configuration selection problem somewhat corresponds to the *Effectively Propositional (EPR)* fragment, also called the *Bernays-Schönfinkel-Ramsey* fragment, which consists of first-order formulas with no occurrences of function symbols other than constants, and which when written in prenex normal form have the quantifier prefix $\exists^*\forall^*$. *EPR* is a decidable fragment of pure first-order logic and very efficient solvers exist [20], and therefore multiple formal verification problems have been encoded into the *EPR* fragment [27], [18], [14], [15], [19].

In our encoding of the configuration selection problem for NNs we require support for reasoning with linear and nonlinear functions: the theory we deal with is quantified linear real arithmetic with ReLU constraints; in addition, for the industrial application that we are dealing with, it is critical for our algorithm to support ordered categorical variables (say integers) and unordered categorical variables. One of the main contributions in this paper is a δ-decision procedure for the relevant fragment of $\exists^*\forall^*$ formulas over these domains, we call *normed GEAR fragment*.

In many real-life applications, for example the ones dealing with analog systems, the value applied to an analog pin, which we usually model as a numeric feature in machine learning and as a real number in the constraint solving world, is not the same as the value sampled by the system. There is always an error, maybe very small, in the value that is applied and in the value that is sampled, and these two errors do not need to add up to 0. Thus when configuring or verifying such a system, it is required to take this error into account. We think that this aspect has been largely neglected in the context of formal methods for quantified formulas, and we will address this problem in this work by considering *stable solutions* for the configuration problem, elaborated upon below.

Neural Networks and the ML models in general do not model the systems with a hundred percent accuracy. In fact, when training a model, it is a bad idea to build a model that exactly matches the output values in the training dataset; this is known in ML literature as *overfitting*, and is considered bad practice because such a model is unlikely to be accurate on the unseen samples (on which the model was not trained). In fact, the data might actually be contradictory in that two completely identical samples might have different labels, because of an error in data collection or because of insufficient precision in the representation of the feature values, thus a function that fully matches the training data might not exist at all. Thus, again, when exploring ML models – configuring them for a safe and close to optimal performance of the systems that they model – one needs to take into account that safely configuring the model does not mean at all that the modelled system itself is safe.

One way of mitigating this safety gap is to look for safe configurations of the NN-ReLU models that are *stable*. A safe configuration is stable if all configurations sufficiently close to it are also safe for all legal inputs. In other words, a stable satisfying assignment to configuration parameters is a Cartesian product of open or close intervals of configuration parameters within their respective legal ranges such that each assignment within the product is a satisfying assignment. In the industrial application where our research results have been applied, for most configuration parameters the radius is actually as large as 10% of the value of the variable in the configuration. This is because the sampling error from analog equipment can be dependent on the intended value itself. For some other configuration parameters, say representing clock ticks, the radius is defined through an absolute value, independently from the value of that variable in the configuration.

It has been shown recently that NNs and several other classification models are vulnerable to *adversarial examples* [30]. That is, these ML models misclassify examples that are only slightly different from correctly classified examples drawn from the data distribution. This is another reason why building stable safe configurations is important: we want the configuration to remain safe if the values of configuration parameters are perturbed, this being caused by a malicious adversary or the errors in sampling or sensing data from the equipment or environment. The roundoff errors in the software packages used in training NNs and other ML models are yet another source for the discrepancy between the intended models and the ones that we analyze formally. This list can be continued further.

Work [4] defines a *robustness* measure of an NN at an input vector as the maximal Chebyshev distance L_∞ to the nearest adversarial input vector and proposes an algorithm for estimating it. Work [16] defines a NN-ReLU as δ-*locally-robust* at an input vector if there is no adversarial data point within L_∞-distance smaller than δ, and reports that their Reluplex algorithm can verify whether a NN-ReLU is δ-locally-robust at a given input vector or is globally robust. Work [12] proposes an efficient way to generate adversarial data samples for the purpose of improving the accuracy of classification. For NN-ReLUs with a numeric output, a safety constraint applied to the output straightforwardly converts the model into a classifier of two classes SAT and UNSAT. We note that unlike the robustness, our notion of stability is defined with respect to the configuration parameters rather than the free inputs.

To reiterate, our aim in this work is to safely configure

real, complex systems, not NNs; the NNs are used to approximate the original systems. In this context, we would like to emphasize the following: real systems in many cases have multiple functionalities and depend on many variables but not all variables are equally important for all the properties of the outputs. Specifically in the CAD domain, often accurate models can be built using few variables only. See [24] for an example where only 10 and 30 features out of 10 000 available features were enough to build high quality models for a classification and a regression task, respectively, in the *Signal Integrity* domain where the results of this research have been applied. Our algorithms determine safe and stable regions for the NN approximations which are checked against the original system to see whether these safe regions are safe in the original system. We demonstrate that one can use SMT solvers to guide the NN model refinement not only based on spurious counter examples to the safety constraint on the output but also based on safe regions for a current NN approximation; the latter is a new paradigm in model refinement. Related abstraction refinement techniques such as usage of genetic algorithms, Bayesian optimization, or reinforcement learning are only heuristic methods, without any safety guarantees, and are not guided by a constraint solver.

Main contributions:

- The notion of Safe and Stable Configurations for systems represented by NNs and the corresponding SSC problem.
- The reflexively guarded $\exists^*\forall^*$ fragment (GEAR) and its connection to the SSC problem.
- A general satisfiability algorithm for GEAR, called GEARSAT and its variant GEARSAT$_\delta$ for the SSC problem.
- Proof that GEARSAT$_\delta$ is a δ-decision procedure for the SSC problem.
- Demonstration of the applicability of GEARSAT$_\delta$ to industrial configuration problems modelled using NNs in the CAD domain.

The rest of the paper is organized as follows. We start with preliminaries in Section II. In Section III we define the problem of configuration selection formally and define stable satisfying assignments for configuration parameters. In Section IV we introduce the GEAR fragment of $\exists^*\forall^*$ formulas capturing this problem in a general context and present a sound satisfiability algorithm GEARSAT. In Section V we introduce GEARSAT$_\delta$, an adaptation of this algorithm to normed domains as required in our application and prove that GEARSAT$_\delta$ is a δ-decision procedure for the SSC problem. Experimental results on industrial problems are reported in Section VI. The conclusions appear in Section VII.

II. PRELIMINARIES

We consider systems which have continuous and discrete inputs and outputs. An input domain $\mathbb{D}$ is a Cartesian product of reals $\mathbb{R}$, integers $\mathbb{Z}$ and finite, non-empty sets with elements from $\mathbb{Z}$. Throughout this paper $\|\cdot\|$ denotes a fixed but arbitrary norm on $\mathbb{D}$.

A *real-valued system* defined on $\mathbb{D}$ can be represented as a function $f : \mathbb{D} \to \mathbb{R}$. A *configurable real-valued system* is a system which also has *configuration parameters* $f : \mathbb{D}_{par} \times \mathbb{D}_{in} \to \mathbb{R}$ where $\mathbb{D}_{par}$ is the domain for configuration parameters and $\mathbb{D}_{in}$ is the domain for inputs. We assume $\mathbb{D} := \mathbb{D}_{par} \times \mathbb{D}_{in}$ is not empty and $\|\cdot\|$ is a norm on $\mathbb{D}$.

We assume that a system is given as a black-box function which can be evaluated on a collection of inputs and configuration parameters but its explicit representation is generally unknown. Given a finite collection D of data points from $\mathbb{D}$ we can build approximations of f using neural networks by training them on D.

A (feed-forward) neural network $\mathcal{N}$ consists of layers with inputs and outputs [29]. The input to the first layer is the input to $\mathcal{N}$ and the output of the last layer is the output of $\mathcal{N}$. The input of an intermediate layer is the output of the previous layer. Each layer is a composition of an affine transformation of its inputs with a non-linear activation function. One of the most commonly used activation functions is the rectified linear unit (ReLU), which is defined to be identity for all positive inputs and 0 for non-positive inputs. Even with such simple activation function neural networks can approximate all continuous functions [22].

One of the advantages of neural networks with the ReLU activation functions (NN-ReLU) is that they can be represented in a language amenable to SMT solvers. In particular, one can represent NN-ReLU either in the theory of linear arithmetic with conditionals or directly as a specialised decision procedure [16].

In this paper we are not concerned with particulars of representations of NN-ReLUs. We will consider a theory $\mathcal{T}_{\|\cdot\|}$ (in the SMT-LIB sense [3]) that can be used to specify NNs, and include:

- sorts for reals, integers, finite non-empty domains interpreted as subsets of integers, together with
- operations for linear arithmetic with real coefficients and variables of mixed real and integer sorts,
- usual arithmetic comparison operators $\{\geq, >, =\}$,
- the norm $\|\cdot\|$,
- Boolean operators and
- a collection of activation functions AF.

We will assume that there is a decision procedure for the quantifier-free fragment of $\mathcal{T}_{\|\cdot\|}$.

In our experiments (Section VI) we use only ReLU and linear activation functions (i.e., $AF = \{\text{ReLU}, \text{Lin}\}$) but our approach is applicable to arbitrary activation functions as long as there is a decision procedure for them. We also used Chebyshev norm $\|\cdot\|_\infty$ as this can be expressed using linear constraints. In these cases activation functions and the norm can be covered by standard SMT theories and we can use SMT solvers or mixed integer programming to solve the quantifier-free fragment of $\mathcal{T}_{\|\cdot\|}$. While our focus in this work is on NN models, we remark that the algorithms and decision procedures proposed in this work are also applicable to other ML models, including tree-based models such as random forest and polynomial models.

We will use p, q, x, y possibly with indices to denote variables and boldface p, q, x will denote vectors of variables. When it is not essential we do not specify sorts of the variables. Given an assignment α, we use $[\![\cdot]\!]^\alpha$ to denote the interpretation of variables according to α, which is extended to interpretation of terms and formulas in the standard way.

We assume that NNs are expressible in $\mathcal{T}_{\|\cdot\|}$. In particular, with each neural network $\mathcal{N} : \mathbb{D}_{par} \times \mathbb{D}_{in} \to \mathbb{R}$ we associate a quantifier-free formula $\varphi_{\mathcal{N}}(p, x, y)$ in $\mathcal{T}_{\|\cdot\|}$ such that for every assignment α of variables, $\mathcal{N}([\![p]\!]^\alpha, [\![x]\!]^\alpha) = [\![y]\!]^\alpha$ if and only if $[\![\varphi_{\mathcal{N}}(p, x, y)]\!]^\alpha$ is true. Note that the special case of classification problems when $\mathcal{N} : \mathbb{D}_{par} \times \mathbb{D}_{in} \to \{0, \ldots, n\}$ is covered by our framework as well.

III. Safe and Stable Configurations

Consider a configurable system $f : \mathbb{D}_{par} \times \mathbb{D}_{in} \to \mathbb{R}$. We distinguish between parameters and inputs in order to be clear about their quantification, which is existential and universal, respectively. Let f be modelled by a neural network $\mathcal{N}$. Let $\varphi_{\mathcal{N}}(p, x, y)$ be a formula in $\mathcal{T}_{\|\cdot\|}$ defining $\mathcal{N}$ as described in Section II. A specification for the system is a formula $\varphi_{spec}(p, x, y)$ which includes constraints on parameters, inputs and output. If the set of parameters is empty then a system is *safe* if the following formula holds:

$$\forall x y (\varphi_{\mathcal{N}}(x, y) \to \varphi_{spec}(x, y)).$$

This notion is similar to the verification problem in [16], [28]. The main problem we consider in this paper is a different one: finding configuration parameters for the system that are safe and stable for all inputs, as defined below.

A *safe solution to the parameter configuration problem (or just a solution for short)* is an assignment α of parameters p such that the following formula holds:

$$\forall x y (\varphi_{\mathcal{N}}([\![p]\!]^\alpha, x, y) \to \varphi_{spec}([\![p]\!]^\alpha, x, y)).$$

Finding solutions to parametrised systems corresponds to checking satisfiability of $\exists^* \forall^*$ formulas:

$$\exists p \forall x y (\varphi_{\mathcal{N}}(p, x, y) \to \varphi_{spec}(p, x, y)).$$

This is in contrast to safety properties where the problem can be formulated using just one type of quantifiers $\forall^*$.

Let $r \geq 0$ be a rational constant. A solution α is called *r-stable* if all parameter configurations which are r close to α are also solutions to the specification:

$$\forall q (\|[\![p]\!]^\alpha - q\| \leq r \to \forall x y (\varphi_{\mathcal{N}}(q, x, y) \to \varphi_{spec}(q, x, y))).$$

Similarly to above, finding r-stable solutions corresponds to checking satisfiability of $\exists^* \forall^*$ formulas.

$$\exists p \forall q (\|p - q\| \leq r \to \\ \forall x y (\varphi_{\mathcal{N}}(q, x, y) \to \varphi_{spec}(q, x, y))). \quad (1)$$

We call this the Safe and Stable Configuration problem (SSC).

Let us note that the stability condition connects existentially quantified parameters p with introduced universally quantified variables q. In this case even when there are no inputs and only

parameters the formula involves $\exists^* \forall^*$ quantifier alternation (see also Remark 1).

In order to solve the SSC problem we first introduce a general GEAR fragment and a satisfiability algorithm for GEAR called GEARSAT. GEARSAT does not rely on properties of $\mathcal{T}_{\|\cdot\|}$ and is applicable to any theory without uninterpreted symbols and decidable quantifier-free fragment. Then we show that SSC can be expressed in a special fragment of GEAR called *normed GEAR*, for which we modify GEARSAT into a δ-complete decision procedure GEARSAT$_\delta$.

IV. The Reflexively guarded $\exists^* \forall^*$ fragment and GEARSAT

Algorithm 1 (EA-SAT-Basic) Solve $\exists p \forall x \varphi(p, x)$ using a solver for the existential fragment.

---

procedure EA-SAT-BASIC(φ)
  loop
    if $\varphi(p, x)$ is unsat **then**
      return unsat
    end if
    $\alpha \leftarrow$ assignment of p, x satisfying φ
    if $\neg \varphi([\![p]\!]^\alpha, x)$ is unsat **then**
      return α restricted to p
    end if
    $\varphi(p', x) \leftarrow \varphi(p', x) \wedge (p' \neq [\![p]\!]^\alpha)$ ▷ learn lemma
  end loop
end procedure

We start with a general Algorithm 1 for solving $\exists^* \forall^*$ formulas which is inspired by model-based quantifier instantiation procedures [11] and only requires a solver for the existential fragment.

Theorem 1. *Algorithm 1 is sound.*

The theorem follows from the observation that Algorithm 1 only generates lemmas which are implied by its input formula φ, making it a sound procedure.

The downside of Algorithm 1 is that it generates very weak lemmas excluding point-wise counter-examples. In particular, for infinite domains, Algorithm 1 does not terminate in general. To mitigate this, we propose a novel procedure (Algorithm 2) which generates more general lemmas which exclude large regions from the search space and facilitate termination. This procedure assumes that the quantifiers in $\exists^* \forall^*$ formulas are guarded as defined below.

Definition 1. A closed first-order $\exists^* \forall^*$ formula ξ of the form

$$\xi \equiv \exists p [\eta(p) \wedge \forall q (\theta(p, q) \to \forall x (\psi(q, x)))] \quad (2)$$

is in the *reflexively guarded* $\exists^* \forall^*$ fragment, GEAR for short, iff η, θ and ψ are quantifier-free formulas and θ defines a reflexive relation. We say that p is guarded by $\eta(p)$ and q is guarded by $\theta(p, q)$.

Algorithm 2 (GEARSAT) Solve reflexively guarded $\exists^*\forall^*$ formulas based on a solver for the existential fragment.

---

  procedure GEARSAT(η, θ, ψ)
    $E(\boldsymbol{p}) \leftarrow \eta(\boldsymbol{p})$
    loop
      if $\psi(\boldsymbol{p},\boldsymbol{x}) \wedge E(\boldsymbol{p})$ is unsat **then**
        return unsat
      end if
      $\alpha \leftarrow$ assignment of $\boldsymbol{p}, \boldsymbol{x}$ satisfying $\psi(\boldsymbol{p},\boldsymbol{x}) \wedge E(\boldsymbol{p})$
      $\varphi(\boldsymbol{q},\boldsymbol{x}) \leftarrow (\theta([\![\boldsymbol{p}]\!]^\alpha, \boldsymbol{q}) \rightarrow \psi(\boldsymbol{q},\boldsymbol{x}))$
      if $\neg\varphi(\boldsymbol{x},\boldsymbol{q})$ is unsat **then**
        return α restricted to $\boldsymbol{p}$
      end if
      $\beta \leftarrow$ assignment of $\boldsymbol{q}, \boldsymbol{x}$ satisfying $\neg\varphi(\boldsymbol{q},\boldsymbol{x})$
      $E(\boldsymbol{p}) \leftarrow E(\boldsymbol{p}) \wedge \neg\theta(\boldsymbol{p}, [\![\boldsymbol{q}]\!]^\beta)$ ▷ learn guard lemma
    end loop
  end procedure

In order to prove soundness of Algorithm 2, we require the guard θ to define a reflexive relation, i.e., $\forall \boldsymbol{q}(\theta(\boldsymbol{q},\boldsymbol{q}))$ holds true. This can be motivated by the observation that θ connects the existentially and (a subset of the) universally quantified variables. In our application θ usually takes the form $\|\boldsymbol{p}-\boldsymbol{q}\| \leq r$, which is trivially reflexive, however, no properties besides reflexivity are required for soundness. We do not impose any restrictions on the guard η, it can be used to constrain the range of configuration parameters.

Theorem 2. *The Algorithm* GEARSAT *is sound for the GEAR fragment.*

Proof: Let ξ be a formula in the GEAR fragment of the form (2). Assume GEARSAT(η, θ, ψ) performs $N \geq 0$ iterations and terminates in iteration $N + 1$ with result κ. By the construction in Algorithm 2, for each $n = 1, \ldots, N$ there are assignments α_n and β_n satisfying $A_n := \eta(\boldsymbol{p}) \wedge \bigwedge_{i=1}^{n-1} \neg\theta(\boldsymbol{p}, [\![\boldsymbol{q}]\!]^{\beta_i}) \wedge \psi(\boldsymbol{p},\boldsymbol{x})$ and $B_n := \theta([\![\boldsymbol{p}]\!]^{\alpha_n}, \boldsymbol{q}) \wedge \neg\psi(\boldsymbol{q},\boldsymbol{x})$, respectively. We show the cases for κ separately.

Consider $\kappa = $ unsat. If $N = 0$, then by construction $A_1 \equiv \eta(\boldsymbol{p}) \wedge \forall\boldsymbol{x}(\psi(\boldsymbol{p},\boldsymbol{x}))$ is unsat. $\eta(\boldsymbol{p})$ is implied by ξ as is $\forall\boldsymbol{q}(\theta(\boldsymbol{p},\boldsymbol{q}) \rightarrow \forall\boldsymbol{x}(\psi(\boldsymbol{q},\boldsymbol{x})))$. Since θ defines a reflexive relation, ξ also implies $\forall\boldsymbol{x}(\psi(\boldsymbol{p},\boldsymbol{x}))$. Therefore ξ is unsat. Otherwise $N > 0$, then $A_{N+1} := A_N \wedge \neg\theta(\boldsymbol{p}, [\![\boldsymbol{q}]\!]^{\beta_N})$ is unsat. In order to derive a contradiction, assume there is $\boldsymbol{p}^*$ such that $\eta(\boldsymbol{p}^*) \wedge \forall\boldsymbol{q}(\theta(\boldsymbol{p}^*,\boldsymbol{q}) \rightarrow \forall\boldsymbol{x}(\psi(\boldsymbol{q},\boldsymbol{x})))$ holds. By property of θ, so does $\theta(\boldsymbol{p}^*,\boldsymbol{p}^*)$, therefore, $\forall\boldsymbol{x}(\psi(\boldsymbol{p}^*,\boldsymbol{x}))$ is true. Since A_{N+1} is unsat and both $\eta(\boldsymbol{p}^*)$ and $\forall\boldsymbol{x}(\psi(\boldsymbol{p}^*,\boldsymbol{x}))$ are true, there is $n \leq N$ such that $\neg\theta(\boldsymbol{p}^*, [\![\boldsymbol{q}]\!]^{\beta_n})$ is false. Consequently, by assumption, $\forall\boldsymbol{x}(\psi([\![\boldsymbol{q}]\!]^{\beta_n},\boldsymbol{x}))$ holds. However, β_n satisfies B_n and therefore also $\neg\psi(\boldsymbol{q},\boldsymbol{x})$. A contradiction.

Consider $\kappa \neq $ unsat. Then the assignment α is computed which satisfies A_{N+1} and, in particular, $\eta(\boldsymbol{p})$. Thus, if $\theta([\![\boldsymbol{p}]\!]^\alpha, \boldsymbol{q}) \wedge \neg\psi(\boldsymbol{q},\boldsymbol{x})$ is unsat, $\eta([\![\boldsymbol{p}]\!]^\alpha) \wedge \forall\boldsymbol{q}\boldsymbol{x}(\theta([\![\boldsymbol{p}]\!]^\alpha, \boldsymbol{q}) \rightarrow \psi(\boldsymbol{q},\boldsymbol{x}))$ and therefore also $\xi([\![\boldsymbol{p}]\!]^\alpha)$ hold. ∎

Let us note that we can apply GEARSAT to general $\exists^*\forall^*$ formulas $\exists\boldsymbol{p}[\forall\boldsymbol{x}(\psi(\boldsymbol{p},\boldsymbol{x}))]$ which are not explicitly guarded by

first transforming them into a guarded form (2) where θ defines the identity relation and $\eta \equiv$ true. In this case GEARSAT performs the same steps as Algorithm 1.

In contrast to Algorithm 1, however, GEARSAT takes advantage of guards when they define large regions in parameter space. In this case, generated lemmas are negations of partial guard instantiations that exclude large regions from the search space around found counter-examples.

Let us note that GEARSAT terminates whenever the process of generating lemmas $E_n(\boldsymbol{p}) = \eta(\boldsymbol{p}) \wedge \bigwedge_{i=1}^n \neg\theta(\boldsymbol{p}, [\![\boldsymbol{q}]\!]^{\beta_i})$ is guaranteed to result in an unsatisfiable lemma after a finite number of steps. Note, that during the run of GEARSAT we generate strictly stronger lemmas, in particular $\exists\boldsymbol{p}(E_i(\boldsymbol{p}) \wedge \neg E_j(\boldsymbol{p}))$ holds for all $i < j$. From this it follows that GEARSAT is a decision procedure for finite domains and more generally for fragments where there are only finitely many non-equivalent lemmas of the form above.

In many applications including ours, solutions to the SSC problem are required to be stable on their (topological) neighbourhood. In this case the reflexive guard also enables *deciding* satisfiability even when the bounded domain itself is infinite. This statement is made precise in Theorem 4 for normed domains such as $\mathbb{D}_{par}$.

V. A δ-DECISION PROCEDURE FOR THE SAFE AND STABLE CONFIGURATION PROBLEM

The GEARSAT algorithm can be employed to find safe and r-stable solutions to the configuration problem as follows. As described in Section III the SSC problem can be represented using formulas of the form (1). Such formulas are a special case of the GEAR formulas (2) where the guard is $\theta_r \equiv \|\boldsymbol{p} - \boldsymbol{q}\| \leq r$, which we call *stability guard*, and $\psi(\boldsymbol{q},\boldsymbol{x},y) \equiv \varphi_\mathcal{N}(\boldsymbol{q},\boldsymbol{x},y) \rightarrow \varphi_{spec}(\boldsymbol{q},\boldsymbol{x},y)$. Then, safe and r-stable regions can be searched using Algorithm 2 applied to:

$$\varphi_r = \exists\boldsymbol{p}[\eta(\boldsymbol{p}) \wedge \forall\boldsymbol{q}(\theta_r(\boldsymbol{p},\boldsymbol{q}) \rightarrow \forall\boldsymbol{x}y(\psi(\boldsymbol{q},\boldsymbol{x},y)))] \quad (3)$$

We will call $\mathcal{T}_{\|\cdot\|}$ formulas of the form (3) *normed GEAR formulas*. They form a special case of reflexively guarded $\exists^*\forall^*$ formulas, since $\|\boldsymbol{p} - \boldsymbol{p}\| = 0$.

In many applications, including ours, we can tolerate to reject solutions if counter-examples are located within some tolerance of the safe region. To this end we introduce the notion of unsatisfiability under δ-*perturbation*, or δ-*unsatisfiability*.

Let θ_r be a stability guard as given above and $\delta > 0$, then the δ-perturbation of θ_r is $\theta_{r+\delta} = \|\boldsymbol{p} - \boldsymbol{q}\| \leq r + \delta$. Similarly, δ-perturbation $\varphi_{r+\delta}$ of φ_r, is obtained by replacing θ_r with $\theta_{r+\delta}$ in φ_r.

We say that φ_r is δ-*unsatisfiable* if δ-perturbation of φ_r is unsatisfiable. The δ-*decision problem for normed GEAR formulas* φ_r is defined as the problem of showing that either φ_r is satisfiable or showing that φ_r is δ-unsatisfiable. This can be seen as an adaptation of the notion of δ-decision from [10] to our setting.

We slightly modify the algorithm GEARSAT to GEARSAT$_\delta(\eta, r, \psi)$ to solve the δ-unsatisfiability problem for normed GEAR formulas as follows. First, we strengthen the lemmas by δ to:

$$E(\boldsymbol{p}) \leftarrow E(\boldsymbol{p}) \wedge \|\boldsymbol{p} - [\![\boldsymbol{q}]\!]^\beta\| > r + \delta$$

Second, "return unsat" is modified to "return δ-unsat".

It is straightforward to generalise Theorem (2) to GEARSAT_δ. Next we show that GEARSAT_δ terminates when we consider bounded domains.

Theorem 3. *Let $\delta > 0$ and $r \geq 0$ be rational numbers. Consider a normed GEAR formula of the form (3) where η defines a bounded subset of $\mathbb{D}$. Then $\text{GEARSAT}_\delta(\eta, r, \psi)$ terminates.*

Proof: Towards a contradiction, assume GEARSAT_δ invoked on (η, r, ψ) does not terminate. Then there is no bound on the number of iterations since the individual steps are computable. Using the notations $A_n := \eta(\boldsymbol{p}) \wedge \bigwedge_{i=1}^{n-1} \neg\theta_{r+\delta}(\boldsymbol{p}, [\![\boldsymbol{q}]\!]^{\beta_i}) \wedge \psi(\boldsymbol{p}, \boldsymbol{x})$ and $B_n := \theta_r([\![\boldsymbol{p}]\!]^{\alpha_n}, \boldsymbol{q}) \wedge \neg\psi(\boldsymbol{q}, \boldsymbol{x})$ similar to those in the proof of Theorem 2, let $(\alpha_n)_n$ and $(\beta_n)_n$ be the sequences of assignments satisfying A_n and B_n, respectively, computed by $\text{GEARSAT}_\delta(\eta, r, \psi)$ in iteration $n \in \mathbb{N}$. Let $\boldsymbol{p}_n := [\![\boldsymbol{p}]\!]^{\alpha_n}$, $\boldsymbol{q}_n := [\![\boldsymbol{q}]\!]^{\beta_n}$ be elements of $\mathbb{D}_{par}$ for each $n \in \mathbb{N}$. We first show a lower bound on the distance between candidates $\boldsymbol{p}_n$. Let $k, n \in \mathbb{N}$ with $k < n$. The triangle inequality for $\|\cdot\|$ implies

$$\|\boldsymbol{p}_n - \boldsymbol{p}_k\| \geq \|\boldsymbol{p}_n - \boldsymbol{q}_k\| - \|\boldsymbol{p}_k - \boldsymbol{q}_k\|. \qquad (*)$$

Each assignment β_k satisfies B_k, in particular, $\theta_r(\boldsymbol{p}_k, \boldsymbol{q})$, i.e., $\|\boldsymbol{p}_k - \boldsymbol{q}_k\| \leq r$ holds. Additionally, α_n satisfies A_n, in particular $\neg\theta_{r+\delta}(\boldsymbol{p}, \boldsymbol{q}_k)$ from which we obtain $\|\boldsymbol{p}_n - \boldsymbol{q}_k\| > r + \delta$. These two facts together with $(*)$ imply $\|\boldsymbol{p}_n - \boldsymbol{p}_k\| > (r + \delta) - r = \delta$.

Thus, the pairwise distances between candidates $\boldsymbol{p}_n$ is at least $\delta > 0$. Since η defines a bounded set and is satisfied by α_n for each $n \in \mathbb{N}$, the number of candidates $\boldsymbol{p}_n$ with pairwise distance of at least δ to each other is also bounded by some $N \in \mathbb{N}$. Thus, the set defined by $\eta(\boldsymbol{p})$ is covered by $\{\boldsymbol{z} : \theta_\delta(\boldsymbol{z}, \boldsymbol{p}_n)\} \subseteq \{\boldsymbol{z} : \theta_{r+\delta}(\boldsymbol{z}, \boldsymbol{q}_n)\}$ for $n = 1, \ldots, N$ making A_{N+1} unsatisfiable and therefore GEARSAT_δ returns δ-unsat. A contradiction. ∎

Theorem (2) and Theorem (3) imply the following.

Theorem 4. *The algorithm GEARSAT_δ is a δ-decision procedure for normed GEAR formulas.*

A. Multiple solutions

We can use GEARSAT_δ to enumerate stable solutions in the following way. Maintain a conjunction η of quantifier-free formulas over free variables $\boldsymbol{p}$, initially true. Then, in a loop, first compute $\kappa = \text{GEARSAT}_\delta(\eta, \theta, \psi)$ and record the formula $E(\boldsymbol{p})$ which it constructs internally. Second, replace $\eta(\boldsymbol{p})$ by $E(\boldsymbol{p}) \wedge (\boldsymbol{p} \neq [\![\boldsymbol{p}]\!]^\kappa)$ and repeat until $\kappa = \text{unsat}$. By Theorem 2, every $\kappa \neq \text{unsat}$ computed by this loop corresponds to a box around $[\![\boldsymbol{p}]\!]^\kappa$ of radius r with the property that $\mathcal{N}$ is safe for all parameters $\boldsymbol{p}$ from that box and for all unconstrained inputs $\boldsymbol{x}$. All κ are different, which is ensured by $(\boldsymbol{p} \neq [\![\boldsymbol{p}]\!]^\kappa)$.

If, for instance, disjoint safe and r-stable regions are sought, this predicate can be adjusted to maintain a concrete distance between solutions which guarantees disjointness, i.e., $\|\boldsymbol{p} - [\![\boldsymbol{p}]\!]^\kappa\| > 2r$. Instead of η being empty initially, it can also be used to define a subset of the domain to be searched. This is presented in Algorithm 3. Let us note that in Algorithm 3 the lemmas are shared during the search for different solutions.

Algorithm 3 Enumerates r-stable pairwise disjoint solutions

> **function** $\text{GEARREGIONS}_\delta(\eta, r, \psi)$
> $R \leftarrow \varnothing$
> $\eta_1(\boldsymbol{p}) \leftarrow \eta(\boldsymbol{p})$
>   **for** $i = 1, 2, \ldots$ **do**
> $\kappa \leftarrow \text{GEARSAT}_\delta(\eta_i, r, \psi)$
>   **if** $\kappa = \delta$-unsat **then**
>   **break**
>   **end if**
> $R \leftarrow R \cup \{[\![\boldsymbol{p}]\!]^\kappa\}$
> $E \leftarrow \text{GEARSAT}_\delta.E$ ▷ lemmas from GEARSAT_δ
> $\eta_{i+1}(\boldsymbol{p}) \leftarrow E(\boldsymbol{p}) \wedge \|\boldsymbol{p} - [\![\boldsymbol{p}]\!]^\kappa\| > 2r$
>   **end for**
>   **return** R
> **end function**

B. Optimisation

In our application we want to find safe and stable configurations such that for all inputs the output of the neural network is greater than a specified threshold th. In this case the specification is of the form $\mathcal{N}(\boldsymbol{q}, \boldsymbol{x}) \geq th$ and ψ will be

$$\psi(\boldsymbol{q}, \boldsymbol{x}, y) \equiv (\varphi_\mathcal{N}(\boldsymbol{q}, \boldsymbol{x}, y) \rightarrow y \geq th).$$

Moreover we want to find configurations with high or close to optimal values of th.

For this we use GEARSAT_δ to find close to optimal solutions by incrementally increasing threshold th or by performing a binary search for close to optimal th. Similarly, for enumeration of solutions we can reuse lemmas generated by those calls to GEARSAT_δ that return satisfying assignments.

Remark 1. It is possible in GEAR formulas (2) (and (3) as a special case) to encode all universally quantified variables in $\forall\boldsymbol{x}(\psi(\boldsymbol{q}, \boldsymbol{x}))$ (which include all inputs and outputs) as parameters under stability conditions resulting in the following normalised form:

$$\exists\boldsymbol{p}[\eta(\boldsymbol{p}) \wedge \forall\boldsymbol{q}(\theta(\boldsymbol{p}, \boldsymbol{q}) \rightarrow \psi(\boldsymbol{q}))]$$

where $\boldsymbol{p}$ and $\boldsymbol{q}$ are of same shape, as follows. Let ξ, η, θ, ψ be as in Definition 1. For every variable x_i in $\boldsymbol{x}$ introduce an existentially quantified variable y_i and a universally quantified variable z_i. Next, define $\eta'(\boldsymbol{p}, \boldsymbol{y}) \equiv \eta(\boldsymbol{p})$ and $\theta'(\boldsymbol{p}, \boldsymbol{y}, \boldsymbol{q}, \boldsymbol{z}) \equiv \theta(\boldsymbol{p}, \boldsymbol{q})$. Then the formula

$$\exists\boldsymbol{p}\boldsymbol{y}[\eta'(\boldsymbol{p}, \boldsymbol{y}) \wedge \forall\boldsymbol{q}\boldsymbol{z}(\theta'(\boldsymbol{p}, \boldsymbol{y}, \boldsymbol{q}, \boldsymbol{z}) \rightarrow \psi(\boldsymbol{q}, \boldsymbol{z}))]$$

has the same solutions as ξ and is in the above normalised form.

This transformation has the effect of eliminating the (universally quantified) input/output variables and replacing them with existentially quantified parameters under stability conditions which require the solution to hold over entire input/output domains. In this way we can uniformly treat inputs as parameters under stability conditions. We adopted this approach in our experiments.

VI. EXPERIMENTAL EVALUATION

We evaluated our configuration selection algorithm on 10 training datasets collected in an Electrical Validation Lab at Intel. The output is an analog signal measuring the quality of a transmitter or a receiver of a channel to a peripheral device. Each channel is divided into eight bytes, and we treat each channel as an unordered categorical variable with eight levels. The integer variable in the data models clock ticks.

The datasets are freely available at http://www.cs.man.ac.uk/~korovink/fmcad2020: 5 transmitter (TX) datasets *s2_tx, m2_tx, h1_tx, h1_iter_tx, mu_tx* and 5 receiver (RX) counterparts *s2_rx, m2_rx, h1_rx, h1_iter_rx, mu_rx*. To avoid IP disclosure, the numeric features including the output are normalized to $[0, 1]$; the integer features are kept intact. We refer to [23], [24] for details on the design of closely related applications dealing with TX/RX/IO systems.

Our aim is to find safe and stable regions where the output o, normalized to $[0, 1]$, satisfies the constraint $o \geq th$ with as high $th \leq 1$ as possible in the grid ranging from 0.7 to 0.95 with an increment of 0.05. In addition, we aim at finding stable safe regions that are reusable across multiple bytes, with as high th as possible. We built NN-ReLUs using the tensorflow [1] and Keras [8] software packages. The different versions of *RX* and *TX* datasets have five to eight input features (not including the channel and bytes parameters). We use NN-ReLUs with two internal layers, 14 nodes in the first layer and 7 nodes in the second layer, which is in line with rule-of-thumb guidelines for selecting the number of internal nodes for a given number of inputs. As stability criterion for solutions we employed a radius of 10% of the value around a safe solution for the numerical variables and ± 5 clock ticks for the integer feature. These radii are measured in the Chebyshev-norm $\| \cdot \|_\infty$.

We implemented our GEARSAT algorithms using Z3 [26] as a backend for solving the quantifier-free fragment of $\mathcal{T}_{\|\cdot\|}$, which can be encoded in QF_LIRA in the SMT-Lib format [3].

Let us first remark that although it is possible to directly encode the SSC problem as a quantified SMT formula without our algorithms, e.g., Z3-v4.8.8 fails to solve a single problem despite many state-of-the-art quantifier elimination procedures are integrated in Z3; the same holds also for CVC4-v1.7 [2] which is another top SMT solver. We included examples of quantified SMT encoding on the website with datasets. In our approach we only resort to quantifier free SMT calls to solve quantified normed GEAR formulas. We believe the main reason our algorithms perform well on these problems is due to strong lemmas that take advantage of the guarded form to exclude large regions from the search space.

C:B	th	safe	lb-ce	lb-time	ub-ce	ub-time
\multicolumn{7}{c}{RX}
0:0	0.9	100	54	319.05	–	–
0:1	0.85	100	69	700.42	0	54.25
0:2	0.9	29	2867	3034.49	–	–
0:3	0.85	100	251	512.31	0	111.00
0:4	0.9	100	128	830.72	–	–
0:5	0.85	100	82	627.68	0	254.81
0:6	0.85	100	121	680.75	0	123.89
0:7	0.85	41	2620	3409.79	0	102.07
1:0	0.8	100	762	606.90	134	290.40
1:1	0.8	1	188	264.75	0	61.46
1:2	0.9	100	369	700.23	–	–
1:3	0.8	100	3449	1328.61	2056	958.96
1:4	0.85	100	16	381.11	0	73.08
1:5	0.85	35	287	769.73	0	53.59
1:6	0.8	100	1088	980.34	0	68.65
1:7	0.9	100	84	405.49	–	–

C:B	th	safe	lb-ce	lb-time	ub-ce	ub-time
\multicolumn{7}{c}{TX}
0:0	0.9	100	156	131.59	–	–
0:1	0.9	51	1006	372.19	–	–
0:2	0.9	100	69	114.17	–	–
0:3	0.9	100	120	78.29	–	–
0:4	0.9	100	315	211.75	–	–
0:5	0.9	100	221	135.44	–	–
0:6	0.9	20	110	41.84	–	–
0:7	0.9	100	176	129.64	–	–
1:0	0.9	100	84	89.81	–	–
1:1	0.85	100	467	226.88	0	11.42
1:2	0.9	100	360	128.06	–	–
1:3	0.9	100	169	82.60	–	–
1:4	0.9	100	304	79.81	–	–
1:5	0.85	100	357	205.29	0	20.24
1:6	0.9	100	259	68.61	–	–
1:7	0.9	100	60	60.01	–	–

TABLE I
BENCHMARKS OF FINDING UP TO 100 SAFE AND STABLE REGIONS FOR DATA SET *s2*.

The results of computing stable safe regions along with their optimal thresholds in the grid of thresholds described above, for the receiver and transmitter datasets *s2_rx, s2_tx* and *h1_rx, h1_tx*, respectively, are shown in Tables I and III. The results are representative for all the datasets used in our experiments. For each combination of channel and byte values, a maximum number of regions was computed – up to a threshold of 100 regions. During the run, the algorithm generates candidate configuration parameters and checks for counter-examples. The system can be used for both finding safe and stable regions, and for checking that such regions do not exist for a given th. For the cases when there are no safe regions, the algorithm relaxes the safety constraint on the output by lowering the threshold value th.

For each combination of channel-byte pair (C:B), the tables give the best threshold (th), the number of safe regions found by the algorithm (safe), and the number of counter-examples (lb-ce) to the safety which are eliminated during the search, along with the computation time for the lower and upper bound of the threshold, respectively; these bounds are defined in the next paragraph. The stable safe regions in the tables have not only been constructed by Algorithm 2, but also by checking each region against samples from the training dataset: the

C 0	0	1	2	3	4	5	6	7
0	–	77	28	16	70	67	22	38
1	20	–	7	10	14	58	32	12
2	0	0	–	0	3	0	2	0
3	0	3	0	–	0	13	0	1
4	6	5	6	0	–	0	0	11
5	0	7	0	7	0	–	5	16
6	0	12	25	9	15	87	–	37
7	0	1	0	0	7	0	0	–

C 1	0	1	2	3	4	5	6	7
0	–	0	0	15	0	34	35	0
1	0	–	0	0	0	0	0	0
2	8	0	–	0	0	2	1	23
3	0	0	0	–	0	2	5	0
4	7	1	0	39	–	60	86	3
5	0	0	0	1	0	–	1	0
6	5	0	0	13	16	4	–	0
7	39	0	1	17	0	54	5	–

TABLE II

SHARED SAFE AND STABLE REGIONS ACROSS MULTIPLE BYTES PER CHANNEL IN DATA SET *s2_rx*: NUMBER OF REGIONS IN BYTE *column* IS SAFE WITH RESPECT TO BYTE *row*.

RX

C:B	th	safe	lb-ce	lb-time	ub-ce	ub-time
0:0	0.9	100	1584	26376.50	–	–
0:1	0.9	100	230	4780.70	–	–
0:2	0.9	100	723	9084.00	–	–
0:3	0.9	100	933	9596.69	–	–
0:4	0.9	100	195	4924.51	–	–
0:5	0.9	100	206	3511.69	–	–
0:6	0.85	100	525	5213.19	636	6213.53
0:7	0.8	100	44	2854.15	0	434.43
1:0	0.9	100	51	2887.82	–	–
1:1	0.85	100	81	1665.96	3	622.37
1:2	0.85	100	81	2758.16	33	651.10
1:3	0.85	100	149	3228.21	0	741.07
1:4	0.9	100	640	5713.27	–	–
1:5	0.85	100	274	3532.65	0	398.29
1:6	0.9	100	90	2691.84	–	–
1:7	0.9	100	336	4378.93	–	–

TX

C:B	th	safe	lb-ce	lb-time	ub-ce	ub-time
0:0	0.9	100	215	1597.45	–	–
0:1	0.9	100	341	1839.79	–	–
0:2	0.9	100	523	3045.20	–	–
0:3	0.9	100	186	1639.23	–	–
0:4	0.9	100	100	635.99	–	–
0:5	0.9	100	206	1544.68	–	–
0:6	0.9	100	157	873.79	–	–
0:7	0.9	76	186	694.96	–	–
1:0	0.9	100	80	607.82	–	–
1:1	0.9	10	269	843.37	–	–
1:2	0.9	100	245	1809.32	–	–
1:3	0.9	77	552	3206.61	–	–
1:4	0.9	100	151	657.32	–	–
1:5	0.85	100	152	681.89	0	42.05
1:6	0.9	100	42	376.40	–	–
1:7	0.9	100	726	5759.01	–	–

TABLE III

BENCHMARKS OF FINDING UP TO 100 SAFE AND STABLE REGIONS FOR DATA SET *h1*. TIMES ARE IN SECONDS, 'CE' IS THE NUMBER OF COUNTER-EXAMPLES, 'LB' AND 'UB' REFER TO THE PROOF OF LOWER AND UPPER BOUND ON THE THRESHOLD, RESPECTIVELY.

regions violated by the samples in the data were not considered safe even if the model output was safe on these samples. The algorithm has been run on the normalized form of the respective formulas as described in Remark 1.

If $th < 0.9$, then at least 2 searches for safe stable regions were performed, one with threshold th, which succeeded in finding some stable safe regions, and another with threshold $th + 0.05$, which did not find any and, in fact, did prove there are none above $th + 2 \cdot 0.05$. The factor 2 here comes from the heuristic used by the solver that the center of a candidate region should evaluate to $th + 0.05$. So we enumerated only regions with $center \geq th + 0.05$. If there are none, it proves the upper bound $th + 0.05$ on the safety threshold. If $th = 0.9$, no upper bound check with threshold 0.95 has been performed, since it could only prove the bound 1, which is clear by construction. Tables I and III also provide the number of counter-examples found during the proof and the computation time.

As can be seen from Algorithms 2 and 3, for a region proven safe two SMT calls were made and for each counter-example (lb-ce and ub-ce) up to two SMT calls were performed. In order to verify that the threshold th is minimal, one additional call per C:B combination was required. As can be seen from the tables, the total of these numbers in order to produce the results for each C:B range between 233 and 11 211 Z3 calls.

In addition, Table II shows the count of stable safe regions shared across multiple bytes of the same channel – from the safe regions reported in Table I. Note that this table is not symmetric because training samples falling in a shared stable safe region can violate the output constraint for some of the bytes (but not all the bytes) for which this region is safe.

As mentioned in the introduction, proving a safety constraint on an NN output does not mean the modelled system itself is safe. One reason for that is that it is very difficult to generate high-quality training samples to build accurate models when little is known about the behavior of the modelled system. It therefore takes a number of iterations to improve the training data and thereby improve the model. One can use the stable safe regions to generate new training samples within the safe regions in order to refine the current model. We have performed such *proof-based abstraction refinement* of the NN models on *h1_rx* and *h1_tx* datasets. We generated 100 random samples in each stable safe region and asked the Lab to measure the output. Interestingly, 790 out of 1600 stable safe regions for *h1_rx* remained safe in the sense that the system output still satisfies the output constraint; and 1106 out of the 1463 safe regions of *h1_tx* remained safe. This matched the user input that the *RX* model was much harder to analyze and configure safely.

VII. CONCLUSIONS AND FUTURE WORK

We have defined the problem of configuration selection for NN models in its general form and demonstrated the feasibility of our proposed algorithms on a real-life industrial application. Our work leverages the recent research on verifying inequality constraints on NN-ReLU output when the inputs are also constrained with inequalities, which can be seen as an atomic black-box operation in our algorithms. In the current implementation we use the Z3 solver for performing this operation in order to support real, integer and categorical variables. As immediate future work, we intend to integrate and evaluate other solvers that might be significantly faster for NN-ReLU with only real-valued inputs (LP) or real and integer valued inputs (MILP). In order to support NNs with transcendental activation functions (such as Sigmoid or Softmax), as well as transcendental constraints on safe and stable solutions, we are extending the implementation to work with solvers such as ksmt [5], dReal [10] and others. We will also integrate other machine learning models such as random forest and polynomial models which can be covered by our framework.

It is important to note that for many CAD applications, in NN models used to model complex systems, there rarely is a need for more than 5 to 20 input features; this is confirmed by our experience of using NN and other models for a wide range of CAD applications at Intel. Indeed, the state of the art is to apply advanced feature selection [13] techniques to the input features in the labeled dataset measured on the system, and to select a subset consisting of highly relevant and highly independent features that provide a high coverage of the variation that exists in the data. Thus computational complexity of the problem that we are dealing with is not preventing usage in real-life CAD applications. For applications in computer vision and related areas where very large NN models are required and the inputs are real variables, we believe that integration of fast decision procedures such as LP will help our algorithms to scale, especially when the number of configuration parameters is a relatively small fraction of the system's interface.

Besides selection of safe and stable regions, our algorithms addresses also the problem of selecting such regions where the performance of the output is close to optimal. As a future work, it would be interesting to adapt our algorithms to multi-objective optimisation problems where the validity of output constraints cannot be compromised for the benefit of optimisation and at the same time Pareto-optimal regions can be selected; besides the application domain discussed in this work, relevant examples include joint optimisation of power, performance and area, as well joint optimisation of voltage, frequency and temperature, without compromising safe operation. Currently multi-objective optimisation tasks are handled in our framework via reduction to single-objective optimisation using a weighted average over the optimisation objectives.

Acknowledgement

This research was supported by a grant from Intel Corporation.

References

[1] M. Abadi, A. Agarwal, P. Barham, E. Brevdo, Z. Chen, C. Citro, G. S. Corrado, A. Davis, J. Dean, M. Devin, S. Ghemawat, I. Goodfellow, A. Harp, G. Irving, M. Isard, Y. Jia, R. Jozefowicz, L. Kaiser, M. Kudlur, J. Levenberg, D. Mane, R. Monga, Sh. Moore, D. Murray, C. Olah, M. Schuster, J. Shlens, B. Steiner, Il. Sutskever, K. Talwar, P. Tucker,
V. Vanhoucke, V. Vasudevan, F. Viegas, O. Vinyals, P. Warden, M. Wattenberg, M. Wicke, Y. Yu, X. Zhengi. Large-Scale Machine Learning on Heterogeneous Systems, https://www.tensorflow.org/, 2015.
[2] C. Barrett, C. L. Conway, M. Deters, L. Hadarean, D. Jovanović, T. King, A. Reynolds, and C. Tinelli. CVC4. Conference on Computer Aided Verification, CAV 2011.
[3] C. Barrett, P. Fontaine, C. Tinelli. The Satisfiability Modulo Theories Library (SMT-LIB). 2016, http://smtlib.cs.uiowa.edu/.
[4] O. Bastani, Y. Ioannou, L. Lampropoulos, D. Vytiniotis, A. Nori, and A. Criminisi. Measuring Neural Net Robustness with Constraints. Neural Information Processing Systems, NIPS 2016.
[5] F. Brauße, K. Korovin, M. V. Korovina, and N. Th. Müller. A CDCL-style calculus for solving non-linear constraints. Frontiers of Combining Systems, FroCoS 2019.
[6] R. Bunel, I. Turkaslan, P.H.S. Torr, P. Kohli, M. Pawan Kumar. A Unified View of Piecewise Linear Neural Network Verification. Neural Information Processing Systems, NIPS 2018.
[7] C.-H. Cheng, G. Nührenberg, C.-H. Huang, H. Ruess. Verification of Binarized Neural Networks via Inter-Neuron Factoring. arXiv:1710.03107, 2017.
[8] F. Chollet. Keras. https://github.com/fchollet/keras, 2015.
[9] S. Dutta, T. Kushner, S. Jha, S. Sankaranarayanan. Sherlock: A Tool for Verification of Deep Neural Networks, https://github.com/souradeep-111/sherlock
[10] S. Gao, J. Avigad, E. M. Clarke. δ-complete decision procedures for satisfiability over the reals. In Automated Reasoning - 6th International Joint Conference, IJCAR 2012.
[11] Y. Ge, L. de Moura. Complete Instantiation for Quantified Formulas in Satisfiabiliby Modulo Theories, CAV 2009.
[12] I. J. Goodfellow, J. Shlens, C. Szegedy, Explaining and harnessing adversarial examples, ICLR 2015.
[13] I. Guyon, A. Elisseeff. An Introduction to Variable and Feature Selection. Journal of Machine Learning Research 3, 2003.
[14] M. Emmer, Z. Khasidashvili, K. Korovin, A. Voronkov. Encoding Industrial Hardware Verification Problems into Effectively Propositional Logic, FMCAD 2010.
[15] M. Emmer, Z. Khasidashvili, K. Korovin, C. Sticksel, A. Voronkov. EPR-Based Bounded Model Checking at Word Level, IJCAR 2012.
[16] G. Katz, Cl. Barrett, D. Dill, K. Julian M. Kochenderfer. Reluplex: An Efficient SMT Solver for Verifying Deep Neural Networks , CAV 2017.
[17] Y. Kazak, C. Barrett, G. Katz, M. Schapira. Verifying Deep-RL-Driven Systems. Network Meets AI & ML, NetAI 2019.
[18] Z. Khasidashvili, M. Kinanah, A. Voronkov. Verifying Equivalence of Memories Using a First Order Logic Theorem Prover, FMCAD 2009.
[19] Z. Khasidashvili, K. Korovin, D. Tsarkov. EPR-based k-induction with Counterexample Guided Abstraction Refinement, GCAI 2015.
[20] K. Korovin. iProver–an instantiation-based theorem prover for first-order logic (system description), IJCAR 2008.
[21] S. Liang, R. Srikant. Why Deep Neural Networks For Function Approximation? ICLR 2017.
[22] Z. Lu, H. Pu, F. Wang, Z. Hu, L. Wang. The Expressive Power of Neural Networks: A View from the Width. Neural Information Processing Systems, 6231–6239, 2017.
[23] A. Manukovsky, Y. Juniman, Z. Khasidashvili. A Novel Method of Precision Channel Modeling for High Speed Serial 56Gb Interfaces, DesignCon'18, 2018.
[24] A. Manukovsky, Z. Khasidashvili, A.J. Norman, Y. Juniman, R. Bloch. Machine Learning Applications for Simulation and Modeling of 56 and 112 Gb SerDes Systems, DesignCon'19, 2019.
[25] G. F. Montúfar, R. Pascanu, K. Cho, and Y. Bengio. On the number of linear regions of deep neural networks. In Advances in Neural Information Processing Systems 27: Annual Conference on Neural Information Processing Systems, 2014.
[26] L. de Moura, N. Bjørner. Z3: An Efficient SMT Solver. TACAS 2008.
[27] J.A. Navarro-Perez, A. Voronkov. Encodings of Bounded LTL Model Checking in Effectively Propositional Logic, CADE 2007.
[28] L. Pulina, A. Tacchella. An Abstraction-Refinement Approach to Verification of Artificial Neural Networks. CAV 2010.
[29] D.E. Rumelhart, G.E. Hinton, R. J. Williams. Learning representations by back-propagating errors, Nature, vol. 323, 1986.
[30] C. Szegedy, W. Zaremba, I. Sutskever, J. Bruna, D. Erhan, I. Goodfellow, R. Fergus. Intriguing properties of neural networks, 2014.

14

Runtime Verification on FPGAs with LTLf Specifications

Tommy Tracy II
iD
University of Virginia
Charlottesville, Virginia 22904
Email: tjt7a@virginia.edu

Lucas M. Tabajara
iD
Rice University
Houston, Texas 77005
Email: lucasmt@rice.edu

Moshe Vardi
iD
Rice University
Houston, Texas 77005
Email: vardi@rice.edu

Kevin Skadron
iD
University of Virginia
Charlottesville, Virginia 22904
Email: skadron@virginia.edu

Abstract—**Runtime verification is a technique that evaluates a system's execution trace at runtime against a formal specification. This approach is particularly useful for safety-critical and autonomous systems to verify system functionality and allow for graceful recovery or intervention in the case of system faults. Specifications are often provided in a high-level form using some type of temporal logic, which can then be compiled into an automaton to be used as a monitor for the system. Existing work has mainly focused on implementing such monitors in software. In recent years there has been extensive research, however, in hardware acceleration of automata applications, which can potentially be extended to runtime monitoring. In this paper, we introduce an open-source framework for translating formulas in Linear Temporal Logic over finite traces (LTL_f) into automata implementations on FPGAs for high-efficiency and high-performance runtime monitoring. By using the spatial dimension of FPGAs, we run many of these automata in parallel, significantly reducing the latency between violation and monitor report and achieving significant throughput. We compare the performance of four different architectures corresponding to the combinations of deterministic or nondeterministic automata with an explicit or symbolic representation, and determine the design parameters that result in efficient hardware utilization and higher clock frequencies. We found that explicit automata tend to use more hardware resources, in particular Lookup Tables (LUTs), than symbolic automata. An exception to this is in the case of Flip-Flop (FF) usage, where symbolic DFAs tend to use more FF resources than explicit NFAs for smaller designs. We also found that explicit NFAs can run at higher clock frequencies, except for very large automata with high edge densities. Symbolic NFAs use fewer Look-Up Table resources and run at higher clock frequencies than symbolic DFAs, whereas symbolic DFAs required fewer Flip-Flop resources, except in the case of very simple small automata with lower edge densities. Finally, we found that explicit automata hardware utilization significantly increases with input signal widths, motivating the use of symbolic automata for wide input signals.**

I. INTRODUCTION

While other types of formal verification seek to verify a system before it is deployed, the goal of runtime verification is to monitor the execution of a system in real time in order to detect behavior that violates the system's formal specification [1], [2], [3]. This gives the system a chance to mitigate, recover from, or document the error. Runtime verification is particularly valuable for safety-critical and autonomous systems [4], where errors that are not immediately dealt with can have catastrophic consequences. Such systems also often operate in physical environments, which are hard to model accurately and often behave in unexpected and unpredictable ways. Therefore, even if the system has been formally verified beforehand, it is possible that it might still display errors during runtime due to assumption violations.

Most existing work on runtime verification has focused on monitors implemented in software [1], [2]. Motivated by the slowing down of Moore's Law and the end of Dennard Scaling [5], there has been a recent trend to use specialized hardware [6]. Specialized hardware that is designed to perform a particular task can be optimized for that task much more than it would be possible for general-purpose hardware. Furthermore, the application can benefit directly from the natural parallelism that hardware provides. For runtime verification, an on-board hardware implementation translates to more efficient real-time monitoring with lower latency.

Monitors used for runtime verification usually take the form of (deterministic or nondeterministic) finite-state automata. Automata applications have already been a target of hardware acceleration, as exemplified by Micron's Automata Processor [7], [8] and subsequent work targeting FPGAs [9], [10]. Specialized architectures for simulating automata have been employed for a number of data- and string-processing applications, including bioinformatics [11], [12], machine learning [13], [14], and natural language processing (NLP) [15]. As an application that also runs automata over streaming data - in this case traces of the system's execution - the extension to runtime verification is a natural one.

Unlike data- and string-processing applications, automata used for formal verification, including runtime verification, are often generated from formal specifications given as formulas in a temporal logic [16], [17], rather than directly as finite automata. A major difference between automata constructed from temporal-logic formulas and those obtained for other applications is the alphabet construction. Data- and string-processing application usually assume a static and relatively small symbol alphabet. For example, an NLP automaton would likely use ASCII as the symbol alphabet, and bioinformatics applications may only need four symbols corresponding to the four nucleotide bases A, T, C and G.

In the case of automata used for formal verification, the symbol alphabet consists of propositional interpretations of the atomic propositions in the formula. The number of possible such interpretations, and therefore the size of the symbol alphabet, is exponential in the number of propositions, leading to potentially much larger alphabets. The problem of the exponential alphabet is usually solved in formal-methods applications by not explicitly representing the transitions on each symbol, but instead labeling transitions by Boolean expressions, with the understanding that a transition is activated by an interpretation if that interpretation satisfies the expression.

Tools that construct automata from temporal formulas [18], [19] often represent transitions in this way. While being very natural when the automaton is generated from a logic formula, this symbolic representation of the transition relation is not supported by Micron's Automata Processor, for example, which uses eight bits per symbol in the alphabet and a memory column of 256 bits per state to recognize the unique symbols in the alphabet. Sadredini et al. [20], with their Flexamata compiler and subsequent Grapefruit [10] FPGA implementation, which integrates Flexamata into a full-stack automata processing framework, addressed this concern by converting among automata of differing symbol alphabet sizes. They do this by trading off symbol alphabet size with automata size and throughput. Unfortunately, this requires temporal multiplexing, where the system signals would need to be buffered and serialized at the reduced width. This approach could work for lower sampling rates of the system signals, but could also bottleneck the system for some applications.

Our main contribution in this work is an investigation among four possible architectures for implementing automata-based monitors for temporal-logic properties on a field-programmable gate array (FPGA). These four architectures are defined by two axes: deterministic vs. nondeterministic and explicit vs. symbolic. The first axis specifies whether the temporal logic specification is converted into a deterministic finite automaton (DFA) or a nondeterministic finite automaton (NFA). It is difficult to predict a priori which of these representations is more efficient in terms of the number of states. Although NFAs have an exponentially smaller worst-case size, DFAs have an exact minimization algorithm that runs in polynomial time, while for NFA minimization, which is PSPACE-complete [21], we are forced to rely on heuristics. The second axis determines whether the state space of the automaton should be represented explicitly or symbolically. In an explicit representation, each state has its own hardware component, called a State Transition Element (STE), that is activated when the automaton moves into that state. Each STE has its own state memory and logic to match the input to the matching symbol set of that state. In this architecture, hardware parallelism allows nondeterminism to be simulated at no additional cost, as multiple STE can be active at the same time. In a symbolic representation, the current state (or set of states, in the case of an NFA) is represented by a bitvector, which is given along with the current input to a logic circuit that computes the bitvector representing the next state. An advantage of DFAs in the symbolic representation is that the current state can be represented in a logarithmic number of

bits, while NFAs require a bit per state. On the other hand, the logarithmic encoding in the DFA might lead to more complex (deeper) combinational logic.

We evaluate each of these four options on a set of randomly-generated formulas in Linear Temporal Logic over Finite Traces (LTL_f) [22], formed by taking random conjunctions of common temporal patterns [23]. LTL_f was chosen because it is a convenient way of specifying events that happen in a finite time, such as the ones that runtime verification seeks to detect, and a lot of machinery exists for translating such formulas into finite automata [24], [25]. The formula set is converted into separate automata, which are then implemented on one FPGA. Each automaton monitors a different property, but the set shares input signals corresponding to shared propositions between the formulas. We scale our benchmarks by varying the number of formulas, the number of different variables across all formulas (number of unique system signals), and the number of conjuncts per formula (formula complexity).

The results of our evaluation provide insight on the different tradeoffs that emerge when considering solutions implemented directly in hardware as opposed to software. We found that symbolic automata tend to use less hardware than explicit automata and that explicit NFAs tend to run at higher clock frequencies, except in the case of very small formulas or very complex formulas. Overall, we find that symbolic NFAs tend to perform best of all of our evaluated architectures across most experiments with the lowest hardware utilization.

Finally, we found that explicit automata hardware utilization significantly increases with the size of the symbol alphabet, motivating the use of symbolic automata for wide input signals, which happens when the formula has a high number of propositions. Our investigation allows us to better understand the considerations that must be taken into account when implementing runtime monitors in hardware, and concludes that, while no particular approach dominates, each one has its own pros and cons that should be considered when deciding how to accelerate runtime verification for a specific application.

II. BACKGROUND

A. Linear Temporal Logic

Linear Temporal Logic over Finite traces (LTL_f) is a variant of Linear Temporal Logic that is interpreted over finite rather than infinite traces. Its syntax is identical to LTL over infinite traces, and is defined as follows for a set of propositions $\mathcal{P}$:

$$ ::= \quad p \quad \mathcal{P} \quad (\quad) \quad (_1 \quad _2) \quad (\mathbf{X}\ ) \quad (_1 \mathcal{U}\ _2) $$

Lichtenstein, Pnueli, and Zuck showed in [26] that every LTL formula is equivalent to a formula of the form $\bigwedge_i^n (GF\rho_i \quad FG\ _i)$, where ρ_i and $_i$ contain only past operators. In other words, ρ_i and $_i$ are finite-trace formulas. Thus, finite-trace monitors are the foundation on which one can build a monitoring framework for LTL [27], which motivates our focus on LTL_f.

$\mathbf{X}$ and $\mathcal{U}$ are the temporal connectives "next" and "until". We can define other temporal connectives such as $\mathbf{F}$

("eventually"), **G** ("always") and $\mathcal{W}$ ("weak until") in terms of those. A *propositional interpretation* $\tau \in 2^{\mathcal{P}}$ is a set of propositions representing the propositions that are true at a given time. A *trace* is a finite sequence $\rho \in (2^{\mathcal{P}})^*$ of propositional interpretations $\rho_0, \rho_1, \ldots, \rho_n$, where ρ_i is the set of propositions that are true at time i. We denote that an LTL_f formula φ is satisfied by a trace ρ at time i by $\rho, i \models \varphi$, and shorten $\rho, 0 \models \varphi$ to $\rho \models \varphi$. Refer to [22] for the semantics of LTL_f formulas. The *language* of an LTL_f formula φ, denoted by $\mathcal{L}(\varphi)$, is the set of finite traces that satisfy φ. The *reverse* of a trace $\rho = \rho_0, \ldots, \rho_n$, denoted by ρ^R, is the trace $\rho_n, \ldots, \rho_0$. The *reverse* of the language of a formula φ, denoted by $\mathcal{L}^R(\varphi)$, is the set of traces ρ^R for $\rho \in \mathcal{L}(\varphi)$.

B. Finite State Automata

A Finite State Automaton (FSA) is a mathematical model of the form $A = (S, \Sigma, I, \Delta, F)$, where: S is a finite set of states, Σ is a finite set of symbols called the input alphabet, $I \subseteq S$ is a set of initial states, $\Delta \subseteq S \times \Sigma \times S$ is a transition relation indicating the successor states of a given state when the automaton reads an input symbol in Σ, and $F \subseteq S$ is a set of accepting states. FSA are often represented by a graph of nodes connected by edges. Figure 1.A shows an example FSA, where the left-most state is an initial state, and the right-most is an accepting state. Edges represent transitions, and are labeled by the corresponding transition symbols from the input alphabet. FSAs process input signals by transitioning between states. The computation begins at the initial state and proceeds at every time interval, evaluating an input symbol. If that input symbol matches a transition symbol, a transition is made to the next state, and so forth. If an accepting state is reached, then the automaton has accepted the input; if not, the input is not accepted. The set of finite traces accepted by an FSA A is the *language* of the FSA, and denoted by $\mathcal{L}(A)$.

FSAs can be deterministic or nondeterministic. Deterministic Finite Automata (DFAs) have at most one initial state, and at most one transition from each given state on a given input symbol. Nondeterministic Finite Automata (NFAs), on the other hand, are more general and can have multiple transitions from each state on the same input symbol. As a consequence, when running an NFA over a sequence of inputs, multiple transitions can be taken at once, and multiple states can be active at the same time. Every NFA can be determinized into a DFA that recognizes the same language, but in the worst case the smallest DFA for a given language may be exponentially larger than the smallest NFA. Because of this, DFAs potentially yield a significant increase in memory utilization, while NFAs are memory-bandwidth bounded by potentially many parallel transitions. However, DFAs have an efficient and exact minimization algorithm, while NFAs can practically only be minimized heuristically [28].

Previous work has demonstrated how finite state automata can be used to accelerate a variety of applications that go beyond the usual string matching applications, including bioinformatics [11], [12], machine learning [13], [14], and natural language processing [15]. These works represent FSAs in

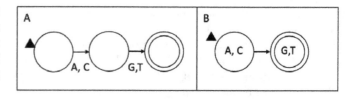

Fig. 1.   Non-homogeneous (A) vs. Homogeneous automaton (B).

a *homogeneous* representation, where matching computations are done on the states, rather than the edges. More specifically, a homogeneous automaton is one where all transitions into a state have the same symbol set [29], [30]. We depict such automata by placing the symbol sets on the states rather than on the edges. Figure 1 depicts a non-homogeneous automaton and its equivalent homogeneous automaton. Homogeneity is used in hardware implementations to simplify the mapping of automata to hardware for parallel transition computation on the nodes, as demonstrated in Micron's Automata Processor [7]. This transformation also comes at a significant increase in the number of states in the automata, scaling with the edge density of the non-homogeneous representation.

Every LTL_f formula φ over a set of propositions $\mathcal{P}$ can be converted into a (deterministic or nondeterministic) FSA A_φ with alphabet $2^{\mathcal{P}}$, such that $\mathcal{L}(A_\varphi) = \mathcal{L}(\varphi)$. In the worst case, the smallest NFA for an LTL_f formula may be at most exponential in the size of the formula, while the smallest DFA may be doubly-exponential. The tool MONA [18] implements an algorithm for constructing a minimal DFA from a formula in Monadic Second-Order Logic (MSO). Since every LTL_f formula can be converted into MSO [22], MONA can be used to generate minimal DFAs for LTL_f formulas. As part of our framework, we present a solution to using MONA for generating NFAs as well.

C. Automata Acceleration with FPGAs

Field Programmable Gate Arrays (FPGAs) are used in computing systems to implement reconfigurable hardware. Existing automata engines including REAPR [9], REAPRpp [31], and Grapefruit [10] accelerate a variety of applications with explicit automata on FPGAs. Figure 2 illustrates how *explicit automata* are represented in hardware by these explicit engines, with constituent states of the automata instantiated with separate memory and logic resources. This requires that the spatial resources used by the design grow in the size of the automata, but also allows all automata states to make transitions in parallel, making this approach particularly efficient for processing NFAs, where the number of active states can be variable and for evaluating multiple automata in parallel.

REAPR works by generating Verilog from ANML [7] automata description files, an XML-like homogeneous FSA representation, and generates an architecture that is very similar to Micron's Automata Processor (AP) [7], using the homogeneous automata representation. One limitation REAPR inherited from the AP is the static 8-bit symbol width. AP-like automata processing assumes an input symbol of 8 bits and a

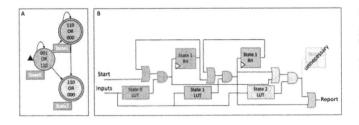

Fig. 2.   Architecture of explicit automata.

corresponding 256-bit matching column for representing the full 8-bit symbol alphabet. Although useful when considering pattern matching on ASCII or byte-level data, when implementing runtime verification, this limits the number of system signals that our formulas could process in one cycle to 8.

Rahimi et al. [10] implement the Flexamata [20] compiler in their Grapefruit full-stack automata engine. They overcome the symbol-width limitation by extending ANML and allowing for arbitrary bitwidths by trading off symbol alphabet size with automata size and throughput. In addition to this, Grapefruit also includes heuristic-based NFA minimization, which allows the tool to reduce the size of explicit finite state automata in hardware. We utilize Grapefruit and extend its functionality to also include symbolic automata (see Section III-B.

D. Runtime Monitors

Although there are many types of runtime monitors with different semantics, in this work we define a monitor for an LTL_f formula φ as an FSA (NFA or DFA) that accepts a finite trace iff this trace satisfies φ. As the monitor reads the trace produced by the system, it continuously reports whether the finite trace observed from the beginning of the execution until the current time step satisfies the formula.

Previous work on runtime monitors has focused on automatically generating runtime system monitors on CPUs as well as on FPGAs. Drusinsky [32] introduces a verification tool that generates code from LTL and MTL assertions written into C, C++, Java, Verilog and VHDL code to evaluate runtime systems against the formulas at runtime.

Tabakov et al. [2] introduce a technique for automatically generating SystemC runtime monitors from LTL formulas. They identify four important components that they optimize to minimize runtime overhead: state minimization, alphabet representation, alphabet minimization, and monitor encoding. They then identify the configurations that offer the best monitor performance in terms of runtime overhead. Pike et al. [33] introduce Copilot, a domain-specific language built on top of Haskell for programming runtime monitors for distributed real-time systems. Boule and Zilic [34] use a recursive technique that breaks properties into syntax trees. Each node in the tree is used to create a sub-property automaton which are concatenated with the rest in an automata generation algorithm.

Geist et al. [35] implement runtime observers in their system on processors implemented on their FPGA. Meredith et al. [36] with MOP and Pellizzoni et al. [37] with BusMOP use the Monitoring Oriented Programming (MOP) framework to synthesize hardware monitors for runtime verification. BusMOP generates monitor blocks from temporal logic specifications. These monitor blocks use symbolic DFAs to verify system properties at runtime.

Jaksic et al. [38] translate Signal Temporal Logic (STL) assertions into hardware runtime monitors on FPGAs. They synthesize *temporal testers*, or transducers, that output a signal if a specification has been satisfied. Selyunin et al. [39] translate Signal Temporal Logic (STL) and Timed Regular Expressions (TRE) into hardware monitors on FPGAs. They demonstrate a High-Level Synthesis (HLS) and automata-based approach for temporal tester transducers.

Selyunin et al. [40] apply runtime monitoring for automata systems and use HLS to synthesize monitors for FPGAs. Baumeister et al. [41] compile RTLola, a stream-based specification language used for real-time properties, into VHDL for FPGA deployment. Convent et al. [42] introduce the Temporal Stream-based Specification Language (TeSSLa) used to specify constraints on railway cyber-physical systems. Their approach differs considerably from previous approaches, because they allow for runtime reconfigurability. They do this by creating a set of event processing units that can be combined at runtime to monitor for complex properties.

Schumann et al. [4] introduce R2U2, a monitoring and diagnosis framework for unmanned aerial systems. R2U2 is implemented on an FPGA and monitors streams of data from the GPS and ground control station, flight software status, sensor readings, and actuator outputs. They implement their runtime monitors in logic as presented by Reinbacher et al. [3].

While previous work has implemented runtime monitors on FPGAs, our work differentiates itself in a few ways. First, we take advantage of recent progress made in hardware acceleration of automata by using state-of-the-art approaches from that field. We also focus on LTL_f as a specification language for runtime properties, allowing us to also use recently-developed techniques for converting LTL_f formulas into automata. Finally, as far as we are aware we are the first to perform an experimental comparison between deterministic and non-deterministic as well as symbolic and explicit automata, in order to determine the advantages and disadvantages of each representation in an FPGA implementation.

III. Implementing LTL_f Monitors in Hardware

We present an open-source software pipeline[43] for converting LTL_f formulas into automata-based runtime monitors implemented on a cloud-deployed FPGA. We explore four possible automata representations placed along two axes: deterministic/non-deterministic and explicit/symbolic. Each representation is described later in this section.

For generating the automata from the temporal formulas, we employ an approach centered on the tool MONA [18], which can construct finite automata from formulas in Monadic Second-order Logic (MSO), a logic strictly more expressive than LTL_f. We chose this tool based on its performance and versatility. Other possible options for converting LTL_f to automata would be the tools SPOT [19] and LISA [44]. Previous comparisons, however, have shown MONA to perform better than SPOT [24], while LISA only has support for DFAs. Because MONA is based on MSO, we can use a technique based on reversing the formula to construct NFAs as well, as described in Section III-A.

Although there are several existing tools for deploying automata on FPGAs, most focus on memory-based DFA solutions. We found the FPGA automata processing framework Grapefruit [10] to be the best solution that provides both DFA and NFA functionality as well as a full end-to-end solution. Grapefruit also demonstrated higher performance over previous work such as REAPR. Grapefruit generates an explicit Hardware Description Language (HDL) module from a description of a homogeneous automaton. We extend Grapefruit to also generate HDL modules that represent logic transitions for symbolic non-homogeneous DFAs and NFAs.

A. Generating Finite Automata from LTL_f Formulas

The first half of our pipeline takes in an LTL_f formula φ and constructs an abstract non-homogeneous representation of a finite automaton that recognizes the language of φ. As previously mentioned, we explore two different constructions, one which produces a deterministic and another which produces a non-deterministic automaton. We start by describing the deterministic construction:

1) Translate the LTL_f formula φ into a formula $fol(\varphi)$ in First-Order Logic (FOL) over finite traces. This is possible since FOL has the same expressive power as LTL_f. A translation algorithm can be found in [22].
2) Use the tool MONA to convert $fol(\varphi)$ into a DFA A that recognizes the same language. This is possible because MONA accepts inputs in MSO, which is a superset of FOL.

It is important to point out that the DFA constructed by MONA is minimal, meaning that it is the smallest DFA that recognizes the language.

Because the construction algorithm implemented in MONA heavily relies on the fact that DFAs can be efficiently minimized, the automaton output by the tool is always deterministic. Yet, it is known that there are languages for which the smallest DFA is exponentially larger than the smallest NFA [45]. Therefore, if our construction algorithm can exploit non-determinism, we may obtain an exponentially smaller automaton. Furthermore, recall that non-determinism allows us to take advantage of the natural parallelism among multiple active states in each automaton, as well as parallelism across multiple automata, and leverages the high degree of parallelism afforded by FPGAs. In order to use MONA to generate an NFA instead, we make use of a technique introduced in [46]:

1) Convert the LTL_f formula φ into a $PastLTL$ formula φ^R such that $\mathcal{L}(\varphi^R) = \mathcal{L}^R(\varphi)$, i.e., φ^R is satisfied by exactly those traces that are the reverse of a trace that satisfies φ. To do this, it is enough to replace all future temporal operators in φ with past temporal operators. See [25] for details.

2) Translate φ^R into a FOL formula $fol(\varphi^R)$ describing the same language. See [25] for a translation algorithm.
3) Use MONA to construct a DFA A^R for $fol(\varphi^R)$. Note that this DFA accepts the reverse language of φ.
4) Reverse A^R by turning initial states into accepting states and vice versa, and swapping the source and destination states of each transition. The result is an NFA A that accepts the reverse language of A^R, and therefore the same language of φ [46].

The minimal DFA for the reverse language of an LTL_f formula is guaranteed to be at most exponential in the size of the formula (see [22] on converting an LTL_f formula to a linear-sized alternating automaton, and [47] on obtaining an exponential-sized DFA for the reverse language of an alternating automaton). In contrast, the DFA for the formula itself can be doubly-exponential. Therefore, the NFA generated by this approach has the potential to be exponentially smaller than the DFA that would be constructed by simply using MONA directly.

B. Implementing Monitors in FPGA

Having obtained an automaton from the LTL_f formula, we explore two ways to implement them on an FPGA: *explicitly* or *symbolically*. In either case, each input signal of the circuit corresponds to a proposition in the formula, and multiple LTL_f formulas can be processed in parallel, up to the capacity of the FPGA.

The *explicit implementation* follows a similar architecture to REAPR and Grapefruit as presented in Section II-C. In this architecture, each state of the automaton is represented by a separate hardware module called a State Transition Element (STE). The STE consists of an activation bit and logic corresponding to the transition condition of this state (the explicit implementation is based on homogeneous automata, so the transition condition is associated with the state, not the edge). The activation bit for a state is set to 1 if any of its predecessors were active in the previous step and the current input satisfies the state's transition condition. Note that if the automaton is an NFA, multiple STEs can be active at the same time. The STE for an accepting state also generates a report bit. Given an automaton (DFA or NFA) A generated by MONA, we perform the following operations to implement A explicitly:

1) Convert A from a non-homogeneous representation given in the output format of MONA into a homogeneous automaton in the ANML format.
2) Use Grapefruit to heuristically minimize the automaton (and remove unreachable states) and generate HDL.
3) Synthesize and target FPGA.

It is important to note that the conversion algorithm to homogeneous automaton may turn a non-homogeneous DFA into a homogeneous NFA, and may come at an increase in automata size. Therefore, when we refer to an "explicit DFA" implementation, we only mean that the automaton was initially constructed and minimized as a DFA, but the

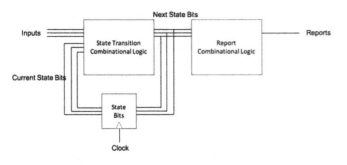

Fig. 3. Architecture of symbolic automata.

homogeneous automaton implemented in the FPGA may be non-deterministic. As a result, the main difference between the explicit DFA and explicit NFA approaches is that they produce automata with a different number of states and transition logic.

The *symbolic implementation* instead encodes the current state by a bitvector stored in an internal memory, and uses a single logic circuit to compute the next state as a function of the current state and inputs. For NFAs, the bitvector includes one bit for each automaton state, representing whether that state is active or not. For DFAs, since only one state is active at a given time, this representation would be inefficient. Instead, each state is given a binary encoding in a logarithmic number of bits. Since symbolic automata do not require separate components for each state, their hardware utilization is expected to be less than explicit automata. In order to capture transitions into accepting (or reporting) states, we use a separate piece of combinational logic to determine if the next state is accepting and generate a report signal that is set to 1 if the state is accepting and 0 otherwise. Figure 3 shows how we represent symbolic automata. The steps for implementing symbolic automata in an FPGA are the following:

1) Remove unreachable states if they exist (since MONA generates minimal DFAs, this may only happen in NFA construction),
2) Convert automaton representation given by MONA into truth tables, one for each state bit and one for the reporting bit. Each table maps the value of the current state and the current input to the new value of the state or reporting bit.
3) Use modified Grapefruit to convert truth tables into synthesizable HDL.
4) Synthesize and target FPGA.

We extend Grapefruit to generate symbolic DFAs and NFAs. We do this in two steps. In the first step, we generate an intermediate Truth Table representation (IR) from the MONA output. We generate a separate truth table for each of the state bits. Recall that the number of state bits for NFAs is linear, while for DFAs it is logarithmic. We found that when comparing DFAs to NFAs, the DFAs have fewer truth tables, but these truth tables required deeper logic circuits. Finally, we generate a separate truth table for the bits reporting the accepting states. This shallow truth table checks the state bits of the DFAs and NFAs and generates an output report signal if any of the accepting states are active.

We then generate Verilog lookup table modules from these IRs, to be synthesized into logical circuits in the FPGA. For state transitions, we use sequential logic with case statements. Each bit in the automaton state maps to its own module with a case statement mapping inputs and current state bits to next state bits. For the report truth tables, we use combinational case statements to map current state bits to a report signal. We use Grapefruit's hardware generator to connect all of the truth table modules to the shared input signals including a system clock, reset, and input symbol, as well as a unique output report signal for each accept state in the automata.

IV. EXPERIMENTAL SETUP

A. Generating LTLf Formulas

In order to evaluate the effectiveness of our pipeline and different approaches for implementing runtime monitors in hardware, we generate a diverse set of LTL_f formulas of differing complexities. The FPGA synthesis and optimization tools optimize circuitry, including removing redundant hardware, and therefore it is not sufficient to duplicate the same formulas to evaluate scalability. To that end, we generate multiple different formulas by taking random combinations of the 18 LTL_f patterns from [23]. Each pattern is a simple formula with one or two variables. We take conjunctions of multiple small patterns, merging like variables among them, in order to generate more complex formulas. This process is repeated several times to create multiple formulas, which all draw randomly from a pool of common variables. That way, different formulas may have shared variables. All formulas are then converted to automata and implemented on the same FPGA. The four possible combinations described in the previous section (deterministic/explicit, non-deterministic/explicit, deterministic/symbolic, non-deterministic/symbolic) give us four quadrants for our experimental evaluation. We evaluate the performance of the formulas we generate for each of these four quadrants and compare among them.

In more detail, the LTL_f formulas used in our evaluation are generated in the following way:

1) Draw n random formulas from the pool of patterns.
2) For each variable of each pattern, draw an associated pattern variable from a pool of k shared input variables. Different variables in the same pattern are mapped to different shared input variables from the pool, but variables from different patterns can be mapped to the same input variable.
3) Take the conjunction of all n formulas, forming a more complex LTL_f formula.
4) Repeat this process m times with the same pool of shared input variables, producing m complex formulas with shared variables between them.

Each complex formula is then separately converted to an automaton and implemented on the FPGA, according to each of the four quadrants described previously. To evaluate how the architecture defined by each of the quadrants scales as the number and complexity of each rule increases, we vary the three parameters n, k and m above:

Number of formulas (n): Number of separate LTL_f formulas implemented on the FPGA. We vary this parameter from 10-10,000.

Number of variables (k): Size of the total pool of variables to be drawn from by the LTL_f formulas. We select 10 and 100.

Formula size (m): Number of conjuncts per formula. We select 1, 3, and 5.

We experimentally determine the range of values for each of the three parameters. In the case of the number of formulas, we used AutomataZoo [48] as a reference with number of states up to approximately one million. We also determined that explicit automata hardware utilization scales rapidly with the number of variables, which maps to the number of input signals; for this reason we ran experiments for 10 and 100 variables. Finally, we tried to keep automata to a few thousand states, and therefore set a formula size cap to 5. We repeat each of these experiments three times, each time generating a new set of formulas, and we report the average of the three runs.

B. Hardware Setup

We target Amazon's cloud-deployed FPGAs to standardize on a publicly-available platform. Amazon provides Xilinx Ultrascale+ FPGAs in their F1 EC2 instances. In order to synthesize and place-and-route our HDL into a bitstream to configure the FPGA, we used Amazon's FPGA developer Amazon Machine Image (AMI), which provides us the FPGA software tools. For our experiments, we used Amazon FPGA Developer AMI version 1.6.0, which includes Vivado 2018.3. We deployed this AMI on Amazon EC2 c4.8xlarge instances.

V. Experimental Results

A. Comparisons Among Automata Implementations

We report the average results of the three runs in Figures 4, 5 and 6. Although transition density has low variance across these three runs, the variance in automaton sizes increases with the size of the formula. We leave a more detailed analysis of the distribution of automaton sizes to future work and focus here on a general analysis based on the average results.

Figures 4 and 5 show the number of Flip-Flops (FFs) and Look-Up Tables (LUTs) utilized by the FPGA for our randomly-generated formulas, composed of the conjunction of multiple patterns over random variables drawn from 10 binary system signals. FFs are used in the explicit implementations to store the bits indicating whether a state is active, and in the symbolic implementations to store the bitvector encoding the current state. LUTs correspond to logic gates and are used to implement transition and reporting logic. The Xilinx Virtex UltraScale+ VU9P has a total 1,181,768 LUTs and 2,363,536 Flip-Flops. Our results show that explicit automata, both DFAs and NFAs, tend to use more LUT hardware resources than symbolic automata. Our explicit NFAs tend to use fewer Flip-Flop and LUT resources than their DFA counterparts.

We determined that transforming the MONA-generated automata to homogeneous automata came at a significant cost in terms of number of states. For our 10-variable, explicit

automata, we saw an increase in number of states from 2x in the case of 1-pattern automata to 10x for 5-pattern automata. This increase in states is due to the increase in edge density as automata become more complex. We found the homogeneous state increase to be be a flat multiplier as we scaled our number of formulas. When comparing to the majority of AutomataZoo benchmarks, which have edge/node densities below 2, our conjunctive LTL formula automata had average edge/node densities of 1.36 edges/node for 1 pattern, 4.53 edges/node for 3 patterns, and 8.89 edges/node for 5 patterns, with explicit DFAs and NFAs having approximately the same edge densities. We repeated this analysis with formulas composed of disjunctions instead of conjunctions and found edge/node densities of 1.36 edges/node for 1 pattern, 5.45 edges/node for 3 patterns, and 12.67 edges/node for 5 patterns.

In the case of symbolic automata, we found that symbolic NFAs tend to use more Flip-Flop resources but fewer LUT resources than deterministic implementations. This is due to symbolic NFAs being represented with a lookup-table module per bit in a linear bit-vector ($\mathcal{O}(n)$) representation of the automata, while the DFA implementation represented each bit in a logarithmic bit-vector ($\mathcal{O}(\log n)$) representation. While the implementation does parallelize the bit logic, the DFA logic depth tended to be deeper than NFA logic, resulting in higher clock frequency support for symbolic NFAs. Finally, Vivado was unable to place-and-route 10,000 automata of formula size 5 for any automata type. Each of these automata of formula size five were composed of 100s of states, and we ran out of resources for many of them.

Figure 6 shows the maximum clock frequencies at which the generated hardware monitors can process input signals. We implement our automata in out-of-context mode, which means that our solutions do not include input or output (I/O) circuitry. We removed I/O complications from our analysis as those decisions are application dependent, and can vary significantly in complexity as shown by I/O work by Bo et al [49] and in Grapefruit [10]. These results show that for a larger number of automata (100-10000), the explicit automata maintain a higher clock frequency than their symbolic counterparts. In the case of very small formulas or for very complex formulas, the explicit automata get larger faster and the symbolic implementations can be run at higher frequencies.

Our results are summarized in Figure 7. We find that if hardware utilization is a primary concern, symbolic automata tend to use less hardware than explicit automata. If minimizing Flip-Flip usage, symbolic DFAs are the best option, except in the case of smaller formulas. We see this behavior, because our NFA implementation uses a logic circuit per state in the automaton, while our DFA representation only needs a number of circuits that is the log of the number of states. This larger number of state bits results in a higher FF usage. If minimizing LUT usage, symbolic NFAs are the best option. Symbolic NFAs have more logic circuits, but each of these logic circuits are shallower than the DFA circuits, resulting in a reduced LUT usage. For our experiments, we found that the difference between architectures can result in up to a 5x increase in

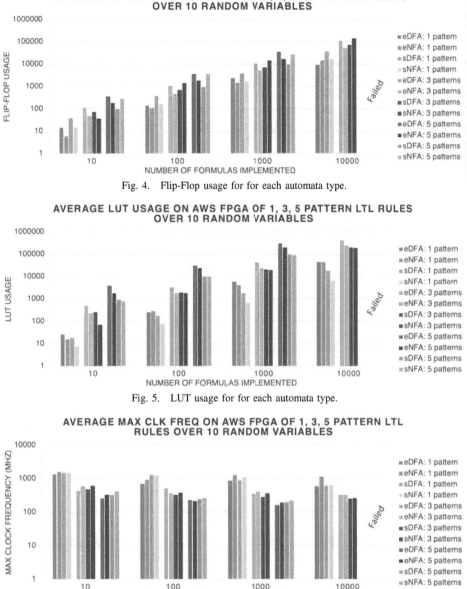

Fig. 4. Flip-Flop usage for for each automata type.

Fig. 5. LUT usage for for each automata type.

Fig. 6. Maximum clock frequency for each automata type.

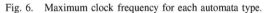

	Deterministic FSA	Non-Deterministic FSA
Explicit		• Lower LUT and FF than eDFA • Higher Clk than eDFA, sDFA, sNFA
Symbolic	• Lower FF than sNFA, eNFA for larger automata • Matching LUT with sNFA for larger automata	• Lower LUT than sDFA, eDFA, eNFA • Lower FF than sDFA for smaller automata • Higher Clk than sDFAs

Fig. 7. Comparing explicit vs. symbolic and deterministic vs. non-determinstic automata implemented in hardware.

LUT and FF usage. If max clock frequency (throughput) is the primary concern, explicit NFAs maintain higher clock frequencies than symbolic automata for a larger number of automata. In the case of very small formulas or very complex formulas, symbolic implementations tend to run at higher frequencies likely due to the clock delay imposed by edges between explicit nodes. Across all of our experiments, we find that symbolic NFAs tend to perform best of all of our evaluated options, and that the difference between architectures can result in up to a 63% reduction in throughput. Similar results were obtained when we repeated the experiments replacing the conjunctions with disjunctions, and the same general conclusions apply. The most significant difference was that, likely due to the steeper scaling of edge/node density, disjunctions failed for 10,000 automata even with only 10 shared variables (k) and a formula size (m) of 3.

B. The Importance of NFA Minimization

Grapefruit includes a series of heuristic minimization techniques that allow us to significantly decrease the number of states in our explicit NFAs. FPGA optimization tools are also applied by Vivado during the synthesis and place-and-route phases. We wanted to determine the effect of higher-level automata optimization on hardware utilization and performance, and synthesized and place-and-routed 3-pattern automata with and without Grapefruit optimizations. We observed that our generated explicit DFAs have fewer states than our generated explicit NFAs across most of our formulas, even post-minimization. We find that during the Cross Boundary and Area Optimization steps of synthesis that the NFA states were merged much more than the DFAs, resulting in a net result of less hardware utilization than DFAs. Although we did use Grapefruit's minimization functionality, the resulting automata are not necessarily minimal. We found that Grapefruit heuristics reduced our state count by between 4.5% and 11.0%, with LUT reductions from 4.3% to 8.2% as we scaled the number of automata from 10 to 10,000.

C. Wide Input Signals

One limitation of our explicit automata implementations is the required distribution of input signals to all of the states that make up the automata. FPGA optimization tools only route signals required by the transition logic for each state, but as formula complexity increases, more signals need to be routed to each state, resulting in significant hardware utilization.

We repeated our experiment with 100 input signals and found that even with simple single-pattern formulas, we were able to synthesize 10,000 symbolic automata formula, but only 1000 explicit automata. When moving complexity up to 3 patterns, we could still support over 10,000 symbolic automata, but fewer than 100 explicit automata. With 5 pattern complexity, we could only support 1000 symbolic automata, and could not synthesize even 10 explicit automata.

Wide input signals require serialization on the input, and handling report identification requires serialization on the output. Our analysis does not investigate I/O because it is implementation dependent. When monitors are monitoring an implementation on the FPGA, there may not be a need to transfer signals off the chip. Also, in the case of output signals, there are many approaches to handling monitoring solutions. If the application and monitoring resolution implementation is on chip, there may not be a need to remove report information off the chip. If this information does need to leave the chip, it might be sufficient to send off a single bit of information, as opposed to the entire report bit vector, as demonstrated with other FPGA-based automata implementations.

VI. CONCLUSIONS AND FUTURE WORK

In this work, we introduce a framework for generating FPGA-deployed runtime monitors based on LTL_f formulas with four different architectures: explicit DFA, explicit NFA, symbolic DFA, symbolic NFA. We use our framework to determine performance tradeoffs among these. Our results show that there is no single best hardware representation for automata-based runtime verification, and that there are trade-offs between hardware utilization and the maximum

clock frequency for automata transitions. Across all of our experiments, we find that symbolic automata tend to use less hardware (FFs and LUTs) than explicit automata, that explicit automata tend to run at higher frequencies (except in the case of very small or very complex formulas), and that symbolic NFAs tend to perform best of all of our evaluated architectures across the widest range of scenarios. Our experiments also showed us that differences between architectures can result in up to a 5x increase in LUT and FF usage, as well as result in up to a 63% reduction in runtime verification throughput.

We extended Grapefruit to also generate symbolic hardware automata. Although Grapefruit includes many other features including targeting Block RAM, full-stack support with I/O, and support for variable symbol width and striding, we did not use these functions in our experiments. Application-side research could further investigate concerns related to I/O and moving signal data to the automata as well as handling reporting data communication.

We targeted Amazon's F1, cloud-deployed FPGAs to standardize on one FPGA platform. Application-side research could utilize our work for integrating runtime monitors into high performance cloud-deployed applications, including machine learning and bioinformatics workloads. Our framework generates HDL that can target smaller and lower power FPGAs for other applications, including embedded systems. Because our explicit automata use the standard ANML format, automata engines built for other architectures can also be used.

We chose to keep the width of input signals constant across our experiments to determine the performance of our solution when all input signals are processed simultaneously. With flexibility in timing, or with slower sampling, future work could utilize Grapefruit's variable symbol-width functionality to handle many more input signals, albeit at a slower rate, thus making it possible to handle formulas with a much larger number of propositional variables. This would also significantly reduce hardware utilization.

In the future, it would also be interesting to compare with existing frameworks for implementing monitors in FPGA, such as [34], [39]. Since these works use different specification languages (e.g. PSL for [34] and STL and TRE for [39]), this would require establishing a unified set of benchmarks for these different formalisms and separating in the experimental evaluation the impact of the differences between specification languages from the performance of the FPGA framework.

During our analysis, we found that the average automata edges/node density scaled differently for conjunctions vs. disjunctions of patterns. We found that edge density for disjunctions tended to scale with a steeper slope than conjunctions. Future work could explore this relationship between compositions of LTL formulas and automata parameters.

ACKNOWLEDGMENTS

Work funded by the NSF XPS and CRISP, one of six centers in JUMP, a Semiconductor Research Corporation (SRC) program, NSF grants IIS-1527668, CCF-1704883, IIS-1830549, and an award from the Maryland Procurement Office.

REFERENCES

[1] K. Havelund, "Runtime verification of C programs," in *Testing of Software and Communicating Systems, 20th IFIP TC 6/WG 6.1 International Conference, TestCom 2008, 8th International Workshop, FATES 2008, Tokyo, Japan, June 10-13, 2008, Proceedings*, ser. Lecture Notes in Computer Science, K. Suzuki, T. Higashino, A. Ulrich, and T. Hasegawa, Eds., vol. 5047. Springer, 2008, pp. 7–22.

[2] D. Tabakov, K. Y. Rozier, and M. Y. Vardi, "Optimized temporal monitors for systemc," *Formal Methods in System Design*, vol. 41, no. 3, pp. 236–268, 2012.

[3] T. Reinbacher, K. Y. Rozier, and J. Schumann, "Temporal-logic based runtime observer pairs for system health management of real-time systems," in *International Conference on Tools and Algorithms for the Construction and Analysis of Systems*. Springer, 2014, pp. 357–372.

[4] J. Schumann, P. Moosbrugger, and K. Y. Rozier, "R2u2: monitoring and diagnosis of security threats for unmanned aerial systems," in *Runtime Verification*. Springer, 2015, pp. 233–249.

[5] J. Dean, D. Patterson, and C. Young, "A new golden age in computer architecture: Empowering the machine-learning revolution," *IEEE Micro*, vol. 38, no. 2, pp. 21–29, 2018.

[6] J. L. Hennessy and D. A. Patterson, "A new golden age for computer architecture," *Commun. ACM*, vol. 62, no. 2, p. 48–60, Jan. 2019. [Online]. Available: https://doi.org/10.1145/3282307

[7] P. Dlugosch, D. Brown, P. Glendenning, M. Leventhal, and H. Noyes, "An efficient and scalable semiconductor architecture for parallel automata processing," *IEEE Transactions on Parallel and Distributed Systems*, vol. 25, no. 12, pp. 3088–3098, 2014.

[8] K. Wang, K. Angstadt, C. Bo, N. Brunelle, E. Sadredini, T. T. II, J. Wadden, M. R. Stan, and K. Skadron, "An overview of micron's automata processor," in *Proceedings of the Eleventh IEEE/ACM/IFIP International Conference on Hardware/Software Codesign and System Synthesis, CODES 2016, Pittsburgh, Pennsylvania, USA, October 1-7, 2016*, 2016, pp. 14:1–14:3.

[9] T. Xie, V. Dang, J. Wadden, K. Skadron, and M. Stan, "Reapr: Reconfigurable engine for automata processing," in *2017 27th International Conference on Field Programmable Logic and Applications (FPL)*. IEEE, 2017, pp. 1–8.

[10] R. Rahimi, E. Sadredini, M. Stan, and K. Skadron, "Grapefruit: An open-source, full-stack, and customizable automata processing on fpgas."

[11] C. Bo, V. Dang, E. Sadredini, and K. Skadron, "Searching for potential grna off-target sites for crispr/cas9 using automata processing across different platforms," in *2018 IEEE International Symposium on High Performance Computer Architecture (HPCA)*. IEEE, 2018, pp. 737–748.

[12] I. Roy and S. Aluru, "Discovering motifs in biological sequences using the micron automata processor," *IEEE/ACM transactions on computational biology and bioinformatics*, vol. 13, no. 1, pp. 99–111, 2015.

[13] T. Tracy, Y. Fu, I. Roy, E. Jonas, and P. Glendenning, "Towards machine learning on the automata processor," in *International Conference on High Performance Computing*. Springer, 2016, pp. 200–218.

[14] M. Putic, A. Varshneya, and M. R. Stan, "Hierarchical temporal memory on the automata processor," *IEEE Micro*, vol. 37, no. 1, pp. 52–59, 2017.

[15] E. Sadredini, D. Guo, C. Bo, R. Rahimi, K. Skadron, and H. Wang, "A scalable solution for rule-based part-of-speech tagging on novel hardware accelerators," in *Proceedings of the 24th ACM SIGKDD International Conference on Knowledge Discovery & Data Mining*, 2018, pp. 665–674.

[16] A. Bauer, M. Leucker, and C. Schallhart, "Comparing ltl semantics for runtime verification," *J. Log. Comput.*, vol. 20, no. 3, pp. 651–674, 2010.

[17] A. Bauer, M. Leucker, and C. Schallhart, "Runtime verification for LTL and TLTL," *ACM Transactions on Software Engineering and Methodology (TOSEM)*, vol. 20, no. 4, pp. 1–64, 2011.

[18] J. G. Henriksen, J. L. Jensen, M. E. Jørgensen, N. Klarlund, R. Paige, T. Rauhe, and A. Sandholm, "Mona: Monadic second-order logic in practice," in *Tools and Algorithms for Construction and Analysis of Systems, First International Workshop, TACAS 95, Proceedings*, 1995, pp. 89–110.

[19] A. Duret-Lutz, A. Lewkowicz, A. Fauchille, T. Michaud, E. Renault, and L. Xu, "Spot 2.0 — A Framework for LTL and ω-automata Manipulation," in *ATVA*, 2016.

[20] E. Sadredini, R. Rahimi, M. Lenjani, M. Stan, and K. Skadron, "Flexamata: A universal and efficient adaption of applications to spatial automata processing accelerators," in *Proceedings of the Twenty-Fifth International Conference on Architectural Support for Programming Languages and Operating Systems*, 2020, pp. 219–234.

[21] H. Gruber and M. Holzer, "Computational complexity of nfa minimization for finite and unary languages." *LATA*, vol. 8, pp. 261–272, 2007.

[22] G. De Giacomo and M. Y. Vardi, "Linear temporal logic and linear dynamic logic on finite traces," in *IJCAI 2013, Proceedings of the 23rd International Joint Conference on Artificial Intelligence, Beijing, China, August 3-9, 2013*, 2013, pp. 854–860.

[23] G. De Giacomo, R. De Masellis, and M. Montali, "Reasoning on LTL on Finite Traces: Insensitivity to Infiniteness," in *Proceedings of the Twenty-Eighth AAAI Conference on Artificial Intelligence*, 2014, pp. 1027–1033.

[24] S. Zhu, L. M. Tabajara, J. Li, G. Pu, and M. Y. Vardi, "Symbolic ltlf synthesis," in *Proceedings of the Twenty-Sixth International Joint Conference on Artificial Intelligence, IJCAI 2017, Melbourne, Australia, August 19-25, 2017*, 2017, pp. 1362–1369.

[25] S. Zhu, G. Pu, and M. Y. Vardi, "First-order vs. second-order encodings for ltlf-to-automata translation," in *Theory and Applications of Models of Computation - 15th Annual Conference, TAMC 2019, Kitakyushu, Japan, April 13-16, 2019, Proceedings*, 2019, pp. 684–705.

[26] O. Lichtenstein, A. Pnueli, and L. Zuck, "The glory of the past," in *Logics of Programs*, ser. Lecture Notes in Computer Science, vol. 193. Springer, 1985, pp. 196–218.

[27] M. d'Amorim and G. Rosu, "Efficient monitoring of omega-languages," in *Proc, 17th Intl Conf. on Computer Aided Verification*, ser. Lecture Notes in Computer Science, vol. 3576. Springer, 2005, pp. 364–378.

[28] H. Björklund and W. Martens, "The Tractability Frontier for NFA Minimization," in *Automata, Languages and Programming, 35th International Colloquium, ICALP 2008, Reykjavik, Iceland, July 7-11, 2008, Proceedings, Part II - Track B: Logic, Semantics, and Theory of Programming & Track C: Security and Cryptography Foundations*, 2008, pp. 27–38.

[29] V. M. Glushkov, "The Abstract Theory of Automata," *Russian Math. Surveys*, vol. 16, pp. 1–53, 1961.

[30] R. McNaughton and H. Yamada, "Regular expressions and state graphs for automata," *IRE Trans. Electronic Computers*, vol. 9, no. 1, pp. 39–47, 1960.

[31] T. Tracy II, J. Wadden, T. Xie, K. Skadron, and M. Stan, "Accelerating design convergence of automata processing designs with a tiled hierarchy," in *FSP Workshop 2019; Sixth International Workshop on FPGAs for Software Programmers*. VDE, 2019, pp. 1–8.

[32] D. Drusinsky, "The temporal rover and the atg rover," in *International SPIN Workshop on Model Checking of Software*. Springer, 2000, pp. 323–330.

[33] L. Pike, N. Wegmann, S. Niller, and A. Goodloe, "Copilot: monitoring embedded systems," *Innovations in Systems and Software Engineering*, vol. 9, no. 4, pp. 235–255, 2013.

[34] M. Boulé and Z. Zilic, "Automata-based assertion-checker synthesis of psl properties," *ACM Transactions on Design Automation of Electronic Systems (TODAES)*, vol. 13, no. 1, pp. 1–21, 2008.

[35] J. Geist, K. Y. Rozier, and J. Schumann, "Runtime observer pairs and bayesian network reasoners on-board fpgas: flight-certifiable system health management for embedded systems," in *International Conference on Runtime Verification*. Springer, 2014, pp. 215–230.

[36] P. O. Meredith, D. Jin, D. Griffith, F. Chen, and G. Roşu, "An overview of the mop runtime verification framework," *International Journal on Software Tools for Technology Transfer*, vol. 14, no. 3, pp. 249–289, 2012.

[37] R. Pellizzoni, P. Meredith, M. Caccamo, and G. Rosu, "Hardware runtime monitoring for dependable cots-based real-time embedded systems," in *2008 Real-Time Systems Symposium*. IEEE, 2008, pp. 481–491.

[38] S. Jaksvic, E. Bartocci, R. Grosu, R. Kloibhofer, T. Nguyen, and D. Nickovié, "From signal temporal logic to fpga monitors," in *2015 ACM/IEEE International Conference on Formal Methods and Models for Codesign (MEMOCODE)*. IEEE, 2015, pp. 218–227.

[39] K. Selyunin, S. Jaksic, T. Nguyen, C. Reidl, U. Hafner, E. Bartocci, D. Nickovic, and R. Grosu, "Runtime monitoring with recovery of the sent communication protocol," in *International Conference on Computer Aided Verification*. Springer, 2017, pp. 336–355.

[40] K. Selyunin, T. Nguyen, E. Bartocci, and R. Grosu, "Applying runtime monitoring for automotive electronic development," in *International Conference on Runtime Verification*. Springer, 2016, pp. 462–469.

[41] J. Baumeister, B. Finkbeiner, M. Schwenger, and H. Torfah, "Fpga stream-monitoring of real-time properties," *ACM Transactions on Embedded Computing Systems (TECS)*, vol. 18, no. 5s, pp. 1–24, 2019.

[42] L. Convent, S. Hungerecker, T. Scheffel, M. Schmitz, D. Thoma, and A. Weiss, "Hardware-based runtime verification with embedded tracing units and stream processing," in *International Conference on Runtime Veri cation*. Springer, 2018, pp. 43–63.

[43] T. Tracy II and L. Tabajara, "Ltlfautomata," https://github.com/tjt7a/LTLfAutomata, 2020.

[44] S. Bansal, Y. Li, L. M. Tabajara, and M. Y. Vardi, "Hybrid compositional reasoning for reactive synthesis from finite-horizon specifications," in *The Thirty-Fourth AAAI Conference on Arti cial Intelligence, AAAI 2020, The Thirty-Second Innovative Applications of Arti cial Intelligence Conference, IAAI 2020, The Tenth AAAI Symposium on Educational Advances in Arti cial Intelligence, EAAI 2020, New York, NY, USA, February 7-12, 2020*. AAAI Press, 2020, pp. 9766–9774.

[45] M. Sipser, *Introduction to the theory of computation*. PWS Publishing Company, 1997.

[46] S. Zhu, L. M. Tabajara, G. Pu, and M. Y. Vardi, "On the Power of Automata Minimization in Temporal Synthesis," *CoRR*, 2020, [Online].

[47] A. Chandra, D. Kozen, and L. Stockmeyer, "Alternation," *J. ACM*, vol. 28, no. 1, pp. 114–133, 1981.

[48] J. Wadden, T. Tracy, E. Sadredini, L. Wu, C. Bo, J. Du, Y. Wei, J. Udall, M. Wallace, M. Stan *et al.*, "Automatazoo: A modern automata processing benchmark suite," in *2018 IEEE International Symposium on Workload Characterization (IISWC)*. IEEE, 2018, pp. 13–24.

[49] C. Bo, V. Dang, T. Xie, J. Wadden, M. Stan, and K. Skadron, "Automata processing in reconfigurable architectures: In-the-cloud deployment, cross-platform evaluation, and fast symbol-only reconfiguration," *ACM Transactions on Recon gurable Technology and Systems (TRETS)*, vol. 12, no. 2, pp. 1–25, 2019.

15

The Proof Checkers Pacheck and Pastèque for the Practical Algebraic Calculus

Daniela Kaufmann(iD), Mathias Fleury(iD) and Armin Biere(iD)
Johannes Kepler University Linz, Altenbergerstr. 69, 4040 Linz, Austria
daniela.kaufmann@jku.at   mathias.fleury@jku.at   armin.biere@jku.at

Abstract—Generating and checking proof certificates is important to increase the trust in automated reasoning tools. In recent years formal verification using computer algebra became more important and is heavily used in automated circuit verification. An existing proof format which covers algebraic reasoning and allows efficient proof checking is the practical algebraic calculus. In this paper we present two independent proof checkers PACHECK and PASTÈQUE. The checker PACHECK checks algebraic proofs more efficiently than PASTÈQUE, but the latter is formally verified using the proof assistant Isabelle/HOL. Furthermore, we introduce extension rules to simulate essential rewriting techniques required in practice. For efficiency we also make use of indices for existing polynomials and include deletion rules too.

I. INTRODUCTION

Formal verification aims to guarantee the correctness of a given system with respect to a certain specification. However, the verification process might contain errors. In order to increase the trust in verification results, it is common to generate proof certificates, which can be checked by a stand-alone proof checker. For example, in the SAT competition certificates of unsatisfiability are required since 2013 and different resolution and clausal proof formats [1], such as DRUP [2], [3], DRAT [4], and LRAT [5] are available.

Automated reasoning based on computer algebra has a long history [6]–[8] with renewed recent interest; e.g., it provides the state of the art in verifying gate-level multipliers [9]–[12]. Furthermore, algebraic reasoning in combination with satisfiability checking (SAT) is succesfully used to solve complex combinatorial problems [13]–[16] with possible future applications in cryptanalysis [17]–[19].

The practical algebraic calculus (PAC) [20] is a proof format to represent certificates for validating results of such algebraic techniques. It is based on the polynomial calculus (PC) [21] and allows to dynamically capture that a polynomial can be derived from a given set of polynomials using algebraic ideal theory. In contrast to PC, PAC proofs can be checked efficiently, for example using our tool PACTRIM [20].

In this paper we add an indexing scheme to PAC and also propose deletion and extension rules. Our paper contains no new theory, except for the more technical formalization of extensions. This allows us to merge and check proofs obtained from SAT and computer algebra [22], the current state-of-the-art, in a uniform (and now precise) manner. The purpose of this system description is to define the new version of PAC and present our new checkers PACHECK and PASTÈQUE. Furthermore, PASTÈQUE in contrast to PACHECK is verified

in Isabelle/HOL, but PACHECK is faster and more memory efficient (also compared to PACTRIM). A preliminary version of this paper is included in the first author's PhD thesis [23].

II. PRACTICAL ALGEBRAIC CALCULUS

In this section we briefly introduce the algebraic notion following [24]. Let X be the set of variables $\{x_1, \ldots, x_n\}$ and further let $G \subseteq \mathbb{Z}[X]$ and $f \in \mathbb{Z}[X]$.

Algebraic proof systems reason about polynomial equations. The aim is to show that the equation $f = 0$ is implied by the equations $g = 0$ for every $g \in G$; i.e., every common root of the polynomials $g \in G$ is also a root of f. In algebraic terms, this question means to derive whether f belongs to the ideal generated by G. A nonempty subset $I \subseteq \mathbb{Z}[X]$ is called an *ideal* if $\forall u, v \in I : u + v \in I$ and $\forall w \in \mathbb{Z}[X], \forall u \in I : wu \in I$. If $G = \{g_1, \ldots, g_m\} \subseteq \mathbb{Z}[X]$, then the ideal generated by G is defined as $\langle G \rangle = \{q_1 g_1 + \cdots + q_m g_m \mid q_1, \ldots, q_m \in \mathbb{Z}[X]\}$.

For a given set of polynomials $G \subseteq \mathbb{Z}[X]$, a *model* is a point $u = (u_1, \ldots, u_n) \in \mathbb{Z}^n$ such that $\forall g \in G : g(u_1, \ldots, u_n) = 0$. Here, by $g(u_1, \ldots, u_n)$ we mean the element of $\mathbb{Z}$ obtained by evaluating the polynomial g for $x_1 = u_1, \ldots, x_n = u_n$.

PAC proofs [20] are sequences of proof rules. We introduce the semantics of PAC as a transition system. Let P denote a sequence of polynomials, which can be accessed via indices. We write $P(i) = \perp$ to denote that the sequence P at index i does not contain a polynomial, and $P(i \mapsto p)$ to determine that P at index i is set to p.

The initial state is $(X = \mathrm{Var}(G \cup \{f\}), P)$ where P maps indices to polynomials of G. For bit-level verification [20] only models of the Boolean domain $\{0, 1\}^n$ are of interest. In previous work, we added the set of Boolean-value constraints $B(X) = \{x^2 - x \mid x \in X\}$ to G and had to include steps in the proofs that operate on these Boolean-value constraints. Instead, we now handle operations on Boolean-value constraints implicitly to reduce the number of proof steps. That is, when checking the correctness, we immediately reduce exponents greater than one in the polynomials. The following two rules model the properties of ideals as introduced above.

[ADD (i, j, k, p)] $\qquad (X, P) \implies (X, P(i \mapsto p))$

provided that $P(j) \neq \perp$, $P(k) \neq \perp$, $P(i) = \perp$, $p \in \mathbb{Z}[X]/\langle B(X) \rangle$, and $p = P(j) + P(k) \mod \langle B(X) \rangle$.

[MULT (i, j, q, p)] $\qquad (X, P) \implies (X, P(i \mapsto p))$

provided $P(j) \neq \perp$, $P(i) = \perp$, $p, q \in \mathbb{Z}[X]/\langle B(X) \rangle$, and $p = q \cdot P(j) \mod \langle B(X) \rangle$.

```
   letter    ::=   'a' | 'b' | ... | 'z' | 'A' | 'B' | ... | 'Z'
  number     ::=   '0' | '1' | ... | '9'
 constant    ::=   (number)⁺
 variable    ::=   letter (letter | number)*
    term     ::=   variable ('*' variable)*
 monomial    ::=   constant | [constant '*'] term
polynomial   ::=   ['-'] monomial ('+' | '-' monomial)*
   index     ::=   constant
   input     ::=   (index polynomial ';')*
 add_rule    ::=   index '+' index ',' index ',' polynomial ';'
 mul_rule    ::=   index '*' index ',' polynomial ',' polynomial ';'
 del_rule    ::=   index 'd' ';'
 ext_rule    ::=   index '=' variable ',' polynomial ';'
   proof     ::=   (add_rule | mul_rule | del_rule | ext_rule)*
  target     ::=   polynomial ';'
```

Figure 1. Syntax of input polynomials, target, and proofs in PAC-format

If in either one of the above rules p is also the target polynomial f, it holds that $f \in \langle G \rangle$. In the original PAC format introduced in [20], it was necessary to explicitly provide the antecedents $P(i)$ and $P(j)$. In our new format, we use indices i and j to access polynomials, similar to LRAT [5]. The new syntax is given in Fig. 1 and an example is provided with our tools [25]. Naming polynomials by indices reduces the proof size and makes parsing more efficient, because only the conclusion polynomials of each rule and the initial polynomials of G are stated explicitly. However, introducing indices for polynomials has the effect that the semantics of P changes from sets to multisets, as in DRAT [3], and it is possible to introduce the same polynomial under different names. Checking the result of each rule allows pinpointing the first error, instead of claiming that the proof is wrong somewhere in one of the (usually millions) of steps.

We extend our original proof rules [20] by adding a deletion and an extension rule. In the deletion rule we remove polynomials from P which are not needed anymore in subsequent steps to reduce the memory usage of our tools.

$$[\text{DELETE}(i)] \qquad (X, P) \implies (X, P(i \mapsto \bot))$$

A. Extension

In our previous work [22], we converted DRUP proofs to the PAC format and encountered the need to extend the initial set of polynomials G to reduce the size of the polynomials in the PAC proof. We included polynomials of the form $-f_x + 1 - x$, similar to the negation rule in the polynomial calculus with resolution [26], which introduced the variable f_x as the negation of the Boolean variable x.

However, at that point we did not use proper extension rules, but simply added these extension polynomials to the initial polynomials G. This may affect the models of the constraint set, because any arbitrary polynomial can be added as initial constraints. For example, we could simply add the constant polynomial 1 to G, which makes any PAC proof obsolete. To prevent this issue we add an extension rule to PAC, which allows to add further polynomials to the knowledge base with new variables while preserving the original models on the original variable set of variables X.

$$[\text{EXT}(i, v, p)] \qquad (X, P) \implies (X \cup \{v\}, P(i \mapsto -v + p))$$

provided that $P(i) = \bot$ and $v \notin X$ and $p \in \mathbb{Z}[X]/\langle B(X) \rangle$, and $p^2 - p \equiv 0 \mod \langle B(X) \rangle$.

With this extension rule, variables v can act as placeholders for polynomials p, i.e., $-v + p = 0$, which enables more concise proofs. The variables v are not allowed to occur earlier in the proof. Furthermore, to preserve Boolean models, we require $p^2 - p \equiv 0 \mod \langle B(X) \rangle$. Without this condition v might take non-Boolean solutions and thus force us to calculate in the ring $\mathbb{Z}[X, v]/\langle B(X) \rangle$ instead of $\mathbb{Z}[X, v]/\langle B(X, v) \rangle$.

Consider for example $P = \{-y + x - 1\}$. The only Boolean model is $(x, y) = (1, 0)$. If we extend P by $-v + x + 1$ we derive $v = 2$, because $x = 1$ for all models of P. Thus $v^2 - v = 0$ does not hold.

Proposition 1. EXT *preserves the original models on* X.

Proof. We show that adding $p_v := -v + p$ does not affect the models of $P \subseteq \mathbb{Z}[X]/\langle B(X) \rangle$. Let "$<$" be a lexicographic ordering, H a Gröbner basis [27] of $\langle P \rangle$ w.r.t. "$<$", and "$<_v$" be an extension of "$<$" with v as largest element. Thm. 3 of [28] shows that $H \cup \{p_v\}$ is a Gröbner basis w.r.t. "$<_v$" for $\langle P_v \rangle := \langle P(i \mapsto p_v) \rangle \subseteq \mathbb{Z}[X \cup \{v\}]/\langle B(X \cup \{v\}) \rangle$, the extended ideal, and $\langle P_v \rangle \cap \mathbb{Z}[X]/\langle B(X) \rangle = \langle H \cup \{p_v\} \rangle \cap \mathbb{Z}[X]/\langle B(X) \rangle = \langle H \rangle = \langle P \rangle$ follows. $\square$

III. PACHECK

We implemented PACHECK as an extension of our previous checker PACTRIM [20]. It consists of approximately 1 700 lines of C code and is published [25] under MIT license. The default mode of PACHECK supports the extended version of PAC, as presented in this paper, for the new syntax using indices. PACHECK is backwards compatible to our original format of PAC [20] and all features including reasoning with exponents are supported. However, extension rules are only supported for Boolean models.

PACHECK reads three input files `<input>`, `<proof>`, and `<target>` and then verifies that the polynomial in `<target>` is contained in the ideal generated by the polynomials in `<input>` using the rules provided in `<proof>`. The polynomial arithmetic needed for checking the proof rules is implemented from scratch. In PACHECK polynomials are stored as ordered linked lists of monomials, where a monomial consists of a coefficient and a term. The coefficients are represented using the GMP library [29]. Terms are ordered linked list of variables that are identified as strings.

In the default mode of PACHECK we order variables in terms lexicographically using `strcmp`. All internally allocated terms in linked lists are shared using a hash table. It turns out that the order of variables has an enormous effect on memory usage, since different variable orderings induce different terms. For example, given the monomials xyz and $x'yz$, sharing of yz is possible for the order $x' > x > y > z$, whereas no sharing occurs for $y > x > z > x'$. For one example with more than 7 million proof steps, using `-1*strcmp` as sorting function leads to an increase of 50% in memory usage. A further option for sorting the variables is to use the same variable ordering as in the given proof files. That is, we assign increasing `level` values to new variables and sort according to this value. However, the best ordering that maximizes internal sharing cannot be determined in advance from the original constraint set, as it highly depends on the applied operations in the proof rules. PACHECK supports the orderings `strcmp`, `-1*strcmp`, `level`, and `-1*level`. Terms in polynomials are sorted using the same order as for the variables.

In the initial phase of PACHECK each polynomial from `<input>` is sorted and stored as an inference. Inferences consist of a given index and a polynomial and are stored in a hash table. In the default mode, the index acts as the hash value. Thus it is possible to add the same polynomial twice. If the original format of PAC is used, a hash value is computed based on the input polynomial. Proof checking is applied on-the-fly. We parse each rule of `<proof>` and immediately apply the necessary checks discussed in Sect. II. If the rule is either ADD or MULT, we have to compute whether the conclusion polynomial of the rule is equal to the arithmetic operation performed on the antecedent polynomials.

We modified the algorithm of polynomial addition in PACTRIM and now assume the monomials of polynomials to be sorted. Addition of polynomials is performed by merging their monomials in an interleaved way. In PACTRIM we pushed the monomials of both polynomials on a stack and then sorted and merged them. Normalization of the exponents is not necessary in the ADD rule, but we still use this technique for multiplication of polynomials, where we multiply each monomial of the first polynomial with each monomial of the second monomial. In the MULT rule we normalize exponents larger than one, before testing equality. Furthermore, we check whether the conclusion polynomial of the rules ADD or MULT matches the polynomial in `<target>` in order to identify whether the target polynomial was derived.

The original version of PACTRIM [20] did not allow to delete inferences. As a consequence the set of polynomials increased with each proof rule, leading to memory exhaustion for very large proofs. In PACHECK we now support deletion of inferences. A partial solution for deletion was used in [9] to reduce memory usage. However, in contrast to our new version, individual inferences could not be deleted (only both antecedents of a proof step could be). Extension variables were not supported in PACTRIM [20] either.

IV. PASTÈQUE

To further increase trust in the verification, we implemented a verified checker called PASTÈQUE in the proof assistant Isabelle/HOL [30]. It follows a "refinement" approach, starting with an abstract specification of ideals, which we then refine with the Isabelle Refinement Framework [31] to the transition system from Sect. II, and further down to executable code using Isabelle's code generator [32]. The Isabelle files have been made available [33]. The generated code consists of 2 800 lines Standard ML (2 400 generated by Isabelle, 400 for the parser) and is also available [25] under MIT license.

On the most abstract level, we start from Isabelle's definition of ideals. The specification states that if "success" is returned, the target is in the ideal. Then we formalize PAC and prove that the generated ideal is not changed by the rules. Proving that PAC respects the specification on ideals was not obvious due to limited automation and development of the Isabelle library of polynomials (e.g., neither "$\mathrm{Var}\,(1) = \emptyset$" nor "$p \neq 0 \implies X \in \mathrm{Var}\,(X \times p)$" are present). However, Sledgehammer [34] automatically proved many of these simple lemmas.

While the input format identifies variables as strings, Isabelle only supports natural numbers as variables. Therefore, we use an injective function to convert between the abstract specification of polynomials (with natural numbers as variables) and the concrete manipulations (with strings as variables). The code does not depend on this function, only the correctness theorem does. Injectivity is only required to check that extension variables did not occur before.

In the third refinement stage, SEPREF [35] changes data structures automatically, such as replacing the set of variables X by a hash-set. Finally, we use the code generator to produce code. This code is combined with a trusted parser and can be compiled using the Standard ML compiler MLTON [36].

The implementation is not backwards compatible and less sophisticated than PACHECK's. In particular, even if terms are sorted, sharing is not considered (neither of variables or of monomials) as it can be executed partially by the compiler, although not guaranteed by Standard ML semantics. Some sharing could be performed by the garbage collector. We tried to enforce sharing by using MLTON's `shareAll` function and by using a hash map during parsing, i.e., using a hash map that assigns a variable to "itself" (the same string, but potentially at a different memory location) and normalize every occurrence. However, performance became worse.

PASTÈQUE is four times slower than PACHECK. First, this is due to Standard ML. While Isabelle's code generator to LLVM [37] produces much faster code, we need integers of arbitrary large size, which is currently not supported. Also achieving sharing is entirely manual, which is challenging due to the use of separation logic SEPREF. Second, there is no axiomatization of file reading and hence parsing must be applied *entirely* before calling the checker in order for the correctness theorem to apply. This is more memory intensive and less efficient than interleaving parsing and checking. PASTÈQUE can be configured via the `uloop` option to either use the main loop generated by Isabelle (parsing before calling the generated checker) or instead use a hand-written copy of the main loop, the *unsafe loop*, where parsing and checking is interleaved. The performance gain is large (on `sp-ar-cl-64` with 32 GB RAM, the garbage collection time went from 700 s down to 25 s), but only the checking functions are verified, not the main loop.

V. TOOL DEMONSTRATION

In this section we show an example of a PAC proof and the output of our new checkers, which demonstrates the usage of our tools PACHECK and PASTÈQUE.

Example 1. *Let $\bar{x} \vee \bar{y}$ and $y \vee z$ be two clauses. From these clauses we are able to derive the clause $\bar{x} \vee z$ using resolution. We show how this derivation can be covered in PAC.*

The clauses are translated into polynomial equations using De Morgan's laws and using the fact that a logical AND can be represented by multiplication. For example, from $\bar{x} \vee \bar{y} = \top \Leftrightarrow x \wedge y = \bot$ we derive the polynomial equation $xy = 0$.

We translate the given clauses, which builds our input `<res.input>` and the target `<res.target>`. For the PAC proof in `<res.proof>` we introduce an extension variable f_z, which models the negation of z, i.e. $-f_z + 1 - z = 0$. We use this extension to reduce the size of the conclusion polynomials. The PAC proof shows only some possible deletion rules, adding more deletion rules is possible. The files of this example are available [25].

```
<res.input>        <res.proof>
 1  x*y;            3  = fz,  -z+1;
 2  y*z-y-z+1;      4  *  3,  y-1, -fz*y+fz-y*z+y+z-1;
                    5  +  2,      4, -fz*y+fz;
                    2  d;
                    4  d;
<res.target>        6  *  1,  fz, fz*x*y;
 -x*z+x;            1  d;
                    7  *  5,   x, -fz*x*y+fz*x;
                    8  +  6,   7, fz*x;
                    9  *  3,   x, -fz*x-x*z+x;
                   10  +  8,   9, -x*z+x;
```

We give these files to PACHECK *and* PASTÈQUE *and the results are provided in the Figs 2 and 3.*

```
$ pacheck res.input res.proof res.target
[pacheck] Pacheck Version 001
[pacheck] Practical Algebraic Calculus Proof Checker
[pacheck] Copyright (C) 2020, Daniela Kaufmann, JKU
[pacheck] compressed mode with indices assumed
[pacheck] checking target enabled
[pacheck] reading target polynomial from 'res.target'
[pacheck] read 8 bytes from 'res.target'
[pacheck] reading original polynomials from 'res.input'
[pacheck] found 2 original polynomials in 'res.input'
[pacheck] read 20 bytes from 'res.input'
[pacheck] reading polynomial algebraic calculus proof from
↪ 'res.proof'
[pacheck] found and checked 8 inferences in 'res.proof'
[pacheck] read 219 bytes from 'res.proof'
[pacheck] found 1 target polynomial inference
[pacheck] proof length 10 (number of polynomials)
[pacheck] proof size 25 (on average 2.5 terms per
↪ polynomial)
[pacheck] proof degree 3 (internal maximum degree 3)
[pacheck] searched 32 inferences 0.1 average collisions
[pacheck] 10 inferences, 3.2 average searches
[pacheck] original inferences 2 (20% of total rules)
[pacheck] inference rules 8 (80% of total rules)
[pacheck] addition inference rules 3 (38% of inference
↪ rules)
[pacheck] multiplication inference rules 4 (50% of inference
↪ rules)
[pacheck] extension rules 1 (12% of inference rules)
[pacheck] deletion inference rules 3 (30% of total rules)
[pacheck] maximum 9 of total 10 terms (90%)
[pacheck] searched 52 terms 81% hits 0.3 average collisions
[pacheck] maximum 2229 bytes allocated (0.0 MB)
[pacheck] maximum resident set size 4481024 bytes (4.3 MB)
[pacheck] process time 0.000 seconds
[pacheck] TARGET CHECKED
```

Figure 2. Output of PACHECK on the example from Ex. 1.

```
$ pasteque res.input res.proof res.target
c polys parsed
c *******************
c pac parsed
c spec parsed
c Now checking
s SUCCESSFULL
c
c ***** stats *****
c parsing polys file init (nonGC): 0.000 s = 0.000 s (usr)
↪ 0.000 s (sys)
c parsing pac file init (nonGC): 0.000 s = 0.000 s (usr)
↪ 0.000 s (sys)
c full init (nonGC): 0.000 s = 0.000 s (usr) 0.000 s (sys)
c time solving (nonGC): 0.000 s = 0.000 s (usr) 0.000 s
↪ (sys)
c time GC: 0.000 s = 0.000 s (usr) 0.000 s (sys)
c time solving(full): 0.000 s
c Overall (nonGC): 0.001 s = 0.001 s (usr) 0.000 s (sys)
c overall GC: 0.000 s = 0.000 s (usr) 0.000 s (sys)
c Overall(full): 0.001 s
```

Figure 3. Output of PASTÈQUE on the example from Ex. 1.

VI. EVALUATION

In our experiments we used an Intel Xeon E5-2620 v4 CPU at 2.10 GHz (with turbo-mode disabled) with a memory limit of 128 GB. The time is listed in rounded seconds (wall-clock time). We measure the wall-clock time from starting the tools until they are finished. In our experiments we aim to highlight the benefits of the new proof format and provide a comprehensive comparison between our two tools. Source code, benchmarks and experimental data are available [25].

For the experiments of Table I we generated PAC proofs as in previous work [9], [22] to validate the correctness of multipliers with input bit-width n. The circuits are either generated with AMG [38], BOOLECTOR [39] or GENMUL [40].

For the upper part of Table I we generated proof certificates with AMULET [9] to validate the correctness of simple multiplier circuits [9]. We modified AMULET to generate proofs in our new PAC format.

Our previous approach [9] to tackle complex multipliers also relies on SAT solving. We substitute complex final-stage adders in multipliers by simple ripple-carry adders. A bit-level miter is generated, which is passed on to a SAT solver to verify the equivalence of the adders. Computer algebra techniques are used to verify the rewritten multiplier. Since two different solving techniques are used, two proof certificates in distinct formats are generated. SAT solvers generate a DRUP proof and computer algebra techniques produce a PAC proof. In order to obtain a single proof certificate we translate DRUP proofs into PAC [22]. In the experiments of [22] all gate constraints of the given multiplier, the equivalent ripple-carry adder, and the bit-level miter are assumed as initial set of constraints G. We even added polynomials that define Boolean negation to the initial constraint set (cf. Sect. II-A). All these polynomials are now added using extension rules. This preserves the models of the gate constraints of the given multiplier. Experiments for these proof certificates are shown in the lower part of Table I. The second column shows the input bit-width, the third column shows the number of generated proof steps and the fourth the highest degree of the polynomials.

Table I
PROOF CHECKING (IN BOLD THE FASTEST VERSION)

multiplier	n	steps (10^6)	deg	PACTRIM		PACHECK						PASTÈQUE			
						no delete		no index		default		default		uloop	
				sec	MB	sec	MB	sec	MB	sec	MB	sec	MB	sec	MB
btor	128	0.4	3	10	105	**5**	273	11	100	**5**	92	22	3 886	17	1 773
btor	256	1.6	3	60	459	**25**	1 144	62	435	**25**	364	105	21 157	79	4 364
btor	512	6.3	3	395	2 066	**138**	4 956	402	1 972	141	1 461	531	64 412	416	22 292
sp-ar-rc	128	0.6	4	16	156	**6**	454	16	148	**6**	136	31	5 002	23	1 608
sp-ar-rc	256	2.3	4	92	687	29	1 858	96	651	**27**	541	139	32 525	102	8 769
sp-ar-rc	512	9.4	4	587	3 107	146	7 683	617	2 965	**134**	2 171	608	64 412	471	25 632
sp-ar-cl	32	1.6	256	31	405	23	773	36	354	**21**	353	121	40 654	113	9 492
sp-dt-lf	32	0.3	46	3	82	**2**	122	3	73	**2**	73	11	1 679	11	886
bp-ct-bk	32	0.2	25	2	57	**1**	86	2	52	**1**	51	8	1 600	7	1 068
bp-wt-cl	32	5.6	764	242	1 716	193	4 324	302	1 430	**181**	1 428	786	58 867	774	64 404

The columns PACTRIM show the time and memory usage of our previous proof checker PACTRIM. For that we reproduce proofs of [9], [22] in the original PAC format. These proofs are also used in the column "no index" to show the backward compatibility of PACHECK. It can be seen that PACTRIM and PACHECK behave similar on the original PAC format.

The effect of deletion rules and indices in PACHECK can also be seen in Table I. Deletion rules reduce the memory usage by at least a factor two, although the effect on runtime is limited. Using indices reduces the runtime by 30 to 80%. Note that in our earlier experiments [22] the proof checking time is slightly faster than in the column "no index", because we did not use proper extension rules, which requires the additional checks $p \in \mathbb{Z}[X]/\langle B(X)\rangle$ and $p^2 - p \equiv 0 \mod \langle B(X)\rangle$.

Furthermore, we can compare the performance of PACHECK and PASTÈQUE. The memory usage for PASTÈQUE depends on the garbage collector, which likely explains the peak around 64 GB (half of the available memory). The verified checker PASTÈQUE is less efficient. It is both much slower and more memory hungry. Verified checkers of SAT certificates [41], [42] have the same level of efficiency as state-of-the-art checkers [43], likely because of the imperative style (unlike our pure functional code) and the more efficient memory usage by managing most memory directly (e.g., for clauses) instead of relying on the garbage collector.

VII. CONCLUSION AND FUTURE WORK

We presented our proof checkers PACHECK and PASTÈQUE which are able to check PAC proofs efficiently. Our new proof format includes an extension rule, which is able to capture rewriting techniques. Furthermore, we added a deletion rule and used indices for polynomials. Our experiments showed that these optimizations cut memory usage in half and reduce the runtime by around 30–80%. PACHECK was four times faster than PASTÈQUE and used an order of magnitude less memory, whereas PASTÈQUE was formally verified in Isabelle.

In the future we want to capture more general extension rules in PAC as the calculus from Section II allows. We imagine that it can be extended in two ways. First, we could relax the condition $p^2 = p$. This condition is necessary to have $v^2 = v$, but could be lifted even if it means that v^n cannot be simplified to v anymore, requiring to manipulate exponents. Second, we currently restrict the extension to the form $v = p$ where p contains no new variables. The correctness theorem does not rely on that and we leave it as future work to determine whether lifting one of these restrictions can lead to shorter proofs.

In the newest version of our tools [9] no redundant proof steps are generated, hence no backward proof checking is necessary unlike SAT certificates. This might still be interesting in other applications. Another idea for future work is to bridge the gap between C and Isabelle, either by imperative code or by verifying the C code directly.

Acknowledgement: This work is supported by Austrian Science Fund (FWF), NFN S11408-N23 (RiSE), and LIT AI Lab funded by the State of Upper Austria.

REFERENCES

[1] M. J. H. Heule and A. Biere, "Proofs for satisfiability problems," in *All about Proofs, Proofs for All*, vol. 55, 2015, pp. 1–22.

[2] A. Van Gelder, "Verifying RUP proofs of propositional unsatisfiability," in *ISAIM*, 2008.

[3] ——, "Producing and verifying extremely large propositional refutations – have your cake and eat it too," *Ann. Math. Artif. Intell.*, vol. 65, no. 4, pp. 329–372, 2012.

[4] M. J. H. Heule, W. A. Hunt, Jr., and N. Wetzler, "Trimming while checking clausal proofs," in *Formal Methods in Computer-Aided Design, FMCAD 2013*. IEEE, 2013, pp. 181–188. [Online]. Available: http://ieeexplore.ieee.org/document/6679408/

[5] L. Cruz-Filipe, M. J. H. Heule, W. A. Hunt, Jr., M. Kaufmann, and P. Schneider-Kamp, "Efficient certified RAT verification," in *CADE 26*, ser. LNCS, L. de Moura, Ed., vol. 10395. Springer, 2017, pp. 220–236.

[6] D. Kapur, "Geometry theorem proving using Hilbert's Nullstellensatz," in *SYMSAC*. ACM, 1986, pp. 202–208.

[7] ——, "Using Gröbner bases to reason about geometry problems," *J. Symb. Comput.*, vol. 2, no. 4, pp. 399–408, 1986.

[8] D. Kapur and P. Narendran, "An equational approach to theorem proving in first-order predicate calculus," in *IJCAI*. Morgan Kaufmann, 1985, pp. 1146–1153.

[9] D. Kaufmann, A. Biere, and M. Kauers, "Verifying large multipliers by combining SAT and computer algebra," in *FMCAD 2019*. IEEE, 2019, pp. 28–36.

[10] A. Mahzoon, D. Große, and R. Drechsler, "RevSCA: Using reverse engineering to bring light into backward rewriting for big and dirty multipliers," in *DAC*. ACM, 2019, pp. 185:1–185:6.

[11] M. J. Ciesielski, T. Su, A. Yasin, and C. Yu, "Understanding algebraic rewriting for arithmetic circuit verification: a bit-flow model," *IEEE TCAD*, pp. 1–1, 2019.

[12] A. Mahzoon, D. Große, C. Scholl, and R. Drechsler, "Towards formal verification of optimized and industrial multipliers," in *DATE 2020*. IEEE, 2020, pp. 544–549.

[13] C. Bright, I. Kotsireas, and V. Ganesh, "Applying computer algebra systems and SAT solvers to the Williamson conjecture," *Journal of Symbolic Computation*, 04 2018.

[14] M. J. H. Heule, "Computing small unit-distance graphs with chromatic number 5," *CoRR*, vol. abs/1805.12181, 2018.

[15] M. J. H. Heule, M. Kauers, and M. Seidl, "Local search for fast matrix multiplication," in *SAT 2019*, ser. LNCS, vol. 11628. Springer, 2019, pp. 155–163.

[16] ——, "New ways to multiply 3 × 3-matrices," *CoRR*, vol. abs/1905.10192, 2019.

[17] C. Condrat and P. Kalla, "A gröbner basis approach to cnf-formulae preprocessing," in *TACAS 2007*, ser. LNCS, vol. 4424. Springer, 2007, pp. 618–631.

[18] M. Soos and K. S. Meel, "BIRD: engineering an efficient CNF-XOR SAT solver and its applications to approximate model counting," in *AAAI 2019*. AAAI Press, 2019, pp. 1592–1599.

[19] D. Choo, M. Soos, K. M. A. Chai, and K. S. Meel, "Bosphorus: Bridging ANF and CNF solvers," in *DATE 2019*, J. Teich and F. Fummi, Eds. IEEE, 2019, pp. 468–473.

[20] D. Ritirc, A. Biere, and M. Kauers, "A practical polynomial calculus for arithmetic circuit verification," in *SC2'18*, A. Bigatti and M. Brain, Eds. CEUR-WS, 2018, pp. 61–76.

[21] M. Clegg, J. Edmonds, and R. Impagliazzo, "Using the Groebner basis algorithm to find proofs of unsatisfiability," in *STOC*. ACM, 1996, pp. 174–183.

[22] D. Kaufmann, A. Biere, and M. Kauers, "From DRUP to PAC and back," in *DATE 2020*. IEEE, 2020, pp. 654–657. [Online]. Available: http://fmv.jku.at/drup2pac/

[23] D. Kaufmann, "Formal verification of multiplier circuits using computer algebra," Ph.D. dissertation, Informatik, Johannes Kepler University Linz, 2020.

[24] D. Cox, J. Little, and D. O'Shea, *Ideals, Varieties, and Algorithms*. Springer-Verlag New York, 1997.

[25] D. Kaufmann and M. Fleury, "The PAC checkers Pacheck and Pastèque," accessed: 2020-05-06. [Online]. Available: http://fmv.jku.at/pacheck_pasteque

[26] M. Alekhnovich, E. Ben-Sasson, A. A. Razborov, and A. Wigderson, "Space complexity in propositional calculus," *SIAM J. Comput.*, vol. 31, no. 4, pp. 1184–1211, 2002.

[27] B. Buchberger, "Ein Algorithmus zum Auffinden der Basiselemente des Restklassenringes nach einem nulldimensionalen Polynomideal," Ph.D. dissertation, University of Innsbruck, 1965.

[28] D. Lichtblau, "Effective computation of strong Gröbner bases over Euclidean domains," *Illinois Journal of Mathematics*, vol. 56, 11 2013.

[29] T. Granlund *et al.*, "GNU Multiple Precision Arithmetic Library," January 2020. [Online]. Available: http://gmplib.org/

[30] T. Nipkow, L. C. Paulson, and M. Wenzel, *Isabelle/HOL: A Proof Assistant for Higher-Order Logic*, ser. LNCS. Springer, 2002, vol. 2283.

[31] P. Lammich, "Refinement based verification of imperative data structures," in *CPP 2016*, J. Avigad and A. Chlipala, Eds. ACM Press, 2016, pp. 27–36.

[32] F. Haftmann and T. Nipkow, "Code generation via higher-order rewrite systems," in *FLOPS 2010*, ser. LNCS, M. Blume, N. Kobayashi, and G. Vidal, Eds., vol. 6009. Springer, 2010, pp. 103–117.

[33] M. Fleury and D. Kaufmann, "Isabelle pac formalization," theory files at https://bitbucket.org/isafol/isafol/src/master/PAC/, Accessed: 2020-05-06. [Online]. Available: http://people.mpi-inf.mpg.de/~mfleury/IsaFoL/current/PAC_Checker/PAC_Checker/index.html

[34] J. C. Blanchette, S. Böhme, M. Fleury, S. J. Smolka, and A. Steckermeier, "Semi-intelligible Isar proofs from machine-generated proofs," *J. Autom. Reasoning*, vol. 56, no. 2, pp. 155–200, 2016.

[35] P. Lammich, "Refinement to Imperative/HOL," in *ITP 2015*, ser. LNCS, C. Urban and X. Zhang, Eds., vol. 9236. Springer, 2015, pp. 253–269.

[36] S. Weeks, "Whole-program compilation in MLton," in *Proceedings of the ACM Workshop on ML, 2006, Portland, Oregon, USA, September 16, 2006*. ACM Press, 2006, p. 1.

[37] P. Lammich, "Generating verified LLVM from Isabelle/HOL," in *ITP 2019*, A. Tolmach, J. Harrison, and J. O'Leary, Eds., 2019.

[38] N. Homma, Y. Watanabe, T. Aoki, and T. Higuchi, "Formal design of arithmetic circuits based on arithmetic description language," *IEICE Transactions*, vol. 89-A, no. 12, pp. 3500–3509, 2006.

[39] A. Niemetz, M. Preiner, C. Wolf, and A. Biere, "BTOR2 , BtorMC and Boolector 3.0," in *CAV*, ser. LNCS, vol. 10981. Springer, 2018, pp. 587–595.

[40] A. Mahzoon, D. Große, and R. Drechsler, "Multiplier generator GenMul," http://www.sca-verification.org/, 2019.

[41] P. Lammich, "The GRAT tool chain - efficient (UN)SAT certificate checking with formal correctness guarantees," in *SAT*, ser. LNCS, vol. 10491. Springer, 2017, pp. 457–463.

[42] M. J. H. Heule, W. A. Hunt, Jr., M. Kaufmann, and N. Wetzler, "Efficient, verified checking of propositional proofs," in *ITP*, ser. LNCS, vol. 10499. Springer, 2017, pp. 269–284.

[43] A. Rebola-Pardo and J. Altmanninger, "Frying the egg, roasting the chicken: Unit deletions in DRAT proofs," in *CPP*, J. Blanchette and C. Hritcu, Eds. ACM, 2020.

16

On Optimizing a Generic Function in SAT

Alexander Nadel (ID)
Intel Corporation, P.O. Box 1659, Haifa 31015 Israel
Email: alexander.nadel@intel.com

Abstract—**The goal of this study is to improve the scalability of today's SAT-based solutions for optimization problems and to pave the way towards extending the range of optimization problems solvable with SAT in practice. Let OptSAT be the problem of optimizing a generic Pseudo-Boolean function, given a satisfiable propositional formula F. We introduce an incremental and anytime incomplete algorithm for solving OptSAT, called** `Polosat`. **We show that integrating** `Polosat` **into a state-of-the-art open-source anytime MaxSAT solver significantly improves the solver's performance. Furthermore, we demonstrate that** `Polosat` **substantially improves the solution quality of an industrial placement tool, where placement is a sub-stage of the physical design stage of chip design.**

I. INTRODUCTION

Given a propositional formula $F(V)$ in Conjunctive Normal Form (CNF), a Boolean satisfiability (SAT) solver either returns a model to $F(V)$ or proves that none exists. Modern SAT solvers are useful for a diverse range of purposes [8]. We are interested in solving optimization problems with SAT, which requires extending the basic SAT formulation.

MaxSAT is the most widely used extension of SAT to optimization. Given a set of hard propositional clauses $H(V)$ and a *target bit-vector (target)* $T = \{t_n, t_{n-1}, \ldots, t_1\}$, where each *target bit* t_i is a Boolean variable associated with a strictly positive integer weight w_i, MaxSAT finds a model to $H(V)$ that minimizes the following objective function: $\sum_{i=1}^{n} t_i \times w_i$. The objective function to minimize is *Linear Pseudo-Boolean*, that is, a linear combination of Boolean variables which, in our case, represents the overall weight of the satisfied target bits. MaxSAT has a diverse plethora of applications in various domains, including computer-aided design [41], [43], [27], [22], [16], [30], artificial intelligence [34], [7], planning and scheduling [10] and bioinformatics [17]. However, MaxSAT is restricted to linear optimization. How can one extend SAT to optimize a generic Pseudo-Boolean function?

In the broadest sense, a Pseudo-Boolean (PB) function is a function that maps every full assignment to a real number (see, e.g., [37]). Hence, the following formulation of a problem, we call OptSAT, is a natural extension of SAT to generic optimization. Given a satisfiable formula $F(V)$ in CNF and an objective PB function Ψ, *OptSAT* returns a model μ to F, such that for every model μ' to F, it holds that $\Psi(\mu) \leq \Psi(\mu')$. Our definition is suitable for any objective function. In particular, the objective function can be *black-box*, where a black-box PB function is not required to have an algebraic representation [25]. Consider the API of an OptSAT solver. How can one supply a black-box function to the solver? One can simply provide it as a callback function parameter. The solver can then query the callback function at any time. Such an API makes the solver independent of the representation of the objective function, which is a desired property, even if an algebraic representation of the function is available to the user.

In this paper, we introduce a new SAT-based OptSAT algorithm, called `Polosat` (*Polarity-Fixing-based Optimization in SAT*). `Polosat` is an anytime algorithm, that is, it generates a series of models improving w.r.t the objective function. `Polosat` can be used incrementally under assumptions, similarly to modern SAT solvers [15], [32]. Our algorithm is incomplete; it works until a fixed-point, but does not guarantee that the eventual solution is optimal. Internally, `Polosat` is based on the ability of modern SAT solvers to look for a solution near a given full assignment μ by fixing the polarities of the variables to μ [2], [29], [1]. Furthermore, we present a version of `Polosat` adjusted for strictly monotone objective functions. We demonstrate the efficiency of `Polosat` in the context of the following two applications.

First, we integrated `Polosat` into our open-source anytime MaxSAT solver `TT-Open-WBO-Inc` [31], which won both of the weighted, incomplete tracks of MaxSAT Evaluation 2019 (MSE19) [5]. The integration was carried out by replacing incremental SAT invocations by `Polosat` invocations in `TT-Open-WBO-Inc`'s SAT-based flow. `Polosat` makes `TT-Open-WBO-Inc` significantly more efficient on the MSE19 instances. This result is evidence that `Polosat` is empirically useful, even when integrated into an already elaborated algorithm for the well-studied problem of linear PB optimization in SAT (that is, MaxSAT).

Second, we integrated `Polosat` into our proprietary industrial SAT-based placement tool, where placement is an essential sub-stage of the physical design stage of chip design [40]. We show that `Polosat` helps the tool to generate placements of a consistently and significantly better quality, thus providing evidence that `Polosat` can improve the scalability of SAT for a critical industrial optimization problem.

While *unconstrained* PB optimization of black-box functions has been studied [25], we are not aware of any previous work on optimizing a black-box PB function, given a CNF formula or other constraints. If the objective function Ψ is provided algebraically, the following flow can be applied to solve OptSAT: 1) linearize Ψ, if not already linear (see [37] for further information about linearization), and 2) invoke a MaxSAT solver. However, it is unclear whether such a flow can be implemented efficiently enough so as to help solving real-world problems. Furthermore, apparently, a MaxSAT-based flow cannot be used to speed up MaxSAT itself, whereas

`Polosat` improves the state-of-the-art in MaxSAT solving. Hence, `Polosat` has a clear empirical added value.

The rest of this paper is organized as follows. Sect. II describes the background. Sect. III is about OptSAT and `Polosat`. Sect. IV discusses our applications. Sect. V provides experimental results. Sect. VI concludes our work.

II. PRELIMINARIES

A *literal* l is a Boolean variable v or its negation $\neg v$. Given a variable v_i and a Boolean value $b_i \in \{0, 1\}$, $v_i^{b_i}$ stands for either the literal v_i if $b_i = 1$ or the literal $\neg v_i$ if $b_i = 0$. We assume that the sets V and L contain all the Boolean variables and literals, respectively. A *clause* is a disjunction of literals. A formula F is in *Conjunctive Normal Form (CNF)* if it is a conjunction (set) of clauses.

A SAT solver [8] receives a CNF formula F and returns a satisfying assignment (aka, model or solution), if one exists. In *incremental SAT solving under assumptions* [15], [32], the user may invoke the SAT solver multiple times, each time with a different set of *assumption literals* (called, simply, the *assumptions*) and, possibly, additional clauses. The solver then checks the satis ability of all the clauses provided so far, while enforcing the values of the current assumptions.

A *bit-vector variable (bit-vector)* of width $n = |B|$, $B = \{v_n, v_{n-1}, \ldots, v_1\}$, is a sequence of n variables, called *bits*. Bit v_1 is the Least Signi cant Bit (LSB) and v_n is the Most Signi cant Bit (MSB). A *bit-vector constant* is a bit-vector (BV) each one of whose bits is substituted by 0 or 1. A BV solver decides the satis ability of BV formulas, that is, formulas built on top of BV variables and BV constants. The only assumption this paper makes about BV formulas is that any BV formula can be translated (aka, synthesized or bit-blasted) to CNF and solved with a SAT solver. This assumption holds for the BV language as de ned in the SMT-LIB standard [6].

A MaxSAT instance comprises a set of *hard* satis able clauses H and a *target bit-vector (target)* $T = \{t_n, t_{n-1}, \ldots, t_1\}$, where each *target bit* t_i is a Boolean variable associated with a strictly positive integer weight w_i. The *weight of a variable assignment* μ is $O(T, \mu) = \sum_{i=1}^{n} \mu(t_i) \times w_i$, that is, the overall weight of T s bits, satis ed by μ. Given a MaxSAT instance, a MaxSAT solver is expected to return a model having the minimum possible weight.

In the standard MaxSAT de nition, the target T contains clauses, called the *soft clauses*, where the MaxSAT solver is required to maximize the overall weight of the satis ed soft clauses. The standard de nition is reducible to ours (which we use for convenience) as follows: every soft clause C is transformed into a target bit v', where v' is a fresh variable, by adding the clause $v' \lor C$ to H.

In the rest of this paper, *assignment* stands for a full variable assignment. We assume that an assignment $\theta = \{\theta(v_{|V|}) = b_{|V|}, \theta(v_{|V-1|}) = b_{|V-1|}, \ldots, \theta(v_1) = b_1\}$, where $b_i \in \{0, 1\}$ for every b_i, is represented as the bit-vector constant $\{b_{|V|}, \ldots, b_1\} \in \{0, 1\}^{|V|}$. Sometimes, it is more convenient to think of an assignment as of a set of literals $\left\{ v_{|V|}^{b_{|V|}}, \ldots, v_1^{b_1} \right\}$. Given an assignment θ and a literal l, we denote by $\theta^{\neg l}$ the assignment created by ipping the value of l s variable in θ. Given a target T, an assignment μ is *ideal* if $\mu(t_i) = 0$ for every target bit $t_i \in T$.

A. Polarity-Fixing in SAT and Anytime MaxSAT

Fixing the polarity of a variable v to a Boolean value σ during SAT solver s invocation means assigning v the value σ, whenever v is chosen by the solver s decision heuristic (whereas the *variable* selection heuristic is not changed).

Given a CNF formula $F(V)$, let θ be a (not-necessarily-satisfying) assignment to V. Consider the problem of nding a model μ *near* θ, that is, a model that minimizes the number of 1s in $\mu \oplus \theta$ (where $\oplus$ stands for bit-vector xor). The following approximate polarity- xing-based algorithm has emerged as a surprisingly ef cient solution to this problem in several contexts. The algorithm xes the polarity of all the variables to their values in θ and runs a SAT solver. This approach carries out a local search near θ (as observed in [11] in the context of Constraint Programming), hence any encountered model is likely to be highly similar to θ.

To the best of our knowledge, polarity- xing for nding a nearby model was rst used in the context of diverse solution generation [2], [29]. A variation was suggested independently in [1] for generating a new model close to a given model.

Anytime MaxSAT algorithms are expected to nd an *improving* set of models $\{\mu_1, \mu_2, \ldots, \mu_n\}$ over time, that is, for every $j > i$, it must hold that $O(T, \mu_j) < O(T, \mu_i)$. Polarity- xing has been found extremely ef cient in the context of anytime MaxSAT. Speci cally, the following three approaches to xing the polarities when trying to improve the best model so far have been successfully applied within different SAT-based anytime MaxSAT algorithms (see [30] for further details):

1) The *conservative* approach [36], [3], [12] xes the polarities of all the variables to their values in the latest best model μ_i. It causes the SAT solver to look for a solution near μ_i, which normally results in nding the next solution quicker.

2) The *optimistic* approach [13] xes the polarity of the target bits to 0, so as to bias the search towards an ideal assignment.

3) The *combined* `Target-Optimum-Rest-Conservative` (TORC) polarity selection heuristic [30] combines the conservative and the optimistic approaches, so as to nd the next model quicker, yet increasing the likelihood of the model being closer to an ideal assignment. Before the initial SAT invocation, TORC xes the polarity of all the target bits to 0. Then, after each new improving model μ_i is encountered, the polarity of all the variables other that the target bits is xed to their values in μ_i. TORC was shown to outperform the other polarity selection heuristics [30]. `TT-Open-WBO-Inc` uses TORC [31].

III. GENERIC OPTIMIZATION IN SAT

Recall our de nition of the OptSAT problem. Given a propositional satis able formula $F(V)$ in CNF and a PB function $\Psi: \{0,1\}^{|V|} \to \mathbb{R}$, *OptSAT* returns a model μ to F, such that for every model μ' to F, it holds that $\Psi(\mu) \leq \Psi(\mu')$.

Our OptSAT algorithm `Polosat` is shown in Alg. 1. Similarly to modern SAT solvers, `Polosat` is incremental under assumptions. It receives three parameters: 1) A satis able CNF formula F (if the invocation is incremental, assume that F contains all the clauses, provided by the user so far); 2) A (possibly empty) set of assumptions *Asmp*. The assumptions are guaranteed to hold for one particular invocation of the algorithm; 3) The objective PB function $\Psi: [0,1]^{|V|} \to \mathbb{R}$.

The algorithm maintains an instance of an incremental SAT solver throughout its execution and the best model so far μ. `Polosat` starts with initializing μ with a model by invoking the SAT solver (line 2). Then, it operates in iterations, where each iteration is called an *epoch* (lines 4 to 14). Each epoch tries to improve μ. An epoch is *good* if it manages to improve μ, otherwise it is *bad*. Our incomplete algorithm nishes whenever a bad epoch is completed.

Each epoch tries to improve the best model so far μ in a loop (lines 7 to 14) by looking for a better solution near μ when, for each loop iteration, one of the variables is forced to ip its value. Speci cally, the loop goes over a set of literals B, initialized by all the literals assigned to 1 by μ (line 5; note that one literal is selected for every variable). For each literal l, `Polosat` tries to nd a model near μ with l s variable ipped. This is carried out by xing the polarities of all the variables to their values in μ (line 9), followed by a SAT invocation with $\neg l$ as a hard assumption (line 10). If the problem is satis able and a model σ better than μ is found, then: 1) μ is updated to σ, 2) the epoch is marked as good, and 3) any literal $l : l \notin \mu$ is removed from B to ensure that one of the literals in B is always ipped w.r.t μ in the subsequent SAT invocations.

`Polosat` may resemble local search algorithms [21], such as GSAT [38] for SAT or `SatLike` [24] for anytime MaxSAT. Local search algorithms maintain an assignment and modify it iteratively. In the context of anytime MaxSAT, they start with a full assignment, choose a variable and ip it in each subsequent step, targeting to nd an assignment which satis es the formula and improves the best model so far. The key algorithmic difference between local search and `Polosat` is that `Polosat` is fully based on incremental SAT solving. Speci cally, `Polosat` takes advantage of polarity- xing to look for a solution *near* a given assignment with a single quick SAT invocation. Hence, `Polosat` never has to handle unsatisfying assignments. Our approach can be thought of as a purely SAT-based version of local search. It is surprisingly ef cient, yet simple to implement. Furthermore, the fact that `Polosat` is SAT-based, makes its integration into any existing SAT-based optimization ow seamless. It is an open question whether traditional local search can solve OptSAT ef ciently.

A. Optimizing a Strictly Monotone Function

Often, the objective function in optimization problems only depends on a subset of the variables, which we call the *observable variables (observables)*. Moreover, the function decreases whenever one of the observables decreases (that is,

---

Algorithm 1 `Polosat`

1: **function** SOLVE(CNF F; Literals *Asmp*; $\Psi: [0,1]^{|V|} \to \mathbb{R}$)
Require: F is satis able
2:     $\mu := \text{SAT}(Asmp)$ $\triangleright$ μ: the best model so far
3:     *is_good_epoch* := 1
4:     **while** *is_good_epoch* **do** $\triangleright$ One loop is an epoch
5:        $B := \{l : l \in L, \mu(l) = 1\}$
6:        *is_good_epoch* := 0
7:        **while** B is not empty **do**
8:           $l := B.front(); B.dequeue()$
9:           Fix the polarities of all the variables to μ
10:          $\sigma := \text{SAT}(Asmp \cup \{\neg l\})$
11:          **if** SAT and $\Psi(\sigma) < \Psi(\mu)$ **then**
12:             $\mu := \sigma$ $\triangleright$ Update the best model so far
13:             *is_good_epoch* := 1 $\triangleright$ Good epoch!
14:             $B := \{l : l \in B, \mu(l) = 1\}$

---

 ipped from 1 to 0). We formalize the property of strict monotonicity for a PB function, to capture the above-mentioned properties, as follows. Let $Obs \subseteq V$ be a set of *observables* and $\Psi: [0,1]^{|V|} \to \mathbb{R}$ be a PB function. Then:

1) Ψ is *restrictable* to Obs, iff for every two assignments θ and λ, such that $\theta(v) = \lambda(v)$ for every $v \in Obs$, it holds that $\Psi(\theta) = \Psi(\lambda)$.

2) Ψ is *strictly monotone in observables Obs*, iff: a) Ψ is restrictable to Obs, and b) For every assignment θ and every variable $v \in Obs$, such that $\theta(v) = 1$, it holds that $\Psi(\theta^{\neg v}) < \Psi(\theta)$.

For example, consider the MaxSAT problem. The objective function $O(T, \mu)$ depends only on the target bits. When one of the target bits decreases, $O(T, \mu)$ decreases too, hence $O(T, \mu)$ is strictly monotone in the target T.

Below, we re ne `Polosat` to functions that are strictly monotone in a subset of variables, targeting empirical ef ciency. Alg. 2 is a version of Alg. 1, applicable when the objective function is strictly monotone in Obs. In fact, Alg. 2 is identical to Alg. 1, but for the following two adjustments:

1) The polarity of the observables is always xed to 0 (lines 2 and 10 in Alg. 2). The intuition behind this adjustment is similar to the intuition behind the TORC polarity selection strategy for anytime MaxSAT. We would like to encourage any encountered model to be close to both: a) the best model so far μ (to generate the solutions rapidly), and b) an ideal assignment, that is, an assignment in which all the observables are assigned 0 (to bias the algorithm towards the ideal).

2) During every epoch, `Polosat` restricts the set B of the literals it considers for ipping to observable variables, which: a) are assigned 1 in the best model so far (line 6 in Alg. 2), and b) have not been assigned 0 in *any* new model, since the beginning of the current epoch (lines 12 to 16 in Alg. 2). Our intuition is as follows. For strictly monotone functions, the only way to improve the objective function is by ipping observables from 1 to

0. Hence, flipping only such observables that have never been assigned 0 in the span of one epoch, is expected to result in improving the best model so far more frequently and in reducing the number of fruitless SAT invocations.

Algorithm 2 Strictly-Monotone `Polosat`

1: **function** SOLVE(CNF F; Literals *Asmp*; Variables *Obs*; $\Psi: [0,1]^{|V|} \to \mathbb{R}$)

Require: F is satisfiable and Ψ is strictly monotone in *Obs*

2:     Fix the polarities of the observables *Obs* to 0
3:     $\mu := $ SAT(*Asmp*)   ▷ μ: the best model so far
4:     *is_good_epoch* := 1
5:     **while** *is_good_epoch* **do**   ▷ One loop is an epoch
6:         $B := \{v : v \in Obs, \mu(v) = 1\}$
7:         *is_good_epoch* := 0
8:         **while** B is not empty **do**
9:             $v := B.front(); B.dequeue()$
10:             Fix the polarities of the observables *Obs* to 0 and all the other variables (that is, $V \setminus Obs$) to μ
11:             $\sigma := $ SAT(*Asmp* $\cup \{\neg v\}$)
12:             **if** SAT **then**   ▷ Satisfiable
13:                 **if** $\Psi(\sigma) < \Psi(\mu)$ **then**
14:                     $\mu := \sigma$ ▷ Update the best model so far
15:                     *is_good_epoch* := 1   ▷ Good epoch!
16:             $B := \{v : v \in B, \sigma(v) = 1\}$

B. `Polosat` Enhancements

We apply two enhancements to `Polosat` (applicable also to the strictly-monotone `Polosat`). As we shall see, they yield a moderate improvement to `Polosat`'s performance.

1) Conflict Threshold for SAT Invocations: It makes sense to cut off difficult SAT invocations in the context of our incomplete algorithm. Hence, we stop all the SAT invocations, except for the initial one (line 2 in Alg. 1 and line 3 in Alg. 2), after 1000 conflicts.

2) Mutation Combination: This enhancement is based on the following empirical observation from [14], made in the context of the `QuickSampler` algorithm for random sampling in SAT.

Let μ_0 be a model to a given formula $F(V)$. Let μ_i be a model to F *near* μ_0, except for one variable v_i, which must be flipped (few other variables might be flipped as well). In other words, the so-called *mutation* $\delta_i = \mu_0 \oplus \mu_i$, representing the difference between μ_0 and μ_i, is expected to be close to the constant 0 with the exception of v_i. (In [14], such a model is found by reduction to MaxSAT.) Let $\mu_{j:j\neq i}$ be another model to F near μ_0, except for one flipped variable v_j. Then, the observation is that the assignment $\theta = \mu_0 \oplus (\delta_i \vee \delta_j)$, generated by flipping in μ_0 only the variables in which μ_0 differs from either μ_i or μ_j (or both), is empirically likely to be a model. We call θ the result of applying the *mutation combination* of μ_i and μ_j to μ_0. `QuickSampler` quickly finds new models by applying mutation combinations to existing models.

In `Polosat`, we apply mutation combination to generate more models at the end of each epoch. Let μ_0 be the best

model at the beginning of a certain epoch. Let R be the set of all the models which improve μ_0 during that epoch (if any). Then, for every two models $\mu_i, \mu_j \in R$, we try to find a model near $\theta = \mu_0 \oplus (\delta_i \vee \delta_j)$, but only if θ is better than the current best model μ (that is, if $\Psi(\theta) < \Psi(\mu)$). Specifically, we apply the following algorithm at the end of each epoch:

1: **for** $(\mu_i \in R, \mu_j \in R)$, where $\mu_i \neq \mu_j$ **do**
2:     $\delta_i := \mu_0 \oplus \mu_i$ ▷ $\delta_i(l) = 1$ iff $\mu_0(l) \neq \mu_i(l)$
3:     $\delta_j := \mu_0 \oplus \mu_j$ ▷ $\delta_j(l) = 1$ iff $\mu_0(l) \neq \mu_j(l)$
4:     $\theta := \mu_0 \oplus (\delta_i \vee \delta_j)$
5:     **if** $\Psi(\theta) < \Psi(\mu)$ **then**
6:         Fix the polarities of all the variables to θ
7:         $\sigma := $ SAT(*Asmp*)
8:         **if** SAT and $\Psi(\theta) < \Psi(\mu)$ **then**
9:             $\mu := \sigma$ ▷ Update the best model so far

IV. APPLYING `Polosat`

We deliberately designed `Polosat` to be incremental in the same sense SAT solvers are. Hence, `Polosat` can be integrated into any existing incremental SAT-based optimization flow by replacing every SAT invocation by a `Polosat` invocation over the same CNF formula and the same assumptions. The two other parameters to `Polosat` are the objective function and the set of observables *Obs* (for functions which are strictly monotone in *Obs*).

As we have mentioned, the objective function can be provided as a callback parameter; it can also be implemented ad-hoc in any specific SAT-based optimization flow.

The set of observables is induced by the optimization problem. However, the order of the observables might matter. This is because the strictly-monotone `Polosat` goes over the observables in the user-given order. Hence, it makes sense to order the observables according to their projected impact on the value of the objective function, if only because a time-out might stop `Polosat`'s execution. For example, for MaxSAT it makes sense to sort the observables according to their weight (that is, the weight w_i for every $t_i \in T$) in decreasing order.

Sect. IV-A below is about integrating `Polosat` into our anytime MaxSAT solver `TT-Open-WBO-Inc` [31]. Sect. IV-B is dedicated to our industrial placement flow.

A. `Polosat` for Anytime MaxSAT

We have integrated `Polosat` into the Bounded Multi-level Optimization (BMO) [4]-based anytime MaxSAT algorithm [19], which we call *BMO-based Clustering (BC)*, implemented in our open-source anytime MaxSAT solver `TT-Open-WBO-Inc` [31]. `TT-Open-WBO-Inc` won both of the weighted, incomplete tracks of MaxSAT Evaluation 2019. It is a spin-off of `Open-WBO-Inc` [20].

1) Integrating `Polosat` into BC: BC [19] clusters all the target bits to disjoint classes based on their weight. That is, all the targets of the same weight w belong to the same class. Then, the algorithm sorts the classes according to their weight and goes over them one-by-one starting with the class associated with the highest weight. BC tries to falsify as many target bits in each class as possible with incremental SAT invocations. After BC completes processing one class, it fixes the overall number of falsified target bits in that class.

Our implementation simply replaces every SAT invocation with a strictly-monotone `Polosat` invocation in BC with the target T as the observables and $O(T, \mu)$ as the objective function. However, there are several subtleties: *a*) We exclude from the set of observables the bits which belong to the fixed classes; *b*) As we have already mentioned, we sort the observables by their weight in decreasing order; *c*) We randomly shuffle the observables within each class before every `Polosat` invocation to diversify `Polosat`'s execution.

2) Adaptive Strategy for `Polosat`*:* Our initial empirical results showed that `TT-Open-WBO-Inc` with `Polosat` outperforms the baseline solver on a significant majority of the benchmarks, however it yields a severe performance degradation on some of them. Further study of this phenomenon showed that `Polosat` tends to be empirically efficient whenever it manages to generate a high number of models per second. This empirical observation lead us to introducing the following adaptive strategy.

We modified `Polosat` to keep track of the number of *Models Per Second* (MPS) throughout its execution starting immediately after the initial SAT invocation. MPS is updated and tested after each SAT invocation. If MPS is lower than 1, the current invocation of `Polosat` is terminated, and the high-level BC algorithm falls backs to invoking a plain SAT solver instead of `Polosat` for the rest of its execution. Falling back to SAT makes sense, since SAT/`Polosat` queries tend to become more difficult as the algorithm advances towards the ideal, hence MPS is unlikely to increase.

B. `Polosat` *for Placement in Physical Design*

1) The Placement Problem: During the *placement* sub-stage of the physical design stage of chip design [40], the standard cells (that is, atomic units of the design) are placed in a bigger design block under various hard constraints and optimization requirements.

More specifically, placement is about placing without overlap a set of rectangles with fixed orientations $R = \{R_1, R_2, \ldots, R_m\}$ on a fixed-sized $2^n \times 2^n$ grid under the following optimization requirement. The user provides a pre-defined set of nets $N = \{N^1, N^2, \ldots, N^k\}$, where each net $N^j = \{R_{j_1}, R_{j_2}, \ldots, R_{j_{|N^j|}}\}$ is a set of rectangles. The intersection between the nets is *not* expected to be disjoint. Let P^j be the *perimeter* of the rectangle, enclosing all the rectangles of net N^j. P^j is called the *perimeter of the net*. The objective function in placement is minimizing the overall sum of the perimeters of all the nets $P = \sum_{j=1}^{k} P^j$, called, simply, the *perimeter* of the placement solution. An example is shown in Fig. 1. The problem is non-trivial as even the decision version of the placement problem is NP-complete [23].

Routing is a sub-stage of physical design, which follows the placement stage, in which each net is inter-connected by wires without intersection between the nets. Empirically, generating placements that minimize the perimeter significantly increases

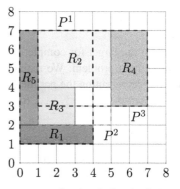

Fig. 1: Placement example. A solution is shown to the problem of placing without overlap five rectangles R_1, R_2, R_3, R_4 and R_5 of the sizes $4 \times 1, 4 \times 3, 2 \times 2, 2 \times 4$ and 1×5, respectively, on a $2^3 \times 2^3$ grid, given the following three nets: $N^1 = \{R_1, R_3, R_5\}$, $N^2 = \{R_2, R_3\}$ and $N^3 = \{R_2, R_4\}$. The lengths of the perimeters of the nets are 20, 18 and 20, for the nets N^1, N^2 and N^3, respectively. The overall perimeter's length is $20 + 18 + 20 = 58$. The solution is an optimal one, that is, no solution with a smaller perimeter exists.

the likelihood that the generated placement is *routable* and the subsequent routing solution has a short wire-length.

Furthermore, any placement solution must meet additional requirements, essential for manufacturing, such as aligning some of the input rectangles, enforcing parity constraints (i.e., the user might require the y coordinates of some of the rectangles to be either even or odd) [33], ensuring a minimal distance between some of the rectangles, keeping some rectangles out of certain regions and others. In practice, all the requirements can be expressed as a bit-vector formula. We omit further details, since they are outside of the scope of this paper and are currently restricted due to IP considerations.

Various algorithms to solve the placement problem, such as, simulated annealing and numerical optimization, have been tried [39], but industrial placement tools are typically heuristical [42]. However, while such tools scale to big designs, they often generate placements that are far from the optimal solution, hence are not routing-friendly. In addition, they might violate some of the manufacturing-driven requirements. Furthermore, conforming to any new requirements might require non-trivial changes to the tool. A scalable SAT-based placer would help to alleviate the above-mentioned issues.

2) Reducing Placement to OBV: Recall the formulation of the problem of *Bit-Vector Optimization (OBV)* [33]. In OBV, also known as Optimization Modulo Bit-Vectors (OMT(BV)), given a bit-vector (or a propositional) formula F and the target bit-vector T, the algorithm has to minimize the value of T, where T is interpreted as an unsigned integer. Placement is directly reducible to OBV as follows.

We associate each rectangle R_i with two bit-vector variables R_i^x and R_i^y of bit-width n, where (R_i^x, R_i^y) represents the location of R_i's bottom-left corner. Let s_i^x and s_i^y be the user-given fixed length and width, respectively, of the rectangle R_i, for each i. Then, constructing and asserting the following formula R, along with the additional requirements we have mentioned, is sufficient to encode placement's decision problem: $R = \bigwedge_{1 \le i < j \le m}((R_i^x + s_i^x \le R_j^x) \vee (R_j^x + s_j^x \le R_i^x) \vee (R_i^y + s_i^y \le R_j^y) \vee (R_j^y + s_j^y \le R_i^y))$. (Here and below, some extra constraints, omitted for simplicity, must be added to prevent over ow.)

It is left to construct the target for completing an OBV formulation for the placement problem. We maintain a BV variable P^j of bit-width n representing the perimeter per every net N^j, where $P^j = 2 \times ((\max(R^x_{j_1} + s^x_{j_1}, \ldots, R^x_{j_{|N^j|}} + s^x_{j_{|N^j|}}) - \min(R^x_{j_1}, \ldots, R^x_{j_{|N^j|}})) + (\max(R^y_{j_1} + s^y_{j_1}, \ldots, R^y_{j_{|N^j|}} + s^y_{j_{|N^j|}}) - \min(R^y_{j_1}, \ldots, R^y_{j_{|N^j|}})))$. The overall perimeter $T = \sum_{j=1}^{k} P^j$ serves as the OBV target in our formulation.

OBV can be reduced to MaxSAT with the same target T, where each bit t_i associated with the weight $w_i = 2^{i-1}$ [9]. Moreover, in [33], we introduced two dedicated SAT-based OBV algorithms. Our anytime algorithm OBV-BS, based on binary search with SAT, turned out to be a robust and scalable solution to the problem of xing an existing placement, if last-minute design changes are introduced; OBV-BS performed substantially better than the reduction to MaxSAT [33]. Unfortunately, in our experience, OBV-BS does not scale when it comes to generating a routable placement from scratch. Typically, a SAT solver can quickly nd a valid placement, but it fails to solve the optimization problem. Why is there such a difference in performance between xing an existing placement and generating a placement from scratch? This is because, in xing, the target comprises lexicographically ordered bits, where each bit is a result of a separate calculation, while, in placement, the target is the result of bit-vector addition operations, thus all the target bits are interconnected.

3) Applying Polosat *for Placement:* PLC is our proprietary industrial placement tool, intended to solve the placement problem by reduction to BV and then bit-blasting to SAT. PLC uses the following simple linear search algorithm as its baseline, since it outperforms the OBV algorithms we have mentioned. PLC starts with invoking the SAT solver to nd a solution μ to the placement problem. The solution represents a valid placement. Then, it asserts that the perimeter P is smaller than its value in μ and runs the incremental SAT solver once again to nd a new μ. If no time-out occurs, the process is repeated until it nishes when the formula is unsatis able, in which case the latest solution is an optimal one.

We have integrated Polosat into PLC by replacing all the SAT invocations with Polosat, where the objective function returns the current value of the perimeter: $\Psi(\mu) = \sum_{j=1}^{k} \mu(P^j)$. Note that Ψ is not linear PB, since P^js are bit-vectors. Ψ is strictly monotone in the bits of the net perimeters. Hence, we use the strictly-monotone Polosat with the following observables: $Obs = \{P^1_n, P^2_n, \ldots, P^k_n, P^1_{n-1}, P^2_{n-1}, \ldots, P^k_{n-1}, \ldots, P^1_1, P^2_1, \ldots, P^k_1\}$ (where, for every j, the bits $\{P^j_n, \ldots, P^j_2, P^j_1\}$ are P^js bits). Note that we ordered Obs to give preference to the more signi cant bits: P^q_k comes before P^w_{k-1} for any q, w and k. We found no need to apply the adaptive strategy in PLC.

V. Experimental Results

In this section, we study the performance of Polosat within both our MaxSAT solver TT-Open-WBO-Inc and our

industrial placement tool PLC. We used machines with 32Gb of memory running Intel® Xeon® processors with 3Ghz CPU frequency for all the experiments.

A. Polosat *in* TT-Open-WBO-Inc *on MSE19 Instances*

This section studies the performance of the following anytime MaxSAT solvers and solver con gurations on the benchmarks used in both the 60-second and 300-second weighted, incomplete categories of MaxSAT Evaluation 2019:

1) loandra [12]: the runner-up in both of the weighted, incomplete categories at MSE19.
2) TT-Open-WBO-Inc [31]: the winner in both of the weighted, incomplete categories at MSE19 and the baseline solver for our Polosat implementation.
3) Polosat: TT-Open-WBO-Inc with the strictly-monotone Polosat integrated as presented in Sect. IV-A.
4) NoAdapt: Polosat without the adaptive strategy (Sect. IV-A2).
5) NoCC: Polosat without the con ict threshold for SAT invocations (Sect. III-B1).
6) NoComb: Polosat without the mutation combination algorithm (Sect. III-B2).

The criterion for comparing anytime MaxSAT solvers at MaxSAT Evaluation 2019 was their *score*, de ned as follows for a particular solver S and i instances: $\sum_i (1 +$ the minimal weight of the unsatis ed target bits found by any participating solver) / (1 + the weight of the unsatis ed target bits found by S). This criterion depends on the participating solvers. Following [30], we decided to calculate an absolute score against the best result, achieved by the top two anytime solvers in MaxSAT Evaluation 2019, that is, TT-Open-WBO-Inc and loandra, as well as the two best-performing complete solvers rc2b [26], [28], [18] and UWrMaxSAT [35], in 24 hours. Hence, we de ne the score as follows: $\sum_i (1 +$ the best result of the four solvers in 24 hours) / (1 + the weight of the unsatis ed target bits found by S).

We ran the solvers for 30 minutes and measured the average score at the following intervals: 60, 180, 300, 600, 900, 1200, 1500 and 1800 seconds. This approach allowed us to study the performance of the solvers over time. We updated both TT-Open-WBO-Inc and loandra to print out the time of discovery of each new model.

The code of the solvers we used as well as instructions on how to reproduce our experiments are publicly available at http://tiny.cc/9fk4rz.

The results are presented in Fig. 2, Table I, Table II and Table III. Some observations are in place.

First, Fig. 2 and Table I show that Polosat signi cantly improves the average score of its baseline TT-Open-WBO-Inc solver for every considered timeout. Furthermore, Table III demonstrates that, for the timeout of 300 sec., Polosat improves the quality on 127 instances and deteorates it only on 42 instances. Moreover, Table II provides evidence that Polosat exhibits a better performance on the majority of the families. In particular, for the timeout of 300

Time	Polo	NoAdapt	NoCC	NoComb	TT	loandra
1800	0.8501	0.8174	0.8464	0.8501	0.8308	0.8097
1500	0.8494	0.8158	0.846	0.8494	0.8302	0.8084
1200	0.849	0.814	0.8441	0.848	0.8292	0.8028
900	0.8486	0.8093	0.8436	0.8467	0.8269	0.8011
600	0.8393	0.7981	0.8333	0.8355	0.8169	0.7975
300	0.8312	0.7829	0.8236	0.8295	0.8089	0.7828
180	0.8231	0.7731	0.8147	0.8213	0.8028	0.7738
60	0.7756	0.7443	0.7656	0.7734	0.7567	0.7352

TABLE I: Comparing the average score (rounded to 4 digits) over time (in seconds). The best result per timeout is highlighted. `TT` stands for `TT-Open-WBO-Inc`; `Polo` stands for `Polosat`.

Family	#Inst	60 sec.		300 sec.		1800 sec.	
		TT	Polo	TT	Polo	TT	Polo
abstr-ref	10	0.900	0.899	0.984	0.992	0.986	0.992
af-synthesis	16	0.994	0.996	1.000	1.000	1.000	1.000
BTBNSL	14	0.982	0.987	0.988	0.991	0.988	0.991
causal-disc	16	0.710	0.904	0.847	0.917	0.879	0.947
corr-clust	23	0.858	0.894	0.887	0.958	0.891	0.960
drmx-crypt	1	0.871	0.876	0.884	0.902	0.915	0.914
hs-timetab	10	0.490	0.533	0.503	0.553	0.514	0.562
lisbon-wed	14	0.714	0.714	0.714	0.714	0.714	0.714
max-real	13	0.904	1.013	0.904	1.013	0.911	1.013
metro	2	1.000	1.000	1.000	1.000	1.000	1.000
MinWDST	7	0.504	0.504	0.932	0.932	0.933	0.933
min-width	17	0.848	0.848	0.848	0.848	0.848	0.848
mpe	15	0.611	0.620	0.611	0.620	0.611	0.620
railway-tr	4	0.902	0.805	0.913	0.919	0.983	0.983
ramsey	12	0.867	0.934	0.894	0.953	0.933	0.953
rel-inf	2	0.015	0.015	0.114	0.111	0.165	0.150
shiftdesign	11	0.805	0.664	1.000	1.000	1.000	1.000
staff-sched	11	0.856	0.775	0.926	0.938	0.971	0.987
tcp	13	1.000	1.000	1.000	1.000	1.000	1.000
timetabling	16	0.303	0.279	0.536	0.507	0.640	0.610
ParRBACM	15	0.000	0.000	0.000	0.000	0.000	0.000
MaxSQIC	15	0.831	0.922	0.905	0.954	0.940	0.974
maxcut	16	0.926	0.949	0.926	0.949	0.926	0.949
pseudoB	7	0.651	0.687	0.660	0.687	0.952	0.980
set-covering	12	0.967	0.968	0.974	0.970	0.978	0.977
spot5	5	0.956	0.957	0.958	0.964	0.964	0.967
Overall	297	0.757	0.776	0.809	0.831	0.831	0.850

TABLE II: `TT-Open-WBO-Inc` (abrr. `TT`) vs. `Polosat` (abrr. `Polo`): average score per family (names abbreviated) for 3 timeouts.

S1	S2	#Inst S1 outperformed S2 {by at least 2 times}
Polosat	TT	127 {1}
TT	Polosat	42 {1}
NoAdapt	TT	117 {4}
TT	NoAdapt	69 {19}

TABLE III: A pairwise solver comparison on the 297 MSE19 instances for the timeout of 300 seconds. Every row shows the number of instances on which the solver `S1` achieves a better quality than the solver `S2`, followed, in braces, by the number of instances on which the score of `S1` is at least 2 times better than that of `S2`. `TT` stands for `TT-Open-WBO-Inc`.

Metric	Minimum	Maximum	Average	Std. Dev.
Variables in CNF	5,580	1,144,731	212,416	217,472
Clauses in CNF	22,155	4,309,253	865,231	912,927

TABLE IV: Placement Problems Statistics

B. Polosat in PLC

We compared the baseline `PLC` placement tool vs. `PLC` enhanced by `Polosat`, on 156 proprietary industrial designs of various sizes and different complexity. Some statistics about the resulting CNF formulas are shown in Table IV. Unfortunately, further details about the input problems are IP-restricted.

Similarly to the MSE19 experiments, we ran the solvers for 30 minutes and measured the average score at the following intervals: 60, 180, 300, 600, 900, 1200, 1500 and 1800 seconds, where the absolute score is the score achieved by the default `PLC` in 24 hours.

Fig. 3 and Fig. 4 show the results. `Polosat` improves the average score for every considered timeout. In fact, for the timeout of 1800 seconds, `Polosat` improves the score for 77.5% of the instances and deteriorates the score only for 15.3% of the instances. In addition, Fig. 4 demonstrates that `Polosat` s score is higher than 1 for a signi cant portion of the instances (38.5%), which means that, on these instances, `Polosat` obtains a better placement in 30 minutes than the default `PLC` in 24 hours.

All in all, `Polosat` is an enabler for successfully producing `PLC`.

sec., `Polosat` improves the average score on 15 out of 26 families and deteriorates the average score on 3 families only.

Second, consider the impact of the adaptive strategy. Table III shows that `NoAdapt` outscores `TT-Open-WBO-Inc` on 117 instances, while `TT-Open-WBO-Inc` outscores `NoAdapt` on 69 instances only, yet Fig. 2 and Table I are evidence that, on average, `NoAdapt` is inferior to `TT-Open-WBO-Inc` for every timeout. The reason is that, as Table III shows, there are 19 instances on which the score of `NoAdapt` is inferior to that of `TT-Open-WBO-Inc` by at least 2 times (in fact, 18 out of these 19 instances belong to only 3 families: shiftdesign, timetabling an hs-timetabling). Fortunately, the adaptive strategy takes care of these benchmarks as `Polosat` is inferior to `TT-Open-WBO-Inc` by at least 2 times on only one benchmark.

Third, Fig. 2 and Table I show that applying the con ict threshold for SAT invocations makes `Polosat` moderately, but consistently more ef cient for every timeout. Mutation combination has a positive, yet minor effect, canceled for the two longest timeouts of 1500 and 1800 sec. The reason might be that, with the time, it becomes dif cult for mutation combination to improve the best model (while, in its original usage in `QuickSampler`, it is suf cient to nd *any* model).

VI. Conclusion

We formulated the problem of generic optimization in SAT (OptSAT) and proposed an ef cient anytime and incremental incomplete OptSAT algorithm, `Polosat`. We integrated `Polosat` into the state-of-the-art open-source anytime MaxSAT solver `TT-Open-WBO-Inc`, which won both of the weighted, incomplete tracks of MaxSAT Evaluation 2019, and demonstrated that `Polosat` signi cantly improves `TT-Open-WBO-Inc` s performance. Furthermore, we showed that integrating `Polosat` into our industrial placement tool is highly advantageous.

Our encouraging empirical results lead us to believe that integrating `Polosat` into other optimization ows as well as further studying both the theoretical and the empirical aspects of OptSAT is a promising long-term research direction, expected to extend the range of optimization problems that can be ef ciently solved with SAT.

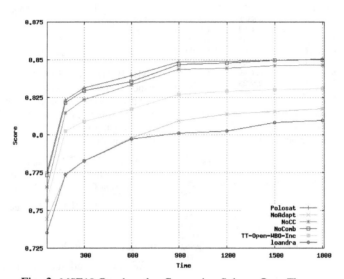

Fig. 2: MSE19 Benchmarks: Comparing Solvers Over Time

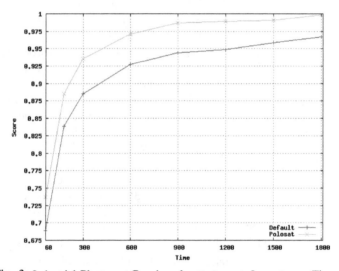

Fig. 3: Industrial Placement Benchmarks: Polosat Impact over Time

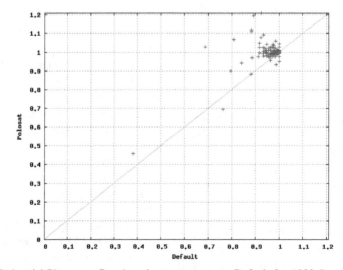

Fig. 4: Industrial Placement Benchmarks: Polosat vs. Default for 1800 Sec. Timeout

References

[1] I. Ab'o, M. Deters, R. Nieuwenhuis, and P. J. Stuckey. Reducing chaos in sat-like search: Finding solutions close to a given one. In *SAT 2011*, pages 273–286, 2011.

[2] S. Agbaria, D. Carmi, O. Cohen, D. Korchemny, M. Lifshits, and A. Nadel. SAT-based semiformal veri cation of hardware. In *FMCAD 2010*, pages 25–32, 2010.

[3] C. Ansótegui and J. Gabas. WPM3: an (in)complete algorithm for weighted partial MaxSAT. *Artif. Intell.*, 250:37–57, 2017.

[4] J. Argelich, I. Lynce, and J. P. M. Silva. On solving Boolean multilevel optimization problems. In *IJCAI 2009*, pages 393–398, 2009.

[5] F. Bacchus, M. Järvisalo, and R. Martins, editors. *MaxSAT Evaluation 2019: Solver and Benchmark Descriptions*, Department of Computer Science Report Series B, Finland, 2019. Department of Computer Science, University of Helsinki.

[6] C. Barrett, A. Stump, and C. Tinelli. The SMT-LIB Standard: Version 2.0. In A. Gupta and D. Kroening, editors, *Proceedings of the 8th International Workshop on Satisfiability Modulo Theories (Edinburgh, UK)*, 2010.

[7] J. Berg, A. Hyttinen, and M. Järvisalo. Applications of maxsat in data analysis. In *Proceedings of Pragmatics of SAT 2015, Austin, Texas, USA, September 23, 2015 / Pragmatics of SAT 2018, Oxford, UK, July 7, 2018.*, pages 50–64, 2018.

[8] A. Biere, M. Heule, H. van Maaren, and T. Walsh, editors. *Handbook of Satisfiability*, volume 185 of *Frontiers in Artificial Intelligence and Applications*. IOS Press, 2009.

[9] N. Bjørner, A. Phan, and L. Fleckenstein. νz - an optimizing SMT solver. In *TACAS 2015*, pages 194–199, 2015.

[10] M. C. Cooper, S. Cussat-Blanc, M. de Roquemaurel, and P. Régnier. Soft arc consistency applied to optimal planning. In *Principles and Practice of Constraint Programming - CP 2006, 12th International Conference, CP 2006, Nantes, France, September 25-29, 2006, Proceedings*, pages 680–684, 2006.

[11] E. Demirov'c, G. Chu, and P. J. Stuckey. Solution-based phase saving for CP: A value-selection heuristic to simulate local search behavior in complete solvers. In *CP 2018*, pages 99–108, 2018.

[12] E. Demirovic and P. J. Stuckey. Techniques inspired by local search for incomplete maxsat and the linear algorithm: Varying resolution and solution-guided search. In *CP 2019, Stamford, CT, USA, September 30 - October 4, 2019, Proceedings*, pages 177–194, 2019.

[13] E. Di Rosa and E. Giunchiglia. Combining approaches for solving satisability problems with qualitative preferences. *AI Commun.*, 26(4):395–408, 2013.

[14] R. Dutra, K. Laeufer, J. Bachrach, and K. Sen. Ef cient sampling of SAT solutions for testing. In *Proceedings of the 40th International Conference on Software Engineering, ICSE 2018, Gothenburg, Sweden, May 27 - June 03, 2018*, pages 549–559, 2018.

[15] N. Eén and N. Sörensson. An extensible SAT-solver. In *SAT*, pages 502–518, 2003.

[16] Y. Feng, O. Bastani, R. Martins, I. Dillig, and S. Anand. Automated synthesis of semantic malware signatures using maximum satis ability. In *24th Annual Network and Distributed System Security Symposium, NDSS 2017, San Diego, California, USA, February 26 - March 1, 2017*, 2017.

[17] A. Graça, I. Lynce, J. Marques-Silva, and A. L. Oliveira. Ef cient and accurate haplotype inference by combining parsimony and pedigree information. In *ANB 2010, Hagenberg, Austria, Revised Selected Papers*, pages 38–56, 2010.

[18] A. Ignatiev, A. Morgado, and J. Marques-Silva. RC2: a python-based MaxSAT solver. In *MaxSAT Evaluation 2018: Solver and Benchmark Descriptions*, volume B-2018-2 of *Department of Computer Science Series of Publications B*, page 22. University of Helsinki, 2018.

[19] S. Joshi, P. Kumar, R. Martins, and S. Rao. Approximation strategies for incomplete MaxSAT. In *CP 2018*, pages 219–228, 2018.

[20] S. Joshi, P. Kumar, S. Rao, and R. Martins. Open-wbo-inc: Approximation strategies for incomplete weighted maxsat. *J. Satisf. Boolean Model. Comput.*, 11(1):73–97, 2019.

[21] H. A. Kautz, A. Sabharwal, and B. Selman. Incomplete algorithms. In Biere et al. [8], pages 185–203.

[22] S. Khoshnood, M. Kusano, and C. Wang. Concbugassist: constraint solving for diagnosis and repair of concurrency bugs. In *Proceedings of the 2015 International Symposium on Software Testing and Analysis,*

[23] ISSTA 2015, Baltimore, MD, USA, July 12-17, 2015, pages 165–176, 2015.

[23] R. E. Korf. Optimal rectangle packing: Initial results. In *Proceedings of the Thirteenth International Conference on Automated Planning and Scheduling (ICAPS 2003), June 9-13, 2003, Trento, Italy*, pages 287–295, 2003.

[24] Z. Lei and S. Cai. Solving (weighted) partial maxsat by dynamic local search for SAT. In *Proceedings of the Twenty-Seventh International Joint Conference on Artificial Intelligence, IJCAI 2018, July 13-19, 2018, Stockholm, Sweden.*, pages 1346–1352, 2018.

[25] I. S. Masich and L. A. Kazakovtsev. A branch-and-bound algorithm for a pseudo-boolean optimization problem with black-box functions. *Facta Universitatis, Series: Mathematics and Informatics*, 33(2):337 – 360, 2018.

[26] A. Morgado, C. Dodaro, and J. Marques-Silva. Core-guided MaxSAT with soft cardinality constraints. In *Principles and Practice of Constraint Programming - 20th International Conference, CP 2014, Lyon, France, September 8-12, 2014. Proceedings*, pages 564–573, 2014.

[27] A. Morgado, F. Heras, M. H. Lif ton, J. Planes, and J. Marques-Silva. Iterative and core-guided MaxSAT solving: A survey and assessment. *Constraints*, 18(4):478–534, 2013.

[28] A. Morgado, A. Ignatiev, and J. Marques-Silva. MSCG: robust core-guided MaxSAT solving. *JSAT*, 9:129–134, 2014.

[29] A. Nadel. Generating diverse solutions in SAT. In *SAT 2011*, pages 287–301, 2011.

[30] A. Nadel. Anytime weighted MaxSAT with improved polarity selection and bit-vector optimization. In *2019 Formal Methods in Computer Aided Design, FMCAD 2019, San Jose, CA, USA, October 22-25, 2019*, pages 193–202, 2019.

[31] A. Nadel. Polarity and variable selection heuristics for SAT-based anytime MaxSAT. *J. Satisf. Boolean Model. Comput.*, 12:17–22, 2020.

[32] A. Nadel and V. Ryvchin. Ef cient SAT solving under assumptions. In *Theory and Applications of Satisfiability Testing - SAT 2012 - 15th International Conference, Trento, Italy, June 17-20, 2012. Proceedings*, pages 242–255, 2012.

[33] A. Nadel and V. Ryvchin. Bit-vector optimization. In *TACAS 2016*, pages 851–867, 2016.

[34] J. D. Park. Using weighted MAX-SAT engines to solve MPE. In *Proceedings of the Eighteenth National Conference on Artificial Intelligence and Fourteenth Conference on Innovative Applications of Artificial Intelligence, July 28 - August 1, 2002, Edmonton, Alberta, Canada.*, pages 682–687, 2002.

[35] M. Piotrów. UWrMaxSat -a new MiniSat+-based Solver in MaxSAT Evaluation 2019. In Bacchus et al. [5].

[36] I. A. Roig. *Solving hard industrial combinatorial problems with SAT*. Dissertation, Polytechnic University of Catalonia, 2013. Chapter 7.8.4.

[37] O. Roussel and V. M. Manquinho. Pseudo-boolean and cardinality constraints. In Biere et al. [8], pages 695–733.

[38] B. Selman, H. J. Levesque, and D. G. Mitchell. A new method for solving hard satis ability problems. In *Proceedings of the 10th National Conference on Artificial Intelligence, San Jose, CA, USA, July 12-16, 1992.*, pages 440–446, 1992.

[39] K. Shahookar and P. Mazumder. VLSI cell placement techniques. *ACM Comput. Surv.*, 23(2):143–220, 1991.

[40] N. A. Sherwani. *Algorithms for VLSI physical design automation*. Kluwer, 3 edition, November 1998.

[41] X. Si, X. Zhang, R. Grigore, and M. Naik. Maximum satis ability in software analysis: Applications and techniques. In *Computer Aided Verification - 29th International Conference, CAV 2017, Heidelberg, Germany, July 24-28, 2017, Proceedings, Part I*, pages 68–94, 2017.

[42] A. F. Tabrizi, N. K. Darav, L. M. Rakai, A. A. Kennings, W. Swartz, and L. Behjat. A detailed routing-aware detailed placement technique. In *2015 IEEE Computer Society Annual Symposium on VLSI, ISVLSI 2015, Montpellier, France, July 8-10, 2015*, pages 38–43, 2015.

[43] C. S. Zhu, G. Weissenbacher, and S. Malik. Post-silicon fault localisation using maximum satis ability and backbones. In *International Conference on Formal Methods in Computer-Aided Design, FMCAD '11, Austin, TX, USA, October 30 - November 02, 2011*, pages 63–66, 2011.

17

Model Checking Software-Defined Networks with Flow Entries that Time Out

Vasileios Klimis(iD), George Parisis(iD) and Bernhard Reus(iD)

University of Sussex, UK

{v.klimis, g.parisis, bernhard}@sussex.ac.uk

Abstract—Software-defined networking (SDN) enables advanced operation and management of network deployments through (virtually) centralised, programmable controllers, which deploy network functionality by installing rules in the flow tables of network switches. Although this is a powerful abstraction, buggy controller functionality could lead to severe service disruption and security loopholes, motivating the need for (semi-)automated tools to find, or even verify absence of, bugs. Model checking SDNs has been proposed in the literature, but none of the existing approaches can support dynamic network deployments, where flow entries expire due to timeouts. This is necessary for automatically refreshing (and eliminating stale) state in the network (termed as *soft-state* in the network protocol design nomenclature), which is important for scaling up applications or recovering from failures. In this paper, we extend our model (MoCS) to deal with timeouts of flow table entries, thus supporting soft state in the network. Optimisations are proposed that are tailored to this extension. We evaluate the performance of the proposed model in UPPAAL using a load balancer and firewall in network topologies of varying size.

I. INTRODUCTION

Software-defined networking (SDN) [1] revolutionised network operation and management along with future protocol design; a virtually centralised and programmable controller 'programs' network switches through interactions (standardised in OpenFlow [2]) that alter switches' flow tables. In turn, switches push packets to the controller when they do not store state relevant to forwarding these packets. Such a paradigm departure from traditional networks enables the rapid development of advanced and diverse network functionality; e.g., in designing next-generation inter-data centre traffic engineering [3], load balancing [4], firewalls [5] and Internet exchange points (IXPs) [6]. Although this is a powerful abstraction, buggy controller functionality could lead to severe service disruption and security loopholes. This has led to a significant amount of research on SDN verification and/or bug finding, including static network analysis [7], [8], [9], dynamic real-time bug finding [10], [11], [12], [13], and formal verification approaches, including symbolic execution [14], [15], [16] and model checking [17], [10], [16], [18] methods. A comprehensive review of existing approaches along with their shortcomings can be found in [19].

Model checking is a renowned automated technique for hardware and software verification and existing model checking approaches for SDNs have shown promising results with respect to scalability and model expressivity, in terms of supporting realistic network deployments and the OpenFlow standard. However, a key limitation of all existing approaches is that they cannot model forwarding state (added in network switches' flow tables by the controller) that expires and gets deleted. Without this, one cannot model nor verify the correctness of SDNs with soft-state which is prominent in the design of protocols and systems that are resilient to failures and scalable; e.g., as in [20], where flow scheduling is on a per-flow basis, and numerous network protocols where in-network state is not explicitly removed but expires, so that overhead is minimised [21].

In this paper, we extend our model (MoCS) [17] to support soft-state, complying with the OpenFlow specification, by allowing flow entries to time out and be deleted. We propose relevant optimisations (as in [17]) in order to improve verification performance and scalability. We evaluate the performance of the proposed model extensions in UPPAAL using a load balancer and firewall in network topologies of varying size.

II. MoCS SDN MODEL

The MoCS model [17] is formally defined by means of an action-deterministic transition system. We parameterise the model by the underlying network topology, λ, and the controller program, CP, in use. The model is a 6-tuple $\mathcal{M}_{(\lambda, \text{CP})} = (S, s_0, A, \hookrightarrow, AP, L)$, where S is the set of all states the SDN may enter, s_0 the initial state, A the set of actions which encode the events the network may engage in, $\hookrightarrow \subseteq S \times A \times S$ the transition relation describing which execution steps the system undergoes as it perform actions, AP a set of atomic propositions describing relevant state properties, and $L : S \to 2^{AP}$ is a labelling function, which relates to any state $s \in S$ a set $L(s) \in 2^{AP}$ of those atomic propositions that are true for s. Such an SDN model is composed of several smaller systems, which model network components (hosts[1], switches and the controller) that communicate via queues and, combined, give rise to the definition of $\hookrightarrow$. A detailed description of MoCS' components and transitions can be found in [17]. Due to lack of space, in this paper, we only discuss aspects of the model that are required to understand and verify the soundness of the proposed model extensions, and examples used in the evaluation section. Figure 1 illustrates a high-level view of OpenFlow interactions, modelled actions and queues, including the proposed extensions discussed in Section III.

---

[1]A host can act as a client and/or server.

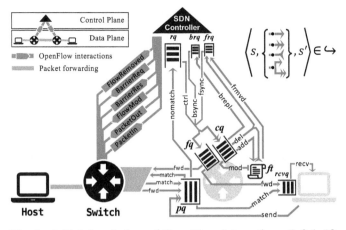

Fig. 1: A high-level view of OpenFlow interactions (left half) and modelled actions (right half). A red solid-line arrow depicts an action which, when fired, (1) dequeues an item from the queue the arrow begins at, and (2) (possibly) adds an item in the queue the arrowhead points to (or multiple items if the arrow is double-headed). Deleting an item from the target queue is denoted by a reverse arrowhead; modifying in, by a hammerhead. A forked arrow denotes (possibly) multiple targeted queues.

States and queues: A *state* is a triple (π, δ, γ), where π is a family of hosts, each consisting of a receive queue (*rcvq*); δ is a family of switches, consisting of a switch packet queue (*pq*), switch forward queue (*fq*), switch control queue (*cq*), switch flow table (*ft*); γ consists of the local controller program state $cs \in CS$, and a family of controller queues: request queue (*rq*), barrier-reply queue (*brq*) and flow-removed queue (*frq*). So π and δ describe the *data-plane*, and γ the *control plane*. The network components communicate via the shared queues. Each transition models a certain network event that will involve some of the queues, and maybe some other network state. Concurrency is modelled through interleavings of those events.

Transitions: Each transition is labelled with an action $\alpha \in A$ that indicates the nature of the network event. We write $s \xrightarrow{\alpha} s'$ and $(s, \alpha, s') \in \hookrightarrow$ interchangeably to denote that the network moved from state s to s' by executing transition α. The parts of the network involved in each individual α, i.e. *packets, rules, barriers, switches, hosts, ports* and *controller states*, are included in the transition label as parameters; e.g., $match(sw, pkt, r) \in A$ denotes the action that switch sw matches packet pkt by rule r and, as a result, forwards it accordingly, leading to a new state after transition.

Atomic propositions: The propositions in AP are statements on (1) controller program states, denoted by $Q(q)$ which expresses that the controller program is in state $q \in CS$, allowing one to reason about the controller's internal data structures, and (2) packet header fields – those packets may be in any switch buffer pq or host buffer $rcvq$ (but no other buffers). For instance, $\exists pkt \in sw.pq \,.\, P(pkt)$ is a legitimate atomic proposition that states that there is a packet in sw's packet queue that satisfies packet pkt property P.

Topology: λ describes the network topology as a bijective map

which associates one network interface (a pair of networking device and physical port) to another.

Specification Logic: The properties of the SDNs to be checked in this paper are safety properties, expressed in linear-time temporal logic without 'next-step' operator, $LTL_{\backslash \{\bigcirc\}}$. We have enriched the logic by modal operators of *dynamic logic* [22], allowing formula construct of the form $[\alpha(\vec{x})]P$ stating that whenever an event $\alpha(\vec{x})$ happened, P must hold. Note that P may contain variables from x. This extension is syntax sugar in the sense that the formulae may be expressed by additional state; e.g., $[match(sw, pkt, r)](r.fwdPort = \texttt{drop})$ states that if *match* happened, it was via a rule that dropped the packet. This permits specification formulae to be interpreted not only over states, but also over actions that have happened. The model checking problem then, for an SDN model $\mathcal{M}_{(\lambda, \text{CP})}$ with a given topology λ, a control program CP and a formula φ of the specification logic as described above, boils down to checking whether all runs of $\mathcal{M}_{(\lambda, \text{CP})}$ satisfy φ, short $\mathcal{M}_{(\lambda, \text{CP})} \models \Box \varphi$.

SDN Operation: End-hosts send and receive packets (*send* and *recv* actions in Figure 1) and switches process incoming packets by matching them (or failing to) with a flow table entry (rule). In the former case (*match* action), the packet is forwarded as prescribed by the rule. In the opposite case (*nomatch* action), the packet is sent to the controller (*PacketIn* message on the left side of Figure 1). The controller's packet handler is executed in response to incoming *PacketIn* messages; as a result of its execution, its local state may change, a number of packets (*PacketOut* message) and rule updates (*FlowMod* message), interleaved with barriers (*BarrierReq* message), may be sent to network switches. Network switches react to incoming controller messages; they forward packets sent by the controller as specified in the respective *PacketOut* message (*fwd* action), update their own forwarding tables (*add/del* actions), respecting set barriers and notifying the controller (*BarrierRes* message) when said barriers are executed (*brepl* action). Finally, upon receiving a *BarrierRes* message, the controller executes the respective handler (*bsync* action), which can result in the same effects as the *PacketIn* message handler.

Abstractions: To obtain finitely representable states, all queues in the model must be finitely representable. For packet queues we use multisets, subject to $(0, \infty)$ abstraction [23]; a packet either does not appear in the queue or appears an unbounded number of times. The other queues are simply modelled as finite sets. Modelling queues as sets means that entries are not processed in the order of arrival. This is intentional for packet queues but for controller queues this may limit behaviour unless the controller program is order-insensitive. We focus on those controller programs in this paper.

III. MODELLING FLOW ENTRY TIMEOUTS

In order to model soft-state in the network, we enrich our model with two new actions that model flow entry timeouts and subsequent handling of these timeouts by the controller program. Note that in our model, timeouts are not triggered by any kind of clock; instead, they are modelled through the interleaving of actions in the underlying transition system that ensure that flow removal (and subsequent handling by the controller program) will appear as it would for any possible value of a timeout in a real system.

The new actions are defined as follows: $frmvd(sw, r)$ models the timeout event, as an action in the transition system that removes the flow entry (rule) r from switch sw and notifies the controller by placing a *FlowRemoved* message (see Figure 1) in the respective queue (frq). The $fsync(sw, r, cs)$ action models the call to the *FlowRemoved* message handler. As a result of the handler execution, the controller's local state (cs) may change, a number of packets (*PacketOut* messages) and rule updates (*FlowMod* messages), interleaved with barriers (*BarrierReq* message), may be sent to network switches. In order to model timeouts, rules are augmented with a *timeout* bit which, when true, signals that the installed rule can be removed at any time, i.e., the *frmvd*-action can be interleaved, in any order, with any other action that is enabled at any state later than the installation of this rule.

To support our examples, we add to the set of *FlowMod* messages a *modify flow entry* instruction. In [17] we only used $add(sw, r)$ and $del(sw, r)$ messages, for installing and deleting rule r at switch sw, respectively. We now add $mod(sw, f, a)$ to these messages. This instructs switch sw that if a rule is found in $sw.ft$ that matches field f, its forwarding actions are modified by a. If no such rule exists, $mod(\cdot)$ does not do anything.

Optimisation: To tackle the state-space explosion, we exploit the fact that some traces are observationally (w.r.t. the property to be proved) equivalent, so that only one of those needs to be checked. This technique, referred to as *partial-order reduction* (POR) [24], reduces the number of interleavings (traces) one has to check. To prove equivalence of traces, one needs actions to be permutable and invisible to the property at hand. This is the motivation for the following definition:

Definition 1 (SAFE ACTIONS) Given a context CTX = (CP, λ, φ), and SDN model $\mathcal{M}_{(\lambda, CP)} = (S, A, \hookrightarrow, s_0, AP, L)$, an action $\alpha(\cdot) \in A(s)$ is called *safe* if it is (1) *independent* of any other action β in A, i.e. executing α after β leads to the same state as running β after α, and (2) *unobservable* for φ (also called φ-*invariant*), i.e., $s \models \varphi$ iff $\alpha(s) \models \varphi$ for all $s \in S$ with $\alpha \in A(s)$.

The following property of controller programs is needed to show safety:

Definition 2 (ORDER-SENSITIVE CONTROLLER PROGRAM) A controller program CP is order-sensitive if there exists a state $s \in S$ and two actions α, β in $\{ctrl(\cdot), bsync(\cdot), fsync(\cdot)\}$ such that $\alpha, \beta \in A(s)$ and $s \xrightarrow{\alpha} s_1 \xrightarrow{\beta} s_2$ and $s \xrightarrow{\beta} s_3 \xrightarrow{\alpha} s_4$ with $s_2 \neq s_4$.

In [17] we already showed that certain actions are safe and can be used for PORs. We now show that the new $fsync(\cdot)$ action is safe on certain conditions.

Lemma 1 (SAFENESS PREDICATES FOR *fsync*) For transition system $\mathcal{M}_{(\lambda, CP)} = (S, A, \hookrightarrow, s_0, AP, L)$ and a formula $\varphi \in \text{LTL}_{\backslash \{\bigcirc\}}$, $\alpha = fsync(sw, r, cs)$ is safe iff the following two conditions are satisfied:

Independence CP is not order-sensitive
Invisibility if $Q(q)$ in AP occurs in φ, then α is φ-invariant

Proof. See [25] Appendix A.   □

Given a context CTX = (CP, λ, φ) and an SDN network model $\mathcal{M}_{(\lambda, CP)} = (S, A, \hookrightarrow, s_0, AP, L)$, for each state $s \in S$ define $ample(s)$ as follows: if $\{\alpha \in A(s) \mid \alpha \text{ safe}\} \neq \varnothing$, then $ample(s) = \{\alpha \in A(s) \mid \alpha \text{ safe}\}$; otherwise $ample(s) = A(s)$. Next, we define $\mathcal{M}^{fr}_{(\lambda, CP)} = (S^{fr}, A, \hookrightarrow_{fr}, s_0, AP, L^{fr})$, where $S^{fr} \subseteq S$ the set of states reachable from the initial state s_0 under $\hookrightarrow_{fr}$, $L^{fr}(s) = L(s)$ for all $s \in S^{fr}$ and $\hookrightarrow_{fr} \subseteq S^{fr} \times A \times S^{fr}$ is defined inductively by the rule:

$$\frac{s \xrightarrow{\alpha} s'}{s \xrightarrow{\alpha}_{fr} s'} \quad \text{if } \alpha \in ample(s)$$

Now we can proceed to extend the POR Theorem of [17]:

Theorem 1 (FLOW-REMOVED EQUIVALENCE) Given a property $\varphi \in \text{LTL}_{\backslash \{\bigcirc\}}$, it holds that $\mathcal{M}^{fr}_{(\lambda, CP)}$ satisfies φ iff $\mathcal{M}_{(\lambda, CP)}$ satisfies φ.

The proof is a consequence of Lemma 1 applied to the proof of Theorem 2 in [17]. See [25] Appendix A for a detailed proof.

IV. EXPERIMENTAL EVALUATION

In this section we experimentally evaluate the proposed extensions in terms of verification performance and scalability. We use a realistic controller program that enables a network switch to act both as a load balancer and stateful firewall (see §V-CP1). The load balancer keeps track of the active sessions between clients and servers in the cluster (see Figure 2), while, at the same time, only allowing specific clients to access the cluster. Soft state is employed here so that flow entries for completed sessions (that were previously admitted by the firewall) time out and are deleted by the switch without having to explicitly monitor the sessions and introduce unnecessary signalling (and overhead). In the underlying SDN model, the *frmvd* action is fired, which, in turn, deletes the flow entry from the switch's table and notifies the controller of that. This enables the *fsync* action that calls the flow removal handler.

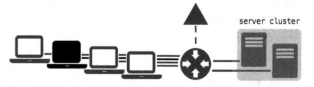

Fig. 2: Four clients and two servers connecting to an OF-switch. ■ is not white-listed.

A session is initiated by a client which sends a packet (*pkt* in §V-CP1) to a known cluster address; servers are not directly visible to the client. Sessions are bi-directional therefore the controller must install respective rules to the switch to allow traffic to and from the cluster. The property that is checked here is that (1) the traffic (i.e. number of sessions, assuming they all produce similar traffic patterns), and resulting load, is uniformly distributed to all available servers, and (2) that traffic from non-whitelisted clients is blocked. More concretely, "*a packet from a 'dodgy' address should never reach the servers, and the difference between the number of assigned sessions at each server should never be greater than 1*", formally,

$$\square \left(\forall s_i, s_j \in Servers \; \forall pkt \in s_i.rcvq \, . \right.$$
$$\left. \neg pkt.src = dodgy \; \wedge \; \left| sLoad[s_i] - sLoad[s_j] \right| < \; 2 \right) \quad (\varphi)$$

where $sLoad$ stores the active session count for each server.

In the first (buggy) version of the controller's packet handler (shaded grey in §V-CP1) and flow removal handler §V-CP2, the controller program assigns new sessions to servers in a round-robin fashion and keeps track of the active sessions (array *deplSessions* in the provided pseudocode). When a session expires, the respective flow table entry is expected to expire and be deleted by the switch without any signalling between the controller, clients or servers[2]. As stated above, this controller program does not satisfy safety property φ because the controller does nothing to rebalance the load when a session expires. Our model implementation[3] discovered the bug in the topology shown in Figure 2 with 3 sessions in 11ms exploring 202 states.

In the second (still buggy) version of the controller, session scheduling is more sophisticated (shaded blue in §V-CP1); a session is assigned to the server with the least number of active sessions. Although the updated load balancing algorithm does keep track of the active sessions per server, this controller is still buggy because no rebalancing takes place when sessions expire. In a topology of 4 clients and 2 servers, we were able to discover the bug in 52ms after exploring 714 states.

We fix the bug by allowing the controller program to rebalance the active sessions, when (1) a session expires and (2) the load is about to get out of balance, by moving one session from the most-loaded to the least-loaded server (§V-CP3). In the same topology as above, we verified the property in 625ms after exploring 15068 states.[4]

Next, we evaluate the performance of the proposed model and extensions for verifying the correctness of the property in a given SDN. We do that by verifying φ with the correct controller program, discussed above, and scaling up the topology in terms of clients, servers and active sessions. Results are listed in Table I and state exploration is illustrated in Figure 4.

Table I lists performance of the model checker for verifying the correct controller program with PORs disabled on the

left and with PORs enabled on the right, respectively. For each chosen topology we list the number of states explored, CPU time used, and memory used. The topology is shaped as in Figure 2, and parametrised by the number of clients (ranging from 3 to 5) and servers (ranging from 2 to 5), as indicated in Table I. The number of required packets and rules, respectively, is shown in grey. These numbers are always uniquely determined by the choice of topology. Where there are no entries in the table (indicated by a dash) the verification did not terminate within 24 hours.

The results clearly show that the verification scales well with the number of servers but not with the number of clients. The reason for the latter is that for each additional client an additional packet is sent, which, according to programs §V-CP1 and CP3, leads to 7 additional actions without timeouts and to 12 with timeouts. The causal ordering of these actions is shown in Fig. 3. The sub-branch in red shows the actions that appear due to a timeout of the added rule. Thus, the number of states is exponential in the number of clients: every new action in Fig. 3 leads to a new change of state, thus doubling the possible number of states. This exponential blow-up happens whether we have timeouts or not. With timeouts, however, we have worse exponential complexity as there are more new states generated.

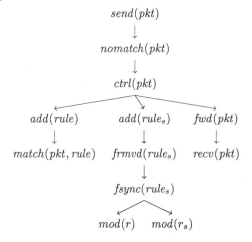

Fig. 3: The causal enabling relation between actions for an additional packet *pkt*; only the relevant arguments are shown using the same nomenclature as in the pseudocode.

The results also demonstrate that, for network setups with three clients, the POR optimisation reduces the state space – and thus the verification time – by about half. For more clients the reduction is far more significant, given that the verification of the unoptimised model did not terminate within 24 hours. This is not surprising as the number of possible interleavings is massively increased by the non-deterministic timeout events.

V. CONTROLLER PROGRAMS

CP1 implements the *PacketIn* message handler that processes packets sent by switches when the *nomatch* action is fired. The two different versions of functionality discussed in the paper are defined by the *leastConnectionsScheduling*

---

[2]It is worth stressing that modelling such functionality is not supported by existing model checking approaches, such as [17] and [18], where flow table entries can only be explicitly deleted by the controller.

[3]UPPAAL [26] is the back-end verification engine for MoCS and all experiments were run on an 18-Core iMac pro, 2.3GHz Intel Xeon W with 128GB DDR4 memory.

[4]Note that the *fsync*-optimisation was not enabled in the examples above.

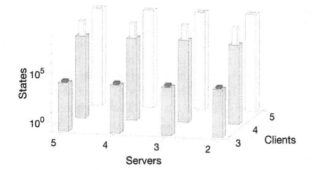

States

10^5

10^0

5   4   3   2   3

Servers

5

4

3

Clients

Fig. 4: Explored States (logarithmic scale). Wide bars represent the optimised model and narrow ones (inside) the unoptimised model. Uncoloured bars represent non-termination.

TABLE I: Performance by number of clients and servers

Clients	Servers	Packets	Rules	without POR			with POR		
				States	CPU user time	Resident memory [KiB]	States	CPU user time	Resident memory [KiB]
3	2	3	13	15,068	553ms	9,516	8,264	317ms	9,016
3	3	3	19	15,068	700ms	10,688	8,264	322ms	8,792
3	4	3	25	15,068	841ms	11,936	8,264	483ms	10,488
3	5	3	31	15,068	987ms	15,280	8,264	563ms	12,844
4	2	4	17	–	–	–	13,244,474	13.2m	2,508,528
4	3	4	25	–	–	–	24,623,435	30.77m	5,432,004
4	4	4	33	–	–	–	24,623,435	37.23m	13,129,916
4	5	4	41	–	–	–	24,623,435	42.64m	15,443,136
5	2	5	21	–	–	–	–	–	–

constant. When *leastConnectionsScheduling* is false, server selection is done in a round-robin fashion, whereas, in the opposite case, the controller assigns the new session to the server with the least number of active sessions.

CP2 implements the naive (and buggy) *FlowRemoved* message handler. When soft state expires in the network, the handler merely updates its local state to reflect the update in the load.

CP3 implements a more sophisticated (and correct) *FlowRemoved* message handler. When soft state expires in the network, the handler updates its local state to reflect the update in the load and re-assigns active sessions from the most to the least loaded server, by updating the flow table of the switch accordingly.

VI. CONCLUSION AND FUTURE WORK

We have proposed model checking of SDN networks with flow entries (rules) that time out. Timeouts pose problems due to the great number of resulting interleavings to be explored. Our approach is the first one to deal with timeouts, exploiting partial-order reductions, and performing reasonably well for small networks. We demonstrated that bug finding works well for SDN networks in the presence of flow entry timeouts. Future work includes exploring flow removals with timeouts that are constrained by integer to *enforce certain orderings* of timeout messages as well as improvements in performance, for instance, by using bounded model checking tools for concurrent programs.

Controller Program CP 1: *PacketIn* Message Handler

```
1:  handler pktIn(pkt, sw)
2:      if pkt.srcIP ≠ dodgy_client then
3:          if ¬deplSessions[pkt.srcIP] then
4:              if ¬leastConnectionsScheduling then
                    // Round-Robin rotation
5:                  server ← server mod 2 + 1
6:              else
                    // Least-Connections scheduling
7:                  server ← min(sLoad[])
8:              end if
                // Initialisation of flow to server
9:              rule.srcIP        ← pkt.srcIP
10:             rule.in_port      ← pkt.in_port
11:             rule.fwdPort      ← server
                // Initialisation of symmetric rule_s
12:             rule_s.srcIP      ← server
13:             rule_s.destIP     ← pkt.srcIP
14:             rule_s.fwdPort    ← pkt.in_port
15:             rule_s.timeout    ← true
                // Initialisation of drop rule rule_d
16:             rule_d.srcIP      ← dodgy_client
17:             rule_d.fwdPort    ← drop
                // Deployment of rules
18:             send_message(FlowMod(add(rule)), sw)
19:             send_message(FlowMod(add(rule_s)), sw)
20:             send_message(FlowMod(add(rule_d)), sw)
                // Update firewall state table
21:             sLoad[server]++
22:             deplSessions[pkt.srcIP] ← true
23:         end if
            // PacketOut: sending pkt out through sw
24:         send_message{PacketOut(pkt, server), sw)
25:     end if
26: end handler
```

Controller Program CP 2: Naive *FlowRemoved* message handler

```
1:  handler flowRmvd(rule_s, sw)
2:      sLoad[rule_s.srcIP]--
3:      deplSessions[rule_s.destIP] ← false
4:  end handler
```

Controller Program CP 3: Correct *FlowRemoved* message handler

```
1:  handler flowRmvd(rule_s, sw)
2:      sLoad[rule_s.srcIP]--
3:      deplSessions[rule_s.destIP] ← false
4:      if max(sLoad[]) − min(sLoad[]) > 1 then
5:          r ← the rule in sw.ft with fwdPort = max(sLoad[])
6:          r_s ← symmetric rule of r
7:          cm ← mod(r, fwdPort ← min(sLoad[]))
8:          cm_s ← mod(r_s, srcIP ← min(sLoad[]))
9:          send_message(FlowMod(cm, sw))
10:         send_message(FlowMod(cm_s, sw))
11:         sLoad[max(sLoad[])]--
12:         sLoad[min(sLoad[])]++
13:     end if
14: end handler
```

References

[1] N. Feamster, J. Rexford, and E. Zegura, "The road to SDN," *SIGCOMM Computer Communication Review*, 2014.

[2] N. McKeown, T. Anderson, H. Balakrishnan, G. Parulkar, L. Peterson, J. Rexford, S. Shenker, and J. Turner, "OpenFlow: Enabling Innovation in Campus Networks," *SIGCOMM Comput. Commun. Rev.*, 2008.

[3] A. R. Curtis, J. C. Mogul, J. Tourrilhes, P. Yalagandula, P. Sharma, and S. Banerjee, "DevoFlow: scaling flow management for high-performance networks," *SIGCOMM*, 2011.

[4] N. Handigol, S. Seetharaman, M. Flajslik, N. McKeown, and R. Johari, "Plug-n-Serve: Load-balancing web traffic using OpenFlow," *SIGCOMM*, 2009.

[5] H. Hu, G.-J. Ahn, W. Han, and Z. Zhao, "Towards a Reliable SDN Firewall," in *ONS*, 2014.

[6] N. Feamster, J. Rexford, S. Shenker, R. Clark, R. Hutchins, D. Levin, and J. Bailey, "SDX: A software-defined Internet exchange," *Open Networking Summit*, 2013.

[7] H. Mai, A. Khurshid, R. Agarwal, M. Caesar, P. B. Godfrey, and S. T. King, "Debugging the data plane with anteater," in *SIGCOMM*, 2011.

[8] P. Kazemian, G. Varghese, and N. McKeown, "Header space analysis: Static checking for networks," in *NSDI*, 2012.

[9] T. Ball, N. Bjørner, A. Gember, S. Itzhaky, A. Karbyshev, M. Sagiv, M. Schapira, and A. Valadarsky, "VeriCon: Towards Verifying Controller Programs in Software-defined Networks," in *PLDI*, 2014.

[10] J. McClurg, H. Hojjat, P. Černý, and N. Foster, "Efficient synthesis of network updates," in *PLDI*, 2015.

[11] G. D. Plotkin, N. Bjørner, N. P. Lopes, A. Rybalchenko, and G. Varghese, "Scaling network verification using symmetry and surgery," in *POPL*, 2016.

[12] A. Horn, A. Kheradmand, and M. R. Prasad, "Delta-net: Real-time Network Verification Using Atoms," in *NSDI*, 2017.

[13] P. Kazemian, M. Chang, H. Zeng, G. Varghese, N. McKeown, and S. Whyte, "Real Time Network Policy Checking Using Header Space Analysis," in *NSDI*, 2013.

[14] R. Stoenescu, M. Popovici, L. Negreanu, and C. Raiciu, "SymNet: Scalable symbolic execution for modern networks," in *SIGCOMM*, 2016.

[15] M. Canini, D. Venzano, P. Perešíni, D. Kostić, and J. Rexford, "A NICE Way to Test Openflow Applications," in *NSDI*, 2012.

[16] Y. Jia, "NetSMC : A Symbolic Model Checker for Stateful Network Verification," in *NSDI*, 2020.

[17] V. Klimis, G. Parisis, and B. Reus, "Towards Model Checking Real-World Software-Defined Networks," in *CAV*, 2020.

[18] R. Majumdar, S. Deep Tetali, and Z. Wang, "Kuai: A model checker for software-defined networks," in *FMCAD*, 2014.

[19] Y. Li, X. Yin, Z. Wang, J. Yao, X. Shi, J. Wu, H. Zhang, and Q. Wang, "A survey on network verification and testing with formal methods: Approaches and challenges," *IEEE Surveys & Tutorials*, 2019.

[20] M. Al-Fares, S. Radhakrishnan, and B. Raghavan, "Hedera: Dynamic Flow Scheduling for Data Center Networks." in *NSDI*, 2010.

[21] P. Ji, Z. Ge, J. Kurose, and D. Towsley, "A comparison of hard-state and soft-state signaling protocols," *IEEE/ACM Transactions on Networking*, 2007.

[22] V. R. Pratt, "Semantical considerations on Floyd-Hoare logic," in *FOCS*, 1976.

[23] A. Pnueli, J. Xu, and L. Zuck, "Liveness with $(0, 1, \infty)$-counter abstraction," in *CAV*, 2002.

[24] D. Peled, "All from one, one for all: on model checking using representatives," in *CAV*, 1993.

[25] V. Klimis, G. Parisis, and B. Reus, "Model Checking Software-Defined Networks with Flow Entries that Time Out (version with appendix)," *arXiv: 2008.06149 [cs.NI]*, 2020.

[26] G. Behrmann, A. David, K. G. Larsen, P. Pettersson, and W. Yi, "Developing UPPAAL over 15 years," *Software: Practice and Experience*, 2011.

18

Parallelization Techniques for Verifying Neural Networks

Haoze Wu[1] , Alex Ozdemir[1] , Aleksandar Zeljić[1], Kyle Julian[1], Ahmed Irfan[1], Divya Gopinath[2],
Sadjad Fouladi[1], Guy Katz[5], Corina Pasareanu[3,4], and Clark Barrett[1]
[1]Stanford University, USA. [2]NASA Ames, KBR Inc. [3]NASA Ames, Moffett Field, CA.
[4]Carnegie Mellon University, USA. [5]The Hebrew University of Jerusalem, Israel.

Abstract—**Inspired by recent successes of parallel techniques for solving Boolean satisfiability, we investigate a set of strategies and heuristics to leverage parallelism and improve the scalability of neural network verification. We present a general description of the Split-and-Conquer partitioning algorithm, implemented within the Marabou framework, and discuss its parameters and heuristic choices. In particular, we explore two novel partitioning strategies, that partition the input space or the phases of the neuron activations, respectively. We introduce a branching heuristic and a direction heuristic that are based on the notion of polarity. We also introduce a highly parallelizable pre-processing algorithm for simplifying neural network verification problems. An extensive experimental evaluation shows the benefit of these techniques on both existing and new benchmarks. A preliminary experiment ultra-scaling our algorithm using a large distributed cloud-based platform also shows promising results.**

I. INTRODUCTION

Recent breakthroughs in machine learning, specifically the rise of *deep neural networks (DNNs)* [1], have expanded the horizon of real-world problems that can be tackled effectively. Increasingly, complex systems are created using machine learning models [2] instead of using conventional engineering approaches. Machine learning models are trained on a set of (labeled) examples, using algorithms that allow the model to capture their properties and generalize them to unseen inputs. In practice, DNNs can significantly outperform hand-crafted systems, especially in fields where precise problem formulation is challenging, such as image classification [3], speech recognition [4] and game playing [5].

Despite their overall success, the black-box nature of DNNs calls into question their trustworthiness and hinders their application in safety-critical domains. These limitations are exacerbated by the fact that DNNs are known to be vulnerable to *adversarial perturbations*, small modifications to the inputs that lead to wrong responses from the network [6], and real-world attacks have already been carried out against safety-critical deployments of DNNs [7, 8]. One promising approach for addressing these concerns is the use of formal methods to certify and/or obtain rigorous guarantees about DNN behavior. Early work in DNN formal verification [9, 10] focused on translating DNNs and their properties into formats supported by existing verification tools like general-purpose *Satis ability Modulo Theories* (SMT) solvers (e.g., Z3 [11], CVC4 [12]). However, this approach was limited to small toy networks (roughly tens of nodes).

More recently, a number of DNN-specific approaches and solvers, including Reluplex [13], ReluVal [14], Neurify [15], Planet [16], and Marabou [17], have been proposed and developed. These techniques scale to hundreds or a few thousand nodes. While a significant improvement, this is still several orders of magnitude fewer than the number of nodes present in many real-world applications. Scalability thus continues to be a challenge and the subject of active research.

Inspired by recent successes with parallelizing SAT solvers [18, 19], we propose a set of strategies and heuristics for leveraging parallelism to improve the scalability of neural network verification. The paper makes the following contributions: 1) We present a divide-and-conquer algorithm, called Split-and-Conquer (S&C), for neural network verification that is parameterized by different partition strategies and constraint solvers (Sec. III). 2) We describe two partitioning strategies for this algorithm (Sec. III-B): one that works by partitioning the input domain and a second one that performs case splitting based on the activation functions in the neural network. The first strategy was briefly mentioned in the Marabou tool paper [17]; we describe it in detail here. The second strategy is new. 3) We introduce the notion of *polarity* and use it to refine the partitioning (Sec. III-C); 4) We introduce a highly parallelizable pre-processing algorithm that significantly simplifies verification problems (Sec. III-D); 5) We show how polarity can additionally be used to speed up satisfiable queries (Sec. III-E); and 6) We implement the techniques in the Marabou framework and evaluate on existing and new neural network verification benchmarks from the aviation domain. We also perform an *ultra-scalability* experiment using cloud computing (Sec. IV). Our experiments show that the new and improved Marabou can outperform the previous version of Marabou as well as other state-of-the-art verification tools such as Neurify, especially on perception networks with a large number of inputs. We begin with preliminaries, review related work in Sec. V, and conclude in Sec. VI.

II. PRELIMINARIES

In this section, we briefly review neural networks and their formalization, as well as the Reluplex algorithm for verification of neural networks.

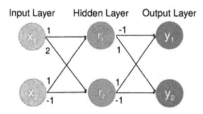

Fig. 1: A small feed-forward DNN $\mathcal{N}$.

A. Formalizing Neural Networks

Deep Neural Networks. A feed-forward *Deep Neural Network* (DNN) consists of a sequence of layers, including an input layer, an output layer, and one or more hidden layers in between. Each non-input layer comprises multiple *neurons*, whose values can be computed from the outputs of the preceding layer. Given an assignment of values to inputs, the output of the DNN can be computed by iteratively computing the values of neurons in each layer. Typically, a neuron's value is determined by computing an affine function of the outputs of the neurons in the previous layer and then applying a non-linear function, known as an *activation function*. A popular activation function is the Rectified Linear Unit (ReLU), defined as $ReLU(x) = max(0, x)$ (see [3, 20, 21]). In this paper, we focus on DNNs with ReLU activation functions; thus the output of each neuron is computed as $ReLU(w_1 \cdot v_1 + \ldots w_n \cdot v_n + b)$, where $v_1 \ldots v_n$ are the values of the previous layer's neurons, $w_1 \ldots w_n$ are the weight parameters, and b is a bias parameter associated with the neuron. A neuron is *active* or in the *active phase*, if its output is positive; otherwise, it is *inactive* or in the *inactive phase*.

Verification of Neural Networks. A neural network verification problem has two components: a neural network N, and a property P. P is often of the form $P_{in} \Rightarrow P_{out}$, where P_{in} is a formula over the inputs of N and P_{out} is a formula over the outputs of N. Typically, P_{in} defines an input region I, and P states that for each point in I, P_{out} holds for the output layer. Given a query like this, a verification tool tries to find a counter-example: an input point i in I, such that when applied to N, P_{out} is false over the resulting outputs. P holds only if such a counter-example does not exist.

The property to be verified may arise from the specific domain where the network is deployed. For instance, for networks that are used as controllers in an unmanned aircraft collision avoidance system (e.g., the ACAS Xu networks [13]), we would expect them to produce sensible advisories according to the location and the speed of the intruder planes in the vicinity. On the other hand, there are also properties that are generally desirable for a neural network. One such property is *local adversarial robustness* [22], which states that a small norm-bounded input perturbation should not cause major spikes in the network's output. More generally, a property may be an arbitrary formula over input values, output values, and values of hidden layers—such problems arise for example in the investigation of the neural networks' explainability [23], where one wants to check whether the activation of a certain

ReLU r implies a certain output behavior (e.g., the neural network always predicts a certain class). The verification of neural networks with ReLU functions is decidable and NP-Complete [13]. As with many other verification problems, scalability is a key challenge.

VNN Formulas. We introduce the notion of VNN (Verification of Neural Network) formulas to formalize Neural Network verification queries. Let $\mathcal{X}$ be a set of variables. A *linear constraint* is of the form $\sum_{x_i \in \mathcal{X}} a_i x_i \bowtie b$, where a_i, b are rational constants, and $\bowtie \in \{\leq, \geq, =\}$. A *ReLU constraint* is of the form $ReLU(x_i) = x_j$, where $x_i, x_j \in \mathcal{X}$.

Definition 1. *A VNN formula ϕ is a conjunction of linear constraints and ReLU constraints.*

A feed-forward neural network can be encoded as a VNN formula as follows. Each ReLU r is represented by introducing a pair of input/output variables r_b, r_f and then adding a ReLU constraint $ReLU(r_b) = r_f$. We refer to r_b as the *backward-facing variable*, and it is used to connect r to the preceding layer. r_f is called the *forward-facing variable* and is used to connect r to the next layer. The weighted sums are encoded as linear constraints.

In general, a property could be any formula P over the variables used to represent $\mathcal{N}$. To check whether P holds on $\mathcal{N}$, we simply conjoin the representation of $\mathcal{N}$ with the negation of P and use a constraint solver to check for satisfiability. P holds iff the constraint is unsatisfiable.

Note that a solver for VNN formulas can solve a property P only if the negation of P is also a VNN formula. We assume this is the case in this paper, but more general properties can be handled by decomposing $\neg P$ into a disjunction of VNN formulas and checking each separately (or, equivalently, using a DPLL(T) approach [24]). This works as long as the atomic constraints are linear. Non-linear constraints (other than ReLU) are beyond the scope of this paper.

B. The Reluplex Procedure

The Reluplex procedure [13] is a sound, complete and terminating algorithm that decides the satisfiability of a VNN formula. The procedure extends the Simplex algorithm—a standard efficient decision procedure for conjunctions of linear constraints—to handle ReLU constraints. At a high level, the algorithm iteratively searches for an assignment that satisfies all the linear constraints, but treats the ReLU constraints lazily in the hope that many of them will be irrelevant for proving the property. Once a satisfying assignment for linear constraints is found, the ReLU constraints are evaluated. If all the ReLU constraints are satisfied, a model is found and the procedure concludes that the VNN formula is satisfiable. However, some ReLU constraints may be violated and need to be fixed. There are two ways to fix a violated ReLU constraint r: 1) *repair the assignment* by updating the assignment of forward-facing r_f or backward-facing variable r_b to satisfy r, or 2) *case split* by considering separate cases for each phase of r (adding the appropriate constraints in each case). In both cases, the search continues using the Simplex algorithm, in the first with

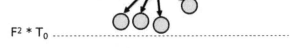

Fig. 2: An execution of the S&C algorithm.

Algorithm 1 Split-and-Conquer

Input: query ϕ, initial partition size N_0, initial timeout T_0, partition size N, timeout factor F
Output: SAT/UNSAT
for $\psi \in \textbf{partition}(\phi, N_0)$ **do**
   $Q.\text{enqueue}(\langle \psi, T_0 \rangle)$
while $Q.\text{notEmpty}()$ **do**
   $\langle \phi', t \rangle \leftarrow Q.\text{dequeue}()$
   $result \leftarrow \textbf{solve}(\phi', t)$
   if $result = $ SAT **then**
      return SAT
   else if $result = $ TIMEOUT **then**
      for $\psi \in \textbf{partition}(\phi', N)$ **do**
         $Q.\text{enqueue}(\langle \psi, t \cdot F \rangle)$
return UNSAT

---

a soft correction via assignment update and in the second by adding hard constraints to the linear problem. Lazy handling of ReLUs is achieved by the threshold parameter t — the number of times a ReLU is repaired before the algorithm performs a case split. In [13], this parameter was set to 20, but even more eager splitting is beneficial in some cases. The Reluplex algorithm also uses bound propagation to fix ReLUs to one phase whenever possible.

In this paper, we explore heuristic choices behind the two options to handle violated ReLU constraints. In the case of assignment repair, the question is which variable assignment, r_f or r_b, to modify (often both are possible). We refer to the strategy used to make this decision as the *direction heuristic*, and we discuss direction heuristics, especially in the context of parallel solving in Sec. III-E. For case splitting, the question is which ReLU constraint to choose. We refer to the strategy used for making this decision as the *branching heuristic*. We explore branching heuristics and their application to parallelizing the algorithm in Sec. III-B and Sec. III-C.

III. S&C: PARALLELIZING THE RELUPLEX PROCEDURE

In this section, we present a parallel algorithm called *Split-and-Conquer* (or simply S&C) for solving VNN formulas, using the Reluplex procedure and an iterative-deepening strategy. We discuss two partitioning strategies: input interval splitting and ReLU case splitting.

Remark. A divide-and-conquer approach with an input-splitting strategy was described in the Marabou tool paper [17], albeit briefly and informally. We provide here a more general framework, which includes new techniques and heuristics, described in detail below.

A. The S&C algorithm

The S&C algorithm partitions an input problem into several sub-problems (that are ideally easier to solve) and tries to solve each sub-problem within a given time budget. If solving a problem exceeds the time budget, that problem is further partitioned and the resulting sub-problems are allocated an increased time budget. Fig. 2 shows solving of problem ϕ as a tree, where the root of the tree denotes the original problem. Sub-problems that exceed their allotted time budget

are partitioned, becoming inner nodes, and leaves are sub-problems solved within their time budget. A formula ϕ is satisfiable if some leaf is satisfiable. If the partitioning is *exhaustive*, that is: $\phi := \bigvee_{\phi_i \in \textbf{partition}(\phi, n)} \phi_i$, for any $n > 1$, then ϕ is unsatisfiable iff all the leaves are unsatisfiable.

The pseudo-code of the S&C algorithm is shown in Algorithm 1, which can be seen as a framework parameterized by the partitioning heuristic and the underlying solver. Details of these parameters are abstracted away within the **partition** and **solve** functions respectively and will be discussed in subsequent sections. The S&C algorithm takes as input the VNN formula ϕ and the following parameters: initial number of partitions N_0, initial timeout T_0, number of partitions N, and the timeout factor F. During solving, S&C maintains a queue Q of ⟨query, timeout⟩ pairs, which is initialized with the partition $N_0 := \langle \phi, T_0 \rangle$. While the queue is not empty, the next pair $\langle \phi', t \rangle$ is retrieved from it, and the query ϕ' is solved with time budget t. If ϕ' is satisfiable, then the original query ϕ is satisfiable, and SAT is returned. If ϕ' times out, **partition**(ϕ', N) creates N sub-problems of ϕ', each of which is enqueued with an increased time budget $t \cdot F$. If the sub-problem ϕ' is unsatisfiable, no special action needs to be taken. If Q becomes empty, the original query is unsatisfiable and the algorithm returns UNSAT. Note that the main loop of the algorithm naturally lends itself to parallelization, since the **solve** calls are mutually independent and query-timeout pairs can be asynchronously enqueued and dequeued.

We state without proof the following result, which is a well-known property of such algorithms.

Theorem 1. *The Split-and-Conquer*(ϕ, N_0, T_0, N, F) *algorithm is sound and complete if the following holds: 1) the* **solve** *function is sound and complete; and 2) the* **partition** *function is exhaustive.*

In addition, with modest assumptions on **solve** and **partition**, and with $F > 1$, the algorithm can be shown to be terminating. In particular, it is terminating for the instantiations we consider below. The S&C algorithm can be tailored to the available computing resources (e.g., number of processors) by specifying the number of initial splits N_0. The other three search parameters of S&C specify the dynamic behavior of the algorithm, e.g. if T_0 and F are small, or if N is large, then new sub-queries are created frequently, which entails a more aggressive S&C strategy (and vice versa). Notice that we can completely discard the dynamic aspect of S&C by setting the initial timeout to be ∞.

A potential downside of the algorithm is that each call to **solve** that times out is essentially wasted time, overhead above and beyond the useful work needed to solve the problem. Fortunately, as the following theorem shows, the number of wasted calls is bounded.

Theorem 2. *When Algorithm 1 runs on an unsatisfiable formula with $N \geq N_0$, the fraction of calls to* **solve** *that time out is less than $\frac{1}{N}$.*

Proof. Consider first the case when $N = N_0$. We can view S&C's UNSAT proof as constructing an N-ary tree, as shown in Fig. 2. The ℓ leaf nodes are calls to **solve** that do not time out. The t non-leaves are calls to **solve** that do time out. Since this is a tree, the total number of nodes n is one more than the number of edges. Since each query that times out has an edge to each of its N sub-queries, the number of edges is Nt. Thus we have $n = Nt + 1$ which can be rearranged to show the fraction of queries that time out: $\frac{t}{n} = \frac{1 - \frac{1}{n}}{N} < \frac{1}{N}$. If $N < N_0$, then let $k = N_0 - N$. The number of nodes is then $n = Nt + k + 1$, and the result follows as before. $\square$

B. Partitioning Strategies

A partitioning strategy specifies how to decompose a VNN formula to produce (hopefully easier) sub-problems.

A ReLU is *fixed* when the bounds on the backward-facing or forward-facing variable either imply that the ReLU is active or imply that the ReLU is inactive. Fixing as many ReLUs as possible reduces the complexity of the resulting problem.

With these concepts in mind, we present two strategies: 1) *input-based partitioning* creates case splits over the ranges of input variables, relying on bound propagation to fix ReLUs, whereas 2) *ReLU-based partitioning* creates case splits that fix the phase of ReLUs directly. Both strategies are exhaustive, ensuring soundness and completeness of the S&C algorithm (by Theorem 1). The *branching heuristic* which determines the choice of input variable, respectively ReLU, on which to split, can have a significant impact on performance. The branching heuristic should keep the total runtime of the sub-problems low as well as achieve a good *balance* between them. To illustrate, suppose the sub-problems created by splitting ReLU$_1$ take 10 and 300 seconds to solve, whereas those created by splitting ReLU$_2$ take 150 and 160 seconds to solve. Though the total solving time is the same, the more balanced split, on ReLU$_2$, results in shorter wall-clock time (given two parallel workers).

If most splits led to easier and balanced sub-formulas, then S&C would perform well, even without a carefully-designed branching heuristic. However, we have observed that this is not the case for many possible splits: the time taken to solve one (or both!) of the sub-problems generated by such splits is comparable to that required by the original formula (or even

worse). Therefore, an effective branching heuristic is crucial. We describe two such heuristics below.

Input-based Partitioning. This simple partitioning strategy performs case splits over the range of an input variable. As an example, consider a VNN formula $\phi := (-2 \leq x_1 \leq 1) \wedge (-2 \leq x_2 \leq 2)$, where x_1 and x_2 are the two input variables of a neural network encoded by ϕ. Suppose we call **partition**(ϕ, 2) using the input-splitting strategy. The choice is between splitting on the range of x_1 or the range of x_2. If we choose x_1, the result is two sub-formulas, ϕ_1 and ϕ_2, where: $\phi_1 := (-2 \leq x_1 < -0.5) \wedge (-2 \leq x_2 \leq 2)$ and $\phi_2 := (-0.5 \leq x_1 \leq 1) \wedge (-2 \leq x_2 \leq 2)$. An obvious heuristic is to choose the input with largest range. A more complex heuristic was introduced in [17]. It samples the network repeatedly, which yields considerable overhead. In fact, both of these heuristics perform reasonably well on benchmarks with only a few inputs (the ACAS Xu benchmarks, for example). Unfortunately, regardless of the heuristic used, this strategy suffers from the "curse of dimensionality" — with a large number of inputs it becomes increasingly difficult to fix ReLUs by splitting the range of only one input variable. Thus, the input-partitioning strategy does not scale well on such networks (e.g., perception networks), which often have hundreds or thousands of inputs.

ReLU-based Partitioning. A complementary strategy is to partition the search space by fixing ReLUs directly. Consider a VNN formula $\phi := \psi \wedge (\text{ReLU}(x) = y)$. A call to **partition**(ϕ, 2) using the ReLU-based strategy results in two sub-formulas ϕ_1 and ϕ_2, where $\phi_1 := \psi \wedge (x \leq 0) \wedge (y = 0)$ and $\phi_2 := \psi \wedge (x > 0) \wedge (x = y)$. Note that here, ϕ_1 is capturing the inactive and ϕ_2 the active phase of the ReLU. Next, we consider a heuristic for choosing a ReLU to split on.

C. Polarity-based Branching Heuristics

We want to estimate the difficulty of sub-problems created by a partitioning strategy. One key related metric is the number of bounds that can be tightened as the result of a ReLU-split. As a light-weight proxy for this metric, we propose a metric called *polarity*.

Definition 2. *Given the ReLU constraint $\text{ReLU}(x) = y$, and the bounds $a \leq x \leq b$, where $a < 0$, and $b > 0$, the polarity of the ReLU is defined as: $p = \frac{a+b}{b-a}$.*

Polarity ranges from -1 to 1 and measures the symmetry of a ReLU's bounds with respect to zero. For example, if we split on a ReLU constraint with polarity close to 1, the bound on the forward-facing variable in the active case, $[0, b]$, will be much wider than in the inactive case, $[a, 0]$. Intuitively, forward bound tightening would therefore result in tighter bounds in the inactive case. This means the inactive case will probably be much easier than the active case, so the partition is unbalanced and therefore undesirable. On the other hand, a ReLU with a polarity close to 0 is more likely to have balanced sub-problems. We also observe that ReLUs in early hidden layers are more likely to produce bound tightening by forward bound propagation (as there are more ReLUs that depend on them).

Algorithm 2 Iterative Propagation

Input: VNN query ψ, timeout t
Output: preprocessed query ψ.
$progress$; ψ ψ
while $progress =$ **do**
  $progress$
  for r in **getUnfixedReLUs**(ψ) **do**
      choosePhase(r)
  $result = $ **solve**(ψ t)
  if $result = $ UNSAT **then**
      flipPhase( )
    ψ ψ
    $progress$
return ψ

We thus propose a heuristic that picks the ReLU whose polarity is closest to 0 among the first $k\%$ unfixed ReLUs, where k is a configurable parameter. Note that, in order to compute polarities, we need all input variables to be bounded, which is a reasonable assumption.

D. Fixing ReLU Constraints with Iterative Propagation

As discussed earlier, the performance of S&C depends heavily on ReLU splits that result in balanced sub-formulas. However, sometimes a considerable portion of ReLUs in a given neural network cannot be split in this way. To eliminate such ReLUs we propose a preprocessing technique called *iterative propagation*, which aims to discover and fix ReLUs with unbalanced partitions.

Concretely, for each ReLU in the VNN formula, we temporarily fix the ReLU to one of its phases and then attempt to solve the problem with a short timeout. The goal is to detect unbalanced and (hopefully) easy unsatisfiable cases. Pseudocode is presented in Algorithm 2. The algorithm takes as input the formula ◁ and the timeout t, and, if successful, returns an equivalent formula ◁ which has fewer unfixed ReLUs than ◁. The outer loop computes the fixed point, while the inner loop iterates through the as-of-yet unfixed ReLUs. For each unfixed ReLU, the **choosePhase** function yields constraints of the easier (i.e. smaller) phase. If the solver returns UNSAT, then we can safely fix the ReLU to its other phase using the **flipPhase** function. We ignore the case where the solver returns SAT, since in practice this only occurs for formulas that are very easy in the first place.

Iterative propagation complements S&C, because the likelihood of finding balanced partitions is increased by fixing ReLUs that lead to unbalanced partitions. Moreover, iterative propagation is highly parallelizable, as each ReLU-fixing attempt can be solved independently. In Section IV, we report results using iterative propagation as a preprocessing step, though it is possible to integrate the two processes more closely, e.g., by performing iterative propagation after every **partition** call.

E. Speeding Up Satis able Checks with Polarity-Based Direction Heuristics

In this section, we discuss how the polarity metric introduced in Sec. III-C can be used to solve satisfiable instances quickly. When splitting on a ReLU, the Reluplex algorithm faces the same choice as the S&C algorithm. For unsatisfiable cases, the order in which ReLU case splits are done make little difference on average, but for satisfiable instances, it can be very beneficial if the algorithm is able to hone in on a satisfiable sub-problem. We refer to the strategy for picking which ReLU phase to split on first as the *direction heuristic*.

We propose using the polarity metric to guide the direction heuristic for S&C. If the polarity of a branching ReLU is positive, then we process the active phase first; if the polarity is negative, we do the reverse. Intuitively, formulas with wider bounds are more likely to be satisfiable, and the polarity direction heuristic prefers the phase corresponding to wider bounds for the ReLU's backward-facing variable.

Repairing an assignment when a ReLU is violated can also be guided by polarity (recall the description of the Reluplex procedure from Sec. II), as choosing between forward- or backward-facing variables amounts to choosing which ReLU phase to explore first. Therefore, we use this same direction heuristic to guide the choice of forward- or backward-facing variables when repairing the assignment. For example, suppose constraint $\text{ReLU}(x_b) = x_f$ is part of a VNN formula ◁. Suppose the range of x_b is [2 1], $A(x_b) =$ 1 and $A(x_f) = 1$, where A is the current variable assignment computed by the Simplex algorithm. To repair this violated ReLU constraint, we can either assign 0 to x_f or assign 1 to x_b. In this case, the ReLU has negative polarity, meaning the negative phase is associated with wider input bounds, so our heuristic chooses to set $A(x_f) = 0$.

We will see in our experimental results (Sec. IV) that these direction heuristics improve performance on satisfiable instances. Interestingly, they also enhance performance on unsatisfiable instances.

IV. EXPERIMENTAL EVALUATION

In this section, we discuss our implementation of the proposed techniques and evaluate its performance on a diverse set of real-world benchmarks – safety properties of control systems and robustness properties of perception models.

A. Implementation

We implemented the techniques discussed above in Marabou [17], which is an open-source neural network verification tool implementing the Reluplex algorithm. Marabou is available at https://github.com/NeuralNetworkVerification/Marabou/[1]. The tool also integrates the symbolic bound tightening techniques introduced in [14]. We refer to Marabou running the S&C algorithm as S&C-Marabou. Two partitioning strategies are supported: the original input-based partitioning

---

[1]The version of the tool used in the experiments is available at https://github.com/NeuralNetworkVerification/Marabou/releases/tag/FMCAD20.

strategy and our new ReLU-splitting strategy. All S&C configurations use the following parameters: the initial partition size N_0 is the number of available processors; the initial timeout T_0 is 10% of the network size in seconds; the number of online partitions N is 4; and the timeout factor F is 1 5. The k parameter for the branching heuristic (see Sec. III-C) is set to 5. The per-ReLU timeout for iterative propagation is 2 seconds. When the input dimension is low (10), symbolic bound tightening is turned on, and the threshold parameter t (see Sec. II) is reduced from 20 to 1. The parameters were chosen using a grid search on a small subset of benchmarks.

B. Benchmarks

The benchmark set consists of network-property pairs, with networks from three different application domains: aircraft collision avoidance (ACAS Xu), aircraft localization (Tiny-TaxiNet), and digit recognition (MNIST). Properties include robustness and domain-specific safety properties.

ACAS Xu. The ACAS Xu family of VNN benchmarks was introduced in [13] and uses prototype neural networks trained to represent an early version of the ACAS Xu decision logic [2]. The ACAS Xu benchmarks are composed of 45 fully-connected feed-forward neural networks, each with 6 hidden layers and 50 ReLU nodes per layer. The networks issue turning advisories to the controller of an unmanned aircraft to avoid near midair collisions. The network has 5 inputs (encoding the relation of the ownship to an intruder) and 5 outputs (denoting advisories: e.g., weak left, strong right). Proving that the network does not produce erroneous advisories is paramount for ensuring safe aviation operation. We consider four realistic properties expected of the 45 networks. These properties, numbered 1–4, are described in [13].

TinyTaxiNet. The TinyTaxiNet family contains perception networks used in vision-based *autonomous taxiing*: the task of predicting the position and orientation of an aircraft on the taxiway, so that a controller can accurately adjust the position of the aircraft [25]. The input to the network is a downsampled grey-scale image of the taxiway captured from a camera on the aircraft. The network produces two outputs: the lateral distance to the runway centerline, and the heading angle error with respect to the centerline. Proving that the networks accurately predict the location of the aircraft even when the camera image suffers from small noise is safety-critical. This property can be captured as local adversarial robustness. If the kth output of the network is expected to be b_k for inputs near $\mathbf{a}$, we can check the unsatisfiability of the following VNN formula:

$$(y_k \quad b_k +) \bigwedge_{i=1}^{N} (a_i \quad x_i \quad a_i +)$$

where $\mathbf{x}$ denotes the actual network input, N the number of network inputs, and y_k the actual k^{th} output. The network is ( )-locally robust on $\mathbf{a}$, only if the formula is unsatisfiable. The training images are compressed to either 2048 or 128 pixels, with value range [0,1]. We evaluate the local adversarial robustness of two networks. TaxiNet1 has 2048

inputs, 1 convolutional layer, 2 feedforward layers, and 128 ReLUs. TaxiNet2 has 128 inputs, 5 convolutional layers, and a total of 176 ReLUs. For each network, we generate 100 local adversarial robustness queries concerning the first output (distance to the centerline). For each model, we sample 100 uniformly random images from the training data, and sample ( ) pairs uniformly from the set 0 004 3 0 004 9 0 008 3 0 008 9 0 016 9 . Setting = 0 004 allows a 1 pixel-value perturbation in pixel brightness along each input dimension, and the units of are meters. We chose the values of the perturbation bounds such that the resulting set contains a mixture of SAT and UNSAT instances with more emphasis on the latter – UNSAT problems are considered more interesting in the verification domain.

MNIST. In addition to the two neural network families with safety-critical real-world applications, we evaluate our techniques on three fully-connected feed-forward neural networks (MNIST1, MNIST2, MNIST3) trained on the MNIST dataset [26] to classify hand-written digits. Each network has 784 inputs (representing a grey-scale image) with value range [0,1], and 10 outputs (each representing a digit). MNIST1 has 10 hidden layers and 10 neurons per layer; MNIST2 has 10 hidden layers and 20 neurons per layer; MNIST3 has 20 hidden layers and 20 neurons per layer. While shallower and smaller networks may be sufficient for identifying digits and are also easier to verify, we evaluate on deeper and larger architectures because we want to 1) stress-test our techniques, and 2) evaluate the effect of moving towards larger perception network sizes like those used in more challenging applications. We consider *targeted robustness* queries, which asks whether, for an input $\mathbf{x}$ and an incorrect output y , there exists a point in the -ball around x that is classified as y . We sample 100 such queries for each network, by choosing random training images and random incorrect labels. We choose values evenly from 0 004 0 008 0 0016 0 0032 .

C. Experimental Evaluation

We present the results of the following experiments: 1) Evaluation of each technique's effect on run-time performance of Marabou on the three benchmark sets. We also compare against Neurify, a state-of-the-art solver on the same benchmarks. 2) An analysis of trade-offs when running iterative propagation pre-processing. 3) Exploration of S&C scalability at a large scale, using cloud computing.

1) Evaluation of the techniques on ACAS Xu, TinyTaxiNet, MNIST : We denote the ReLU-based partitioning strategy as **R**, polarity-based direction heuristics as **D**, and iterative propagation as **P**. We denote as **S** a hybrid strategy that uses input-based partitioning on ACAS Xu networks, and ReLU-based partitioning on perception networks. We run four combinations of our techniques: 1) **R**; 2) **S+D**; 3) **S+P**; 4) **S+D+P**, and compare them with two baseline configurations: 1) the sequential mode of Marabou (denoted as **M**); 2) S&C-Marabou with its default input-based partitioning strategy (denoted as **I**).

We compare with Neurify [15], a state-of-the-art solver, on the same benchmarks. Neurify derives over-approximations of

TABLE I: Evaluation of the Techniques on ACAS Xu, TinyTaxiNet, MNIST

Bench. [# inst.]	M		I		R		S		S+D		S+P		S+D+P		Neurify	
	#S	Time	#S	Time	#S	Time	#S	Time	#S	Time	#S	Time	#S	Time	#S	Time
ACAS	40	17224	**45**	**4884**	**45**	5009	**45**	**4884**	**45**	5480	**45**	8419	**45**	7244	39	4167
[180]	101	57398	130	48954	125	45036	130	48954	131	51413	130	50828	131	53717	**133**	1438
TinyTaxi.	34	4591	34	1815	34	433	34	433	34	419	34	533	**35**	1172	**35**	**88**
[200]	141	33909	110	24088	147	23079	147	23079	147	22345	**149**	**20583**	**149**	21949	146	7158
MNIST	11	2349	19	13032	22	9680	22	9680	26	11727	20	9956	**29**	19351	27	151
[300]	140	64418	78	27134	181	52776	181	52776	183	59195	184	67625	**185**	68307	153	10640
All	85	24164	98	19731	101	15122	101	14997	105	17626	99	18908	**109**	27767	101	4406
[680]	382	155725	318	100176	453	120891	458	124809	461	132953	463	139036	**465**	143973	432	19236

Number of solved instances (#S) and run-time in seconds of different configurations. For each benchmark set, top and bottom rows show data for satisfiable (SAT) and unsatisfiable (UNSAT) instances respectively. The results for configuration **S** are computed virtually from **R** and **I**.

the output bounds using techniques such as symbolic interval analysis and linear relaxation. On ACAS Xu benchmarks, it operates by iteratively partitioning the input region to reduce error in the over-approximated bounds (to prove UNSAT) and by randomly sampling points in the input region (to prove SAT). On other networks, Neurify uses off-the-shelf solvers to handle ReLU-nodes whose bounds are potentially overestimated. Neurify also leverages parallelism, as different input regions or linear programs can be checked in parallel.

We run all Marabou configurations and Neurify on a cluster equipped with Intel Xeon E5-2699 v4 CPUs running CentOS 7.7. 8 cores and 64GB RAM are allocated for each job, except for the **M** configuration, which uses 1 processor and 8GB RAM per job. Each job is given a 1-hour wall-clock timeout.

Results. Table I shows a breakdown of the number of solved instances and the run-time for all Marabou configurations and for Neurify. We group the results by SAT and UNSAT instances. For each row, we highlight the entries corresponding to the configuration that solves the most instances (ties broken by run-time). Here are some key observations:

– On ACAS Xu benchmarks, both input-based partitioning (**I**) and ReLU-based partitioning (**R**) yield performance gain compared with the sequential solver (**M**), with **I** being more effective. On perception networks, **I** solves significantly fewer instances than **M** while **R** continues to be effective.
– Comparing the performance of **S**, **S+D**, and **S+P** suggests that the polarity-based direction heuristics and iterative propagation each improve the overall performance of S&C-Marabou. Interestingly, the polarity-based heuristic improves the performance on not only SAT but also UNSAT instances, suggesting that by affecting how ReLU constraints are repaired, direction heuristics also favorably impact the order of ReLU-splitting. On the other hand, iterative propagation alone only improves performance on UNSAT instances. **S+D+P** solves the most instances among all the Marabou configurations, indicating that the direction heuristics and iterative propagation are complementary to each other.
– **S+D+P** solves significantly more instances than Neurify overall. While Neurify's strategy on Acas Xu benchmarks allows it to dedicate more time on proving UNSAT by rapidly partitioning the input region (thus yielding much shorter run-times than **S+D+P** on that benchmark set), its performance

on SAT instances is subject to (un)lucky guesses. When it comes to perception neural networks that are deeper and have higher input dimensions, symbolic bound propagation, on which Neurify heavily relies, becomes more expensive and less effective. In contrast, Marabou does not rely solely on symbolic interval analysis, but in addition uses interval bound-tightening techniques (see [17] for details).

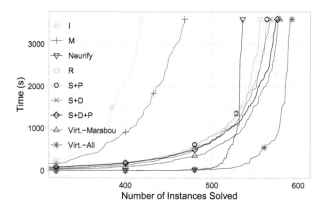

Fig. 3 Cactus plot: all solvers + two virtual best configurations.

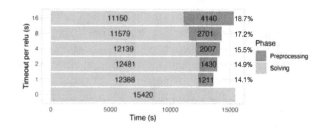

Fig. 4 The effect of varying per-ReLU timeout in preprocessing.

Fig. 3 shows a cactus plot of the 6 Marabou configurations and Neurify on all benchmarks. In this plot, we also include two virtual portfolio configurations: **Virt.-Marabou** takes the best run-time among all Marabou configurations for each benchmark, and **Virt.-All** includes Neurify in the portfolio. Interestingly, **S+D+P** is outperformed by **S+D** in the beginning but surpasses **S+D** after 500 seconds. This suggests that iterative propagation creates overhead for easy instances, but benefits the search in the long run. We also observe that Neurify can solve a subset of the benchmarks very rapidly, but solves very few benchmarks after 1500 seconds. One possible explanation is that Neurify splits the input region and makes solver calls eagerly. While this allows it to resolve some queries quickly, it also results in rapid (exponential) growth of the number of sub-regions and solver calls. By contrast, Marabou splits lazily. While it creates overhead sometimes, it results in more solved instances overall. The **Virt.-All** configuration solves significantly more instances than **Virt.-Marabou**, suggesting that the two procedures are complementary to each other. We note that the bound tightening techniques presented in Neurify can be potentially integrated into Marabou, and the polarity-based heuristics and iterative propagation could also be used to improve Neurify and other VNN tools.

2) Costs of Iterative Propagation: As mentioned in Sec. 2, intuitively, the longer the time budget during iterative propagation, the more ReLUs should get fixed. To investigate this trade-off between the number of fixed ReLUs and the overhead, we choose a smaller set of benchmarks (40 ACAS Xu benchmarks, 40 TinyTaxiNet benchmarks, and 40 MNIST benchmarks), and vary the timeout parameter t of iterative propagation. Each job is run with 32 cores, and a wall-clock timeout of 1 hour, on the same cluster as in Experiment IV-C1.

Results. Fig. 4 shows the preprocessing time + solving time of different configurations on commonly solved instances. The percentage next to each bar represents the average percentage of ReLUs fixed by iterative propagation. Though the run-time and unfixed ReLUs continue to decrease as we invest more in iterative propagation, performing iterative propagation no longer provides performance gain when the per-ReLU-timeout exceeds 8 seconds.

3) Ultra-Scalability of S&C: S&C-Marabou runs on a single machine, which intrinsically limits its scalability to the number of hardware threads. To investigate how the S&C algorithm scales with much higher degrees of parallelism, we implemented it on top of the gg platform [27].

The gg platform facilitates expressing parallelizable computations and executing them. To use it, the programmer expresses their computation as a dependency graph of tasks, where each task is an executable program that reads and writes files. The output files can encode the result of the task, or an extension to the task graph that must be executed in order to produce that result. The gg platform includes tools for executing tasks in parallel. Tasks can be executed *locally*, using different processes, or *remotely*, using cloud services such as AWS Lambda [28]. Since these cloud services offer a high degree of concurrency with little setup or administration, gg is a convenient tool for executing massively parallel computations [27].

In our implementation of the S&C algorithm on top of gg, each task runs the base solver with a timeout. If the solver completes, the task returns the result; otherwise it returns a task graph extension encoding the division of the problem into sub-queries. We call this implementation of the S&C algorithm, *gg-Marabou.*

We measure the performance of S&C and gg-Marabou at varying levels of parallelism to establish that they perform

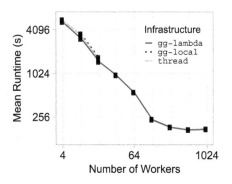

Fig. 5: Ultra-Scalability of S&C.

similarly and to evaluate the scalability of the S&C algorithm. Our experiments use three underlying infrastructures: S&C-Marabou (denoted `thread`), gg-Marabou executed locally (`gg-local`), and gg-Marabou executed remotely on AWS Lambda [28] (`gg-lambda`). We vary the parallelism level, p, from 4 to 16 for the local infrastructures and from 4 to 1000 for `gg-lambda`. For `gg-lambda`, we run 3 tests per benchmark, taking the median time to mitigate variation from the network. From the UNSAT ACAS Xu benchmarks which S&C-Marabou can solve in under two hours using 4 cores, we chose 5 of the hardest instances. We set $T_0 = 5\,\mathrm{s}$, $F = 15$, $N = 2^{(5+\log_2 p)}3$ and use the input-based partitioning strategy.

Results. Fig. 5 shows how mean runtime (across benchmarks) varies with parallelism level and infrastructure. Our first conclusion from Fig. 5 is that gg does **not** introduce significant overhead; at equal parallelism levels, all infrastructures perform similarly. Our second conclusion is that gg-Marabou scales well up to over a hundred workers. This is shown by the constant slope of the runtime/parallelism level line up to over a hundred workers. We note that the slope only flattens when total runtime is small: a few minutes.

V. RELATED WORK

Over the past few years, a number of tools for verifying neural network have emerged and broadly fall into two categories — precise and abstraction-based methods. Precise approaches are complete and usually encode the problem as an SAT/SMT/MILP constraint [13, 16, 17, 29, 30]. Abstraction-based methods are not necessarily complete and abstract the search space using intervals [14, 15] or more complex abstract domains [31]–[33]. However, most of these approaches are sequential, and for details, we refer the reader to the survey by Liu et al. [34]. To the best of our knowledge, only Marabou [17] and Neurify [15] (and its predecessor Relu-Val [14]) leverage parallel computing to speed up verification.

As mentioned in Sec. IV, Neurify combines symbolic interval analysis with linear relaxation to compute tighter output bounds and uses off-the-shelf solvers to derive more precise bounds for ReLUs. These interval analysis techniques lend themselves well to parallelization, as independent linear programs can be created and checked in parallel. By contrast, S&C-Marabou creates partitions of the original query and solves them in parallel. Neurify supports a selection of hard-coded benchmarks and properties and often requires modifications to support new properties, while Marabou provides verification support for a wide range of properties.

Split-and-Conquer is inspired by the *Cube-and-Conquer* algorithm [18], which targets very hard SAT problems. Cube-and-Conquer is a divide-and-conquer technique that partitions a Boolean satisfiability problem into sub-problems by conjoining cubes —a cube is a conjunction of propositional literals— to the original problem and then employing a conflict-driven SAT solver [35] to solve each sub-problem in parallel. The propositional literals used in cubes are chosen using look-ahead [36] techniques. Divide-and-conquer techniques have also been used to parallelize SMT solving [37, 38]. Our approach uses similar ideas to those in previous work, but is optimized for the VNN domain.

Iterative propagation is, in part, inspired by the look-ahead techniques. While the latter is used to partition the search space, the former is used to reduce the overall complexity of the problem.

VI. Conclusions and Future Work

In this paper, we presented a set of techniques that leverage parallel computing to improve the scalability of neural network verification. We described an algorithm based on partitioning the verification problem in an iterative manner and explored two strategies that work by partitioning the input space or by splitting on ReLUs, respectively. We introduced a branching heuristic and a direction heuristic, both based on the notion of polarity. We also introduced a highly parallelizable pre-processing algorithm for simplifying neural network verification problems. Our experimental evaluation shows the benefit of these techniques on existing and new benchmarks. A preliminary experiment with ultra-scaling using the gg platform on Amazon Lambda also shows promising results.

Future work includes: i) Investigating more dynamic strategies for choosing hyper-parameters of the S&C framework. ii) Investigating different ways to interleave iterative propagation with S&C. iii) Investigating the scalability of ReLU-based partitioning to high levels of parallelism. iv) Improving the performance of the underlying solver, Marabou, by integrating conflict analysis (as in CDCL SAT solvers and SMT solvers) and more advanced bound propagation techniques such as those used by Neurify. v) Extending the techniques to handle other piecewise-linear activation functions such as hard tanh and leaky ReLU, to which the notion of polarity applies.

Acknowledgements

The project was partially supported by grants from the Binational Science Foundation (2017662), the Defense Advanced Research Projects Agency (FA8750-18-C-0099), Ford Motor Company, the Israel Science Foundation (683/18), and the National Science Foundation (1814369).

References

[1] I. Goodfellow, Y. Bengio, and A. Courville, *Deep Learning*. MIT Press, 2016, http://www.deeplearningbook.org.

[2] K. D. Julian, M. J. Kochenderfer, and M. P. Owen, "Deep neural network compression for aircraft collision avoidance systems," *Journal of Guidance, Control, and Dynamics*, vol. 42, no. 3, pp. 598–608, 2019. [Online]. Available: https://doi.org/10.2514/1.G003724

[3] A. Krizhevsky, I. Sutskever, and G. E. Hinton, "Imagenet classification with deep convolutional neural networks," in *NIPS*, 2012, pp. 1106–1114.

[4] G. Hinton, L. Deng, D. Yu, G. E. Dahl, A.-r. Mohamed, N. Jaitly, A. Senior, V. Vanhoucke, P. Nguyen, T. N. Sainath *et al.*, "Deep neural networks for acoustic modeling in speech recognition: The shared views of four research groups," *IEEE Signal processing magazine*, vol. 29, no. 6, pp. 82–97, 2012.

[5] D. Silver, A. Huang, C. J. Maddison, A. Guez, L. Sifre, G. Van Den Driessche, J. Schrittwieser, I. Antonoglou, V. Panneershelvam, M. Lanctot *et al.*, "Mastering the game of go with deep neural networks and tree search," *nature*, vol. 529, no. 7587, p. 484, 2016.

[6] C. Szegedy, W. Zaremba, I. Sutskever, J. Bruna, D. Erhan, I. J. Goodfellow, and R. Fergus, "Intriguing properties of neural networks," in *ICLR (Poster)*, 2014.

[7] M. Cissé, Y. Adi, N. Neverova, and J. Keshet, "Houdini: Fooling deep structured prediction models," *CoRR*, vol. abs/1707.05373, 2017.

[8] A. Kurakin, I. J. Goodfellow, and S. Bengio, "Adversarial examples in the physical world," in *ICLR (Workshop)*. OpenReview.net, 2017.

[9] L. Pulina and A. Tacchella, "An abstraction-refinement approach to verification of artificial neural networks," in *CAV*, ser. Lecture Notes in Computer Science, vol. 6174. Springer, 2010, pp. 243–257.

[10] ——, "Challenging SMT solvers to verify neural networks," *AI Commun.*, vol. 25, no. 2, pp. 117–135, 2012.

[11] L. M. de Moura and N. Bjørner, "Z3: an efficient SMT solver," in *TACAS*, ser. Lecture Notes in Computer Science, vol. 4963. Springer, 2008, pp. 337–340.

[12] C. W. Barrett, C. L. Conway, M. Deters, L. Hadarean, D. Jovanovic, T. King, A. Reynolds, and C. Tinelli, "CVC4," in *CAV*, ser. Lecture Notes in Computer Science, vol. 6806. Springer, 2011, pp. 171–177.

[13] G. Katz, C. Barrett, D. Dill, K. Julian, and M. Kochenderfer, "Reluplex: An Efficient SMT Solver for Verifying Deep Neural Networks," in *Proc. 29th Int. Conf. on Computer Aided Veri cation (CAV)*, 2017, pp. 97–117.

[14] S. Wang, K. Pei, J. Whitehouse, J. Yang, and S. Jana, "Formal security analysis of neural networks using symbolic intervals," in *27th {USENIX} Security Symposium ({USENIX} Security 18)*, 2018, pp. 1599–1614.

[15] ——, "Efficient formal safety analysis of neural networks," in *Advances in Neural Information Processing Systems 31: Annual Conference on Neural Information Processing Systems 2018, NeurIPS 2018, 3-8 December 2018, Montréal, Canada*, 2018, pp. 6369–6379. [Online]. Available: http://papers.nips.cc/paper/7873-efficient-formal-safety-analysis-of-neural-networks

[16] R. Ehlers, "Formal verification of piece-wise linear feed-forward neural networks," in *International Symposium on Automated Technology for Veri cation and Analysis*. Springer, 2017, pp. 269–286.

[17] G. Katz, D. A. Huang, D. Ibeling, K. Julian, C. Lazarus, R. Lim, P. Shah, S. Thakoor, H. Wu, A. Zeljić *et al.*, "The marabou framework for verification and analysis of deep neural networks," in *International Conference on Computer Aided Veri cation*, 2019, pp. 443–452.

[18] M. Heule, O. Kullmann, S. Wieringa, and A. Biere, "Cube and conquer: Guiding CDCL SAT solvers by lookaheads," in *Haifa Veri cation Conference*, ser. Lecture Notes in Computer Science, vol. 7261. Springer, 2011, pp. 50–65.

[19] M. J. H. Heule, O. Kullmann, and V. W. Marek, "Solving and verifying the boolean pythagorean triples problem via cube-and-conquer," in *SAT*, ser. Lecture Notes in Computer Science, vol. 9710. Springer, 2016, pp. 228–245.

[20] V. Nair and G. E. Hinton, "Rectified linear units improve restricted boltzmann machines," in *ICML*. Omnipress, 2010, pp. 807–814.

[21] A. L. Maas, A. Y. Hannun, and A. Y. Ng, "Rectifier nonlinearities improve neural network acoustic models," in *Proc. icml*, vol. 30, no. 1, 2013, p. 3.

[22] G. Katz, C. W. Barrett, D. L. Dill, K. Julian, and M. J. Kochenderfer, "Towards proving the adversarial robustness of deep neural networks," in *FVAV@iFM*, ser. EPTCS, vol. 257, 2017, pp. 19–26.

[23] D. Gopinath, H. Converse, C. Pasareanu, and A. Taly, "Property inference for deep neural networks," in *2019 34th IEEE/ACM International Conference on Automated Software Engineering (ASE)*, Nov 2019, pp. 797–809.

[24] R. Nieuwenhuis, A. Oliveras, and C. Tinelli, "Solving sat and sat modulo theories: From an abstract davis– putnam–logemann–loveland procedure to dpll(*t*)," *J. ACM*, vol. 53, no. 6, pp. 937–977, 2006.

[25] K. D. Julian, R. Lee, and M. J. Kochenderfer, "Validation of image-based neural network controllers through adaptive stress testing," *arXiv preprint arXiv:2003.02381*, 2020.

[26] "The MNIST database of handwritten digits Home Page," http://yann.lecun.com/exdb/mnist/.

[27] S. Fouladi, F. Romero, D. Iter, Q. Li, S. Chatterjee, C. Kozyrakis, M. Zaharia, and K. Winstein, "From laptop to lambda: Outsourcing everyday jobs to thousands of transient functional containers," in *2019 USENIX Annual Technical Conference, USENIX ATC 2019, Renton, WA, USA, July 10-12, 2019*, 2019, pp. 475–488. [Online]. Available: https://www.usenix.org/conference/atc19/presentation/fouladi

[28] "AWS lambda," https://docs.aws.amazon.com/lambda/index.html.

[29] N. Narodytska, S. Kasiviswanathan, L. Ryzhyk, M. Sagiv, and T. Walsh, "Verifying properties of binarized deep neural networks," in *Thirty-Second AAAI Conference on Arti cial Intelligence*, 2018.

[30] E. Botoeva, P. Kouvaros, J. Kronqvist, A. Lomuscio, and R. Misener, "Efficient verification of relu-based neural networks via dependency analysis." in *AAAI*, 2020, pp. 3291–3299.

[31] T. Gehr, M. Mirman, D. Drachsler-Cohen, P. Tsankov, S. Chaudhuri, and M. Vechev, "Ai2: Safety and robustness certification of neural networks with abstract interpretation," in *2018 IEEE Symposium on Security and Privacy (SP)*. IEEE, 2018, pp. 3–18.

[32] G. Singh, T. Gehr, M. Mirman, M. Püschel, and M. Vechev, "Fast and effective robustness certification," in *Advances in Neural Information Processing Systems*, 2018, pp. 10 802–10 813.

[33] G. Singh, T. Gehr, M. Püschel, and M. Vechev, "An abstract domain for certifying neural networks," *Proceedings of the ACM on Programming Languages*, vol. 3, no. POPL, pp. 1–30, 2019.

[34] C. Liu, T. Arnon, C. Lazarus, C. Barrett, and M. J. Kochenderfer, "Algorithms for verifying deep neural networks," 2019.

[35] J. P. M. Silva, I. Lynce, and S. Malik, "Conflict-driven clause learning SAT solvers," in *Handbook of Satis ability*, ser. Frontiers in Artificial Intelligence and Applications. IOS Press, 2009, vol. 185, pp. 131–153.

[36] M. Heule and H. van Maaren, "Look-ahead based SAT solvers," in *Handbook of Satis ability*, ser. Frontiers in Artificial Intelligence and Applications. IOS Press, 2009, vol. 185, pp. 155–184.

[37] A. E. Hyvärinen, M. Marescotti, and N. Sharygina, "Search-space partitioning for parallelizing smt solvers," in *International Conference on Theory and Applications of Satis ability Testing*. Springer, 2015, pp. 369–386.

[38] M. Marescotti, A. E. Hyvärinen, and N. Sharygina, "Clause sharing and partitioning for cloud-based smt solving," in *International Symposium on Automated Technology for Veri cation and Analysis*. Springer, 2016, pp. 428–443.

19

Effective System Level Liveness Verification

Alexander Fedotov*[iD], Jeroen J.A. Keiren*[iD], Julien Schmaltz[†]

Eindhoven University of Technology
Eindhoven, The Netherlands
{a.fedotov, j.j.a.keiren}@tue.nl
[†]*ICT Group*
Eindhoven, The Netherlands
julien.schmaltz@ict.nl

Abstract—The language xMAS has been designed by Intel with the purpose of modelling and verification of hardware. Recently, the language was extended with finite state machines to make it more expressive [19]. Furthermore, it was shown how to prove liveness of such extended xMAS networks [19]. Unfortunately, we demonstrate that the proof technique is unsound. We provide an alternative approach which we have carefully proven to be correct. Moreover, we show that our approach scales very well, which makes it possible to prove liveness properties at the system level. In particular, we show that using our approach, it is possible to verify a power control architecture composed of 1299 state machines representing 50 power domains where each domain contains 5 master and 5 slave devices. Proving liveness of this system takes less than 10 minutes.

Index Terms—Formal verification, liveness, communication networks, finite state machines

I. INTRODUCTION

Formal verification has been successfully introduced in many design flows of hardware and software systems. More and more often, the sign-off decision for hardware blocks is taken solely on the results of formal proofs, the so-called *formal sign-off*. However, scaling formal verification to the system level remains a challenge.

Originally proposed by researchers at Intel, the xMAS language [7] and associated techniques for invariant generation [6], property checking [6], and deadlock hunting [12, 16][1] have been developed to address this challenge. These techniques are very efficient and were extended to performance validation [15], asynchronous circuits [4], progress verification [8], generalized to language families [17], and directly related to the Register Transfer Level [11, 13, 14].

Regarding liveness analysis, the key contribution of Gotmanov *et al.* [12] is to encode the existence of a deadlock state as a satisfiability problem. This technique is sound and can prove the absence of deadlock states. It is incomplete because a satisfiable solution does not necessarily represent a reachable state of the xMAS network. Checking reachability of potential xMAS deadlock states is efficient [20].

Verbeek *et al.* introduced state machines into xMAS together with extensions of liveness analysis techniques [19].

Their extension enables the modeling and analysis of complex cooperating state machines under the constraints imposed by micro-architectural choices. They demonstrated the verification of large systems consisting of nodes running cache coherence protocols and communicating via a Network-on-Chip. Inspired by Gotmanov *et al.*, Verbeek *et al.* encode liveness verification of xMAS extended with (finite) state machines to satisfiability. As we will show in this paper, their method is *unsound*.

We present a counter-example that is composed of a network with a deadlock that is not found by the technique of Verbeek *et al.* [19]. Subsequently, we propose an alternative encoding of liveness into a satisfiability problem. We carefully prove that if an xMAS network has a path to a state with a deadlock, there exists a satisfying assignment to the satisfiability problem we generate, i.e., our encoding is sound. Finally, we introduce two sets of benchmarks including a simplified power control architecture inspired by industrial case-studies.

The benchmarks and our implementation are publicly available [2]. A network with 1299 state machines can be proven live in less than 10 minutes.

We introduce xMAS, liveness of channels and idle and block equations in Section II. In Section III we introduce xMAS finite state machines, and show why the approach from [19] is unsound. Our approach using idle and block equations is described in Section IV. Our implementation is evaluated in Section V. We conclude in Section VI.

II. PRELIMINARIES

A. xMAS syntax

xMAS [7] is a graphical language aimed at modeling and verifying communication fabrics. An xMAS network comprises a set of primitives connected by typed channels. The progress of messages between primitives is controlled by a simple handshake protocol. Each channel consists of three signals, one for data and two boolean control signals, **irdy** and **trdy**. Consider the transfer of data from primitive A to primitive B via channel x. When primitive A is ready to transfer datum d through channel x, it sets $x.\textbf{data}$ to d, and $x.\textbf{irdy}$ to true, indicating the *initiator* is ready to transfer data. Whenever B is ready to accept data, it sets $x.\textbf{trdy}$ to true, indicating the *target* is ready to receive. The data transfer happens if and only if $x.\textbf{irdy} \wedge x.\textbf{trdy}$, i.e., the initiator is

---

[1]Note that in the literature related to liveness verification of xMAS networks, it is common to call states with non-live channels deadlock states. We adhere to this terminology, although it is different from the conventional notion of deadlock.

ready to send and the target is ready to receive. The core xMAS primitives are shown in Figure 1.

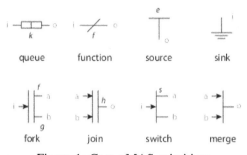

Figure 1: Core xMAS primitives

We provide detailed descriptions of the source, sink and queue primitives as they are used directly in this paper. For details of the other primitives the reader is referred to [7].

A source non-deterministically injects data into the network infinitely often. This is modelled using the unconstrained primary input **oracle**. Once a source decides to transfer datum d, it will keep trying until the transfer succeeds. This is modelled using the standard synchronous operator **pre** that returns the value of its argument in the previous clock cycle, and *false* in the very first cycle. Formally, the source is described as follows:

$$o.\mathbf{irdy} := \mathbf{oracle} \vee \mathbf{pre}(o.\mathbf{irdy} \wedge \neg o.\mathbf{trdy})$$
$$o.\mathbf{data} := d.$$

A sink consumes data from the network infinitely often:

$$i.\mathbf{trdy} := \mathbf{oracle} \vee \mathbf{pre}(i.\mathbf{trdy} \wedge \neg i.\mathbf{irdy}).$$

A queue is a FIFO buffer with k places. A queue is ready to write data to the output when it is not empty. The data the queue is ready to write is the head of the queue. A queue is ready to accept data when it is not full. Formally,

$$o.\mathbf{irdy} := \neg \mathbf{is\_empty}, \qquad o.\mathbf{data} := \mathbf{head},$$
$$i.\mathbf{trdy} := \neg \mathbf{is\_full},$$

where i and o are the input and output channels of the queue respectively.

Example 1. Consider the simple xMAS network depicted in Figure 2. We use this network as a running example. The network consists of a source, a queue, and a sink. The source produces tokens t. The source controls the $x.\mathbf{irdy}$ and $x.\mathbf{data}$ signals of its output channel x. The queue controls the $x.\mathbf{trdy}$ signal of channel x, and $y.\mathbf{irdy}$ and $y.\mathbf{data}$ of its output

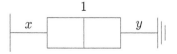

Figure 2: xMAS example

channel y. The sink controls the $y.\mathbf{trdy}$ signal of channel y. The signals are defined as follows.

$$x.\mathbf{irdy} := \mathbf{oracle}_{src} \vee \mathbf{pre}(x.\mathbf{irdy} \wedge \neg x.\mathbf{trdy})$$
$$x.\mathbf{data} := t$$
$$x.\mathbf{trdy} := \neg \mathbf{is\_full}$$
$$y.\mathbf{irdy} := \neg \mathbf{is\_empty}$$
$$y.\mathbf{data} := \mathbf{head}$$
$$y.\mathbf{trdy} := \mathbf{oracle}_{snk} \vee \mathbf{pre}(y.\mathbf{trdy} \wedge \neg y.\mathbf{irdy}).$$

The semantics of an xMAS network consists of a combinatorial and a sequential phase. In the first, all **data**, **irdy** and **trdy** signals are updated. In the second all components with state update their state. The global state of an xMAS network is the product of the local states of all components. We write $\vec{s} \xrightarrow{X} \vec{s'}$ for the transition between global states $\vec{s}$ and $\vec{s'}$, where X is a set of (channel,data) pairs representing the simultaneous data transfers in the current clock cycle.

B. Liveness of channels

Liveness of channels is defined using linear temporal logic (LTL). LTL and its semantics are considered standard, and we refer to text books such as [3] for the details. To interpret LTL on xMAS networks, we first define paths and maximal paths in such networks. In the rest of this paper, we implicitly fix an xMAS network $N = (P, G)$, where P is the set of primitives, and G is the set of channels. Given a channel $x \in G$, by $C(x)$ we denote the set of all possible values of $x.\mathbf{data}$. By C we denote the set of all data of N, that is $C = \bigcup_{x \in G} C(x)$.

Definition 1. A *path* is a possibly infinite sequence of global states $\pi = \vec{s}_0, \vec{s}_1, \vec{s}_2, \dots$ such that for all $j > 0$, $\vec{s}_{j-1} \xrightarrow{X} \vec{s}_j$ for some X. The set of paths starting in a state $\vec{s}$ is denoted using $\mathsf{Paths}(\vec{s})$, and for xMAS network N we write $\mathsf{Paths}(N)$ to denote $\mathsf{Paths}(\vec{s}_0)$, where $\vec{s}_0$ is the initial state of the network N. For finite paths $\pi = \vec{s}_0, \dots, \vec{s}_n$ we define $\mathsf{last}(\pi) = \vec{s}_n$. A path π is called *maximal* if and only if it is infinite, or it is finite and $\mathsf{last}(\pi)$ has no outgoing transitions.

A channel is *live* whenever, always when its initiator is ready to transfer data, the transfer will eventually be successful.

Definition 2 ([12][2]). Channel $x \in G$ is *live* for $d \in C(x)$ iff

$$N \models \mathsf{G}((x.\mathbf{irdy} \wedge x.\mathbf{data} = d)$$
$$\implies \mathsf{F}(x.\mathbf{irdy} \wedge x.\mathbf{trdy} \wedge x.\mathbf{data} = d)).$$

We henceforth make the (standard) assumption that channels are (forward) persistent. This means that whenever the initiator is ready to send d along x, it will remain ready to do so until the transfer is successful. Formally, the network satisfies $\mathsf{G}((x.\mathbf{irdy} \wedge x.\mathbf{data} = d \wedge \neg x.\mathbf{trdy}) \implies \mathsf{X}(x.\mathbf{irdy} \wedge x.\mathbf{data} = d))$. Under this assumption, channel x is live if and only if it is live for all $d \in C(x)$.

---

[2]Gotmanov et al. [12] use property $\mathsf{G}(x.\mathbf{irdy} \implies \mathsf{F}\, x.\mathbf{trdy})$, which does not guarantee that the transfer eventually succeeds if persistency is not assumed.

We recall the notions *idle* and *block* from [12]. A channel is *idle* for d if eventually the initiator will never send message d along that channel, and it is *blocked* if eventually the target will never be able to receive a message along that channel.

Definition 3 ([12]). Let $x \in G$ and $d \in C(x)$. We define

$$\mathbf{idle}(x(d)) := \mathsf{FG}(\neg x.\mathbf{irdy} \vee x.\mathbf{data} \neq d)$$
$$\mathbf{block}(x) := \mathsf{FG}\neg x.\mathbf{trdy}$$

A local deadlock is defined as a *dead* channel, where a channel is dead for value d if and only if it is not live for d. This means there exists a path in the xMAS network to a state that satisfies $\neg\mathbf{idle}(x(d)) \wedge \mathbf{block}(x)$. In other words, a channel is dead whenever its initiator is ready to transfer datum d and its target will never be ready to accept the data.

Definition 4. Let N be an xMAS network, with x a forward persistent channel in N, and $d \in C(x)$. We define

$$\mathbf{live}(x(d)) := \mathbf{idle}(x(d)) \vee \neg\mathbf{block}(x)$$
$$\mathbf{dead}(x(d)) := \neg\mathbf{live}(x(d))$$
$$\mathbf{live}(x) := \bigwedge_{d \in C(x)} \mathbf{live}(x(d))$$
$$\mathbf{dead}(x) := \bigvee_{d \in C(x)} \mathbf{dead}(x(d))$$

Persistency now allows us to simplify the definition of liveness using the following theorem adapted from [12].

Theorem 1. *For all channels $x \in G$ and $d \in C(x)$, let*

$$\mathbf{live}(x(d)) := \mathbf{idle}(x(d)) \vee \neg\mathbf{block}(x)$$
$$\mathbf{dead}(x(d)) := \neg\mathbf{live}(x(d)).$$

Then, for all persistent channels $x \in G$ and $d \in C(x)$,

1) *x is live for d iff $N \models \mathbf{live}(x(d))$, and*
2) *x is dead for d iff $\exists \pi \in \mathsf{Paths}(N).\pi \models \mathbf{dead}(x(d))$.*

Note that the formula for *live* channels is evaluated over the *network* (i.e., over *all* paths), and the formula for *dead* channels is evaluated over a *path* due to the LTL semantics.

In Definition 3, we only defined $\mathbf{block}(x)$. We can refine this definition by introducing $\mathbf{block}(x(d))$ as follows.

$$\mathbf{block}(x(d)) := \mathsf{FG}(\neg x.\mathbf{trdy} \vee x.\mathbf{data} \neq d)$$

It is easy to see that $\mathbf{block}(x)$ implies $\mathbf{block}(x(d))$ for any $d \in C(x)$. The following then follows immediately.

Lemma 1. *For all persistent channels $x \in G$, $d \in C(x)$, and all paths $\pi \in \mathsf{Paths}(N)$, $\pi \models \mathbf{dead}(x(d))$ implies $\pi \models \bigwedge_{e \in C(x)} \mathbf{block}(x(e))$.*

C. Idle and block equations

The main contribution of Gotmanov *et al.* [12] is to express deadlock conditions for each primitive using equations over boolean variables. If these *idle and block equations* are satisfiable, a (possible) deadlock has been detected; otherwise, the network is guaranteed to be deadlock free. The method

is sound but incomplete: if the equations are satisfiable, the assignment to the boolean variables may constitute an unreachable deadlock state. This is alleviated to some extent by using invariants to approximate the reachable states.

The boolean variables express the conditions under which a primitive will eventually never try to output value d, denoted using variable $\mathbf{idle}_x^d$, or eventually never try to read from channel x, denoted using variable $\mathbf{block}_x$. The encoding essentially approximates the LTL specifications of idle and block defined before. In particular, if there exists a path π in the xMAS network such that $\pi \models \mathbf{dead}(x(d))$, then there is a satisfying assignment to the variables in the idle and block equations in which $\mathbf{idle}_x^d$ is *false*, and $\mathbf{block}_x$ is *true*.

Example 2. Recall the network from Example 1. Sources are never idle, and sinks are never blocked. The input channel of the queue, x, is blocked when the queue is full and its output channel y is blocked. The output channel of the queue is idle when the queue is empty and its incoming channel x is idle. This results in the following equations.

$$\mathbf{idle}_x \equiv \bot \qquad\qquad \mathbf{block}_x \equiv \mathbf{full} \wedge \mathbf{block}_y$$
$$\mathbf{idle}_y \equiv \mathbf{empty} \wedge \mathbf{idle}_x \qquad \mathbf{block}_y \equiv \bot$$
$$\mathbf{dead}_x \equiv \neg\mathbf{idle}_x \vee \mathbf{block}_x \qquad \mathbf{dead}_y \equiv \neg\mathbf{idle}_y \vee \mathbf{block}_y$$

We can conclude that neither x nor y is dead.

III. LIFE AND DEATH OF STATE MACHINES IN xMAS

A. xMAS finite state machines

Verbeek *et al.* describe an extension of xMAS with finite state machines for the integrated verification of, for instance, cache coherence protocols together with their underlying communication fabric [18, 19]. The xMAS automata allow for the symbolic description of the channels and data read and written along transitions. However, every transition reads and writes (at most) one channel. In this paper we require explicit definition of every datum read/written on a transition to simplify the presentation. The results could equally be expressed using symbolic notation as in [18, 19]. However, since the number of channels and the data transferred are typically assumed to be finite, they can be expanded in the FSM, and this change does not alter the expressive power.

Definition 5. A *finite state machine (FSM)* is a tuple (S, s_0, I, O, T), where S is a finite set of states; $s_0 \in S$ is an initial state; I is a finite set of input channels; O is a finite set of output channels; and $T \subseteq S \times (I \times C) \times (O \times C) \times S$ is the total transition relation.

Since T is total, every state has at least one outgoing transition. We use names $s, s', s_1, \ldots$ for states. We write $s \xrightarrow{x(d)/y(e)} s'$ for $(s, (x, d), (y, e), s') \in T$. We sometimes write $?x(d)$ and $!y(e)$ to stress d is read from channel x, and e is written to y. For state $s \in S$, $in(s)$ and $out(s)$ denote the sets of incoming and outgoing transitions of s, respectively. Likewise, for channels $x \in (I \cup O)$, and data $d \in C(x)$, $read(x, d)$ and $write(x, d)$ represent the sets of transitions reading d from x and writing d to x, respectively.

Note that the requirement that every transition reads from and writes to exactly one channel is not fundamental. Transitions $t = s \xrightarrow{!y(e)} s'$ that do not read from an input channel can be modeled by introducing a new channel x_t that is connected to a source and the FSM, and be replaced by $s \xrightarrow{?x_t/!y(e)} s'$. Transitions that do not write to an output channel and transitions that do not read or write any channel can be modeled in a similar way.

In an FSM, exactly one state is current at a time, this state is denoted $cur(s)$. A transition $s \xrightarrow{x(d)/y(e)} s'$ is enabled if and only if s is the current state, the input channel x is ready to send d, and the output channel y is ready to receive. Note that whether the input and output channels are ready depends on the environment of the FSM.

Definition 6. Given FSM (S, s_0, I, O, T), transition $s \xrightarrow{x(d)/y(e)} s' \in T$ is enabled, denoted $enabled(s \xrightarrow{x(d)/y(e)} s')$ iff $cur(s) \wedge x.\mathbf{irdy} \wedge x.\mathbf{data} = d \wedge y.\mathbf{trdy}$.

In any state, there can be multiple enabled transitions. To resolve this non-determinism, a scheduler sel is introduced that, at every clock cycle, selects an enabled transition. If transition t is selected, this is denoted $sel = t$.

The FSM needs to indicate to its environment whether it is ready to send along an outgoing channel, or to read along an incoming channel. This is defined in terms of **irdy**, **trdy** and **data** as follows.

Definition 7. Given FSM (S, s_0, I, O, T), for $x \in I, y \in O$:

$$x.\mathbf{trdy} := \exists s \xrightarrow{x(d)/y(e)} s' \in T.sel = s \xrightarrow{x(d)/y(e)} s'$$

$$y.\mathbf{irdy} := \exists s \xrightarrow{x(d)/y(e)} s' \in T.sel = s \xrightarrow{x(d)/y(e)} s'$$

$$y.\mathbf{data} := \begin{cases} e & \text{if } \exists s \xrightarrow{x(d)/y(e)} s' \in T.sel = s \xrightarrow{x(d)/y(e)} s' \\ \bot & \text{otherwise} \end{cases}$$

Since the scheduler non-deterministically chooses between enabled transitions, and **irdy** is only set for the output channel of a selected transition, whenever **irdy** is set for an output channel of an FSM, the target of that channel is ready to receive, i.e., **trdy** is set. Non-determinism of the scheduler could lead to an enabled transition being ignored for an infinite amount of time. However, we assume scheduler sel to be fair, i.e., if state s is visited infinitely often with $s \xrightarrow{x(d)/y(e)} s'$ enabled, then $s \xrightarrow{x(d)/y(e)} s'$ will be selected infinitely often. We therefore only verify liveness of the xMAS network along fair paths. Such paths are defined as follows.

Definition 8. Given a path π, we say that π is fair if and only if for all FSM primitives $M = (S^M, s_0^m, I^M, O^M, T^M)$ and local transitions $t \in T^M$, we have $\pi \models (\mathbf{GF} enabled(t)) \implies (\mathbf{GF} sel = t)$

B. Idle and block equations by Verbeek et al.

Verbeek *et al.* define a SAT encoding using idle and block equations for xMAS automata as follows. Given $M =$

(S, s_0, I, O, T), for $s \xrightarrow{x(d)/y(e)} s' \in T$, $x \in I$, $y \in O$, $d \in C(x)$, $e \in C(y)$, they define the following.

$$\mathbf{dead}_{s \xrightarrow{x(d)/y(e)} s'} \equiv \mathbf{idle}_x^d \vee \mathbf{block}_y$$

$$\mathbf{dead}_s \equiv cur_s \wedge \bigwedge_{t \in out(s)} \mathbf{dead}_t$$

$$\mathbf{dead}_M \equiv \bigvee_{s \in S} \mathbf{dead}_s$$

$$\mathbf{block}_x^d \equiv \mathbf{dead}_M \vee (read(x, d) = \emptyset)$$

$$\mathbf{idle}_y^e \equiv \mathbf{dead}_M \vee (write(y, e) = \emptyset)$$

Here, cur_s are boolean variables, aimed at reflecting the current state of the FSM.

Intuitively, Verbeek *et al.* propose to encode that input (output) channels of an FSM are blocked (idle) as follows. An input channel x is blocked for d if either the FSM has no transition which reads d from x or the FSM is dead. Likewise, an output channel y is idle for e if either the FSM has no transition which writes e to y or the FSM is dead. With the notion of dead FSM, Verbeek *et al.* intend to encode the existence of a state (a dead state, using the terminology of the authors), which can eventually be reached, and at the same time cannot be left anymore, since all outgoing transitions are dead. In such a situation, the FSM can neither read from its inputs nor write to its outputs.

C. Life and death of state machines: a counter-example

Unfortunately, there are xMAS networks with FSMs that are deadlock free according to these idle and block equations that do contain a deadlock. This is illustrated by the following example.

Example 3. Consider the state machine, depicted in Figure 3. It has two input channels x and y, connected to sources, and two output channels o and z, connected to sinks. All channels only transfer datum d. Initially, in s_0, the FSM can either read d from channel x and produce d on channel o, and stay in s_0, or it can read d from y *once* and produce d on z, and go to s_1. In s_1, the FSM never reads from y nor writes to o, and only reads from x, writes to z, and stays in s_1.

According to the definition by Verbeek *et al.*, the FSM is not *dead*: channels o and z are not blocked, and since channel x is not idle, neither of the self-loops is dead. Consequently, neither s_0 nor s_1 is dead, and the FSM is not dead. However, once s_1 is reached, messages waiting on channel y will never be read, so y should be blocked.

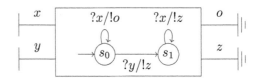

Figure 3: Counterexample to method by Verbeek et al.

The example shows that, although channel y is dead for d, since $\mathbf{block}_y^d$ is false, this is not detected using the idle and block equations. The encoding from [19] is therefore unsound.

Generally, the issue lies in the definition of $\mathbf{dead}_M$. Even when none of the input channels are idle, and no output channel is blocked, a state machine can block an input channel. This happens, *e.g.*, when source states of transitions reading from a particular channel are reached only *finitely many times*. Output channels can become idle for similar reasons.

IV. IDLE AND BLOCK EQUATIONS FOR xMAS FSMs

We propose alternative idle and block equations for FSMs in the spirit of [12]. An input channel x of an FSM is dead, when eventually all transitions reading x become disabled. There are two possible causes for this. First, the source state of the transition can eventually never be reached anymore. Second, whenever the source state of the transition is current, the environment disables the transition since the output channel is blocked. We capture this intuition by saying that states that are eventually never reached again are idle, and transitions that are eventually never enabled are dead.

Definition 9 (Idle states and dead transitions). Consider FSM (S, s_0, I, O, T). For $s \in S$ and $t \in T$ we define the following.

$$\mathbf{idle}(s) := \mathsf{FG} \neg cur(s)$$
$$\mathbf{dead}(t) := \mathsf{FG} \neg enabled(t)$$

Formally, transitions eventually never become enabled along a path if and only if either the source state or the input channel of the transition is idle, or the output channel is blocked.

Lemma 2. *Let $M = (S, s_0, I, O, T)$ be an FSM in N. For all $t = s \xrightarrow{x(d)/y(e)} s' \in T$, global states $\vec{s}$, and paths $\pi \in \mathsf{Paths}(\vec{s})$,*

$$\pi \models \mathsf{FG} \neg enabled(t) \text{ iff } \pi \models \mathbf{idle}(s) \vee \mathbf{idle}(x(d)) \vee \mathbf{block}(y).$$

Proof sketch (for the full proof see [10]). Fix an arbitrary transition $t = s \xrightarrow{x(d)/y(e)} s'$, global state $\vec{s}$, and path $\pi \in \mathsf{Paths}(\vec{s})$. We prove both directions separately.

$\Rightarrow$ Assume that $\pi \models \mathsf{FG} \neg enabled(t)$. Towards a contradiction, suppose $\pi \not\models \mathbf{idle}(s) \vee \mathbf{idle}(x(d)) \vee \mathbf{block}(y(e))$. We know that $\neg \mathbf{idle}(s) \equiv \mathsf{GF} cur(s)$, $\neg \mathbf{idle}(x(d)) \equiv \mathsf{GF}(x.\mathbf{irdy} \wedge x.\mathbf{data} = d)$, $\neg \mathbf{block}(y) \equiv \mathsf{GF} y.\mathbf{trdy}$. From this, using the semantics of LTL formulas we derive that $\pi \models \mathsf{GF} enabled(t)$, which is a contradiction.

$\Leftarrow$ Suppose $\pi \models \mathbf{idle}(s) \vee \mathbf{idle}(x(d)) \vee \mathbf{block}(y)$. We split the three cases and use Definitions 3, 6, and 8 to show that $\pi \models \mathsf{FG} \neg enabled(t)$ in each of these cases. $\square$

Due to the way the semantics of FSMs resolve nondeterminism, output channels of an FSM are never dead.

Lemma 3. *Given FSM (S, s_0, I, O, T) in N, for all global states $\vec{s}$ and for channels $y \in O$ and $e \in C(y)$, we have for all paths $\pi \in \mathsf{Paths}(\vec{s})$, $\pi \not\models \mathbf{dead}(y(e))$.*

We now specify the idle and block equations for FSMs used in a SAT encoding. The equations refer to variables $\mathbf{idle}$ of

incoming channels and $\mathbf{block}$ of outgoing channels that are defined in other components.

Definition 10 (Idle and block equations for FSMs). Consider an FSM $M = (S, s_0, I, O, T)$. For $s \in S$, $x \in I$, $y \in O$, $d \in C(x)$, $e \in C(y)$, and $s \xrightarrow{x(d)/y(e)} s' \in T$ we define the following equations.

$$\mathbf{dead}_s \xrightarrow{x(d)/y(e)} s' \equiv \mathbf{idle}_s \vee \mathbf{idle}_x^d \vee \mathbf{block}_y$$
$$\mathbf{idle}_s \equiv \neg cur_s \wedge \bigwedge_{t \in in(s)} \mathbf{dead}_t$$
$$\mathbf{block}_x^d \equiv \bigwedge_{t \in read(x,d)} \mathbf{dead}_t$$
$$\mathbf{block}_x \equiv \bigwedge_{d \in C(x)} \mathbf{block}_x^d$$
$$\mathbf{idle}_y^e \equiv \bigwedge_{t \in write(y,e)} \mathbf{dead}_t$$
$$\mathbf{idle}_y \equiv \bigwedge_{e \in C(y)} \mathbf{idle}_y^e$$

$\mathrm{SAT}(M)$ consists of the conjunction of all the idle and block equations for all states, transitions and channels in FSM M. Similarly we write $\mathrm{SAT}(N)$ for network N, which is the conjunction of all formulas for all the primitives of N, where for non-FSM components, the encoding from [12] is used.

We additionally use the invariants from [19] to reduce the number of false deadlocks. For example, $\sum_{s \in S} cur_s = 1$ dictates that the FSM is always in exactly one state.

The intuition behind the encoding is as follows. If a state is not current, and eventually none of its incoming transitions can ever become enabled, the state is effectively unreachable, thus the state is idle. In turn, a transition is dead if it ultimately never becomes enabled. This is the case if either its source state or its incoming channel is idle, or its outgoing channel is blocked. An input channel is blocked for a given datum if no transition will read that datum from the channel. Likewise an output channel is idle for a datum if that datum is never written to it. An output channel is idle if it is idle for all values, meaning that no value will ever be written to it. An input channel is blocked if it is blocked for all values. This follows from Lemma 1: a dead channel is blocked for all data.

We say assignment σ is *consistent* with path π and a set of components if for all input channels x, output channels y and data e of these components, $\sigma(\mathbf{block}_x) = \top$ iff $\pi \models \mathbf{block}(x)$ and $\sigma(\mathbf{idle}_y^e) = \top$ iff $\pi \models \mathbf{idle}(y(e))$.

We finally prove our idle and block equations are sound: if there is a channel that is dead for a particular value, then there is a satisfying assignment to the boolean equations showing this. We only consider input channels of FSMs, since output channels of FSMs cannot be dead as shown in Lemma 3.

Recall that a maximal path can either be finite or infinite, and in an infinite path in an xMAS network, the FSM can be stuck in a state locally. We construct assignments for each of these cases, and prove that each of the assignments is a satisfying assignment. We first construct assignment σ_s for the case where a (fair) maximal path in a network containing the FSM is such that the FSM is stuck locally in state s.

Definition 11. Let $M = (S, s_0, I, O, T)$ be an FSM that appears in an xMAS network N, $\pi \in \mathsf{Paths}(M)$ and $s \in S$. Assignment σ_s is defined as follows, where we write $v := w$ if σ_s assigns w to v. For states $s' \in S$, transitions $t \in T$, channels $x \in I$, $y \in O$, and $d \in C(x)$, $e \in C(y)$, let:

$$cur_{s'} := s = s' \qquad idle_{s'} := s \neq s' \qquad dead_t := \top$$

$$\mathbf{block}_x^d := \top \qquad \mathbf{block}_x := \top \qquad \mathbf{block}_y := \top$$

$$\mathbf{idle}_y^d := \top \qquad \mathbf{idle}_y := \top \qquad \mathbf{idle}_x^d := \bot$$

and σ_s is consistent with π for all components other than M.

Whenever the FSM is stuck locally, σ_s gives a satisfying assignment for the encoding to SAT.

Lemma 4. Let $M = (S, s_0, I, O, T)$ be an FSM that appears in an xMAS network N and $s \in S$. If $\pi \in \mathsf{Paths}(N)$ is a fair maximal path *such that either*

- π *is finite and* $\mathsf{last}(\pi) \models cur(s)$, *or*
- $\pi \models \mathsf{FG}\left(cur(s) \wedge \bigwedge_{t \in out(s)} \neg enabled(t)\right)$

then σ_s *is a satisfying assignment for* $\mathsf{SAT}(N)$.

The proof of this lemma and Lemma 5 are omitted due to space restrictions. Details can be found in [10].

For a fair maximal path π on which the FSM is not stuck locally, we construct a satisfying assignment σ_π based on π.

Definition 12. Let $M = (S, s_0, I, O, T)$ be an FSM that appears in an xMAS network N and $\pi \in \mathsf{Paths}(N)$. Assignment σ_π is defined as follows. For states $s' \in S$, transitions $t \in T$, channels $x \in I$, $y \in O$, and $d \in C(x)$, $e \in C(y)$, let:

$$cur_{s'} := s = s'$$

$$\mathbf{idle}_{s'} := \forall 0 \leq k \leq n.\pi[i+k] \models \neg cur(s')$$

$$\mathbf{dead}_t := \forall 0 \leq k \leq n.\pi[i+k] \models \neg enabled(t)$$

$$\mathbf{block}_x^d := \forall t \in read(x, d).\forall 0 \leq k \leq n.$$
$$\pi[i+k] \models \neg enabled(t)$$

$$\mathbf{block}_x := \forall d \in C(x).\forall t \in read(x, d).\forall 0 \leq k \leq n.$$
$$\pi[i+k] \models \neg enabled(t)$$

$$\mathbf{idle}_y^d := \forall t \in write(y, e).\forall 0 \leq k \leq n.$$
$$\pi[i+k] \models \neg enabled(t)$$

$$\mathbf{idle}_y := \forall e \in C(y).\forall t \in write(y, e).\forall 0 \leq k \leq n.$$
$$\pi[i+k] \models \neg enabled(t)$$

and σ_π is consistent with π for all components other than M.

Whenever the FSM is not stuck locally, σ_π gives a satisfying assignment for the encoding to SAT.

Lemma 5. Let $M = (S, s_0, I, O, T)$ be an FSM that appears in an xMAS network N. If $\pi \in \mathsf{Paths}(N)$ is an infinite fair maximal paths *such that for all* $s \in S$, $\pi \models \mathsf{GF}\left(cur(s) \implies \bigvee_{t \in out(s)} enabled(t)\right)$, the assignment σ_π is a satisfying assignment for $\mathsf{SAT}(N)$.

We finally prove soundness of our encoding, assuming that idle and block equations for non-FSM components are sound.

Theorem 2. *Let* $M = (S, s_0, I, O, T)$ *be an FSM in xMAS network* N. *For all channels* $x \in I$ *and data* $d \in C(x)$, *if there exists a fair maximal path* $\pi \in \mathsf{Paths}(N)$ *such that* $\pi \models \mathbf{dead}(x(d))$, *then* $\mathsf{SAT}(N) \wedge \neg\mathbf{idle}_x^d \wedge \mathbf{block}_x$ *is satisfiable.*

Proof. Fix arbitrary channel $x \in I$, and datum $d \in C(x)$, and let $\pi \in \mathsf{Paths}(N)$ be a fair maximal path such that $\pi \models \mathbf{dead}(x(d))$. We distinguish three cases:

- π is finite. Let $\mathsf{last}(\pi) \models cur(s)$ for some $s \in S$. According to Lemma 4, σ_s is a satisfying assignment for $\mathsf{SAT}(N)$. Note that $\mathbf{block}_x = \top$ and since σ_s is consistent with π for non-FSM components, $\mathbf{idle}_x^d = \bot$. So σ_s is a satisfying assignment for $\mathsf{SAT}(N) \wedge \neg\mathbf{idle}_x^d \wedge \mathbf{block}_x$.

- π is infinite and $\pi \models \mathsf{FG}(cur(s) \wedge \bigwedge_{t \in out(s)} \neg enabled(t))$ for some $s \in S$. Let s be such. According to Lemma 4, σ_s is consistent with $\mathsf{SAT}(N)$. Using similar reasoning as in the previous case, we can conclude that σ_s is a satisfying assignment for $\mathsf{SAT}(N) \wedge \neg\mathbf{idle}_x^d \wedge \mathbf{block}_x$.

- π is infinite and for all $s \in S$, we have $\pi \not\models \mathsf{FG}(cur(s) \wedge \bigwedge_{t \in out(s)} \neg enabled(t))$, i.e., $\pi \models \mathsf{GF}(cur(s) \implies \bigvee_{t \in out(s)} enabled(t))$. According to Lemma 5, σ_π is consistent with $\mathsf{SAT}(N)$. Note that since $\pi \models \mathbf{dead}(x(d))$, $\pi \models \mathbf{block}(x(e))$ for all $e \in C(x)$, according to Lemma 1. Consider arbitrary $e \in C(x)$, we show that the assignment satisfies $\mathbf{block}_x^e$. From this and the definition it immediately follows that it satisfies $\mathbf{block}_x$.
  Let i be the index that signals the start of the loop of the lasso on π. Since $\pi \models \mathbf{block}(x(e))$, $\pi \models \mathsf{FG}(\neg x.\mathbf{trdy} \vee x.\mathbf{data} \neq e)$. By definition of *enabled*, this implies $\pi \models \mathsf{FG}(\neg enabled(t))$ for all $t \in read(x, e)$. Hence, for all $0 \leq k \leq n$, $\pi[i+k] \models \neg enabled(t)$ for all $t \in read(x, e)$. By definition of σ_π, we then have $\mathbf{block}_x^e = \top$. Since this holds for all e, by definition also $\mathbf{block}_x = \top$, and σ_π is a satisfying assignment for $\mathsf{SAT}(N) \wedge \neg\mathbf{idle}_x^d \wedge \mathbf{block}_x$. $\qquad\square$

We illustrate our approach using an example.

Example 4. Recall the FSM from Example 3. The environment guarantees $\mathbf{idle}_x = \mathbf{idle}_y = \mathbf{block}_o = \mathbf{block}_z = \bot$. The idle and block equations are as follows.

$$\mathbf{idle}_{s_0} \equiv \neg cur_{s_0} \wedge \mathbf{dead}_{s_0 \xrightarrow{x/o} s_1}$$

$$\mathbf{idle}_{s_1} \equiv \neg cur_{s_1} \wedge \mathbf{dead}_{s_0 \xrightarrow{y/z} s_1} \wedge \mathbf{dead}_{s_1 \xrightarrow{x/z} s_1}$$

$$\mathbf{dead}_{s_0 \xrightarrow{x/o} s_1} \equiv \mathbf{idle}_{s_0} \vee \mathbf{idle}_x \vee \mathbf{block}_o$$

$$\mathbf{dead}_{s_0 \xrightarrow{y/z} s_1} \equiv \mathbf{idle}_{s_0} \vee \mathbf{idle}_y \vee \mathbf{block}_z$$

$$\mathbf{dead}_{s_1 \xrightarrow{x/z} s_1} \equiv \mathbf{idle}_{s_1} \vee \mathbf{idle}_x \vee \mathbf{block}_z$$

$$\mathbf{block}_x \equiv \mathbf{dead}_{s_0 \xrightarrow{x/o} s_1} \wedge \mathbf{dead}_{s_1 \xrightarrow{x/z} s_1}$$

$$\mathbf{block}_y \equiv \mathbf{dead}_{s_0 \xrightarrow{y/z} s_1}$$

$$\mathbf{idle}_o \equiv \mathbf{dead}_{s_0 \xrightarrow{x/o} s_1}$$

$$\mathbf{idle}_z \equiv \mathbf{dead}_{s_1 \xrightarrow{x/z} s_1}$$

We correctly detect that y is dead. This is witnessed by the following satisfying assignment for these equations, that also satisfies $\mathbf{block}_y = \top$, and thus $\neg\mathbf{idle}_y \wedge \mathbf{block}_y$.

$$cur_{s_0} := \bot \qquad\qquad cur_{s_1} := \top$$
$$\mathbf{idle}_{s_0} := \top \qquad\qquad \mathbf{idle}_{s_1} := \bot$$
$$\mathbf{dead}_{s_0} \xrightarrow{x/o} s_1 := \top \qquad \mathbf{dead}_{s_0} \xrightarrow{y/z} s_1 := \top$$
$$\mathbf{dead}_{s_1} \xrightarrow{x/z} s_1 := \bot$$
$$\mathbf{block}_x := \bot \qquad\qquad \mathbf{block}_y := \top$$
$$\mathbf{idle}_o := \top \qquad\qquad \mathbf{idle}_z := \bot$$

V. Experiments

We have implemented the idle and block equations described in Section IV. Given an xMAS model as input, our tool automatically generates a SAT problem that incorporates the idle and block equations [2]. The SAT problem is solved using Z3 [9] to verify liveness. Our tool can also generate an SMV model that encodes the xMAS network and its behaviour. This model uses idle and block equations as invariants. Reachability of a state in which a channel of the given xMAS model is checked using the NUXMV model-checker [5].

A. Experimental setup

We evaluate our implementation using two sets of models: one inspired by "go/no go" testing, the other inspired by power domains architectures. All models also have a version in which deadlocks have been introduced. A detailed description of the models can be found in [1].

Go/no go models are balanced binary trees of go/no go blocks. Each block has two binary inputs and one binary output, and consists of a pair of interconnected FSMs. The output of the block is *ok* if the data consumed from both input channels are *ok*, and it is *nok* otherwise.

Models of n levels of go/no go blocks (each block consists of two FSMs) are constructed by composing $2^n - 1$ go/no go blocks as a balanced binary tree. The output channels of two adjacent blocks on one level are used as input channels of a block on the next level in the tree.

Go/no go models with deadlocks are obtained by modifying one FSM in a go/no go block whose inputs are not connected to another block as follows. We add a new state with a self-loop reading *ok* from the first input channel i. We add a transition that reads *nok* from i from the initial state of the FSM to this new state. The new state is reachable, channel i is blocked for *nok*, and all output channels are idle.

Power domains are used to improve power efficiency of systems on chip. A power control architecture turns power domains on and off depending on the needs of an application. We model a dynamic power management policy that is an abstraction of industrial practice.

Our models consist of a number of power domains, each of which has a domain power controller. If the model has multiple power domains it also has a top power controller. Every power domain contains a number of device-controller pairs. In Figure 4a, we depict a device controller, which turns

on its device (depicted in Figure 4b) if the device indicates activity (generated by the FSM depicted in Figure 4c). If a device shows no activity, its device controller requests to turn off the device, and the device can non-deterministically accept the request or decline it. A domain power controller powers on the domain when one of the devices in the domain shows activity. It powers off the domain when all device controllers in the power domain indicate their devices are turned off. The top power controller powers on if one of the domain power controllers indicates it needs power. It powers off if all domain power controllers indicate that all devices are turned off.

To obtain power domain models with a deadlock, one of the device controller FSMs is changed such that in its *off* state it expects to read $act(0)$, and in its *on* state, it expects to read $act(1)$, which leads to synchronisation issues and deadlocks.

All experiments were executed on a MacBook Pro 2015, 2,7GHz Intel Core i5, 16Gb RAM, running MacOS Catalina 10.15.4. For SAT solving, we use the Z3 solver, version 4.8.0 64-bit [9]. For reachability checks, we use NUXMV, version 2.0.0 64-bit [5]. Instructions to reproduce the experiments and the script used to obtain our results are available at [1].

B. Results

Model	#FSMs	Live	SAT		Reachability	
			Res.	Time (s)	Res.	Time (s)
gonogo_1	2	✓	✓	0.1	✓	0.2
gonogo_1_dl	2	✗	✗	0.1	✗	0.3
gonogo_2	6	✓	✓	0.1	✓	0.5
gonogo_2_dl	6	✗	✗	0.1	✗	2.4
gonogo_3	14	✓	✓	0.3	✓	1.5
gonogo_3_dl	14	✗	✗	0.3	✗	5.9
gonogo_4	30	✓	✓	0.6	✓	5.5
gonogo_4_dl	30	✗	✗	0.6	✗	18.0
gonogo_5	62	✓	✓	2.0	✓	21.2
gonogo_5_dl	62	✗	✗	1.9	✗	54.9
gonogo_6	126	✓	✓	7.9	✓	92.7
gonogo_6_dl	126	✗	✗	6.7	✗	221.7
power1_5	25	✓	✓	0.4	✓	1.6
power1_5_dl	25	✗	✗	0.2	✗	2.1
power10_5	259	✓	✓	14.0	✓	120.0
power10_5_dl	259	✗	✗	10.1	✗	104.2
power20_5	519	✓	✓	57.5	✓	564.8
power20_5_dl	519	✗	✗	50.3	✗	451.1
power30_5	779	✓	✓	352.5	✓	1597.4
power30_5_dl	779	✗	✗	262.9	✗	1107.3
power40_5	1039	✓	✓	410.2	✓	n/a
power40_5_dl	1039	✗	✗	245.6	✗	n/a
power50_5	1299	✓	✓	542.2	✓	n/a
power50_5_dl	1299	✗	✗	481.1	✗	n/a

Table I: Experimental results

The times required for the experiments are reported in Table I. The *Model* column indicates the model that is evaluated. For go/no go models, the number in the name signifies the number of blocks. For power domain models, the first and second number in the name denote the number of power domains and device-controller pairs in every domain, respectively. *#FSMs* reports the number of FSMs in the model. In the *Live* column, ✓ indicates that the model is deadlock free, ✗ indicates it is not. For each instance, we list the result

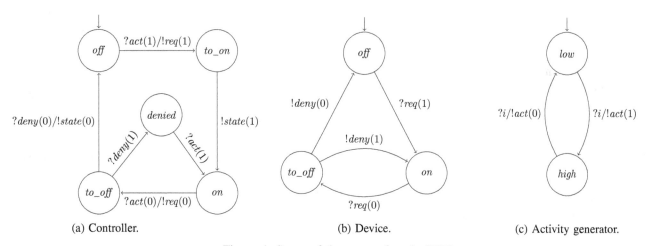

Figure 4: Some of the power domain FSMs

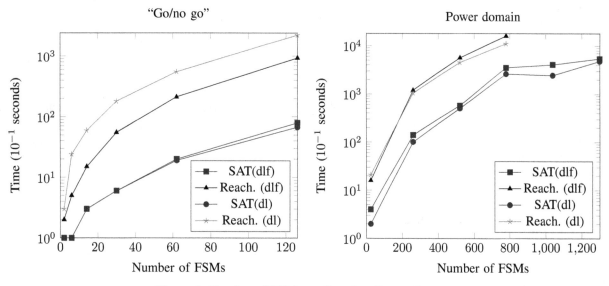

Figure 5: Number of FSMs vs time for all experiments.

reported by the tool (*Res.*), where ✓ and ✗ represent absence and presence of deadlocks, respectively. Running time for each instance is reported in seconds.

For both sets of models, SAT and reachability correctly report absence and existence of deadlocks in all models. The largest go/no go models contain 126 FSMs. Liveness of the largest deadlock free go/no go model is proven using SAT in 7 seconds. Reachability analysis takes 1 minute 32 seconds for the same go/no go model. For the largest go/no go model with a deadlock, a deadlock is reported using SAT in 6 seconds. Using reachability it can be proven that a deadlock state is reachable in 3 minutes 41 seconds. As for the power domain experimental set, the largest models (both with and without deadlock) contain 1299 FSMs. For the largest model without a deadlock, SAT proves liveness in 9 minutes and 2 seconds. Analysis of the largest power domain model with a deadlock takes 8 minutes and 1 second using SAT. Reachability analysis for the power domain models with numbers of power domains larger than 30 was not possible in our case. This was caused by NUXMV exceeding the maximum allowed stack on MacOS.

C. Discussion

The results show that using our technique we can prove liveness of large xMAS models with FSMs. We plot the performance results on both sets of models in Figure 5. Note that we use the log-scale for the y-axis. In addition, we use deciseconds instead of seconds in order to avoid values less than 1 for the y-axis. The results show that both methods scale exponentially in the number of FSMs. However, using SAT for liveness verification significantly outperforms reachability for xMAS extended with FSMs. This is in line with our expectations, and aligns with results for standard xMAS [12].

Although we do not encounter false deadlocks in our experiments, the fact that our method is incomplete implies that finding false deadlocks using SAT is possible. If SAT reports a deadlock, it is not known if the deadlock is reachable or not. In that case, reachability analysis is necessary.

VI. Conclusions

We demonstrated that the approach to verify liveness of xMAS networks with FSMs proposed by Verbeek *et al.* [19] is unsound. We proposed new idle and block equations for xMAS networks containing FSMs, and proved their soundness. Our experimental evaluation shows that deadlock detection using satisfiability outperforms reachability analysis using symbolic model checking in NUXMV. In case deadlocks are found, the latter can, however, verify their reachability reasonably efficiently. Although our method is incomplete, this was not observed during the experiments.

As future work, we plan to investigate ways to make the method complete. In particular, an alternative encoding to SAT based on bounded model checking, could make the method complete provided an appropriate bound can be derived. Additionally, the FSMs presented in this paper always read from and write to exactly one channel. This restriction could be relaxed to read and write multiple channels on a single transition to enable more compact modeling of some FSMs.

References

[1] Description of go/no go and power domain models (MaDL github wiki). https://github.com/MaDL-DVT/madl-dvt/wiki/FMCAD20-Experiments.

[2] MaDL design and verification tools. https://github.com/MaDL-DVT/madl-dvt.

[3] C. Baier and J.-P. Katoen. *Principles of Model Checking*. The MIT Press, 2008.

[4] F. Burns, D. Sokolov, and A. Yakovlev. GALS synthesis and verification for xMAS models. In *DATE 2015*, pages 1419–1424. EDA Consortium, 2015.

[5] R. Cavada, A. Cimatti, M. Dorigatti, A. Griggio, A. Mariotti, A. Micheli, S. Mover, M. Roveri, and S. Tonetta. The nuXmv symbolic model checker. In *CAV 2014*, pages 334–342, 2014.

[6] S. Chatterjee and M. Kishinevsky. Automatic generation of inductive invariants from high-level microarchitectural models of communication fabrics. In *CAV 2010*, pages 321–338. Springer, Berlin, Heidelberg, 2010.

[7] S. Chatterjee, M. Kishinevsky, and U. Y. Ogras. xMAS: Quick formal modeling of communication fabrics to enable verification. *IEEE Design Test of Computers*, 29(3):80–88, 2012.

[8] S. Das, C. Karfa, and S. Biswas. xMAS based accurate modeling and progress verification of NoCs. In *VLSI Design and Test*, pages 792–804. Springer, Singapore, 2017.

[9] L. de Moura and N. Bjørner. Z3: An efficient SMT solver. In C. R. Ramakrishnan and J. Rehof, editors, *TACAS 2008*, LNCS, pages 337–340, Berlin, Heidelberg, 2008. Springer.

[10] A. Fedotov, J. J. A. Keiren, and J. Schmaltz. *Sound idle and block equations for finite state machines in xMAS*. Computer science reports. Technische Universiteit Eindhoven, 11 2019.

[11] A. Fedotov and J. Schmaltz. Automatic generation of hardware checkers from formal micro-architectural specifications. In *DATE 2018*, pages 1568–1573, 2018.

[12] A. Gotmanov, S. Chatterjee, and M. Kishinevsky. Verifying deadlock-freedom of communication fabrics. In *VMCAI 2011*, pages 214–231. Springer, Berlin, Heidelberg, 2011.

[13] S. J. C. Joosten and J. Schmaltz. Generation of inductive invariants from register transfer level designs of communication fabrics. In *Proc. MEMOCODE 2013*, pages 57–64, 2013.

[14] S. J. C. Joosten and J. Schmaltz. Automatic extraction of micro-architectural models of communication fabrics from register transfer level designs. In *Proc. DATE 2015*, pages 1413–1418, 2015.

[15] Z. Lu and X. Zhao. xMAS-based QoS analysis methodology. *IEEE Transactions on Computer-Aided Design of Integrated Circuits and Systems*, 37(2):364–377, 2018.

[16] F. Verbeek and J. Schmaltz. Hunting deadlocks efficiently in microarchitectural models of communication fabrics. In *Proc. FMCAD 2011*, pages 223–231, 2011.

[17] F. Verbeek and J. Schmaltz. Automatic generation of deadlock detection algorithms for a family of microarchitecture description languages of communication fabrics. In *Proc. HLDVT 2012*, pages 25–32. IEEE, 2012.

[18] F. Verbeek, P. M. Yaghini, A. Eghbal, and N. Bagherzadeh. ADVOCAT: Automated deadlock verification for on-chip cache coherence and interconnects. In *DATE 2016*, pages 1640–1645, 2016.

[19] F. Verbeek, P. M. Yaghini, A. Eghbal, and N. Bagherzadeh. Deadlock verification of cache coherence protocols and communication fabrics. *IEEE Transactions on Computers*, 66(2):272–284, 2017.

[20] S. Wouda, S. J. C. Joosten, and J. Schmaltz. Process algebra semantics & reachability analysis for micro-architectural models of communication fabrics. In *Proc. MEMOCODE 2015*, pages 198–207. IEEE, 2015.

20

Incremental Verification by SMT-Based Summary Repair

Sepideh Asadi*, Martin Blicha*†, Antti Hyvärinen*, Grigory Fedyukovich‡, Natasha Sharygina*

*Universita della Svizzera italiana, Lugano, Switzerland

†Charles University, Faculty of Mathematics and Physics, Czech Republic

‡Florida State University, Tallahassee, USA

* asadis,blicham,hyvaeria,sharygin @usi.ch, ‡grigory@cs.fsu.edu

Abstract—We present UPPROVER, a bounded model checker designed to incrementally verify software while it is being gradually developed, refactored, or optimized. In contrast to its predecessor, a SAT-based tool EVOLCHECK, our tool exploits rst-order theories available in SMT solvers, offering two more levels of encoding precision: linear arithmetic and uninterpreted functions, thus allowing a trade-off between precision and performance. Algorithmically UPPROVER is based on the reuse and repair of interpolation-based function summaries from one software version to another. UPPROVER leverages tree-interpolation systems in SMT to localize and speed up the checks of new versions. UPPROVER demonstrates an order of magnitude speedup on large-scale programs in comparison to EVOLCHECK and HIFROG, a non-incremental bounded model checker.

I. INTRODUCTION

Software is always in a state of constant change. While verifying a large amount of closely related programs, a significant portion of efforts is repeated. One approach to overcome this issue is to operate incrementally by attempting to maximally reuse the results of previous computations. Furthermore, the performance and scalability of verification depends on the way software is encoded. To avoid the expensive bit-blasting during SAT-based verification, a variety of encodings offered by Satisfiability Modulo Theories (SMT) are successfully used in state-of-the-art tools. For instance, checking arithmetic properties about software might often be performed by a solver for Linear Real Arithmetic. While automatically identifying a proper level of encoding is difficult (and not a subject of this paper), tools at least should offer various encoding options to the user.

This paper presents a new tool allowing for the trade-off between efficiency and precision for the incremental analysis of pairs of software versions. *Over-approximating function summaries* are useful to enable such an analysis [1]. Summaries compactly represent all safe function behaviors, can be computed by *Craig interpolation* [2] from safety proofs of one software version, then validated on another version, and repaired if needed. An existing implementation of this idea, EVOLCHECK [3], uses a SAT solver and scales poorly on benchmarks that can be modeled using first-order theories. Our new Bounded Model Checking (BMC) [4] tool, called UPPROVER, supports several state-of-the-art SMT algorithms

for interpolation [5] and allows the user to choose more efficient algorithms. In addition to the purely propositional encoding UPPROVER generates models with fragments of quantifier-free first-order logic, in particular in Linear Real Arithmetic (LRA) and Equality with Uninterpreted Functions (EUF). Overall, UPPROVER distinguishes itself by:

- Reusing the efforts invested in the verification runs of previous program versions in verification of new versions;
- Providing an ability to maintain and to repair previously computed summaries on-the-fly and to use them in the subsequent verification runs;
- Allowing for a more succinct summary representation in first-order logic as opposed to purely propositional logic;
- Leveraging the power of SMT solvers by symbolic encodings of program versions and function summaries using first-order theories (the encoding is flexible and provides an ability to adjust precision and efficiency with different levels of encoding); and
- Demonstrating a competitive performance experimentally compared to both EVOLCHECK and a non-incremental BMC engine while verifying gradual changes in large-scale programs.

II. ALGORITHMIC BACKGROUND

UPPROVER is an incremental model checker which operates on loop-free programs that are seen as a set of functions F, each $f \in F$ expressed in their Static Single Assignment form. The behavior of a program is captured by the conjunction of the SMT encodings $enc(f)$ of each $f \in F$. The program respects a safety property Q if and only if the *safety query* $\bigwedge_{f \in F} enc(f) \wedge enc(Q)$ is unsatisfiable.

We use *Craig interpolation* from the proof of unsatisfiability of the safety query to construct *function summaries*, that is, relations over the input and output variables of a function that over-approximate the precise function behavior [6], [5], [7].

In UPPROVER, the problem of determining whether a changed program still meets the safety property, w.r.t. which the summaries were created, is reduced to the problem of validating these summaries on the changed program. To guarantee algorithmic correctness, the process requires a specialization of Craig interpolants called *tree interpolants* (see [8], [1]). The tree structure of the interpolation problem corresponds to the call tree of the program. We use approaches that guarantee the

This work was supported by Swiss National Science Foundation grant 200021_185031 and by Czech Science Foundation grant 20-07487S.

Algorithm 1: Summary validation in UPPROVER
___
Input: function summaries of the old version,
    tree = call-tree of the new version, Δ = set
    of changed functions in the new version;
Result: new version is *Safe* or *Unsafe*;

1 **while** *all Δ are not processed* **do**
2   choose the first f in the reverse postorder of tree
      such that $f \in \Delta$;
3   **if** *f has a summary* **then**
4   **if** *the summary is invalid* **then**
5   Remove the summary;
6   **if** *f has a parent (f is not root)* **then**
7   Add the parent to Δ to be processed;
8   **else**
9   **return** *Unsafe*, error trace;
10   **else**
11   Repair summaries from subtree of f by
          interpolation;
12 **return** *Safe*, set of valid and repaired summaries;
___

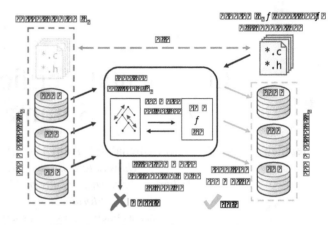

Figure 1: Overview of the UPPROVER architecture.

tree-interpolation property by construction [9], as opposed to, for instance, checking it on-the-fly.

Summary validation and repair, shown in Alg. 1, consists of a series of local validation checks for all changed function calls and their possibly affected callers, beginning at the deepest node. If a local validation succeeded, but for some function call in the subtree, a summary was invalidated, UPPROVER *repairs* the summary (line 11) using interpolation. Note that this local validation continues until there are no more functions to be processed, and if it succeeds, the new version is reported as *Safe*, potentially along with a set of repaired summaries that are made available for checking the next version.

It is worth noting that when the validation check propagates to the call tree root, i.e., *main* function, it corresponds to the pure BMC check where all functions are inlined. Thus in the worst case, since the programs that we check are bounded (a decidable problem), the algorithm fall backs to pure BMC.

III. Overview of UPPROVER

The overview of UPPROVER's architecture is shown in Fig. 1. UPPROVER implements Alg. 1 by maintaining three levels of precision—*linear real arithmetic* (LRA), *uninterpreted functions with equality* (EUF), and purely *propositional logic* (PROP)—to check the validity of summaries of program P_1 against the encodings of the function bodies of program P_2. Repaired function summaries are produced by the range of interpolation algorithms available in the underlying SMT solver. Next we describe UPPROVER's key features.

a) Efficiency / precision trade-off: A key enabler of UPPROVER's ability to adjust to user's needs in precision and efficiency is the safe over-approximation of programs with different SMT encodings. The high-level approach is to use linear or uninterpreted versions of the bit-precise program instructions whenever possible. The user selects the precision

of the overall encoding (i.e., LRA, EUF, and PROP) which uniquely determines the precision of summaries that are available after the preceding verification of P_1.

If the user is interested in checking program properties that are likely sensitive to some bit operators in software, he/she might prefer PROP encoding. The tool then bit-blasts the program together with summaries and uses its most expensive theory (essentially, a SAT solver). However, to accelerate the process, the user might choose instead a light-weight theory, forcing the tool to pick summaries appropriately. The program statements outside of the chosen theory will be modeled nondeterministically in this case. Thus, if a bug is detected, it might be due to the theory usage, and the user is encouraged to repeat the analysis with a more precise theory (and thus, more precise summaries). Note that there is no way in general to predict the best level of encoding for each program: even if a program has seemingly bit-sensitive statements, they might be sliced out or treated nondeterministically, allowing for a successful use of a light-weight theory.

b) Summary repair: Summaries of P_1 (of the selected level of precision) are taken as input and used in the incremental analysis on demand. The tool iteratively checks if the summaries are valid for P_2 and repairs them if needed. In the best-case scenario, all summaries of P_1 are validated for P_2, copied to the persistent storage, and become available for the future analysis of P_2. When some of the summaries need repair, the tool generates new interpolants from the successful validity checks of the parent functions and stores them as the corresponding summaries. No summaries are produced when the tool returns *Unsafe*.

c) Difference annotations / validation scope: UPPROVER does not take P_1 as input, but relies on annotating the lines of code changed between P_1 and P_2. The user may choose an inexpensive syntax-level difference, or a more expensive and precise semantic-level difference that compares programs after some normalization and translation to an intermediate representation [3]. The functions that have been identified as changed are stored in Δ in Alg. 1. Note that if a function f is introduced in P_2, the caller of f is marked as changed by our difference-checker. When no summary exists for f, the algorithm continues to check the caller. A successful validation with inlined f generates a summary for f.

d) SMT solving and interpolation engine: For answering BMC queries and the subsequent Craig interpolation, UP-PROVER uses the SMT solver OPENSMT [10]. The solver generates a quantifier-free first-order interpolant as a combination of interpolants from resolution refutations [11], proofs obtained from a run of a congruence closure algorithm [12], and Farkas coefficients obtained from the Simplex algorithm in linear real arithmetic [13].

e) Implementation: UPPROVER is available as an open-source software. Each component, from difference checker to modeling to solving procedures, has been significantly optimized compared to its earlier version EVOLCHECK. As a front-end of UPPROVER, we use the infrastructure from CPROVER v5.10 to transform C program to obtain a basic unrolled BMC representation that we use as a basis for producing the final logical formula.

f) Compatibility: The summaries computed by UP-PROVER are compatible with the input to HIFROG [5], another tool for incremental verification of different assertions in a *single program*. Note the difference in the use of summaries in HIFROG and UPPROVER: the former does not validate the summaries, but takes them as granted (even from the user, thus not guaranteeing the tree-interpolation property), and uses them to accelerate the verification of several new assertions.

IV. EXPERIMENTAL EVALUATION

In this section, we present an experimental evaluation of UPPROVER. We demonstrate two key features of our tool: (i) the usefulness of summary reuse in verifying program revisions, and (ii) the usefulness of different levels of modeling precision, i.e., LRA, EUF, and PROP. To this end, we compare UPPROVER against our current implementation of its predecessor EVOLCHECK and a bounded model checker HIFROG.[1] Then, we compare UPPROVER with CPACHECKER [14] a tool that uses intermediate results called *abstraction precision* for caching and reusing.

Our benchmarks, containing one or more assertions, originate from different revisions of Linux kernel device drivers from [14].[2] After excluding cases where CPROVER had frontend issues, we shortlisted 1679 revision pairs (LOC on average 16K). We also included 92 pairs hand-crafted benchmarks that stress-test our implementation. All experiments were run with a 30 GB memory limit and a 600 s time limit. The complete experimental results, benchmarks, and the source code are available at http://verify.inf.usi.ch/upprover.

A. Demonstrating the effect of summary reuse in UPPROVER

In the first set of experiments, we compare UPPROVER (incremental verification) against HIFROG (non-incremental verification). The results of the experiment within the same theory encodings by LRA and EUF are displayed in Fig. 2.

[1]The tools share the same front-end for parsing C programs, thus the comparison is not affected by unrelated implementation differences.
[2]https://www.sosy-lab.org/research/RegressionVerification/.

A large amount of points (that represent pairs of runs) on the upper triangle reveals that UPPROVER is an order of magnitude faster than the non-incremental verification in HIFROG.

Table I gives further details on 11 randomly selected pairs of benchmarks comparing the non-incremental HIFROG and incremental UPPROVER, both using the EUF encoding. Our results in LRA are very similar and therefore omitted. Each row in Table I refers to a pair (P_1, P_2) of programs. We use acronyms F for number of functions in P_1, for number of changed functions in P_2, *diff* for the time to construct between P_1 and P_2, *itp* for the time for generating all summaries after successful bootstrapping of P_1, and *result* for reporting whether the second version was safe or unsafe. The columns *total* in HIFROG and UPPROVER show the total verification time for non-incremental and incremental verification of P_2 respectively. Even though UPPROVER's total time includes overhead such as summary repair for the subsequent runs and the difference check, in many benchmarks UPPROVER convincingly outperforms non-incremental HIFROG.

The *speedup* column demonstrates the relative speedup of UPPROVER over non-incremental verification in HIFROG. In the majority of cases, UPPROVER gains a significant speedup when reusing EUF summaries (typeset in bold). This occurs especially when the two versions have the same intermediate representation (e.g., pair 3) and the validation check is omitted. Slowdowns typically happen when both the number of changed functions and the iterative validation checks are big (e.g., pair 9), or when the verification task is relatively trivial in non-incremental verification (e.g., pairs 2 and 5). Slowdowns are demonstrated on average of 0.6x for 30% of our benchmarks in UPPROVER. On the other hand, the positive effect of summary reuse in UPPROVER was very evident, with notable speedup of 10.7x on 70% of benchmarks in LRA and EUF on average, and with an impressive max value of 109x in EUF and 104x in LRA summary reuse.

B. Demonstrating the effect of theory encoding in UPPROVER

Figure 3 illustrates the trade-off between the precision and run time of incremental verification by comparing the LRA/EUF-based encodings in UPPROVER against the PROP-based encoding in EVOLCHECK. Each point corresponds to an incremental verification run on P_2. Almost universally, whenever run time exceeds one second, it is an order of magnitude faster to verify with LRA and EUF than

Table I: UPPROVER using EUF summary vs. non-incremental HIFROG.

pair	F	boot itp(s)	HiFrog total(s)	diff(s)		valid	UpProver total(s)	speedup	result
1	2124	0.5	36.6	0.2	80	92	8.9	**4.1**	Safe
2	25	0.1	0.8	0.1	1	2	1.8	0.4	Unsafe
3	2291	1.3	41.8	0.2	0	0	0.5	**92.9**	Safe
4	2148	0.6	41.4	0.2	4	4	0.8	**55.2**	Safe
5	544	0.1	2.4	0.1	95	105	4.7	0.5	Unsafe
6	4350	0.7	32.1	0.5	415	552	58.1	0.6	Safe
7	665	0.1	2.5	0.1	1	1	0.2	**10.8**	Safe
8	357	0.1	3.8	0.1	10	13	0.4	**9.9**	Safe
9	5417	0.6	43.2	0.5	750	1201	101.1	0.4	Safe
10	2121	0.5	37.6	0.2	4	4	0.8	**49.5**	Safe
11	31246	3.2	83.2	12.1	30	41	78.2	**1.1**	Safe

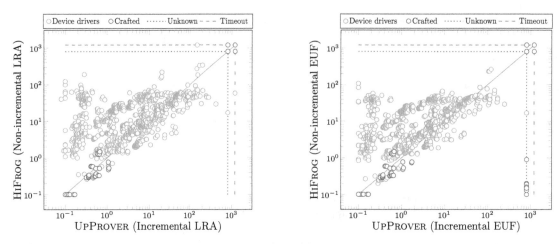

Figure 2: Demonstrating the impact of summary reuse by comparing verification time of UPPROVER versus HIFROG on LRA (*left*) and EUF (*right*).

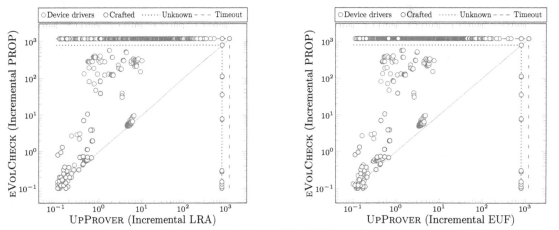

Figure 3: Demonstrating the impact of theory encoding by comparing timings of LRA/EUF encodings in UPPROVER vs. PROP encoding in EVOLCHECK.

Table II: A comparison of different encodings in UPPROVER on device drivers (light gray) and crafted benchmarks (dark gray).

results	PROP P_1	PROP P_2	LRA P_1	LRA P_2	EUF P_1	EUF P_2	Regret PROP P_1+P_2	Regret LRA P_1+P_2	Regret EUF P_1+P_2
Safe	353	353	1591	1589	1591	1590	0+0	0+0	0+0
Unsafe	0	0	78*	1*	85*	1*	n/a	n/a	n/a
TO	1326	2	10	1	3	0	n/a	n/a	n/a
Total	1679								
Safe	57	38	73	57	35	28	2+2	16+17	4+6
Unsafe	6	12	16*	12*	53*	6*	n/a	n/a	n/a
TO	27	3	3	0	4	0	n/a	n/a	n/a
MO	2	0	0	0	0	0	n/a	n/a	n/a
Total	92								

with PROP. In addition, a large number of benchmarks on the top horizontal lines suggests that it is possible to solve many more instances with LRA/EUF-based encoding than with PROP-based encoding. However, the loss of precision is seen on the benchmarks on the vertical line labeled Unknown, indicating if the incremental result using LRA/EUF is unsafe, the result might be spurious because of abstraction.

More statistics are shown in Table II. For each encoding within the time and memory limits, the benchmarks are reported as *Safe* or *Unsafe*. The unsafe results might be spurious on theory encodings (indicated by an asterisk). We use acronyms *TO* for time out, *MO* for memory out, and P_1, P_2 for two versions of a program. We notice that PROP times out in 76% of the benchmarks, while LRA and EUF time out for less than 1%. The last three columns (the first number refers to P_1 and the second to P_2) indicate how many benchmarks can be solved exclusively in a single encoding. This can be interpreted as the *regret* of not including a solver in an imaginary portfolio.

The results for crafted benchmarks show that the theories are complementary, with LRA having the biggest regret. This can be contrasted to the plot in Fig. 4 showing that LRA encoding has a constant 30% time overhead compared to EUF due to the more expensive decision procedure.

Our extensive experimentation reveals that LRA and EUF encodings are crucial for scalability. At the same time, there is a small number of benchmarks that require PROP. While it is unsurprising that bit-blasted models are more expensive to check than the EUF and LRA models, we find it surprising that the light-weight encodings work so often. In effect, the encodings complement each other, and the results suggest an approach where the user gradually tries different precisions until one is found that suits the benchmarks at hand.

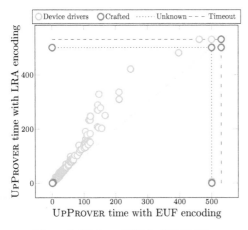

Figure 4: LRA vs. EUF in UPPROVER.

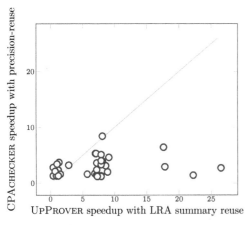

Figure 5: Speedup in UPPROVER vs. CPACHECKER.

C. Comparison of UPPROVER and CPACHECKER

Finally, we compare UPPROVER with a widely-used tool CPACHECKER that is able to perform incremental verification by reusing abstraction precisions. It is an orthogonal technique to ours, i.e., it is an unbounded verifier and aims at finding loop invariants. Thus, comparing running times does not make sense since running times in UPPROVER crucially depend on the chosen bound.[3] Instead, we concentrate on comparing the speedups obtained with the two methods since the change of a bound affects a speedup less.

Here we report the results only on device driver instances which both tools could handle. Among the 250 device drivers categories reported in https://www.sosy-lab.org/research/cpa-reuse/predicate.html, we matched 34 categories which are suitable for UPPROVER.[4] These categories contain in total 903 verification tasks.

Fig. 5 depicts the comparison of speedup in UPPROVER and CPACHECKER. A large amount of points on the lower triangle

[3]For instance, the average running times in CPACHECKER is 285.3 seconds and in UPPROVER with LRA is 13.4 seconds for chosen bound 5. For other bounds UPPROVER would have different average running times.

[4]The reported version of UPPROVER is constrained by its dependency on the CPROVER framework which impedes its frontend from processing some benchmarks.

lets us conclude that summary reuse in UPPROVER achieves superior speedup than the precision reuse in CPACHECKER. The average speedup in UPPROVER was 7.3 with standard-deviation of 6 and in CPACHECKER the average speedup was 2.9 with standard-deviation of 1.7. There were 4 slowdowns in UPPROVER whereas CPACHECKER did not report any slowdowns on these 34 categories. The detailed results are available at http://verify.inf.usi.ch/upprover/experimentation.

V. RELATED WORK

The trend towards constructing efficient tools for incremental formal verification exists since last two decades [15]. We identify here two main approaches to incremental verification of different revisions of a program:

a) Differential program reasoning: Reasoning over multiple programs (to, e.g., prove program equivalence) is usually performed by creating a so-called *product program* [16], [17], [18], [19], [20], [21] and analyzing this product program using the general-purpose tools. These approaches, however, do not usually consider properties about isolated programs. A modular approach that works by simultaneously traversing the call trees of both programs is proposed in [16], but it does not use function summaries. A probabilistic framework has been recently proposed in [22], but it is applicable to differential bug finding, rather than to proving the absence of bugs.

b) Incremental Verification: A number of approaches accelerate verification by reusing previous efforts. Program changes are extensively used in incremental modal μ-calculus [23], solving of Constrained Horn Clauses [24], [25], predicate abstraction [14], [26], automata-based approaches [27], reusing the results from constraint solving [28], and state-space graph for checking temporal safety properties [29]. However these groups of techniques are orthogonal to our approach as we store and reuse the interpolation-based function summaries in the context of BMC for verifying revisions of programs. In addition, our tool outputs a *certificate of correctness* in the form of a function summary that can be used as a function specification.

VI. CONCLUSION AND FUTURE WORK

We presented UPPROVER, an SMT-based incremental BMC tool for different revisions of a program. Its key innovation is in several SMT-level encodings and the corresponding SMT-level summarization algorithms that allow the user to adjust the precision or efficiency of verification. UPPROVER enables LRA and EUF theories (and in the future, more) thus allowing a trade-off between precision and performance. Furthermore, our approach not only extracts function summaries but provides a capability of repairing them on-the-fly and reusing them in the subsequent verification runs. Our experimentation reveals that UPPROVER is more efficient than its predecessor and the two orthogonal approaches: non-incremental bounded model checker [5] and precision reuse [14].

In future we extend the tool to handle summaries from different theories simultaneously in the style of [7] and [30], possibly by allowing checks for the tree-interpolation property on-the-fly.

References

[1] O. Sery, G. Fedyukovich, and N. Sharygina, "Incremental upgrade checking by means of interpolation-based function summaries," in *Proc. FMCAD 2012*. IEEE, 2012, pp. 114–121.

[2] W. Craig, "Three uses of the Herbrand-Gentzen theorem in relating model theory and proof theory," *J. Symb. Log.*, vol. 22, no. 3, pp. 269–285, 1957.

[3] G. Fedyukovich, O. Sery, and N. Sharygina, "eVolCheck: Incremental upgrade checker for C," in *Proc. TACAS 2013*, ser. LNCS, vol. 7795. Springer, 2013, pp. 292–307.

[4] A. Biere, A. Cimatti, E. M. Clarke, and Y. Zhu, "Symbolic model checking without BDDs," in *Proc. TACAS 2003*, ser. LNCS, vol. 1579. Springer, 1999, pp. 193–207.

[5] L. Alt, S. Asadi, H. Chockler, K. Even-Mendoza, G. Fedyukovich, A. E. J. Hyvärinen, and N. Sharygina, "HiFrog: SMT-based function summarization for software verification," in *Proc. TACAS 2017*, ser. LNCS, vol. 10206. Springer, 2017, pp. 207–213.

[6] O. Sery, G. Fedyukovich, and N. Sharygina, "Interpolation-based function summaries in bounded model checking," in *Proc. HVC 2011*, ser. LNCS, vol. 7261. Springer, 2011, pp. 160–175.

[7] S. Asadi, M. Blicha, G. Fedyukovich, A. E. J. Hyvärinen, K. Even-Mendoza, N. Sharygina, and H. Chockler, "Function summarization modulo theories," in *Proc. LPAR-22*, ser. EPiC Series in Computing, vol. 57. EasyChair, 2018, pp. 56–75.

[8] S. Asadi, M. Blicha, A. E. J. Hyvärinen, G. Fedyukovich, and N. Sharygina, "Farkas-based tree interpolation," in *Proc. SAS 2020 (to appear)*, ser. LNCS. Springer.

[9] J. Christ and J. Hoenicke, "Proof tree preserving tree interpolation," *J. Autom. Reasoning*, vol. 57, no. 1, pp. 67–95, 2016.

[10] A. E. J. Hyvärinen, M. Marescotti, L. Alt, and N. Sharygina, "OpenSMT2: An SMT solver for multi-core and cloud computing," in *Proc. SAT 2016*, ser. LNCS, vol. 9710. Springer, 2016, pp. 547–553.

[11] L. Alt, G. Fedyukovich, A. E. J. Hyvärinen, and N. Sharygina, "A proof-sensitive approach for small propositional interpolants," in *Proc. VSTTE 2015*, ser. LNCS, vol. 9593. Springer, 2016, pp. 1–18.

[12] L. Alt, A. E. J. Hyvärinen, S. Asadi, and N. Sharygina, "Duality-based interpolation for quantifier-free equalities and uninterpreted functions," in *Proc. FMCAD 2017*. IEEE, 2017, pp. 39–46.

[13] M. Blicha, A. E. J. Hyvärinen, J. Kofron, and N. Sharygina, "Decomposing Farkas interpolants," in *Proc. TACAS 2019*, ser. LNCS, vol. 11427. Springer, 2019, pp. 3–20.

[14] D. Beyer, S. Löwe, E. Novikov, A. Stahlbauer, and P. Wendler, "Precision reuse for efficient regression verification," in *Proc. ESEC/FSE 2013*. ACM, 2013, pp. 389–399.

[15] R. H. Hardin, R. P. Kurshan, K. L. McMillan, J. A. Reeds, and N. J. A. Sloane, "Efficient regression verification," in *Proc. WODES 96*. IEEE, 1996, pp. 147–150.

[16] B. Godlin and O. Strichman, "Regression verification," in *Proc. DAC 2009*. ACM, 2009, pp. 466–471.

[17] G. Barthe, J. M. Crespo, and C. Kunz, "Relational verification using product programs," in *Proc. FM 2011*, ser. LNCS, vol. 6664. Springer, 2011, pp. 200–214.

[18] S. K. Lahiri, K. L. McMillan, R. Sharma, and C. Hawblitzel, "Differential assertion checking," in *Proc. FSE 2013*. ACM, 2013, pp. 345–355.

[19] L. Pick, G. Fedyukovich, and A. Gupta, "Exploiting synchrony and symmetry in relational verification," in *Proc. CAV 2018, Part I*, ser. LNCS, vol. 10981. Springer, 2018, pp. 164–182.

[20] R. Shemer, A. Gurfinkel, S. Shoham, and Y. Vizel, "Property directed self composition," in *CAV 2019, Part I*, vol. 11561. Springer, 2019, pp. 161–179.

[21] D. Mordvinov and G. Fedyukovich, "Property directed inference of relational invariants," in *Proc. FMCAD 2019*. IEEE, 2019, pp. 152–160.

[22] K. Heo, M. Raghothaman, X. Si, and M. Naik, "Continuously reasoning about programs using differential Bayesian inference," in *Proc. PLDI 2019*. ACM, 2019, pp. 561–575.

[23] O. Sokolsky and S. A. Smolka, "Incremental model checking in the modal mu-calculus," in *Proc. CAV 1994*, ser. LNCS, vol. 818. Springer, 1994, pp. 351–363.

[24] G. Fedyukovich, A. Gurfinkel, and N. Sharygina, "Incremental verification of compiler optimizations," in *Proc. NFM 2014*, ser. LNCS, vol. 8430. Springer, 2014, pp. 300–306.

[25] ——, "Property directed equivalence via abstract simulation," in *Proc. CAV 2016*, vol. 9780, Part II. Springer, 2016, pp. 433–453.

[26] F. He, Q. Yu, and L. Cai, "When regression verification meets CEGAR," *CoRR*, vol. abs/1806.04829, 2018. [Online]. Available: http://arxiv.org/abs/1806.04829

[27] B. Rothenberg, D. Dietsch, and M. Heizmann, "Incremental verification using trace abstraction," in *Proc. SAS 2018*, ser. LNCS, vol. 11002. Springer, 2018, pp. 364–382.

[28] W. Visser, J. Geldenhuys, and M. B. Dwyer, "Green: reducing, reusing and recycling constraints in program analysis," in *20th ACM SIGSOFT Symposium on the Foundations of Software Engineering (FSE-20), SIGSOFT/FSE 12,*. ACM, 2012, p. 58.

[29] T. A. Henzinger, R. Jhala, R. Majumdar, and M. A. A. Sanvido, "Extreme model checking," in *Verification: Theory and Practice, Essays Dedicated to Zohar Manna on the Occasion of His 64th Birthday*, 2003, pp. 332–358.

[30] A. E. J. Hyvärinen, S. Asadi, K. Even-Mendoza, G. Fedyukovich, H. Chockler, and N. Sharygina, "Theory refinement for program verification," in *Proc. SAT 2017*, ser. LNCS, vol. 10491. Springer, 2017, pp. 347–363.

21

Smart Induction for Isabelle/HOL (Tool Paper)

Yutaka Nagashima (iD)
CIIRC, Czech Technical University in Prague
University of Innsbruck
Email: yutaka.nagashima@cvut.cz

Abstract—Proof assistants offer tactics to facilitate inductive proofs; however, deciding what arguments to pass to these tactics still requires human ingenuity. To automate this process, we present `smart_induct` for Isabelle/HOL. Given an inductive problem in any problem domain, `smart_induct` lists promising arguments for the `induct` tactic without relying on a search. Our in-depth evaluation demonstrate that `smart_induct` produces valuable recommendations across problem domains. Currently, `smart_induct` is an interactive tool; however, we expect that `smart_induct` can be used to narrow the search space of automatic inductive provers.

I. INTRODUCTION

Proof by induction lies at the heart of verification of computer programs that involve recursive data-structures, recursion, or iteration [1]. To facilitate proofs by induction, interactive theorem provers, such as Isabelle/HOL [2], Coq [3], and HOL[4], offers tactics. Yet, it requires prover specific expertise to be familiar with such tactics, and human developers have to manually investigate each inductive problem to decide how to apply such tactics.

Unfortunately, the automation of proof by induction is considered as a long standing challenge in computer science, for which Gramlich [1] presented the following conjecture in 2005:

> in the near future, inductive theorem proving will only be successful for very specialised domains for very restricted classes of conjectures. Inductive theorem proving will continue to be a very challenging engineering process [1].

We challenge his conjecture with `smart_induct`, a recommendation tool for proof by induction in Isabelle/HOL. Given an inductive problem in *any* domain, `smart_induct` suggests how one should apply the `induct` tactic to attack that problem.

II. PROOF BY INDUCTION IN ISABELLE/HOL

Given the following two simple reverse functions defined in Isabelle/HOL [2], how do you prove their equivalence [5]?

```
primrec rev::"α list => α list" where
  "rev  []      = []"
| "rev (x # xs) = rev xs @ [x]"

fun itrev::"α list => α list => α list"
where
  "itrev  []    ys = ys"
| "itrev (x#xs) ys = itrev xs (x#ys)"
```

```
lemma "itrev xs ys = rev xs @ ys"
```

where # is the list constructor, and @ appends two lists. Using the `induct` tactic of Isabelle/HOL, we can prove this inductive problem in multiple ways:

```
lemma prf1: "itrev xs ys = rev xs @ ys"
  apply(induct xs arbitrary: ys) by auto
lemma prf2: "itrev xs ys = rev xs @ ys"
  apply(induct xs ys rule:itrev.induct)
  by auto
```

`prf1` applies structural induction on `xs` while generalising `ys` before applying induction by passing `ys` to the `arbitrary` field. It is worth noting that the `induct` tactic determines the default induction principle in `prf1` from the induction term, `xs`. On the other hand, `prf2` applies functional induction (also known as computation induction) on `itrev` by the induction principle, `itrev.induct`, to the `rule` field.

There are other lesser-known techniques to handle difficult inductive problems using the `induct` tactic, and sometimes users have to develop useful auxiliary lemmas manually; however, for most cases the problem of how to apply induction boils down to the the following three questions:

- On which terms to apply induction?
- Which variables to generalise using the `arbitrary` field?
- Which rule to use for functional induction or rule inversion (as known as rule induction) in the `rule` field?

To answer these questions automatically, we previously developed a proof strategy language, `PSL` [6]. Given an inductive problem, `PSL` produces various combinations of induction arguments for the `induct` tactic and conducts an extensive proof search based on a given strategy. If `PSL` completes a proof search, it identifies the appropriate combination of arguments for the problem and presents the combination to the user; however, when the search space becomes enormous, `PSL` cannot find a proof within a realistic timeout and fails to provide any recommendation, even if `PSL` produces the right combination of induction arguments. For further automation of proof by induction, we need a tool that satisfies the following two criteria:

- The tool suggests right induction arguments without completing a proof search.
- The tool suggests right induction arguments for any inductive problems.

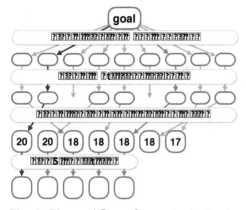

Fig. 1: The workflow of `smart_induct`.

In this paper we present `smart_induct`, a recommendation tool that addresses these criteria. `smart_induct` is available at GitHub [7] together with our running example and the evaluation files discussed in Section IV.

The implementation of `smart_induct` is specific to Isabelle/HOL; however, the underlying concept is transferable to other tactic-based proof assistants including HOL4 [4], Coq [3], and Lean [8]. We developed `smart_induct` as an interactive tool, but one can take its approach to narrow the search space for automatic inductive provers, such as ACL2 [9] and Imandra [10].

To the best of our knowledge `smart_induct` is the first recommendation tool that uses a logic to analyze the syntactic structures of proof goals and advises how to apply the `induct` tactic across problem domains without completing to a proof search.

III. GENERATING AND FILTERING TACTICS

Fig. 1 illustrates the internal workflow of `smart_induct`: when invoked by a user, the first step produces many variants of the `induct` tactic with different combinations of arguments. Secondly, the multi-stage screening step filters out less promising combinations of induction arguments. Thirdly, the scoring step evaluates each combination to a natural number using logical feature extractors implemented in `LiFtEr` [11] and reorder the combinations based on their scores. Lastly, the short-listing step takes the best 10 candidates and prints them in the Output panel of Isabelle/jEdit as shown in Fig. 2. In this section, we explore details of Step 1 to Step 3.

A. Step 1: Creation of Many Induction Tactics.

`smart_induct` inspects the given proof goal and produces a number of combinations of arguments for the `induct` tactic taking the following procedure: `smart_induct` collects variables and constants appearing in the goal. If a constant has an associated induction rule in the underlying proof context, `smart_induct` also collects that rule. From these variables and induction rules, `smart_induct` produces the power set of combinations of arguments for the `induct` tactic. Then, for each member of the power set `smart_induct` computes the permutation of the induction variables since

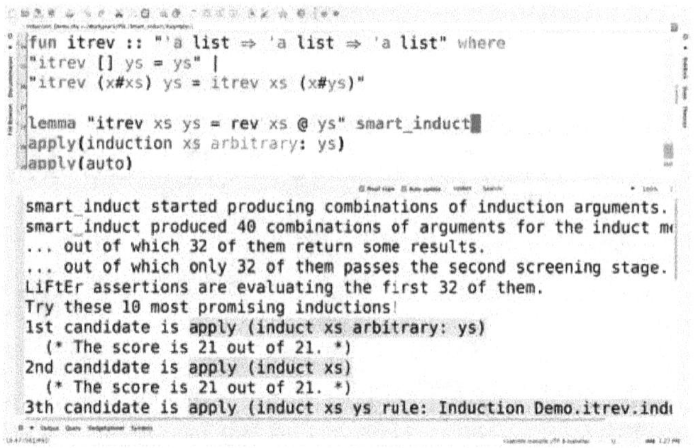

Fig. 2: The user-interface of `smart_induct`.

the `induct` tactic behaves differently for different orders of induction variables. Finally, `smart_induct` produces a tactic for each well-typed permutation of induction variables for each member of the power set.

In our example, `smart_induct` picks up `xs` and `ys` as variables and `itrev` and `rev` as constants, from which it finds `itrev.induct` as an induction rule, which Isabelle derived automatically when defining `itrev`. From these variables and rule, `smart_induct` produces 40 combinations of induction arguments.

If the size of this set is enormous, we cannot store all the produced induction tactics in our machines. Therefore, `smart_induct` produces this set as a lazy sequence and takes only the first 10,000 combinations for further processing.

B. Step 2: Multi-Stage Screening.

10,000 is still a large number, and feature extractors used in Step 3 often involve nested traversals of nodes in the syntax tree representing a proof goal, leading to high computational costs. Fortunately, the application of the `induct` tactic itself is not computationally expensive in most cases: we can apply the `induct` tactic to a proof goal and have intermediate sub-goals at a low cost. Therefore, in Step 2, `smart_induct` applies the `induct` tactic to the given proof goal using the various combinations of arguments from Step 1 and filter out some of them through the following two stages.

Stage 1 focuses on the `induct` tactics that return some results: in the first stage, `smart_induct` filters out those combinations of induction arguments, with which Isabelle/HOL does not produce an intermediate goal. Since we have no known theoretical upper bound for the computational cost for the `induct` tactic, we also filter out those combinations of arguments, with which the `induct` tactic does not return a result within a pre-defined timeout. In our running example, this stage filters out 8 combinations out of 40.

Stage 2 discards the `induct` tactic tactics that return unpromising results: taking the results from the previous stage, Stage 2 scans both the original goal and the newly introduced intermediate sub-goals at the same time to further filter out less promising combinations. More concretely, this stage filters out all combinations of arguments if they satisfy any of the following conditions.

- Some of newly introduced sub-goals are identical to each other.
- A newly introduced sub-goal contains a schematic variable even though the original first sub-goal did not contain a schematic variable.

In our example, Stage 2 does not filter out any combination. Note that these tests on the original goal and resulting sub-goals do not involve nested traversals of nodes in the syntax tree representing goals. For this reason, the computational cost of this stage is often lower than that of Step 3.

C. Step 3: Scoring Induction Arguments using LiFtEr.

Step 3 carefully investigates the remaining candidates using heuristics implemented in LiFtEr [11]. LiFtEr is a domain-specific language to encode induction heuristics in a style independent of problem domains. Given a proof goal and combination of induction arguments, the LiFtEr interpreter mechanically checks if the combination is appropriate for the goal in terms of a heuristic written in LiFtEr. The interpreter returns True if the combination is compatible with the heuristic and False if not. We illustrated the details of LiFtEr in our previous work [11] with many examples. In this paper, we focus on the essence of LiFtEr and show one example heuristic used in smart_induct.

LiFtEr supports four types of variables: natural numbers, induction rules, terms, and term occurrences. An induction rule is an auxiliary lemma passed to the rule field of the induct tactic. The domain of terms is the set of all sub-terms appearing in a given goal. The logical connectives ($\vee$, $\wedge$, $\rightarrow$, and $\neg$) correspond to the connectives in the classical logic. LiFtEr offers atomic assertions, such as is_rule_of, to examine the property of each atomic term. Quantifiers bring the power of abstraction to LiFtEr, which allows LiFtEr users to encode induction heuristics that can transcend problem domains. Quantification over term can be restricted to the induction terms used in the induct tactic.

We encoded 19 heuristics in LiFtEr for smart_induct and assign weights to these heuristics. Some of them examine a combination of induction arguments in terms of functional induction or rule inversion, whereas others check the combination for structural induction. Program 1, for example, encodes a heuristic for functional induction. In English this heuristic reads as follows:

> if there exists a rule, $r1$, in the rule field of the induct tactic, then there exists a term $t1$ with an occurrence $to1$, such that $r1$ is derived by Isabelle when defining $t1$, and for all induction terms $t2$, there exists an occurrence $to2$ of $t2$ such that, there exists a number n, such that $to2$ is the nth argument of $to1$ and that $t2$ is the nth induction terms passed to the induct tactic.

If we apply this heuristic to our running example, prf2, the LiFtEr interpreter returns True: there is an argument,

Program 1 A LiFtEr heuristic used in smart_induct.

```
∃ r1 : rule. True
→
∃ r1 : rule.
  ∃ t1 : term.
   ∃ to1 : term_occurrence ∈ t1 : term.
    r1 is_rule_of to1
   ∧
    ∀ t2 : term ∈ induction_term.
     ∃ to2 : term_occurrence ∈ t2 : term.
      ∃ n : number.
       is_nth_argument_of (to2, n, to1)
      ∧
       t2 is_nth_induction_term n
```

itrev.induct, in the rule field, and the occurrence of its related term, itrev, in the proof goal takes all the induction terms, xs and ys, as its arguments in the same order.

Attentive readers may have noticed that Program 1 is independent of any types or constants specific to prf2. Instead of handling specific constructs explicitly, Program 1 analyzes the structure of the goal with respect to the arguments passed to the induct tactic in an abstract way using quantified variables and logical connectives. This power of abstraction let smart_induct evaluate whether a given combination of arguments to the induct tactic is appropriate for a user-defined proof goal consisting of user-defined types and constants, even though such constructs are not available to the smart_induct developers. In fact, none of the LiFtEr heuristics used in smart_induct relies on constructs specific to any problem domain except for one heuristic, which involves a heuristic about Set.member. We developed this particular heuristic for conjectures involving Set.member since Set.member appears in the standard library of Isabelle/HOL and is used by many Isabelle users.

In Step 3, smart_induct applies these heuristics to the results from Step 2. For each heuristic, smart_induct gives certain predefined points to each combination of induct arguments if the LiFtEr interpreter returns True for that combination. Then, smart_induct reorders these combinations based on their scores and presents the most promising combinations to the user in Step 4.

D. User-Interface

Fig. 2 shows a screenshot of Isabelle/jEdit interface with smart_induct. The seamless integration into Isabelle's ecosystem makes smart_induct easy to install and easy to use: smart_induct is free from any dependency to external tools except for Isabelle/HOL itself, and we have incorporated smart_induct into Isabelle/Isar [12], Isabelle's proof language, and Isabelle/jEdit, its standard editor. This allows Isabelle users to invoke smart_induct by typing smart_induct within their proof document and to copy a recommended use of the induct tactic to the right location in the document with one click.

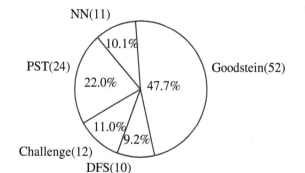

Fig. 3: Breakdown of the evaluation dataset.

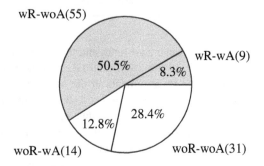

Fig. 4: Use of `rule` and `arbitrary` fields.

Since `smart_induct` is a meta-tool to use Isabelle's default induction tactic, once `smart_induct` has been called and the tactic inserted, one can remove the `smart_induct` call.

IV. EVALUATION

We evaluated `smart_induct` by measuring its performance. We conducted all evaluations using a MacBook Pro (15-inch, 2019) with 2.6 GHz Intel Core i7 6-core memory 32 GB 2400 MHz DDR4.

A. Database for evaluation.

As our evaluation target, we chose five Isabelle theory files with many inductive problems developed by various researchers from the Archive of Formal Proofs [13]. In the following, we use the following short names to denote these files:

1) *Challenge* stands for `Challenge1A.thy`, which is a part of the solution for VerifyThis2019, a program verification competition associated with ETAPS2019 [14],
2) *DFS* stands for `DFS.thy`, which is a formalisation of depth-first search [15],
3) *Goodstein* is for `Goodstein_Lambda.thy`, which is an implementation of the Goodstein function in lambda-calculus [16],
4) *NN* stands for `Nearest_Neighbors.thy`, which is from the formalisation of multi-dimensional binary search trees [17], and

TABLE I: Scope of `smart_induct`.

-	w/ handwritten rule	w/o handwritten rule
w/ compound term	1 (0.9%)	1 (0.9%)
w/o compound term	5 (4.6%)	102 (93.6%)

5) *PST* stands for `PST_RBT.thy`, which is from the formalisation of priority search tree [18].

As a whole these files contain 109 calls of the `induct` tactic. Fig. 3 shows the demographics of our dataset. For example, NN(11) 10.1% mean that `Nearest_Neighbor.thy` contains 11 invocations of the `induct` tactic, which accounts for 10.1% of all invocations of the `induct` tactic in our dataset.

Fig. 4, on the other hand, shows how often proof authors used the `rule` and `arbitrary` fields. In the labels of Fig. 4, "w" and "wo" stand for "with" and "without", respectively; whereas "R" and "A" stand for "Rule" and "Arbitrary". For example, "wR-woA(55) 50.5%" represents that among the 109 applications of the `induct` tactic 55 of them have an argument in the `rule` field but have no argument in the `arbitrary` field, and this amounts to 50.5%. We greyed the area corresponding to the applications of the `induct` tactic with an argument in the `rule` field.

This figure illustrates that in our dataset

- more than half of applications come with a `rule`, and
- applications of the `induct` tactic with a `rule` are less likely to involve generalisation.

Table I shows how many proofs by induction in the evaluation dataset reside within the scope of `smart_induct`. For example, 102(93.6%) for "w/o compound term" and "w/o handwritten rule" means the following: for 102 proofs by induction out of 109, developers of this dataset used the `induct` tactic without applying induction on a compound term nor using an induction rule in the `rule` field that was conjectured and proved manually by a human developer.

These 102 proofs by induction are the only ones that reside within the scope of `smart_induct` because Step 1 of `smart_induct` does not create the `induct` tactics on compound terms or the `induct` tactics with induction principles that were not derived by Isabelle automatically when defining a constant appearing in the proof goal at hand.

Conversely, the remaining three entries in Table I correspond to the invocations of the `induct` tactic that lie outside the scope of `smart_induct`. And such invocations amount to 7 (6.4%) out of 109.

B. Coincidence Rate.

The most important aspect of this tool would be the accuracy of its recommendation. Unfortunately, it is in general not possible to measure if a combination of induction arguments is correct for a goal because many proofs by induction can be valid for one inductive problem. For our running example, we have two proofs, `prf1` and `prf2`, and both of them are equally good. In this particular case, we can confirm

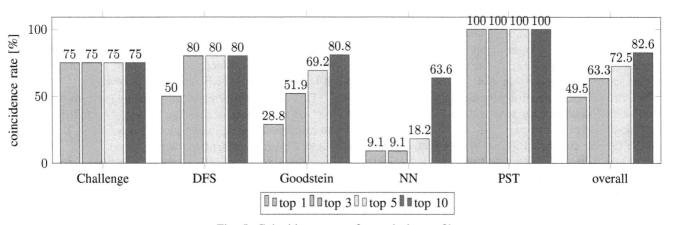

Fig. 5: Coincidence rates for each theory file.

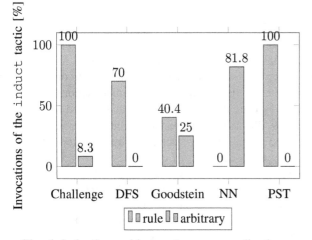

Fig. 6: Inductions with a `rule` or generalization.

the correctness of these combinations of induction arguments by completing the corresponding proof attempts; however, the necessary proof scripts that follow the `induct` tactic, in general, can be arbitrarily long, and for this reason it is not possible to mechanically check whether a combination of induction arguments is correct or not.

Since we cannot directly measure the true success rate of `smart_induct`, we evaluated the trustworthiness of `smart_induct` s recommendations using *coincidence rates*: we counted how often its recommendation coincides with the choices of Isabelle experts. Since we often have multiple equally valid combinations of induction arguments for a given proof goal, we should regard a coincidence rate as a conservative estimate of true success rate.

On the other hand, we can safely consider our coincidence rates as the lower bound for the true success rates since we collected our evaluation targets from the Archive of Formal Proofs [13], which accepts Isabelle proof documents only after the peer-reviewing process by Isabelle experts.

Fig. 5 shows coincidence rates for each theory file and the entire dataset separately. The four bars for each theory file represent the corresponding success rates among top n

recommendations, where n is 1, 3, 5, and 10 from left to right. For example, top 3 for Goodstein is 51.9%. This means the following: when `smart_induct` recommends three most promising combinations induction arguments to 52 inductive problems in `Goodstein_Lambda.thy`, for 51.9% out of 52 problems in this file one of the three combinations of induction arguments recommended by `smart_induct` *coincides* with the choice of human proof author.

As mentioned earlier, we should regard a coincidence rate as a conservative estimate of true success rate. Therefore, 51.9% mentioned above should be interpreted as following: `smart_induct` s recommendation coincides with the choice of experienced Isabelle user for 51.9% of times when it is allowed to recommend three combinations of arguments, but the real success rate of `smart_induct` s recommendation can be higher than 51.9%.

Notably the rightmost group of bars in Fig. 5 shows that `smart_induct` can recommend the choice of human engineer as the most promising application of the `induct` tactic for at least roughly half of the cases (49.5%).

A quick glance over Fig. 5 would give the impression that `smart_induct` s performance depends heavily on problem domains: `smart_induct` demonstrated the perfect result for PST, whereas the coincidence rate for NN remains at 18.2% for top_5.

However, a closer investigation of the results reveals that the different coincidence rates come from the style of induction rather than domain specific items such as the types or constructs appearing in goals.

To corroborate this claim, we illustrate how each proof author used the `induct` tactic to develop each theory file in Fig. 6. In this figure each pair of bars presents how often the `induct` tactic comes with an argument in the `rule` field and `arbitrary` field, respectively. For example, the left bar for Goodstein is 40.4% whereas its right bar is 25.0%. This means that the `induct` tactic is applied with an argument in the `rule` field for 40.4% of times in Goodstein, and the `induct` tactic generalises a variable using the `arbitrary` field for 25.0% of times in the same file.

Together with Fig. 5, Fig. 6 shows that `smart_induct`

tends to show a higher coincidence rate for theory files with a high proportion of the `induct` tactics with an argument in the `rule` field and a lower proportion of the tactics with generalisation using the `arbitrary` field. NN and PST are two extreme examples: In NN, 81.8% of applications of the `induct` tactic involve generalisation while no application of the tactic has an argument in the `rule` field in Fig. 6, and `smart_induct`s coincidence rates are lowest for NN. On the contrary, PST has no application involving generalisation while all applications use the `rule` field, and `smart_induct`s showed the perfect result for PST.

To further investigate how the style of induction affects the coincidence rate of `smart_induct`, we measured coincidence rates based on the use of the `rule` and `arbitrary` fields in Fig. 7 where "w" and "wo" stand for "with" and "without", respectively. For example, the leftmost group labelled with "w-rule-w-arb" represents the coincidence rates among the applications of the `induct` tactic that have arguments in both the `rule` and `arbitrary` fields.

The two right most groups of bars represent the coincidence rates based on the use of `rule` field regardless of the use of the `arbitrary` field. These two groups show that `smart_induct` tends to perform better in predicting how human engineers use the `induct` tactic when the `induct` tactic has an argument in the `rule` field, which correspond to functional induction and rule inversion.

Interestingly, the two groups in the middle of Fig. 7 show that if we focus on the cases without generalisation we can see that the trend among the gaps between the coincidence rates for rule-based inductions (function induction and rule inversion) and the corresponding rates for structural inductions is less clear: we have a wider gap for "top 1", but narrower gaps for "top 3" and "top 5". And for "top 10" we even have a lower coincidence rate for rule-based inductions. Moreover, if we focus on the `induct` tactics involving generalisation, `smart_induct` shows even *lower* coincidence rates for rule-based inductions as shown by the two leftmost groups in Fig. 7; even though `smart_induct` overall tends to show *higher* coincidence rates for rule-based inductions.

This seemingly paradoxical phenomenon is best explained by Fig. 4, which shows that rule-based inductions less often involve generalisation (14.0%) than structural induction (31.1%) in the dataset: it is still difficult for `smart_induct` to predict which variable to generalise, especially for rule-based inductions, but rule-based inductions tend not to involve variable generalisation to begin with.

To investigate how far generalisation of variables leads to poor coincidence rates, we computed the coincidence rates for NN again based on a different criterion: this time we ignored the `arbitrary` fields and took only induction terms and arguments in the `rule` into consideration to measure coincidence rates presented in Fig. 8. In Fig. 8, the coincidence rate among top 1 is still as low as 9.1% since `smart_induct` often chooses a rule-based induction for the most promising candidate, but the overall trend is much better and similar to the rates for w-rule-wo-arb in Fig 7. The large discrepancies

between the numbers for NN in Fig. 5 and those in Fig. 8 show that even for the most problematic theory file, NN, which contains many structural inductions `smart_induct` is often able to predict on which variables experts apply induction, but it fails to predict which variables to generalise.

The limited performance in predicting experts use of the `arbitrary` field stems from `LiFtEr`s limited capability to examine semantic information of proof goals. Even though `LiFtEr` offers quantifiers, logical connectives, and atomic assertions to analyze the syntactic structure of a goal in an abstract way, `LiFtEr` does not offer enough supports to analyze the semantics of the goal. For more accurate prediction of variable generalisation, `smart_induct` needs a language to analyze not only the structure of a goal itself but also the structure of the definitions of types and constants appearing in the goal abstractly.

C. Pruning.

Section III showed how `smart_induct` produces many candidates of the `induct` tactic and prunes less promising ones step by step. We measured how each of these steps contributes to the production of recommendations by counting how many candidates are produced and pruned at each step.

Fig. 9 illustrates how many candidates `smart_induct` produced at each step for each proof by induction. The vertical axis denotes the number of candidates after each step for the corresponding proof by induction. White circles and "+"es represent the number of remaining candidates for invocations of `smart_induct` when the choice of induction arguments by human authors coincides with one of the 10 most promising combinations recommended by `smart_induct`. For such *successful* cases, we also used a white diamond to depict the corresponding "rank" given by `smart_induct`. For example, if `smart_induct` gives a rank of 3, this means `smart_induct` recommended the choice of human engineer as the third most promising combination of arguments to the `induct` tactic.

Along the horizontal axis in Fig. 9, we sorted proofs by induction based on the number of candidates after Step 1. For example, at the right-end of the horizontal axis, we have a circle, a plus, and a diamond. This means for the proof by induction represented by these three points Step 1 produced 10,000 candidates, and Step 2 pruned them down to 128 candidates, and Step 3 ranked the choice of human engineer as the most promising candidate.

On the other hand, black circles and "x"es represent the number of candidates for *failed* cases where the choice of induction arguments by human authors did not appear among the top 10 recommendations by `smart_induct`.

One can see that black circles are broadly distributed along the horizontal axis, indicating that the number of initial candidates after Step 1 does not have a strong influence on the accuracy of `smart_induct`.

The use of the logarithmic scale for the vertical axis makes it clear that the number of candidates after Step 1 differs wildly.

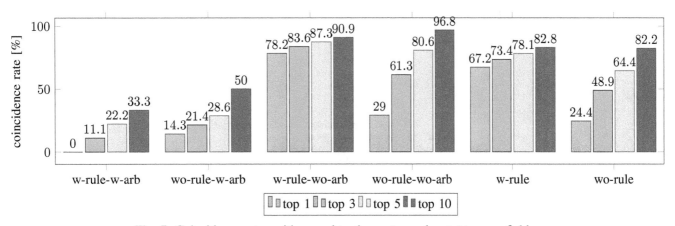

Fig. 7: Coincidence rates with regard to the `rule` and `arbitrary` fields.

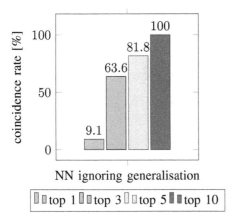

Fig. 8: Coincidence rates when ignoring `arbitrary`.

On the other hand, the number of candidates after Step 2 are mostly contained under 200 with a single exception of 592.

Fig. 9 also shows that we had 6 cases where Step 1 reached its upper limit, 10,000. Interestingly, all these cases are successful and 5 of them have the rank of 1. From this, we can judge that the pre-defined upper limit of 10,000 is a descent compromise, which excludes some possible combinations of induction arguments without seriously damaging the coincidence rates of `smart_induct`.

Finally the wide gaps between each "+" and its corresponding diamond in Fig. 9 indicate that `smart_induct`s heuristics written in `LiFtEr` effectively nailed down the combination of induction arguments used by human engineers out of many plausible options.

D. Execution Time.

For `smart_induct` to be useful, it has to be able to provide valuable recommendations within a realistic time out.

Fig. 10 illustrates the distribution of `smart_induct`s execution time necessary to produce recommendations. The vertical axis represents the execution times in second for each data point, which are sorted along the horizontal axis. As is the case in Section IV-C, we filled circles for unsuccessful cases with black.

Similarly to Fig. 9, Fig. 10 also shows that the unsuccessful cases are spread along the horizontal axis, meaning there is no clear correlation between execution time and the accuracy of recommendation.

We again used the logarithmic scale for the vertical axis. This means that execution times vary largely for different proofs by induction, even though the numbers of candidates after Step 2 are mostly kept below 200, as we saw in Section IV-C, This is because the computational cost for each `LiFtEr` heuristic in Step 3 depends on the syntactic structure of each inductive problem, `smart_induct`s execution time varies for different problems.

The overall median value is 25.5 seconds, which means `smart_induct` can produce a recommendation within 25.5 seconds for half of the problems. In the future we plan to identify and discard less valuable heuristics in Step 3 to speed up `smart_induct`.

V. CONCLUSION

We presented `smart_induct`, a recommendation tool for proof by induction in Isabelle/HOL. Our evaluation showed `smart_induct`s excellent performance in recommending how to apply functional induction and rule inversion and good performance at identifying induction variables for structural induction for various inductive problems across problem domains. This partially refutes Gramlichs bleak conjecture from 2005. However, recommendation of variable generalisation remains as a challenging task.

It remains as an open question how far we can improve the accuracy and speed of `smart_induct` by combining it with search based systems [6], [19] and approaches based on evolutionary computation [20] or statistical machine learning [21].

Related Work: The most well-known approach for inductive problems is called the Boyer-Moore waterfall model [22]. This approach was invented for a first-order logic on Common Lisp. ACL2 [23] is a commonly used waterfall model based prover. When deciding how to apply induction, ACL2 computes a score, called *hitting ratio*, to estimate how good each induction scheme is for the term which it accounts

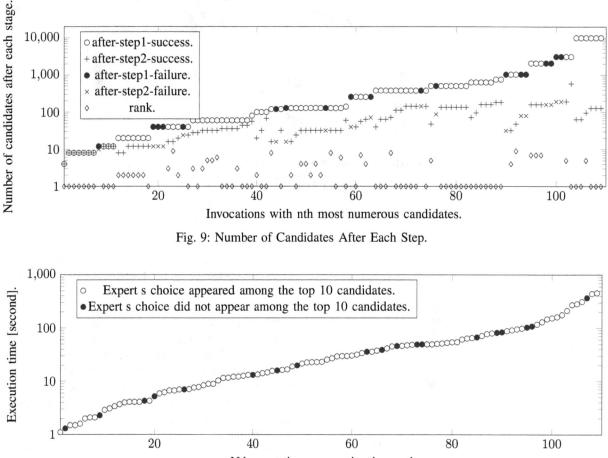

Fig. 9: Number of Candidates After Each Step.

Fig. 10: Execution Time of `smart_induct`.

for and proceeds with the induction scheme with the highest hitting ratio [9], [24].

Instead of computing the hitting ratios, `smart_induct` analyzes the structures of proof goals directly using LiFtEr. While ACL2 produces many induction schemes and computes their hitting ratios, `smart_induct` does not directly produce induction schemes but analyzes the given proof goal, the arguments passed to the `induct` tactic, and the emerging sub-goals.

Jiang *et al.* ran multiple waterfalls [25] in HOL Light [26]. However, when deciding induction variables, they naively picked the first free variable with a recursive type and left the selection of appropriate induction variables as future work.

Machine learning applications to tactic-based provers [27], [28], [29], [30], [31], [32] focus on selections of tactics, and the selections of tactic arguments are restricted to premise selections for general-purpose tactics; even though one often has to choose terms for induction arguments to use the `induct` tactic effectively.

Sometimes it is not enough to apply the `induct` tactic to discharge an inductive problem in Isabelle/HOL but we have to conjecture useful auxiliary lemmas, which we can use to prove the original problem effectively. There are two schools to automate such conjecturing step: bottom-up approach known as theory exploration [33], [34] and top-down approach known as goal-oriented conjecturing [19]. For both cases, conjectured lemmas themselves are often inductive problems, which one has to prove by applying proof by induction. For this reason, we plan to achieve complementary strengths by incorporating `smart_induct` into a conjecturing tool.

There was a series of attempts to automate proof by induction in Isabelle/HOL in the style of *rippling* [35], [36]. Compared to their approach, we built `smart_induct` on top of the default `induct` tactic, which allowed us to exploit the widely used existing framework for proof by induction in Isabelle/HOL and made the resulting proof scripts maintainable without `smart_induct`.

Reger *et al.* incorporated lightweight automated induction into Vampire [37] for saturation-based automated first-order theorem proving [38], while we built `smart_induct` for Isabelle/HOL, a tactic-based interactive theorem prover for higher-order logic.

ACKNOWLEDGMENT

This work was supported by the European Regional Development Fund under the project AI & Reasoning (reg.no. CZ.02.1.01/0.0/0.0/15_003/0000466) and by NII under NII-Internship Program 2019-2nd call.

REFERENCES

[1] B. Gramlich, "Strategic issues, problems and challenges in inductive theorem proving," *Electr. Notes Theor. Comput. Sci.*, vol. 125, no. 2, pp. 5–43, 2005. [Online]. Available: https://doi.org/10.1016/j.entcs.2005.01.006

[2] T. Nipkow, L. C. Paulson, and M. Wenzel, *Isabelle/HOL - a proof assistant for higher-order logic*, ser. Lecture Notes in Computer Science. Springer, 2002, vol. 2283.

[3] The Coq development team, "The Coq proof assistant." [Online]. Available: https://coq.inria.fr

[4] K. Slind and M. Norrish, "A brief overview of HOL4," in *Theorem Proving in Higher Order Logics, 21st International Conference, TPHOLs 2008, Montreal, Canada, August 18-21, 2008. Proceedings*, 2008, pp. 28–32. [Online]. Available: https://doi.org/10.1007/978-3-540-71067-7_6

[5] T. Nipkow and G. Klein, *Concrete Semantics - With Isabelle/HOL*. Springer, 2014. [Online]. Available: https://doi.org/10.1007/978-3-319-10542-0

[6] Y. Nagashima and R. Kumar, "A proof strategy language and proof script generation for Isabelle/HOL," in *Automated Deduction - CADE 26 - 26th International Conference on Automated Deduction, Gothenburg, Sweden, August 6-11, 2017, Proceedings*, ser. Lecture Notes in Computer Science, L. de Moura, Ed., vol. 10395. Springer, 2017, pp. 528–545. [Online]. Available: https://doi.org/10.1007/978-3-319-63046-5_32

[7] Y. Nagashima, "data61/psl." [Online]. Available: https://github.com/data61/PSL/releases/tag/0.1.7-alpha

[8] L. M. de Moura, S. Kong, J. Avigad, F. van Doorn, and J. von Raumer, "The Lean Theorem Prover (System Description)," in *Automated Deduction - CADE-25 - 25th International Conference on Automated Deduction, Berlin, Germany, August 1-7, 2015, Proceedings*, 2015, pp. 378–388. [Online]. Available: https://doi.org/10.1007/978-3-319-21401-6_26

[9] R. S. Boyer and J. S. Moore, *A computational logic handbook*, ser. Perspectives in computing. Academic Press, 1979, vol. 23.

[10] G. O. Passmore, S. Cruanes, D. Ignatovich, D. Aitken, M. Bray, E. Kagan, K. Kanishev, E. Maclean, and N. Mometto, "The imandra automated reasoning system (system description)," *CoRR*, vol. abs/2004.10263, 2020. [Online]. Available: https://arxiv.org/abs/2004.10263

[11] Y. Nagashima, "LiFtEr: Language to encode induction heuristics for Isabelle/HOL," in *Programming Languages and Systems - 17th Asian Symposium, APLAS 2019, Nusa Dua, Bali, Indonesia, December 1-4, 2019, Proceedings*, 2019, pp. 266–287. [Online]. Available: https://doi.org/10.1007/978-3-030-34175-6_14

[12] M. Wenzel, "The Isabelle/Isar reference manual," 2011.

[13] G. Klein, T. Nipkow, L. Paulson, and R. Thiemann, *The Archive of Formal Proofs*, 2004. [Online]. Available: https://www.isa-afp.org/

[14] P. Lammich and S. Wimmer, "Verifythis 2019 – polished isabelle solutions," *Archive of Formal Proofs*, Oct. 2019, http://isa-afp.org/entries/VerifyThis2019.html, Formal proof development.

[15] T. Nishihara and Y. Minamide, "Depth first search," *Archive of Formal Proofs*, Jun. 2004, http://isa-afp.org/entries/Depth-First-Search.html, Formal proof development.

[16] B. Felgenhauer, "Implementing the goodstein function in lambda-calculus," *Archive of Formal Proofs*, Feb. 2020, http://isa-afp.org/entries/Goodstein_Lambda.html, Formal proof development.

[17] M. Rau, "Multidimensional binary search trees," *Archive of Formal Proofs*, May 2019, http://isa-afp.org/entries/KD_Tree.html, Formal proof development.

[18] P. Lammich and T. Nipkow, "Priority search trees," *Archive of Formal Proofs*, Jun. 2019, http://isa-afp.org/entries/Priority_Search_Trees.html, Formal proof development.

[19] Y. Nagashima and J. Parsert, "Goal-oriented conjecturing for Isabelle/HOL," in *Intelligent Computer Mathematics - 11th International Conference, CICM 2018, Hagenberg, Austria, August 13-17, 2018, Proceedings*, 2018, pp. 225–231. [Online]. Available: https://doi.org/10.1007/978-3-319-96812-4_19

[20] Y. Nagashima, "Towards evolutionary theorem proving for Isabelle/HOL," in *Proceedings of the Genetic and Evolutionary Computation Conference Companion, GECCO 2019, Prague, Czech Republic, July 13-17, 2019*, 2019, pp. 419–420. [Online]. Available: https://doi.org/10.1145/3319619.3321921

[21] *Towards Machine Learning Mathematical Induction*, 2018. [Online]. Available: http://arxiv.org/abs/1812.04088

[22] J. S. Moore, "Computational logic : structure sharing and proof of program properties," Ph.D. dissertation, University of Edinburgh, UK, 1973. [Online]. Available: http://hdl.handle.net/1842/2245

[23] *Symbolic Simulation: An ACL2 Approach*, 1998. [Online]. Available: https://doi.org/10.1007/3-540-49519-3_22

[24] J. S. Moore and C. Wirth, "Automation of mathematical induction as part of the history of logic," *CoRR*, vol. abs/1309.6226, 2013. [Online]. Available: http://arxiv.org/abs/1309.6226

[25] Y. Jiang, P. Papapanagiotou, and J. D. Fleuriot, "Machine learning for inductive theorem proving," in *Artificial Intelligence and Symbolic Computation - 13th International Conference, AISC 2018, Suzhou, China, September 16-19, 2018, Proceedings*, 2018, pp. 87–103. [Online]. Available: https://doi.org/10.1007/978-3-319-99957-9_6

[26] J. Harrison, "HOL light: A tutorial introduction," in *Formal Methods in Computer-Aided Design, First International Conference, FMCAD 96, Palo Alto, California, USA, November 6-8, 1996, Proceedings*, 1996, pp. 265–269. [Online]. Available: https://doi.org/10.1007/BFb0031814

[27] Y. Nagashima and Y. He, "PaMpeR: proof method recommendation system for isabelle/hol," in *Proceedings of the 33rd ACM/IEEE International Conference on Automated Software Engineering, ASE 2018, Montpellier, France, September 3-7, 2018*, 2018, pp. 362–372. [Online]. Available: https://doi.org/10.1145/3238147.3238210

[28] Y. Nagashima, "Simple dataset for proof method recommendation in isabelle/hol," in *Intelligent Computer Mathematics*, C. Benzmüller and B. Miller, Eds. Cham: Springer International Publishing, 2020, pp. 297–302.

[29] K. Bansal, S. M. Loos, M. N. Rabe, C. Szegedy, and S. Wilcox, "HOList: An environment for machine learning of higher order logic theorem proving," in *Proceedings of the 36th International Conference on Machine Learning, ICML 2019, 9-15 June 2019, Long Beach, California, USA*, 2019, pp. 454–463. [Online]. Available: http://proceedings.mlr.press/v97/bansal19a.html

[30] T. Gauthier, C. Kaliszyk, and J. Urban, "TacticToe: Learning to reason with HOL4 tactics," in *LPAR-21, 21st International Conference on Logic for Programming, Artificial Intelligence and Reasoning, Maun, Botswana, May 7-12, 2017*, ser. EPiC Series in Computing, T. Eiter and D. Sands, Eds., vol. 46. EasyChair, 2017, pp. 125–143. [Online]. Available: http://www.easychair.org/publications/paper/340355

[31] L. Blaauwbroek, J. Urban, and H. Geuvers, "Tactic learning and proving for the Coq proof assistant," in *LPAR 2020: 23rd International Conference on Logic for Programming, Artificial Intelligence and Reasoning, Alicante, Spain, May 22-27, 2020*, ser. EPiC Series in Computing, E. Albert and L. Kovács, Eds., vol. 73. EasyChair, 2020, pp. 138–150. [Online]. Available: https://easychair.org/publications/paper/JLdB

[32] L. Blaauwbroek *et al.*, "The Tactician," in *Intelligent Computer Mathematics*, C. Benzmüller and B. Miller, Eds. Cham: Springer International Publishing, 2020, pp. 271–277.

[33] B. Buchberger, "Theory exploration with theorema," 2000.

[34] M. Johansson, D. Rosén, N. Smallbone, and K. Claessen, "Hipster: Integrating theory exploration in a proof assistant," in *Intelligent Computer Mathematics CICM 2014*.

[35] A. Bundy, A. Stevens, F. van Harmelen, A. Ireland, and A. Smaill, "Rippling: A heuristic for guiding inductive proofs," *Artif. Intell.*, vol. 62, no. 2, pp. 185–253, 1993. [Online]. Available: https://doi.org/10.1016/0004-3702(93)90079-Q

[36] A. Bundy, D. A. Basin, D. Hutter, and A. Ireland, *Rippling - meta-level guidance for mathematical reasoning*, ser. Cambridge tracts in theoretical computer science. Cambridge University Press, 2005, vol. 56.

[37] G. Reger and A. Voronkov, "Induction in saturation-based proof search," in *Automated Deduction - CADE 27 - 27th International*

Conference on Automated Deduction, Natal, Brazil, August 27-30, 2019, Proceedings, ser. Lecture Notes in Computer Science, P. Fontaine, Ed., vol. 11716. Springer, 2019, pp. 477–494. [Online]. Available: https://doi.org/10.1007/978-3-030-29436-6_28

[38] L. Kovács and A. Voronkov, "First-order theorem proving and Vampire," in *Computer Aided Veri cation - 25th International Conference, CAV 2013, Saint Petersburg, Russia, July 13-19, 2013. Proceedings*, ser. Lecture Notes in Computer Science, N. Sharygina and H. Veith, Eds., vol. 8044. Springer, 2013, pp. 1–35. [Online]. Available: https://doi.org/10.1007/978-3-642-39799-8_1

22

Angelic Checking within Static Driver Verifier: Towards High-Precision Defects without (Modeling) Cost

Shuvendu K. Lahiri*, Akash Lal*, Sridhar Gopinath§, Alexander Nutz‡, Vladimir Levin†,
Rahul Kumar*, Nate Deisinger†, Jakob Lichtenberg†, and Chetan Bansal*
*Microsoft Research
†Microsoft
‡University of Freiburg
§University of Texas at Austin

Abstract—Microsoft's Static Driver Verifier (SDV) pioneered the use of software model checking for ensuring that device drivers correctly use operating system (OS) APIs. However, the verification methodology has been difficult to extend in order to support either (*a*) new classes of drivers for which SDV does not already have a harness and stubs, or (*b*) memory-corruption properties. Any attempt to apply SDV out-of-the-box results in either *false alarms* due to the lack of environment modeling, or *scalability issues* when finding deeply nested bugs in the presence of a very large number of memory accesses.

In this paper, we describe our experience designing and shipping a new class of checks known as *angelic checks* through SDV with the aid of *angelic verification* (AV) [1] technology, over a period of 4 years. AV pairs a precise inter-procedural assertion checker with automatic inference of *likely specifications* for the environment. AV helps compensate for the lack of environment modeling and regains scalability by making it possible to find deeply nested bugs, even for complex memory-corruption properties. These new rules have together found over a hundred confirmed defects during internal deployment at Microsoft, including several previously unknown high-impact potential security vulnerabilities. AV considerably increases the reach of SDV, both in terms of drivers as well as rules that it can support effectively.

I. INTRODUCTION

Microsoft's Static Driver Verifier (SDV) [2], [3] is a formal software verification tool that checks Windows device drivers against a set of rules on the correct usage of operating system (OS) APIs. These Windows OS APIs, which are published on MSDN, and exported for writing Windows drivers are commonly referred to as the Driver Development Interface (DDI) [4]. SDV is shipped to driver developers in the Windows ecosystem through the Windows Driver Development Kit (WDK). Running SDV is a mandated check for a driver to obtain certification for Windows Server OS [5].

Examples of SDV rules range from checking that a driver calls a DDI function at a particular Interrupt Request Level (IRQL), to ensuring that locks are acquired and released in correct sequence. Given: (*a*) a rule, written in SDV's specification language SLIC [6], (*b*) a *harness* for the driver class (e.g. storage or networking) that determines how the driver can be invoked by the OS, and (*c*) *stubs* for OS DDI functions that can be invoked by the driver, SDV uses a software verification tool to look for driver executions that violate the rule. SDV also has a detailed defect viewer to aid

in debugging. The viewer allows stepping through (interprocedural) counterexample traces reported by the verifier. The trace contains not just control-flow information but also values of various variables along the trace. The verification "engine" powering the analysis has transformed from SLAM [7] to SLAM-2 [8] to YOGI [9] and then finally to Corral [10], [11], each time improving performance, accuracy and scalability. SDV establishes a high bar for precision of each of its supported rules; typically false-positives rate is below 5% [8].

However, despite a decade of investment in the technology and advances in the underlying verification engines [10], [12], it has been difficult to adapt the tool to new verification challenges, even within the world of device drivers. Specifically,

Memory safety: Checking for memory corruption bugs within the driver code.

Unsupported drivers: Performing verification of DDI compliance rules for unsupported driver classes whose frameworks are not modeled accurately by harnesses and stubs.

Memory safety violation is broadly interpreted as an unchecked invalid access to a piece of memory during a program's execution. These issues are prevalent in low-level languages such as C and C++ that trade off performance for automatic memory management overheads. Memory safety violations can be either (i) *temporal*, which pertains to a type-state on a memory address such as being `allocated`, `freed`, or `null`, or (ii) *spatial*, which pertains to checking bounds of an allocated buffer. Such violations can have serious implications on both the reliability and, more importantly, on the security of the entire system. Recent studies attribute as much as 70% of all security bugs in Microsoft products can be attributed to memory safety issues [13]. Static analysis tools such as SDV are particularly attractive for the domain of kernel-mode drivers due to the poor coverage of dynamic tools in this space (because of System issues in setting up dynamic tools for kernel-mode components, as well as the large input space).

On the other hand, SDV currently supports environments for certain general purpose drivers (WDM, WDF) as well as two driver classes (storage, networking). However, there are several important driver classes that SDV doesn't support, including file system filters, audio drivers, kernel streaming (in particular, camera) drivers. For such drivers, SDV environment is insufficient, which results in partial coverage at best (lack of a harness that calls the entry points) and false alarms (as DDIs implemented by a driver class library are not modeled by stubs).

In other words, SDV enjoys a very high *precision* on the rules and driver classes it supports, but has a relatively poor *recall* (or *coverage*) on the set of all possible bugs discovered in Windows drivers, particularly those that affect memory safety. In this paper, we therefore focus on the following problem in the context of SDV:

> *Can we improve the coverage (or recall) of reliability and security bugs in Windows drivers using SDV without sacrificing the high precision bar?*

Note that retaining the high precision bar is necessary for SDV; customers will push back if SDV slowed down the development process due to the need to deal with spurious alarms. We are careful to pose the problem as that of "improving the coverage" rather than "full coverage" (or ensuring the absence of) of newer class of defects not detected by SDV. At the same time, it is desirable that the approach is able to leverage additional modeling (if present) to achieve higher coverage[1].

We studied the main technical difficulties to adapt SDV to new verification challenges, and narrowed it down to a combination of two reasons:

1) **Precision due to un(der)-constrained environment models:** Creating models for a new class of drivers requires upfront investment that ranges from several weeks to months of effort and close interaction with domain experts. Furthermore, even the existing models for DDIs may leave most behaviors unspecified, focussing on just the ones that matter for the current set of rules. This is especially troublesome for memory-safety rules because existing models leave out pointer-related behaviors. For example, it was very common for existing stubs to non-deterministically return a `null` pointer as output; this was fine for existing SDV rules, until we started checking for `null`-safety and got numerous false alarms.

2) **Scalability:** Software verifiers face a path-explosion problem when large parts of a program cannot be abstracted with *summaries*. Although there has been progress in performing modular software verification for simple properties, performing summarization for memory safety with SMT solvers is still an open research problem. This is primarily due to the need to summarize the state of the heap including state in linked data structures. Secondly, the path explosion problem worsens with the depth of nesting of procedure calls. Even when a bug is *localized* to a procedure, e.g., the procedure sets a pointer to `null` and then dereferences it, the verifier could still fail (timeout) in trying to enumerate feasible paths from a driver entrypoint to the procedure. This search is unnecessary because a user can immediately

---

[1]One can view this as the principle of *pay-as-you-go verification*.

Rule	Bugs
NULLCHECK	68
USEAFTERFREE	7
DOUBLEFETCH	11
IRQLCHECK	26
Total	112

Fig. 1. A count of true bugs found by SDV using angelic checks.

identify the bug without looking at the rest of the code. This indicates a shortcoming of the SDV approach.

This paper describes how we significantly extended the reach of SDV through a set of *angelic checks*. We distinguish these checks from the currently supported (*demonic*) checks, where the expectation was that SDV does due diligence to provide accurate harnesses and stubs with full path coverage for loop-free programs. We observed that we can address both the issues of (a) spurious alarms from under-constrained environment, and (b) scalability to find defects in deeply-nested methods, by using angelic verification technology [14], [1].

Angelic verification equips a precise *interprocedural* verifier (such as Corral) with automatic inference of *likely specifications* for the unknowns that correspond to values controlled by the environment. AV suppresses alarms from the verifier if it can infer a *reasonable* environment specification to rule out the alarm. Furthermore, because AV can also tolerate an unconstrained initial state, AV can start exploration from any driver procedure, not just the harness. This is beneficial for catching deeply-nested bugs.

Since the AV technology works on programs written in Boogie [15], we also developed an instrumentation framework called AVP for Boogie programs that we used to instrument the new class of memory safety properties. We have used the new framework to successfully add several angelic checks to SDV with the goal of realizing the above vision. These include the following:

1) NULLCHECK: checks that a `null`-valued pointer is not dereferenced,

2) USEAFTERFREE: checks that a freed pointer is not used (or freed again),

3) DOUBLEFETCH: checks that a *userland* pointer is not dereferenced twice in any execution within the kernel [16],

4) IRQLCHECK: checks that DDI calls are made only at an acceptable IRQL state.

The first three rules above pertain to memory safety (or memory corruption) rules. Moreover, a violation of USE-AFTERFREE and DOUBLEFETCH rules can expose a serious security vulnerability.

We report our experience developing these checks and specifically comment on the trade-offs between increasing recall at the cost of sacrificing precision. These rules have been evaluated on close to a thousand drivers within Microsoft, including drivers outside SDV's supported list. These new rules have together found over a hundred confirmed defects during an internal deployment at Microsoft, including several

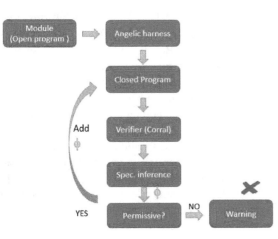

Fig. 2. AV tool flow

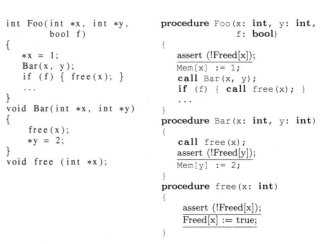

Fig. 3. A program in C and its encoding in Boogie.

previously unknown high-impact potential security vulnerabilities. The exact counts are summarized in Figure 1. All bugs, except one for DOUBLEFETCH, were previously unknown. AV was able to suppress tens of thousands of spurious traces in total over all these examples, indicating that these bugs could not have been discovered without the angelic checks.

At the time of writing this paper, all the rules except DOUBLEFETCH are available with Windows 10 WDK. The DOUBLEFETCH rule is currently a part of *preview* versions of the WDK for co-engineering partners. Furthermore, we note that the AV tool is available open-source[2]. We hope that the experience captured in this paper, in conjunction with open-source AV, allows the development of similar tools in domains other than device drivers.

The rest of the paper is organized as follows. Section II presents background on the AV technology. Section III describes the angelic checks for memory safety, which incudes NULLCHECK, USEAFTERFREE as well as DOUBLEFETCH. Section IV covers the role of IRQL in device drivers and the corresponding angelic check for it (IRQLCHECK). Section V describes related work and Section VI concludes.

II. ANGELIC CHECKS

In this section, we describe background on angelic verification (Section II-A) and some details of the AVP property instrumentation language (Section II-B).

A. Angelic Verification

Angelic verification [1] (AV) is a technique for leveraging automatic static assertion checkers for finding high-confidence defects in open programs. The technique pairs a precise assertion checker (AC) (that can find interprocedural traces for assertion violations in closed programs) with the inference of *angelic specifications* on the environment. The latter is used to push back on the AC verifier from reporting "dumb" false alarms in open programs.

[2] https://github.com/boogie-org/corral/tree/master/AddOns/AngelicVerifierNull

Figure 2 describes the high-level flow of the algorithm. Given an open program with a set of assertions in Boogie [15], we first close the program with an *angelic harness*. The angelic harness helps to create a unified representation of unknown values resulting from both the input state (value of parameters and the heap state when program execution begins) as well as the output state of an external call (return value as well as side-effects). We refer the readers to earlier work for further details [1]. The harness non-deterministically calls into all procedures of the input program. (For the purpose of this section, we make the simplifying assumption that the program contains no external methods.) AV invokes a whole-program verifier (CORRAL) in a loop to enumerate traces that violate an assertion in the input program. For each such failure trace τ starting at a procedure p with unconstrained inputs over X that violates an assertion, AV infers a precondition ϕ over X that ensures $\phi \Rightarrow wp(true, \tau)$, where wp stands for the *weakest liberal precondition* [17]. AV then checks if the precondition is consistent with the previously inferred specifications (starting with $true$). If so, it suppresses the trace τ, else it marks τ as an *angelic trace* to be displayed to the user.

AV provides several *knobs* to the rule developer in order to control the expressiveness of the inferred specifications ϕ, which in turn helps determine the scalability and the precision of AV on that rule. Among other things, an angelic check is parameterized by a *vocabulary V* of predicates that constitutes the atoms in the preconditions (the pool of candidate predicates are automatically mined from the trace). For example, we can require the vocabulary to only consist of non-aliasing predicates, connected with arbitrary Boolean connectives. Further, AV allows the analysis to only suppress the *data flow* (i.e. consider wp while treating all conditionals in a path as non-deterministic) or consider the *control flow* of the defect as well [14], [1]. For the checks presented in this paper, AV only considered blocking the data flow.

Figure 3 shows AV's working on a simplified version of the USEAFTERFREE rule. The figure shows the program in C, as well as its encoding in Boogie, where the heap is modeled using an array Mem that maps a pointer to its contents. (A more detailed explanation on the encoding of C semantics in Boogie can be found in previous work [18], [11].) The underlined statements in the Boogie encoding denote the instrumentation performed for checking UseAfterFree on the code. This instrumentation happens via the AVP tool described in Section II-B. We introduce a map Freed to track the allocated-ness of a pointer, and add assertions before the use of a pointer (either a dereference or a free of the pointer).

AV requires two verification queries for this program, one that starts program execution at Foo and other that starts at Bar. The analysis of Bar produces two error traces due to unconstrained inputs, which can be blocked using preconditions !Freed[x] and !Freed[y] && x != y respectively. Note the role of the vocabulary V here; if we disallow equality predicates in our vocabulary, then there are no permissive specifications to block the second trace. However, the only specification for Foo to block the trace that frees x twice by descending into Bar is !f, which creates dead code and is not permissive. For the angelic checks in SDV, we decided to not block the trace based on control flow as described earlier. Thus, in this case, AV will report one angelic trace for Foo that will be displayed to the user. Next we briefly describe the property instrumentation tool for creating the input to AV.

B. AVP Instrumentation Language

Since AV operates on Boogie programs, we designed a custom domain-specific language (DSL) called AVP[3] that describes a source-to-source instrumentation of Boogie programs. The language is a collection of *LHS-to-RHS* rules. A rule can pattern-match on Boogie AST nodes like expressions, statements or procedures and present a rewriting of the match.

Each angelic check is described as an AVP file whose purpose is to add ghost state (such as Freed in Figure 3) and instrument the necessary assertions and updates to ghost variables into the program. The NULLCHECK rule, for instance, matches on the base pointer p of a dereference (such as $*(p+4)$) and adds the following assertion right before the dereference:

```
assert (!aliases(p, NULL) || p != NULL)
```

The aliases function triggers AV's alias analysis as a pre-pass. If the analysis finds that an expression e1 cannot alias e2, then it replaces the occurrence aliases(e1, e2) syntactically with false; otherwise, it is replaced with true. The ability to refer to alias analysis allows us to express not just syntactic, but a more semantic program instrumentation to add a property. We leverage this feature for all the memory safety properties. But it is important to note that we use alias analysis only as an optimization to prune the space of assertions. It does not affect precision given an interprocedural checker that reasons precisely about aliasing within the module and the specification inference takes care of possible spurious aliasing due to the environment.

III. Angelic Memory Safety Checks

In this section, we describe the different angelic checks related to memory safety. Recall that such issues arise primarily in low-level languages such as C and C++ that rely on the programmer to ensure that a program does not access invalid memory. Examples of invalid accesses include: accessing a null pointer, accessing a pointer after it has been freed, or accessing a pointer outside the bounds of an allocated object. In recent years, many of these invalid memory accesses have lead to security exploits, where an attacker can trick a system to perform information leak or remote code execution [19], [13]. Some of the classical memory safety issues can be mitigated by programming in *managed* languages such as Rust, where accesses to invalid addresses lead to runtime exceptions with clear semantics (unlike the undefined behaviors for programs written in *unmanaged* languages). However, other security relevant memory safety issues (e.g. DoubleFetch) that result from the kernel-user boundary [16], [20], [21], [22] may be applicable even when the drivers are authored in memory safe languages such as Rust.

In this section, we describe the different rules and our experience with deploying them. These properties were developed and tested over various points over the course of four years, so we report our evaluation of the rules as they were developed and tested before being rolled out to customers. Note that we did not change the internals of AV tool for supporting these multiple properties. Each property is completely contained in its own AVP file.

A. Nullcheck

In our earlier work [1], we presented an evaluation of the angelic NULLCHECK rule on 10 modules in Windows, totaling over 300K lines of code, and compared it with a mature tool PREfix. We briefly summarize our findings. PREfix is an industrial strength tool being used at Microsoft for over a decade, and has custom algorithms for null-checking as well as accurate models for many OS components. Over a set of 68 defects that PREfix reported in these 10 modules, we managed to confirm over 80% of the defects, found several false alarms in the PREfix defects due to imprecise modeling of C semantics, and also discovered new true alarms not reported by PREfix. AV also reported less than 10% of false positives on this set (leaving aside frontend translation issues that have subsequently been addressed).

These results were seen as encouraging by the SDV product team and lead to the integration of NULLCHECK as the first angelic check in SDV. The rule now appears documented on MSDN[4] since its release in 2018. This section outlines the further insights that were needed to take NULLCHECK from a research prototype to a push-button check available to the entire Windows driver ecosystem.

First, we performed several improvements on the precision and usability of the check when evaluating on Windows drivers. The chief among them are the following.

---

[3]https://github.com/boogie-org/corral/wiki/AV-Property-(AVP)-Language

[4]https://docs.microsoft.com/en-us/windows-hardware/drivers/devtest/nullcheckw?redirectedfrom=MSDN

1) **Improved alias analysis:** We designed an alias analysis that works on a Boogie program and use it to prune away `null` checks on pointers that cannot alias `null`. The analysis implements the usual Andersen's may-alias analysis [23], however it is optimized to track the flow of `null`-value very precisely [24]. The analysis is able to prune away almost 98% of all `null`-checks.

2) **Changes to existing SDV models:** We needed to modify SDV's harness and stubs even for supported driver frameworks. These modifications consisted of the following major changes. (*a*) First, we found that several existing OS models mistakenly left an output pointer unallocated even when the return `NT_STATUS` error code denoted successful allocation. This leads to a false alarm because AV will discover a `null`-dereference in the caller; the alarm cannot be suppressed without creating dead code. (*b*) Second, we did not use SDV's harness even when present. Recall that a harness calls the driver APIs in a sequence in order to mimic how an actual OS would invoke the driver. Using the harness would cause the analysis to time out even when driver had simple bugs but were embedded deep inside the driver. Instead of using the harness, we run AV on all methods of the driver in parallel. This allows SDV to get much better coverage on the driver. However, dropping the harness does cause us to miss bugs that can only be triggered by calling several driver APIs in sequence.

3) **Side-effects of external methods:** Finally, we realized that AV suppresses spurious alarms arising from external methods only when it can estimate the side-effects of the external method. We currently use the signature of an external method to automatically determine the side effects in addition to the return value. For example, if an external method takes an argument e of static type `int **`, then we assume that the values of e and e may be modified. This in turn allows AV to infer angelic specifications on these unknown modified values. However, this heuristic does not work when the external method (*a*) modifies some global variable, or (*b*) exits under some condition. Of these, the former happens frequently when the external method sets up a global function pointer that is invoked later in the driver. We, therefore, manually added models for such DDI functions driven by the false alarms we saw during our evaluation.

We evaluated the NULLCHECK rule on a set of 192 real-world drivers that constitute the *Integration Test Pass* (ITP), the regression test suite for the SDV product. These constitute drivers from *Storport*, *KMDF*, *WDM* and *NDIS* classes of drivers. Of these, we found 61 defects over 27 drivers and 3 drivers timed out after 3000 seconds. Several of the authors spent a few months (of 2016) to inspect these traces, and consulted with driver experts to determine the ground truth on their validity. We finally determined that 58 out of the 61 defects were *true defects* (95% precision). Several of these bugs (after removing duplicates that require the same underlying

fix) were filed and fixed. The bugs that were confirmed but not fixed mainly came from two categories: (*a*) the driver was no longer being maintained or shipped externally, or (*b*) there was a runtime assertion `NT_ASSERT(FALSE)` in debug mode that would cause the driver to crash if the pointer was `null`, eliminating any security implications (12 such cases). These runtime assertions indicate that the driver developers suspected these pointers could be `null` at runtime although there is no proof of their absence. The 3 false alarms came from the absence of two models of external functions and 1 modeling issue for C arrays in the front end; the latter has since been fixed. The two OS models required modeling of linked lists `ExInterlockedRemoveHeadList` and additional ghost state in `IoAttachDeviceToDeviceStack`, neither of which were deemed cost effective to add.

In addition to the 58 bugs in ITP, at least 10 more true bugs have been found and confirmed by SDV team during internal deployment. The rule has found a couple of potential security bugs in Windows drivers, of which at least one was classified by a security review as critical, (hence) immediately fixed and the fix was taken to an OS security update (in 2016).

B. Use After Free

Figure 3 showed an example of the USEAFTERFREE angelic check. The ability to use a pointer after it has been freed has serious implications ranging from corruption of valid data to remote code execution vulnerabilities [25]. In this section, we describe the rule in more detail and present our experience with deploying it internally in Microsoft.

The rule ensures that a non-null pointer that has been *freed* by calling a DDI function (either `free` or variants such as `IoFreeMdl`, etc.), is not *used*[5]. A pointer is used if it is an argument to a routine that frees the pointer (special case signifying *double-free*), or is dereferenced. To specify the rule, we leverage our alias analysis to guard the check to only those pointers that can potentially be aliased with a freed-pointer within the module. This is achieved by tracking a global variable `freedp` that can be non-deterministically assigned one of the pointers that is freed, and weakening the assertion to only consider pointers that could be aliased with `freedp`. We refined the rule to allow freeing of `null`, which is a valid behavior. In fact, it is a common practice to set a freed pointer to `null`, and not check for a pointer to be non-null before freeing it.

We performed an extensive evaluation on 65 drivers that contain at least one call to a method named "free". Our initial rule was more aggressive than the final rule described above in two aspects to not miss defects during evaluation:

1) We considered any external method with a substring *free* as a method that could potentially free a pointer, and

2) We considered a pointer argument to any external procedure as a use; our intuition was that it is a bad practice to pass a freed pointer externally.

[5]The property file is located here: https://github.com/boogie-org/corral/blob/master/AddOns/PropInst/PropInst/ExampleProperties/useafterfree-razzle.avp

```
void Foo(x) {                    void Bar() {
  Increment(&x->RefCnt);           Decrement(x->RefCnt);
  Bar(x);   // may free x          if(x->RefCnt == 0) {
  x->f = 1; // use                     free(x);
}                                    }
                                 }
```

Fig. 4. False alarm for USEAFTERFREE.

We obtained a total of 69 traces in 22 drivers that we carefully inspected after removing duplicates. We filed 7 new bugs with developers and most of them were either fixed or confirmed but not fixed due to the lack of support for the driver. Many of these bugs were due to cleanups along exception paths, making them difficult to reach during regular testing.

A majority of the spurious alarms resulted from the two decisions above. For example, routines such as RtlFreeUnicodeString take a pointer to a structure as an argument, but only free the Buffer field of that structure. Similarly, we found several low-level print functions such as TracePrint that never dereference the pointer and therefore safe. In addition to these, there was one class of false alarms in 3 traces that demonstrates a fundamental limitation of the angelic choice that we adopted. We discuss this in more detail.

Consider a simplified program in Figure 4. AV performs two checks, starting at each of the two procedures. When analyzing Foo, there is a path where x is freed and later dereferenced. This is a false alarm as callers of Foo ensure that x->RefCount is always greater than 1 on entry. However, the default configuration of AV does not infer a specification on RefCount values because we treat path conditions as non-deterministic. In other words, we only treat the data-flow in an angelic manner, not the control flow. We are working on improving AV to push the traces all the way to module entry points in such cases to remove this class of false alarms.

C. Double Fetch

Consider the method Foo below that marks an entry point into the kernel and consider a pointer parameter x that can be controlled by the user from a user-mode application or driver (referred to as *userland* pointers). Consider an execution when the pointer is "fetched" twice, in lines 2 and 5.

```
1  NT_STATUS Foo(A *x, ..) {
2      int len = x->Length;
3      if (len > 0) {
4          char *y = malloc(len);
5          RtlCopyMemory(y, x->Length, x->Buffer);
6      }
7  }
```

A malicious user may alter the value of x->Length between the two lines, resulting in a buffer overflow of the kernel memory, which can be exploited for information disclosure or remote code execution. These bugs have lead to several security vulnerabilities in both Linux and Windows kernels and therefore of great concern to kernel-mode driver developers.

The double-fetch property is encoded as an angelic check[6]. Similar to USEAFTERFREE, we maintain a map hasBeenRead that maps each address to the number of times it has been read, and ensure that a userland pointer is never read twice. However, *userland* pointers cannot be distinguished from kernel-allocated pointers without precisely marking the kernel entry points. Instead, we approximate it by assuming that that driver developer at least *probes* userland pointers before accessing them in the kernel. We use a similar trick as USEAFTERFREE where we consider a pointer as userland if it aliases with the argument of either ProbeForRead or ProbeForWrite.

We have currently evaluated this rule on one driver where a violation was detected by security pen-testers manually over a year ago. The bug was present in a C++ module, and spanned several method calls between the site of probe and the two fetches. Further, one of the fetches was directly inside a condition statement. To recover the bug, we had to fix some issues in the SDV front end for C++ as well as set a high timeout of 9000 seconds for the angelic check. Not only did we recover the *precise* bug, but we also discovered 10 more variants of the bug (all confirmed by the pen-testers) on other pointers and procedures on the same version of the driver (the driver was already rewritten substantially after previous bugs). There has not been any false alarms from this rule to date on either this or other drivers that we have tested so far, although further evaluation starting with the ITP suite is still pending. The DOUBLEFETCH rule is currently a part of preview versions of the WDK for co-engineering partners, and will be made available to broader ecosystem in the near future.

IV. ANGELIC IRQL CHECKS

This section starts by describing the concept of IRQLs in Windows device drivers, followed by the design of the IRQLCHECK angelic rule and our experience with it on internal drivers.

A. IRQL

IRQL (Interrupt Request Level) is a number, ranging from 0 to 31 on x86, which is used to assign priorities to interrupts. An IRQL value is associated with each CPU processor of a system as well as incoming interrupt requests. If a processor is currently at an IRQL value v_1 and an interrupt arrives at level v_2, then the interrupt waits if v_2 v_1. Otherwise, the processor's current task is interrupted, its IRQL is raised to v_2 and it starts processing the interrupt.

Some of the important IRQL levels are PASSIVE_LEVEL (0), APC_LEVEL (1) and DISPATCH_LEVEL (2). User-level threads and most kernel-mode operations execute at PASSIVE_LEVEL. Since this is the lowest level, all interrupts are accepted at this level. Asynchronous procedure calls (APCs) and the page fault handler execute at APC_LEVEL. The Windows thread scheduler and deferred procedure calls (DPCs) execute at DISPATCH_LEVEL. When executing at

---

[6]https://github.com/boogie-org/corral/blob/master/AddOns/PropInst/PropInst/ExampleProperties/doubleFetch.avp

this level, a thread cannot be pre-empted by other threads because an interrupt request from the thread scheduler gets masked (but higher-level interrupts can still be scheduled as they arrive).

Windows provides kernel routines to manipulate the IRQL value of a processor. Driver developers use these routines to control which interrupts should be masked during the execution of the driver. However, the developer must use these routines carefully. For instance, code running at APC_LEVEL should not access pageable memory due to the possibility of a page fault, which cannot be served at APC_LEVEL. Running at DISPATCH_LEVEL further rules out context-switching to other threads. Thus, a thread must not wait on any synchronization objects at this level. Furthermore, the amount of time spent at DISPATCH_LEVEL should be limited to a minimum to keep the system responsive. In order to guard against these errors, Windows restricts invoking certain kernel routine at an unacceptable IRQL value. Doing so can cause a kernel panic at runtime. The IRQL requirements of each kernel routine are very clearly specified in the MSDN documentation. For instance, expensive safe-string routines like RtlEqualString[7] should only be invoked at PASSIVE_LEVEL, etc. It is important to weed out incorrect IRQL violations statically.

B. AV rules

Development of the AV property specification for checking correct IRQL usage required modest effort; a majority of it was completed in one person month. The IRQL requirements of each kernel routine was already well documented. Often, the effort was simply to codify the documentation. For instance, the KeAcquireSpinLock[8] routine requires that current IRQL be less than DISPATCH_LEVEL. It then raises the IRQL to DISPATCH_LEVEL and stashes the old IRQL value in the pointer argument supplied to it. Calls to this routine are instrumented as shown below.

```
procedure KeAcquireSpinLock(x0: int, x1: int);
{
    assert irql <= 2;
    Mem[x1] := irql;
    irql := 2;
}
```

This uses a single global variable irql that records the current IRQL value of the processor. Note that SDV performs sequential verification only; correspondingly, we only need to track the IRQL of a single processor.

Any behavior that was unrelated to IRQLs, e.g., actually acquiring a lock, was left unspecified, limiting the amount of work that was required to design the AV property file. The entire property specification consists of 476 such rules. Out of these, only 65 routines actually change the IRQL value, whereas the rest simply assert a precondition. Each rule was at most 4 lines of instrumentation.

---

[7]https://docs.microsoft.com/en-us/windows-hardware/drivers/ddi/ntddk/nf-ntddk-rtlequalstring

[8]https://docs.microsoft.com/en-us/windows-hardware/drivers/ddi/wdm/nf-wdm-keacquirespinlock

```
int DriverRoutine (...)

    if (...)  // branch B

        // Requires irql <= 1, sets irql to 1
        ExAcquireFastMutex (...);
        // Requires irql == 0
        RtlEqualString (...);

    else

        // Requires irql == 2
        KeTryToAcquireSpinLockAtDpcLevel (...)

    ...
```

Fig. 5. Program snippet illustrating AV for checking correct IRQL usage.

The AV vocabulary is set to arbitrary arithmetic constraints (equality, disequality and comparisons) over the variable irql and any constant. This vocabulary is different from the vocabulary used for memory safety rules, where we do not permit equality predicates over the pointers. For instance, for NULLCHECK, the vocabulary only allows disequality constraints to model non-aliasing and non-nullness. This illustrates the flexibility of the AV framework to adapt to new classes of rules with relative easy.

We illustrate the behavior of AV for checking correct IRQL usage using the example shown in Figure 5. This program shows a simple driver routine that calls three different kernel routines. The requirements of each of the kernel routines are shown in comments, along with any side-effects they have on changing the IRQL value. This information is instrumented into the program by property instrumentation tool.

We describe a sample run of AV on DriverRoutine. AV will start analysis on this routine with an unconstrained initial value for irql, because of which it will detect a possible failure of the assertion irql ≤ 1 at the call to ExAcquireFastMutex. AV will suppress this failure by installing an angelic precondition on DriverRoutine, namely that irql ≤ 1. Next, AV restarts the analysis with this new pre-condition. In this case, it will report another possible failure: the assert irql == 0 fails on the call to RtlEqualString. This failure has no dependence on the initial value of irql (because ExAcquireFastMutex always sets irql to 1); thus, it cannot be suppressed by AV and it will correspondingly show the violation to the user as a single trace of execution of DriverRoutine. This kind of analysis also has a pleasant side-effect: the user can inspect this trace in isolation from the callers of DriverRoutine because the initial value of irql is immaterial.

C. Inconsistency Violations

There is a second class of violations that AV can report that we call *inconsistency violations*. Such a violation consists of multiple (2 or more) traces. Consider the assertion at the call to KeTryToAcquireSpinLockAtDpcLevel. AV will try to suppress this violation as well by installing the precondition irql == 2 to DriverRoutine. However, this precondition *conflicts* with the previous precondition irql ≤ 1, i.e., their conjunction is *unsatisfiable* (and therefore rejected by the permissiveness check in Figure 2). AV detects this conflict and shows a violation to the user consisting of two traces: the first trace is the one that ends in a call to `ExAcquireFastMutex` and the second one ends in a call to `KeTryToAcquireSpinLockAtDpcLevel`. This violation tells the user that at least one of the calls (maybe, both) is potentially buggy.

Note that it is possible for AV to report false inconsistency violations. For instance, if the branch B in the code had a condition dependent on some flags passed to `DriverRoutine` that were set by its callers to indicate different IRQL levels, then it is possible for `DriverRoutine` to be correct. AV only includes inferring preconditions on the `irql` variable, so it does not pick up the branch condition B. This allows AV to scale at the cost of some precision. In our experiments, however, AV did not report any false positives because of this reason.

D. Evaluation

During the development of the IRQLCHECK rule, we conducted an initial set of experiments on internal driver code. We picked 797 driver modules that each had some usage of IRQL levels, i.e., ones that called at least one kernel routine that manipulated the IRQL value. The average running time of AV on these modules was 180 seconds. A distribution of the AV running times, shown in Figure 6, indicates that a majority of modules take little time, however there are a few that take much longer.

AV reported a total of 29 violations in these modules. Manual inspection revealed that 26 of these were true violations; of these 18 were single-trace defects and the rest 8 were inconsistency violations consisting of two traces each. There were 3 false positives. In two of these, AV reported a violation assuming an initial IRQL value of -1. This is not possible. We fixed it by constraining the `irql` variable to always be between 0 and 31 and the corresponding false positives went away. One false positive was due to imprecision in aliasing where the value stored under a global variable was overwritten by a write through an unconstrained pointer. The code did not contain any evidence that the pointer could alias the global. This is currently a limitation of AV but happens very rarely; usually the pointer analysis is good at ruling out such possibilities.

V. RELATED WORK

Memory safety of C/C++ applications has naturally received a lot of attention, both in academia and industry, because of their security implications. Microsoft has invested in tools such as Esp [26], Espx [27] and Prefix [28] that have all targeted the Windows Operating System. As opposed to SDV, these tools are not shipped externally. They are used in-house and for that reason they have been heavily tuned for internal Windows code through the use of custom analyses (often a form of pointer analysis), annotations (SAL [29]) or extensive models. Such investment makes the tools expensive to maintain (dependence

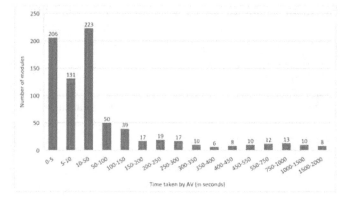

Fig. 6. Histogram of AV running times on multiple Windows modules.

on annotations/models also implies a constant maintenance struggle) or extend to new properties (which requires a new custom analysis).

Facebook supports the open-source tool Infer [30]. Infer performs a bottom-up pointer-based analysis of C/C++ programs (even Java) looking for null-safety, use-after-free violations, etc. Infer is designed to be incredibly fast so that developers get immediate feedback as they make code changes. SDV is much more heavy-weight with the use of its SMT-based engine so it cannot provide immediate feedback. Instead, SDV finds its place in a certification process for drivers where it has more time to perform the analysis. On the other hand, Infer is not as readily extensible as SDV for new checks as it requires the creation of a new abstract domain for summarizing behaviors relevant to the property of interest. Besides, the presence of overapproximate summaries can lead to false alarms even for closed programs, especially when summaries need to capture complex arithmetic conditions. Unfortunately, we cannot perform a direct comparison with Infer on the common rules, as Infer cannot be integrated into the build environment for these Windows drivers that use the Microsoft C/C++ compiler toolchain.

The angelic checks in SDV has two key contributions over the tools mentioned above. First, the use of a precise SMT-based backend allows AV-SDV to be easily tuned to support multiple different rules, simply as a new AVP instrumentation file. For instance, IRQLCHECK is not a pointer-based rule; instead it requires arithmetic reasoning of the IRQL value. Yet, AV-SDV supports it without any changes to the tool flow. Second, AV can tolerate imprecise models, thus considerably reducing the maintenance effort.

The core idea of angelic verification is related to research on *abduction* [31] and maximal specification inference [32]. These techniques use novel yet expensive quantifier elimination algorithms to find permissive specifications on the environment. Further these techniques can be used to infer loop invariants for unbounded executions. The main differences lie in the use of AV in SDV to detect high quality bugs instead of finding the maximally permissive or inductive specifications. Although this may result in AV failing to infer a permissive specification even when it exists, AV's lightweight predicate abstraction allows us to scale to modules with hundreds of thousands of lines of code in the presence of a heap. Finally, the idea of starting exploration from functions other than entrypoints is also explored in recent scalable pointer analysis approaches [33], [34].

VI. CONCLUSION

In this paper, we described our experience integrating angelic checking with the Static Driver Verifier tool, over a period of several years. We described the limitations of SDV for checking unsupported drivers as well as memory safety properties before this work, and provide evidence that the angelic checks provide a cost-effective solution to finding high-quality defects in drivers with very low upfront investment. For future work, we are currently working on: (a) making AV more scalable by pruning state space already explored from transitive callees, and (b) providing support for writing other security critical angelic checks that require *taint* tracking through values in the heap.

REFERENCES

[1] A. Das, S. K. Lahiri, A. Lal, and Y. Li, "Angelic verification: Precise verification modulo unknowns," in *Computer Aided Verification - 27th International Conference, CAV 2015, San Francisco, CA, USA, July 18-24, 2015, Proceedings, Part I*, vol. 9206. Springer, 2015, pp. 324–342.

[2] T. Ball, V. Levin, and S. K. Rajamani, "A decade of software model checking with slam," *Communications of the ACM*, vol. 54, no. 7, pp. 68–76, 2011.

[3] Microsoft, "Static driver verifier," https://docs.microsoft.com/en-us/windows-hardware/drivers/devtest/static-driver-verifier, 2012.

[4] ——, "Programming reference for windows device driver interface (ddi)," https://docs.microsoft.com/en-us/windows-hardware/drivers/ddi, 2019.

[5] "Windows hardware lab kit," https://docs.microsoft.com/en-us/windows-hardware/test/hlk/, 2018.

[6] T. Ball, E. Bounimova, V. Levin, R. Kumar, and J. Lichtenberg, "The Static Driver Verifier research platform," in *Computer Aided Verification*. Springer, 2010, pp. 119–122.

[7] T. Ball, R. Majumdar, T. D. Millstein, and S. K. Rajamani, "Automatic predicate abstraction of C programs," in *Proceedings of the 2001 ACM SIGPLAN Conference on Programming Language Design and Implementation (PLDI), Snowbird, Utah, USA, June 20-22, 2001*, M. Burke and M. L. Soffa, Eds. ACM, 2001, pp. 203–213.

[8] T. Ball, E. Bounimova, R. Kumar, and V. Levin, "SLAM2: static driver verification with under 4% false alarms," in *Proceedings of 10th International Conference on Formal Methods in Computer-Aided Design, FMCAD 2010, Lugano, Switzerland, October 20-23*, R. Bloem and N. Sharygina, Eds. IEEE, 2010, pp. 35–42.

[9] A. V. Nori, S. K. Rajamani, S. Tetali, and A. V. Thakur, "The yogiproject: Software property checking via static analysis and testing," in *Tools and Algorithms for the Construction and Analysis of Systems, 15th International Conference, TACAS 2009, Held as Part of the Joint European Conferences on Theory and Practice of Software, ETAPS 2009, York, UK, March 22-29, 2009. Proceedings*, 2009, pp. 178–181.

[10] A. Lal, S. Qadeer, and S. K. Lahiri, "A solver for reachability modulo theories," in *Computer Aided Verification - 24th International Conference, CAV 2012, Berkeley, CA, USA, July 7-13, 2012 Proceedings*, vol. 7358. Springer, 2012, pp. 427–443.

[11] A. Lal and S. Qadeer, "Powering the static driver verifier using corral," in *Proceedings of the 22nd ACM SIGSOFT International Symposium on Foundations of Software Engineering, (FSE-22), Hong Kong, China, November 16 - 22, 2014*, 2014, pp. 202–212.

[12] L. De Moura and N. Bjørner, "Z3: An efficient smt solver," in *Tools and Algorithms for the Construction and Analysis of Systems*. Springer, 2008, pp. 337–340.

[13] "Microsoft: 70 percent of all security bugs are memory safety issues," https://www.zdnet.com/article/microsoft-70-percent-of-all-security-bugs-are-memory-safety-issues, 2019.

[14] S. Blackshear and S. K. Lahiri, "Almost-correct specifications: a modular semantic framework for assigning confidence to warnings," in *ACM SIGPLAN Conference on Programming Language Design and Implementation, PLDI 13, Seattle, WA, USA, June 16-19, 2013*. ACM, 2013, pp. 209–218.

[15] M. Barnett, K. R. M. Leino, M. Moskal, and W. Schulte, "Boogie: An intermediate verification language," 2009, https://github.com/boogie-org/boogie/.

[16] "Microsoft: The case of the kernel mode double-fetch," https://msrc-blog.microsoft.com/tag/double-fetch/, 2008.

[17] K. R. M. Leino, "Efficient weakest preconditions," *Inf. Process. Lett.*, vol. 93, no. 6, pp. 281–288, 2005.

[18] J. Condit, B. Hackett, S. K. Lahiri, and S. Qadeer, "Unifying type checking and property checking for low-level code," in *ACM SIGPLAN Notices*, vol. 44, no. 1. ACM, 2009, pp. 302–314.

[19] "Openssl tls heartbeat extension read overflow discloses sensitive information," https://www.kb.cert.org/vuls/id/720951/, 2014.

[20] "Cwe-367: Time-of-check time-of-use (toctou) race condition," https://cwe.mitre.org/data/definitions/367.html, 2008.

[21] M. Xu, C. Qian, K. Lu, M. Backes, and T. Kim, "Precise and scalable detection of double-fetch bugs in OS kernels," in *2018 IEEE Symposium on Security and Privacy, SP 2018, Proceedings, 21-23 May 2018, San Francisco, California, USA*. IEEE Computer Society, 2018, pp. 661–678.

[22] P. Wang, J. Krinke, K. Lu, G. Li, and S. Dodier-Lazaro, "How double-fetch situations turn into double-fetch vulnerabilities: A study of double fetches in the linux kernel," in *26th USENIX Security Symposium (USENIX Security 17)*. USENIX Association, 2017, pp. 1–16.

[23] L. O. Andersen, "Program analysis and specialization for the C programming language," Ph.D. dissertation, DIKU, University of Copenhagen, May 1994.

[24] A. Das and A. Lal, "Precise null-pointer analysis using global value numbering," in *Automated Technology for Verification and Analysis (ATVA)*, July 2017.

[25] "Cwe-416: Use after free," https://cwe.mitre.org/data/definitions/416.html, 2008.

[26] M. Das, S. Lerner, and M. Seigle, "ESP: path-sensitive program verification in polynomial time," in *Proceedings of the 2002 ACM SIGPLAN Conference on Programming Language Design and Implementation (PLDI), Berlin, Germany, June 17-19, 2002*, J. Knoop and L. J. Hendren, Eds. ACM, 2002, pp. 57–68.

[27] B. Hackett, M. Das, D. Wang, and Z. Yang, "Modular checking for buffer overflows in the large," in *28th International Conference on Software Engineering (ICSE 2006), Shanghai, China, May 20-28, 2006*, L. J. Osterweil, H. D. Rombach, and M. L. Soffa, Eds. ACM, 2006, pp. 232–241.

[28] W. R. Bush, J. D. Pincus, and D. J. Sielaff, "A static analyzer for finding dynamic programming errors," *Softw. Pract. Exp.*, vol. 30, no. 7, pp. 775–802, 2000.

[29] "Using sal annotations to reduce c/c++ code defects," https://docs.microsoft.com/en-us/cpp/code-quality/using-sal-annotations-to-reduce-c-cpp-code-defects?view=vs-2019, 2016.

[30] C. Calcagno, D. Distefano, P. W. O'Hearn, and H. Yang, "Compositional shape analysis by means of bi-abduction," in *Proceedings of the 36th ACM SIGPLAN-SIGACT Symposium on Principles of Programming Languages, POPL 2009, Savannah, GA, USA, January 21-23, 2009*, Z. Shao and B. C. Pierce, Eds. ACM, 2009, pp. 289–300.

[31] I. Dillig, T. Dillig, and A. Aiken, "Automated error diagnosis using abductive inference," in *ACM SIGPLAN Conference on Programming Language Design and Implementation, PLDI 12, Beijing, China - June 11 - 16, 2012*, J. Vitek, H. Lin, and F. Tip, Eds. ACM, 2012, pp. 181–192.

[32] A. Albarghouthi, I. Dillig, and A. Gurfinkel, "Maximal specification synthesis," in *Proceedings of the 43rd Annual ACM SIGPLAN-SIGACT Symposium on Principles of Programming Languages, POPL 2016, St. Petersburg, FL, USA, January 20 - 22, 2016*, R. Bodk and R. Majumdar, Eds. ACM, 2016, pp. 789–801.

[33] Q. Shi, X. Xiao, R. Wu, J. Zhou, G. Fan, and C. Zhang, "Pinpoint: Fast and precise sparse value flow analysis for million lines of code," *SIGPLAN Not.*, vol. 53, no. 4, 2018.

[34] H. Yan, Y. Sui, S. Chen, and J. Xue, "Spatio-temporal context reduction: A pointer-analysis-based static approach for detecting use-after-free vulnerabilities," in *Proceedings of the 40th International Conference on Software Engineering*, ser. ICSE 18.   Association for Computing Machinery, 2018.

23

Learning Properties in LTL ∩ ACTL from Positive Examples Only

Rüdiger Ehlers*, Ivan Gavran[†], and Daniel Neider[†]

*Clausthal University of Technology, Clausthal-Zellerfeld, Germany

Email: ruediger.ehlers@tu-clausthal.de

[†]Max Planck Institute for Software Systems, Kaiserslautern, Germany

Email: {gavran, neider}@mpi-sws.org

Abstract—Inferring correct and meaningful specifications of complex (black-box) systems is an important problem in practice, which arises naturally in debugging, reverse engineering, formal verification, and explainable AI, to name just a few examples. Usually, one here assumes that both positive and negative examples of system traces are given—an assumption that is often unrealistic in practice because negative examples (i.e., examples that the system cannot exhibit) are typically hard to obtain.

To overcome this serious practical limitation, we develop a novel technique that is able to infer specifications in the form of universal very-weak automata from positive examples only. This type of automata captures exactly the class of properties in the intersection of Linear Temporal Logic (LTL) and the universal fragment of Computation Tree Logic (ACTL), and features an easy-to-interpret graphical representation. Our proposed algorithm reduces the problem of learning a universal very-weak automaton to the enumeration of elements in the Pareto front of a specifically-designed monotonous function and uses classical automaton minimization to obtain a concise, finite-state representation of the learned property. In a case study with specifications from the Advanced Microcontroller Bus Architecture, we demonstrate that our approach is able to infer meaningful, concise, and easy-to-interpret specifications from positive examples only.

I. INTRODUCTION

The engineering process of reactive systems requires a good understanding of the *specification* that the system should fulfill. For instance, while model checking can prove a system design to be correct with respect to a specification, the resulting proof is only meaningful if the specification captures the requirements of the application. Similarly, while the process of *synthesizing* reactive systems from their specifications is well-researched, both the system specification and the specification of the environment in which the system needs to operate must be correct in order for synthesis to be useful.

Writing correct and complete specifications is hard. Crucial properties of an application are easy to miss, and formalizing the specification as automata or in a logic such as linear temporal logic (LTL) is difficult. The problem can be addressed in multiple ways. Easier to use specification formalisms can support the writing process of specifications. Alternatively, approaches for *inferring* specifications from existing system implementations or examples can avoid the burden of manually writing the specifications. Such *specification learning* techniques are especially useful when a design is already available, so that its implicit specification can be documented

by examining the set of its traces. Furthermore, a set of human-given examples may be available from which the wanted requirements should be distilled. Classical specification mining requires both examples that violate the (implicit) specification and examples that satisfy it, as with only one of these classes, either *false* or *true* can be valid specifications, making the problem ill-defined.

Unfortunately, both negative *and* positive examples are not always available. For instance, when inferring the specification of a system that is too big to be fully analyzed, but whose implementation is given, we can extract input/output traces that represent possible executions of the system. Proving that a certain input/output trace is not a possible execution of the system is however a model checking problem, which can be infeasible to solve for complex designs. Similarly, we may want to deduce an environment specification to be used in synthesis from observing the environment. For a black-box environment, we can never know that some behavior observation sequence cannot occur. These observations give rise to the question if there is some way to learn from positive (or negative) example traces only.

To make this problem well-posed, we need to introduce some kind of measure of how *tight* the specification should be that we want to obtain. For the case of positive examples, there is a spectrum of possible specification solutions ranging from *true* all the way to the specification that only allows exactly the set of traces in the example set. Both extremes make little sense, and a learning procedure to solve the problem should be parameterized by a *tightness value* n. At the same time, the intuitive idea of tightness with respect to some parameter n must be concretized in a way such that an efficient learning procedure to learn n-tight specifications can be given *and* we can observe that in practice, the learned specifications capture some relevant specification parts of systems while being easy enough to understand by an engineer.

In this paper, we give such a learning procedure for specifications from positive examples only. We identified *universal very-weak word automata* (UVWs) over infinite words as a specification representation that has a natural definition of tightness, lends itself to an efficient learning procedure, and leads to easily readable learned specifications. This automaton class has been identified as characterizing the class of properties representable both in linear temporal logic (LTL) and in the universal fragment of computation tree logic (ACTL) [1]. While this implies that there are some ω-regular properties that cannot be learned by our framework, the intersection of LTL and ACTL includes the vast majority of specifications found in case studies on specification shapes [2]. By trading away the full ω-regular expressivity, we get multiple advantages that make learning from only positive examples feasible: UVWs can be decomposed into *simple chains* [3] that each represent a scenario and how the system satisfying the specification is required to react. Thus, they are easy to examine by a specification engineer. We will demonstrate that the maximum length of such a chain is also a natural notion of the complexity of a specification part, making it a good candidate for the concretization of the concept of tightness of a learned specification. Most importantly, simple chains have a natural approximation of language inclusion that enables us to efficiently learn a specification by enumerating all strictest chains that are not in contradiction to any example trace.

The algorithm for learning tight UVWs in this paper starts from a representation of the set of positive traces as *ultimately periodic words*, i.e., words of the form uv^{ω} for some finite words u and v. It is well-known that ω-regular specifications (or automata) are precisely characterized by the set of ultimately periodic words that satisfy the specification (or are included in the language of the automaton). Since ultimately periodic words can be encoded in a finite format, they are a natural choice of representation for the positive examples that are input to our algorithm.

We evaluate our approach on benchmarks from a case study on the AMBA AHB protocol [4]. Starting from LTL formulas describing the allowed behavior of the AMBA bus clients, we randomly generate sets of positive examples. We run our algorithm on the generated sets of different sizes and note how big the learned UVW is and how long it takes to compute it with our prototype implementation. Our experiments show that if the set of positive examples to learn from is big enough, the algorithm computes a UVW representation of the right LTL formula. The experiments also show that if too few positive examples are available, the UVWs grow quite large to capture the automaton language with the desired tightness value n.

Related Work

The problem of automata learning from data traditionally comes in two different settings: *active* [5]–[7] and *passive* [8]–[10]. In an active setting, the learning algorithm interacts with a *teacher*. The teacher answers two kinds of queries: membership queries (whether a proposed word is in the language of the automaton) and equivalence queries (whether a proposed automaton is the correct one). Learning stops once the teacher answers an equivalence query positively. Having a teacher that is able to answer equivalence queries is a strong assumption. Our work focuses on the passive setting, where the learning algorithm only has access to data, a set of classified examples.

The standard problem formulation of passive learning is that a sample consisting of positive and negative examples

is given. For such a setup, several methods have been proposed for learning not only automata [9], [10], but also LTL formulas [11]–[13], or STL formulas [14], [15]. None of these methods provides good results when they are presented with only one class of examples—they return a trivial solution, one that accepts (or rejects) all possible examples.

Our problem—learning a specification from system traces—fits into the process mining framework (see Aalst et al. [16] for an overview): given an event log from a process, find a process model that satisfies certain properties. The properties are *fitness* (the model should be consistent with the examples from the log), *precision* (the model should not be overly general, e.g., modeling arbitrary examples), *generalization* (the model should not be overly tight, e.g., consistent only with the examples from the log), and *simplicity* (the model should be simple). Different operationalizations of the four properties give rise to different problem formulations and solutions. By choosing UVWs as our model, we get (structural) simplicity and connect it to the generalization property by the tightness value n, for which we require the tightest possible UVW consistent with the data.

Closely related to our approach is an algorithm by Avellaneda and Petrenko [17] for inferring deterministic automata over finite words (DFAs) from positive finite-word examples alone. Their algorithm searches for an automaton $\mathcal{A}$ with a given number of states n that is consistent with the given positive examples and for which no n-state DFA $\mathcal{A}'$ exists such that the language of $\mathcal{A}'$ is a strict subset of the language of $\mathcal{A}$. Both their approach and ours identify the language to be learned in the limit and use a single additional parameter for choosing the complexity of the language to be learned. Unlike in our approach, the resulting language in their algorithm is not unique for a given value of n. Furthermore, while our approach is relatively simple to adapt to the finite-word setting, their approach is difficult to adapt to the infinite-word setting, which we support in our work. This observation is rooted in the fact that their approach employs a SAT solver to search for candidate solutions, where clauses for the positive examples not found in previous solutions are added step-by-step. For the case of automata over infinite words, this requires the encoding of product runs between the deterministic automaton and the words to be accepted in SAT clauses (as described in [18], [19]). Every positive example requires additional clauses and variables, and for large numbers of positive examples, this easily leads to prohibitive sizes of the SAT instances.

Another direction of previous work is the identification of Live Sequence Charts (LSCs) [20], [21] from system runs. Live Sequence Charts [22] are a specification formalism that is popular for its compliance to the UML standard and the corresponding tools (e.g., IBM RSA). The set of properties representable as Live Sequence Charts, when not using free variables, was shown to be contained in the intersection of LTL and ACTL [23], which is characterized by UVWs (the version with free variables is characterized as a subset of first-order CTL* [24]). The existing work on mining LSCs [20], [21] borrows the concepts of *support* and *consistency* from data mining [25]. With user-defined thresholds for support and consistency, charts are enumerated until one exceeding that threshold is found. Rather than giving more credibility to patterns occurring most often in the example traces (as it is the case when using the notion of support), our method prefers semantically stronger UVWs, controlled by their size. This lets our approach converge to the same property regardless of the distribution of the traces, as long as all traces (in the form of ultimately periodic words) have a non-zero probability of occurring.

A problem related to ours by the fact that the learning happens over (positive) demonstrations only, is inverse reinforcement learning [26]. There, however, it is the reward function that is being learned. Obtaining only the reward function does not provide a human-understandable task specification. Inspired by inverse reinforcement learning, Vazquez-Chanlatte et al. [27] learn LTL-like temporal specifications from demonstrations. In order to do so, they have to pre-compute the implication lattice between the possible specifications, which limits the applicability of their approach. This is not necessary in our work, as we take advantage of the syntactic approximation of language inclusion between simple chains of UVWs. On the other hand, they successfully handle noise in the sample.

II. PRELIMINARIES

a) Basics: Given an alphabet Σ, the expression Σ^* represents the set of finite words with characters in Σ, and Σ^ω represents the set of words of infinite length in which each element is in Σ.

Let $\mathbb{B} = \{1, 0\}$ denote the set of Boolean values, with 1 representing **true** and 0 representing **false**. Moreover, let $S_1, \ldots, S_m$ be sets and $\sqsubseteq_i$ for $i \in \{1, \ldots, m\}$ be a partial order over the set S_i. Then, we call a function $f \colon S_1 \times \cdots \times S_m \to \mathbb{B}$ monotone if $s_i \sqsubseteq_i s_i'$ for each $i \in \{1, \ldots, m\}$ implies $f(s_1, \ldots, s_m) \leq f(s_1', \ldots, s_m')$. Adopting terminology from multicriteria optimization, we say that some tuple $(s_1, \ldots, s_m)$ is a *Pareto optimum* for f if $f(s_1, \ldots, s_m) = 1$ and for no $(s_1', \ldots, s_m') \neq (s_1, \ldots, s_m)$ with componentwise inequality $(s_1', \ldots, s_m') \leq (s_1, \ldots, s_m)$, we have $f(s_1', \ldots, s_m') = 1$. The set of Pareto optima is called the *Pareto front*. Likewise, we say that some tuple $(s_1, \ldots, s_m)$ is an element of the *co-Pareto front* if $f(s_1, \ldots, s_m) = 0$ and for all $(s_1', \ldots, s_m') \neq (s_1, \ldots, s_m)$ with $(s_1', \ldots, s_m') \geq (s_1, \ldots, s_m)$, we have $f(s_1', \ldots, s_m') = 1$.

b) Automata over infinite words: Given an alphabet Σ, an automaton over infinite words is a tuple $\mathcal{A} = (Q, \Sigma, \delta, Q_I, F)$, where Q is a finite set of *states*, $\delta \subseteq Q \times \Sigma \times Q$ is a *transition relation*, $Q_I \subseteq Q$ is a set of initial states, and F is a set of *final states*.

Given an infinite word $w = a_0 a_1 \ldots \in \Sigma^\omega$, we say that $\mathcal{A}$ induces a *run* $\pi = \pi_0 \pi_1 \ldots \in Q^\omega$ if $\pi_0 \in Q_I$ and for every $i \in \mathbb{N}$, we have that $(\pi_i, a_i, \pi_{i+1}) \in \delta$. An automaton defines a *language* $\mathcal{L}(\mathcal{A})$, i.e., a subset of Σ^ω that it *accepts*. Universal co-Büchi automata accept all words w for which all (infinite) runs $\pi = \pi_0 \pi_1 \ldots$ induced by the word w visit states from

F only finitely often, i.e., there exists an $i \in \mathbb{N}$ such that for every $j \in \mathbb{N}$ with $i \leq j$ we have $\pi_j \notin F$. The final states are also called *rejecting* states in this case.

Another type of automaton over infinite words are *non-deterministic Büchi automata*, which accept all words that have runs that visit F infinitely often. Such an automaton is furthermore called *deterministic* if for each $(q, a) \in Q \times \Sigma$, we have at most one $q' \in Q$ with $(q, a, q') \in \delta$.

We say that a automaton is *one-weak* or *very weak* if there exists a ranking function $r \colon Q \to \mathbb{N}$ such that for every $(q, a, q') \in \delta$, we have that either $r(q') < r(q)$ or q and q' are identical. More intuitively, this means that all loops in $\mathcal{A}$ are self-loops.

c) Linear Temporal Logic: The logic LTL (Linear Temporal Logic) [28] extends propositional Boolean logic with temporal modalities, which allow reasoning about sequences of events. Formulas of LTL are inductively defined as follows:

- each atomic proposition is an LTL formula;
- if ψ and φ are LTL formulas, so are $\neg\psi$, $\psi \vee \varphi$, $\mathsf{X}\,\psi$ ("next"), and $\psi \,\mathsf{U}\, \varphi$ ("until").

As syntactic sugar we add to the set of formulas *true*, *false*, $\psi \wedge \varphi$ and $\psi \to \varphi$, which are defined as usual for propositional logic. Moreover, we add the derived temporal operators $\mathsf{F}\,\psi := true \,\mathsf{U}\, \psi$ ("finally") and $\mathsf{G}\,\psi := \neg\,\mathsf{F}\,\neg\psi$ ("globally").

The semantics of propositional operators is defined as usual and here we describe the semantics of temporal modalities.

An LTL formula over some set of atomic propositions AP is evaluated on a word $w = a_0 a_1 \ldots \in (2^{\mathsf{AP}})^\omega$ and a time point $i \in \mathbb{N}$ of the sequence.

- $w, i \models p$ for $p \in \mathsf{AP}$ if $p \in a_i$
- $w, i \models \mathsf{X}\varphi$ if $w, i+1 \models \varphi$
- $w, i \models \varphi \,\mathsf{U}\, \psi$ if $\exists j \geq i.\ w, j \models \psi$ and $\forall k. i \leq k < j \Rightarrow w, k \models \varphi$

d) Universal very weak automata: Universal very-weak automata (UVW) are universal co-Büchi automata that are also very-weak. While universal co-Büchi automata are as expressive as Linear Temporal Logic (LTL) [29], universal very-weak automata are less expressive and only capture the properties whose satisfaction by a reactive system can be expressed both in computational tree logic with only universal path quantifiers (ACTL) and linear temporal logic [1], [30].

The language represented by a finite ω-automaton (such as a UVW) is uniquely determined by the set of *ultimately periodic words* uv^ω with $u, v \in \Sigma^*$ in the language of the automaton.

A universal very-weak automaton can be decomposed into *simple chains* [3], i.e., such that no state is directly reachable from more than one other state (apart from possibly itself). More formally, a simple chain is a sequence of different states $q_1, \ldots, q_n$ such that for all $i \in \{1, \ldots, n-1\}$, there exists some $a \in \Sigma$ with $(q_i, a, q_{i+1}) \in \delta$.

A simple chain is called *longest* (or *maximal*) in an automaton if it cannot be extended by an additional state at the beginning or the end of the sequence without losing the property that it is contained in the automaton. We say that a UVW is in decomposed form if there are no transitions between the maximal simple chains of the UVW and for every such simple chain $q_1, \ldots, q_n$, there are no "jumping transitions", i.e., for no $i, j \in \mathbb{N}$ and $a \in \Sigma$, we have $(q_i, a, q_j) \in \delta$ with $j > i + 1$. Without loss of generality, we can assume that in a decomposed UVW, every chain has an initial state and the last state is rejecting, as otherwise the whole chain or the last state, respectively, can be removed.

III. LEARNING UNIVERSAL VERY-WEAK AUTOMATA

In this section, we describe our approach to learn universal very weak automata (UVW) from positive examples alone. We first define the notion of n-tightness of a UVW, which specifies what languages we want to learn from positive examples alone. We prove that the languages of n-tight automata are unique, which ensures that the learning problem is well-posed.

We then establish in Section III-B how the simple chains of n-tight automata can be learned. As per the acceptance definition of UVW, the chains describe the words to be rejected. Hence, learning n-tight automata amounts to enumerating all simple chains of length up to n that do not reject any of the positive examples. We show that enumerating them all can be posed as the problem of enumerating the *co-Pareto front elements* of a monotone function.

In Section III-C, we then show how this insight leads to an efficient learning process: we show that the monotone function can be evaluated by solving a relatively simple model checking problem, and for enumerating all chains, we can use a Pareto optima enumeration algorithm from existing work, which outputs the co-Pareto front as a byproduct. To obtain reasonably-sized UVW, the last step is then to run the usual simulation-based automaton minimization steps.

A. Defining tight universal very-weak automata

Given a set of *positive* examples $P \subset \Sigma^\omega$, we want to compute (learn) an automaton $\mathcal{A}$ such that $P \subseteq \mathcal{L}(\mathcal{A})$, where we assume that for each $p \in P$, we have that $p = u_p(v_p)^\omega$ for some finite words $u_p, v_p \in \Sigma^*$ with $|v_p| \geq 1$.

Since there are infinitely many automata $\mathcal{A}$ satisfying this condition, we need an optimization criterion for finding the automaton $\mathcal{A}$. Minimizing the number of states of the solution is not a meaningful optimization criterion in this context, as the smallest automaton is always the one with 0 states – such an automaton does not visit final states, and by the acceptance definition of UVW, this means that all words are accepted.

To permit learning from positive examples only, we hence define an alternative learning criterion: we learn the strictest automaton (i.e., with the smallest language) that satisfies some syntactic cut-off criterion. For UVWs, there is a natural such criterion: the size of the co-domain of the ranking function, or equivalently, the length of the longest chain in a UVW.

Definition 1: Let $P \subset \Sigma^\omega$ be a set of positive examples and $\mathcal{A}$ be a UVW with $\mathcal{L}(\mathcal{A}) \supseteq P$. We say that $\mathcal{A}$ is n-tight for some $n \in \mathbb{N}$ if the following conditions hold:

1) There does not exist a simple chain of states longer than n in $\mathcal{A}$ (or equivalently, there exists a ranking function proving the very-weakness with co-domain $\{1, \ldots, n\}$),

2) For no other UVW $\mathcal{A}'$ with $P \subseteq \mathcal{L}(\mathcal{A}') \subset \mathcal{L}(\mathcal{A})$, we have that all simple chains of states in $\mathcal{A}'$ are of length at most n.

Lemma 1: Given a set of positive examples P and some value $n \in \mathbb{N}$, there exists an n-tight UVW $\mathcal{A}$ with $P \subseteq \mathcal{L}(\mathcal{A})$. All other n-tight UVWs have the same language.

Proof: We construct a universal very weak automaton in its decomposed form, i.e., where the UVW consists of a finite set of simple chains without transitions between them. Let C be a set of all possible simple chains of length up to n. We ignore the state identities/names, so that a chain of length n is characterized completely by transitions between the states, of which there are fewer than $2^{|\Sigma| \cdot (2n-1)}$ many different ones (as there can be at most $2^{|\Sigma|}$ different self-loops on n states and fewer than $2^{|\Sigma| \cdot (n-1)}$ many transitions between different states). This makes the set C finite. We choose an automaton $\mathcal{A}$ to consist of the set of all chains $c \in C$ such that $P \subseteq \mathcal{L}(c)$. We claim that this is an n-tight UVW accepting all words from P and that its language is the language of all n-tight automata.

Indeed, for a tighter UVW $\mathcal{A}'$ (i.e., such that $P \subseteq \mathcal{L}(\mathcal{A}') \subset \mathcal{L}(\mathcal{A})$) with maximal chain length n, there must exist $\alpha \in \Sigma^\omega$ such that $\alpha \in \mathcal{L}(\mathcal{A}) \setminus \mathcal{L}(\mathcal{A}')$. The fact that $\alpha \notin \mathcal{L}(\mathcal{A}')$ means that a run of $\mathcal{A}'$ on α will end up in one of its final (rejecting) states going through a chain of up to n states. But by $P \subseteq \mathcal{L}(\mathcal{A}')$ and by our definition of $\mathcal{A}$, this chain should be a part of $\mathcal{A}$. Therefore, $\alpha \notin \mathcal{L}(\mathcal{A})$, which yields a contradiction.

Let now $\mathcal{A}$ and $\mathcal{A}'$ be two n-tight automata. If they are not equivalent, then there exists a word $\alpha \in \Sigma^\omega \setminus P$ accepted by one of them but not by the other. Wthout loss of generality, let $a \notin \mathcal{L}(\mathcal{A})$. Since all chains in $\mathcal{A}$ and $\mathcal{A}'$ are of length at most n, this means that the word is rejected by one of such chains in $\mathcal{A}$. As the chain can be added to $\mathcal{A}'$ without making it reject a word in P, this proves that $\mathcal{A}'$ is not n-tight, yielding a contradiction. Hence, the assumption that the two automata $\mathcal{A}$ and $\mathcal{A}'$ are not equivalent but both n-tight cannot be fulfilled. $\square$

The lemma shows that for a given set of positive examples P, n-tight automata have a unique language. It also shows how such an automaton can be computed: we first enumerate all simple chains of length n that a decomposed automaton accepting all elements from P could have. Taking these chains together, we obtain an n-tight UVW.

B. Enumerating All Simple Chains of a UVW to be Learned

The n-tightness definition of the previous subsection states what language the automaton that we want to learn from a set of positive examples should have. However, enumerating all simple chains that are consistent with the given positive examples is computationally inefficient as their number grows exponentially with n and the size of the alphabet. We show in this subsection how this problem can be mitigated.

To do so, we represent simple chains syntactically by so-called *chain strings*. Then, we define a partial order over these strings that is consistent with language inclusion between automata consisting only of the represented chains. In order

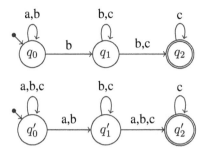

Fig. 1. Two example simple chains, where the lower one is syntactically stronger than the first one.

to obtain n-tight UVWs, we then only need to enumerate all chain strings that are *strongest* according to this partial order.

We visualize this idea in Figure 1 for the case of $n = 3$ and $\Sigma = \{a, b, c\}$. The simple chains given there are represented by the chain strings $(\{a, b\}, \{b\}, \{b, c\}, \{b, c\}, \{c\})$ and $(\{a, b, c\}, \{a, b\}, \{b, c\}, \{a, b, c\}, \{c\})$, which denote the edge labels along the chain, alternating between self-loops and edges between states. Assuming that both chains are compatible with some set of positive examples over the alphabet $\Sigma = \{a, b, c\}$, the lower one is *stronger* than the upper one in the sense that it rejects strictly more words.

This can be seen from the fact that both chains have the same length, and at each self-loop and each edge between the states, the labels for the lower chain are supersets of the respective labels for the upper automaton. On the chain string level, we can easily see that by looking at every pair of elements in the string and comparing the respective sets for set inclusion. Hence, every rejecting run for the upper chain is a rejecting run for the lower one as well. Chain strings induce a natural order by element-wise inclusion, and as already mentioned, the main idea of our approach is to enumerate only the largest chain strings with respect to the partial order that are consistent with the set of positive examples, which decreases the number of chains to be enumerated.

To simplify the presentation henceforth, the formal chain string definition also permits interrupted chains of states, which are not simple chains according to their definition in Section II. Furthermore, we only care about chains in which exactly the first state is initial and exactly the last state is rejecting. The generality is, however, not lost: if a simple chain does not have this form (so it has additional initial or rejecting states), then it contains another shorter simple chain of this form. This shorter simple chain can be extended to a chain of length n by duplicating the last (rejecting) state and rerouting the outgoing transitions of the previously last state to the new last state. This yields another chain of length n that is not missed when enumerating *all* maximal (w.r.t. their partial order) chain strings of length n that are compatible with P according to the definitions to follow. Figure 2 depicts this observation. The leftmost chain is split into a chain for the rejecting state q_2 and a chain for the rejecting state q_3. The now shorter chain is post-processed to a longer chain by

duplicating the last state.

Definition 2: Let Σ and n be given. A *chain string* for Σ and n is of the form $s = (l_1, m_1, l_2, m_2, \ldots, l_n) \in (2^\Sigma \times 2^\Sigma)^{n-1} \times 2^\Sigma$. Such a string s induces a chain-like automaton $\mathcal{A} = (Q, \Sigma, \delta, Q_I, F)$ with

- $Q = \{q_1, \ldots, q_n\}$;
- $Q_I = \{q_1\}$;
- $\delta = \{(q_i, x, q_i) \mid x \in l_i, i \in \{1, \ldots, n\}\} \cup \{(q_i, x, q_{i+1}) \mid x \in m_i, i \in \{1, \ldots, n-1\}\}$; and
- $F = \{q_n\}$.

Note that the induced automaton $\mathcal{A}$ consists of at most one single simple chain that is reachable from an initial state.

The main idea of the following enumeration procedure is to cast the problem of finding all strongest simple chains as a problem of finding the *co-Pareto front* of a monotonous function f_n over chain strings. This enables the use of a Pareto front enumeration algorithm [31] for monotone functions to enumerate all simple chains that are consistent with the given positive examples.

The said algorithm however finds the Pareto front elements of a rectangular finite subset of $\mathbb{N}^u$ for some $u \in \mathbb{N}$. To make it compatible with the problem of finding simple chains, we have to encode chain strings into $\mathbb{N}^u$. The fact that all chain string elements are powersets enables a relatively simple encoding. We set $u = |\Sigma| \cdot (2n - 1)$ and for every chain string $s = (l_1, m_1, l_2, m_2, \ldots, l_n) \in (2^\Sigma \times 2^\Sigma)^{n-1} \times 2^\Sigma$, the corresponding encoded string in $\mathbb{N}^u$ is of the form $s' = (l_1^1, \ldots, l_1^{|\Sigma|}, m_1^1, \ldots, m_1^{|\Sigma|}, l_2^1, \ldots, l_2^{|\Sigma|}, \ldots, l_n^1, \ldots, l_n^{|\Sigma|})$, where every every element l_j^i and m_j^i is either 0 or 1, depending on whether the ith element of Σ is part of the encoded l_j. The order of the elements of Σ used in this encoding is arbitrary but fixed.

A Pareto-front enumeration algorithm necessarily also enumerates the co-Pareto front to be sure it found all Pareto front points [31], which we exploit to find all strongest chain strings, as these form the co-Pareto front. The monotone function itself implements a *model checking* step of all elements in P against the chain, which due to the lasso-like structure of the examples is relatively easy to solve.

Lemma 2: Let P be a set of positive examples over the alphabet Σ, $n \in \mathbb{N}$, and $f_n \colon (2^\Sigma \times 2^\Sigma)^{n-1} \times 2^\Sigma \to \mathbb{B}$ be a function that maps a chain string over Σ and n to 1 if and only if the automaton induced by the string rejects some element in P. Then, the function f_n is monotone.

Proof: Let $s = (l_1, m_1, l_2, \ldots, m_{n-1}, l_n)$ and $s' = (l_1', m_1', l_2', \ldots, m_{n-1}', l_n')$ be two chain strings with $l_i \subseteq l_i'$ for each $i \in \{1, \ldots, n\}$ and $m_i \subseteq m_i'$ for each $i \in \{1, \ldots, n-1\}$. Furthermore, let $\mathcal{A}_s = (Q_s, \Sigma, \delta_s, Q_{I,s}, F_s)$ and $\mathcal{A}_{s'} = (Q_{s'}, \Sigma, \delta_{s'}, Q_{I,s'}, F_{s'})$ be the corresponding UVWs as in Definition 2 with $Q_s = Q_s' = \{q_1, \ldots, q_n\}$.

As $l_i \subseteq l_i'$ for each $i \in \{1, \ldots, n\}$ and $m_i \subseteq m_i'$ for each $i \in \{1, \ldots, n-1\}$, by the fact that by Definition 2, the transition relation of $\mathcal{A}_s$ is monotone in $l_1 \ldots l_n$ and $m_1 \ldots m_n$, we have that $\delta_s \subseteq \delta_{s'}$. Hence, every run π of $\mathcal{A}_s$ for some word $w \in \Sigma^\omega$ is also a run of $\mathcal{A}_{s'}$ for the same word.

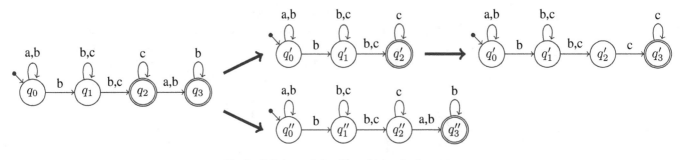

Fig. 2. Splitting a chain with multiple rejecting states

As universal automata accept all words that do not induce any rejecting run, this means that all words rejected by $\mathcal{A}_s$ will also be rejected by $\mathcal{A}_{s'}$, and hence, we have $\mathcal{L}(\mathcal{A}_{s'}) \subseteq \mathcal{L}(\mathcal{A}_s)$.

To show that f_n is monotone, recall that the function f_n maps a chain string t to whether the UVW $\mathcal{A}_t$ rejects a word in P. Towards a contradiction, assume that $f_n(\mathcal{A}_s) = 1$ but $f_n(\mathcal{A}_{s'}) = 0$. This means that there exists a word $w \in P$ such that $w \notin \mathcal{L}(\mathcal{A}_s)$ and $w \in \mathcal{L}(\mathcal{A}_{s'})$. Thus, w witnesses $\mathcal{L}(\mathcal{A}_{s'}) \not\subseteq \mathcal{L}(\mathcal{A}_s)$, which is a contradiction to the previous part of the proof. In conclusion, we obtain that f_n is monotone. $\square$

We obtain the following corollary:

Corollary 1: Let P be a set of positive examples over the alphabet Σ, $n \in \mathbb{N}$, and A be the set of automata induced by the co-Pareto front elements of the function f_n. The automaton for the language $\bigcap_{\mathcal{A} \in A} \mathcal{L}(\mathcal{A})$ is n-tight for P and Σ.

The automaton from this corollary can be built easily, as universal very-weak automata are closed under language intersection by just merging the state sets, transition relations, and initial states [3]. This enables us to simply merge all chains found together into a single UVW.

C. Engineering Considerations of the Learning Algorithm

After the co-Pareto front of strongest chains has been enumerated, the last step in the construction of the UVWs is merging them to a single UVW. We add the chains one-by-one to a solution UVW. After every such step, we use the automaton minimization techniques described in [2] to reduce the size of the automaton. If the process is stopped prematurely, the result is still useful—a UVW that accepts a subset of the language that the final automaton (given sufficient computation resources) would accept. This property makes it possible to use the algorithm in the *anytime* fashion, stopping it when a given resource budget is exceeded.

It remains to be described how f_n can be computed efficiently. We implemented this process as follows: let $P = \{(u_1, v_1), \ldots, (u_m, v_m)\}$ and $\mathcal{A} = (Q, \Sigma, \delta, Q_I, F)$ with $Q = \{q_1, \ldots, q_n\}$ be an automaton induced by a chain string to be checked. For every $j \in \{1, \ldots, m\}$, we translate (u_j, v_j) to a deterministic Büchi automaton $\mathcal{A}'$ accepting exactly $u_j(v_j)^\omega$. Such an automaton has $|u_j| + |v_j| + 1$ states. We then check if $\mathcal{A}'$ admits a word rejected by $\mathcal{A}$, i.e., if $\mathcal{L}(\mathcal{A}') \cap \overline{\mathcal{L}(\mathcal{A})} \neq \emptyset$. Since the complement of a universal co-Büchi word automaton can be obtained in the form of a non-deterministic Büchi automaton by just interpreting $\mathcal{A}$ as such, the standard product

construction from linear-time model checking can be applied to test if $\mathcal{L}(\mathcal{A}') \cap \overline{\mathcal{L}(\mathcal{A})} \neq \emptyset$. The function f_n can then simply iterate over all examples $j \in \{1, \ldots, m\}$ and test if this is the case for any of them. Whenever it finds that $\mathcal{L}(\mathcal{A}') \cap \overline{\mathcal{L}(\mathcal{A})} \neq \emptyset$ for some automaton $\mathcal{A}'$ built from a positive example, the function f_n returns 1. Otherwise, it returns 0 after iterating through all values for $j \in \{1, \ldots, m\}$.

Note that in an actual implementation of f_n, there is no need to explicitly build $\mathcal{A}'$ or construct the product Büchi automaton. Rather, the implementation can make use of the fact that only the last state of the simple chain is rejecting. So it can compute the states of the product that are reachable and then check if state q_n in the $\mathcal{A}$ component of the product is reachable while at the same time, all characters in v_j are contained in the self-loop label of state q_n. If and only if that is the case, positive example number j is rejected by $\mathcal{A}$.

IV. Empirical Evaluation

We implemented the approach from this paper in a prototype toolchain [32], which is available on Github. The enumeration of the simple chains is performed by a tool written in C++, while the subsequent minimization of the resulting UVWs is implemented in Python 3.

In order to assess the performance of our approach on practically relevant properties, we considered the specification of the industrial on-chip bus arbiter of the AMBA AHB bus [33]. Specifically, we considered ten assumptions made for the master of the AHB bus, as described in [4]. For simplicity we abstracted from the concrete variable names and rewrote predicates over categorial values into individual propositions. For instance, the original property A8 from [4] referring to a burst sequence of unspecified length (denoted by the value INCR) is $\mathsf{G}[\mathsf{HLOCK} \wedge (\mathsf{HBURST} = \mathsf{INCR}) \rightarrow \mathsf{X}\,\mathsf{F}(\neg\mathsf{REQ\_VLD})]$. It is rewritten into $\mathsf{G}[(a \wedge b) \rightarrow \mathsf{X}\,\mathsf{F}(\neg c)]$. All the resulting formulas are shown on the left-hand-side of Table I.

Except for Property 3, all properties can be represented in UVW form by a single simple chain with two states each. For Property 3, we need two chains of length 3. The properties employing *two to four* atomic propositions have been learned over words with characters that encode this number of propositions. Propery 6 has been learned over positive examples in which each character has three proposition values, while for Property 9, we used two propositions. This deviation was necessary to

TABLE I
MEAN COMPUTATION TIMES FOR UVW LEARNING FOR THE TEN LTL
PROPERTIES CONSIDERED IN SECTION IV

	Property	Time in s	
		chain len. 2	chain len. 3
1)	$G[a \rightarrow (b \vee c \vee d)]$	0.763	timeout
2)	$G[a \rightarrow (b \vee c)]$	0.517	1.029
3)	$G[X \neg a \rightarrow (\neg b \leftrightarrow X(\neg b))]$	0.493	1.184
4)	$G[a \rightarrow \neg b]$	0.408	0.713
5)	$G[a \rightarrow (\neg b \wedge \neg c)]$	0.533	1.059
6)	$G\,a$	0.526	1.057
7)	$G[a \rightarrow F\,b]$	0.442	0.870
8)	$G[(a \wedge b) \rightarrow X\,F(\neg c)]$	0.634	119.123
9)	$G\,F\,a$	0.423	0.685
10)	$G\,F(\neg a \wedge \neg b)$	0.428	0.702

ensure that there are enough distinct positive examples for these properties.

For each property, we computed 50,000 different ultimately periodic words uv^{ω} that satisfy the property, where $|u|$ is of length 0, 1, 2, 3, or 4, while $|v|$ is of length 1, 2, 3, or 4. The characters of the words are the subsets of propositions holding, and all word part lengths are equally likely to be chosen. We also use a uniform probability distribution over the characters when computing the positive examples. Whenever a non-positive example for the property is found during the positive example computation, it is discarded and another example word is computed instead. We ran every experiment on 10 different example sets generated in this way and report the mean values obtained in the following.

The experiments were conducted on a computer with four AMD EPYC 7251 processors running at 2,1 GHz and an x64 version of Linux. The available main memory per run of the learner was restricted to 3 GB. We used a computation time limit of 600 s per learning problem.

Table I contains the mean computation times for all properties when using all 50,000 positive examples as input in each case. It can be seen that for most combinations, our approach computes a UVW rather quickly. Only for one property with a higher number of atomic propositions and an unnecessarily long chosen chain length, the toolchain times out.

Figure 3 shows for nine of the ten properties how big the computed UVW are, where sizes for both chain lengths of 2 and 3 are reported. Here, we varied the number of positive examples provided to the learner along the X axis (minimum: 100, in steps of 100). For very low number of examples, our toolchain often times out. This is rooted in the fact that the tightest UVW is often very large when not enough positive examples are available. It can also be observed that for a lower chain length, the computed UVW converges to a small one much earlier.

Figure 4 depicts the relationship between computation time and the sizes of the computed UVWs in more detail, using Property 3, the one that was left out of Figure 3. It can be observed that computation times are very short when enough positive examples are available, and they grow only very

mildly with additional positive examples. When, however, not enough examples are available, the approach computes a much larger number of simple chains, which also increases the workload of the UVW minimization heuristic.

Finally, Figure 5 depicts the UVWs learned for Property 3. The property can only be learned correctly with a chain length of 3, and the two paths through the UVW on the right-hand side show the two conjunctive requirements that the LTL property $G[X \neg a \rightarrow (\neg b \leftrightarrow X(\neg b))]$ imposes, namely that (1) after a character with $b = true$ is seen, b needs to retain a value of $true$ until a gets a $false$ value afterwards and (2) after a character with $b = false$ is seen, b needs to retain a value of $false$ until a gets a $false$ value afterwards. The automaton has a simple structure and is quite easy to read. The computed UVW for a chain length of 2 is, as expected, an overapproximation of the language to be learned. Interestingly, the encoded language is a liveness language, even though the approximated LTL property is not.

For all ten LTL properties considered in our experiments, the learned UVWs for the correct chain lengths represent the correct languages and have a minimal number of states. Moreover, the resulting UVWs are fairly easy to understand (we refer the reader to the extended version of the experiments, available in the code repository [32] for their depiction), which underpins the use of UVWs as an easy-to-understand specification formalism.

V. DISCUSSION OF THE PROPOSED APPROACH

In this section, we discuss potential challenges for the application of our approach as well as strategies to mitigate them.

First, our learning algorithm depends on a well-chosen tightness value n: if the value is too small, then the resulting UVW is too permissive and imprecise; if the value is chosen too large, on the other hand, the computational effort for learning an UVW can become prohibitive. Determining an appropriate value for n remains an open question. A potential strategy to find such a value in practice—apart from relying on domain knowledge—could be to perform a search that starts with a reasonably small tightness value and then increments the value until the resulting UVW does no longer change. As Table I suggest, our learning algorithm is fast enough (less than 1 s given sufficiently many examples) so that such a search is a viable approach. On a more general note, however, we would like to reiterate that without such a parameter, the problem of learning from only positive examples is ill-defined.

Second, as our experimental evaluation has shown, our learning algorithm requires a fair amount of positive examples (several thousands) to perform well. However, compared to most other learning algorithms, which require negative examples, we believe that this is not a major restriction in practice because (a) positive examples are usually much easier to obtain than negative examples and (b) positive examples are often readily available (e.g., from log files) or can be generated automatically (e.g., by means of simulations).

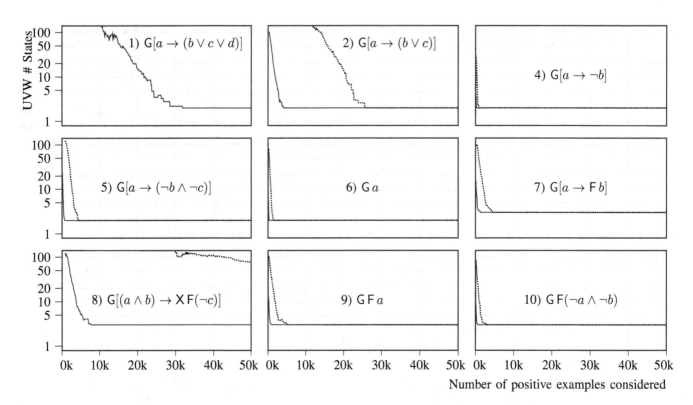

Fig. 3. UVW sizes for nine of the ten examples. The dotted lines are for a UVW chain length of 3, while the solid lines are for a UVW chain length of 2. The number of positive examples given to the learner ranges between 100 and 50,000 and is displayed on the x axis of each chart. Parts in the charts with absent lines represent timeouts, which were common for low numbers of positive examples.

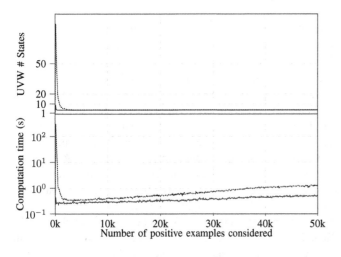

Fig. 4. Joint plot for the computation time and UVW sizes for Property 3).

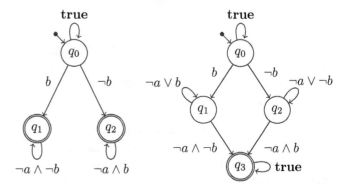

Fig. 5. Learned UVW (for chain lengths of 2 on the left and 3 on the right) from the positive examples for the LTL property $G[X \neg a \rightarrow (\neg b \leftrightarrow X(\neg b))]$.

obtained from observing an existing system without access to its internal state, one can use acceleration-like techniques [34] to detect cycles based on repeating patterns in the observations.

VI. CONCLUSION AND DIRECTION FOR FUTURE WORK

We have developed an effective method for learning formal specifications in the form of universal very-weak automata from positive examples only. Our learning algorithm reduces the problem of learning such an automaton to the enumeration of elements in a Pareto front and uses an effective minimization technique to obtain a unique finite-state representation of the learned property. Experiments with properties from

Finally, our learning algorithm is designed to learn properties of infinite words and, hence, requires infinite words (in the form of ultimately periodic words uv^ω) as input. In practice however, one will only be able to observe or simulate finite executions. To mitigate this challenge, we propose two strategies. If the examples are obtained from simulations, it is fairly easy to detect repetitions of system states that can be used to partition the execution into an initial fragment u and a repeating part v. On the other hand, if the examples are the Advanced Microcontroller Bus Architecture (AMBA) have demonstrated that our approach is able to infer concise and easy-to-interpret specifications from positive examples.

For future work, we plan to adapt our learning algorithm to be able to learn from finite rather than infinite words. A relatively straightforward way to do this would be to restrict the chain enumeration to only consider chains that have $\bigcirc\!\!\!\!\!\sim$ **true** as final state. The class of languages learnable by this approach would then exactly be the set of languages that can be accepted by so-called universal very-weak finite automata, studied, for instance, by Bojańczyk [30].

Finally, we are interested in determining an appropriate tightness value automatically from the sample, which seems to be a non-trivial problem.

REFERENCES

[1] M. Maidl, "The common fragment of CTL and LTL," in *FOCS 2000, Proceedings*, 2000, pp. 643–652. [Online]. Available: https://doi.org/10.1109/SFCS.2000.892332

[2] K. Adabala and R. Ehlers, "A fragment of linear temporal logic for universal very weak automata," in *Automated Technology for Verification and Analysis - 16th International Symposium, ATVA 2018, Los Angeles, CA, USA, October 7-10, 2018, Proceedings*, 2018, pp. 335–351.

[3] R. Ehlers, "ACTL ∩ LTL synthesis," in *Computer Aided Verification - 24th International Conference, CAV 2012, Berkeley, CA, USA, July 7-13, 2012 Proceedings*, 2012, pp. 39–54.

[4] Y. Godhal, K. Chatterjee, and T. A. Henzinger, "Synthesis of AMBA AHB from formal specification: a case study," *International Journal on Software Tools for Technology Transfer*, vol. 15, no. 5, pp. 585–601, Oct 2013.

[5] D. Angluin, "Learning regular sets from queries and counterexamples," *Inf. Comput.*, vol. 75, no. 2, pp. 87–106, 1987.

[6] M. J. Kearns and U. V. Vazirani, *An Introduction to Computational Learning Theory*. MIT Press, 1994.

[7] R. L. Rivest and R. E. Schapire, "Inference of finite automata using homing sequences," *Inf. Comput.*, vol. 103, no. 2, pp. 299–347, 1993.

[8] J. Oncina and P. Garcia, "Inferring regular languages in polynomial updated time," in *Pattern recognition and image analysis: selected papers from the IVth Spanish Symposium*. World Scientific, 1992, pp. 49–61.

[9] M. Heule and S. Verwer, "Exact DFA identification using SAT solvers," in *ICGI*, ser. Lecture Notes in Computer Science, vol. 6339. Springer, 2010, pp. 66–79.

[10] D. Neider and N. Jansen, "Regular model checking using solver technologies and automata learning," in *NASA Formal Methods*, ser. Lecture Notes in Computer Science, vol. 7871. Springer, 2013, pp. 16–31.

[11] D. Neider and I. Gavran, "Learning linear temporal properties," in *FMCAD*. IEEE, 2018, pp. 1–10.

[12] A. Camacho and S. A. McIlraith, "Learning interpretable models expressed in linear temporal logic," in *ICAPS*. AAAI Press, 2019, pp. 621–630.

[13] J. Kim, C. Muise, A. Shah, S. Agarwal, and J. Shah, "Bayesian inference of linear temporal logic specifications for contrastive explanations," in *IJCAI*. ijcai.org, 2019, pp. 5591–5598.

[14] G. Bombara, C. I. Vasile, F. Penedo, H. Yasuoka, and C. Belta, "A decision tree approach to data classification using signal temporal logic," in *Proceedings of the 19th International Conference on Hybrid Systems: Computation and Control, HSCC 2016, Vienna, Austria, April 12-14, 2016*. ACM, 2016, pp. 1–10.

[15] S. Mohammadinejad, J. V. Deshmukh, A. G. Puranic, M. Vazquez-Chanlatte, and A. Donzé, "Interpretable classification of time-series data using efficient enumerative techniques," in *HSCC*. ACM, 2020, pp. 9:1–9:10.

[16] W. M. P. van der Aalst, J. Carmona, T. Chatain, and B. F. van Dongen, "A tour in process mining: From practice to algorithmic challenges," *Trans. Petri Nets Other Model. Concurr.*, vol. 14, pp. 1–35, 2019.

[17] F. Avellaneda and A. Petrenko, "Inferring DFA without negative examples," in *Proceedings of the 14th International Conference on Grammatical Inference, ICGI 2018, Wrocław, Poland, September 5-7, 2018*, 2018, pp. 17–29. [Online]. Available: http://proceedings.mlr.press/v93/avellaneda19a.html

[18] R. Ehlers, "Minimising deterministic Büchi automata precisely using SAT solving," in *Theory and Applications of Satisfiability Testing - SAT 2010, 13th International Conference, SAT 2010, Edinburgh, UK, July 11-14, 2010. Proceedings*, ser. Lecture Notes in Computer Science, O. Strichman and S. Szeider, Eds., vol. 6175. Springer, 2010, pp. 326–332.

[19] S. Baarir and A. Duret-Lutz, "SAT-based minimization of deterministic ω-automata," in *Logic for Programming, Artificial Intelligence, and Reasoning - 20th International Conference, LPAR-20 2015, Suva, Fiji, November 24-28, 2015, Proceedings*, 2015, pp. 79–87.

[20] D. Lo and S. Maoz, "Specification mining of symbolic scenario-based models," in *Proceedings of the 8th ACM SIGPLAN-SIGSOFT Workshop on Program Analysis for Software Tools and Engineering, PASTE'08, Atlanta, Georgia, November 9-10, 2008*, 2008, pp. 29–35.

[21] ——, "Mining scenario-based triggers and effects," in *23rd IEEE/ACM International Conference on Automated Software Engineering (ASE 2008), 15-19 September 2008, L'Aquila, Italy*, 2008, pp. 109–118.

[22] W. Damm and D. Harel, "LSCs: Breathing life into message sequence charts," *Formal Methods Syst. Des.*, vol. 19, no. 1, pp. 45–80, 2001.

[23] H. Kugler, D. Harel, A. Pnueli, Y. Lu, and Y. Bontemps, "Temporal logic for scenario-based specifications," in *Tools and Algorithms for the Construction and Analysis of Systems, 11th International Conference, TACAS 2005, Held as Part of the Joint European Conferences on Theory and Practice of Software, ETAPS 2005, Edinburgh, UK, April 4-8, 2005, Proceedings*, ser. Lecture Notes in Computer Science, N. Halbwachs and L. D. Zuck, Eds., vol. 3440. Springer, 2005, pp. 445–460. [Online]. Available: https://doi.org/10.1007/b107194

[24] W. Damm, T. Toben, and B. Westphal, "On the expressive power of live sequence charts," in *Program Analysis and Compilation, Theory and Practice, Essays Dedicated to Reinhard Wilhelm on the Occasion of His 60th Birthday*, 2006, pp. 225–246.

[25] J. Han, M. Kamber, and J. Pei, *Data Mining: Concepts and Techniques, 3rd edition*. Morgan Kaufmann, 2011. [Online]. Available: http://hanj.cs.illinois.edu/bk3/

[26] A. Y. Ng and S. J. Russell, "Algorithms for inverse reinforcement learning," in *ICML*. Morgan Kaufmann, 2000, pp. 663–670.

[27] M. Vazquez-Chanlatte, S. Jha, A. Tiwari, M. K. Ho, and S. A. Seshia, "Learning task specifications from demonstrations," in *Advances in Neural Information Processing Systems 31, NeurIPS*, 2018, pp. 5372–5382. [Online]. Available: http://papers.nips.cc/paper/7782-learning-task-specifications-from-demonstrations

[28] A. Pnueli, "The temporal logic of programs," in *18th Annual Symposium on Foundations of Computer Science, Providence, Rhode Island, USA, 31 October - 1 November 1977*. IEEE Computer Society, 1977, pp. 46–57.

[29] O. Kupferman and M. Y. Vardi, "Safraless decision procedures," in *46th Annual IEEE Symposium on Foundations of Computer Science (FOCS 2005), 23-25 October 2005, Pittsburgh, PA, USA, Proceedings*. IEEE Computer Society, 2005, pp. 531–542.

[30] M. Bojańczyk, "The common fragment of ACTL and LTL," in *Foundations of Software Science and Computational Structures, 11th International Conference, FOSSACS*, ser. Lecture Notes in Computer Science, R. M. Amadio, Ed., vol. 4962. Springer, 2008, pp. 172–185.

[31] R. Ehlers, "Computing the complete pareto front," *CoRR*, vol. abs/1512.05207, 2015. [Online]. Available: http://arxiv.org/abs/1512.05207

[32] I. Gavran, R. Ehlers, and D. Neider, "unite - Uvw learNer from posITive Examples," Aug. 2020. [Online]. Available: https://github.com/TUC-ES/unite

[33] "ARM Ltd. Amba specification (rev. 5)," 2019. [Online]. Available: http://infocenter.arm.com/help/index.jsp?topic=/com.arm.doc.ihi0033/index.html

[34] B. Jonsson and M. Saksena, "Systematic acceleration in regular model checking," in *CAV*, ser. Lecture Notes in Computer Science, vol. 4590. Springer, 2007, pp. 131–144.

24

Distributed Bounded Model Checking

Prantik Chatterjee*, Subhajit Roy*, Bui Phi Diep†, Akash Lal‡

*IIT Kanpur, {prantik, subhajit}@cse.iitk.ac.in
†Uppsala University, bui.phi-diep@it.uu.se
‡Microsoft Research, akashl@microsoft.com

Abstract—Program verification is a resource-hungry task. This paper looks at the problem of parallelizing SMT-based automated program verification, specifically bounded model-checking, so that it can be distributed and executed on a cluster of machines. We present an algorithm that dynamically unfolds the call graph of the program and frequently splits it to create sub-tasks that can be solved in parallel. The algorithm is adaptive, controlling the splitting rate according to available resources, and also leverages information from the SMT solver to split where most complexity lies in the search. We implemented our algorithm by modifying CORRAL, the verifier used by Microsoft's Static Driver Verifier (SDV), and evaluate it on a series of hard SDV benchmarks.

I. INTRODUCTION

Program verification has a long history of over five decades and it has been consistently challenged over this entire duration by the continued increase in the size and complexity of software. As the efficiency of techniques and solvers has increased, so has the amount of software that is written. For this reason, *scalability* remains central to the applicability of program verification in practice.

This paper studies the problem of automated program verification. In particular, we consider Bounded Model Checking (BMC) [1]: the problem of reasoning over the entire space of program inputs but only over a subset of program paths, typically up to a bound on the number of loop iterations and recursive calls. BMC side-steps the need for (expensive and undecidable) inductive invariant generation and instead directly harnesses the power of SAT/SMT solvers in a decidable fragment of logic. BMC techniques are popular; they are implemented in most program verification tools today [2, Table 5].

Our goal is to scale BMC by parallelizing the verification task and distributing it across multiple machines to make use of larger compute and memory resources. The presence of several public cloud providers has made it easy to set up and manage a cluster of machines. While this distributed platform is available to us, there is a shortage of verification tools that can exploit it.

Parallelizing BMC. BMC works by generating logical encodings, often called *verification conditions* or VCs, for a subset of program paths that are then fed to an SMT solver to look for potential assertion violations in the program. We aim to retain the same architecture, where we continue to use the SMT solver as a black-box, but generate multiple different VCs in parallel to search over disjoint sets of program paths. This allows us to directly consume future improvements in SMT solvers, retaining one of the key advantages of BMC.

Our technique works by *splitting* the set of program paths into disjoint subsets that are then searched independently in parallel. The splitting is done by simply picking a control node and considering (*a*) the set of paths that go through the node, and (*b*) the set of paths that do not. Splitting can happen multiple times. The decisions of *what* node to split and *when* to split are both taken dynamically by our technique. We refer to the BMC problem restricted to a set of splitting decisions (i.e., nodes that must be taken, and nodes that must be avoided) as a *verification partition*.

Verification starts by creating multiple processes, each of which have access to the input program and are connected over the network. One process is designated as the *server* while the rest are called *clients*. The search starts sequentially on one of the clients that applies standard BMC on the input program. At some point in time, which is controlled by the *splitting rate*, the client chooses a splitting node, thus creating two partitions. The client continues verification on one of the partitions, and sends the other partition to the server. The server is only responsible for coordination; it does not do verification itself. It accumulates the partitions (represented as a set of splitting decisions) coming in from the clients and farms them off to idle clients for verification. Clients can split multiple times. This continues until a client reports a counterexample (in which case, it must be a counterexample in the original program) or the server runs out of partitions and all clients become idle (in which case, the BMC problem is concluded as *safe*).

The splitting rate is adjusted according to the current number of idle client: it is reduced when all clients are busy, and then increased as more clients becomes available.

Splitting has some challenges that we illustrate using the following snippet of code.

```
procedure main() {
    var x := 0;
    if (...) { call foo(); x := 1; }
    if (...) { call bar(); }
    if (...) { call baz(); }
    assert(x == 1 || expr);
}
```

Suppose that the assertion at the end of `main` is the one that we wish to verify (or find a counterexample) and all uses of variable `x` are shown in the snippet. The `main` procedure calls multiple other procedures, each of which can manipulate global variables of the program (not shown). In this case, if we split on the call to `foo`, then one partition (the one that must take `foo`) becomes trivial: it is easy to see that the assertion holds in that partition, irrespective of what happens in the rest of the program. We refer to this as a *trivial* split. Each split incurs an overhead when a partition is shipped to another client where the verification context for that partition must be set up from scratch. Trivial splits are troublesome because they accumulate this overhead without any real benefits in trimming down the search. Unfortunately, it is hard to avoid trivial splits altogether because it can involve custom (solver specific) reasoning (e.g., the fact that variable x is not modified outside of `main`). Our technique instead aims to reduce the overhead with splitting when possible. The server prioritizes sending a partition back to the client that generated it. Each client uses the incremental solving APIs of SMT solvers to remember backtracking points of previous splits that it had produced. This allows a client to get setup for one of its previous partitions much faster, thus reducing overhead.

Next, consider splitting on the call to `bar`. In this case, both of the generated partitions must still reason about `baz` because taking or avoiding `bar` has no implications on the call to `baz`. If `bar` turns out to be simple, while most of the complexity lies inside `baz`, then both partitions will end up doing the same work and diminish the benefits of parallelization. In this case, we rely on extracting information from the solver (via an unsat core) to make informed splitting choices and avoid duplicating work across partitions.

Implementation. We have implemented our technique in a tool called HYDRA[1]. The sequential BMC technique used by HYDRA is *stratified inlining* (SI) [3]. SI incrementally builds the VC of a program by lazily inlining procedure calls. HYDRA keeps track of the expanding VC, and frequently splits it by picking a splitting node that has already been inlined in the VC.

We evaluated HYDRA on Windows Device Driver benchmarks obtained using the Static Driver Verifier [4], [5]. These benchmarks extensively exercise the various features of C such as heaps, pointers, arrays, bit-vector operations, etc. [6] and collective require more than 11 CPU days to verify in a sequential setting.

The contributions of this paper are as follows:

- We propose a distributed design to enable solving large verification problems on a cluster of machines (Section IV-A and Section IV-B);
- We design a *proof-guided* splitting strategy that enables a lazy, semantic division of the verification task (Section III-B and Section IV-C);
- We implemented our design in a tool called HYDRA that achieves a $20\times$ speedup on 32 clients, solving 30% additional benchmarks on which the sequential version timed out (Section V).

The rest of the paper is organized as follows. Section II covers background on VC generation and the stratified inlining algorithm. Section III discusses on how the search is decomposed for parallel exploration while Section IV presents the

[1]HYDRA is available in the *hydra* branch of https://github.com/boogie-org/corral.git.

```
procedure main() {
  int x, y, z; bool c;
  L0: goto L1, L2;
  L1: assume c;
      call foo(x,z);
      goto L3;
  L2: assume !c;
      call bar(x,z);
      goto L3;
  L3: call baz(y);
      goto L4;
  L4: assume z != 0
      return;
}
procedure baz(int y) {
  L10: assume y == 3;
       return;
}

procedure foo(int x, int z) {
  bool d;
  L5: goto L6, L7;
  L6: assume d;
      assume z == x + 1;
      goto L8;
  L7: assume !d;
      assume z == x - 1;
      goto L8;
  L8: return;
}

procedure bar(int x, int z) {
  L9: assume z == x + 5;
      return;
}
```

Fig. 1: An Example of a Passified Program

design of HYDRA. Section V presents an evaluation of HYDRA and Section VI discusses related work.

II. BACKGROUND

We describe our techniques on a class of *passified* imperative programs. Such a program can have multiple procedures. Each procedure has a set of labelled basic blocks, where each block contains a list of statements followed by a **goto** or a **return**. A statement can only be an **assume** or a procedure **call**. A procedure can have any number of formal input arguments and local variables. Local variables are assumed to be non-deterministically initialized, i.e., their initial value is unconstrained. An **assume** statement takes an arbitrary expression over the variables in scope. An example program is shown in Figure 1. A **goto** statement takes multiple block labels and non-deterministically jumps to one of them.

Passified programs do not have global variables, return parameters of procedures, or assignments. These restrictions are without loss of generality because programs with these features can be easily converted to a passified program [7]; such conversion is readily available in tools like BOOGIE [8]. We also leave the expression syntax unspecified: we only require that expressions can be directly encoded in SMT. Our implementation uses linear arithmetic, fixed-size bit-vectors, uninterpreted functions, and extensional arrays. This combination is sufficient to support C programs [6], [9].

We aim to solve the following safety verification problem: given a passified program P, is the end of `main` reachable, i.e., is there an execution of `main` that reaches its **return** statement? This question is answered YES (or UNSAFE) by producing such an execution and the answer is NO (or SAFE) if there is no such execution. Furthermore, we only consider a *bounded* version of problem where P cannot have loops or recursion. (In other words, loops and recursive calls must be unrolled up to a fixed depth.) This problem is decidable with NEXPTIME complexity [7]. We next outline VC generation for single-procedure (Section II-A) and multi-procedure (Section II-B) programs.

A. VC generation for a single procedure

Let $p(\vec{x})$ be a procedure that takes a sequence of arguments $\vec{x}$. Further, assume that p does not include procedure calls. In that case, we construct a formula $VC(p)(\vec{x})$ such that p has a terminating execution starting from arguments $\vec{c}$ if and only if $VC(p)(\vec{c})$ is satisfiable.

The VC is constructed as follows. For each block labelled l, let b_l be a fresh Boolean variable and i_l be a unique integer constant. Let $succ(l)$ be the set of successor blocks of l (mentioned in the **goto** statement at the end of block l, if any). Further, let e_l be a conjunction of all assumed expressions in the block. Let φ_l be $(b_l \Rightarrow e_l)$ if the block l ends in a return statement, otherwise let it be:

$$b_l \Rightarrow \left(e_l \wedge \bigvee_{s \in succ(l)} (b_s \wedge (i_s == f(i_l))) \right) \tag{1}$$

where f is an uninterpreted function $\mathbb{Z} \to \mathbb{Z}$ called the *control-flow function*.

The variables b_l are collectively referred to as *control variables*. Intuitively, b_l is *true* when control reaches the beginning of block l during the procedure's execution. The constraint φ_l means that if the control reaches block l, then it must satisfy the assumed constraints on the block (e_l) and pick at least one successor block to jump to. The function f records the chosen successor for each block.

Let l_p be the label of the first block of p (where procedure execution begins). Let $blocks(p)$ be the set of block labels in p. Then, $VC(p)$ is $b_{l_p} \wedge \bigwedge_{l \in blocks(p)} \varphi_l$. If the VC is satisfiable, then one can read-off the counterexample trace from a satisfying assignment by looking at the model for f. As an example, the VC of procedure foo of Figure 1 is given in Figure 2.

The arguments of a procedure are its *interface* variables and we make these explicit in the VC. For instance, we will write $VC(\text{foo})(x,z)$ to make it explicit that x and z are the interface variables (free variables) and the rest of the variables are implicitly existentially quantified.

B. Stratified Inlining

Inlining all procedure calls can result in an exponential blowup in program size. For that reason, the *stratified inlining* (SI) algorithm [3] constructs the VC of a program in a lazy fashion. For ease in description, assume that each block can have at most one procedure call. For a procedure p, let $\text{pVC}(p)$, called the *partial VC*, be the VC of the procedure constructed as described in the previous section where each procedure call is replaced with an "**assume** *true*" statement.

Given that programs can only have assume statements, the partial VC of a procedure represents an over-approximation of the procedure's behaviors, one where it optimistically assumes that each callee simply returns. Similarly, for a procedure p, if we replace each call with an "**assume** *false*" statement, then we get an under-approximation of p. The VC of this under-approximation can be obtained by setting the control variables b_l to false for each block l with an "**assume** *false*" statement. For instance, pVC(main) is an over-approximation

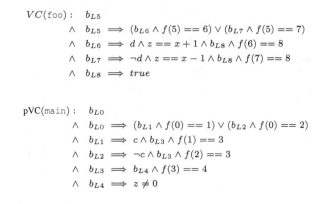

Fig. 2: VCs of procedures foo and main from Figure 1

of main (shown in Figure 2), whereas the following is an under-approximation: $pVC(\text{main}) \wedge \neg b_{L1} \wedge \neg b_{L2} \wedge \neg b_{L3}$.

A *static callsite* is defined as the pair (l, p) that represents the (unique) call of procedure p in block l. For instance, main of Figure 1 has three callsites: $(L1, \text{foo})$, $(L2, \text{bar})$, $(L3, \text{baz})$. A *dynamic callsite* is a stack of static callsites that represents the runtime stack during a program's execution. We assume that main is always present at the bottom of the stack for any dynamic callsite. For instance, $[\text{main}, (L1, \text{foo})]$ represents the call stack where main executed to reach L1 and then called foo.

For a procedure p, let *callsites(p)* be the set of static callsites in p. Given a static callsite s, and dynamic callsite c, let $s :: c$ be the dynamic callsite where s is pushed on the top of the stack c. SI can require to inline the same procedure multiple times. Suppose that a procedure p calls p' twice, once in block l_1 and once in block l_2. Dynamic callsites will help distinguish between the two instances of p': the first will have (l_1, p') on top of the stack and the latter will have (l_2, p') on top of the stack.

We must take care to avoid variable name clashes between different VCs as we inline procedures. For a dynamic callsite c and procedure p that is at the top of c, let $\text{pVC}(p, c)$ be the partial VC of p (as described earlier in the section), however for the construction of the partial VC, we use globally fresh control variables (variables b_l of Equation 1), globally fresh block identifiers (constants i_l of Equation 1) as well as globally fresh instances for the local variables. In $\text{pVC}(p, c)$, the argument c is only used for bookkeeping purposes: let *control-variable(l, c)* refer to the control variable used for block l when constructing $\text{pVC}(p, c)$. If c is $(l, p) :: c'$, then let *control-variable(c)* be *control-variable(l', c')*. Similarly, if p' is called from procedure p in block l', then let *interface-variables((l', p') :: c)* be the set of interface variables (actuals) for the call to procedure p' in block l' in $\text{pVC}(p, c)$.

The SI algorithm is shown in Algorithm 1. The algorithm requires an SMT solver with the usual interface. We use the *Push* API to set a backtracking point and a *Pop* API that backtracks by removing all asserted constraints until a matching *Push* call. Further, we assume that a counterexample

Algorithm 1: The Stratified Inlining algorithm.

> **Input:** A Program P with starting procedure `main`
> **Input:** An SMT solver S
> **Output:** SAFE, or UNSAFE(τ)
> 1 $C \leftarrow \{[\text{main}, s] \mid s \in \textit{callsites}(\text{main})\}$
> 2 $S.\text{Assert}(\text{pVC}(\text{main}, [\text{main}]))$
> 3 **while** *true* **do**
> 4 $\quad$ *outcome* $\leftarrow$ SISTEP(P, C, S)
> 5 $\quad$ **if** *outcome* == SAFE $\lor$ *outcome* == UNSAFE(τ) **then**
> 6 $\quad\quad$ **return** *outcome*
> 7 $\quad$ **else**
> 8 $\quad\quad$ **let** NODECISION($\_, \_, C'$) = *outcome*
> 9 $\quad\quad$ $C \leftarrow C'$

Algorithm 2: SISTEP(P, C, S)

> **Input:** A Program P, a set of callsites C
> **Input:** An SMT solver S
> **Output:** SAFE, UNSAFE(τ), NODECISION(uc, I, C)
> 1 // *Under-approximate check*
> 2 $S.\text{Push}()$
> 3 **forall** $c \in C$ **do**
> 4 $\quad$ $S.\text{Assert}(\neg \textit{control-variable}(c))$
> 5 **if** $S.Check()$ == SAT **then**
> 6 $\quad$ **return** UNSAFE($S.\text{Model}()$)
> 7 **else**
> 8 $\quad$ $uc \leftarrow S.\text{UnsatCore}()$
> 9 $S.\text{Pop}()$
> 10 // *Over-approximate check*
> 11 **if** $S.Check()$ == UNSAT **then**
> 12 $\quad$ **return** SAFE
> 13 **else**
> 14 $\quad$ $\tau \leftarrow S.\text{Model}()$
> 15 $\quad$ $I \leftarrow C \cap \textit{callsites}(\tau)$
> 16 $\quad$ $C' \leftarrow \emptyset$
> 17 $\quad$ **forall** $c \in I$ **do**
> 18 $\quad\quad$ $C' \leftarrow$ INLINE(c)
> 19 $\quad$ $C \leftarrow (C - I) \cup C'$
> 20 $\quad$ **return** NODECISION(uc, I, C)

trace can be extracted from a model returned by the solver.

The algorithm works by iteratively refining over-approximations of the program (in hope of getting an early SAFE verdict) and under-approximations of the program (in hope of getting an early UNSAFE verdict). Both these approximations are refined by inlining procedures.

Line 1 initializes a set C of *open* dynamic callsites. This set represents procedure calls that have not been inlined yet. The partial VC of `main` is asserted on the solver in Line 2.

SI, then, iteratively calls the SISTEP routine (Algorithm 2) that returns one of three possible answers: conclusive verdicts SAFE or UNSAFE, or an inconclusive verdict NODECISION.

The SISTEP routine is shown in Algorithm 2. It does an under-approximate check (Line 5) by assuming that calls at each of the open callsites cannot return (Line 4). If it finds a counterexample trace, SI returns UNSAFE, along with the model that can be used to construct the trace. This trace is guaranteed to only go through inlined procedure calls because

Algorithm 3: INLINE(c, S)

> **Input:** A dynamic callsite c, An SMT solver S
> **Output:** A set of open callsites C'
> 1 **let** $(l, p) :: c' = c$
> 2 $S.\text{Assert}(\textit{control-variable}(c) \implies$
> $\quad$ pVC(p, c)(*interface-variables*(c)))
> 3 $C' \leftarrow C' \cup \{s :: c \mid s \in \textit{callsites}(p)\}$
> 4 **return** C'

SISTEP	Action	Open Callsites	Inlined Callsites
Step-0	Assert pVC(main)	[main, (L1,foo)], [main, (L2,bar)], [main, (L3,baz)]	[main]
Step-1	Underapprox check: UNSAT Overapprox check: SAT Assert pVC(foo) Assert pVC(baz)	[main, (L2,bar)]	[main, (L1,foo)] [main, (L3,baz)]
Step-3	Underapprox check: SAT Return UNSAFE	[main, (L2,bar)]	

TABLE I: Execution of SI on the program of Fig. 1

all the open ones were blocked. Ignore the call to gather the unsat core shown on Line 8 for now; we use this information in the next section.

Next, SISTEP does an over-approximate check (Line 11). If this is UNSAT, then SI returns SAFE. If the check was satisfiable, then we construct the counterexample trace from the model provided by the solver (Line 14). This trace is guaranteed to go through at least one open call site (because the under-approximate check was UNSAT). The SI algorithm proceeds to inline the procedures called at each of the open callsites that the trace goes through. Such callsites are recorded in variable I (Line 15); these get returned for bookkeeping purposes (used in the next section). Callsites in I are inlined by asserting the partial VC of the callee, as shown in Line 2 in Algorithm 3. Read the asserted constraint as follows: if the control variable of the calling block is set to *true* then the VC of the procedure must be satisfied. The use of *interface-variables* ensures that formals are substituted with actuals for the procedure call. New callsites that are created as a result of the inlining are recorded in C' and then eventually added back to C (Line 19). Finally, SISTEP returns NODECISION back to SI with the set of callsites that it inlined, and the process repeats. An example illustrating the execution of SI is shown in Table I.

Define a *call tree* to be a (prefix-closed) set of dynamic callsites that represents all dynamic callsites that have been inlined by the SI algorithm at any point in time. We call this set as a tree because it can be represented as an unfolding of the program's call graph.

III. SPLITTING THE SEARCH

HYDRA employs a *decomposition*-based strategy to achieve parallelism. During the course of execution of the SI algorithm, HYDRA *splits* the current verification task by picking a dynamic callsite c that has already been inlined by SI. This generates two *partitions*: one that requires executions to pass through c (referred to as the *must-reach* partition), and the other that requires executions to avoid c (referred to as the *must-avoid* partition). This strategy provides for an exhaustive and *path-disjoint* partitioning of the search space.

Formally, a *partition* is a pair (T, D) where T is a call tree (i.e., set of inlined callsites) and D is a set of *decisions* (either *must-avoid*(c) or *must-reach*(c) for $c \in T$). As a notation shorthand, for a partition $\rho = (T, D)$ and callsite c, let $\rho + c$ be the partition $(T \cup \{c\}, D)$. Similarly, for a decision d, let $\rho + d$ be the partition $(T, D \cup \{d\})$. Further, let *calltree*$(\rho) = T$ and *decisions*$(\rho) = D$. One can also see the above strategy as dividing the proof obligation (correctness theorem) on the complete program into a set of *lemmas* corresponding to each of the partitions.

This section addresses two primary concerns: (a) how to enforce splitting decisions during search? (Section III-A), and (b) how to choose a callsite for splitting? (Section III-B).

A. Encoding splitting decisions in SI as constraints

The constraint for *must-avoid*(c) is relatively straightforward. It is simply $\neg$*control-variable*(c). Asserting this constraint any time after SI has inlined c will ensure that control cannot go through c, thus SI will avoid c altogether.

We next describe the encoding of the *must-reach* constraint by first looking at the single-procedure case. For a procedure p, we introduce *must-reach* control variables r_l, one for each basic block l of p. Intuitively, setting r_l to *true* should mean that control must go through block l. Recall from Section II that the VC of a procedure uses i_l as a unique integer constant for block l and f as the control-flow function. We define *must-reach*(p) as the following constraint:

$$\bigwedge_{l \in blocks(p)} (r_l \Rightarrow \bigvee_{n \in pred(l)} (r_n \wedge f(i_l) == i_n)) \quad (2)$$

This constraint enforces that if a block l must be reached, then one of its predecessors must be reached. The use of the control-flow function ties this constraint with the procedure's VC. For any block l, asserting $r_l \wedge$ *must-reach*(p), in addition to the VC of p will enforce the constraint that control *must* pass through block l. The proof is straightforward and we omit it from this paper.

For multi-procedure programs, we construct the *must-reach* constraint inductively. Let *must-reach*(p, c) be the constraint *must-reach*(p), but where the block identifiers $\{i_l\}$ are the same as the ones used in pVC(p, c). We construct *must-reach*(c) inductively over the length of c. If $c = [\text{main}]$, then *must-reach*(c) is *true*. Otherwise, if $c = (l, p) :: c'$, then *must-reach*(c) is $r_l \wedge$ *must-reach*$(p, c') \wedge$ *must-reach*(c').

B. Choosing a splitting candidate

Given an unsatisfiable formula Φ, expressed as a conjunction set of clauses $\{\phi_i\}$, a *minimal unsatisfiable core (min-unsatcore)* is a subset of clauses $\Psi \subseteq \Phi$ whose conjunction is still unsatisfiable and every proper subset of Ψ is satisfiable.

Consider the under-approximate check made by SI (Line 5 of Algorithm 2) where it blocks open-callsites and attempts to find a counterexample in the currently inlined portion of the program. This check is a conjunction of constraints, passed

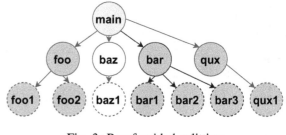

Fig. 3: Proof-guided splitting

via $\mathcal{S}$.Assert, of two forms. First is the (partial) VCs of inlined callsites (Line 2 of Algorithm 3) and second is the blocked open callsites (Line 4 of Algorithm 2). If the check is unsatisfiable, then we extract its *min-unsatcore* and represent it as a set of callsites uc (that may be inlined or may be open). The set uc represents the current proof of safety of the program. Inlined callsites that are not part of uc are deemed *search-irrelevant* because whether they were inlined or not is immaterial to conclude safety of the program (at this point in the search). Formally, those callsites could have been left open (i.e., over-approximated) and the check would still be unsatisfiable. Therefore, the solver is likely to spend its energy searching and expanding the uc portion of the calltree as the search proceeds further. Consequently, we restrict splitting to a callsite chosen from uc so that we split where the search complexity lies.

Consider the inlining tree shown in Figure 3, where the open callsites appear as dotted circles and the inlined ones are shown as solid circles; the shaded nodes are the callsites that appear on the *min-unsatcore* (uc). In this case, both baz and baz1 are ruled out for falling outside uc. If we pick some other callsite to split, say qux, then the *must-reach*(qux) partition of that split is likely to search in the subtree rooted at qux, whereas the *must-avoid*(qux) partition will search the uc portion excluding the subtree rooted at qux. We use a simple heuristic that roughly balances these partitions. Let the current inlined calltree be T and let subtree(T, c) be the subtree rooted at c. We choose the splitting callsite as the one that has maximum number of relevant callsites in its subtree (excluding main because that would be a trivial split). Formally, the splitting callsite is:

$$\underset{c \in uc}{\arg\max} \{|\text{subtree}(T, c) \cap uc|\}$$

In our example, we will pick bar for splitting.

We note that this choice of balancing the partitions is just a heuristic. In general, there may be dependencies between callsites. For instance, blocking one callsite can block others or make others be *must-reach* because of control-flow dependencies in the program. Our heuristic does not capture these dependencies. Furthermore, in our implementation, we do not insist on obtaining a *minimal* unsat core in order to reduce the time spent in computing it. Solvers generally provide a best-effort unsat core minimization (e.g., the core.minimize option in Z3).

Algorithm 4: Client-side verification algorithm

Input: A Program P
Input: An SMT solver $\mathcal{S}$

1 **while** *true* **do**
2      $\rho \leftarrow SendSync(\text{GET\_PARTITION})$
3   outcome $\leftarrow$ VERIFY$(P, \rho, \mathcal{S})$
4      $SendAsync(\text{OUTCOME}, \text{outcome})$

IV. HYDRA DESIGN AND IMPLEMENTATION

HYDRA employs a client-server distributed architecture with a single server and multiple clients. The server (Section IV-B) is responsible for coordination while verification happens on the clients (Section IV-A). A client can decide to split its current search, at which point it sends one partition to the server while it continues on the other partition. If a client finishes its current search with a SAFE verdict, it contacts the server to borrow a new partition and starts solving it.

A. Client Design

All clients implement Algorithm 4. We use $SendSync$ as a message-response interaction with the server. $SendAsync$ is the asynchronous version where a message is sent to the server but a response is not expected. A client repeatedly requests the server for a partition (Line 2), solves it (Line 3) and sends the result back to the server on completion. Each client uses its own dedicated SMT solver ($\mathcal{S}$) for verification.

VERIFY (Algorithm 5) maintains a stack of decisions $dstack$ and a set of open callsites C. It starts off by preparing the input partition (Lines 3 to 7): it inlines the calltree of ρ and asserts all its splitting decisions. The client then enters a verification loop (Line 8) that repeatedly uses SISTEP (Line 9) to expand its search. If a counterexample is found (Line 10), the client returns an UNSAFE verdict back to the server. If SISTEP returns NODECISION, it implies that some more procedures were inlined but the search remained inconclusive; in this case, we perform the necessary bookkeeping on the set of currently open callsites (C'), new procedures inlined (I), and the minunsatcore from the unsat query (uc').

If SISTEP returned SAFE, then the search on the current partition has finished and the client must pick another partition to solve. This is done by returning the SAFE verdict (Line 22). The check on Line 15 is an optimization that we describe later in this section.

After checking the outcome of SISTEP, the client decides if it is time to split its search. This is referred to abstractly as "*TimeToSplit*" on Line 23: the exact time is communicated by the server to client (see Section IV-C). For splitting, the client picks a callsite c in accordance with our proof-guided splitting heuristic (from Section III-B) using the stored unsatcore uc. We note that the correctness of our technique does not rely on when a split happens or what splitting callsite is chosen. Therefore, these decisions can be guided by heuristics and tuned to optimized performance.

After splitting, the client continues along the partition with the MUSTAVOID(c) decision (let's call this partition ρ_1). The

---

Algorithm 5: VERIFY$(P, \rho, \mathcal{S})$

Input: A Program P, A partition ρ of P, A solver $\mathcal{S}$
Output: SAFE, or UNSAFE(τ)

1 $\mathcal{S}.\text{reset}()$, $dstack \leftarrow [\,]$, $C \leftarrow \emptyset$ $uc \leftarrow \emptyset$
2 // Setup input partition
3 **forall** $c \in calltree(\rho)$ **do**
4      $C' \leftarrow$ INLINE(c), $C \leftarrow (C - \{c\}) \cup C'$
5 **forall** $d \in decisions(\rho)$ **do**
6   **if** $d ==$ MUSTAVOID(c) **then** $\mathcal{S}.\text{Assert}(must\text{-}avoid(c))$
7   **if** $d ==$ MUSTREACH(c) **then** $\mathcal{S}.\text{Assert}(must\text{-}reach(c))$
8 **while** *true* **do**
9   outcome $\leftarrow$ SISTEP$(P, C, \mathcal{S})$
10   **if** $outcome ==$ UNSAFE(τ) **then**
11   **return** outcome
12   **else if** $outcome ==$ NODECISION(uc', I, C') **then**
13         $uc \leftarrow uc'$, $C \leftarrow C'$, $\rho \leftarrow \rho + I$
14   **else**
15   **if** $SendSync(POP)==YES$ **then**
16   **repeat**
17   **let** $d(c) :: ds = dstack$
18                 $\mathcal{S}.\text{Pop}()$, $dstack \leftarrow ds$, $\rho \leftarrow \rho - d(c)$
19   **until** $d ==$ MUSTAVOID
20             $\mathcal{S}.\text{Push}()$, $\mathcal{S}.\text{Assert}(must\text{-}reach(\text{c}))$,
                $dstack \leftarrow$ MUSTREACH$(c) :: dstack$,
                $\rho \leftarrow \rho +$ MUSTREACH(c)
21   **else**
22   **return** outcome
23   **if** *TimeToSplit* **then**
24         $c \leftarrow$ **choose**$(calltree(\rho), uc)$
25         $\mathcal{S}.\text{Push}()$
26         $\mathcal{S}.\text{Assert}(must\text{-}avoid(c))$
27         $SendAsync(\text{SEND\_PARTITION},$
            $\rho +$ MUSTREACH$(c))$
28         $dstack \leftarrow$ MUSTAVOID$(c) :: dstack$,
            $\rho \leftarrow \rho +$ MUSTAVOID(c)

---

other partition (ρ_2) is sent to the server (Line 27). Note further that on Line 25, the client creates a backtracking point that is *just before* the decision on c is asserted. This backtracking point is exploited in Lines 15 to 20. When the client finishes search on ρ_1, it pings the server to know if ρ_2 has already been solved by a different client or not. If not, it simply backtracks the solver state and asserts the flipped decision MUSTREACH(c) to immediately get set up for search on ρ_2. This way, the client avoids the expensive setup of initializing a new partition. Because splitting can happen multiple times, the loop on Line 19 is necessary to follow along the recorded stack of decisions.

B. Server Design

We assume that each client has an associated unique identifier. Each message coming from a client is automatically tagged with the client's identifier. The server maintains two data structures. The first is an array Q of double-ended queues. The queue $Q[id]$ stores all partitions produced by client id. The second is a queue wt of clients that are currently idle.

The server processes incoming messages as follows. On receiving the message $\langle$SEND_PARTITION$, \rho\rangle$ from client id, it

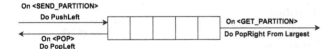

Fig. 4: Maintaining the double-ended queues

does a `push-left` to insert ρ into $Q[id]$. (The manipulation of Q is depicted in Figure 4.) This ensures that later partitions (which have a larger number of decisions and a larger call tree) from a particular client id appear on the left of $Q[id]$.

On receiving message $\langle$GET_PARTITION$\rangle$ from client id, the server needs to reply with a partition because id has just become idle. If all queues $Q[i]$ are empty, then id is inserted into wt and the client is kept waiting for a reply. Otherwise, the server picks the longest queue $Q[i]$, does a `pop-right` and replies to the client. This strategy attempts to avoid skew in queue sizes. Further, the rightmost partition is the smallest in that queue, which minimizes the setup time for that partition for the client that will get it. As more partitions are reported to the server (via a SEND_PARTITION), the server loops through wt, replying to as many idle clients as possible with partitions popped-right from the currently longest queue.

The message $\langle$POP$\rangle$ from client id implies that the client wishes to backtrack to its previously reported partition. Because reported partitions are pushed-left, and other clients (on GET_PARTITION) steal from the right, the previously reported partition from client id is exactly the leftmost one in $Q[id]$, if any. Thus, the server replies YES back to the client if $Q[id]$ is non-empty, followed by a `pop-left`. Otherwise, the server replies NO.

The server additionally listens to OUTCOME messages. If any client reports UNSAFE, all clients are terminated and the UnSafe verdict is returned to the user. The server returns SAFE verdict to the user when all queues in Q are empty and all clients are idle (i.e., wt consists of all clients).

Our design of the work-queue Q, as an array of sorted (by size) work-queues, is in contrast with using a centralized queue that is standard in classical work-stealing algorithms. It is useful for avoiding skew in queue sizes, distributing smaller partitions first, and enabling the client-backtracking optimization.

C. Adaptive rate of splitting

While a low splitting rate inhibits parallelism, a high rate increases the partition-initialization overhead on the clients. HYDRA uses a dynamic split-rate determined by the number of idle clients and the number of partitions available at the server. Each client maintains a *split time interval* δ (in seconds) and splits the search ("*TimeToSplit*" of Algorithm 5), if δ seconds have elapsed since the last split. The value of δ starts as a constant δ_c and is updated by the server as follows:

$$\delta_i = \begin{cases} \frac{Q[i].count}{wt.count} \times \delta_c & \text{if } wt.count \neq 0 \\ K \times \delta_c, & \text{otherwise.} \end{cases} \quad (3)$$

In the first case, a client's splitting is slowed down in proportion to its queue size (divided by the number of idle

clients). The second case applies when there are no idle clients. Increasing δ by a factor of K reduces the rate of splitting drastically. We use $\delta_c = 0.5s$ and $K = 20$ in our experiments.

V. EXPERIMENTAL RESULTS

We evaluated HYDRA on SDV benchmarks [10]. SDV is used by Windows driver developers to statically check various rules on correct usage of kernel APIs in a driver. SDV comes packaged with a set of rules[2] that typically establish that kernel APIs are called in the correct temporal sequence; for instance, that a lock must be released before it can be acquired again.

The SDV benchmarks are obtained from a run of SDV on set of real-world device drivers that exercise all features of the C language: loops and recursion (up to a bounded depth), pointers, arrays, heap, bit-vector operations, etc. Each instance in the benchmark suite is a device driver paired with one of the SDV rules, i.e., it checks for the correct usage of the rule in the driver. SDV compiles the drivers, instruments the property and produces a program in Boogie [8]. The process of compilation to Boogie has been described in detail in previous work [6]. Each Boogie program has a well-defined entry point that is annotated with the tag {:entrypoint} and multiple assertions. The verification objective is to find an execution that starts at the entry procedure and ends with an assertion failure. Note that although these benchmarks are all compiled from C, HYDRA itself is source-language agnostic and can accept Boogie programs obtained from any source language.

We compared the performance of HYDRA against CORRAL [3] that implements the sequential Stratified Inlining algorithm. CORRAL forms a good baseline because it has been optimized heavily for SDV over the years [6].

We only selected hard benchmarks (where CORRAL took at least 200 seconds to solve or timed out). We ran HYDRA with 32 clients. Timeout was set to 1 hour. We conducted our experiments with the server running on one machine (16 core, 64 GB RAM) and the 32 clients running on another machine (72-core with Intel Xeon Platinum 8168 CPU and 144 GB RAM), communicating via HTTP calls. As clients never communicate amongst themselves, this setup is equivalent to running clients on different machines.

Both CORRAL and HYDRA use Z3 [11] as the underlying SMT solver. While we used the default setting of a fixed random seed for Z3, we verified that the results reported here do not depend on the random seed. In fact, the behavior of the SI algorithm, which underlies both CORRAL and HYDRA, is not impacted by the choice of the random seed in any statistically significant way.

A. HYDRA versus CORRAL

Instances Solved. There were a total of 333 programs. HYDRA solved 99 instances (30%) on which CORRAL timed out (34 of these were SAFE and the rest 65 were UNSAFE). Conversely, CORRAL solved 12 (4%) instances on which HYDRA timed out. We did not investigate these cases in detail;

---

[2]https://docs.microsoft.com/en-us/windows-hardware/drivers/devtest/static-driver-verifier

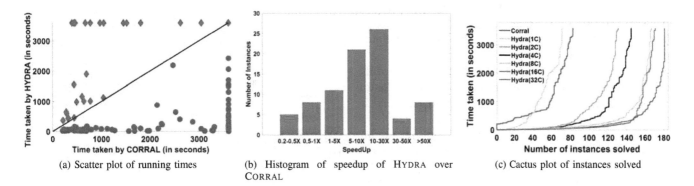

(a) Scatter plot of running times

(b) Histogram of speedup of HYDRA over CORRAL

(c) Cactus plot of instances solved

Fig. 5: Comparison of HYDRA against CORRAL on SDV benchmarks

in a practical scenario one can simply dedicate a single client to run CORRAL and get the best of both tools. Overall, HYDRA solved 183 (55%) instances while CORRAL solved only 96 (29%) instances. Interestingly, there were 138 instances (41%) that were unsolved by both HYDRA and CORRAL indicating the need for further improvements.

Verification Time. In terms of running time, HYDRA was significantly faster than CORRAL in most (84%) cases: Figure 5a shows the scatter plot of running times. Figure 5b is a histogram of the speedup of HYDRA over CORRAL. For example, there were 8 instances where HYDRA was more than $50\times$ faster than CORRAL. A small fraction of instances had slowdowns as well, but the worst among these was $0.2\times$, i.e., CORRAL was $5\times$ faster than HYDRA. Over all instances, the mean speedup is $20.4\times$ and median speedup is $9.7\times$. Speedup excludes cases in which one of the tools timed out.

Scalability. Figure 5c is a cactus plot illustrating the scalability of HYDRA with the number of clients. CORRAL is able to solve only 58 instances within 1000 seconds. Running HYDRA with only a single client results in worse performance than CORRAL (solves only 46 instances within 1000 seconds). However, the performance improves significantly with the number of clients (solves 166 instances with 32 clients within 1000 seconds).

B. Effectiveness of proof-guided splitting

Empirical Analysis. We define *dissimilarity* $\eta(i,j)$ of a client i with respect to client j as $1 - \frac{|\mathcal{L}_i \cap \mathcal{L}_j|}{|\mathcal{L}_i|}$, where $\mathcal{L}_i$, $\mathcal{L}_j$ denote the set of callsites that i and j have inlined, respectively, when HYDRA finishes. A high value of $\eta(i,j)$ implies that the clients did a different search. Note, however, that $\eta(i,j)$ will never be 1 because certain callsites (like `main`) will always need to be inlined by each client.

Across all benchmarks and all client pairs, the average dissimilarity value was 0.55. This indicates sufficient difference among the inlined calltrees across clients.

Statistical Analysis. We implemented a randomized splitting algorithm that (1) decides to split/not-to-split at each inlining step uniformly at random, (2) if it has decided to split, it selects the splitting call-site uniformly at random.

We ran this randomized splitting algorithm 5 times for each program and compared the minimum verification time of these 5 runs for each instance against that of HYDRA. Using the Wilcoxon Sign Rank test, we found that HYDRA is statistically better than the randomized splitting algorithm with a p-value of 0.0012, indicating that the performance of the splitting heuristic is not accidental.

C. Server optimizations

We measured the performance impact of the server-side queue implementation on HYDRA. We compared our double-ended queues Q from Section IV-B against a classical work-stealing queue implementation. Our implementation allowed HYDRA to complete on 40% more cases where using the classical version made HYDRA time out. Further, HYDRA's performance was 8.5 times faster when both implementations terminated with a verdict.

In terms of controlling the splitting rate, both the performance (p-value of 5.27×10^{-5}) and the number of splits (p-value of 5.43×10^{-33}) were found to be statistically better with split-rate feedback.

VI. RELATED WORK

Parallelizing SAT/SMT solvers. In contrast to parallelizing verification tasks, parallelizing SAT/SMT solvers has attracted wider attention. There have been two popular, incomparable [12], approaches to parallelizing satisfiability problems: portfolio-based techniques [13], [14], [15] and divide and conquer techniques (decomposition [16], [17] or partitioning [18], [19], [20], [21]). Portfolio-based strategies either run multiple different algorithms or multiple instances of a randomized algorithm. They tend to work well in the presence of heavy-tailed distribution of problem hardness.

Divide and conquer strategies are most similar to our work. They either use static partitioning, based on the structure of the problem [22], or dynamic partitioning [19] based on run-time heuristics. However, unlike partitioning on individual variables at the logical-level, we split at the program-level based on its call graph. In our setting, the VC of a program can be exponential in the size of the program. This makes it hard to directly use parallelized solvers; we must split even before the entire VC is generated. Furthermore, parallelized solvers are still not as mainstream as sequential solvers. Using solvers as a black-box allows us to directly leverage continued improvements in solver technology

Parallelizing program verification. Saturn [23] is one of the earlier attempts at parallelizing program verification. Saturn performs a bottom-up analysis on the call graph, generating summaries of procedures in parallel. While the intraprocedural analysis of Saturn is precise, it only retains *abstractions* of function summaries, thus cannot produce precise refutations of assertions like BMC.

There have been attempts at parallelizing a top-down abstraction-based verifier [24] as well as the property-directed reachability (PDR) algorithm [25], [26], [22], [13] and k-induction [27], [28]. These all rely on the discovery of inductive invariants for proof generation, a fundamentally different problem than BMC. It would be interesting future work to study the relative speedups obtained for parallelization in these respective domains.

Closer to BMC, parallelization has been proposed by a partitioning of the control-flow graph [29]. This approach does static partitioning (based on program slicing) and does not consider procedures at all (hence, must rely on inlining all procedures). Further, it has only been evaluated on a single benchmark program. Our technique, on the other hand, performs dynamic partitioning, supports procedures and has been much more extensively evaluated.

In a recent work, Inverso et al. [30] propose a parallelization technique for the verification of concurrent programs by partitioning the verification task such that each partition considers a subset of the interleavings of the input program. Next, it uses sequentialization to generate a sequential program for each partition and then verifies the sequential program. The partitioning is static and done up-front. This work is complementary to HYDRA: it addresses the complexity arising from many interleavings, whereas HYDRA addresses complexity arising from many (sequential) procedures calling each other.

REFERENCES

[1] E. M. Clarke, D. Kroening, and K. Yorav, "Behavioral consistency of C and Verilog programs using Bounded Model Checking," in *Proceedings of the 40th Design Automation Conference, DAC 2003, Anaheim, CA, USA, June 2-6, 2003*, 2003, pp. 368–371.

[2] D. Beyer, "Automatic verification of C and Java programs: SV-COMP 2019," in *Tools and Algorithms for the Construction and Analysis of Systems - 25 Years of TACAS: TOOLympics, Held as Part of ETAPS 2019, Prague, Czech Republic, April 6-11, 2019, Proceedings, Part III*, 2019, pp. 133–155.

[3] A. Lal, S. Qadeer, and S. K. Lahiri, "A solver for reachability modulo theories," in *Computer Aided Verification - 24th International Conference, CAV 2012, Berkeley, CA, USA, July 7-13, 2012 Proceedings*, 2012, pp. 427–443, https://github.com/boogie-org/corral/.

[4] T. Ball, E. Bounimova, V. Levin, R. Kumar, and J. Lichtenberg, "The Static Driver Verifier research platform," in *Computer Aided Verification*. Springer, 2010, pp. 119–122.

[5] Microsoft, "Static Driver Verifier," http://msdn.microsoft.com/en-us/library/windows/hardware/ff552808(v=vs.85).aspx.

[6] A. Lal and S. Qadeer, "Powering the Static Driver Verifier using Corral," in *Proceedings of the 22nd ACM SIGSOFT International Symposium on Foundations of Software Engineering, (FSE-22), Hong Kong, China, November 16 - 22, 2014*, 2014, pp. 202–212.

[7] ——, "Reachability modulo theories," in *Reachability Problems - 7th International Workshop, RP 2013, Uppsala, Sweden, September 24-26, 2013 Proceedings*, 2013, pp. 23–44.

[8] M. Barnett, K. R. M. Leino, M. Moskal, and W. Schulte, "Boogie: An intermediate verification language," 2009, https://github.com/boogie-org/boogie/.

[9] S. K. Lahiri and S. Qadeer, "Back to the future: revisiting precise program verification using SMT solvers," in *POPL '08: Proc. 35th ACM SIGPLAN-SIGACT Symposium on Principles of Programming Languages*. ACM, 2008, pp. 171–182.

[10] Microsoft, "Static Driver Verifier Benchmarks," https://github.com/boogie-org/sdvbench.

[11] L. De Moura and N. Bjørner, "Z3: An efficient smt solver," in *International conference on Tools and Algorithms for the Construction and Analysis of Systems*. Springer, 2008, pp. 337–340.

[12] M. Marescotti, A. Hyvärinen, and N. Sharygina, "SMTS: Distributed, visualized constraint solving," in *LPAR-22. 22nd International Conference on Logic for Programming, Artificial Intelligence and Reasoning*, ser. EPiC Series in Computing, G. Barthe, G. Sutcliffe, and M. Veanes, Eds., vol. 57. EasyChair, 2018, pp. 534–542. [Online]. Available: https://easychair.org/publications/paper/k7BQ

[13] S. Chaki and D. Karimi, "Model checking with multi-threaded IC3 portfolios," in *Verification, Model Checking, and Abstract Interpretation*, B. Jobstmann and K. R. M. Leino, Eds. Berlin, Heidelberg: Springer Berlin Heidelberg, 2016, pp. 517–535.

[14] A. E. J. Hyvärinen, T. Junttila, and I. Niemelä, "Incorporating learning in grid-based randomized SAT solving," in *Artificial Intelligence: Methodology, Systems, and Applications*, D. Dochev, M. Pistore, and P. Traverso, Eds. Berlin, Heidelberg: Springer Berlin Heidelberg, 2008, pp. 247–261.

[15] C. M. Wintersteiger, Y. Hamadi, and L. Moura, "A concurrent portfolio approach to SMT solving," in *Proceedings of the 21st International Conference on Computer Aided Verification*, ser. CAV '09. Berlin, Heidelberg: Springer-Verlag, 2009, p. 715–720.

[16] N. Eén and N. Sörensson, "An extensible SAT-solver," in *Theory and Applications of Satisfiability Testing*, E. Giunchiglia and A. Tacchella, Eds. Berlin, Heidelberg: Springer Berlin Heidelberg, 2004, pp. 502–518.

[17] Y. Hamadi, J. Marques-Silva, and C. M. Wintersteiger, "Lazy decomposition for distributed decision procedures," *Electronic Proceedings in Theoretical Computer Science*, vol. 72, p. 43–54, Oct 2011. [Online]. Available: http://dx.doi.org/10.4204/EPTCS.72.5

[18] H. Zhang, M. P. Bonacina, and J. Hsiang, "PSATO: a distributed propositional prover and its application to quasigroup problems," *Journal of Symbolic Computation*, vol. 21, no. 4, pp. 543 – 560, 1996. [Online]. Available: http://www.sciencedirect.com/science/article/pii/S0747717196900309

[19] R. Martins, V. Manquinho, and I. Lynce, "Improving search space splitting for parallel SAT solving," in *2010 22nd IEEE International Conference on Tools with Artificial Intelligence*, vol. 1, Oct 2010, pp. 336–343.

[20] M. Böhm and E. Speckenmeyer, "A fast parallel SAT-solver — efficient workload balancing," *Annals of Mathematics and Artificial Intelligence*, vol. 17, no. 2, pp. 381–400, Sep 1996. [Online]. Available: https://doi.org/10.1007/BF02127976

[21] B. Jurkowiak, C. M. Li, and G. Utard, "Parallelizing Satz using dynamic workload balancing," *Electronic Notes in Discrete Mathematics*, vol. 9, pp. 174 – 189, 2001, IICS 2001 Workshop on Theory and Applications of Satisfiability Testing (SAT 2001). [Online]. Available: http://www.sciencedirect.com/science/article/pii/S157106530400321X

[22] M. Marescotti, A. Gurfinkel, A. E. J. Hyvärinen, and N. Sharygina, "Designing parallel PDR," in *Proceedings of the 17th Conference on Formal Methods in Computer-Aided Design*, ser. FMCAD '17. Austin, Texas: FMCAD Inc, 2017, p. 156–163.

[23] A. Aiken, S. Bugrara, I. Dillig, T. Dillig, B. Hackett, and P. Hawkins, "An overview of the Saturn project," in *Proceedings of the 7th ACM SIGPLAN-SIGSOFT workshop on Program analysis for software tools and engineering*, 2007, pp. 43–48.

[24] A. Albarghouthi, R. Kumar, A. V. Nori, and S. K. Rajamani, "Parallelizing top-down interprocedural analyses," *ACM SIGPLAN Notices*, vol. 47, no. 6, pp. 217–228, 2012.

[25] A. R. Bradley, "SAT-based model checking without unrolling," in *Proceedings of the 12th International Conference on Verification, Model*

Checking, and Abstract Interpretation, ser. VMCAI'11.   Berlin, Heidelberg: Springer-Verlag, 2011, p. 70–87.

[26] N. Een, A. Mishchenko, and R. Brayton, "Efficient implementation of property directed reachability," in *Proceedings of the International Conference on Formal Methods in Computer-Aided Design*, ser. FMCAD '11.   Austin, Texas: FMCAD Inc, 2011, p. 125–134.

[27] T. Kahsai and C. Tinelli, "PKIND: A parallel k-induction based model checker," *EPTCS*, vol. 72, 11 2011.

[28] M. Blicha, A. Hyvärinen, M. Marescotti, and N. Sharygina, "A co-operative parallelization approach for property-directed k-induction," in *VMCAI*, 01 2020, pp. 270–292.

[29] M. K. Ganai and W. Li, "D-TSR: Parallelizing SMT-Based BMC using tunnels over a distributed framework," in *Haifa Verification Conference*. Springer, 2008, pp. 194–199.

[30] O. Inverso and C. Trubiani, "Parallel and distributed bounded model checking of multi-threaded programs," in *Proceedings of the 25th ACM SIGPLAN Symposium on Principles and Practice of Parallel Programming*, 2020, pp. 202–216.

25

Accelerating Parallel Verification via Complementary Property Partitioning and Strategy Exploration

Rohit Dureja* ⓘ, Jason Baumgartner[†], Robert Kanzelman[†], Mark Williams[†] and Kristin Y. Rozier* ⓘ
*Iowa State University, [†]IBM Corporation

Abstract—**Industrial hardware verification tasks often require checking a large number of properties within a testbench. Verification tools often utilize parallelism in their solving orchestration to improve scalability, either in *portfolio* mode where different solver strategies run concurrently, or in *partitioning* mode where disjoint property subsets are verified independently. While most tools focus solely upon reducing end-to-end wall-time, reducing overall CPU-time is a comparably-important goal influencing power consumption, competition for available machines, and IT costs. Portfolio approaches often degrade into highly-redundant work across processes, where similar strategies address properties in nearly-identical order. Partitioning should take *property affinity* into account, atomically verifying high-affinity properties to minimize redundant work of applying identical strategies on individual properties with nearly-identical logic cones. In this paper, we improve multi-property parallel verification with respect to both wall- and CPU-time. We extend affinity-based partitioning to guarantee *complete* utilization of available processes, with provable *partition quality*. We propose methods to minimize redundant computation, and dynamically optimize work distribution. We deploy our techniques in a sequential redundancy removal framework, using *localization* to solve non-inductive properties. Our techniques offer a median 2.4 speedup yielding 18.1% more property solves, as demonstrated by extensive experiments.**

I. INTRODUCTION

Practical hardware and software verification often mandates checking a large number of properties on a given design. For example, *functional verification* involves checking a suite of low-level assertions and higher-level encompassing properties. *Equivalence checking* compares pairwise equality of each output across two designs, yielding a distinct property per output. *Redundancy removal* requires proving many gate-equalities throughout a design, each comprising a distinct property. Redundancy removal is the core procedure of equivalence checking, and is widely-used to boost verification scalability.

Each property has a distinct minimal *cone of influence* (COI), or fan-in logic of the signals referenced in the property. Verification of a group of properties requires resources proportional to the collective COI size, which is often exponential (after lighter logic reductions). Each property adds distinct logic to the group's collective COI; *affinity* refers to the degree of common vs. distinct logic in the COI. *Atomic verification*[1] of a group of low-affinity properties is

---

[1]*Atomic verification* refers to running a set of single-process verification engines (called a *strategy*) on a group of properties. *Serial verification* refers to beginning one atomic task after another finishes, using a single process. *Concurrent* or *parallel verification* refers to dispatching multiple atomic tasks on concurrently-running parallel processes.

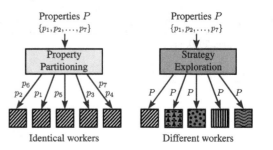

Fig. 1. Parallel verification: property partitioning vs. strategy exploration.

thus often significantly slower than solving them one-at-a-time. Conversely, atomic verification of a high-affinity group saves considerable verification resource, as the effort expended for one property can benefit the others without significantly slowing them down [1, 2]. Parallel verification resource can be optimized to leverage these facts using affinity-based *property partitioning* [3], where each parallel process, or *worker*, runs the same strategy on a different property group.

An alternate way to accelerate verification is by using a parallel portfolio (*strategy exploration*), where the same property group is concurrently verified using a different strategy per worker, as depicted in Fig. 1. However, portfolio approaches often degrade into highly-redundant work across processes, where similar algorithms address properties in nearly-identical order. Existing tools often independently use these modes in different contexts, particularly strategy exploration first running qualitatively-different strategies in available workers (e.g., BMC, IC3, interpolation) then padding differently-configured identical strategies in the remaining processes (e.g., IC3 with different heuristics). The latter yields increasingly-redundant CPU-time for diminishing gains in wall-time. These modes need not be mutually-exclusive: a strategy could partition within a worker, and partitioning could use different strategies for different groups. We explore the mutual optimization between property partitioning and strategy exploration, addressing the following challenges:

Property partitioning →

P1 Some workers are not utilized if the number of high-affinity groups is less than available workers.

P2 Some workers finish their tasks and idle (no more partitions to dispatch) while others degrade wall-time solving large or difficult groups, or run on slower machines.

Strategy exploration →

P3 Nearly-identical strategies verify the same properties concurrently yielding redundant computation; two or more workers would solve the same property at nearly the same time.

P4 A worker gets stuck on the first difficult property inhibiting progress; easy properties go unexplored.

P5 When using a round-robin resource-constrained approach to avoid **P4**, a worker fails to solve a difficult property in the allocated time even after several repetitions.

Contributions: We optimize parallel verification using complementary *property partitioning* and *strategy exploration*, in terms of both wall- and CPU-time. **(1)** We present a scalable property partitioning algorithm (Sect. III-A), extending [3] to guarantee *complete* utilization of available processes with provable partition quality. **(2)** We propose parallel scheduling improvements (Sect. III-B), such as resource-constrained irredundant group iteration, incremental repetition, and group decomposition to dynamically cope with more-difficult groups or slower workers. **(3)** We address irredundant strategy exploration of a localization portfolio in a sequential redundancy removal framework (Sect. IV), which we have found to be the most-scalable strategy to prove non-inductive redundancies. **(4)** We additionally propose improvements to *semantic group partitioning* within localization (Sect. IV-C). To our knowledge, this is the first published approach to mutually-optimize property partitioning and strategy exploration within a multi-property localization portfolio.

A. Related Work

Despite the prevalence of parallel verification tools and multi-property testbenches, little research has addressed mutual optimization of parallel partitioning and strategy exploration. Furthermore, most approaches optimize wall-time alone without considering CPU-time, treating additional CPUs as free horsepower to fill with slightly-modified strategies without attempting to minimize redundant computation.

Methods to group properties based on COI similarity are either computationally-prohibitive [1, 2, 4], or do not optimally utilize available parallel processes [3]. They may generate fewer groups than processes, or lose affinity guarantees when requiring *number of groups* as an algorithmic parameter.

Much prior work addresses ways to parallelize specific algorithms in a *single-property* context [5]–[7]. Other work incrementally reuses information between properties to accelerate specific algorithms [8]–[11]. These are complementary to our work, and can be used as strategies therein.

Much complementary research has addressed sequential redundancy removal, using scalability-boosting strategies including induction [12]–[14], simulation [15, 16], and synergistic transformation and verification algorithms [16, 17]. The benefit of parallelizing inductively-provable redundancies has been noted in [18, 19], though little work addresses parallelizing non-inductive redundancies. Localization is a powerful scalability boost to redundancy removal [14, 16, 20] and property checking [21]–[24]. Prior work is focused mostly upon single-property single-process contexts [21]–[24], or solely upon parallel property partitioning [3]. This work is complementary to ours: we extend state-of-the-art solutions for both, to mutually-optimized parallel verification.

II. Preliminaries

The design under verification is represented as a *netlist* N, which is a tuple $\langle V, E, F \rangle$ where $\langle V, E \rangle$ is a directed graph with vertices V representing *gates*, and edges $E \subseteq V \times V$ representing interconnections between gates. Function $F : V \to types$ assigns vertices to gate types: constants, primary inputs, combinational logic such as *AND* gates, and sequential logic such as *registers*. A *state* is a valuation to the registers. Certain gates are labeled as *properties*. The *fan-in* (*fan-out*) of gate u is the set of gates which may be reached by traversing edges backward (forward) from u. The fan-in of property p is called the *cone of influence* (COI) of p. Registers and inputs in the COI are called *support variables*. The number of support variables in the COI is its *size*. A *strongly connected component* (SCC) is a set of interconnected gates such that there is a non-empty directed path between every pair of gates in the same SCC. A *merge* of gate u onto gate v consists of moving the output edges of u onto v, then eliminating u from the netlist by treating u as a rename for v.

A. Affinity Analysis

Property grouping algorithms represent support variable information as a *Boolean bitvector* per property [25]. Every support variable in the netlist is indexed to a unique position in the bitvector, set to "1" if and only if the support variable is in the COI of the property. The length of such a bitvector is equal to the total number of support variables in the netlist, and all bitvectors have the same length. The COI size of the property is the number of bits set to "1". These bitvectors may be compared to determine relative property *affinity*. Properties p_1, p_2 with bitvectors bv_1, bv_2 respectively have

$$0 \le \text{affinity}(p_1, p_2) = 1 - \frac{\text{hamming}(bv_1, bv_2)}{\text{length}(bv_1)} \le 1.0$$

where $\text{hamming}(bv_1, bv_2)$ is the Hamming distance between bv_1 and bv_2, and $\text{length}(bv_1)$ is the number of support variables in the netlist [3]. The *distance* between p_1, p_2 equals the Hamming distance between their bitvectors, i.e., $\text{dist}(p_1, p_2) = \text{hamming}(bv_1, bv_2)$. A *group* g is a set of properties, with a single property g^* therein representing its *center*. The *quality* $Q(g)$ of a group is the minimum affinity between any property in g vs. its center g^*:

$$Q(g) = \min(\text{affinity}(p, g^*) \mid p \in g)$$

It is desirable that property partitioning algorithms guarantee group quality to be greater than a specifiable threshold.

B. High-Affinity Property Grouping

Three-leveled grouping [3] (Fig. 2) utilizes support bitvectors of properties to generate high-affinity groups. The algorithm takes the desired grouping level (l) and affinity threshold (t). It groups properties based upon: a) *Level-1*: identical bitvectors (identical support variables); b) *Level-2*: common large SCCs (containing t% netlist support variables) in the COI; and c) *Level-3*: small Hamming distance between support bitvectors, scalably identified by equivalence-classing *mapped*

structural_grouping (**Properties** P, **Netlist** N, **Level** l, **Affinity** t)
1: **Groups** $G = P$ # each property in singleton group
2: **if** l 1 : grouping_level_1 (G, N) # identical COI
3: **if** l 2 : grouping_level_2 (G, N, t) # large SCCs in COI
4: **if** l 3 : grouping_level_3 (G, N, t) # Hamming distance
5: **return** G # return high-affinity groups

Fig. 2. Algorithm to group properties based on structural affinity [3].

bitvectors using threshold-aware mapping functions. Higher levels yield progressively fewer but larger groups.

Straightforward grouping approaches such as pairwise comparison are computationally prohibitive [25], requiring at least quadratic resource with respect to number of properties. Despite being conceptually a quadratic-resource algorithm, bitvector equivalence-classing [3] consumes near-linear runtime and memory in practice, enabling scalable online partitioning with provable quality bounds [3]. Bitvectors are computed during a linear sweep of the netlist, and have size proportional to the number of SCCs plus non-SCC support variables. SCC computation has linear runtime [26]. With efficient implementation, this entire process consumes a few seconds on netlists with millions of support variables and properties: e.g. computing bitvectors in topological netlist order, and garbage-collecting bitvectors as soon as all fanout references have been processed [25].

A priori knowledge of solvers may dictate the ideal grouping level. For example, BDD-based reachability is highly sensitive to COI size, and thus may prefer level=1. BMC may prefer level=3 with lower affinity. Localization may prefer level=1, =2, or =3 depending on subsequent solvers. In many contexts, the caller can set level=3 and allow Fig. 2 to determine group count and size, especially when using the techniques of Sect. III-B and Sect. IV-C to decompose difficult groups.

Theorem 1 ([3]). *Level-1 grouping generates property groups* G *such that* g $G : Q(g) = 1.0$.

Theorem 2 ([3]). *Given affinity t, level-2 grouping generates property groups G such that* g $G : Q(g)$ t.

Theorem 3 ([3]). *Given affinity t, level-3 grouping generates property groups G such that* g $G : Q(g)$ 3 t 2.

Note that desired number of property groups is not an algorithmic parameter; affinity analysis determines the optimal number of groups respecting configurable quality bounds. For more details on leveled grouping, we refer the reader to [3].

III. GROUPING FOR PARALLEL VERIFICATION

Many organizations have large clusters of computers for load-balancing of tasks such as verification. The maximum number of available workers for a given task (n) is often known, e.g. the maximum number of organizational job submissions allowed per user, minus how many that user wishes to reserve for other tasks. Existing scalable grouping algorithms [3] may generate fewer high-affinity groups than n (**P1**). While partitioning a high-affinity group may yield redundant

structural_grouping_parallel (**Properties** P, **Netlist** N, **Level** l,
                                                    Affinity t, **Workers** n)
1: **Level** $l_c = 0$ # current grouping level
2: **Groups** $G = $ singletons(P) # initialize to singleton groups
3: **if** G n : **return** G # fewer properties than workers
4: **if** l 1 : grouping_level_1 (G, N), $l_c = 1$ # identical COI
5: **if** l 2 **and** G n : # else fewer groups than workers
6:    grouping_level_2 (G, N, t), $l_c = 2$ # large SCCs in COI
7: **if** l 3 **and** G n : # else fewer groups than workers
8:    grouping_level_3 (G, N, t), $l_c = 3$ # Hamming distance
9: **if** G $< n$: # fewer groups than available workers
10:    rebalance (G, N, l_c, t, n) # distribute groups, see Fig. 4
11: **assert** (G n) # guaranteed to hold
12: **return** G # return high-affinity groups

Fig. 3. Property grouping guaranteed to generate at least $\min(n, P)$ high-affinity groups for n parallel workers.

rebalance (**Groups** G, **Netlist** N, **Level** l_c, **Affinity** t, **Workers** n)
1: **if** $l_c == 1$: # divide large level-1 groups in half
2:    halve_groups (G, n) # see Fig. 5
3: **else** # rollback minimal-quality level-2 & level-3 groups
4:    rollback_groups (G, N, l_c, t, n) # see Fig. 6

Fig. 4. Algorithm to subdivide high-affinity groups for n workers.

CPU-time (similar effort expended on nearly-identical COIs), it may benefit wall-time due to disparate difficulty of properties therein: e.g. one may be inductive, and another require deep sequential analysis. Traditional clustering algorithms can be configured to produce n groups, though are computationally prohibitive for online use and may not yield affinity guarantees if n does not align with the given netlist.

A. Property Grouping Algorithm

Fig. 3 shows our extension to leveled grouping [3] (Fig. 2), guaranteeing generation of at least $\min(n, P)$ provable-affinity groups. Each property is returned as a singleton if there are fewer than n properties. Otherwise, grouping is performed in three levels that iteratively generate fewer, larger groups. Later levels are skipped if the number of generated groups becomes less than n at any level. The algorithm then rebalances as needed by fine-grained affinity analysis: subdividing large or lower-affinity groups to generate at least $\min(n, P)$ property groups. As discussed in Sect. III-B, this procedure is beneficial even after initial partitioning to subdivide a difficult group into provably high-affinity subgroups.

The rebalancing algorithm is shown in Fig. 4. It subdivides groups based on the grouping level l_c that generated fewer groups than n. For level-1, quality is already 100% so division is based on number of properties in the group (Fig. 5). Groups with the most properties are halved until at least $\min(n, P)$ groups are generated. Finer-grained analysis may be integrated if desired, e.g. considering affinity of combinational gates in the combinational fan-in of these properties. Group rollback for higher levels is more intricate (Fig. 6), with the goal of *improving* group quality. A group with minimal quality is conservatively subdivided until at least $\min(n, P)$ groups are generated. A minimal-quality group is split to yield smaller,

```
halve_groups (Groups G, Workers n)
1: while |G| < n :
2:     Group g = pick largest non-singleton group from G
3:     G = (G − g) ∪ halve_group (g)  # see below

halve_group (Group g)
1: return  first half of g, second half of g   # split in half
```

Fig. 5. Algorithm for subdividing large level-1 groups in half.

```
rollback_groups (Groups G, Netlist N, Level l_c, Affinity t, Workers n)
1: while |G| < n :
2:     Group g = pick minimal-quality non-singleton group from G
3:     G = (G − g) ∪ rollback_group (g, N, l_c, t)  # see below

rollback_group(Group g, Netlist N, Level l_c, Affinity t)
1: Groups G = singletons(g) # split g to singletons
2: grouping_level_1 (G, N)  # level-1
3: if |G| == 1 : G = halve_group (g ∈ G) return G # |G| == 2
4: else if |G| == 2 : return G  # g had two 100% quality subgroups
5: rollback_group_level (G, N, t, 2)  # level-2
6: if |G| == 2 : return G
7: if l_c == 3 : rollback_group_level (G, N, t, 3)  # level-3
8: return G  # |G| == 2

rollback_group_level (Groups G, Netlist N, Affinity t, Level l)
1: Groups G_c = G  # local copy of G
2: Group g_0, g_1 = ∅  # temporary groups, initially empty
3: if l == 2 : grouping_level_2 (G_c, N, t)  # level-2
4: else : grouping_level_3 (G_c, N, t)  # level-3
5: if |G_c| == 1 :  # G_c is one group containing all properties in G
6:     g_0 = g ∈ G containing center property g_c*
7:     # extract most-distant property into distinct subgroup
8:     g_1 = g ∈ G s.t. dist(g_0*, g*) == max( dist(g_0*, g_i*) ∀ g_i ∈ G )
9:     for each group g ∈ G : # merge groups to minimize distance
10:        if dist(g_0*, g*) ≤ dist(g_1*, g*) : add properties in g to g_0
11:        else : add properties in g to g_1
12:     G = {g_0, g_1}  # note Q(g_0), Q(g_1) ≥ Q(g_c), see Thm. 4
13: else : G = G_c  # |G| ≥ 2
```

Fig. 6. Algorithm for subdividing minimal-quality groups.

higher-quality subgroups. This process has negligible runtime, reuses precomputed support bitvectors and requires only a few milliseconds on the largest netlists.

The rebalancing procedure generates groups with quality bounds per Theorems 1, 2 and 3. Note that arbitrarily subdividing level-2,-3 groups without careful affinity consideration might violate affinity thresholds, because the quality of group g is measured with respect to its center property g^*. Assume that we generate subgroups g_0 and g_1 from g. If g^* is in g_0, we trivially have $Q(g_0^*) \geq Q(g^*)$ for any properties subgrouped with g^*. However, no such claim can be made about g_1; its properties might have been nearer to g^* than to each other. It is thus desirable to subdivide the most-distant property g_1^* from g^* to improve vs. risk degrading the resulting quality of both subgroups. Moreover, simply rolling back a higher level group to lower-level subgroups risks generating more groups than necessary, e.g., one level-2 group rolled back to ten level-1 groups. The algorithm in Fig. 3 generates *a minimal number $|G|$* of high-affinity groups with provable affinity bounds, where $|G| \leq min(n, |P|)$.

Theorem 4. *Given a group g, the rollback_group procedure*

subdivides g into two disjoint subgroups g_0 and g_1 such that $Q(g_0) \geq Q(g)$ and $Q(g_1) \geq Q(g)$.

Proof. (Sketch) The algorithm returns two 100% affinity groups when properties in g generate at most two level-1 subgroups. Otherwise, the greatest-Hamming-distance property $g_1^* \in g$ from g's center property g^* is identified. Subgroup g_0 inherits g^* as its center, and g_1 inherits g_1^* as its center. Remaining properties in g are added to g_0 vs. g_1 to minimize distance from g_0^* vs. g_1^*, ensuring provable quality bounds. □

Corollary 4.1. *Given affinity t and level l, grouping for parallelism (Fig. 3) generates groups G such that $\forall g \in G$:* a) $Q(g) = 1.0$ if $l = 1$, b) $Q(g) \geq t$ if $l = 2$, and c) $Q(g) \geq 3 \cdot t − 2$ if $l = 3$.

Proof. The proof follows per Theorems 1, 2 and 3 when no rebalancing occurs. Otherwise, rebalancing divides group g into smaller groups based on: (i) $l = 1$, level-1 subgroups are generated and $Q(g) = 1.0$ per Theorem 1; (ii) $l = 2$, levels-1 or 2 subgroups are generated and $Q(g) \geq t$ per Theorems 2 and 4; and (iii) $l = 3$, levels-1, 2 or 3 subgroups are generated and $Q(g) \geq 3 \cdot t − 2$ per Theorems 3 and 4. □

Theorem 5. *Given groups G over a set of properties P, and workers n with $|G| < n$ and $|P| \geq n$, rebalancing generates property groups G' such that $|G'| = n$.*

Proof. Both halve_group and rollback_group subdivide a non-singleton group g into exactly two subgroups, and iterate until $|G'| \geq n$. Therefore, the number of groups increases by exactly one in every iteration, unless all groups become singleton which cannot happen until $|G'| = |P| \geq n$. □

Corollary 5.1. *Given a set of properties P and n workers, grouping for parallelism (Fig. 3) generates groups G from P such that $|G| \leq min(n, |P|)$.*

Proof. The proof trivially holds when $\leq n$ groups or $|P| \leq n$ singletons are generated without rebalancing. Otherwise, the proof holds per Theorem 5 when rebalancing occurs. □

B. Group Distribution Heuristics

We propose three heuristics to optimally utilize parallel workers, used on-the-fly by a *manager* that dispatches property groups and dynamically adjusts based upon worker feedback. When partitioning is supported by an engine within a strategy (e.g. a localization engine [3]), there might be multiple managers partitioning an identical or overlapping set of properties. It is sometimes beneficial to use a hierarchy of managers: the *root* might use lower-affinity partitioning onto parallel strategies, with higher-affinity partitioning within a strategy.

Iteration order (I): Fig. 3 orders groups deterministically, and thus distributed managers within a strategy will likely verify common properties in the same order. This results in redundant CPU-time, where two or more strategies may solve the same property at nearly the same time (**P3**). The root manager could instead dispatch disjoint properties to different workers, though there are motivations for building

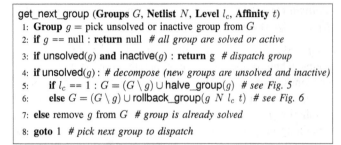

```
get_next_group (Groups G, Netlist N, Level l_c, Affinity t)
1: Group g = pick unsolved or inactive group from G
2: if g == null : return null  # all group are solved or active
3: if unsolved(g) and inactive(g) : return g  # dispatch group
4: if unsolved(g) :  # decompose (new groups are unsolved and inactive)
5:     if l_c == 1 : G = (G \ g) ∪ halve_group(g)  # see Fig. 5
6:     else G = (G \ g) ∪ rollback_group(g N l_c t)  # see Fig. 6
7: else remove g from G  # group is already solved
8: goto 1  # pick next group to dispatch
```

Fig. 7. *Manager* routine to dispatch unsolved groups using decomposition.

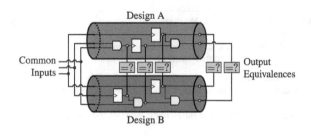

Fig. 8. Sequential equivalence checking uses redundancy removal to eliminate gate-equivalences between two logic designs. Each speculated gate-equality requires verifying a property called a *miter* (depicted as green box =?).

intelligence into distributed managers working on the entire property set, such as enabling incrementality and data sharing across properties [8]–[11]. To minimize redundant work, the manager may be augmented with options to iterate common groups in different orders: 1) smallest to largest COI (*forward*); 2) largest to smallest COI (*backward*); and 3) *random* to heuristically minimize concurrent solving of the same group while more groups than workers remain unsolved. If all properties are of comparable difficulty, running two identical strategies with opposite group ordering effectively halves wall-time with almost no redundant CPU-time. This approach can yield superlinear irredundant speedup when different strategies are tailored for easier vs more-difficult properties: a lighter strategy can iterate *forward* heuristically addressing easier properties first (the heavier strategy would be slower for these), while the heavier strategy can iterate *backward* addressing more-difficult properties first (the lighter strategy might be unable to solve these).

Controlled repetition (R): Each worker solves groups one-at-a-time. Encountering a difficult group inhibits overall progress (**P4**). Easier groups might follow, which when solved might speed-up incremental verification of the previous difficult group. Furthermore, solving easy properties sooner benefits other workers, allowing them to focus on fewer difficult groups. It is thus beneficial to impose time-limits per group within certain *fast* strategies. The manager must be capable of pruning already-solved properties (possibly solved by different workers), and repeating groups up to a configurable maximum allowed repetitions (to reduce redundant CPU-time). It may be beneficial to increase resource limits between repetitions, possibly after *n* repetitions with no progress. Engine incrementality is fairly important when imposing time-limits and repetition, to minimize redundant CPU-time.

Decomposition (D): Some groups are more difficult than others, either because they are large (e.g., many properties), or because individual properties therein are more difficult (e.g., having a very-deep counterexample). Some workers might be slower than others, possibly due to varying machine load. A common wall-time degradation occurs when fewer difficult groups than workers remain, and previously-active workers become idle (**P2**). This heuristic decomposes unsolved groups and dispatches them to idle workers, to accelerate convergence despite imposing some redundant CPU-time. Rather than redundantly dispatching an entire unsolved group, this

heuristic utilizes the algorithms of Fig. 5 and Fig. 6 to subdivide unsolved groups to smaller and higher-affinity groups, eventually becoming singletons. Smaller groups are easier for idle workers to redundantly solve (**P5**), benefiting but not preempting active workers (which might be on the verge of solves). The corresponding manager with decomposition is shown in Fig. 7. A group is *inactive* when no worker is currently verifying it. Solved properties and groups are discarded; groups with *unsolved* properties are subdivided and redundantly dispatched. Singleton groups are not redundantly dispatched, being *inactive* after the first dispatch.

IV. LOCALIZATION FOR REDUNDANCY REMOVAL

Industrial hardware designs are often rife with redundancy, e.g. to boost the performance of semiconductor devices, and to implement features such as error resilience, security, initialization logic and post-silicon observability. Verification testbenches yield additional netlist redundancies, due to *input constraints* restricting the set of stimulus applied to the design, and due to redundancies arising between the design and synthesized properties. Equivalence checking can be viewed as verifying a *composite netlist* comprising two designs as per Fig. 8. *Sequential redundancy removal* [12]–[14, 16]–[18, 27] (Fig. 9) is the process of proving that equivalence-classes of gates evaluate to equal or opposite values in all reachable states; each speculated redundancy entails solving a property called a *miter*. When a miter is proven, the corresponding redundant gates can be merged. This COI reduction is highly beneficial to verification scalability, and is the core procedure of sequential equivalence checking (SEC).

Various heuristics control the scope of equivalence-class candidates affecting runtime vs. reduction (Fig. 9 Step 1): e.g. whether to consider only registers vs. all gate types; whether to prune classes to reflect *corresponded signal names* or require per-class candidates spanning both designs in an equivalence-checking context (Fig. 8) [14, 20]. A *speculatively-reduced netlist* (Steps 2-3) accelerates verification of the miters. Techniques such as BMC and guided simulation are typically used to falsify miters; then induction proves the easier miters; and finally multi-engine strategies prove the difficult miters or find difficult counterexamples (Steps 4,5). Failed proofs (falsified miters or inconclusive results) cause a *refinement* of the equivalence classes to separate unproven miters' gates, then another expensive proof iteration is performed. Our goal is to minimize inconclusive proofs to achieve maximum netlist reduction with

```
redundancy_removal (Netlist N)
 1: Guess the redundancy candidates - sets of equivalence classes of gates
    in N, where gate u in class Q(u) is suspected equivalent to every other
    gate v in the same equivalence class.
 2: Select a representative gate R(Q(u)) from each class Q(u).
 3: Construct the speculatively-reduced netlist by replacing source gate u
    of every edge (u, v) ∈ E by R(Q(u)). Additionally, for each gate v,
    add a miter property asserted when v ≠ R(q(v)).
 4: Attempt to prove that each miter is unassertable.
 5: If a miter cannot be proven unassertable, refine the equivalence classes
    to separate the corresponding gates, and goto Step 2.
 6: For all unassertable miters, merge the corresponding gates onto the
    representative to eliminate redundancy.
```

Fig. 9. Generic sequential redundancy removal framework [16].

minimal wall- *and CPU*-time, using a parallel localization portfolio. Note that even if a testbench has only a single property, redundancy removal will often create thousands of miters. The large number of miters often tremendously benefit from parallel processing, as noted for combinational redundancy removal [19] and induction [18]. These miters are distributed throughout the netlist, making affinity partitioning particularly beneficial. Since practical netlists comprise a diversity of logic, different miters benefit from different strategies.

The proof or counterexample of a property often only depends on a small subset of logic in its COI. *Localization* [21]–[24] is a powerful abstraction method to reduce COI size by replacing irrelevant gates by *cutpoints* or unconstrained primary inputs. Since cutpoints can simulate the behavior of the original gates and more, the abstracted netlist over-approximates the behavior of the original netlist: abstract proofs imply original proofs, but abstract counterexamples might be spurious. Abstraction *refinement* eliminates cutpoints deemed responsible for spurious counterexamples, re-introducing previously-eliminated logic. It is desirable that the abstract netlist be as small as possible to enable scalable verification, while being immune to spurious counterexamples.

Localization is often essential to solve non-inductive miters, leveraging speculative reduction to abstract nearly all logic except for differently-implemented yet functionally-equivalent logic *between* speculated equivalences [14, 16]. Without localization, the COI of a miter may be very large despite speculative reduction. This large COI size may choke even fairly-scalable provers such as IC3. While the benefits of localization for sequential redundancy removal are well-known [17], prior work considered only single-process miter verification, aside from use of a standard parallel model-checking portfolio to solve miters [20]. Ours is the first to optimize a parallel localization portfolio in this (or any multi-property) context, using property partitioning and irredundant scheduling procedures (Figs. 3 and 7), along with the following complementary strategies tailored for easier vs. difficult properties. Note that substrategies in either may be employed by the other.

A. Fast-and-Lossy Localization

Fast-and-Lossy localization (Fig. 10) attempts to quickly discharge easier property groups, using timeouts to skip diffi-

```
fast_lossy_localization (Group g, unsigned n, Timeout T)
 1: Netlist L = load_incremental_abstraction(g) # initially empty
 2: unsigned k = load_incremental_bmc_depth(g) # initially 0
 3: while elapsed_time() ≤ T and unsolved(g) :
 4:     localize_bmc (g, L, k, unchanged)  # see below
        # check if netlist unchanged for last n bmc steps
 5:     if unchanged < n : k = k + 1, goto 4  # increment depth
 6:     run_proof_strategy(L, g, T - elapsed_time())
 7: save_incremental_data (G, k, L)  # timeout: save incremental data

localize_bmc (Group g, Netlist L, unsigned k, unsigned unchanged)
 1: bool stop = 0  # some properties fail at depth k
 2: while not stop :  # loop until all properties pass at depth k
 3:     Gates c = ∅, stop = 1  # cutpoints to refine, initially empty
 4:     for each Property p ∈ g :
 5:         Result r = run_bmc(L, p, k)  # run bmc with depth k
 6:         if r == unsat : continue  # property passes
 7:         if cex not spurious : report_solved(p, cex), continue
 8:         stop = 0  # property fails
 9:         Gates d = cutpoints_to_refine(), c = c ∪ d
10:     if not stop : refine_abstraction(L, c), unchanged = 0
11:     else unchanged += 1  # no change in abstraction
```

Fig. 10. *Fast-and-Lossy* localization with incremental repetition of high-affinity property groups.

cult groups. If the group is not solved within the allotted time, verification data (e.g., the current abstract netlist and achieved BMC depth) is saved for incremental reuse to accelerate later repetition. Skipped groups can be repeated as-is, or rebalanced (Fig. 7) after several repetitions of no progress. Note that repeating a group as-is may likely proceed further upon repetition, by incrementally skipping earlier processing and since a different worker might have solved some properties therein. *Fast-and-Lossy* localization uses counterexample-based refinement sometimes with quick proof-based abstraction (PBA), possibly yielding larger abstract netlists that are more-difficult to prove but with less time expended in BMC itself [23] for faster performance on easier groups. When ready to prove (i.e., no refinements occur for n consecutive BMC steps), abstracted groups are passed to a sequence of lighter reduction engines then IC3 [5, 28]) under a modest time-limit (e.g. ~300s) which can be increased across repetitions (**R**).

B. Aggressive Localization

Aggressive localization (Fig. 11) is aimed at solving difficult properties, where *Fast-and-Lossy* may fail due to larger-than-necessary abstractions, insufficient reductions prior to IC3, or small group time-limits. *Aggressive* never repeats groups, so either imposes no time limit whatsoever, or a large time-limit as shown applied to semantically-partitioned (Sec. IV-C) sub-groups but iterated and increased until the group is solved. *Aggressive* typically uses a hybrid of counterexample-based refinement and PBA run after every unsatisfiable BMC result, to yield smaller abstractions than the former alone to accelerate subsequent proofs at the expense of more runtime spent in BMC itself [23]. When ready to prove (i.e., no refinements occur for n consecutive BMC steps), abstracted groups are passed to a sequence of heavy reduction engines (including nested induction-only sequential redundancy removal across

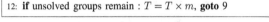
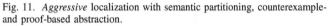

```
aggressive_localization (Group g, unsigned n, bool pba, bool semantic,
                         Affinity t, Timeout T, Multiplier m)
 1:  Netlist L = initial_abstraction(g)  # initially empty
 2:  unsigned k = 0  # bmc depth
 3:  localize_bmc (g, L, k, unchanged)  # see Fig. 10
 4:  if semantic : collect_support_info (...)  # see Sect. IV-C
 5:  if pba : minimize L using proof-based abstraction
         # check if netlist unchanged for last n bmc steps
 6:  if unchanged < n : k = k + 1, goto 3  # increment depth
 7:  Groups G = semantic ? structural_grouping (g, L, 3, t) : G
         # Sort via (I) mode (Sect. III-B): forward, backward, or random
 8:  Sort G by abstract COI size
 9:  for each unsolved group g ∈ G :
10:      while elapsed_time() ≤ T and unsolved(g) :
11:          run_proof_strategy(L, g, T - elapsed_time())
12:  if unsolved groups remain : T = T × m, goto 9
```

Fig. 11. *Aggressive* localization with semantic partitioning, counterexample-
and proof-based abstraction.

all gates, which might be too expensive to converge on large
netlists before localization) followed by IC3 [5, 28]).

C. Semantic Partitioning

Semantic partitioning [3] refers to re-partitioning a group
whose *unabstracted COI* was high-affinity, yielding subgroups of high affinity with respect to *abstract COI* as
correlates to subsequent verification complexity. Abstract COI
information is mined onto support bitvectors on a per-property
basis as cutpoints are refined (Fig. 11 Step 4), considering
minimized counterexamples for individual properties despite
incrementally using the same BMC instance for the entire
group. The group is partitioned into smaller, high-localized-
affinity subgroups (Step 7) before attempting to prove.

Improvements to semantic partitioning vs. [3]: Per-property
abstract-COI bloat may arise during counterexample analysis, because the group must be mutually refined to be free
of spurious counterexamples. Eager partitioning (as soon as
any diverged abstract COI occurs) *could* circumvent this
ambiguous bloat, though often severely hurts performance
since intermediate abstract-COI differences often reconverge.
In practice, lazy partitioning deferred until modest BMC time
limits are exceeded is far superior (particularly since BMC
often benefits from level=3 lower affinity), retaining high-
affinity atomic verification benefits. Abstract-COI ambiguities
can be largely corrected during proof analysis, by analyzing a
distinct proof per property. Incremental data should be saved
when semantically re-partitioning, to minimize restart penalty.

Difficult sub-groups are susceptible to delaying easier later
sub-groups. Subgroups should be ordered as per **(I)** mode
(Sect. III-B): *forward*, *backward*, and *random*, configured
differently in parallel strategies for better portfolio performance with less redundant CPU-time. Subgroups are verified
in the chosen order using controlled repetition **(R)** and large
Aggressive time-limits (Steps 9–11). We recommend T ≥ 1h
multiplying 2× at each iteration (Step 12) and overriding to
unlimited when a single sub-group remains.

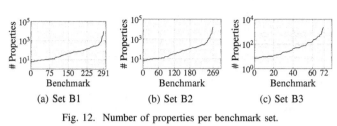

(a) Set B1   (b) Set B2   (c) Set B3

Fig. 12. Number of properties per benchmark set.

V. EXPERIMENTAL RESULTS

We evaluate our techniques within the post-induction
proof strategy of a sequential redundancy removal framework
(Fig. 9). To eliminate *noise* such as different counterexamples
yielding different equivalence-classes (Step 5), we snapshot
the speculatively-reduced netlist after ten minutes of induction,
before the final iteration of a six-hour eight-process semi-
formal bug-hunting [29] and localization portfolio to eliminate most incorrect and easier [27] miters. The following
experiments[2] are run on these snapshotted netlists (pruning
those with fewer miters than processes), yielding three benchmark sets. Set **B1** (Fig. 12a) are the most-difficult 291 of
1822 proprietary SEC benchmarks, where initial equivalence
classes comprise original properties and *name corresponded*
register pairs. Set **B2** (Fig. 12b) has 269 netlists derived from
the former, including a large equivalence class for registers
without name correlation. Set **B3** has 72 netlists from the
SINGLE property HWMCC 2017 benchmarks, comprising a
large initial equivalence class of all registers. Our techniques
are implemented within *RuleBase: Sixthsense Edition* [30].

A. Localization Portfolio

We select our localization portfolio (Table I) from extensive
evaluation of 36 single-process localization configurations and
30 subsequent proof strategies, exploring options such as
enabling vs. disabling PBA [23]; different levels of property grouping vs. no grouping [3]; enabling vs. disabling
semantic partitioning (Sect. IV-C); and different policies for
group iteration **(I)**, repetition **(R)**, and decomposition **(D)**
(Sect. III-B). The best-performing collection is chosen, maxi-
mizing *complementary* unique solves. *Aggressive* localization
(Sect. IV-B) primarily uses both counterexample- and proof-
based abstraction, yielding smallest abstract netlists solved
with a single-process heavy strategy of combinational rewriting; input elimination [31]–[33] which is especially powerful after localization due to inserted cutpoints; min-area
retiming [34]; a nested induction-only gate-based sequential
redundancy removal; then IC3. *Fast-and-Lossy* localization
(Sect. IV-A) uses counterexample-based refinement mainly
with no or lighter PBA for faster BMC, yielding larger
abstract netlists solved using light combinational rewriting,
input elimination, then IC3. The former is fastest for difficult
properties; the latter for easier properties.

We compare four 6-process localization portfolios derived
from Table I. The localization configuration and subsequent
solving strategy of each process is identical across portfolios,

---

[2]Detailed results available at http://temporallogic.org/research/FMCAD20

TABLE I
SIX-PROCESS COMPLEMENTARY LOCALIZATION PORTFOLIO.

#	Localization Strategy	Grouping Level	Semantic	Iteration (I)	Repetition (R)	Decomposition (D)
S1	*Fast-and-Lossy*	Level-1	✗	Forward	✓	✗
S2	*Fast-and-Lossy*	Level-1	✗	Reverse	✓	✓
S3	*Fast-and-Lossy*	Level-3	✓	Forward	✓	✓
S4	*Aggressive*	Level-1	✗	Forward	✗	-
S5	*Aggressive*	Level-1	✗	Reverse	✗	-
S6	*Aggressive*	Level-3	✓	Forward	✗	-

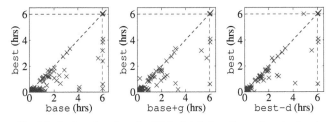

(a) Set B1　　　　　(b) Set B2

Fig. 13. #Properties solved vs. wall-time for **B1** and **B2**; 6-hour time limit.

Fig. 14. **best** vs. baselines for **B1** (points below diagonal are in favor).

except for adherence to the illustrated scheduling differences as discussed below. For greater portfolio value, each process includes localization configuration differences beyond the illustrated scheduling distinction in Table I. **S1** only performs counterexample-based refinement; **S2** and **S3** also perform PBA. **S2** vs. **S3** perform hybrid counterexample-based refinement with light PBA (modest time limit) after every unsatisfiable BMC step vs. only before the subsequent solving strategy, respectively. Abstract-netlist gates remaining after PBA are considered *committed* and cannot be eliminated in later PBA steps [21] in **S2**, but not **S3**. **S3** utilizes a minimal unsatisfiable core to further reduce the abstract netlist. **S4-S6** are identical to **S1-S3**, respectively, without imposed time-limits and modulo the above-mentioned post-localization solving strategy differences. To highlight our individual contributions, we compare four variants of this portfolio:

1) `base`: No property grouping or incremental repetition of properties; all processes iterate properties in forward order. This represents a standard state-of-the-art localization portfolio approach *without property grouping*, e.g., before [3].

2) `base+g` extends `base` with affinity property grouping, including semantic partitioning in one *Fast-and-Lossy* and one *Aggressive* strategy. This represents a state-of-the-art localization portfolio *with property grouping*, e.g., as per [3] though with our semantic refinement improvements of Sect. IV-C.

3) `best-d` extends `base+g` with incremental repetition (**R**) and irredundant iteration order (**I**), to reduce CPU-time.

4) `best` extends `best-d` with decomposition (**D**).

Processes S1-S6 are generic online localization strategies. Multi-property localization *without affinity-partitioning* generally yields poor/noncompetitive performance [3], eroding most of its scalability benefit, especially for difficult miters. (Recall that these benchmarks pre-filter easier miters, using induction and semi-formal bug-hunting.) Therefore, `base` and `base+g` are highly-competitive 6-process localization portfolios, for online "first-run-of-a-testbench." Industrial verification tools may use more processes for large testbenches, and may post-process data from prior/ongoing runs to accelerate future results. This level of sophisticated benchmark-specific orchestration is valuable, though does not readily benefit "first-run-of-a-testbench" and introduces noise in experiments hence are not used herein. We optimize runtime of a generic 6-process localization portfolio without per-benchmark customization.

B. Experiment Setup

Our experiments run on a computing grid with identical x86 Linux nodes. Each benchmark run uses a 6-process portfolio

(Table I); each process **S1-S6** runs on a single identical CPU core on the same host-machine. Each process eagerly cancels solved properties across all processes in that portfolio, to reduce redundant computation.

While most prior research and competitions focus solely upon optimizing wall-time, our techniques additionally benefit CPU-time. Traditionally, Fast-and-Lossy (unlike Aggressive) processes terminate early, leaving unsolved difficult properties. In these experiments, `base` and `base+g` augment Fast-and-Lossy processes to naively repeat identically-configured **S1-S3** with identical resource limits per group (whereas `best-d` and `best` add incremental-repetition (**R**) with resource-doubling across repetitions), until all properties are solved or global timeout. This naive repetition is wasteful in practice, yielding highly-redundant CPU-time for marginal benefit. However, disabling naive repetition in these experiments yielded 3.2% fewer solves in `base` and `base+g` vs. `best-d` and `best`, which arguably unfairly penalized them as state-of-the-art solutions *before our contributions*. Therefore, **S1-S6** in each portfolio continue working until all processes terminate, hence CPU-time is approximately 6× wall-time in these experiments.

C. Proprietary Benchmarks

Fig. 13 shows the number of properties solved vs. wall-time for **B1** and **B2**. `best` is the clear winner, solving 18.1% (15.3%) more properties in 17.2% (22.9%) less time for **B1** (**B2**, respectively) compared to `base`. Affinity-grouping significantly improves performance of `base+g` over `base`. Level-3 grouping with our semantic partitioning improvements (Sect. IV-C) benefits *Aggressive*, atomically solving properties in fewer, larger high-abstract-affinity groups compared to level-1,-2. Incremental repetition and irredundant iteration allows `best-d` to solve 8.1% more properties than `base+g`, less-severely hindered by difficult groups. `best` yields additional solves through decomposition of difficult groups after five incremental repetitions of no progress, solving all properties in 4 vs. 6 benchmarks in **B1** vs. **B2** that time out with

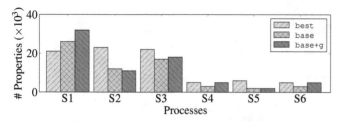

Fig. 15. #Properties solved on **B2** per process of Table I.

TABLE II
UTILITY OF AGGRESSIVE STRATEGY PROCESSES IN A PORTFOLIO.

Portfolio	Set B1		Set B2	
	#Solved	Time (h)	#Solved	Time (h)
3× *Fast-and-Lossy*, 3× *Aggressive*	**46,844**	**236**	**93,806**	**165**
6× *Fast-and-Lossy* (modified best)	41,702	275	91,639	184

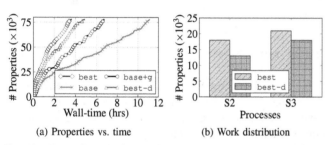

(a) Properties vs. time   (b) Work distribution

Fig. 16. #Properties solved vs. wall-time for **big**: (a) by all portfolios; (b) per process of Table I within best and best-d.

other portfolios. Fig. 14 details per-**B1**-benchmark runtimes of best, yielding a median speedup of 2.4×, 2.0× and 1.5× vs. base, base+g, and best-d, respectively.

Fig. 15 shows the distribution of properties solved per process (Table I) within these portfolios. The percentage solved by each *Fast-and-Lossy* (and *Aggressive*) process is nearly uniform in best, showing near-optimal irredundant work distribution. In contrast, without **(I)** and **(R)**, base and base+g have highly-uneven distributions due largely to parallel processes addressing the same groups concurrently. While the number of solved (easier) miters is considerably larger with *Fast-and-Lossy*, we emphasize how critical the *Aggressive* solution of difficult miters is to the overall redundancy removal process. If any are left unsolved, Fig. 9 Step 5 will forgo attempting to merge the corresponding gates, thereby weakening netlist reductions, risking unsolved SEC, and hurting runtime by requiring yet another expensive proof iteration with refined equivalence classes [14] – where fan-out miters often become more-difficult than those unsolved in prior iterations. Table II shows the number of properties solved by best, and a modified best portfolio with all *Fast-and-Lossy* strategy processes where **S4-S6** are identical to **S1-S3** respectively, but without imposed time-limits and iterating groups in opposite order. Without *Aggressive* processes in the portfolio, modified best solves 10.9% (2.31%) fewer properties in 16.5% (11.51%) more time for **B1** (**B2**).

To further highlight the value of decomposition **(D)**, Fig. 16b illustrates an additional **big** benchmark containing 77728 properties partitioned into 9958 level-1 and level-2, and 2991 level-3 high-affinity groups. Fig. 16a shows the

number of properties solved by each portfolio vs. time. best is 3.0× faster than base. Fig. 16b shows the number of properties solved by two *Fast-and-Lossy* processes of best and best-d; decomposition enables **S2** and **S3** in best to collectively solve 25.2% more properties than best-d.

D. HWMCC Benchmarks

Fig. 17 shows the number of properties solved by each portfolio for set **B3**. best is again the winner, solving 3054 more properties in less time than base. Incremental repetition and irredundant iteration is particularly

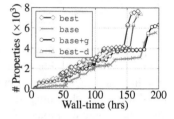

Fig. 17. #Solved vs. wall-time for **B3**.

beneficial in this set: several benchmarks have counterexamples that are discovered in earlier group repetitions, enabling *Aggressive* and later *Fast-and-Lossy* repetitions to direct resource upon more-difficult provable miters.

VI. CONCLUSIONS AND FUTURE WORK

We focus upon boosting the scalability of multi-property parallel verification, with application to sequential redundancy removal using a localization portfolio. Our contributions optimize both wall-time and CPU-time, orchestrating via complementary strategy exploration and property partitioning. **(1)** We extend scalable affinity-based property partitioning to guarantee *complete* utilization of available processes with provable partition affinities. **(2)** We propose improvements to the scheduling of parallel processes, such as resource-constrained irredundant iteration, incremental repetition, and decomposition of difficult groups. **(3)** We deliver a carefully-optimized localization portfolio, self-tailoring to irredundantly address a range of property difficulties through a synergistic balance of *Fast-and-Lossy* vs. *Aggressive* configurations. **(4)** We propose improvements to *semantic group partitioning* within localization, boosting scalability by enabling the BMC within localization to benefit from larger and slightly-lower affinity groups, then optimally sub-dividing those groups before solving the localized properties. To our knowledge, this is the first published approach to optimize both property partitioning and strategy exploration within a multi-property localization portfolio. Experiments confirm that this solution works well across large suites of benchmarks.

Note that our mutually-optimized partitioning vs. strategy-exploration orchestration offers broad insights early in an ongoing verification-tool run, whereas traditional orchestration typically explores only easier (smaller-COI) properties or only a subset of strategies early in the run. Exploring how this insight may enable dynamic benchmark-specific customized orchestration *during* an ongoing run is a promising future direction, e.g. dynamically adjusting which strategy is used per process and partition. Exploring these techniques across a broader set of engines, and exploring incrementality of strategies across localization and equivalence-class refinements, are additional promising research directions.

ACKNOWLEDGMENTS

We thank the anonymous reviewers for their valuable feedback and suggestions. We thank Alexander Ivrii for assistance in implementing various localization features and for feedback on early drafts of this paper. We thank Raj Kumar Gajavelly for providing benchmarks and assistance with experimental evaluation. This work is partially supported by National Science Foundation CAREER Award CNS-1664356.

REFERENCES

[1] G. Cabodi, P. E. Camurati, C. Loiacono, M. Palena, P. Pasini, D. Patti, and S. Quer, "To split or to group: from divide-and-conquer to subtask sharing for verifying multiple properties in model checking," *International Journal on Software Tools for Technology Transfer (STTT)*, vol. 20, pp. 313–325, Jun 2018.

[2] G. Cabodi and S. Nocco, "Optimized model checking of multiple properties," in *Design, Automation and Test in Europe (DATE)*, pp. 1–4, Mar 2011.

[3] R. Dureja, J. Baumgartner, A. Ivrii, R. Kanzelman, and K. Y. Rozier, "Boosting verification scalability via structural grouping and semantic partitioning of properties," in *Formal Methods in Computer Aided Design (FMCAD)*, pp. 1–9, Oct 2019.

[4] R. Dureja and K. Y. Rozier, "More scalable LTL model checking via discovering design-space dependencies (D^3)," in *Tools and Algorithms for the Construction and Analysis of Systems (TACAS)* (D. Beyer and M. Huisman, eds.), (Cham), pp. 309–327, Springer International Publishing, Apr 2018.

[5] A. R. Bradley, "SAT-based model checking without unrolling," in *Verification, Model Checking, and Abstract Interpretation (VMCAI)*, (Berlin, Heidelberg), p. 70–87, Springer-Verlag, 2011.

[6] S. Chaki and D. Karimi, "Model checking with multi-threaded IC3 portfolios," in *Verification, Model Checking, and Abstract Interpretation (VMCAI)* (B. Jobstmann and K. R. M. Leino, eds.), (Berlin, Heidelberg), pp. 517–535, Springer Berlin Heidelberg, Jan 2016.

[7] M. Marescotti, A. Gurfinkel, A. E. J. Hyvärinen, and N. Sharygina, "Designing parallel PDR," in *Formal Methods in Computer-Aided Design (FMCAD)*, (Austin, Texas), p. 156–163, FMCAD Inc, Oct 2017.

[8] Z. Khasidashvili, A. Nadel, A. Palti, and Z. Hanna, "Simultaneous SAT-based model checking of safety properties," in *Hardware and Software, Verification and Testing (HVC)* (S. Ur, E. Bin, and Y. Wolfsthal, eds.), (Berlin, Heidelberg), pp. 56–75, Springer Berlin Heidelberg, 2006.

[9] Z. Khasidashvili and A. Nadel, "Implicative simultaneous satisfiability and applications," in *Hardware and Software: Verification and Testing (HVC)* (K. Eder, J. Lourenço, and O. Shehory, eds.), (Berlin, Heidelberg), pp. 66–79, Springer Berlin Heidelberg, 2012.

[10] R. Dureja and K. Y. Rozier, "FuseIC3: An algorithm for checking large design spaces," in *Formal Methods in Computer Aided Design (FMCAD)*, pp. 164–171, Oct 2017.

[11] J. Marques-Silva, "Interpolant learning and reuse in SAT-based model checking," *Electronic Notes in Theoretical Computer Science*, vol. 174, no. 3, pp. 31 – 43, 2007.

[12] C. A. J. van Eijk, "Sequential equivalence checking without state space traversal," in *Design, Automation and Test in Europe (DATE)*, pp. 618–623, Feb 1998.

[13] P. Bjesse and K. Claessen, "SAT-based verification without state space traversal," in *Formal Methods in Computer-Aided Design (FMCAD)* (W. A. Hunt and S. D. Johnson, eds.), (Berlin, Heidelberg), pp. 409–426, Springer Berlin Heidelberg, Oct 2000.

[14] H. Mony, J. Baumgartner, V. Paruthi, and R. Kanzelman, "Exploiting suspected redundancy without proving it," in *Design Automation Conference (DAC)*, pp. 463–466, Jun 2005.

[15] K. Debnath, R. Murgai, M. Jain, and J. Olson, "SAT-based redundancy removal," in *Design, Automation and Test in Europe (DATE)*, pp. 315–318, Mar 2018.

[16] H. Mony, J. Baumgartner, A. Mishchenko, and R. Brayton, "Speculative reduction-based scalable redundancy identification," in *Design, Automation and Test in Europe (DATE)*, pp. 1674–1679, Apr 2009.

[17] J. Baumgartner, H. Mony, V. Paruthi, R. Kanzelman, and G. Janssen, "Scalable sequential equivalence checking across arbitrary design transformations," in *2006 International Conference on Computer Design*, pp. 259–266, Oct 2006.

[18] A. Mishchenko, M. Case, R. Brayton, and S. Jang, "Scalable and scalably-verifiable sequential synthesis," in *International Conference on Computer-Aided Design*, 2008.

[19] V. N. Possani, A. Mishchenko, R. P. Ribas, and A. I. Reis, "Parallel combinational equivalence checking," in *IEEE Transactions on Computer-Aided Design of Integrated Circuits and Systems*, Oct 2019.

[20] R. Brayton, N. Een, and A. Mishchenko, "Using speculation for sequential equivalence checking," in *International Workshop on Logic and Synthesis (IWLS)*, Jun 2012.

[21] A. Mishchenko, N. Een, R. Brayton, J. Baumgartner, H. Mony, and P. Nalla, "GLA: Gate-level abstraction revisited," in *2013 Design, Automation Test in Europe Conference Exhibition (DATE)*, pp. 1399–1404, March 2013.

[22] K. L. McMillan and N. Amla, "Automatic abstraction without counterexamples," in *Tools and Algorithms for the Construction and Analysis of Systems (TACAS)* (H. Garavel and J. Hatcliff, eds.), (Berlin, Heidelberg), pp. 2–17, Springer Berlin Heidelberg, 2003.

[23] N. Amla and K. L. McMillan, "A hybrid of counterexample-based and proof-based abstraction," in *Formal Methods in Computer-Aided Design (FMCAD)* (A. J. Hu and A. K. Martin, eds.), (Berlin, Heidelberg), pp. 260–274, Springer Berlin Heidelberg, 2004.

[24] P. Chauhan, E. Clarke, J. Kukula, S. Sapra, H. Veith, and D. Wang, "Automated abstraction refinement for model checking large state spaces using SAT based conflict analysis," in *Formal Methods in Computer-Aided Design (FMCAD)* (M. D. Aagaard and J. W. O'Leary, eds.), (Berlin, Heidelberg), pp. 33–51, Springer Berlin Heidelberg, 2002.

[25] G. Cabodi, P. Camurati, and S. Quer, "A graph-labeling approach for efficient cone-of-influence computation in model-checking problems with multiple properties," *Software: Practice and Experience*, vol. 46, no. 4, pp. 493–511, 2016.

[26] R. Tarjan, "Depth first search and linear graph algorithms," in *SIAM Journal on Computing*, 1972.

[27] M. Case, J. Baumgartner, H. Mony, and R. Kanzelman, "Optimal redundancy removal without fixedpoint computation," in *Formal Methods in Computer-Aided Design (FMCAD)*, pp. 101–108, Oct 2011.

[28] N. Een, A. Mishchenko, and R. Brayton, "Efficient implementation of property directed reachability," in *Formal Methods in Computer-Aided Design (FMCAD)*, (Austin, TX), pp. 125–134, FMCAD Inc, 2011.

[29] P. K. Nalla, R. K. Gajavelly, J. Baumgartner, H. Mony, R. Kanzelman, and A. Ivrii, "The art of semi-formal bug hunting," in *International Conference on Computer-Aided Design (ICCAD)*, (New York, NY, USA), ACM, 2016.

[30] H. Mony, J. Baumgartner, V. Paruthi, R. Kanzelman, and A. Kuehlmann, "Scalable automated verification via expert-system guided transformations," in *Formal Methods in Computer-Aided Design (FMCAD)* (A. J. Hu and A. K. Martin, eds.), (Berlin, Heidelberg), pp. 159–173, Springer Berlin Heidelberg, 2004.

[31] J. Baumgartner and H. Mony, "Maximal input reduction of sequential netlists via synergistic reparameterization and localization strategies," in *Correct Hardware Design and Verification Methods*, Oct 2005.

[32] N. Eén and A. Mishchenko, "A fast reparameterization procedure," in *International Workshop on Design and Implementation of Formal Tools and Systems*, 2013.

[33] R. K. Gajavelly, J. Baumgartner, A. Ivrii, R. L. Kanzelman, and S. Ghosh, "Input elimination transformations for scalable verification and trace reconstruction," in *Formal Methods in Computer-Aided Design (FMCAD)*, 2019.

[34] A. Kuehlmann and J. Baumgartner, "Transformation-based verification using generalized retiming," in *Computer Aided Verification (CAV)* (G. Berry, H. Comon, and A. Finkel, eds.), (Berlin, Heidelberg), pp. 104–117, Springer Berlin Heidelberg, 2001.

26

EUFicient Reachability in Software with Arrays

Denis Bueno (ID)
Computer Science and Engineering
University of Michigan
Email: dlbueno@umich.edu

Arlen Cox
Institute for Defense Analyses
Center for Computing Sciences
Email: arlen@super.org

Karem Sakallah (ID)
Computer Science and Engineering
University of Michigan
Email: karem@umich.edu

Abstract—Whether representing strings, heap objects, or numerical vectors, arrays are pervasive in software. Unfortunately, while several software model checkers support arrays, they tend to struggle with many array-manipulating programs due to work expended generating theory lemmas that are ultimately irrelevant or redundant. By judicious abstraction of array operations to the logic of equality with uninterpreted functions (EUF), we show that we can *directly* reason about array reads and *adaptively* learn lemmas about array writes leading to significant performance improvements over existing approaches. We find that our model checker solves more than 100 more SV-COMP benchmarks than SPACER, a leading model checker.

I. INTRODUCTION

Arrays and array-like structures are pervasive in the software world. From C/C++ arrays and vectors to Python lists, it is difficult to find software that doesn't use and manipulate arrays. Despite this, research of software model checkers has largely focused on finding numerical invariants and proving numerical properties of programs. As results of the software verification competition (SV-COMP) show, even when model checkers support arrays, there are a significant number of programs that cannot be automatically verified—some for a lack of expressivity and some for a lack of performance. Our focus is on the latter.

The key challenge that we face is adequately controlling theory reasoning in the SMT solver underlying the model checker. While SMT solvers typically have an array theory and can therefore directly solve array problems, the interface that SMT solvers provide does not provide for adequate incrementality and hinting to enable maximal performance. For instance, we find that, in SV-COMP benchmarks, as many as 90% of the array lemmas that the SMT solver is learning are either redundant or ultimately irrelevant. Most lemmas either do not advance the cause of the model checker or were thrown away by the SMT solver due to imperfect caching. Thus time spent learning those lemmas was wasted effort.

To eliminate this waste, we do incremental inductive model checking on top of an equality with uninterpreted functions (EUF) theory [1]. This removes the need for SMT array theories in the core incremental model checking process, relegating the array theory solely to abstraction refinement operations, and yielding a thousand-fold reduction in the number of operations that do redundant or irrelevant work. Additionally this means that array lemmas are only learned where they are pertinent to proving or disproving the property.

Moreover our strategy addresses a fundamental tension. On the one hand, incremental model checkers [2], which construct a safety proof bit by bit, are particularly scalable because their many individual queries are simple to solve and generalize. On the other hand, these queries lack error path information that could simplify overall checking.

For example, consider model checking the following program, assuming that a, b, and f are distinct constant values:

```
        int[] A; int i, a, b, f;
ℓ₁:   A[3] = f;
ℓ₂:   A[1] = a;
        A[2] = b;
        assume(1 <= i <= 3);
        if (A[i] == f);
ℓ₃:     error();
        else
ℓ₄:     exit();
```

The model checker is trying to find if any values of i lead to the error at location ℓ_3. Of course it can reach ℓ_3 if $i = 3$, which the checker takes two SMT queries to discover. The first query corresponds to reaching ℓ_3, where $A[i] = f$, from ℓ_2. The solver deduces $i \notin \{1, 2\}$, meaning the property may yet be violated, so the checker moves on to the next query, which corresponds to reaching the failure from ℓ_1. The first query involves two array stores and one read; the SMT array theory will generate theory lemmas to deduce that $A[i]$ is not set to f by any assignment from ℓ_2. Several of these lemmas ultimately do not matter, however, since the property is discovered to be violated by the antecedent assignment at ℓ_1.

We study arrays and array abstraction in the context of EUF model checking and make the following contributions:

1) We develop an algorithm for integrating array abstraction into EUFORIA, an EUF-based, incremental, inductive, model checker (Section III).
2) We introduce a refinement procedure for learning relevant array lemmas (Section IV).
3) We evaluate the integration of array abstraction with EUF-based model checking using a variety of device driver benchmarks from SV-COMP (Section V). We find that EUFORIA performs well compared to SPACER and IC3IA.

II. BACKGROUND

a) Equality with Uninterpreted Functions (EUF): We consider a first-order language with equality with signature $\mathcal{S}$ and two common sorts, BOOLs and INTs. Our setting is standard quantifier-free, first-order logic (FOL) with the standard notions of theory, satisfiability, validity, entailment, and models. Much of this background is adapted from previous work [1].

The EUF logic grammar is presented here:

type		production	explanation
term (t)	::=	x | y | z | $\cdots$	0-arity term
	|	$F(t_1, t_2, \ldots, t_n)$	uninterp. function (UF)
	|	$ite(f, t_1, t_2)$	if-then-else
atom (a)	::=	$t_1 = t_2$	equality atom
	|	$x \mid y \mid z \mid \cdots$	Boolean atom
	|	$P(t_1, t_2, \ldots, t_n)$	uninterp. predicate (UP)
formula (f)	::=	a	
	|	$\neg a$	negation
	|	$f_1 \wedge f_2$	conjunction
	|	$f_1 \vee f_2$	disjunction

Atomic formulas (atoms) are made up of Boolean identifiers, uninterpreted predicates (UPs), and equalities between terms. Formulas are made up of terms combined with arbitrary Boolean structure. For simplicity, but without loss of generality, we only consider formulas in negation normal form. A *literal* is a (possibly-negated) atom containing no occurrences of ITE. A *clause* is a disjunction of literals. A *cube* is a conjunction of literals. When convenient, a formula F may be treated as a set of its top-level conjuncts, e.g., $x = 1 \in F$ if $F = (x > 17 \wedge x = 1)$. $a \models b$ means that a entails b. We write uninterpreted objects—terms x, functions F, and predicates P—in sans serif face. The semantics of these formulas is standard.

b) Arrays: We consider a theory of arrays with extensionality and constant-initialized arrays. This theory has the particular function symbols select, store, and const-array. The theory is defined by McCarthy's axioms [3], extended with axioms for extensionality and constant initialization:

$$\forall aije.\ i = j \implies \text{select}(\text{store}(a, i, e), j) = e \quad (1)$$

$$\forall aije.\ i \neq j \implies \text{select}(\text{store}(a, i, e), j) = \text{select}(a, j) \quad (2)$$

$$\forall ab.\ (\forall i.\ \text{select}(a, i) = \text{select}(b, i)) \implies a = b \quad (3)$$

$$\forall ik.\ \text{select}(\text{const-array}(k), i) = k \quad (4)$$

The first two axioms specify array accesses. The third axiom specifies that equal arrays have identical elements at identical indices. The fourth axiom specifies that every index of a constant-initialized array has the initializer value.

We consider this array theory—specifically including equality and constant initialization—because of its utility for software verification. Programs commonly bulk-initialize arrays and array equality allows encodings to be easily composed.

c) Transition Systems for Programs: A transition system [4], [5] is a tuple $\mathcal{T} = (X, Y, I, T)$ consisting of a (non-empty) set of *state variables* $X = \{x_1, \ldots, x_n\}$, a (possibly empty) set of *input variables* $Y = \{y_1, \ldots, y_m\}$, and two formulas: I, the *initial states*, and T, the *transition relation*. Formulas over state variables, or *state formulas*, are identified

with the sets of states they denote; for example, the formula $(x_1 = x_2)$ denotes all states where x_1 and x_2 are equal, and other variables may have any value. The *state space* of $\mathcal{T}$ is the set of all valuations to variables in X. The set of *next-state variables* is $X' = \{x'_1, x'_2, \ldots, x'_n\}$. For a formula σ, $\text{Vars}(\sigma)$ denotes the set of state variables free in σ (respectively, $\text{Vars}'(\sigma)$ denotes the set of next-state variables in σ). We may write σ as $\sigma(X)$ when we wish to emphasize that the free variables in σ are drawn solely from the set X, i.e., $\text{Vars}(\sigma(X)) \subseteq X$; similarly for $\sigma(X')$ (also written σ'). The system's *transition relation* $T(X, Y, X')$ is a formula over the current-state, next-state, and input variables.

A (possibly-infinite) sequence of states $\sigma_0(X), \sigma_1(X), \ldots$ is an *execution* of a transition system if $\sigma_0(X) \models I(X)$ and for every pair $(\sigma_i(X), \sigma_{i+1}(X))$, $\sigma_i(X) \wedge T \models \sigma'_{i+1}(X)$.

A *safety property* is specified by a formula, $P(X)$. The *model checking problem* is to determine whether any state satisfying $\neg P(X)$ is reachable through an execution of T. A *counterexample* to a safety property $P(X)$ is a k-step execution such that $\sigma_k(X) \models \neg P(X)$.

A *concrete transition system* (CTS) is defined over bit vector and array state variables and operations in the quantifier-free logic of bit vectors and arrays (QF_ABV from SMT-LIB [6]).

III. MODEL CHECKING WITH EUF AND ARRAYS

To better understand how arrays are handled within EUF-ORIA, we first review EUFORIA's data abstraction approach. It is the inspiration and basis for our array abstraction.

EUFORIA homomorphically maps bit vector operations into uninterpreted functions in order to avoid potentially expensive reasoning (e.g., nonlinear computations). EUF operation abstraction was introduced by Burch and Dill [7] for checking the equivalence between pipelined computer architectures and their single-step specifications. EUFORIA adopts and extends this abstraction to check for general safety properties. For purposes of this paper, we assume there is an abstraction function $[\![.]\!]$ that homomorphically maps a given concrete transition relation to an EUF transition relation. For instance, $[\![x' = x + 1]\!] = (\widehat{x}' = \text{ADD}(\widehat{x}, \widehat{1}))$. State variables, inputs, and constants are mapped to uninterpreted 0-arity terms with hats (e.g., $x \mapsto \widehat{x}$, and $1 \mapsto \widehat{1}$). Operations are mapped to appropriately-named UFs. The crucial property guaranteed by this abstraction is that executions of the EUF transition system over-approximate the executions of the concrete transition system. The details of EUFORIA's translation are available in previous work [1].

EUFORIA performs an incremental induction reachability search based on IC3 [2], a model checking algorithm for finite, Boolean transition systems. EUFORIA uses a counterexample-guided abstraction refinement (CEGAR) [8] approach that extends IC3 to apply to EUF transition systems while retaining termination.

EUFORIA takes a model checking problem as input, (X, Y, I, T, P). It maps the CTS and property to produce a corresponding EUF abstract transition system (ATS) and property, $(\widehat{X}, \widehat{Y}, \widehat{I}, \widehat{T}, \widehat{P})$. EUFORIA then alternates between two phases: EUF reachability and abstraction refinement. EUF reachability searches for a counterexample in the ATS. If no counterexample is found, soundness of the ATS proves that the property holds in the CTS. Otherwise, abstraction refinement analyzes the counterexample to determine if it is feasible in the CTS and, if not, modifies the EUF abstraction to increase its fidelity to the CTS. We first give a brief review of EUF reachability [1] before focusing on refinement.

As in IC3, EUF reachability operates on an iteratively deepened sequence of reachable sets of formulas, R_i, each denoting an over-approximation of the set of states reachable in i transitions ($0 \leq i \leq N$). The algorithm maintains the following invariants:

$$R_0 = \widehat{I}(\widehat{X}) \tag{5}$$

$$R_i \models R_{i+1} \tag{6}$$

$$R_i \models \widehat{P}(\widehat{X}) \qquad (i < N) \tag{7}$$

$$R_{i+1} \text{ over-approximates the image of } R_i \tag{8}$$

EUF reachability computes an inductive invariant for $\widehat{P}$ or a counterexample to the safety property. An *inductive invariant* $\widehat{S}$ for $\widehat{P}$ has the following properties:

$$\widehat{I} \models \widehat{S}, \qquad \widehat{S} \wedge \widehat{T} \models \widehat{S}', \text{ and } \qquad \widehat{S} \models \widehat{P}.$$

This paper brings arrays into the mix. In order to avoid the overhead of instantiating array axioms, array operations and terms may be abstracted. The operations select, store, and const-array are mapped into corresponding uninterpreted functions, **select**, **store**, and **const-array** by extending the EUF abstraction mapping $[\![\cdot]\!]$ to array terms and operations as follows:

$$[\![a : \text{Array}]\!] = \widehat{a} \tag{9}$$

$$[\![\text{select}(a, i)]\!] = \textbf{select}([\![a]\!], [\![i]\!]) \tag{10}$$

$$[\![\text{store}(a, i, x)]\!] = \textbf{store}([\![a]\!], [\![i]\!], [\![x]\!]) \tag{11}$$

$$[\![\text{const-array}(k)]\!] = \textbf{const-array}([\![k]\!]) \tag{12}$$

The array abstraction fits neatly into EUFORIA's data abstraction approach. In fact, this abstraction approach keeps EUFORIA reasoning at the pure (quantifier-free) uninterpreted function level, for which there are efficient decision procedures.

IV. ABSTRACTION REFINEMENT FOR ARRAYS

EUF reachability may find an abstract counterexample (ACX). Due to EUF abstraction, the concretized abstract counterexample (CACX) may *not* be a counterexample in the CTS. For example, consider the transition system $\mathcal{E} = (X, Y, I, T)$ defined as

$$(\{A, i\}, \emptyset, [\text{select}(A, i) = 3], [A' = \text{store}(A, i, 3)])$$

with the property, $P = [\text{select}(A, i) = 3]$, which is its own safety invariant. Nevertheless, $[\![P]\!]$ does not hold in $\widehat{\mathcal{E}}$, since EUF abstraction does not preserve the relationship between store and select, and yields the two-step CACX $(I, \text{select}(A, i) \neq 3)$ which is infeasible in the QF_ABV

theory. EUFORIA uses this contradictory CACX to *refine*, or increase the fidelity of, the abstraction. Refinement is accomplished by conjoining formulas, called lemmas, to the abstract transition relation.

In this example, EUFORIA learns an instance of McCarthy's axiom (1), to eliminate the spurious behavior caused by the abstraction:

$$\widehat{A}' = \textbf{store}(\widehat{A}, \widehat{i}, \widehat{3}) \Rightarrow \textbf{select}(\widehat{A}', \widehat{i}) = \widehat{3}$$

This lemma constrains the abstract state space of $\widehat{\mathcal{E}}$ and is therefore appropriately called a *constraint lemma*. Constraint lemmas restrict the behavior of uninterpreted functions to make them conform more closely to the behavior of their concrete counterparts. A second type of refinement involves learning *expansion lemmas*, which introduce new terms from CACXs. We will discuss these after we present our implementation of abstraction refinement.

A. Implementation of Abstraction Refinement

Our implementation first attempts to derive constraint lemmas by examining individual states and transitions of the abstract counterexample. If none are found, it performs a bounded model check (BMC) of the entire counterexample. If that check is inconsistent, then EUFORIA calculates interpolants from which it derives expansion lemmas. We use a Horn clause solver (SPACER) for convenience to calculate the interpolants; but the interpolants could be obtained using any interpolating theorem prover for QF_ABV. We will discuss each part of refinement in turn.

An n-step *abstract counterexample* is an execution $\widehat{A}_0, \widehat{A}_1, \ldots, \widehat{A}_n$ in $\widehat{T}$ where each $\widehat{A}_i$ ($0 \leq i \leq n$) is a state formula. An abstract formula $\widehat{\sigma}$ is *feasible* if its concretization σ is satisfiable over QF_ABV; therefore, an abstract counterexample is feasible if its concretization is a counterexample in the CTS.

EUFORIA's refinement procedure, BUILDCX, is given in Figure 1a; it has three stages. The first stage (lines 1–3) checks whether each $\widehat{A}_i$ is feasible ($0 \leq i \leq n$). The second stage (lines 4–6) checks whether each $\widehat{A}_{i-1} \wedge \widehat{T} \wedge \widehat{A}_i'$ is feasible ($0 < i \leq n$). If an infeasible state or transition is found during the first two stages, we compute an UNSAT core, negate it, and abstract it to form a constraint lemma (in LEARNLEMMA). States and transitions are prioritized over the third stage, BMC, because it is advantageous to learn constraint lemmas, since they make the abstract state space smaller.

Nevertheless, EUFORIA must learn across multiple counterexample steps in general. Therefore, the third stage, BUILD-BMCCX, performs a BMC query to learn across multiple steps of the counterexample; this is shown in Figure 1b. This stage of refinement has two phases.

a) BUILDBMCCX phase one, BMC solving: In phase one (lines 1–2), BMCFORMULA constructs the instance as

BUILDCX():

Returns true if counterexample is true, false if abstraction is refined

input: counterexample $(\widehat{A}_0, \widehat{A}_1, \ldots, \widehat{A}_n)$ in $\widehat{T}$

1: **if** $\exists i \in \{0, \ldots, n\}. \neg\mathrm{SAT}[A_i]$ **then**
2:     LEARNLEMMA(UNSATCORE())
3:     **return** false
4: **if** $\exists i \in \{1, \ldots, n\}. \neg\mathrm{SAT}[A_{i-1} \wedge T \wedge A'_i]$ **then**
5:     LEARNLEMMA(UNSATCORE())
6:     **return** false
7: **return** BUILDBMCCX()

(a) The first two stages of refinement: examining concretized states and transitions.

BUILDBMCCX():

1: $\mathcal{B} \leftarrow$ BMCFORMULA()
2: **if** $\neg\mathrm{SAT}[\mathcal{B}]$ **then**
3:     REFINEWITHINTERPOLANTS(UNSATCORE())
4:     **return** false
5: **return** true $\triangleright$ feasible counterexample

(b) The third stage of refinement, bounded model checking and interpolant calculation.

Fig. 1: EUFORIA's refinement procedure, BUILDBMCCX.

1: **procedure** MBPOUTER(M, f)
2:     $S \leftarrow \emptyset; r \leftarrow \mathrm{MBP}(f); \mathbf{return}\ S \cup \{\mathrm{Lit}(r)\}$
3: **procedure** MBP(f)
4:     **switch** f **do**
5:         **case** x $\triangleright x$ a 0-arity term
6:             **return** x
7:         **case** $\mathrm{F}(t_1, t_2, \ldots, t_n)$
8:             **return** $\mathrm{F}(\mathrm{MBP}(t_1), \mathrm{MBP}(t_2), \ldots, \mathrm{MBP}(t_n))$
9:         **case** $\mathrm{ite}(c, t_1, t_2)$ $\triangleright$ traverse satisfied branch
10:            $S \leftarrow S \cup \{\mathrm{Lit}(\mathrm{MBP}(c))\}$
11:            **if** $M \models c$ **then return** $\mathrm{MBP}(t_1)$
12:            **else return** $\mathrm{MBP}(t_2)$
13:        **case** b $\triangleright b$ a Boolean variable or its negation
14:            **return** $\mathrm{Lit}(b)$
15:        **case** $t_1 = t_2$
16:            **return** $\mathrm{Lit}(\mathrm{MBP}(t_1) = \mathrm{MBP}(t_2))$
17:        **case** $\mathrm{P}(t_1, t_2, \ldots, t_n)$
18:            **return** $\mathrm{Lit}(\mathrm{P}(\mathrm{MBP}(t_1), \mathrm{MBP}(t_2), \ldots, \mathrm{MBP}(t_n)))$
19:        **case** $f_1 \wedge f_2$
20:            **if** $M \models f$ **then return** $\mathrm{MBP}(f_1) \wedge \mathrm{MBP}(f_2)$
21:            **else if** $M \models \neg f_1$ **then return** $\mathrm{MBP}(f_1)$
22:            **else return** $\mathrm{MBP}(f_2)$ $\triangleright M \models \neg f_2$
23:        **case** $f_1 \vee f_2$
24:            **if** $M \models f_1$ **then return** $\mathrm{MBP}(f_1)$
25:            **else if** $M \models f_2$ **then return** $\mathrm{MBP}(f_2)$
26:            **else return** $\mathrm{MBP}(f_1) \wedge \mathrm{MBP}(f_2)$ $\triangleright M \models \neg f$

Fig. 2: Model-based projection of a formula f with model M where $M \models f$. MBPOUTER(M, f) $= S_{\mathrm{MBP}}$ computes a set S_{MBP} of constraints for a formula f such that $M \models S_{\mathrm{MBP}}$ and $S_{\mathrm{MBP}} \models f$. Essentially, it justifies the model of f. In the figure, $\mathrm{Lit}(b) = b$ if $M \models b$ and $\mathrm{Lit}(b) = \neg b$ if $M \models \neg b$.

below by explicitly renaming variables and using multiple copies of T:

$$\begin{aligned} \mathcal{B} = {}& A(X_0) \wedge I(X_0) \wedge T(X_0, Y_1, X_1) \wedge \\ & A(X_1) \wedge T(X_1, Y_2, X_2) \wedge \ldots \wedge \\ & A(X_{n-1}) \wedge T(X_{n-1}, Y_n, X_n) \wedge A(X_n) \end{aligned}$$

$\mathcal{B}$ is then checked for feasibility. Solving BMC queries is challenging for several reasons. First, there are multiple copies of T. Second, T is monolithic because it encodes the entire program, even though only part of the program is relevant for a given counterexample step. Third, even if we could reduce T at each step by removing irrelevant parts, using a large-step encoding [9] for T means that the reduced T would likely still contain a whole pile of nested Boolean logic, not all of which is necessarily relevant.

At a high level, we address these difficulties by conjoining extra constraints onto $\mathcal{B}$ that significantly prune its search space. These constraints are derived from abstract models gathered during EUFORIA's EUF reachability (see Section III). We use our model-based projection procedure, MBPOuter, given in Figure 2, to derive these extra constraints from the abstract transition relation. We now detail how we solve $\mathcal{B}$.

Let $\widehat{M}_i^{i+1}$ denote the abstract model for the transition $(\widehat{A}_i, \widehat{A}_{i+1})$ in the abstract counterexample ($0 \leq i < n$). We augment the query $\mathcal{B}$ so that each $T(X_i, Y_{i+1}, X_{i+1})$ is conjoined with the concretization of the constraints in $\mathrm{MBPOuter}(\widehat{M}_i^{i+1}, \widehat{T}(\widehat{X}_i, \widehat{Y}_{i+1}, \widehat{X}_{i+1}))$. The effect of this is that nested logic in $\widehat{T}$ is projected away by justifying the model $\widehat{M}_i^{i+1}$ of the transition. Next, we pre-process $\mathcal{B}$ by an equation solving pass that performs Gaussian elimination and variable elimination.[1] Variables assigned to constants at the top-level will be removed, possibly opening up other elimination opportunities. Linear constraints are solved, leading to further variable elimination. Combining equation-solving with extra constraints addresses difficulties two (T is monolithic) and three (T contains much nested logic). In practice, their combination achieves efficiency far beyond what either does in isolation. Finally, if $\mathcal{B}$ is feasible (BUILDBMCCX line 5), it is a counterexample to the property. If $\mathcal{B}$ is infeasible, BUILDBMCCX enters phase two.

b) BUILDBMCCX phase two, interpolants: Phase two is implemented in REFINEWITHINTERPOLANTS, given in Figure 3. BUILDHORN uses $\mathcal{B}$'s UNSAT core to create a (reduced) inductive interpolant sequence problem $\mathcal{B}_{HC}$ [10] using only the constraints from $\mathcal{B}$ that occur in the core. $\mathcal{B}_{HC}$ is a set of recursion-free Horn clauses in which uninterpreted

---

[1] The `solve-eqs` tactic in Z3.

REFINEWITHINTERPOLANTS($core$):
1: $\mathcal{B}_{HC} \leftarrow$ BUILDHORN($core$)
2: $\mathcal{M} \leftarrow$ HORNSOLVE($\mathcal{B}_{HC}$)
3: **for** $i \in \{1, \ldots, n\}$ **do**
4:    $p_i \leftarrow$ GETINTERPOLANT($\mathcal{M}, i$)
5:    $p_{i+1} \leftarrow$ GETINTERPOLANT($\mathcal{M}, i+1$)
6:    $l \leftarrow p_{i-1}(X) \land body_i(X, Y, X') \land \neg p_i(X')$
7:    LEARNLEMMA(l)

Fig. 3: Constructs lemmas from an inductive interpolant sequence derived from a solution to (satisfiable) Horn clauses. GETINTERPOLANT($\mathcal{M}, i$) returns a formula, the ith interpolant in the interpolant sequence, given a model for $\mathcal{B}_{HC}$.

predicates p_i stand for step-wise interpolants:

$$p_0(X_0) \Leftarrow true$$
$$p_1(X_1) \Leftarrow p_0(X_0) \land A^*(X_0) \land I(X_0) \land T^*(X_0, Y_1, X_1)$$
$$p_2(X_2) \Leftarrow p_1(X_1) \land A^*(X_1) \land T^*(X_1, Y_2, X_2)$$
$$\vdots$$
$$p_n(X_n) \Leftarrow p_{n-1}(X_{n-1}) \land A^*(X_{n-1}) \land T^*(X_{n-1}, Y_n, X_n)$$
$$false \Leftarrow p_n(X_n)$$

where $F^* = \bigwedge \{f \in F \mid f \in \text{UnsatCore}(\mathcal{B})\}$ for $F \in \{A, T\}$.[2] These Horn clauses are satisfiable by construction since $\mathcal{B}$ is infeasible.

For each nontrivial solution to the Horn clauses, we extract a lemma from the corresponding Horn clause as follows:

$$\neg[p_{i-1}(X) \land body_i(X, Y, X') \land \neg p_i(X')] \qquad 0 < i \leq n \quad (13)$$

where $body_i$ stands for the interpreted body predicates from the rule whose head is p_i.

We now return to the topic of expansion lemmas. Consider a program $x = 3; x = x + 3; assert(x < 7)$. Consider an (infeasible) 2-step counterexample $(x = 3, x \geq 7)$ and its corresponding set of Horn clauses:

$$p_0(3) \qquad (14)$$
$$p_1(x') \Leftarrow p_0(x) \land x' = x + 3 \qquad (15)$$
$$false \Leftarrow p_1(x) \land x \geq 7 \qquad (16)$$

A solution is $p_0(x) = (x = 3)$ and $p_1(x) = (x = 6)$ which results in the following lemmas (see (13)):

$$\neg[x = 3 \land y = x + 3 \land y \neq 6] \qquad (17)$$
$$\neg[x = 6 \land x \geq 7] \qquad (18)$$

The key take-away here is that these lemmas introduce the new term 6 into the abstraction, which previously only contained terms from the program text, namely 3, i, 7, and the addition and less-than. These lemmas increase the granularity of the

---

[2]$\mathcal{B}_{HC}$ could be computed without $\mathcal{B}$'s UNSAT core, but using it promotes learning concise lemmas, because it substantially reduces the complexity of the Horn clause bodies. See equation (13).

LEARNLEMMA(f):
Precondition: f is unsatisfiable in QF_ABV
1: $\widehat{f} \leftarrow$ ABSTRACTANDNORMALIZE(f)   ▷ abstract and eliminate input variables
2: **if** f contains no inputs **then**
3:    **if** VARS(f) $\subseteq X$ **then**   ▷ only present-state vars
4:       Simplify and add lemma $\neg\widehat{f}(\widehat{X}')$
5:    **if** VARS(f) $\subseteq X'$ **then**   ▷ only next-state vars
6:       Simplify and add lemma $\neg\widehat{f}(\widehat{X})$
7: Simplify and add lemma $\neg\widehat{f}$

Fig. 4: Learns a lemma by abstracting and conjoining $\neg\widehat{f}$ to $\widehat{T}$

abstraction. This kind of learning is similar to learning new predicates in a predicate abstraction (e.g., [11]).

Lemmas are expansion lemmas only when the interpolants contain new terms. Using our method implies that the interpolation system itself decides whether a particular lemma is expansive or not; EUFORIA does not make this decision explicitly. EUFORIA's back-end uses SPACER to solve $\mathcal{B}_{HC}$.

Refinement is not guaranteed to succeed. We require quantifier-free interpolants but interpolants for arrays in general are not quantifier-free [12]. Moreover, the interpolant back-end may give up.

To sum up, constraint lemmas specialize UFs to particular concrete behaviors. Expansion lemmas increase the granularity of the EUF abstraction. EUFORIA learns array lemmas only if they crop up in a CACX's contradiction, ensuring that the lemmas are directly relevant to the property that is being checked. Empirically speaking, contradictions usually feature a small handful of UFs which are ultimately relevant to the property, resulting in targeted lemmas. Our process avoids most of the expense of array lemma generation, as we will see in the evaluation.

B. Exceptionally Lazy Learning of Array Lemmas

Fundamentally, the procedure LEARNLEMMA (Figure 4) learns its lemmas by negating formulas found to be unsatisfiable in QF_ABV and conjoining them to $\widehat{T}$. It also simplifies the formulas in order to generalize the lemmas as much as possible, specifically by eliminating input variables (line 1). We eliminate input variables from formulas by (1) collecting top-level equalities and computing their equality closure, resulting in equivalence classes of terms; and (2) substituting every input with a member of its equivalence class that doesn't contain inputs (if possible). Next, if the lemma formula is a state formula, then two versions are learned: one on current-state variables and one on next-state variables (lines 2–6).

Consequently, EUFORIA generates property-directed instantiations of array theory axioms. For instance, here is a lemma learned in one of our benchmarks:

$$A \neq \text{const-array}(0) \lor 0 \neq \text{select}(A, i) \qquad (19)$$

This lemma is an instance of axiom (4). We also find instances of McCarthy's axiom (1):

$$\text{select}(A', i) = 0 \vee i' \neq i \vee A' \neq \text{store}(A, i', 0) \qquad (20)$$

Array lemmas may also include bit-vector function symbols to learn targeted lemmas about composite behavior:

$$B \neq \text{store}(A, i, 0) \vee \text{extract}(7, 0, \text{select}(B, i)) \neq 0 \qquad (21)$$

Finally, some lemmas combine multiple array axioms:

$$\text{store}(B, i, 0) \neq A \vee \text{store}(A, i, 0) = A \qquad (22)$$

This lemma relates stores and array extensionality. It is not a direct instance of any axiom (1)–(4), but rather a consequence of several instantiations.

We note that LEARNLEMMA is not specialized to produce array lemmas. Rather, it generalizes formulas from unsatisfiable refinement queries that themselves pinpoint which array lemma instantiations to learn. This design allows LEARNLEMMA to produce lemmas that are property-directed combinations of array theory axiom instantiations.

V. EVALUATION

To evaluate EUFORIA, we rely on benchmarks from SV-COMP'17 [13], as they are widely used and relatively well understood. We evaluate on C programs from the Systems_DeviceDriversLinux64_ReachSafety benchmark set, hereafter abbreviated *DeviceDrivers*. This set contains 64-bit C programs and contains "problems that require the analysis of pointer aliases and function pointers." EUFORIA was originally designed for control properties, so our benchmark set includes benchmarks with control properties and arrays.

We consider two other model checkers, SPACER and IC3IA. SPACER [14], [15], [16] is an over- and under-approximation driven incremental model checker that is tightly integrated with Z3. It computes procedure summaries to support checking programs with recursive functions. It is capable of inferring quantified array invariants and uses model-based projection array procedures to lazily instantiate property-directed array axioms, making the checker particularly efficient. IC3IA [11] is an IC3-style CEGAR model checker that implements implicit predicate abstraction. IC3IA's architecture is quite similar EUFORIA's, more similar than SPACER's. As discussed in Cimatti [11], IC3IA is superior to state-of-the-art bit-level IC3 implementations and can support hundreds of predicates, around an order of magnitude more than what explicit predicate abstraction tools practically support. We also evaluated ELDARICA [17], a predicate-abstraction based CEGAR model checker that supports integers, algebraic data types, arrays, and bit vectors. Unfortunately, ELDARICA either threw errors, ran out of time, or ran out of memory on all of our benchmarks, so we do not consider it further.

We use SeaHorn as a front-end to encode programs into Horn clauses. SeaHorn [18] is a verification condition (VC) generator for C and C++ programs that uses LLVM in order to optimize and generate large-step, Horn clause benchmarks in SMT-LIB declare-rel format [19]. Note that we use the term benchmark to refer both to the C programs and their encoded counterparts. Since SeaHorn is not able to produce bit-vector encoded benchmarks, we modified it to produce bit-vector VCs.[3] Moreover, since EUFORIA does not yet support procedure calls, we instruct SeaHorn to inline all procedures, resulting in linear Horn clauses. We ran SeaHorn on each benchmark, limiting it to one hour of runtime and 8GB of memory. SeaHorn can fail to produce a usable benchmark due to lack of resources or because the input is trivially solved during optimization. All told, SeaHorn produced 948 *DeviceDrivers* Horn clause benchmarks out of 2703 original C programs. 687 are safe and 261 are unsafe.

SPACER natively supports Horn clauses, but EUFORIA and IC3IA take VMT files as input. The VMT format [20] is a syntax-compatible extension of the SMT-LIB format that specifies a syntax for labeling formulas denoting initial state, the transition relation, and property. In order to create comparable benchmarks for EUFORIA and IC3IA, we translate the Horn clause benchmarks into VMT using Horn2VMT [21], resulting in 948 VMT files that correspond to the 948 Horn benchmarks. The benchmarks range in size from 2^9 to more than 2^{23}, with a median size of 2^{19}; this size is the number of distinct SMT-LIB expressions used to define (I, T, P). When compressed with gzip, their sizes range from 2K to 153 MB.

All checkers run on 2.6 GHz Intel Sandy Bridge (Xeon E5-2670) machines with 2 sockets, 8 cores with 64GB RAM, running RedHat Enterprise Linux 7. Each checker run was assigned to one socket during execution and was given a 30 minute timeout. For every benchmark solved by any checker, we verified that its result was consistent with other checkers.

A. EUFORIA *compared with* SPACER

Figure 5 shows a scatter plot of runtime for EUFORIA and SPACER on *DeviceDrivers* benchmarks. Overall, EUFORIA solves 491 benchmarks and SPACER solves 386. EUFORIA times out on 33 benchmarks that SPACER solves. SPACER times out on 138 benchmarks that EUFORIA solves.

a) When SPACER *solves* EUFORIA*'s timeouts:* In the 33 cases where spacer was able to solve a benchmark that EUFORIA could not, we identified several causes:

1) SPACER's preprocessor is able to solve 19 benchmarks without even invoking search. By comparison, EUFORIA's front-end takes excessive time to parse and normalize the benchmarks. EUFORIA parses VMT files using MathSAT5, since it the simplest API to do so. In addition to parsing, MathSAT normalizes and simplifies the resulting formula.

2) Another 12 benchmarks are quite large, and the overhead of a monolithic transition relation dominates EUFORIA's abstract reachability. To explain: SeaHorn produces an *explicitly sliced* transition relation which SPACER exploits by making sliced incremental queries. EUFORIA consumes and queries a monolithic transition relation as produced by Horn2VMT.

---

[3]We worked from SeaHorn commit id 8e51ef84360a602804fce58cc5b7019f1f17d2dc.

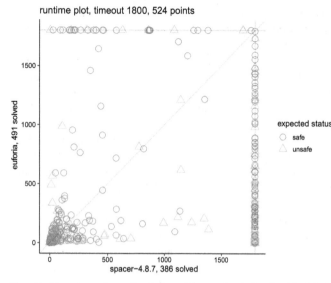

Fig. 5: Benchmarks solved by either solver (or both). Note the points on the right hand side of this plot. Each point is a benchmark that EUFORIA solved within 30 minutes that SPACER did not solve during that time.

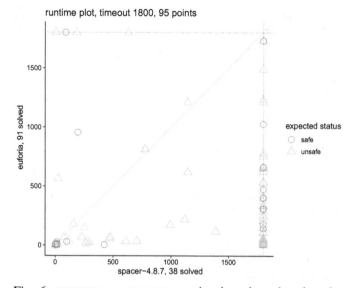

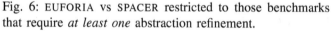

Fig. 6: EUFORIA vs SPACER restricted to those benchmarks that require *at least one* abstraction refinement.

3) In one benchmark EUFORIA gets stuck in a single interpolation query. We suspect this is because some interpolation queries generated by EUFORIA are unexpectedly difficult for SPACER.

In the last un-accounted for benchmark, there was no obvious cause. We believe that front-end improvements would address the issues identified in item 2. For instance, SPACER's preprocessor could be made independent of z_3 so that it could be applied before Horn2VMT.[4] Alternatively, EUFORIA could be integrated into z_3 so that it could exploit the same preprocessing as SPACER, but exploring this remains future work.

b) When EUFORIA *solves* SPACER*'s timeouts:* In the 138 cases where EUFORIA was able to solve a benchmark that SPACER did not, we examined causes. In over half of the cases, SPACER gets stuck solving concrete incremental queries. In the other 52 cases, SPACER gives up before the timeout (it returns unknown). In other words, in every case individual queries were unable to be tackled given the resources constraints. Therefore we emphasize that, in contrast, EUFORIA has the strong benefit of making individual queries predictably fast.

We wondered: is EUFORIA only winning because it hardly needs to do refinement? The answer is no. Figure 6 shows the same scatter plot as Figure 5 but restricted to EUFORIA-solved benchmarks that required at least one abstraction refinement. It shows that EUFORIA requires refinement for many of the benchmarks for which SPACER times out.

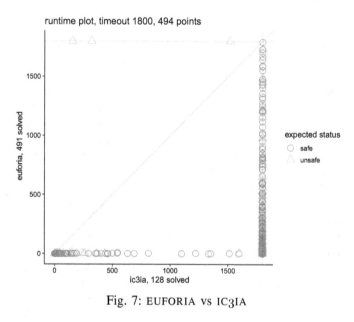

Fig. 7: EUFORIA vs IC3IA

B. EUFORIA *compared with* IC3IA

Figure 7 shows a scatter plot of our results compared with IC3IA. IC3IA solves 128 benchmarks total. Excepting three of these, EUFORIA solves *all* the benchmarks that IC3IA solves, usually in orders of magnitude less time. Our results are significant because IC3IA and EUFORIA are quite similar: both implement a PDR-style [22] algorithm, both operate on *exactly* the same VMT instance encoding, and both are written it C++. They differ in two respects: (1) IC3IA uses (implicit) predicate abstraction and EUFORIA uses EUF abstraction; (2) IC3IA's SMT solver backend is MathSAT5 and EUFORIA's is z_3.

On the benchmarks where EUFORIA times out, two benchmarks get stuck after several seconds in an interpolant query; the other learns a pile of lemmas but doesn't converge in time.

---

[4]We tried dumping the benchmark after SPACER's preprocessing step, but the benchmark was no longer guaranteed to be Horn, so it was not a valid input for encoding to VMT with Horn2VMT.

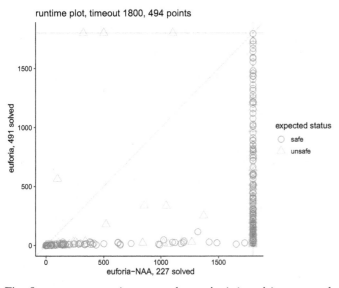

Fig. 8: EUFORIA$_{NAA}$ (no array abstraction) (x axis) compared with EUFORIA (y axis).

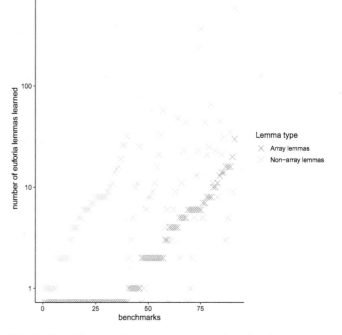

Fig. 9: Breakdown of lemmas as array-related and non array-related on the subset of benchmarks (91) for which any lemma learning was required (y axis is log scale).

C. EUFORIA *and array abstraction*

For solvers that use lazy theory lemma learning or a trigger-based saturation method [23], array lemmas will be learned in response to property-directed queries. Does EUFORIA's array abstraction really provide a benefit over such an approach?

To address this question, we modified EUFORIA to compute a hybrid abstraction using the theory of EUF and arrays. It abstracts bit-vector operations into UFs (as before), but uses array theory operations for arrays. Call this configuration EUFORIA$_{NAA}$, for No Array Abstraction.

As demonstrated in Figure 8, EUFORIA$_{NAA}$ is significantly slower almost everywhere and strictly slower in all cases but four. One important difference between EUFORIA and EUFORIA$_{NAA}$ is an enormous disparity in array theory lemmas learned by the underlying SMT solver. Between configurations, the difference of the number of array theory lemma instantiations is almost two orders of magnitude (1.9), on 95% of the benchmarks; almost four orders of magnitude (3.8), on 50% of the benchmarks; and more than seven orders of magnitude (7.2), on 5%. To calculate this result, we measure the number of array theory axiom instantiations in the underlying SMT solver (z3). Then, for each benchmark, we took the difference of the logs (base 10) between the two configurations; this quantity is proportional to the order of magnitude difference between the numbers.

We conclude that EUFORIA$_{NAA}$ spends a lot of time reasoning about arrays despite the fact that EUFORIA required relatively little array reasoning to solve the same benchmarks. Moreover, compared to SPACER's 386 solves, EUFORIA$_{NAA}$ solves only 227 instances, which (1) shows that array abstraction is critical to performance and (2) gives some additional evidence that SPACER's array projection helps its runtime.

D. EUFORIA *in itself—the role of lemmas*

This section discusses EUFORIA's learned lemmas as detailed in Section IV. Lemmas in general play a relatively minor role; they're only required in 19% of benchmarks that EUFORIA solved (91). Moreover, only 22 benchmarks required interpolants. Figure 9 shows the count of total lemmas learned, broken down by whether EUFORIA learned array lemmas or non-array lemmas. First, we can see that there is a trend that EUFORIA learns fewer array lemmas than data lemmas. Second, all but two benchmarks required fewer than 100 lemmas. These results suggest our benchmarks only depend sparingly on the behavior of memory manipulations, and confirm the suitability of EUFORIA's abstraction. SPACER solves 34 of these benchmarks; out of 34, 14 benchmarks require array lemmas and 20 do not.

VI. RELATED WORK

The relationship between EUF and the theory of arrays has been long recognized [24], [12] and analyzed [25] and exploited in decision procedures [26] and in the implementation of several SMT solvers, including Yices [27] and z3 [28]. Array terms are compiled into EUF or a ground theory to instantiate the needed array axioms. Our approach lifts EUF outside the SMT solver, to the model checking level, and refines it on demand.

Komuravelli *et al.* introduce a model-based projection for pre-images in order to rewrite array operators into terms in a scalar theory [16]; this algorithm is implemented in SPACER [15] used in our evaluation. Predicate abstraction applies to programs with arrays directly [11], with the limitation that quantifier-free interpolants do not exist in general for the theory of arrays [12]. We inherit that limitation, but contribute a different, inexpensive way to place array constraints in pre-images and refine them lazily.

Broadly, SMT solvers solve constraints over arrays in three ways (sometimes combined): (1) by rewriting selects and stores into a finite number of terms and axiom instantiations in a ground theory, possibly combined with EUF [29], [30], [24], [31], [25], [32], [33], [23], [26]; (2) by abstraction-refinement procedures over the array constraints [34], [35]; (3) by rewriting into (non-abstract) representations which are solved with specialized algorithms [36], [37], [38]. The issue addressed by our paper is applicable to each of these: we use an abstraction that inexpensively supports (limited) array reasoning and we only invoke an SMT array solver at the last possible moment.

VII. Conclusion and Future Work

This paper introduces an approach for model checking software with arrays that avoids substantial computational effort spent in reasoning about arrays by using EUF abstraction. We integrated our approach inside a incremental model checker that natively supports EUF abstraction. Our approach bests stiff competition on control-oriented benchmarks, solving over 100 more benchmarks.

We demonstrated that our approach reduces the amount of redundant or irrelevant array reasoning by several orders of magnitude in most cases. We are eager to investigate the possibilities of expanding our universe of target programs. As software size grows, its sheer size begins to overwhelm the checker, even if the property to prove is relatively simple (for a machine). Inlining all functions only exacerbates the problem. In future work we plan to explore compositional reasoning, in particular analyzing programs with procedures by integrating it efficiently with our EUF abstraction.

We find that for some benchmarks, stronger lemmas are required to speed up convergence. We would like to address this by inferring quantified lemmas during search. One issue is how to generalize counterexamples to quantified lemmas. A second issue is how to keep the abstraction tractable in the presence of quantified lemmas. Both of these issues form important future work.

Acknowledgment

We thank Arie Gurfinkel and Nikolaj Bjørner for their help regarding SPACER and Z3 internals. We thank the anonymous reviewers for their helpful feedback.

References

[1] D. Bueno and K. A. Sakallah, "EUFORIA: Complete software model checking with uninterpreted functions," in *Verification, Model Checking, and Abstract Interpretation - 20th International Conference, VMCAI 2019, Cascais, Portugal, January 13-15, 2019, Proceedings*, ser. Lecture Notes in Computer Science, C. Enea and R. Piskac, Eds., vol. 11388. Springer, 2019, pp. 363–385.

[2] A. R. Bradley, "SAT-based model checking without unrolling," in *Verification, Model Checking, and Abstract Interpretation*, ser. Lecture Notes in Computer Science, R. Jhala and D. A. Schmidt, Eds., vol. 6538, Springer. Springer, 2011, pp. 70–87.

[3] J. McCarthy, "Towards a mathematical science of computation," in *Information Processing, Proceedings of the 2nd IFIP Congress 1962, Munich, Germany, August 27 - September 1, 1962*. North-Holland, 1962, pp. 21–28.

[4] E. M. Clarke, O. Grumberg, and D. E. Long, "Model checking and abstraction," *ACM Trans. Program. Lang. Syst.*, vol. 16, no. 5, pp. 1512–1542, 1994.

[5] A. R. Bradley and Z. Manna, "Checking safety by inductive generalization of counterexamples to induction," in *Formal Methods in Computer-Aided Design*. IEEE Computer Society, 2007, pp. 173–180.

[6] C. Barrett, A. Stump, and C. Tinelli, "The SMT-LIB Standard: Version 2.0," in *Workshop on Satisfiability Modulo Theories*, A. Gupta and D. Kroening, Eds., 2010.

[7] J. R. Burch and D. L. Dill, "Automatic verification of pipelined microprocessor control," in *Computer Aided Verification*, ser. Lecture Notes in Computer Science, D. L. Dill, Ed., vol. 818. Springer, 1994, pp. 68–80.

[8] E. M. Clarke, O. Grumberg, S. Jha, Y. Lu, and H. Veith, "Counterexample-guided abstraction refinement," in *Computer Aided Verification*, ser. Lecture Notes in Computer Science, E. A. Emerson and A. P. Sistla, Eds., vol. 1855. Springer, 2000, pp. 154–169.

[9] D. Beyer, A. Cimatti, A. Griggio, M. E. Keremoglu, and R. Sebastiani, "Software model checking via large-block encoding," in *Formal Methods in Computer-Aided Design*. IEEE, 2009, pp. 25–32.

[10] P. Rümmer, H. Hojjat, and V. Kuncak, "Classifying and solving horn clauses for verification," in *Verified Software: Theories, Tools, Experiments*, ser. Lecture Notes in Computer Science, E. Cohen and A. Rybalchenko, Eds., vol. 8164. Springer, 2013, pp. 1–21. [Online]. Available: https://doi.org/10.1007/978-3-642-54108-7_1

[11] A. Cimatti, A. Griggio, S. Mover, and S. Tonetta, "IC3 modulo theories via implicit predicate abstraction," in *Tools and Algorithms for the Construction and Analysis of Systems*, ser. Lecture Notes in Computer Science, E. Ábrahám and K. Havelund, Eds., vol. 8413. Springer, 2014, pp. 46–61.

[12] D. Kapur, R. Majumdar, and C. G. Zarba, "Interpolation for data structures," in *SIGSOFT FSE*, M. Young and P. T. Devanbu, Eds. ACM, 2006, pp. 105–116. [Online]. Available: https://doi.org/10.1145/1181775.1181789

[13] D. Beyer, "Software verification with validation of results - (report on SV-COMP 2017)," in *Tools and Algorithms for the Construction and Analysis of Systems*, ser. Lecture Notes in Computer Science, A. Legay and T. Margaria, Eds., vol. 10206, 2017, pp. 331–349.

[14] A. Komuravelli, A. Gurfinkel, S. Chaki, and E. M. Clarke, "Automatic abstraction in smt-based unbounded software model checking," in *Computer Aided Verification*, ser. Lecture Notes in Computer Science, N. Sharygina and H. Veith, Eds., vol. 8044. Springer, 2013, pp. 846–862. [Online]. Available: https://doi.org/10.1007/978-3-642-39799-8_59

[15] A. Komuravelli, A. Gurfinkel, and S. Chaki, "SMT-Based Model Checking for Recursive Programs," in *Computer Aided Verification*, ser. Lecture Notes in Computer Science, A. Biere and R. Bloem, Eds., vol. 8559. Berlin, Heidelberg: Springer-Verlag, 2014, pp. 17–34. [Online]. Available: https://doi.org/10.1007/978-3-319-08867-9

[16] A. Komuravelli, N. Bjørner, A. Gurfinkel, and K. L. McMillan, "Compositional verification of procedural programs using horn clauses over integers and arrays," in *Formal Methods in Computer-Aided Design*, R. Kaivola and T. Wahl, Eds. IEEE, 2015, pp. 89–96.

[17] H. Hojjat and P. Rümmer, "The ELDARICA horn solver," in *2018 Formal Methods in Computer Aided Design, FMCAD 2018, Austin, TX, USA, October 30 - November 2, 2018*, N. Bjørner and A. Gurfinkel, Eds. IEEE, 2018, pp. 1–7. [Online]. Available: https://doi.org/10.23919/FMCAD.2018.8603013

[18] A. Gurfinkel, T. Kahsai, A. Komuravelli, and J. A. Navas, "The SeaHorn verification framework," in *Computer Aided Verification*, ser. Lecture Notes in Computer Science, D. Kroening and C. S. Pasareanu, Eds., vol. 9206. Springer, 2015, pp. 343–361.

[19] N. Bjørner, K. L. McMillan, and A. Rybalchenko, "Program verification as satisfiability modulo theories," in *Workshop on Satisfiability Modulo Theories*, ser. EPiC Series in Computing, P. Fontaine and A. Goel, Eds., vol. 20. EasyChair, 2012, pp. 3–11. [Online]. Available: https://easychair.org/publications/paper/qGkT

[20] F. B. Kessler, *The VMT format*, 2020 (accessed May 13, 2020). [Online]. Available: https://nuxmv.fbk.eu/index.php?n=Languages.VMT

[21] D. Bueno and K. Sakallah, "Horn2VMT: Translating horn reachability into transition systems," in *Workshop on Horn Clauses for Verification and Synthesis*, 2020, p. To appear.

[22] N. Een, A. Mishchenko, and R. Brayton, "Efficient implementation of property directed reachability," in *Formal Methods in Computer-Aided Design*. IEEE, 2011, pp. 125–134.

[23] L. M. de Moura and N. Bjørner, "Generalized, efficient array decision procedures," in *Formal Methods in Computer-Aided Design*. IEEE, 2009, pp. 45–52. [Online]. Available: https://doi.org/10.1109/FMCAD.2009.5351142

[24] D. Kapur and C. G. Zarba, "A reduction approach to decision procedures," University of New Mexico, Tech. Rep., 2005.

[25] A. Goel, S. Krstić, and A. Fuchs, "Deciding array formulas with frugal axiom instantiation," in *International Workshop on Satisfiability Modulo Theories*, ser. SMT '08. New York, NY, USA: ACM, 2008, pp. 12–17. [Online]. Available: http://doi.acm.org/10.1145/1512464.1512468

[26] A. R. Bradley, Z. Manna, and H. B. Sipma, "What's decidable about arrays?" in *Verification, Model Checking, and Abstract Interpretation*, ser. Lecture Notes in Computer Science, E. A. Emerson and K. S. Namjoshi, Eds., vol. 3855. Springer, 2006, pp. 427–442. [Online]. Available: https://doi.org/10.1007/11609773_28

[27] B. Dutertre and L. M. de Moura, "A fast linear-arithmetic solver for DPLL(T)," in *Computer Aided Verification, 18th International Conference, CAV 2006, Seattle, WA, USA, August 17-20, 2006, Proceedings*, ser. Lecture Notes in Computer Science, T. Ball and R. B. Jones, Eds., vol. 4144. Springer, 2006, pp. 81–94. [Online]. Available: https://doi.org/10.1007/11817963_11

[28] L. M. de Moura and N. Bjørner, "Z3: An efficient SMT solver," in *Tools and Algorithms for the Construction and Analysis of Systems*, ser. Lecture Notes in Computer Science, C. R. Ramakrishnan and J. Rehof, Eds., vol. 4963. Springer, 2008, pp. 337–340.

[29] N. Suzuki and D. Jefferson, "Verification decidability of presburger array programs." CARNEGIE-MELLON UNIV PITTSBURGH PA DEPT OF COMPUTER SCIENCE, Tech. Rep., 1977.

[30] J. Jaffar, "Presburger arithmetic with array segments," *Inf. Process. Lett.*, vol. 12, no. 2, pp. 79–82, 1981. [Online]. Available: https://doi.org/10.1016/0020-0190(81)90007-7

[31] C. Lynch and B. Morawska, "Automatic decidability," in *IEEE Symposium on Logic in Computer Science*. IEEE Computer Society, 2002, p. 7. [Online]. Available: https://doi.org/10.1109/LICS.2002.1029813

[32] A. Armando, M. P. Bonacina, S. Ranise, and S. Schulz, "New results on rewrite-based satisfiability procedures," *ACM Trans. Comput. Log.*, vol. 10, no. 1, pp. 4:1–4:51, 2009. [Online]. Available: https://doi.org/10.1145/1459010.1459014

[33] J. Christ and J. Hoenicke, "Weakly equivalent arrays," in *International Symposium on Frontiers of Combining Systems*, ser. FroCoS 2015. Berlin, Heidelberg: Springer-Verlag, 2015, pp. 119–134.

[34] V. Ganesh and D. L. Dill, "A decision procedure for bit-vectors and arrays," in *Computer Aided Verification*, ser. Lecture Notes in Computer Science, W. Damm and H. Hermanns, Eds., vol. 4590. Springer, 2007, pp. 519–531.

[35] R. Brummayer and A. Biere, "Lemmas on demand for the extensional theory of arrays," *JSAT*, vol. 6, no. 1-3, pp. 165–201, 2009. [Online]. Available: https://satassociation.org/jsat/index.php/jsat/article/view/74

[36] A. Stump, C. W. Barrett, D. L. Dill, and J. R. Levitt, "A decision procedure for an extensional theory of arrays," in *IEEE Symposium on Logic in Computer Science*. IEEE Computer Society, 2001, pp. 29–37.

[37] M. Bofill, R. Nieuwenhuis, A. Oliveras, E. Rodríguez-Carbonell, and A. Rubio, "A write-based solver for SAT modulo the theory of arrays," in *Formal Methods in Computer-Aided Design*, A. Cimatti and R. B. Jones, Eds. IEEE, 2008, pp. 1–8. [Online]. Available: https://doi.org/10.1109/FMCAD.2008.ECP.18

[38] P. Habermehl, R. Iosif, and T. Vojnar, "What else is decidable about integer arrays?" in *Foundations of Software Science and Computational Structures*, ser. Lecture Notes in Computer Science, R. M. Amadio, Ed., vol. 4962. Springer, 2008, pp. 474–489.

[39] *Formal Methods in Computer-Aided Design*. IEEE, 2009.

Permissions

All chapters in this book were first published by TU Wien Academic Press; hereby published with permission under the Creative Commons Attribution License or equivalent. Every chapter published in this book has been scrutinized by our experts. Their significance has been extensively debated. The topics covered herein carry significant findings which will fuel the growth of the discipline. They may even be implemented as practical applications or may be referred to as a beginning point for another development.

The contributors of this book come from diverse backgrounds, making this book a truly international effort. This book will bring forth new frontiers with its revolutionizing research information and detailed analysis of the nascent developments around the world.

We would like to thank all the contributing authors for lending their expertise to make the book truly unique. They have played a crucial role in the development of this book. Without their invaluable contributions this book wouldn't have been possible. They have made vital efforts to compile up to date information on the varied aspects of this subject to make this book a valuable addition to the collection of many professionals and students.

This book was conceptualized with the vision of imparting up-to-date information and advanced data in this field. To ensure the same, a matchless editorial board was set up. Every individual on the board went through rigorous rounds of assessment to prove their worth. After which they invested a large part of their time researching and compiling the most relevant data for our readers.

The editorial board has been involved in producing this book since its inception. They have spent rigorous hours researching and exploring the diverse topics which have resulted in the successful publishing of this book. They have passed on their knowledge of decades through this book. To expedite this challenging task, the publisher supported the team at every step. A small team of assistant editors was also appointed to further simplify the editing procedure and attain best results for the readers.

Apart from the editorial board, the designing team has also invested a significant amount of their time in understanding the subject and creating the most relevant covers. They scrutinized every image to scout for the most suitable representation of the subject and create an appropriate cover for the book.

The publishing team has been an ardent support to the editorial, designing and production team. Their endless efforts to recruit the best for this project, has resulted in the accomplishment of this book. They are a veteran in the field of academics and their pool of knowledge is as vast as their experience in printing. Their expertise and guidance has proved useful at every step. Their uncompromising quality standards have made this book an exceptional effort. Their encouragement from time to time has been an inspiration for everyone.

The publisher and the editorial board hope that this book will prove to be a valuable piece of knowledge for researchers, students, practitioners and scholars across the globe.

List of Contributors

Alessandro Cimatti, Luca Geatti, Nicola Gigante, Angelo Montanari and Stefano Tonetta
Fondazione Bruno Kessler, Trento, Italy
University of Udine, Udine, Italy

Rüdiger Ehlers
Clausthal University of Technology, Clausthal-Zellerfeld, Germany

Ivan Gavran and Daniel Neider
Max Planck Institute for Software Systems, Kaiserslautern, Germany

M. Fareed Arif, Daniel Larraz, Mitziu Echeverria, Andrew Reynolds, Omar Chowdhury and Cesare Tinelli
Department of Computer Science, The University of Iowa

Zichao Zhang, Arthur Azevedo de Amorim and Limin Jia
Carnegie Mellon University

Corina S. Pasareanu
Carnegie Mellon and NASA Ames

Franz Brauße and Konstantin Korovin
Department of Computer Science, University of Manchester, UK

Zurab Khasidashvili
Product Enablement Solutions Group, Intel Israel Development Center

Lauren Pick and Aarti Gupta
Princeton University, Princeton, NJ, USA

Grigory Fedyukovich
Florida State University, Tallahassee, FL, USA

Haoze Wu, Alex Ozdemir, Aleksandar Zeljić, Kyle Julian, Ahmed Irfan, Sadjad Fouladi and Clark Barrett
Stanford University, USA

Divya Gopinath
NASA Ames, KBR Inc., USA

Corina Pasareanu
NASA Ames, Moffett Field, CA, USA
Carnegie Mellon University, USA

Guy Katz
The Hebrew University of Jerusalem, Israel

Xuankang Lin, Roopsha Samanta and Suresh Jagannathan
Purdue University, West Lafayette, IN 47907

He Zhu
Rutgers University, Piscataway, NJ 08854

Shuvendu K. Lahiri, Akash Lal, Rahul Kumar and Chetan Bansal
Microsoft Research

Vladimir Levin, Nate Deisinger and Jakob Lichtenberg
Microsoft

Alexander Nutz
University of Freiburg

Sridhar Gopinath
University of Texas at Austin

Byron Cook
Amazon Web Services
University College London

Daniel Kroening
Amazon Web Services
University of Oxford

Michael Tautschnig
Amazon Web Services
Queen Mary University of London

Björn Döbel, Norbert Manthey, Martin Pohlack and Pawel Wieczorkiewicz
Amazon Web Services

Elizabeth Polgreen
University of Edinburgh
UC Berkeley

Vasileios Klimis, George Parisis and Bernhard Reus
University of Sussex, UK

Vincent Liew and Paul Beame
Allen School of Computer Science & Engineering, University of Washington, Seattle, WA, USA

Jo Devriendt and Jan Elffers
Department of Computer Science, Lund University & University of Copenhagen, Lund, Sweden and Copenhagen, Denmark

Jakob Nordström
Department of Computer Science, University of Copenhagen & Lund University Copenhagen, Denmark and Lund, Sweden

Aina Niemetz, Mathias Preiner, Andres Nötzli and Clark Barrett
Stanford University

Alexander Nadel
Intel Corporation, Haifa 31015, Israel

Andrew Reynolds and Cesare Tinelli
The University of Iowa

Yutaka Nagashima
CIIRC, Czech Technical University in Prague, University of Innsbruck

Pamina Georgiou, Bernhard Gleiss and Laura Kovács
TU Wien, Austria

Daniela Kaufmann, Mathias Fleury and Armin Biere
Johannes Kepler University Linz, Altenbergerstr. 69, 4040 Linz, Austria

Thomas Pani, Georg Weissenbacher and Florian Zuleger
TU Wien, Vienna, Austria

Sepideh Asadi, Antti Hyvärinen and Natasha Sharygina
Universita della Svizzera italiana, Lugano, Switzerland

Martin Blicha
Universita della Svizzera italiana, Lugano, Switzerland Charles University, Faculty of Mathematics and Physics, Czech Republic

Rohit Dureja and Kristin Y. Rozier
Iowa State University

Jason Baumgartner, Robert Kanzelman and Mark Williams
IBM Corporation

Florian Lonsing, Subhasish Mitra and Clark Barrett
Computer Science Department, Stanford University, Stanford, CA 94305, USA

Alexander Fedotov and Jeroen J.A. Keiren
Eindhoven University of Technology, Eindhoven, The Netherlands

Julien Schmaltz
ICT Group, Eindhoven, The Netherlands

Tommy Tracy II
University of Virginia, Charlottesville, Virginia 22904

Lucas M. Tabajara and Moshe Vardi
Rice University, Houston, Texas 77005

Kevin Skadron
University of Virginia, Charlottesville, Virginia 22904

Prantik Chatterjee and Subhajit Roy
IIT Kanpur

Bui Phi Diep
Uppsala University

Akash Lal
Microsoft Research

Denis Bueno and Karem Sakallah
Computer Science and Engineering, University of Michigan

Arlen Cox
Institute for Defense Analyses, Center for Computing Sciences

Index

Printed in the USA
CPSIA information can be obtained
at www.ICGtesting.com
JSHW051412091023
49903JS00006B/390